R. Gupta's®

POPULAR MASTER GUIDE

ESSE

Eklavya Model Residential Schools (EMRS) Staff Selection Exam

PGT

Post Graduate Teacher

Tier-I : Preliminary Exam

by

RPH Editorial Board

2026
EDITION

RAMESH PUBLISHING HOUSE, NEW DELHI

Published by

O.P. Gupta *for* Ramesh Publishing House

Admin. Office

12-H, New Daryaganj Road, Opp. Officers' Mess,
New Delhi-110002 ✆ 23275224, 23245124

E-mail: info@rameshpublishinghouse.com

For Online Shopping: www.rameshpublishinghouse.com

Showroom

- Balaji Market, Nai Sarak, Delhi-110006 ✆ 23282525 📱 9354373464
- 4457, Nai Sarak, Delhi-110006

Book Code: R-2249

ISBN: 978-93-90744-63-3

Price: ₹ 290

Printed at: Deepak Offset, Delhi

CONTENTS

■ ■ ■ ■

SCHEME OF EXAMINATION

FOR PGTs POST

Tier-I : Preliminary (Qualifying) Examination in OMR (Objective) Mode (Total – 100 marks)

Test	Component of the Test	Number of Questions	Total Marks	Duration of the Test
Part-I	General Awareness	10	10	The test will be of 2 hours 30 minutes duration without any time limit for each part of the test individually.
Part-II	Reasoning Ability	15	15	
Part-III	Knowledge of ICT	15	15	
Part-IV	Teaching Aptitude	30	30	
Part-V	Domain Knowledge:			
	(a) Experiential Activity-based Pedagogy and Case Study-based Questions.	20	30	
	(b) NEP-2020	10		
	Total	**100**	**100**	
Part-VI	Language Competency Test (General English and General Hindi-10 marks each subject). This part is qualifying in nature only with minimum 40% marks together i.e., minimum 8 marks out of 20 marks combining English & Hindi. Part-I to V of the candidate will not be evaluated, if he/she fails to attain qualifying marks in Part-VI.	20	20	

Note: • One mark (1) shall be awarded to every correct answer and 1/3 marks shall be deducted for every incorrect answer. Unanswered questions will not be given any marks.

Special Note: This book covers common subjects only. For Subject Knowledge PGTs candidates are advised to read from their own resources.

Previous Years' Paper

ESSE

Eklavya Model Residential School (EMRS) Staff Selection Exam

PGT RECRUITMENT EXAM, 2023

(Exam held on 16-12-2023)

PART-I : GENERAL AWARENESS

1. Which of the following statement(s) is/are **correct** about 'India State of the Forest Report' (ISFR)?

(*a*) The first State of the Forest Report was published in 1947.

(*b*) The report is based on the biennial assessment of India's forests carried out by Forest Survey of India (FSI).

(*c*) Based on the ISFR 2021 report the total forest cover of the country is 21.71% of the total geographical area of the country.

(*d*) The ISFR 2021 report shows a decrease of forest cover as compared to the previous assessment.

Choose the **correct** answer using the codes below:

A. Only (*a*), (*b*) and (*c*) are correct
B. Only (*b*), (*c*) and (*d*) are correct
C. Only (*c*) and (*d*) are correct
D. Only (*b*) and (*c*) are correct

2. Which team won the 2023 Women T20 World Cup?

A. South Africa
B. India
C. Australia
D. England

3. Who was awarded the Sahitya Akademi Bhasha Samman 2022?

A. Uday Nath Jha
B. Krishna Bhattacharya
C. Chungkhan Yashawanta Singh
D. Shashi Nath

4. What do we call the process through which bacterial and fungal enzymes degrade detritus into simpler inorganic substances?

A. Fragmentation
B. Leaching
C. Catabolism
D. Humification

5. According to the National Education Policy 2020, by which year the Gross Enrolment Ratio in higher Education including vocational education is to be increased to 50%?

A. 2050 B. 2030
C. 2040 D. 2035

6. 'Milpa', 'Roca', 'Ladang' are different names of which of the following?

A. Rain water harvesting
B. Shifting cultivation
C. Open-cast mining
D. Earthquake waves

1. D **2.** C **3.** A **4.** C **5.** D **6.** B

7. **Assertion (A):** Both India and the USA have bicameral legislature.

Reason (R): The upper house of the legislature in both the countries has an equal number of seats reserved for different states.

Choose the **correct** answer from the codes below:

A. (A) is correct, but (R) is wrong
B. (A) is wrong, but (R) is correct
C. Both (A) and (R) are correct
D. Neither (A) nor (R) is correct

8. Johann Gutenberg developed the first-known printing press in Germany. Which was the first book he published in that press?

A. The Odyssey B. The Magna Carta
C. The Republic D. The Bible

9. **Assertion (A):** As part of the major reforms to Union Budget, the date of budget was advanced to 1 February for the first time from the Budget for Financial year 2020.

Reason (R): The advancement of Budget date has been done to enable early completion of the Budget cycle.

Choose the **correct** answer from the codes below:

A. (A) is correct, but (R) is wrong
B. (A) is wrong, but (R) is correct
C. Both (A) and (R) are correct and (R) explains (A)
D. Neither (A) nor (R) is correct

10. Students' and Teachers' Holistic Advancement through Quality Education (SARTHAQ) is an ________.

A. Indicative and suggestive NEP implementation plan for Technical Education
B. Indicative and suggestive NEP implementation plan for Legal Education
C. Indicative and suggestive NEP implementation plan for Higher Education
D. Indicative and suggestive NEP implementation plan for School Education

PART-II : REASONING ABILITY

11. Select the letter cluster that will replace the question mark (?) in the following series

BVU, ZXQ, XZM, VBI, TDE, ___?___.

A. RAF
B. RFA
C. FAR
D. FRA

12. A patient has been given a medicine schedule. There are eight medicine capsules. S, T, U, V, W, X, Y and Z.

Which have to be taken each day based on the following conditions:

(*i*) Capsule 'S' must be taken sometimes before 'T' and 'W',

(*ii*) 'T' must be taken immediately before 'V',

(*iii*) Fourth capsule must be 'U',

(*iv*) 'Y' must be taken immediately before 'X',

(*v*) 'Z' must be taken immediately after 'W',

(*vi*) 'Y' is the first capsule to be taken.

Which of the following statements is **false**?

A. 'X' is taken before 'S'.
B. 'U' must be taken between 'S' and 'T'.
C. The sixth capsule must be 'V'.
D. 'T' is taken immediately after 'S'.

7. A	8. D	9. B	10. D	11. B	12. D

13. A statement is given followed by four conclusions numbered I, II, III and IV. Assuming the statement to be true, decide which of the conclusions is/are definitely true.

Statement: $C = R > D \lesseqgtr E = K > P$

Conclusions:

I. $C > D$ II. $K \leq D$
III. $P < E$ IV. $E \geq R$

A. Only conclusions I and II are true.
B. Only conclusions I and III are true.
C. Only conclusions II and IV are true.
D. Only conclusion IV is true.

14. Study the given diagram carefully and answer the question. The numbers in different sections indicate the number of persons.

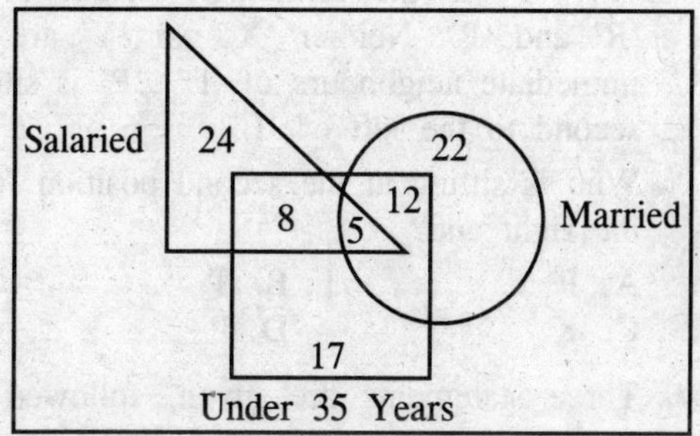

How many 'Under 35 years' people are 'Salaried' but not 'Married'?

A. 5 B. 8
C. 12 D. 13

15. There is a family of six members D, K, L, M, N and P. They are Lecturer, Artist, Businessman, Executive, NGO worker and Singer but not necessarily in the same order. There are two married couples. 'N', a Lecturer, is married to the Artist who is the mother of 'L' and 'P'. 'P' is pursuing singing. 'D' has one son and one grandson who is an Executive. 'K', the Businessman, is married to 'D'. Of the two married ladies, one is a NGO worker.

Which of the following statements is **true**?

A. 'K' is the wife of 'D'
B. 'M' is the Executive.
C. 'M' is the Artist
D. 'L' is son of 'D' and 'K'.

16. Two statements labelled as Assertion (A) and Reason (R) are given. Consider both the statements carefully.

Assertion (A): Fake news spread in world has become a serious problem.

Reason (R): The internet is source of all fake news.

Select **correct** answer with the help of code.

A. Both (A) and (R) are true and (R) is the correct explanation of (A).
B. Both (A) and (R) are true, but (R) is not the correct explanation of (A).
C. (A) is false, but (R) is true.
D. (A) is true, but (R) is false.

17. Lakshmi starts from point 'A' and travels 2 km Southwards to a point 'Z' and then turns right and travels twice that distance to reach 'Y'. She then turns left and travels five times the distance she covered between point 'A' and 'Z' and reaches point 'X'. From there she turns left and travels 4 km to reach destination 'B'. What is the shortest distance between the points 'A' and 'B' and what is B's direction with respect to 'A'?

A. 12 km, North B. 12 km, South
C. 8 km, North D. 8 km, South

18. Sudha is the wife of Anand. Kavita is the mother of Gaurav. Anu is the daughter of Ravi, who is the brother of Aryan, Anu's mother Kavita is the daughter-in-law of Anand. How is Sudha related to Aryan?

A. Sister
B. Mother
C. Paternal grandmother
D. Maternal grandmother

13. B **14.** B **15.** C **16.** D **17.** B **18.** B

19. Three statements are given followed by two conclusions I and II. Assuming the statements to be true decide which of the conclusions is/are definitely true.

Statements:

1. $M > Q$ 2. $P \geq M$
3. $N \leq M$

Conclusions:

I. $Q = N$ II. $Q < P$

A. Only conclusion I is true.
B. Only conclusion II is true.
C. Both conclusions I and II are true
D. Neither conclusion I nor II is true.

20. Which of the following Venn diagram represents the best relationship between Teachers, Sisters, Females?

A. 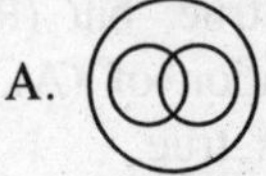
B. 
C.
D. 

21. Given below is a question, followed by two statements I and II, each containing some information. Decide which of the statements is/are sufficient to answer the question.

How is Kushal related to Meenakshi?

Statements:

I. Kushal is only son of Meenakshi's brother-in-law.
II. Garvita is Kushal's only sister.

A. The statement I alone is sufficient to answer the question while the statement II alone is not sufficient.
B. The statement II alone is sufficient to answer the question while the statement I alone is not sufficient.
C. Both statements I and II together are necessary to answer the question.
D. Both the statements I and II together are not sufficient to answer the question.

22. Eight friends J, K, L, M, P, Q, R and S are sitting around a square table in such a way that all are facing towards the centre of the table. 'L' sits in the middle of the side. 'P' is second to the left of 'M'. 'Q' is exact right of 'K' and is sitting in the middle of the side. 'P' doesn't sit with 'L'. 'M' sits exact right of 'J. Two friends are sitting in between 'M' and 'S'. 'R' is second to the left of 'J'. 'S' is exact left of 'L'. 'K' is third to the left of 'L'. Who sits fourth to the right of 'K'?

A. J B. P
C. R D. S

23. Seven children K, L, P, R, T, X and Y are sitting on a straight bench facing towards North. 'X' is sitting immediately left of 'Y'. 'T' is the immediate neighbour of 'R' and 'P'. Neither 'X' nor 'Y' are the immediate neighbours of 'L'. 'P' is sitting second to the left of 'L'.

Who is sitting at the second position from the right end?

A. R B. T
C. K D. P

24. Three statements are given, followed by four conclusions numbered I, II, III and IV. Assuming the statements to be true, even if they seem to be at variance with commonly known facts, decide which of the conclusions logically follow(s) from the statements?

Statements : 1. All boats are fishes.
2. Some fishes are rivers.
3. Some rivers are sailors.

Conclusions : I. Some sailors are fishes.
II. Some boats are sailors.
III. Some rivers are boats.
IV. Some fishes are boats.

A. Only conclusions I and II follow.
B. Only conclusions II and III follow.
C. Only conclusion IV follows.
D. Only conclusions I, II and IV follow.

19. B **20.** D **21.** A **22.** C **23.** C **24.** C

25. If North becomes South-West, then what will West become?

A. East
B. North-East
C. North-West
D. South-East

26. Refer to the following letter sequence and answer the question:

(Left) S B T M R E S I C Z Y O W A P D F H G U L (Right)

Which letter is fifth to the right of the twelfth letter from your right end of the given sequence?

A. R　　B. X
C. P　　D. W

27. Three statements are given, followed by three conclusions numbered I, II and III. Assuming the statements to be true, even if they seem to be at variance with commonly known facts, decide which of the conclusions logically follow(s) from the statements.

Statements:

1. All pinks are scarlets.
2. Some scarlets are blues.
3. No blue is brown.

Conclusions:

I. Some browns are blues.
II. No Pink is brown.
III. Some scarlets are pinks.

A. Only conclusions I and II follow.
B. Only conclusions II and III follow.
C. Only conclusion I follows.
D. Only conclusion III follows.

28. Given below is a question, followed by two statements I and II, each containing some information. Decide which of the statements is/are sufficient to answer the question.

Who is to the immediate right of 'J' among five friends J, K, L, M and N, facing the North?

I. 'L' is third to the left of 'K' and 'J' is second to the right of 'L'.
II. 'K' is to the immediate left of 'N' who is second to the right of 'J'.

A. The statement I alone is sufficient to answer the question while the statement II alone is not sufficient.
B. The statement II alone is sufficient to answer the question while the statement I alone is not sufficient.
C. Both statements I and II together are necessary to answer the question.
D. Either statement I alone or statement II alone is sufficient to answer the question.

29. Two statements labelled as Assertion (A) and Reason (R) are given. Consider both the statements carefully.

Assertion (A): India has the potential to make its Handicrafts industry a very flourishing sector.

Reason (R): India is a home to a very large number of craft forms including textiles.

Select **correct** answer with the help of code.

A. Both (A) and (R) are true and (R) is the correct explanation of (A).
B. Both (A) and (R) are true, but (R) is not the correct explanation of (A).
C. (A) is false, but (R) is true.
D. (A) is true, but (R) is false.

30. 'M + Q' means 'M' is the wife of 'Q';
'M − Q' means 'M' is the father of 'Q';
'M × Q' means 'M' is the daughter of 'Q';
'M ÷ Q' means 'M' is the son of 'Q'.
If A ÷ B × J + U − D, how is 'B' related to 'D'?

A. Mother
B. Brother
C. Sister
D. Aunt

25. D	**26.** C	**27.** D	**28.** D	**29.** A	**30.** C

PART-III : KNOWLEDGE OF ICT

31. Which of the following software you preferred most to design an animated multimedia presentation on the topic 'Benefits of Renewable Energies'?

A. Microsoft Edge
B. Microsoft Word
C. Microsoft Excel
D. Microsoft PowerPoint

32. The power backup device, UPS, stands for:

A. Under-control Power System
B. Under-controlled Power Supply
C. Uninterruptible Power Supply
D. Uninterruptible Power System

33. Which type of network we create when we connect two smartphones to transfer some photos through Bluetooth?

A. MAN B. WAN
C. PAN D. LAN

34. Which of the following does not come under cyber-crime under IT Act 2000?

A. Stealing monitor from a store
B. Distributing child pornography over internet
C. Misusing personal information over internet
D. Using fake email messages to get personal information

35. Which of the following is not a source of the virus entering your system?

A. Email attachment
B. Hard Disk
C. Pen drive
D. Printouts

36. McAfee Plus is an example of:

A. Anti-virus
B. Application software
C. Open source software
D. Programming Language

37. Which of the following cloud storage service owned by Microsoft?

A. iCloud B. One Drive
C. Floppy Drive D. Google Drive

38. Out of the following options, the most popular combination of shortcut keys to copy some selected text in most of the MS windows applications is:

A. Ctrl + C B. Ctrl + O
C. Ctrl + P D. Ctrl + X

39. Which of the following groups of devices are only input devices?

A. Mouse, Monitor, Joystick
B. Mouse, Microphone, Speaker
C. Keyboard, Printer, Light Pen
D. Joystick, Microphone, Scanner

40. Which of the following is an example of an Operating System?

A. Bing B. Edge
C. Word D. Windows

PART-IV : TEACHING APTITUDE

41. Effective teaching, by and large, is a function of:

A. teacher's honesty.
B. teacher's scholarship.
C. teacher's positive attitude towards teaching.
D. teacher's ability to make students learn.

31. D **32.** C **33.** C **34.** A **35.** D **36.** A **37.** B **38.** A **39.** D **40.** D **41.** D

42. Mohan can now think in terms of propositions and deal with propositions instead of objects. He deals with sum total of possibilities rather than empirical situation. He takes final steps towards versatility in thought.

Mohan is at which stage of Piaget's model?

A. Pre-operational stage
B. Sensory-motor stage
C. Concrete operations stage
D. Formal operations stage

43. Which one of the following is not a characteristic of teacher centred approach?

A. Large sized classes are handled very well.
B. Unfamiliar or abstract concepts are directly explained by the teacher.
C. Enough scope for discussion and debate is available.
D. Courses prescribed can be completed in time.

44. If students are not taking interest in their studies, the teacher should:

A. ask them as to why are they not taking interest in their studies.
B. tell them that taking interest in their studies would lead to good result.
C. file a complaint with the principal and parents and seek their indulgence.
D. find out causes for lack of interest and take corrective measures.

45. The ASSURE model of integration of ICT in the learning process has the components:

A. Analyse learners, state the objectives, select the media and materials and evaluate.
B. Activity, state the objectives, support and extend.
C. Analyse the content, state the aim, select method and materials and evaluate.
D. Analyse the learners, state the aim, select the method and materials and extend.

46. What is not an advantage of Discovery method?

A. This method is suitable for the students of lower classes.
B. It develops scientific and critical attitude among students.
C. It provides training to prepare students for life.
D. It develops self confidence and self reliance.

47. Which of the following is not an example of 'Assessment of Learning'?

A. Annual Examination
B. Assessment of Homework
C. Scholarship Examination
D. Anecdotal Records

48. Which characteristic does not belong to Adolescence stage?

A. Pronounced group loyalty
B. Forming groups among members of same sex
C. A period of intense emotions
D. Highly critical of social evils and injustice

49. What should not be a role of a teacher in the construction of knowledge by students?

A. Being sensitive to the previous experience of each and every student in the class
B. Supporting cooperative and collaborative learning in the classroom
C. Focussing on realistic approaches to solve real world problems
D. Discouraging self analysis and self assessment

50. Which one of the following is not associated with a unit test?

A. Standardized Achievement Tests
B. Confined to limited number of competencies
C. Totally controlled by the teacher
D. Used for Remedial purpose

42. D **43.** C **44.** D **45.** A **46.** A **47.** B **48.** B **49.** D **50.** A

EXPLANATORY ANSWERS

1. (D): The correct answer is D. Only statements (*b*) and (*c*) are correct.

(*a*) Incorrect. The first State of the Forest Report was not published in 1947.

(*b*) Correct. The report is based on the biennial assessment of India's forests carried out by the Forest Survey of India (FSI).

(*c*) Correct. Based on the ISFR 2021 report, the total forest cover of the country is 21.71% of the total geographical area of the country.

(*d*) Incorrect. The ISFR 2021 report does not show a decrease in forest cover compared to the previous assessment.

Forest Survey of India (FSI), is a premier national organization under the union Ministry of Environment and Forests, responsible for assessment and monitoring of the forest resources of the country regularly. In addition, it is also engaged in providing the services of training, research and extension. Established on June 1, 1981, the Forest Survey of India succeeded the "Preinvestment Survey of Forest Resources"(PISFR), a project initiated in 1965 by Government of India with the sponsorship of FAO and UNDP.

2. (C): The 2023 Women's T20 World Cup was the eighth edition of Women's T20 World Cup tournament. It was held in South Africa between 10 February and 26 February 2023. The final took place at Cape Town. Australia won their sixth and third consecutive title after beating the hosts South Africa in the final by 19 runs.

3. (A): Dr. Uday Nath Jha was awarded the Sahitya Akademi Bhasha Samman 2022 for his valuable contributions to the field of classical and medieval literature in the eastern region.

The Sahitya Akademi was formally inaugurated by the Government of India on 12 March 1954.

It is India's National Academy of Letters and the central institution for literary dialogue, publication and promotion in the country and the only institution that undertakes literary activities in 24 Indian languages, including English.

4. (C): Catabolism is the process through which bacterial and fungal enzymes degrade detritus (dead organic matter) into simpler inorganic substances. This is a part of the decomposition process, where complex organic materials are broken down, releasing nutrients back into the ecosystem.

Humification: Part of the decomposed organic matter is converted into humus, a stable, dark organic material. Humus improves soil structure, water retention, and fertility.

Fragmentation: Detritus, such as dead leaves and animal remains, is physically broken down into smaller pieces by detritivores (organisms like earthworms and insects). This increases the surface area for microbial action.

Leaching: Water-soluble substances in the detritus are dissolved and carried away by water. This process removes soluble nutrients and makes them available to microorganisms.

5. (D): Effective implementation of National Education Policy, 2020 (NEP) is likely to restore India's glory as a great centre of learning. One of the targets of NEP 2020 is to increase Gross Enrolment Ratio (GER) in higher education to 50% by 2035.

Gross Enrolment Ratio (GER) or Gross Enrolment Index (GEI) is a statistical measure used in the education sector, and formerly by the UN in its Education Index, to determine the number of students enrolled in school at several different grade levels (like elementary, middle school and high school), and use it to show the ratio of the number of students who live in that country to those who qualify for the particular grade level.

6. **(B):** Shifting Cultivation is a form of agricultural practice or a cultivation system in which an area is cleared for vegetation and cultivated for a few years then left abandoned. Shifting cultivation is practised in many areas around the world. It is called by different names in different areas, like:

- **Milpa:** A term used in Mexico and Central America for a system of traditional agriculture, particularly shifting cultivation.
- **Roca:** A term used in Brazil for shifting cultivation, also known as "slash and burn" agriculture.
- **Ladang:** A term used in Indonesia and Malaysia for shifting cultivation, where land is cleared and crops are grown for a few years before moving to a new area.

7. **(A): Assertion (A):** Both India and the USA have bicameral legislatures. This is correct. In India, the two houses are the Rajya Sabha (Council of States) and the Lok Sabha (House of the People). In the USA, the two houses are the Senate and the House of Representatives.

Reason (R): The upper house of the legislature in both countries has an equal number of seats reserved for different states. This is incorrect. In the USA, each state is represented equally in the Senate with two senators per state. However, in India, the representation in the Rajya Sabha is not equal for all states; it is based on the population of each state.

Hence, the correct answer is A. (A) is correct, but (R) is wrong.

8. **(D):** Johann Gutenberg's first major printed work was the Gutenberg Bible, also known as the 42-line Bible or Mazarin Bible. It was printed around 1455 and is considered one of the earliest and most significant books printed using movable type in Europe.

9. **(B): Assertion (A):** The date of the Union Budget was advanced to February 1 for the first time with the Budget for the Financial Year 2017, not 2020.

Reason (R): The advancement of the Budget date was indeed done to enable early completion of the Budget cycle, so that the government can implement its expenditure plans right from the beginning of the financial year (April 1).

Hence, the correct answer is B. (A) is wrong, but (R) is correct.

10. **(D):** Students' and Teachers' Holistic Advancement through Quality Education (SARTHAQ) is an indicative and suggestive NEP implementation plan for School Education.

SARTHAQ was launched as part of the National Education Policy (NEP) 2020 to facilitate the effective implementation of the policy in school education. It aims to achieve the policy's goals and ensure a holistic development of students and teachers through various initiatives, plans, and activities.

11. **(B):**

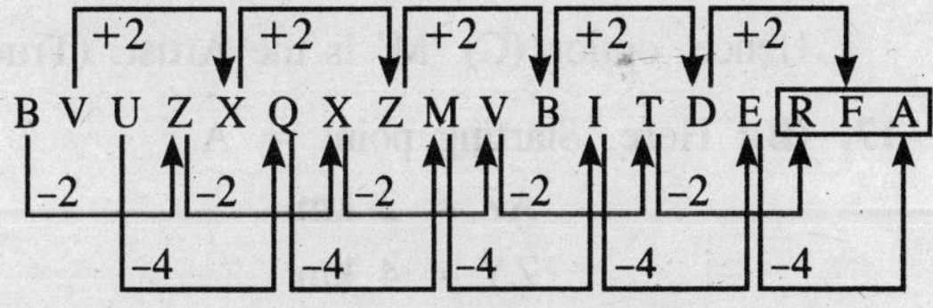

Here, ? = the next letter cluster = **RFA.**

12. (D): A patient has been given a medicine schedule

Y	X	S	U	T	V	W	Z
1	2	3	4	5	6	7	8

Option (D) is false because T is taken immediately after 'U'.

13. (B): Given, Statement:

$C = R > D \leq E = K > P$

$\Rightarrow C > D, K \geq D, P < E,$

Conclusions:

I. $C > D$ (True)

II. $K \leq D$ (False)

III. $P < E$ (True)

IV. $E \geq R$ (False)

Here, Only conclusions I and III are true.

14. (B): From given diagram:

The number of 'under 35 years' People are 'Salaried' but not 'Married'

= Common in under 35 years and salaried

= 8.

15. (C): Given, There is a family of 6 members.

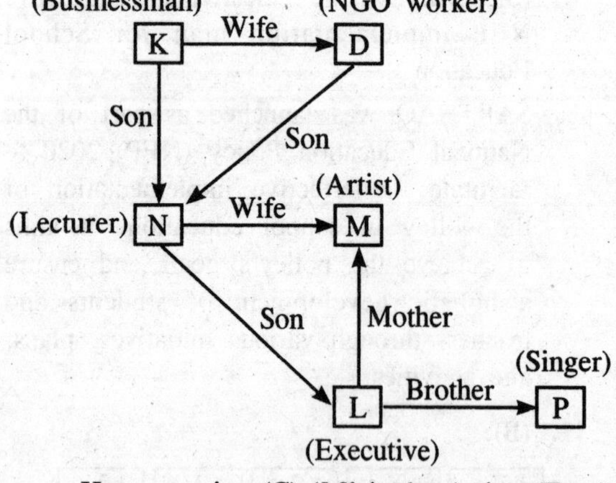

Hence, option (C) 'M' is the Artist. (True)

17. (B): Here, Starting point = A

AZ = 2 km

ZY = 4 km

YX = 10 km

XB = 4 km

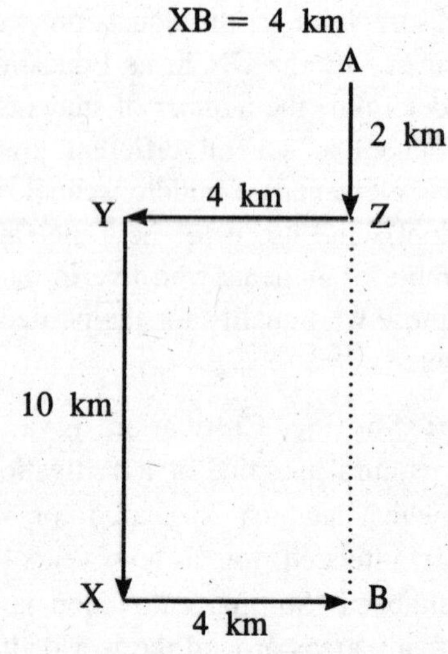

$\therefore$ ZY = XB = 4 km

$\therefore$ YX = ZB = 10 km

$\therefore$ AB = AZ + ZB

= 2 + 10 = 12 km

Hence, the shortest distance between the point 'A' and 'B' is 12 km and B's direction is in South with respect to 'A'.

18. (B):

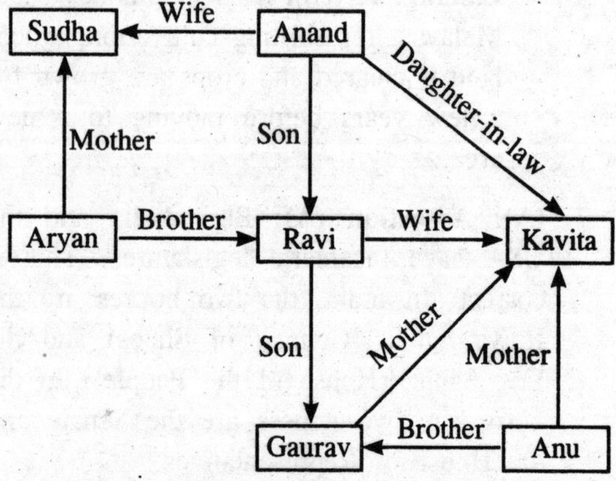

Here, Sudha is the Mother of Aryan.

19. (B): Given, Statements:

1. $M > Q$
2. $P \geq M$
3. $N \leq M$

$\Rightarrow P \geq M > Q$ and $M \geq N$

Conclusions:

I. Q = N (False)

II. Q < P (True)

Hence, Only conclusion II is true.

21. (A): From given statements:

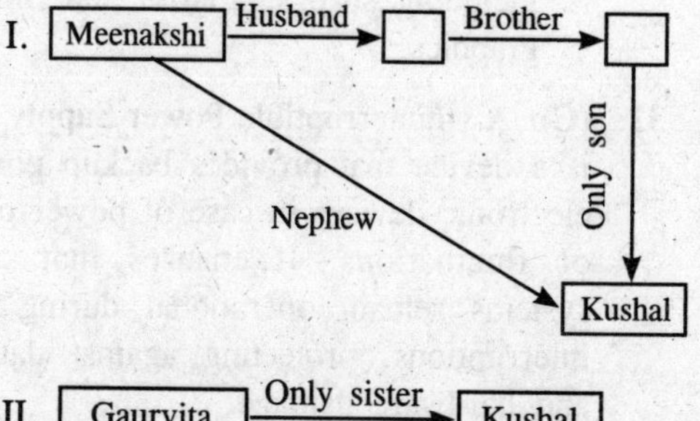

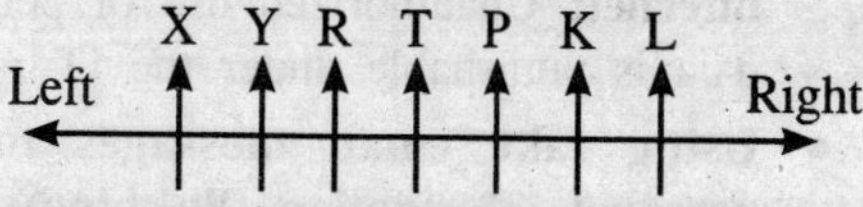

∴ Kushal is the nephew of Meenakshi.

Hence, The Statement-I alone is sufficient to answer the question while II alone is not sufficient.

22. (C): Given, 8 friends are sitting around a square table in such a way that all are facing towards the centre.

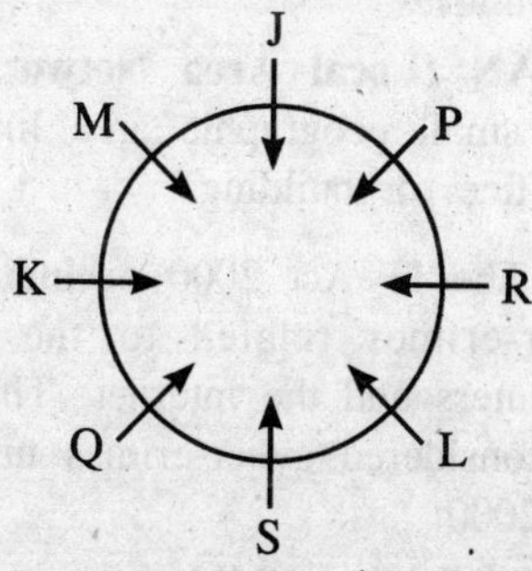

Here, 'R' sits fourth to the right of 'K'.

23. (C): Given, 7 children are sitting on a straight bench facing towards North

X Y R T P K L

Left Right

Here, K is sitting at the second position from the right end.

24. (C): From given statements:

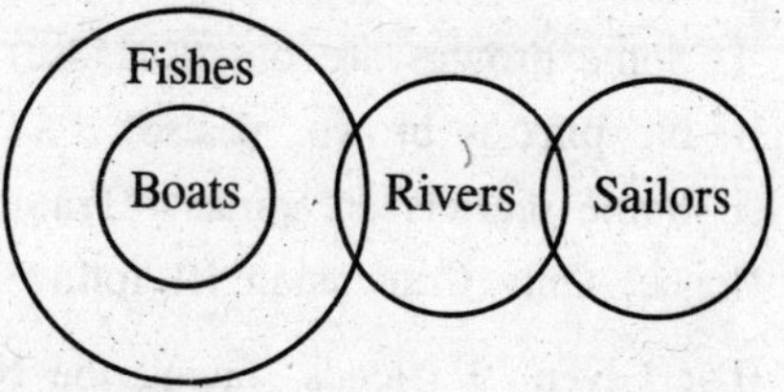

Conclusions:

I. Some sailors are fishes. (False)

II. Some boats are sailors. (False)

III. Some rivers are boats. (False)

IV. Some fishes are boats. (True)

Hence, Only Conclusion IV follows.

25. (D): Given, North becomes South-West
⇒ North move 135° anticlockwise.

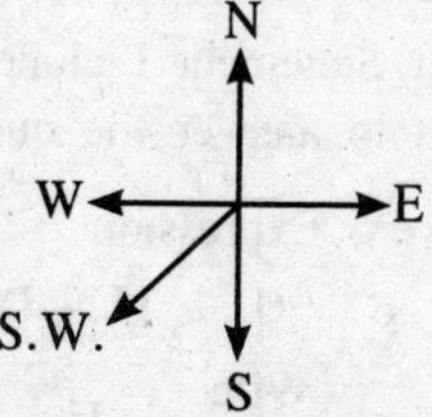

Similarly, West move 135° anticlockwise
⇒ West becomes South-East

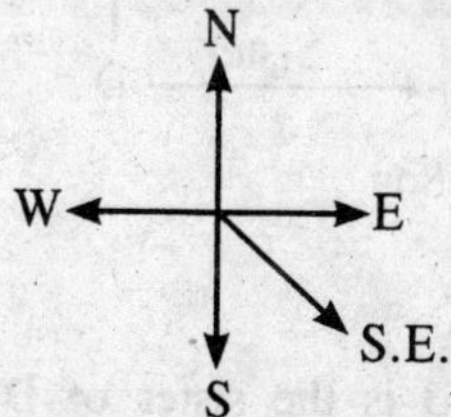

26. (C): From given letter sequence:
The twelfth letter from your right end = Z and fifth letter to the right of Z = P
∴ Required letter = P.

27. (D): From given statements:

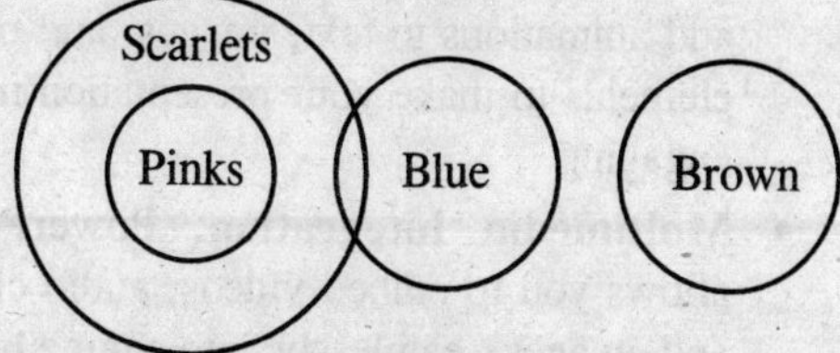

Conclusions:

I. Some browns are blues. (False)

II. No pink is brown. (False)

III. Some scarlets are pinks. (True)

Hence, Only Conclusion III follows.

28. **(D):** Given, 5 friends, facing the North

From Statement-I:

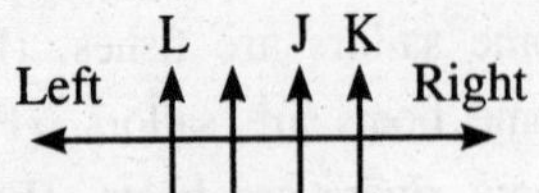

From Statement-II:

Hence, K is the immediate right of J.

∴ Either Statement I alone or II alone is sufficient to answer the question.

30. **(C):** Given, Expression

$= A \div B \times J + U - D$

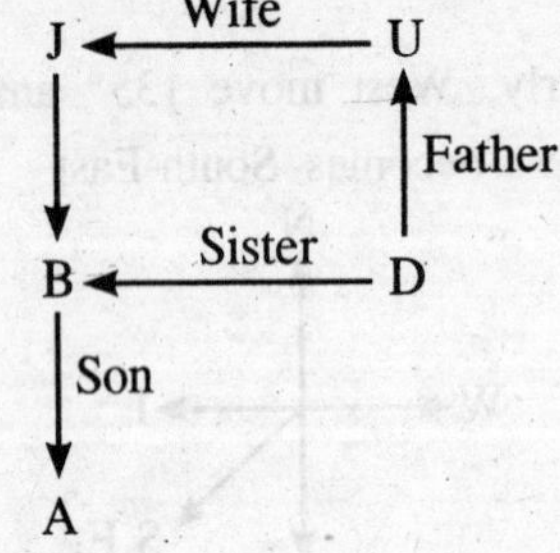

Hence, B is the sister of D.

31. **(D):** Microsoft PowerPoint is the preferred software for designing animated multimedia presentations. It offers a wide range of features for creating visually appealing and interactive presentations, including:

- **Animations and Transitions:** You can add animations to text, images, and other elements to make your presentation more engaging.
- **Multimedia Integration:** PowerPoint allows you to embed videos, audio clips, and images seamlessly into your slides.
- **Templates and Themes:** There are numerous templates and themes available to help you design professional-looking presentations quickly.
- **Customization:** PowerPoint provides various tools to customize your slides, including shapes, charts, and SmartArt graphics.

32. **(C):** A Uninterruptible Power Supply (UPS) is a device that provides backup power to electronic devices in case of power outages or fluctuations. It ensures that critical systems remain operational during power interruptions, protecting against data loss and hardware damage.

33. **(C):** A Personal Area Network (PAN) is a network used for communication among devices close to one person. **When** you connect two smartphones via **Bluetooth** to transfer photos, you are creating a PAN.

- **MAN (Metropolitan Area Network):** Covers a larger geographic area like a city.
- **WAN (Wide Area Network):** Covers a broad area like a country or multiple countries.
- **LAN (Local Area Network):** Covers a small geographic area like a home, office, or building.

34. **(A):** The IT Act 2000 in India addresses cyber-crimes related to the misuse of computers and the internet. The following are considered cyber-crimes under the IT Act 2000:

- **Distributing child pornography over the internet:** This is a serious offense and is prohibited under the IT Act.
- **Misusing personal information over the internet:** Unauthorized use of personal data is punishable under the IT Act.
- **Using fake email messages to get personal information (Phishing):** This is considered fraud and is covered under the IT Act.

- Stealing a monitor from a store is a criminal offense, but it is not classified as a cyber-crime as it does not involve the misuse of technology or the internet.

35. (D): The correct answer is D.

- **Email attachment:** Viruses can be distributed through infected email attachments.
- **Hard Disk:** While viruses typically spread through removable media, an infected hard disk can also harbor viruses that spread to other devices.
- **Pen drive:** Viruses can be easily transmitted through pen drives and other removable storage devices.
- **Printouts:** A printout is a physical copy and cannot carry or transmit a computer virus.

36. (A): McAfee Plus is a type of anti-virus software designed to protect your computer from viruses, malware, and other online threats. It scans your system, detects malicious activities, and helps in removing harmful software to keep your data and devices secure.

37. (B):

- **OneDrive** is a cloud storage service owned by Microsoft. It allows users to store files and access them from any device with an internet connection.
- **iCloud:** Owned by Apple.
- **Floppy Drive:** A type of storage device, not a cloud storage service.
- **Google Drive:** Owned by Google.

38. (A):

- **Ctrl + C:** This is the most common keyboard shortcut for copying selected text or items in most MS Windows applications.
- **Ctrl + O:** This shortcut is typically used to open a file.
- **Ctrl + P:** This shortcut is commonly used to print the current document or page.
- **Ctrl + X:** This shortcut is used to cut selected text or items, removing them from their original location to be pasted elsewhere.

The correct answer is A. Ctrl + C.

39. (D): Input devices are hardware components that allow users to enter data, commands, and other inputs into a computer or other digital systems. They are essential for interacting with and controlling computer systems.

- **Joystick:** A joystick is an input device used to control movement in computer games and simulations. It consists of a stick that pivots on a base and reports its angle or direction to the device it is controlling.

  Use Cases: Commonly used in gaming, flight simulators, and other applications where directional control is required.

- **Microphone:** A microphone captures audio input from the user. It converts sound waves into electrical signals that can be processed by the computer.

  Use Cases: Used for voice recording, voice recognition software, video conferencing, and multimedia applications.

- **Scanner:** A scanner captures images or text from physical documents and converts them into digital form. It uses light to scan the document and create a digital copy.

  Use Cases: Used for digitizing documents, photos, and barcodes.

40. (D): Windows: An operating system developed by Microsoft that manages the hardware and software resources of a computer.

Bing is a search engine that allows users to find information on the internet. Launched by Microsoft in 2009, Bing offers a variety of features to enhance the search experience, making it a powerful tool for discovering and accessing information.

Edge is a modern web browser developed by Microsoft, introduced in 2015 as the successor to Internet Explorer. Initially released with Windows 10, Edge has since evolved and is now available on multiple platforms, including Windows, macOS, iOS, and Android.

Word is a word processing application developed by Microsoft. It is part of the Microsoft Office suite of productivity software.

41. (D): Effective teaching primarily revolves around the ability of a teacher to facilitate learning in students. While honesty, scholarship, and a positive attitude towards teaching are important attributes for a teacher, the ultimate measure of effective teaching is how well a teacher can engage students, make complex concepts understandable, inspire critical thinking, and enable students to retain and apply knowledge.

42. (D): According to Jean Piaget's theory of cognitive development, the Formal Operations Stage is the final stage, typically beginning around age 11 and continuing into adulthood. At this stage, individuals develop the ability to think abstractly, reason logically, and plan systematically. They can consider hypothetical situations and use deductive reasoning, which aligns with Mohan's ability to think in terms of propositions and deal with possibilities rather than just empirical situations.

43. (C): A teacher-centered approach typically emphasizes the teacher's role as the primary authority figure, with students being more passive recipients of information.

Characteristic of teacher centred approach:

- **Large sized classes are handled very well:** In a teacher-centered approach, the teacher directs all activities, which can be efficient for managing large groups.
- **Unfamiliar or abstract concepts are directly explained by the teacher:** The teacher often uses direct instruction to convey new or complex information.
- **Courses prescribed can be completed in time:** A teacher-centered approach can help ensure that the curriculum is covered within the allotted time, as the teacher controls the pace and delivery of content.

The correct answer is C. Enough scope for discussion and debate is available. This is not a characteristic of a teacher-centered approach.

44. (D): The best approach is D. find out causes for lack of interest and take corrective measures.

When students are not taking an interest in their studies, it's important for the teacher to understand the underlying reasons behind their lack of engagement.

This involves identifying any potential issues or challenges the students might be facing, such as:

- **Learning difficulties:** Some students might struggle with the material and need additional support or alternative teaching methods.
- **Personal issues:** Factors outside of school, such as family problems or health issues, can impact a student's ability to focus and engage in their studies.
- **Teaching methods:** The way the material is being presented might not be resonating with the students, and a different approach could be more effective.

45. (A): The ASSURE model is a structured approach to integrating technology and media into the teaching and learning process. It consists of the following components:

- **Analyse Learners:** Understand the characteristics of the learners, including their prior knowledge, skills, and learning preferences.
- **State the Objectives:** Clearly define the learning objectives and outcomes that you aim to achieve.
- **Select the Media and Materials:** Choose appropriate media and materials that will support the achievement of the learning objectives.
- **Utilize Media and Materials:** Effectively use the selected media and materials in the instructional process.
- **Require Learner Participation:** Engage learners in activities that will help them achieve the objectives.
- **Evaluate and Revise:** Assess the effectiveness of the instruction and make necessary revisions based on feedback and outcomes.

The correct answer is A. Analyse learners, state the objectives, select the media and materials and evaluate.

46. (A): The Discovery Method, also known as Discovery Learning, involves students exploring and discovering information on their own, guided by a facilitator or teacher.

Advantages of discovery method:

- **Develops scientific and critical attitude among students:** By exploring and discovering concepts independently, students learn to think critically and scientifically.
- **Provides training to prepare students for life:** This method equips students with problem-solving skills and the ability to apply knowledge in real-life situations.
- **Develops self-confidence and self-reliance:** As students make discoveries on their own, they build confidence in their abilities and learn to rely on themselves.
- **Suitable for the students of lower classes:** This is not typically an advantage. Younger students, especially in lower classes, may find the Discovery Method challenging without the necessary foundational knowledge and skills. Hence, the correct answer is A.

47. (B): Assessment of Learning refers to evaluations that are used to measure what students have learned, typically at the end of a teaching period. These are often summative assessments.

- **Annual Examination:** This is a summative assessment to evaluate students' learning at the end of an academic year.
- **Assessment of Homework:** This can be considered a form of summative assessment if it contributes to the final grade.
- **Scholarship Examination:** This is also a summative assessment to evaluate students' eligibility for scholarships based on their knowledge and performance.
- **Anecdotal Records:** These are informal, narrative accounts of a student's progress, behavior, and learning experiences recorded by the teacher. They are typically used for formative assessment purposes. Hence, the correct answer is D.

48. (B): The characteristic that does not typically belong to the adolescence stage is B. Forming groups among members of same sex.

- **Pronounced group loyalty:** During adolescence, peer relationships become increasingly important, and adolescents often show strong loyalty to their peer groups.

- **A period of intense emotions:** Adolescence is marked by hormonal changes that can lead to heightened emotions and mood swings.
- **Highly critical of social evils and injustice:** Adolescents often develop a sense of idealism and become more aware of social issues, leading them to criticize social injustices.

49. (D): A teacher should encourage self-analysis and self-assessment as they are essential for students to reflect on their learning, identify areas for improvement, and take ownership of their educational journey. Here's a quick breakdown of the roles:

- **Being sensitive to the previous experience of each and every student in the class:** This helps tailor instruction to meet individual needs and build on existing knowledge.
- **Supporting cooperative and collaborative learning in the classroom:** This fosters teamwork, communication skills, and shared understanding.
- **Focussing on realistic approaches to solve real world problems:** This ensures that learning is relevant and applicable to students' lives.

Discouraging self-analysis and self-assessment would hinder students' ability to understand their progress and develop critical thinking skills.

50. (A): Standardized Achievement Tests: These are not typically associated with unit tests. Standardized tests are designed to measure students' performance against a common standard and are administered uniformly across different schools or regions.

- **Confined to limited number of competencies:** Unit tests usually focus on specific competencies or learning objectives covered in a particular unit or chapter.
- **Totally controlled by the teacher:** Unit tests are usually created and administered by the teacher, giving them control over the content and format.
- **Used for Remedial purpose:** Unit tests can be used to identify areas where students need additional support or remediation, helping teachers tailor their instruction to meet students' needs.

Experiential Activity-based Pedagogy and Case Study-based Questions

1. During a discussion on "Cricket", a teacher is posing questions mostly to boys and not to girls. This act of teacher is an example of:
A. Gender Empowerment
B. Gender bias
C. Gender relevance
D. Gender threat

2. You are a teacher who believes that "children learn at varied paces and in different ways". In your class, you will plan assessment which:
A. is same for all students.
B. includes objective type questions only.
C. is not related to how children learn.
D. is based on different methods of assessment.

3. Seeing a horse, a three year old child exclaimed. "Wow! Such a big dog". As per Jean Piaget's theory of cognitive development, this response by child is an example of:
A. assimilation.
B. make-believe.
C. object-permanence.
D. deferred imitation.

4. Classroom environment has a significance on children's learning. To inculcate a culture of mastery oriented learning (learning that focuses on understanding), learning, classroom environment should be:
A. performance oriented.
B. competitive and individualistic.
C. teacher dominated.
D. cooperative and collaborative.

5. Pooja tells her friend that we should follow class rules else the teacher will not allow us to play outside. Pooja is at which stage of moral development according to Lawrence Kohlberg?
A. Obedience and Punishment Oriented
B. Good boy-good girl orientation
C. Authority and social-order maintaining orientation
D. Universal Ethical Principles orientation

6. Identifying the difficulty; setting the goal; exploring possible solution and consequences; acting accordingly and evaluate the outcomes are important steps involved in the process of:
A. Attribution
B. Imitation
C. Problem-solving
D. Passive attention

7. Which of the following is an inappropriate way of using feedback as a motivator?

A. Feedback concentrated on the ability of the student
B. Feedback focused on the process of an activity
C. Feedback in descriptive style related to students' work
D. Feedback without referring to comparisons with other students

8. A teacher always asks boys to do tasks such as moving the furniture and girls to keep the class tidy and decorated. This perception is not appropriate because this is an example of:
A. gender stereotype
B. gender identity
C. gender stability
D. gender equality

9. **Assertion (A) :** Teachers should ask questions that facilitates students to establish relationships between what they are expected to learn and what they already know.
Reason (R) : Prior knowledge doesn't play any role in learning of new concepts.
Choose the correct option.
A. Both (A) and (R) are true and (R) is the correct explanation of (A).
B. Both (A) and (R) are true, but (R) is not the correct explanation of (A).
C. (A) is true, but (R) is false.
D. Both (A) and (R) are false.

10. You are teaching a chapter about the disabilities of deafness and dumbness and how to communicate without speaking. A child asks, "We all can speak. So why are we studying this in EVS?"
Which of the below responses BEST explains the scope of learning this chapter in EVS?
A. Some people are different from you all. They have the specific challenge where they cannot hear or speak. You will need to understand why they are considered as differently abled.
B. All of us have different abilities and constraints. Some people have the specific challenge where they cannot hear or speak. We need to understand how to communicate with them and be inclusive.
C. Some people have the specific challenge where they cannot hear or speak. You need to be careful and alert when you are interacting with them. This chapter will help you in such scenarios.
D. Some of you may want to become doctors when you grow up. Understanding various types of problems and physical challenges is the first step towards that.

11. You have brought 15 chart papers to your classroom for students to use in their projects for an upcoming exhibition. You have told students that the chart papers will not be replaced once finished and they will have to use it wisely.
Which of the below activities would LEAST help students engage on the idea of using resources judiciously that are in limited supply?
A. Discussing projects that do not need chart paper and how they can still be good options for the science exhibition.
B. Conducting a poll on how many chart papers different students require and asking them to compare this with number of chart papers available.
C. Brainstorming on ideas for reducing the use of chart paper in projects.
D. Asking students to write in a common register the quantity of chart paper they took each time, when and why.

12. In order to cater the needs of students with giftedness, which of the following is an effective strategy?
A. Ask them very simple and easy questions
B. Assign them challenging and higher-order tasks
C. Give extra time to comprehend the information
D. Keep low expectations of success from them

13. A teacher is asking students to think about their own thinking processes. Which kind of skills she is focusing to develop among students?

A. Declarative B. Meta-cognitive
C. Procedural D. Semantic

14. Formulating new clarifications, going beyond the simple application of previously learned rules to achieve a goal; and evaluating the outcomes are important parts of:

A. assimilation
B. misconception
C. problem-solving
D. rote-memorisation

15. You have brought 1 large bottle of glue to your classroom for students to use for their projects for an upcoming exhibition. You have told students that the bottle will not be replaced once finished and they will have to use it wisely.

Which of the below activities would MOST help students engage on the idea of conserving resources that cannot be brought back?

A. Put up a poster that displays the projects where glue can be used and where it cannot.
B. Conduct a class survey to find out how many students require glue for their projects and for what.
C. Distribute the glue equally to all students and see who has how much left at the end of the week.
D. Ask students to write in a common register how many spoons of glue they took each time, when and why.

16. A teacher uses a widely accepted computer program that renders a 3D representation of Earth based on satellite imagery to teach her students various aspects of the Earth.

Compared to traditional map books, what advantage does this application have as an instructional tool?

A. It develops the habit of independent study in students.
B. It helps activate student's prior knowledge on the Earth.
C. It helps students in understanding the positions of countries better.
D. It helps students in understanding landscapes better.

17. Amrit reasons that we can change laws if they do not meet the needs of the society but it should be done through mutual agreement and democratic process. According to Lawrence Kohlberg at which stage of moral reasoning does Amrit come under?

A. Social order orientation
B. Social contract orientation
C. Universal ethics principles
D. Good boy-Good girl orientation

18. Which of the following is a correctly matched pair of response and goal orientation?

A. Doing a worksheet to improve one's competence in domain of particular interest: Approach-oriented mastery goals
B. Preparing for a test to win the cash prize: Avoidance-oriented performance goals
C. Taking extra classes for a subject to achieve first rank in class: Avoidance-oriented mastery goals
D. Working hard for not getting outperformed by others: Approach-oriented goals

19. For the topic 'historical monuments', which of these is a specific, measurable and attainable learning objective?

A. Student will know why stone was used to build monuments in the past.
B. Students will draw an architectural plan of the Taj Mahal, to appropriate scale.
C. Students will classify the different materials used in building the Golkonda Fort based on their purpose.
D. Students will help preserve historical monuments, recognizing the importance of these.

20. Assertion (A) : Teachers should involve the students in decision-making and encourage active participation in the classroom.
Reason (R) : Learning is transmitted directly from the teacher to the student.
Choose the correct option.
A. Both (A) and (R) are true and (R) is the correct explanation of (A).
B. Both (A) and (R) are true, but (R) is not the correct explanation of (A).
C. (A) is true, but (R) is false.
D. Both (A) and (R) are false.

21. For successful inclusion of students belonging to diverse cultural backgrounds, which of the following should be **avoided** by the teacher?
A. Acknowledge and respect every student.
B. Give priority to the experiences of dominant groups.
C. Incorporate diversity in the content of teaching.
D. Practice cultural sensitivity in classroom.

22. After answering the questions based on recall of specific information a students is reflecting on what cues helped her. By doing so, the students is developing ________.
A. delayed imitation.
B. ego-centricism.
C. meta-cognition.
D. over-justification.

23. A teacher holds the perception that boys are more intelligent and risk taking and girls are obedient and sincere and treats them accordingly. This is an example of:
A. gender bias
B. gender constancy
C. gender equity
D. gender equality

24. Ruhi is shown three pencils and she observes that pencil A is longer than pencil B and pencil B is longer than pencil C. When Ruhi infers that A is longer pencil than C, which characteristic of Jean Piaget's cognitive development is she demonstrating?
A. Seriation
B. Conservation
C. Transitive thought
D. Hypothetico-deductive reasoning

25. Rohan's response on receiving a toy doll was, 'I don't like this toy because boys do not play with dolls'. This is an example of
A. Gender relevance
B. Gender discrimination
C. Gender stereotype
D. Gender stability

26. To teach a concept, a teacher is giving multiple examples and subsequently ask students to form a rule considering the information gathered through those examples. Which of the following approach is being used here for concept formation among children?
A. Deductive
B. Inductive
C. Imitative
D. Competitive

27. Which of the following is an example of extrinsic motivation?
A. While doing research, Arman consults various sources to be sure about his learnings.
B. Rayon researches from many sources for a project to get a cash prize.
C. To ensure self-satisfaction, Sitara takes regular feedback from her seniors.
D. For personal interest and to improve his capabilities, Kulmeet practices the task regularly.

28. During the Covid-19 Pandemic has negatively affected the performance of students in examination. Which of the following relationship is highlighted in this statement?
A. Competition and Cognition
B. Cognition and Emotions
C. Heredity and Performance
D. Heredity and Environment

29. A child is facing regular difficulty in writing. She also experiences a challenge in formation of alphabets and spacing of words. These characteristics hints towards which of the following learning disability?

A. Dyslexia
B. Dysgraphia
C. Dyscalculia
D. Attention Deficit Hyperactivity Disorder

30. Children often form alternative conceptions and misconceptions about various concepts. Which of the following statement is NOT correct in this context?
A. Alternative conceptions and misconceptions formed by students should be highly discouraged by the teacher.
B. Formation of alternative conceptions and misconceptions is very natural among children as well as adults.
C. A teacher should definitely attend to these alternative conceptions and misconceptions as they are significant in process of teaching-learning.
D. Alternative conceptions and misconceptions are not always baseless rather these represent children's intuitive ideas about world around them.

31. A student of your class faces problems in expressing views and often switches between school mainstream language and the dialect spoken in his/her hometown. As a teacher, you must:
A. emphasize the purity of language usage.
B. recommend the child to a special school.
C. introduce similar word-meanings in the target language gradually.
D. rebuke student for mixing languages.

32. A teacher encourages her students to identify and recognise meaningful words such as 'pen', 'tiger', 'water', to initiate reading. Which principle of learning is this pedagogy situated in?
A. Operant conditioning
B. Classical conditioning
C. Reductionism
D. Constructivism

33. A student in your class feels anxious and concerned about the competitive environment. As a teacher you feel:
(*a*) High academic anxiety keeps people motivated and responsible and helps in having a more sustainable and prosperous life.
(*b*) Increased apprehension and uneasiness of the students can also be accompanied by emotional fear which might interfere with students' concentration power and memory.
A. (*a*) is incorrect, but (*b*) is correct
B. Both (*a*) & (*b*) are incorrect
C. (*a*) is correct, but (*b*) is incorrect
D. Both (*a*) & (*b*) are correct

34. A student feels that she would not be able to achieve success on a test and will never be able to improve her performance. Such beliefs about ability:
A. increases the students' motivation to learn.
B. does not affect the students' motivation in any manner.
C. makes the student feel a sense of giving up on the task and experiencing 'learned helplessness'.
D. helps the student relax.

35. Sachin comes from a socio economically disadvantaged background. Mrs. Khurana his class teacher should help Sachin and create a classroom background/environment which:
A. Values his cultural and social background.
B. Discourages the use of his vernacular language and focuses on English.
C. Categorizes him into a separate group.
D. Teaches him etiquettes and manners which she feels he lacks.

36. As an infant Raghav was deprived of personal affection. In his late childhood he found considerate teachers.Yet, he has issues trusting people and lacks courage to take risks. Which issue of development aptly describes Raghav's case?
A. Continuity-discontinuity issue
B. Early-later experiences issue
C. Nature-nurture issue
D. Uniformity-individuality issue

37. At which stage of moral reasoning in Lawrence Kohlberg's theory do children believe that rules must be enforced in the same manner for everyone and each individual must obey them as his personal duty?
A. Good boy-good girl orientation
B. Punishment and obedience orientation
C. Instrumental purpose orientation
D. Social-order maintaining orientation

38. Pointing out to the level of the lemonade in her taller but thinner glass Sara teases her sister that their father has given her more lemonade. Her sister does not respond since she had seen their father pour the lemonade from her glass to Sara's and knew that both glasses contained equal amount of lemonade. Given this context, Sara exhibits:
A. Centration B. Animation
C. Seriation D. Class inclusion

39. Rashi tried a new method to assess children's understanding of concepts. She asked them to frame as many questions as possible for the given answer. Her approach to teaching-learning is:
A. Child-centred
B. Textbook-centred
C. Didactic
D. Memorisation focussed

40. Anuj teaches EVS to class III and always does 'Brainstorming' immediately after introducing any topic to his students. Which of the following would this strategy promote?
(*i*) rote learning
(*ii*) perspective-taking
(*iii*) critical thinking
(*iv*) inquiry
A. (*i*), (*iv*) B. (*i*), (*iii*), (*iv*)
C. (*ii*), (*iii*) D. (*ii*), (*iii*), (*iv*)

41. In class III chapter 'Flying High' while discussing the topic birds, a teacher Tina asks students to observe bird and their characteristics in their surroundings. The purpose of this activity is to:
A. Develop information base on birds among students
B. Develop knowledge base about birds among students
C. Develop interest of students in birds
D. Develop scientific understanding of birds by students

42. Which principle of development states that motor development proceeds from the centre of the body towards the extremities?
A. Cephalocandal B. Proximodistal
C. Cerebral D. Peripheral

43. Rhea, a 4 year old girl got scolded by her parents when she refused to eat her vegetables. During make-believe play, Rhea repeats this behaviour. Her behaviour depicts:
A. Primary socialization
B. Secondary socialization
C. Maturation
D. Unfolding of genetic programming

44. Anita took Rashmi's pen and in retaliation Rashmi ate Anita's lunch. Pooja was observing all this but did not report these incidents to the teacher as it involved 'equal exchanges'. At which stage of Moral development is Pooja according to Lawrence Kohlberg?
A. The good boy-good girl orientation
B. The social-order maintaining orientation
C. The Punishment and Obedience orientation
D. The instrumental purpose orientation

45. Which of the following is a potential risk factor involved with learning and development of children from the marginalized groups?
A. Teacher's negative beliefs about their abilities and having very low expectations.
B. Representation of marginalized groups as central characters in stories that are included in textbooks.
C. Emphasis on connection between local knowledge with school knowledge wherever possible.
D. Heterogeneous grouping in classrooms.

46. What pedagogical strategies should schools adapt to address individual differences among students?
A. Follow uniform curriculum and assessment for all students.

B. Categorize children based on their cognitive abilities and teach them in separate sections.

C. Cater to the individual needs of children by being flexible.

D. Ensure that all individual differences among the children are removed.

47. As an elementary school teacher, which of the following assessment strategy will you use in the classroom to assist children with learning disability?

A. Construct tests that require maximum writing.

B. Keep handwriting as a creation for evaluating assignments.

C. Avoid spelling as a criterion for evaluating assignments.

D. Decrease the time allowed for writing.

48. Meera practices guitar after school as she loves the activity and finds it very satisfying. She illustrated ________.

A. extrinsic motivation

B. intrinsic motivation

C. deficiency need

D. physiological need

49. A 5 year old child is shown 16 flowers, 4 of which are red and 12 are blue. When a 5 year old child is asked if there are more blue flowers or red flowers, the child is likely to respond that there are more blue flowers. According to Jean Piaget's theory, the reason for this is that the child is yet to master in:

A. seriation.

B. hierarchical classification.

C. transitive inference.

D. propositional thought.

50. A teacher often encourages her students to describe the process which they used in solving a mathematical problem. In context of process of learning, this strategy:

A. is meaningless.

B. should be used rarely.

C. can disrupt pace of learning.

D. helps in development skills.

51. Students have just learnt how equality and justice are inseparable, and are asked to list examples of this in India. The options show the responses of four students.

Which of these students shows the conceptual understanding?

A. Minimum wage for factory workers.

B. Reservations in government offices for women.

C. Mid-day meal program in government schools

D. Tax exemptions for charitable organizations

52. In a classroom students are working in small groups on a task and teacher facilitates each group. Which approach is being followed in the classroom?

A. Behaviouristic

B. Constructivistic

C. Psychoanalytic

D. Expository

53. Which of the following principle of development proposes that children gain muscular control of arms relatively earlier than that of fingers?

A. Proximodistal Principle

B. Cephalocandal Principle

C. Independence of Systems Principle

D. Hierarchical Integration Principle

54. A child made a mental note that all creatures that have wings and can fly are called birds. Later, she saw a bat in a picture book and identifies it as a bird instead of mammal. The process of knowledge construction described here is:

A. Assimilation

B. Accommodation

C. Seriation

D. Conservation

55. Fatima reasons– "You should be honest because then your parents would be proud of you". In which stage of Lawrence Kohlberg's theory of moral reasoning does Fatima come under?

A. Social contract orientation

B. Law and order orientation

C. Good boy-good girl orientation

D. Punishment-obedience orientation

56. Rajan appears to be lost in his world as he avoids eye contact with others and plays alone with a feather throughout the day. Rajan's behaviour is indicating towards which of the following disorder?

A. Muscular dystrophy
B. Autism Spectrum Disorder
C. Dyscalculia
D. Dysphoria

57. A teacher uses a text and some pictures of fruits and vegetables to facilitate discussion with her students. The students link these details with previous knowledge and learn the concepts of nutrition. This approach is based on:

A. Classical conditioning of learning
B. Theory of reinforcement
C. Operant conditioning of learning
D. Construction of knowledge

58. Srija strongly believes that she will fail in the upcoming Math test, just like the previous time and has stopped exerting effort in the subject. Also, her teacher holds low expectation of her. Srija seems to be:

A. lazy and someone who makes excuses
B. experiencing learned helplessness
C. prone to escapism
D. a rational decision maker

59. In Abeer's class, children participate in a wide range of challenging activities along with teacher and peers to jointly construct knowledge. This type of classroom will be called:

A. Social constructivist
B. Individual constructivist
C. Traditional classroom
D. Multilingual classroom

60. A child can throw the ball before holding a pencil and write. Which principle of development this situation illustrates?

A. Cephalo caudal principle
B. Proximo-Distal principle
C. Uniformity of pattern
D. Principle of integration

61. Two glasses hold the same amount of water yet Anu thinks that the taller glass holds more water than the 'wider but shorter' glass. According to Jean Piaget, this reasoning of Anu is due to:

A. Centration B. Seriation
C. Conservation D. Maturation

62. Eight year old Rohit reasons stealing is wrong because stealing behaviour can lead to his rejection by others. As per Lawrence Kohlberg's theory of moral development, which stage is he displaying?

A. 'Good boy-good girl' orientation
B. Punishment and disobedience orientation
C. Social order orientation
D. Universal ethical principles

63. During the lockdown due to COVID-19 pandemic, Rohini likes to read the story books her elder sister had without any promting from anybody. Rohini is a:

A. Competitive learner
B. Intrinsically motivated learner
C. Performance-oriented learner
D. Extrinsically motivated learner

64. A primary teacher asks her students to write all the information at least five times in their notebook. The technique would be:

A. highly effective since rehearsal and repetition helps significantly in meaningful learning of content.
B. effective since repetition of any information less than five times leads to immediate forgetting.
C. ineffective since more rehearsal is not a suitable technique for meaningful learning.
D. ineffective since rehearsal is a complex method of meaningful learning.

65. Sana learnt to hold a glass and a bottle before she could hold a pen or button her shirt. This example indicates that:

A. Development is unidimensional.
B. Direction of development is cephalo-caudal.
C. Direction of development is proximo-distal.
D. Direction follows a random pattern.

66. 9 year old Leela classifies a collection of buttons according to their size. She then combines all groups of buttons and re-distributes them on the basis of holes on them. According to Jean Piaget's theory of cognitive development, Leela is in ______ stage of development.

A. Pre-operational
B. Formal-operational
C. Concrete-operational
D. Sensori-motor

67. When a teacher adjusts the support offered to a child to fit the child's current level of performance and to help her reach her zone of proximal development, the teacher is:

A. using co-operative learning.
B. demonstrating inter-subjectivity.
C. scaffolding the child.
D. inducing cognitive conflict in the child.

68. Mohan provides students with containers of different capacities to help them learn the concept of volume. Farah ask students to brainstorm on possibilities of making waste disposal a mechanical task so that people do not have to do these menial task.

Both of the teachers are employing ______ in their classroom.

A. Behaviourism
B. Constructivism
C. Direct instruction
D. Operant conditioning

69. Anita, a teacher of 4th grade is facing a situation in her class where several students are reporting boredom in ongoing theme. In this scenario, she should:

A. Ignore these students and continue teaching the same content.
B. Punish these students and report this to their parents.
C. Reflect on the content of lesson and method of teaching.
D. Assume that these students are not capable of learning.

70. What should a teacher tell her students to encourage them to be intrinsically motivated for tasks?

A. The students who finishes first will get 5 stars.
B. Let me see who finishes first, who is the smartest.
C. Working on this is so interesting. Let's see what all we can learn in this activity.
D. Those who do not finish quickly will not go out and play the games period.

71. Rashmi uses a variety of tasks to cater to the different learning potential of learners in her class and often makes groups to facilitate peer learning. Which of the following theory supports her actions?

A. Sigmund Freud's psycho-sexual theory
B. Lev Vygotsky's socio-cultural theory
C. Lawrence Kohlberg's moral development theory
D. B.F. Skinner's behaviouristic theory

72. Dolls and pink dresses are usually associated with girls while cars and blue dresses are usually associated with boys. This is a demonstration of:

A. gender constancy
B. gender empowerment
C. gender diversity
D. gender stereotyping

73. Ramneek has a student with visual impairment in her class. In this context, what instructional adaptations should she make in an inclusive classroom?

A. Using a variety of visual presentations
B. Providing lot of print books
C. Making use of tactile materials such as three dimensional maps and charts
D. Giving lot of small print worksheets

74. Anupama, a science teacher, often makes linkages in her classrooms with the concepts students are studying in Mathematics. This kind of pedagogy:

A. would help in transfer of learning and promote inter-disciplinarity.
B. would hinder in acquisition of knowledge.
C. would hinder learning as it would increase the students burden.
D. would promote misconceptions amongst children.

75. Meena has begun to use 'words' and started understanding that words represent objects. She is also beginning to reason logically though she cannot perform conservation. According to Jean Piaget, which stage of cognitive development is Meena in?

A. Pre-operational
B. Formal operational
C. Sensori-motor
D. Concrete operational

76. Paro helps her father in his carpentry shop where she successfully measures wooden blocks using techniques taught by her father. She is recently admitted to a public school under EWS scheme, where she is unable to cope up with the academic demands especially in this situation, the teacher should:

A. tell Paro that she does not have the ability to study.
B. give tests and encourage repeated drill and practice.
C. contextualize the curriculum and study material for Paro integrating her mathematical experiences gained outside the school.
D. ask Paro to keep her knowledge gained at home separate from knowledge gained in school.

77. Choose the example that illustrates intrinsic motivation.

A. Roshni is working hard to score well in exams as her parents have promised her a watch on getting above 90%.
B. Rumi completing her homework so that his parents let him watch T.V.
C. Rama reading more books so that her name is first on the 'reading stars' to win her teacher's appreciation.
D. Ravi exploring various resources for his project because he loves learning new things.

78. Rachita a Mathematics teacher, tries to analyse the errors made by her students in identifying the correct operation to be applied for statement sum. She does this to:

A. segregate students who make more errors in comparison to others.
B. give more questions to them as a punishment.
C. correct the errors by giving them more practice.
D. understand the errors since they are a window to children's thinking.

79. A child is shown a 3-D model of three mountains. Another person is looking at the model from a different position. The child is asked to depict the other person's view of the model but is unable to do so correctly. According to Jean Piaget, this is illustrative of:

A. egocentricism
B. animism
C. object performance
D. hypothetical thinking

80. Responding to Heinz Dilemma Roohi says, 'stealing the drug is wrong under any circumstance because it is wrong to steal. According to Lawrence Kohlberg's Theory of Moral Development, Roohi is at:

A. Pre-conventional level; Punishment Obedience Orientation
B. Pre-conventional level; Personal-reward Orientation
C. Conventional level; Law and Order Orientation
D. Post conventional level; Social-contract Orientation

81. Salma, a 5-years-old girl, started playing the musical instrument Guitar without any outside instruction when she was 3 years old. This talent would characterizes her as a:

A. slow learner
B. child with low IQ
C. gifted
D. Autistic

82. Hardik has low vision. The teacher has not been informed of his condition. Which of the following actions in class can indicate the teacher that he has low vision?

A. Squinting of eyes while reading
B. Standing far away from the blackboard to read it clearly

C. Completing worksheets with fine print quickly

D. Reading physical maps which have minute details

83. A metaphor of 'Jug and the mug' is often used to depict how traditional education views teacher as a big jug pouring knowledge into the mind of a student depicted by a smaller mug. This kind of understanding is problematic because:

A. Students carry valuable experiences with them and learning is constructed with their active participation with teacher & peers.

B. Students are naïve and they can't learn anything without the teacher.

C. There is no need of any content or teacher in the process of learning.

D. Learning happens best if children listen to the teacher passively.

84. Which of the following can enhance critical thinking in middle school students?

A. Asking students to read the textbook on their own and avoid discussion with peers.

B. Asking students to discuss topics in groups and come up with questions.

C. Presentation by the teacher using lecture method.

D. Giving students homework to write the answers to recall the questions given at the end of the textbook.

85. A teacher along with her class VII students is trying to understand how plants grow. They planted a number of tomato seeds at various depths and at various places in their school garden and took care of them. After some time, they observed that a few seeds began to develop as plants while others died out. The teacher asked the students to use their observations and think of the factors to due to which some seeds could not develop. Which process skill is likely to be developed through this exercise?

A. Hypothesising B. Predicting
C. Classifying D. Measuring

86. Read the following paragraph:

In 1822, a man named Alexis St. Martin was badly hit by a shot-gun. The bullet had seriously damaged the chest wall and made a hole in his stomach. He was brought to an American army doctor William Beaumont who saved the patient but could not close the hole properly and left it bandaged. He used this as opportunity to see the inside of the stomach to some gain in understanding about the process of digestion?

Which of the following understanding (s) about development of scientific knowledge is conveyed in this paragraph:

(*a*) Science proceeds systematically according to pre-determined steps.

(*b*) Science requires careful observation and creative response to situations.

A. only (*a*) B. only (*b*)
C. (*a*) & (*b*) D. Neither (*a*) nor (*b*)

87. During discussion on a scientific concept, a teacher found that a few students have certain misconceptions related to that concept. What should the teacher do in such a scenario?

A. Let students talk about the misconceptions and provide opportunities for discovering scientific logic.

B. Outrightly reject those misconceptions and tell them the standard information on that concept.

C. Refer these children to a special educator and recommend assessment for a learning disability.

D. Teacher should not respond on those misconceptions and move ahead towards next concept.

88. A teacher finds that her class VIII students have difficulty in comprehending that non-living objects like a table can exert a force on other objects. She realises that this would cause a difficulty for them in understanding the concept of normal reaction (force). Engaging her students in which of the following activities would be helpful in making them understanding this concept?

A. Playing tug of war
B. Pressing on a spring kept on ground
C. Weighing different objects on a pan balance
D. Pulling a wheeled chair towards oneself.

89. Anita watches a youtube video to understand the process of baking a cake and then bakes a cake following exact steps. Which kind of learning is taking place in this case?

A. Classical conditioning
B. Observational learning
C. Insightful learning
D. Operant conditioning

90. In a school based on progressive principles, school holidays coincide with tribal festivals and the weekly holiday is in tune with the local weekly bazaar. This illustrates ....

A. regressive school practices
B. flexibility of school organization
C. cultural discontinuity between school and home
D. ignorance towards children's education

91. A group of children enact scenes from a popular dance reality show in their play. As a judge, 8 years old Sana gives comments on other children's dances. This situation highlights the important role of .... in the socialization of children.

A. religious institutions
B. family
C. media
D. school

92. Which of the following illustrates a constructivist learning approach in a progressive classroom?

A. Multiple interpretations
B. Rote memorization and verbatim recall
C. Rewards and punishment
D. Repeated drill and practice

93. A student is unable to pay attention in class, becomes distracted easily, can't sit in the assigned seat, fidgets and loses things. These characteristics are indicative of:

A. Attention Deficit Hyperactivity disorder
B. Visual impairment
C. Dyslexia
D. Dysgraphia

94. During the classroom discussion on concept of water, a child responded, "water is not colourless". On enquiring by the teacher, child gave reference of dirty water which he had seen in a drain near his home. A teacher respond to this misconception of the child by:

A. completely discarding this answer.
B. asserting that his logic is baseless.
C. accept the response and explain the logic of calling the water colourless.
D. emphasing on only one correct answer i.e. water is colourless.

95. Seeing that their son Ravi was interested in reading and could read at the age of 3, his parents got him a lot of books. Due to his parents' encouragement Ravi's reading was very advanced as per his age.

Which principle of development can be inferred from the above example?

A. Development does not follow a predictable path.
B. Development is proximodistal.
C. Development is cephalocaudal
D. Development is a result of interaction between heredity and environment.

96. The teacher was dealing with the theme 'population' in her class. She asked students to calculate increase in population using births, deaths, in migration and out migration in a particular region between two points of time. She is giving a task on which of the following concepts?

A. Density of the population.
B. Distribution of the population.
C. Natural growth of population.
D. Rate of Migration in population.

97. A teacher wishes to discuss that the Indian Constitution recognises every person as equal.

Which of the following examples will most likely find a place in the discussion?

A. People standing in a line to cast their vote in an assembly election.

B. A stadium full of people cheering the national cricket team.

C. People standing in a line outside the government hospital.

D. People standing in a line to buy movie tickets.

98. Read the given scenarios carefully. Which among the following provides an opportunity to a teacher to plan a visit to Delhi monuments with her students?

(*a*) Her students askes her what is superstructure, while discussing architecture of Sultanate Era.

(*b*) They were fascinated by the Structure of the "Bangla dome".

(*c*) Her students wanted to paint the pillars of Pietra dura for their upcoming art exhibition.

A. (*a*), (*b*) and (*c*) B. (*a*) and (*b*)

C. (*a*) and (*c*) D. (*b*) and (*c*)

99. When teacher is providing students items like research articles, books, photographs, audio and video recordings, materials and websites etc; for a upper primary school, the objective would be towards ______.

A. facilitating the school projects scientifically.

B. providing background information as a key component of enquiry process.

C. participate on National level seminars, workshops, and conferences.

D. teaching review of literature.

100. A language teacher along with her social science colleague gives an assignment on 'Cultural diversity of India'. Learners are to consult social science books and other books and documents relating to History, Geography, Culture and Politics to write a report and develop a poster on the theme. What would this process of language learning called?

A. Language in Social Science

B. Social Science assignment

C. Language Across the Curriculum

D. Language writing development

101. A learner is able to read a text with limited understanding. She is able to read the text very well and do the comprehension tasks with the support of her elder brother. This practice of learning-teaching is called ....

A. Coaching B. Tutoring

C. Scaffolding D. Input hypothesis

102. Which of the following questions provide opportunities to promote critical thinking skills?

(*a*) What role does the Constitution play in people's struggle for equality?

(*b*) What are the different markets through which cotton travels to become a shirt?

(*c*) Who benefits maximum in the production processes of making a shirt?

(*d*) What is the difference between evergreen forests and deciduous forests?

Choose the correct option.

A. (*a*), (*b*) and (*c*) only

B. (*a*), (*b*), (*c*) and (*d*)

C. (*a*) and (*b*) only

D. (*a*) and (*c*) only

103. Which among the following would one use as a primary source for studying how colonial rule impacted the lives of tribal groups in the Indian sub-continent?

A. A documentary made on the life of Birsa Munda

B. A historical fiction written by writer Amitav Ghosh

C. A chapter in a history textbook dedicated to the situation of tribes under colonial rule

D. Songs that were sung by tribes like the Baigas during that period, and documented by anthropologist Verrier Elwin

104. Which of the following questions assesses the 'application' skill of learners?

(*a*) Which gas creates green house effect in the atmosphere?
(*b*) What is air pressure?
(*c*) Name three types of rainfall.
(*d*) What is literacy? List five states which have literacy levels beyond the national level.
(*e*) Private health facilities can mean many things. Explain with the help of some examples from your area.

Choose the correct option.

A. (*a*), (*b*), (*c*) and (*d*) B. (*a*), (*b*) and (*c*)
C. (*d*) and (*e*) D. (*a*) and (*e*)

105. A geography teacher wants to teach about natural vegetation. Which of the following could she plan for an appropriate classroom based session on the topic?

(*a*) Bringing pictures of various types of trees
(*b*) Asking students to bring few objects made up of softwood
(*c*) Bringing charts comparing the characteristics of various forests and vegetation available in them.
(*d*) Discussing how climate affects the nature of vegetation.

Choose the appropriate option

A. Only (*a*), (*b*) and (*c*)
B. Only (*a*), (*c*) and (*d*)
C. Only (*b*), (*c*) and (*d*)
D. Only (*a*), (*b*), (*c*) and (*d*)

106. Mr. D'Souza wants his students to empirically find out that 'price levels cannot be very different in a competitive market'.

Which of the following would be an appropriate vacation project for this purpose?

A. Collect from news websites the price of 1 litre of petrol over the years and draw a graph.
B. Group different brands of smartphones based on price and derive which brands are competing against each other.
C. Go to a weekly vegetable market and ask different vendors the price of cabbage.
D. Go to a weekly shoe market and note down prices of a few types of shoes at each shop.

107. You are showing your students a documentary and after half of it is over, you come across a scene that paints a particular community in a negative light.

What would be the most responsible way of dealing with this situation?

A. Ignore the scene and move on with the documentary to avoid wasting time on the unnecessary point.
B. Tell students that you were not aware of this scene and they should only use their textbook for learning various topics.
C. Analyse the scene along with students, where they can contest the assumptions and generalizations made about the community.
D. Continue with the documentary but if there are any students from the community mentioned, apologise to them for the negative portrayal.

108. Here is what a teacher does in her classroom. She asks her learners to find ways and means in which water is available and used in their villages and towns. Later she asks them write a report of the same. She also asks them to read stories on water in their languages. Learners present the report and discuss with peers in their classroom. What is this activity known as?

A. Assignment
B. Environmental Science activity
C. Project work
D. Learning activity

109. A teacher wants her students to inquire about development of industries in her social science classroom. Which of the following activities have more chances to be included in her teaching?

(*a*) Asking students to talk to two workers to find out if they are receiving the minimum wages laid down by law.

(*b*) Asking students to find out the changes in land use pattern in their village/city/town.
(*c*) Asking students to perform a role play on issues of social justice taking examples from their experiences.
(*d*) Asking students to write about whether the victims of the Bhopal gas tragedy got justice or not.

Choose the appropriate option.

A. Only (*a*), (*b*) and (*c*)
B. Only (*b*), (*c*) and (*d*)
C. Only (*a*), (*c*) and (*d*)
D. Only (*a*), (*b*) and (*d*)

110. You are showing a documentary to your students where a government school teacher is wearing some religious symbols and the headmaster says, "we should not wear religious symbols inside the school".

A student asked if this is an act of secularism.

What would be a technically correct answer?

A. The headmaster's statement shows religious bias which is against the principles of secularism and right to freedom of religion.
B. The headmaster's statement is not an example of secularism. However, it is aligned with the principles of the Indian Constitution where schools are supposed to not enforce any religion.
C. The headmaster's statement shows secularism and thus it follows the principles of the Indian Constitution.
D. The headmaster's statement shows secularism. However, it is against the interpretation of secularism in the Indian Constitution, which provides the right to freedom of religion.

111. Mr. Justin wanted to test his students' understanding of the 'nature of weekly markets from a seller's point of view'.

Which of the following questions are suited to test this?

(*i*) Can a weekly market address all the needs of a family? Why or why not?
(*ii*) Compare and contrast the characteristics of a weekly market and a permanent shop.
(*iii*) Are you likely to find a well-known brand as part of a weekly market? Why or why not?
(*iv*) Can any seller increase their price a lot compared to other sellers in a weekly market? Why or why not?

A. (*i*), (*ii*), (*iii*) B. (*i*), (*iii*), (*iv*)
C. (*ii*), (*iii*), (*iv*) D. (*i*), (*ii*), (*iv*)

112. Learning Objective: Students will show their understanding of the role of media in a democracy. Which of the following question tests for this learning objective?

A. Why are both government controlled media and private media important?
B. Is the media free from external control?
C. Why should the media write a balanced report of events?
D. Describe instances when the government had censored the media.

113. A newspaper article stated that an employer asked candidates which state they belonged to and accordingly decided whether to proceed with the interview or not.

The above example is in violation of which of the following rights?

A. Right against exploitation
B. Right to employment
C. Right to equality
D. Affirmative action for locals

114. A teacher uses a research article with rich data, as a resource to teach students about India's relations with other nations. However, during the class, the teacher and students come across a paragraph that paints a neighbouring country in a strongly negative light.

Which of the following is the most responsible approach for the Social Science teacher?

A. Tell students that you were not aware of these paragraphs and they should only use their textbook for learning various topics.

B. Switch to another, less useful, source instead, to continue the class. Discussing the controversy would only waste time.
C. Analyse the paragraph along with students, where they can discuss and debate the assumptions made or data given about the country.
D. Continue reading the article as-is, since the students in your class are all from India and it should not hurt their sentiments.

115. Mr. Daljeet asked his students to research and write a short note on "the most important reason which led to the launch of the Civil Disobedience movement in India". He then wants to use the submitted assignments for "assessment as learning".

Which of the following is the relevant question for him to ask students?

A. Who were the notable personalities leading the civil disobedience movement?
B. Describe the academic resources that you used to conduct the research for your assignment
C. What was your thought process when you decided which reason to write about?
D. Pair up with a friend and check if you both have chosen the same reason to be the most important.

ANSWERS

1. (B)	**2. (D)**	**3. (A)**	**61. (A)**	**62. (A)**	**63. (B)**
4. (D)	**5. (A)**	**6. (C)**	**64. (C)**	**65. (C)**	**66. (C)**
7. (A)	**8. (A)**	**9. (C)**	**67. (C)**	**68. (B)**	**69. (C)**
10. (B)	**11. (A)**	**12. (B)**	**70. (C)**	**71. (B)**	**72. (D)**
13. (B)	**14. (C)**	**15. (D)**	**73. (C)**	**74. (A)**	**75. (A)**
16. (D)	**17. (B)**	**18. (C)**	**76. (C)**	**77. (D)**	**78. (D)**
19. (C)	**20. (C)**	**21. (B)**	**79. (A)**	**80. (C)**	**81. (C)**
22. (C)	**23. (A)**	**24. (C)**	**82. (A)**	**83. (A)**	**84. (B)**
25. (C)	**26. (B)**	**27. (B)**	**85. (A)**	**86. (B)**	**87. (A)**
28. (B)	**29. (D)**	**30. (A)**	**88. (C)**	**89. (B)**	**90. (B)**
31. (C)	**32. (D)**	**33. (A)**	**91. (C)**	**92. (A)**	**93. (A)**
34. (C)	**35. (A)**	**36. (B)**	**94. (C)**	**95. (D)**	**96. (C)**
37. (D)	**38. (A)**	**39. (A)**	**97. (A)**	**98. (A)**	**99. (B)**
40. (D)	**41. (C)**	**42. (B)**	**100. (C)**	**101. (C)**	**102. (D)**
43. (A)	**44. (D)**	**45. (A)**	**103. (D)**	**104. (A)**	**105. (D)**
46. (C)	**47. (C)**	**48. (B)**	**106. (C)**	**107. (C)**	**108. (C)**
49. (B)	**50. (D)**	**51. (B)**	**109. (D)**	**110. (D)**	**111. (C)**
52. (B)	**53. (A)**	**54. (A)**	**112. (C)**	**113. (C)**	**114. (C)**
55. (C)	**56. (B)**	**57. (D)**	**115. (C)**		
58. (B)	**59. (A)**	**60. (B)**			

❑❑❑

New Education Policy (NEP)–2020

NEP 2020 is the first education policy of the 21st century and replaces the thirty-four year old National Policy on Education (NPE), 1986. Built on the foundational pillars of Access, Equity, Quality, Affordability and Accountability, this policy is aligned to the 2030 Agenda for Sustainable Development and aims to transform India into a vibrant knowledge society and global knowledge superpower by making both school and college education more holistic, flexible, multidisciplinary, suited to 21st century needs and aimed at bringing out the unique capabilities of each student.

The policy has been formulated after a very detailed consultative process, unprecedented in depth and scale. Consultation involved over 2 lakh suggestions from 2.5 lakhs Gram Panchayats, 6600 Blocks, 6000 ULBs, 676 Districts. The MHRD had initiated a collaborative, inclusive, and highly participatory consultation process from January 2015. In May 2016, '*Committee for Evolution of the New Education Policy*' under the Chairmanship of Late Shri T.S.R. Subramanian, Former Cabinet Secretary, submitted its report. Based on this, the Ministry prepared '*Some Inputs for the Draft National Education Policy, 2016*'. In June 2017 a '*Committee for the Draft National Education Policy*' was constituted under the Chairmanship of eminent scientist **Padma Vibhushan, Dr. K. Kasturirangan**, which submitted the Draft National Education Policy, 2019 to the Hon'ble Human Resource Development Minister on 31st May, 2019.

SCHOOL EDUCATION

Ensure Universal Access at All Levels of schooling from pre-primary school to Grade 12

NEP 2020 aims to achieve 100% Gross Enrollment Ratio in school education by 2030. The initiatives that will be undertaken for this include provision of effective and sufficient infrastructure, alternative and innovative education centres to ensure that children who are dropping out of school are brought back into mainstream education, universal participation in school by carefully tracking students, as well as their learning levels. Counsellors or well-trained social workers connected to schools/school complexes and teachers will continuously work with students and their parents to ensure that all school-age children are attending and learning in school.

Early Childhood Care Education

NEP 2020 emphasises on the criticality of the early years to ensure quality early childhood care and education for all children between 3-6 years by 2025. The children in the ages of 3-5 will be catered to by the current system of anganwadis and pre-schools, and age 5-6 will be included with the schooling system in a seamless integrated manner, with a play-way based curriculum to be prepared by the NCERT. A National Curricular and Pedagogical Framework for Early Childhood Care and Education (NCPFECCE) for children up to the age of 8 will be developed by NCERT. The planning and implementation of early childhood education will be carried out jointly by the Ministries of HRD, Women and Child Development (WCD), Health and Family Welfare (HFW), and Tribal Affairs.

New Curricular and Pedagogical Structure

With emphasis on Early Childhood Care and Education, the 10+2 structure of school curricula is to be replaced by a 5+3+3+4 curricular structure corresponding to ages 3-8, 8-11, 11-14, and 14-18 years respectively. This will bring the hitherto uncovered age group of 3-6 years under school curriculum, which has been recognized globally as the crucial stage for development of mental faculties of a child. The new system will have 12 years of schooling with three years of Anganwadi/pre schooling. The new system will cover four stages:

Foundational Stage (in two parts, that is, 3 years of Anganwadi/pre-school + 2 years in primary school in Grades 1-2; both together covering ages 3-8),

Preparatory Stage (Grades 3-5, covering ages 8-11), **Middle Stage** (Grades 6-8, covering ages 11-14), and **Secondary Stage** (Grades 9-12 in two phases, *i.e.,* 9 and 10 in the first and 11 and 12 in the second, covering ages 14-18).

The curricula will aim for **holistic development of learners,** equipping them with the key 21st century skills, reduction in curricular content to enhance essential learning and critical thinking and greater focus on **experiential learning**. Students will have increased flexibility and choice of subjects so that they choose their own paths according to their talents and interests. There will be **no rigid separations between arts and sciences, between curricular and extra-curricular activities, between vocational and academic streams**. The objective is to give equal emphasis on all subjects-science, social sciences, art, languages, sports, mathematics - with integration of vocational and academic streams in school. A new and comprehen-sive **National Curricular Framework for School Education**, NCFSE 2020-21, will be developed by the NCERT.

High-quality textbook materials will be developed by NCERT and SCERTs. States will prepare their own curricula and prepare textbooks incorporating state flavour and material. The availability of textbooks in all regional languages will be a top priority. Reducing the weight of school bags and textbooks will also be ensured by suitable changes in curriculum load.

Attaining Foundational Literacy and Numeracy

A National Mission on Foundational Literacy and Numeracy will be set-up on priority to focus on early language and mathematical skills from Grades 1 to 3 by 2025. Strategies include: developing school readiness through interim 3-month play-based school preparation module for all Grade 1 students; increased focus on reading, writing, speaking, counting, arithmetic, and mathematical thinking; continuous assessment and adaptive testing; national repository of high-quality resources on foundational literacy and numeracy; filling teacher vacancies; peer-tutoring and volunteer activities; setting up school libraries in every village; A National Book Promotion Policy will be formulated, and initiatives to ensure the availability, accessibility, quality, and readership of books across geographies, languages, levels, and genres will be undertaken.

Multilingualism and the Power of Language

NEP 2020 lays great emphasis on promoting multilingualism so that children know and learn about the rich and vast array of languages of their country. The medium of instruction until at least Grade 5, but preferably till Grade 8 and beyond, will be the home language/ mother tongue/local language/regional language. Every student in the country will participate in a fun project/activity on 'The Languages of India', sometime in Grades 6-8, such as, under the *'Ek Bharat Shrestha Bharat'* initiative. Sanskrit will be offered at all levels of school and higher education as an important, enriching option for students, including as an option in the three-language formula. Other classical languages and literatures of India, including Tamil, Telugu, Kannada, Malayalam, Odia, Pali, Persian, and Prakrit, will also be widely available in schools as options for students. Foreign languages, such as Korean, Japanese, Thai, French, German, Spanish, Portuguese, and Russian, will also be offered at the secondary level. Indian Sign Language (ISL) will be standardized across the country, and National and State curriculum materials developed, for use by students with hearing impairment.

Assessment Reforms

There will be a shift from summative assessment to regular and formative assessment, which is more competency-based, promotes learning and development, and tests higher-order skills, such as analysis, critical thinking, and conceptual clarity. Board exams for Grades 10 and 12 will be continued, but be reformed to eliminate the need for taking coaching classes. Board exams will be redesigned to encourage holistic development; and will also be made 'easier', by testing core capacities/ competencies. All students will be allowed to take Board Exams on up to two occasions during any given school year, one main examination and one for improvement, if desired. All students will take school examinations in Grades 3, 5, and 8 which will be conducted by the appropriate authority.

A new **National Assessment Centre, PARAKH (Performance Assessment, Review, and Analysis of Knowledge for Holistic Development)**, will be set up as a standard-setting body for setting norms, standards, and guidelines for student assessment and evaluation for all recognized school boards of India, guiding the State Achievement Survey (SAS) and undertaking the National Achievement Survey (NAS), monitoring achievement of learning outcomes and encouraging and helping school boards to shift their assessment patterns towards meeting the skill requirements of the 21st century.

Equitable and inclusive education

NEP 2020 aims to ensure that no child loses any opportunity to learn and excel because of the circumstances of birth or background. Special emphasis will be given on Socially and Economically Disadvantaged Groups(SEDGs) which include: gender identities (particularly female and transgender individuals), socio-cultural identities (such as Scheduled Castes, Scheduled Tribes, OBCs, and minorities), geographical identities (such as students from villages, small towns, and aspirational districts), disabilities (including learning disabilities), and socio-economic conditions (such as migrant communities, low income households, children in vulnerable situations, victims of or children of victims of trafficking, orphans including child beggars in urban areas, and the urban poor).

A **separate Gender Inclusion fund** will be created as also **Special Education Zones** for disadvantaged regions and groups.

Every State/District will be encouraged to establish **"Bal Bhavans"** as a special daytime boarding school, to participate in art-related, career-related, and playrelated activities. The unutilized capacity of school infrastructure will be used to promote social, intellectual, and volunteer activities for the community and to promote social cohesion during non-teaching / schooling hours and may be used as a **"Samajik Chetna Kendra"**.

Teacher recruitment and career path

Teachers will be recruited through robust, transparent processes. Promotions will be merit-based, and a mechanism for multi-source periodic performance appraisals will be put in place. Progression paths to become educational administrators or teacher educators will be available for the teachers. A common **National Professional Standards for Teachers (NPST)** will be developed by 2022, by the National Council for Teacher Education, in consultation with NCERT, SCERTs, teachers from across levels and regions, expert bodies in vocational education, and higher education institutions etc.

HIGHER EDUCATION

Quality Universities and Colleges

- Higher education plays an extremely important role in promoting human as well as societal wellbeing and in developing India as envisioned in its Constitution - a democratic, just, socially conscious, cultured, and humane nation upholding liberty, equality, fraternity, and justice for all.
- Higher education must form the basis for knowledge creation and innovation thereby contributing to a growing national economy. The purpose of quality higher education is, therefore, more than the creation of greater opportunities for individual employment. It represents the key to more vibrant, socially engaged, cooperative communities and a happier, cohesive, cultured, productive, innovative, progressive, and prosperous nation.

Problems

Some of the major problems currently faced by the higher education system in India include:

(*a*) a severely fragmented higher educational ecosystem;

(*b*) less emphasis on the development of cognitive skills and learning outcomes;

(*c*) a rigid separation of disciplines, with early specialisation and streaming of students into narrow areas of study;

(*d*) limited access particularly in socio-economically disadvantaged areas, with few HEIs that teach in local languages

(*e*) limited teacher and institutional autonomy;

(*f*) inadequate mechanisms for merit-based career management and progression of faculty and institutional leaders;

(*g*) lesser emphasis on research at most universities and colleges, and lack of competitive peer reviewed research funding across disciplines;

(*h*) suboptimal governance and leadership of HEIs;

(*i*) an ineffective regulatory system; and

(*j*) large affiliating universities resulting in low standards of undergraduate education.

Key Changes

The policy's vision includes the following key changes to the current system:

(*a*) moving towards a higher educational system consisting of large, multidisciplinary universities and colleges, with at least one in or near every district, and with more HEIs across India that offer medium of instruction or programmes in local/Indian languages;

(*b*) moving towards a more multidisciplinary undergraduate education;

(*c*) moving towards faculty and institutional autonomy;

(*d*) revamping curriculum, pedagogy, assessment, and student support for enhanced student experiences;

(*e*) reaffirming the integrity of faculty and institutional leadership positions through merit appointments and career progression based on teaching, research, and service;

(*f*) establishment of a National Research Foundation to fund outstanding peer-reviewed research and to actively seed research in universities and colleges;

(*g*) governance of HEIs by high qualified independent boards having academic and administrative autonomy;

(*h*) "light but tight" regulation by a single regulator for higher education;

(*i*) increased access, equity, and inclusion through a range of measures, including greater opportunities for outstanding public education; scholarships by private/ philanthropic universities for disadvantaged and underprivileged students; online education, and Open Distance Learning (ODL); and all infrastructure and learning materials accessible and available to learners with disabilities.

Institutional Restructuring and Consolidation

- The main thrust of this policy regarding higher education is to end the fragmentation of higher education by transforming higher education institutions into large multidisciplinary universities, colleges, and HEI clusters/Knowledge Hubs, each of which will aim to have 3,000 or more students.
- Moving to large multidisciplinary universities and HEI clusters is thus the highest recommendation of this policy regarding the structure of higher education.
- Autonomous degree-granting College (AC) will refer to a large multidisciplinary institution of higher learning that grants undergraduate degrees and is primarily focused on undergraduate teaching though it would not be restricted to that and it need not be restricted to that and it would generally be smaller than a typical university.
- A stage-wise mechanism for granting graded autonomy to colleges, through a transparent system of graded accreditation, will be established.
- With appropriate accreditations, Autonomous degree-granting Colleges could evolve into Research- intensive or Teaching-intensive Universities, if they so aspire.

Over a period of time, it is envisaged that every college would develop into either an Autono-mous degree-granting College, or a constituent college of a university – in the latter case, it would be fully a part of the university.

In addition to **teaching and research**, HEIs will have **other crucial responsibilities**, which they will discharge through appropriate resourcing, incentives, and structures. These include **supporting other HEIs** in their development, **community engagement** and **service**, contribution to various fields of **practice**, **faculty development** for the higher education system, and **support to school education**.

Curricular Structure

Imaginative and flexible curricular structures will enable creative combinations of disciplines for study, and would offer multiple entry and exit points, thus, removing currently prevalent rigid boundaries and creating new possibilities for life-long learning.

Flexibility in curriculum and novel and engaging course options will be on offer to students, in addition to rigorous specialization in a subject or subjects. This will be encouraged by increased faculty and institutional autonomy in setting curricula. Pedagogy will have an increased emphasis on communication, discussion, debate, research, and opportunities for cross-disciplinary and interdisciplinary thinking.

Environment education will include areas such as climate change, pollution, waste management, sanitation, conservation of biological diversity, management of biological resources and biodiversity, forest and wildlife conservation, and sustainable development and living.

(*a*) *Structure of Degree Programme*

The undergraduate degree will be of either **3 or 4-year duration**, with multiple exit options within this period, with appropriate certifications, e.g., a certificate after completing 1 year in a discipline or field including vocational and professional areas, or a diploma after 2 years of study, or a Bachelor's degree after a 3-year programme.

The **4-year multidisciplinary Bachelor's programme**, however, shall be the preferred option since it allows the opportunity to experience the full range of holistic and multidisciplinary education in addition to a focus on the chosen major and minors as per the choices of the student.

An **Academic Bank of Credit (ABC)** shall be established which would digitally store the academic credits earned from various recognized HEIs so that the degrees from an HEI can be awarded taking into account credits earned. The **4-year programme** may also lead to a degree **'with Research'** if the student completes a rigorous research project in their major area(s) of study as specified by the HEI.

HEIs will have the flexibility to offer different designs of Master's programmes:

(*a*) there may be a 2-year programme with the second year devoted entirely to research for those who have completed the 3-year Bachelor's programme;

(*b*) for students completing a 4-year Bachelor's pro-gramme with Research, there could be a 1-year Master's programme; and

(*c*) there may be an integrated 5-year Bachelor's/Master's programme.

(*d*) Undertaking a Ph.D. shall require either a Master's degree or a 4-year Bachelor's degree with Research.

The M.Phil. programme shall be discontinued.

(*b*) *Model Public Universities*

Model public universities for holistic and multidisciplinary education, at par with IITs, IIMs, etc., called MERUs (Multidisciplinary Education and Research Universities) will be set up and will aim to attain the highest global standards in quality education. They will also help set the highest standards for multidisciplinary education across India.

(*c*) *Research and Innovation*

HEIs will focus on research and innovation by setting up start-up incubation centres; technology development centres; centres in frontier areas of research; greater industry-academic linkages; and interdisciplinary research including humanities and social sciences research. HEIs will develop specific hand holding mechanisms and competitions for promoting innovation among student communities.

Academic Plan

- Each institution will integrate its academic plans ranging from curricular improvement to quality of classroom transaction - into its larger Institutional Development Plan (IDP).
- Each institution will be committed to the holistic development of students and create strong internal systems for supporting diverse student cohorts in academic and social domains both inside and outside formal academic interactions in the classroom.
- Over time, such activities could be incorporated into the curriculum once appropriate faculty expertise and campus student demand is developed.

"Faculty will have the capacity and training to be able to approach students not just as teachers, but also as mentors and guides."

Online Education

- ODL and online education provide a natural path to increase access to quality higher education.
- ODL programmes will aim to be equivalent to the highest quality in-class programmes available.

- Norms, standards, and guidelines for systemic development, regulation, and accreditation of ODL will be prepared, and a framework for quality of ODL that will be recommendatory for all HEIs will be developed.

"Finally, all programmes, courses, curricula, and pedagogy across subjects, including those inclass, *online, and in ODL modes as well as student support will aim to achieve global standards of quality.*"

Internationalization

Courses and programmes in subjects, such as Indology, Indian languages, AYUSH systems of medicine, yoga, arts, music, history, culture, and modern India, internationally relevant curricula in the sciences, social sciences, and beyond, meaningful opportunities for social engagement, quality residential facilities and on-campus support, etc. will be fostered to attain the goal of global quality standards, attract greater numbers of international students, and achieve the goal of 'internationalization at home'.

Credits acquired in foreign universities will be permitted, where appropriate as per the requirements of each HEI, to be counted for the award of a degree.

Student Activity and Participation

Students are the prime stakeholders in the **education system** and hence they will be given plenty of opportunities for participation in sports, culture/arts clubs, eco-clubs, activity clubs, community service projects, etc.

In every education institution, there shall be counselling systems for handling stress and emotional adjustments. Furthermore, a systematized arrangement shall be created to provide the requisite support to students from rural backgrounds, including increasing hostel facilities as needed. All HEIs will ensure quality medical facilities for all students in their institutions.

Teacher Education

Teacher education is vital in creating a pool of school teachers that will shape the next generation. Teacher preparation is an activity that requires multidisciplinary perspectives and knowledge, formation of dispositions and values, and development of practice under the best mentors.

By 2030, only educationally sound, multidisciplinary, and **integrated teacher education programmes** shall be in force. All teacher education programmes must be conducted within composite multidisciplinary institutions. Hence, universities and colleges will also run B.Ed. programmes, in collaboration with other departments such as psychology, philosophy, sociology, neuroscience, Indian languages, arts, music, history, literature, physical education, science and mathematics.

All stand-alone TEIs will be required to convert to multidisciplinary institutions by 2030, since they will have to offer the **4-year integrated** teacher preparation programme.

"The 4-year integrated B.Ed. offered by such multidisciplinary HEIs will, by 2030, become the minimal degree qualification for school teachers."

Reimagining Vocational Education

This policy aims to overcome the social status hierarchy associated with vocational education and requires integration of vocational education programmes into mainstream education in all education institutions in a phased manner.

- Beginning with vocational exposure at early ages in middle and secondary school, quality vocational education will be integrated smoothly into higher education.
- It will ensure that every child learns at least one vocation and is exposed to several more.
- This would lead to emphasizing the dignity of labour and importance of various vocations involving/Indian arts and artisanship.

- By 2025, at least 50% of learners through the school and higher education system shall have exposure to vocational education, for which a clear action plan with targets and timelines will be developed.
- The number of students in vocational education will be considered while arriving at the GER targets. The development of vocational capacities will go hand-in-hand with the development of 'academic' or other capacities.
- Higher education institutions will offer vocational education either on their own or in partnership with industry and NGOs.
- The B.Voc. degrees introduced in 2013 will continue to exist, but vocational courses will also be available to students enrolled in all other Bachelor's degree programmes, including the 4-year multi-disciplinary Bachelor 's programmes.
- HEIs will also be allowed to conduct short-term certificate courses in various skills including soft skills.
- The possibility of offering vocational courses through ODL mode will also be explored.
- Vocational education will be integrated into all school and higher education institutions in a phased manner over the next decade.

Transforming The Regulatory System of Higher Education

The regulatory system of higher education will ensure that the distinct functions of regulation, accreditation, funding, and academic standard setting will be performed by distinct, independent, and empowered bodies.

This is considered essential to create checks-and-balances in the system, minimize conflicts of interest, and eliminate concentrations of power.

- The first vertical of Higher Education Commission of India (HECI) will be the National Higher Education Regulatory Council (NHERC).
- It will function as the common, single point regulator for the higher education sector including teacher education and excluding medical and legal education, thus eliminating the duplication and disjunction of regulatory efforts by the multiple regulatory agencies that exist at the current time.

Accreditation

The primary mechanism to enable above mentioned regulation will be accreditation. The second vertical of HECI will, therefore, be a 'meta-accrediting body', called the **National Accreditation Council (NAC)**.

- Accreditation of institutions will be based primarily on basic norms, public self-disclosure, good governance, and outcomes, and it will be carried out by an independent ecosystem of accrediting institutions supervised and overseen by National Accreditation Council (NAC).
- The task to function as a recognized accreditor shall be awarded to an appropriate number of institutions by NAC.
- In the short term, a robust system of graded accreditation shall be established, which will specify phased benchmarks for all HEIs to achieve set levels of quality, self-governance, and autonomy.
- In turn, all HEIs will aim, through their Institutional Development Plans (IDPs), to attain the highest level of accreditation over the next 15 years, and thereby eventually aim to function as **self-governing degree-granting institutions/clusters**.

General Education Council

The fourth vertical of HECI will be the General Education Council (GEC), which will frame expected learning outcomes for higher education programmes, also referred to as 'graduate attributes'.

- A National Higher Education Qualification Framework (NHEQF) will be formulated by the GEC and it shall be in sync with the National Skills Qualifications Framework (NSQF) to ease the integration of vocational education into higher education.
- Higher education qualifications leading to a degree/diploma/certificate shall be described by the NHEQF in terms of such learning outcomes.
- The GEC shall set up facilitative norms for issues, such as credit transfer, equivalence, etc., through the NHEQF.
- The GEC will be mandated to identify specific skills that students must acquire during their academic programmes.

Professional Standard Setting Bodies (PSSBs)

The professional councils, such as the Indian Council for Agricultural Research (ICAR), Veterinary Council of India (VCI), National Council for Teacher Education (NCTE), Council of Architecture (CoA), National Council for Vocational Education and Training (NCVET) etc., will act as Professional Standard Setting Bodies (PSSBs).

They will play a key role in the higher education system and will be invited to be members of the GEC. These bodies, after restructuring as PSSBs, will continue to draw the curricula, lay down academic standards and coordinate between teaching, research and extension of their domain/ discipline, as members of the GEC.

OTHER KEY AREAS OF FOCUS

Professional Education

Professional education becomes an integral part of the overall higher education system.

Agricultural Education

Stand-alone agricultural universities, legal universities, health science universities, technical universities, and stand-alone institutions in other fields, shall aim to become multi-disciplinary institutions offering holistic and multidiscip-linary education.

All institutions offering either professional or general education will aim to organically evolve into institutions/clusters offering both seamlessly, and in an integrated manner by 2030. Agricultural education with allied disciplines will be revived. Both capacity and quality of agriculture and allied disciplines must be improved in order to increase agricultural productivity through better skilled graduates and technicians, innovative research, and market-based extension linked to technologies and practices.

Legal Education

Legal education needs to be competitive globally. The curricula for legal studies must reflect socio-cultural contexts along with, in an evidence based manner, the history of legal thinking, principles of justice, the practice of jurisprudence, and other related content appropriately and adequately. State institutions offering law education must consider offering bilingual education for future lawyers and judges—in English and in the language of the State in which the institution is situated.

Healthcare Education

Healthcare education needs to be re-envisioned so that the duration, structure, and design of the educational programmes need to match the role requirements that graduates will play.

Students will be assessed at regular intervals on well-defined parameters primarily required for working in primary care and in secondary hospitals. Our healthcare education system must be integrative meaning thereby that all students of allopathic medical education must have a basic understanding of Ayurveda, Yoga and Naturopathy, Unani, Siddha, and Homeopathy (AYUSH), and vice versa. There shall also be a much greater emphasis on preventive healthcare and community medicine in all forms of healthcare education.

Technical Education

Technical education includes degree and diploma programmes in, engineering, technology, management, architecture, town planning, pharmacy, hotel management, catering technology etc., which are critical to India's overall development.

Technical education will also aim to be offered within multidisciplinary education institutions and programmes and have a renewed focus on opportunities to engage deeply with other disciplines. India must also take the lead in preparing professionals in cutting-edge areas that are fast gaining prominence, such as Artificial Intelligence (AI), 3-D machining, big data analysis, and machine learning, in addition to genomic studies, biotechnology, nanotechnology, neuro-science, with important applications to health, environment, and sustainable living that will be woven into undergraduate education for enhancing the employability of the youth.

Adult Education and Lifelong Learning

An outstanding adult education curriculum framework will be developed by a new and well-supported constituent body of the NCERT that is dedicated to adult education, so as to develop synergy with and build upon NCERT's existing expertise in establishing outstanding curricula for literacy, numeracy, basic education, vocational skills, and beyond.

The curriculum framework for adult education will include at least five types of programmes, each with clearly defined outcomes:

(*a*) foundational literacy and numeracy;

(*b*) critical life skills (including financial literacy, digital literacy, commercial skills, health care and awareness, child care and education, and family welfare);

(*c*) vocational skills development (with a view towards obtaining local employment);

(*d*) basic education (including preparatory, middle, and secondary stage equivalency); and

(*e*) continuing education (including engaging holistic adult education courses in arts, sciences, technology, culture, sports, and recreation, as well as other topics of interest or use to local learners, such as more advanced material on critical life skills).

The framework would keep in mind that adults in many cases will require rather different teaching-learning methods and materials than those designed for children.

The NETF

An autonomous body, the **National Educational Technology Forum (NETF)**, will be created to provide a platform for the free exchange of ideas on the use of technology to enhance learning, assessment, planning, administration, and so on, both for school and higher education. The aim of the NETF will be to facilitate decision making on the induction, deployment, and use of technology, by providing to the leadership of education institutions, State and Central governments, and other stakeholders, the latest knowledge and research as well as the opportunity to consult and share best practices.

The NETF will have the following functions:

(*a*) provide independent evidence-based advice to Central and State Government agencies on technology-based interventions;

(*b*) build intellectual and institutional capacities in educational technology;

(*c*) envision strategic thrust areas in this domain; and

(*d*) articulate new directions for research and innovation.

The NETF will maintain a regular inflow of authentic data from multiple sources including educational technology innovators and practitioners and will engage with a diverse set of researchers to analyze the data.

Teaching-Learning

A rich variety of **educational software**, for all the above purposes, will be developed and made available for students and teachers at all levels. All such software will be available in all major Indian languages and will be accessible to a wide range of users including students in remote areas and Divyang students.

Teaching-learning **e-content** will continue to be developed by all States in all regional languages, as well as by the NCERT, CIET, CBSE, NIOS, and other bodies/institutions, and will be uploaded onto the DIKSHA platform. This platform may also be utilized for Teacher's Professional Development through e-content.

CIET will be strengthened to promote and expand **DIKSHA** as well as other education technology initiatives. Suitable equipment will be made available to teachers at schools so that teachers can suitably integrate e-contents into teaching-learning practices. Technology-based education platforms, such as **DIKSHA/SWAYAM**, will be better integrated across school and higher education, and will include ratings/reviews by users, so as to enable content developers create user friendly and qualitative content.

Online and Digital Education : Ensuring Equitable Use of Technology

New circumstances and realities require new initiatives. The National Education Policy, 2020 recognizes the importance of leveraging the advantages of technology while acknowledging its potential risks and dangers. The existing digital platforms and ongoing **ICT-based** educational initiatives must be optimized and expanded to meet the current and future challenges in providing quality education for all. Given the emergence of digital technologies and the emerging importance of leveraging technology for teaching-learning at all levels from school to higher education, this Policy recommends the following key initiatives:

(*a*) **Pilot studies for online education:** Appropriate agencies, such as the NETF, CIET, NIOS, IGNOU, IITs, NITs, etc. will be identified to conduct a series of pilot studies, in parallel, to evaluate the benefits of integrating education with online education while mitigating the downsides and also to study related areas, such as, student device addiction, most preferred formats of e-content, etc. The results of these pilot studies will be publicly communicated and used for continuous improvement.

(*b*) **Digital infrastructure:** There is a need to invest in creation of open, interoperable, evolvable, public digital infrastructure in the education sector that can be used by multiple platforms and point solutions, to solve for India's scale, diversity, complexity and device penetration.

(*c*) **Online teaching platform and tools:** Appropriate existing e-learning platforms such as SWAYAM, DIKSHA, will be extended to provide teachers with a structured, user-friendly, rich set of assistive tools for monitoring progress of learners. Tools, such as, two-way video and two-way audio interface for holding online classes are a real necessity.

(*d*) **Content creation, digital repository, and dissemination:** A digital repository of content including creation of coursework, Learning Games & Simulations, Augmented Reality and Virtual Reality will be developed, with a clear public system for ratings by users on effectiveness and quality.

(*e*) **Virtual Labs:** Existing e-learning platforms such as DIKSHA, SWAYAM and

SWAYAMPRABHA will also be leveraged for creating virtual labs so that all students have equal access to quality practical and hands-on experiment-based learning experiences. The possibility of providing adequate access to SEDG students and teachers through suitable digital devices, such as tablets with pre-loaded content, will be considered and developed.

(f) **Training and incentives for teachers:** Teachers will undergo rigorous training in learner-centric pedagogy and on how to become high-quality online content creators themselves using online teaching platforms and tools. There will be emphasis on the teacher's role in facilitating active student engagement with the content and with each other.

(g) **Online assessment and examinations:** Appropriate bodies, such as the proposed National Assessment Centre or PARAKH, School Boards, NTA, and other identified bodies will design and implement assessment frameworks encompassing design of competencies, portfolio, rubrics, standardized assessments, and assessment analytics. Studies will be undertaken to pilot new ways of assessment using education technologies focusing on 21st century skills.

(h) **Blended models of learning:** While promoting digital learning and education, the importance of face-to-face in-person learning is fully recognized. Accordingly, different effective models of blended learning will be identified for appropriate replication for different subjects.

(i) **Laying down standards:** As research on online/digital education emerges, NETF and other appropriate bodies shall set up standards of content, technology, and pedagogy for online/digital teaching-learning. These standards will help to formulate guidelines for e-learning by States, Boards, schools and school complexes, HEIs, etc.

Dedicated Unit For Digital Education

A dedicated unit for the purpose of orchestrating the building of digital infrastructure, digital content and capacity building will be created in the Ministry to look after the e-education needs of both school and higher education. Since technology is rapidly evolving, and needs specialists to deliver high quality e-learning, a vibrant ecosystem has to be encouraged to create solutions that not only solve India's challenges of scale, diversity, equity, but also evolve in keeping with the rapid changes in technology, whose half-life reduces with each passing year.

This centre will, therefore, consist of experts drawn from the field of administration, education, educational tech-nology, digital pedagogy and assessment, egovernance, etc.

MULTIPLE CHOICE QUESTIONS

1. According to NEP 2020 the Indian education system produced great scholars such as Charaka, Nagarjuna. Find out the odd one from the list.

A. Aryabhata
B. Varahamihira
C. Xenocrates
D. Bhaskaracharya

2. Education is a great leveler and is the best tool for achieving economic and social mobility, inclusion, and ______.

A. disparity
B. discrimination
C. inequality
D. equality

3. How many of the fundamental principles mentioned in National Education Policy 2020?

A. 5 B. 11

C. 22 D. 20

4. National Education Policy 2020 replaced by a new pedagogical and curricular structure. What is the new curricular structure according to NEP 2020?

A. "3 + 4 + 4 + 5" model

B. "5 + 3 + 3 + 4" model

C. "4 + 3 + 3 + 5" model

D. "5 + 4 + 3 + 3" model

5. What is the age group covered in school education according to NEP 2020 new curricular structure?

A. 16-18 B. 3-18

C. 6-18 D. 5-18

6. What are the classes which cover the "Secondary" stage according to NEP 2020 new curricular structure?

A. Class 6 to 9 B. Class 9 to 12

C. Class 6 to 8 D. Class 11 to 12

7. What are the classes which cover the "Middle" stage according to NEP 2020 new curricular structure?

A. Class 6 to 9 B. Class 9 to 12

C. Class 6 to 8 D. Class 11 to 12

8. What are the classes which cover the "Preparatory" stage according to NEP 2020 new curricular structure?

A. Class 6 to 9 B. Class 3 to 5

C. Class 6 to 8 D. Class 1 to 2

9. What are the classes which cover the "Foundational" stage according to NEP 2020 new curricular structure?

A. Covers only (Class 1 & 2)

B. Covers only (Anganwadi/pre-school/Balvatika)

C. Covers (Anganwadi/pre-school/Balvatika) and 2 years (Class 1 & 2)

D. Covers up to class 5

10. How much (per cent %) of a child's cumulative brain development occurs prior to the age of 6 according to NEP 2020?

A. Over 85% B. Over 95%

C. Over 75% D. Over 65%

11. NEP proposed that universal provisioning of quality early childhood development, care, and education must be achieved. What is the timeline for this?

A. 2030 B. 2035

C. 2040 D. 2050

12. What is the timeline to ensure that all students entering Grade 1 are school ready according to National Education Policy 2020?

A. 2035 B. 2040

C. 2025 D. 2030

13. NEP 2020 proposed pedagogical framework for Early Childhood Care and Education. What is the name of ECCE pedagogical framework?

A. NCPFECED B. NCPFECCE

C. NCPFECDE D. NCPOECCE

14. NEP 2020 proposed pedagogical framework for Early Childhood Care and Education. What age group will be covered in the ECCE pedagogical framework?

A. children up to the age of 4

B. children up to the age of 6

C. children up to the age of 5

D. children up to the age of 8

15. Which educational organization will prepare NEP 2020 proposed pedagogical framework for Early Childhood Care and Education?

A. NCERT B. SCERT

C. SEDGC D. NTSC

16. The goal of universal access to high-quality ECCE across the country will be implemented in a phased manner. ECCE shall be delivered through various education institutions. Find out the odd one institution.

A. stand-alone Anganwadis;

B. Anganwadis co-located with primary schools;

C. stand-alone pre-schools
D. Kindergarten Sections of Private schools

17. National Education Policy 2020 proposed establishment of "Preparatory Class" or "Balavatika". What is the age limit for the "Preparatory Class" or "Balavatika"?
A. prior to the age of 6
B. prior to the age of 5
C. prior to the age of 4
D. prior to the age of 3

18. Ministry of Human Resources Development (MHRD) renamed as:
A. Ministry of Human Development
B. Ministry of Education
C. Ministry of Human Rights
D. Ministry of Human Capital

19. Who is the last minister of MHRD and first minister of Education?
A. Piyush Goel B. Kapil Sibbal
C. Ramesh Pokhriyal D. Jairam Ramesh

20. As per the policy public investment in education will be increased from the current 4.3% to:
A. 5% of GDP B. 7% of GDP
C. 6.6% of GDP D. 6% of GDP

21. The new policy aims in the higher education to improve the Gross Enrollment Ratio from 26.3% to 50% by:
A. 2030 B. 2035
C. 2025 D. 2040

22. Consider the following statement relating to the medium of instruction in NEP 2020
I. The medium of instruction until at least Grade 5, but preferably till Grade 8 and beyond, will be the home language/mother tongue/local language
II. Medium of instruction is mandatory
III. It is only for Public School

Select Incorrect answer given code below:
A. I & III Only B. II & III Only
C. III Only D. I & II Only

23. The vocational education will start from:
A. Class 5th B. Class 8th
C. Class 6th D. Class 7th

24. Consider the following statement regarding the foundational pillars in NEP 2020.
I. Accessibility II. Affordability
III. Accountability IV. Quality
V. Equity VI. Access

Select Correct answer given code below:
A. I, II, III Only
B. I, II, III, IV Only
C. I, II, III, IV, V Only
D. I, II, III, IV, V & VI

25. What will be age of Early Childhood Care and Education (ECCE) in NEP 2020?
A. 3-6 years B. 2-6 years
C. 4-7 years D. 3-8 years

26. Ministry of Education plan for attaining universal foundational literacy and numeracy in all primary schools for all learners by grade 3 by:
A. 2022 B. 2025
C. 2027 D. 2030

27. Consider the following statements regarding languages in NEP 2020.
I. It will promote 'Ek Bharat Shrestha Bharat' initiative
II. Three language formula with greater flexibility
III. All Classical languages will be available in school as options.

Select CORRECT code given below:
A. I Only B. II Only
C. I and II Only D. I, II and III

28. Consider the following statements regarding Adult Education in NEP 2020.
I. Policy aim to achieve 100% youth and Adult literacy
II. Public library spaces for adult education courses
III. Quality technology based options for adult learning

Select CORRECT code given below:

A. I and II Only B. II and III Only

C. I, II and II D. III Only

29. Under the chairmanship of whom 'Committee for Evolution of the New Education Policy' submitted its report in May 2016?

A. Late Shri T.S.R. Subramanian

B. Dr. K. Kasturirangan

C. Rina Ray

D. Shri Sanjay Dhotre

30. According to the National Education Policy 2020, teacher will be able to teach lessons in mother tongue or regional language up to Grade ______.

A. Grade 3 B. Grade 4

C. Grade 5 D. None of these

31. Who among the following was the Chairman of newly constituted drafting NEP 2020 in June 2017?

A. Vasudha Kamat

B. Dr. K. Kasturirangan

C. K. J. Alphonse

D. Ram Shankar Kureel

32. According to the National Education Policy 2020 by how much percent the Gross Enrolment Ratio in higher education to be raised?

A. 25% B. 30%

C. 40% D. 50%

33. National Education Policy, 2020 emphasizes:

A. Flexibility of the curriculum

B. Standardization of the curriculum

C. De-contextualization of textbooks

D. Rote memorization of the textbooks

34. National Education Policy 2020 emphasises on:

A. flexible multi-level activity based learning.

B. only the aspects related to cognitive development of children.

C. standardization of a national curriculum.

D. measurement of memorization abilities of children.

35. The purpose of assessment as per the National Education Policy 2020 is to provide information on:

A. how to support the students in and out of the classroom.

B. comparison of the students performance with her classmates.

C. the gaps and deficiencies in student learning to accurately identify her failure.

D. memorization capacities of the student.

36. In the context of languages, National Education Policy 2020 emphasizes on:

A. Multilingualism

B. Monolingualism

C. English as the medium of instruction across the nation

D. Hindi as the medium of instruction across the nation

37. National Education Policy 2020 suggests that assessment:

A. must be undertaken through formal exams taken once in an academic year.

B. is important to find out a child's progress over a certain period of time.

C. must be at the centre of all educational activities.

D. is important to assign ranks to the children in order to merit.

38. Which of the following has **not** been advocated in the National Education Policy 2020?

(*i*) Emphasis on conceptual understanding

(*ii*) Summative assessment

(*iii*) Increasing curriculum content

(*iv*) Decreased use of Technology

A. (*i*) (*ii*) B. (*ii*) (*iv*)

C. (*i*) (*ii*) (*iii*) D. (*ii*) (*iii*) (*iv*)

39. The central focus on National Education Policy 2020 is on

A. Rigid curriculum, pedagogy and assessment.

B. Multidisciplinary and holistic education.

C. Learning towards and for exams.

D. Adoption of summative methods of assessment.

40. Which of the following has NOT been promoted by National Education Policy, 2020 in context of education of students with disabilities?
A. Appropriate infrastructure
B. One-on-one teachers and tutors
C. Compulsory Special Education
D. Suitable technological interventions

41. What is the structure of school education as recommen-ded by the National Education Policy, 2020?
A. 5+3+3+4
B. 2+3+3+4
C. 2+5+3+2+2
D. 5+3+3+2+2

42. National Education Policy 2020, recommends:
A. Multilingualism
B. Monolingualism
C. Standardization of curriculum
D. Standardization of assessment

43. National Education Policy, 2020 recognizes ______.
A. 'multilingualism and the power of languages' as essential for learning in school.
B. English as medium of instruction at the primary stage of schooling for upward mobility.
C. All language learning needs to be in the mother tongue only.
D. Children should learn many languages as per their choices.

44. Which of the following statements is proposed in National Education Policy, 2020?
A. Being educated in one's mother tongue is detrimental to educational and technological advancements.
B. Schools should encourage children to learn and speak English as their first language.
C. Multilingualism has great cognitive benefits for young students.
D. Bilingual approach confuses students and hampers learning.

45. Which of the following features is NOT prescribed in the National Education Policy 2020?
A. It is important to identify and foster the unique capabilities of each student.
B. Emphasis should be placed on conceptual under-standing rather than rote learning and learning for-exams.
C. There should be due focus on creativity and critical thinking to encourage logical decision-making and innovation.
D. Teachers should focus on use of rewards and punishment to promote compliance in children.

ANSWERS

1. (C)	**2. (D)**	**3. (C)**	**25. (D)**	**26. (B)**	**27. (D)**
4. (B)	**5. (B)**	**6. (B)**	**28. (C)**	**29. (A)**	**30. (C)**
7. (C)	**8. (B)**	**9. (B)**	**31. (B)**	**32. (D)**	**33. (A)**
10. (A)	**11. (A)**	**12. (D)**	**34. (A)**	**35. (A)**	**36. (A)**
13. (B)	**14. (D)**	**15. (A)**	**37. (B)**	**38. (D)**	**39. (B)**
16. (D)	**17. (B)**	**18. (B)**	**40. (C)**	**41. (A)**	**42. (A)**
19. (C)	**20. (D)**	**21. (B)**	**43. (A)**	**44. (C)**	**45. (D)**
22. (B)	**23. (C)**	**24. (D)**			

❑❑❑

Teaching Aptitude/Pedagogy

MULTIPLE CHOICE QUESTIONS

1. When a test has a high degree of reliability; we can conclude that
A. there is the likelihood that a pupil will maintain his/her position in the same group of test-takers when he/she takes an equivalent test
B. there is the likelihood that a pupil will get a higher score when he/she takes an equivalent test
C. the test is measuring what it intends to measure
D. the test is highly objective

2. The likelihood that a pupil will maintain his/ her position in the same group of test-takers, when he/she takes an equivalent test, is a measure of the ..... of that test.
A. validity
B. objectivity
C. reliability
D. prognostic ability

3. Out of the following, the most useful step for studying relationships among pupils is the
A. anecdotal record
B. sociogram
C. Rorschah Test
D. Kuder Programme Test

4. The best argument for group intelligence test is that it
A. treats all the children equally
B. provides the teacher with diagnostic information
C. is less tension-producing than an individual test
D. is the least expensive method to determine the IQ

5. The least justifiable use of the results of a standardised reading test is to
A. evaluate the reading instruction programme
B. serve as a basis for report card marks
C. serve as a basis for parent conference
D. serve as a basis for making groups in the class

6. The term "identical elements" is closely associated with
A. group instruction
B. transfer of learning
C. jealousy between twins
D. similar test questions

7. The evaluation of personality is best made through the use of a/an
A. inventory test B. preference test
C. survey test D. projective test

8. Group test that have norms for each grade and that are administered in accordance with uniform procedures listed in a mammal of instruction is called
A. school-wide finals
B. quizzes
C. standardised tests
D. class tests

9. Although pupils in a large elementary school (of a city) have an average value of IQ well below the city's norm, yet the results of a standardised science test fall within the city's tenth percentile. The most probable reason for this is that
A. the science curriculum in this school is better than the curriculum in other parts of the city
B. children cheated during the test

C. teachers are highly proficient in instruction of science
D. teachers were biased while they marked the test

10. The limitation of the five-stage system of Herbart is
A. making the students passive
B. giving less importance to the teacher
C. giving less importance to knowledge
D. giving more importance to planning

11. A lesson, in which examples are given first and then, students are told to delineate a general rule or principle, is known as a/an
A. deductive lesson
B. inductive lesson
C. knowledge lesson
D. developing lesson

12. For knowledge lessons
A. Glover's Scheme is used
B. Herbart's five-stage system is used
C. Garry's scheme is used
D. None of these

13. Who is considered to be the creator of the play-way method of education?
A. Coldwell Cook B. Madam Montessori
C. Froebel D. John Devy

14. The special feature of the play-way method is that
A. games take the place of studies
B. There is no importance of studies in it
C. games are added into studies in order to remove the boredom and monotony of the latter
D. education cannot be complete without games

15. The project education method of teaching is associated with
A. Rousseau B. Frobel
C. Dewey D. Armstrong

16. "This methodology trains the child to search for facts, rules and principles by his own efforts, organise the set of knowledge gained and delineate general rules." The aforementioned statement is about the following methodology of teaching
A. Montessory B. Kindergarten
C. Heuristic D. Play-way

17. In Garry's Plan
A. work is important
B. play is important
C. learning is important
D. all these three have equal importance

18. Under the Wennetka Plan
A. the diversity of interests of the students is recognised
B. the diversities of abilities are accepted
C. the diversities of needs are accepted
D. all of these are recognised

19. The Dalton Scheme of education is useful for which ones of the following?
A. For infants
B. For little children
C. For older children
D. For all of these

20. Why do you not support the five-stage method of Herbart?
A. In this, there is no scope for the individual diversity of students
B. Under this, it is difficult to make coordination between various subjects
C. Under this, generalisation is not required to be done while teaching subjects like language, history, geography etc.
D. All of these

21. "In the school, provisions must be made for free and natural expressions of a child." Who gave this statement?
A. T. Remont B. Ryeburn
C. Montessori D. Lyndon

22. According to Dewey, education is a
A. Social need
B. Personal need
C. Psychological need
D. theoretical need

23. In the context of education, some views of Gandhiji have been appended below. Which one of them is incorrect?
A. In education, experimentation, work and research must be given due places

B. Education must be self-dependent
C. Literacy is education
D. Education must be such as to develop all the powers and inherent qualities of children

24. The theoretical basis of the Montessory educational system is
A. complete freedom of the child to indulge in games of his choice
B. that the child gets inspiration from the teacher
C. freedom of the child in expressing his tastes/orientations
D. that games assist the child in his education

25. According to the Dalton Scheme of education; which one of the following is dominant?
A. The teacher B. The contract
C. The student D. Guidance

26. Who gave the principle of "pupil activity?"
A. Rousseau B. Handerson
C. Comenius D. Binet

27. Personalised System of education
A. does not inculcate a feeling of socialisation in students
B. does not inculcate a feeling of competition in students
C. leads to wastage of time and energy
D. All of these are true

28. Froebel's most important contribution to education was his development of the
A. vocational school B. public high school
C. kindergarten D. Latin school

29. All of the following advocated principles of child development are closely allied to the stimulus-response learning theory, except
A. Hull B. Gesell
C. Pavlov D. Skinner

30. "At least one-third of learning that will determine later levels of school achievement has already taken place by the age of six." This is a statement most closely associated with the writings of
A. Benjamin Bloom B. Martin Mayer
C. Fritz Redl D. Nathan Glazer

31. Of the following items in a pupil's cumulative folder, the one that is least appropriate is
A. "Height 1977-40 in; 1978-42 in"
B. "WISC: 1977 V 96, P92, FS 95"
C. "10-12-77 during a maths test, asked to leave room; 10-19 same; 11-3 same"
D. "Is an emotionally distributed child"

32. As a teacher, what is your opinion about the creation of a students' union in your school?
A. This will waste the time of students
B. The work load of teachers increases
C. Indiscipline is promoted among students
D. The spirit of leadership is developed among students

33. Your opinion about including sex education in the academic curriculum, in order to impart such type of education to students, is that
A. this step would to generation of wrong feelings among students
B. this step is necessary for the enlightenment of the society
C. this would eliminate the delusions prevalent in the society
D. we can protect ourselves from the evils arising due to it

34. If I were given an opportunity in future, I would like to become a/an
A. doctor
B. businesswoman
C. police officer
D. engineer

35. A student of the class is always scared or full of fears. In order to make him brave, the teacher should
A. advise him not to be afraid
B. himself talk to that student with love and affection
C. persuade him to play with other students
D. inform the principal about his problem

36. I am very much pleased when I have
A. all the members of my family around me
B. good magazines and periodicals with me
C. people respect me
D. I have enough of money to help others

37. The major objective of my life is to become a
A. rich woman
B. good teacher
C. journalist
D. successful housewife

38. Any teacher can become favourite among his students by
A. completing their syllabus
B. telling them stories
C. helping them in doing their homework
D. behaving with them in a sympathetic manner

39. An easy method to impress students is to
A. make them feel scared
B. display your knowledge before them
C. keep your conduct ideal
D. take the support of the Principal

40. In order to encourage good students
A. they must be praised
B. they should be allocated tasks of responsibility
C. they should be treated in a friendly manner
D. all of these

41. After beating a student, you realise that he was innocent. In such a situation, you will
A. not worry about the episode
B. repent over your act
C. apologise to the student
D. apologise to the student in privacy

42. If an intelligent student is delaying the norms of discipline in the class, then
A. no notice should be taken of his activities
B. he should be given severe punishment
C. a complaint should be made to his parents/ guardians
D. his problem must be understood and an effort should be made to solve it

43. In the present times, a lady teacher faces the maximum number of problems due to
A. female students
B. parents/guardians
C. the headmistress
D. a fall in the values of life

44. On the day of paying fees, a student forgot to bring the fees you will
A. send a complaint to his parents/guardians
B. tell him to go home and bring fees
C. tell him to bring fees on the next fees day
D. deposit his fees from your pocket, if it is feasible

45. A student has been failing in a class for two years in a row. As his class teacher, you will
A. Scold him severely and try to improve his performance
B. suggest to him to start a business
C. try to identify the reasons of his failure
D. tell him not to study further

46. Some of your students are weak in the subject bring taught by you. In order to improve their academic performance, you will
A. not make any effort because it is not your responsibility
B. tell their parents/guardians to arrange tutors for them
C. motivate them to do extra hard work
D. give them personalised assistance and support and raise their mental levels

47. After becoming a lady teacher, if you have to interact with people of the reputed society, then you will
A. to be reluctant to tell them that you are a teacher
B. like to tell them that you are in administrative services
C. be proud to inform them that you are proud to be a lady teacher
D. move away from the place at such an occasion

48. An example of verbal illustration is
A. simile B. model
C. chart D. graph

49. If a student gives an answer in which there are mistakes of language, grammar and facts, then that (wrong) answer should be written on the blackboard and
A. all the mistakes should be underlined
B. that student should be told to find out mistakes in the answer

C. that student should be told to find out mistakes and rectify them

D. the rectified forms of mistakes should be written by the teacher

50. Which one of the following questions is incorrect?

A. Who is a weak student of our class?

B. Who is the greatest person of India?

C. Which is the best river of China?

D. All of these

51. Some students, who give wrong answers to a question, you should

A. tell them to repeat the correct answer time and again

B. not ask that question time and again

C. not expect the right answer to the question

D. tell those students to repeat the answer

52. A teacher, who is liked by students, is the one who

A. listens to their problems

B. becomes angry quite early

C. does not become angry easily

D. wears gaudy clothes

53. The reason of students not taking interest in studies is that

A. they do not visualise good future in studies

B. they lack good values

C. their parents/guardians are callous towards their academic needs

D. the academic curriculum is not of right contents/quality

54. A normal child of twelve years of age is most likely to

A. have difficulty with gross motor coordination

B. have feelings of anxiety about pleasing adults

C. confine his/her interests to here and now

D. be eager for peer approval

55. Creative writing should be an activity planned for

A. only those children reading on grade level

B. only those children who can spell and also, can write cohesive sentences

C. only those children who want to write for the newspaper of the class

D. all children

56. Of the following, the most promising step for a teacher to take in order to improve class discipline is to

A. note specific infractions of class rules in the marking book

B. evaluate his/her materials, methods and approaches to children

C. consult the class and agree upon a graduated series of punishments

D. call a parent-teacher meeting to discuss the situation

57. A quiet reserved fourth grader brings road-maps to school and looks at them, whenever he gets a chance. The teacher should

A. encourage the pupil to talk about them during a show-and-tell period

B. tell the pupil to leave maps at home

C. take the maps away

D. call the mother of the pupil to determine the reason of his behaviour

58. Lesson planning should be guided primarily by the consideration of

A. meeting the needs of an average child of the class

B. creating a happy classroom environment

C. the curriculum goals

D. providing pupils with work

59. In a kindergarten class, it would be unreasonable to expect a child to

A. care for plants

B. clean up after clay work

C. bring an old shirt for painting activities

D. know when it is time to clean up

60. A male student of eighth grade of your school gives you a letter in which, he has expressed the feeling of his love for you. In this context, your reaction would be

A. You will make fun of him in the presence of all the students the next day

B. You will meet him in privacy and explain to him that you are helpless because you are already married

C. You will give him a piece of your mind and tell him to concentrate more on his studies
D. You will visit his home and tell his parents/guardians about his mental state and also, make combined efforts (along with them) to rectify him

61. Normally students do not study their subjects. In this context
A. punishment should be made compulsory for such students
B. the subject matter should be made more interesting and worth learning
C. the teacher should try to learn why they lack interest in studies
D. the teacher should complain to the Principal about such students

62. Of the following, the statement that is least educationally valid is that
A. heterogeneous grouping is undemocratic
B. drill periods should be brief
C. study habits should be taught
D. overlearning constitutes wastage of time

63. A class of sixth grade includes a group of children reading in the fourth grade. Of the following, the best material to be used with this group is a
A. basal reader of fourth grade
B. tape recorder
C. high-interest low-level book of stories
D. work book of sixth grade

64. A child is active by birth. Therefore, we must motivate him to take interest in
A. sports
B. physical development
C. gaining knowledge
D. creative activities

65. The parent of a fourth grader refuses to give permission to her child to go on a class trip. The teacher should, first of all
A. refer the matter to the guidance counsellor
B. confer with the parent to discuss the educational purpose of the trip
C. send messages to all the parents through their children, giving reasons why each child should go on the trip
D. tell the class that the trip will be cancelled if any child does not receive admission from his/her parents or guardians

66. A fifteen year old student is fond of wearing the same type of sweaters that are worn by his lady teacher. The form of behaviour is known as
A. compensation B. transference
C. identification D. egocentrism

67. When misbehaviour of a pupil persists even though the teacher punishes the child for each infraction, the teacher is probably practising the policy of
A. negative reinforcement
B. corporal punishment
C. retribution
D. sarcasm

68. A teacher notices poor attendance in the class on Fridays, the day on which, weekly tests are given. The teacher should
A. call the parents of the absentees
B. schedule tests throughout the week
C. do nothing
D. tell the pupils that missing two tests will result in a failing mark

69. If a student comes to your class in dirty and crumpled clothes, what type of remedy you will like to implement?
A. You will tell him that he should go home and change his clothes
B. After the class is over, you will advise him to come to the class in clean clothes
C. You will ridicule him because of his clothes in the presence of all the children
D. You will make him sit in the class, totally away from other students of the class

70. In your opinion, arrangement of educationl tours for students in the school is very much important because
A. students and their parents/guardians remain happy due to these excursions
B. teachers get freedom from teaching at least for a few days
C. students are able to get knowledge because of their direct contact (with new environment/people/education institute)

D. students do not have to go to school for some days

71. Our present system of education is the one that creates unemployment because

A. only the knowledge based on principles can be imparted

B. education is imparted on the basis of policies defined by Lord McCaulay

C. education is not vocation oriented

D. All of these

72. Knowledge of child psychology is a must for a primary teacher. That is because

A. it helps in making children disciplined

B. the examination result is improved

C. it becomes a convenient mode for motivating children

D. it helps the teacher in understanding the behaviour of children

73. Why Navodaya Vidyalayas have been created under the aegis of National Education Policy?

A. Rural children will be able to learn in these schools

B. Students with good abilities and hailing from cities and villages will be able to study in such schools

C. So that children of cities as well as villages may be able to study in such schools

D. For educating Urban students

74. "The schools of the future will be organised along more flexible lines to permit students to move at their own rate rather than remain in fixed groups." Of the following, the one that is not an example of this philosophy is

A. non-graded primary classes

B. achievement grouping

C. pre-kindergarten classes

D. team teaching

75. Teachers are likely to play an intelligent role in curriculum improvement when they

A. implement new courses of study prepared by well-qualified supervisors

B. devise their own curriculum for their class

C. utilise the latest text books as the basis for what they teach

D. participate with other staff members in devising the curriculum for the school

76. How should the subjects be distributed in the time table?

A. According to the convenience of the school

B. According to the tastes/interests of students

C. According to the level of difficulty of subjects

D. There should be no criterion

77. Of the following, the most unreliable predictor of educational achievement is

A. inherited biological potential for learning

B. ethnic origin of parents

C. classroom experiences

D. family background and training

78. In comparing lectures and developmental lessons, all of the following are true except that

A. there are more activities of the pupil in a development lesson

B. it is more difficult to ascertain pupil learning in a lecture session

C. the lecture method is more conducive and useful for larger classes

D. slow children derive benefit from a lecture than brighter children do

79. A non-traditional method of education is

A. public school teaching

B. kindergarten teaching

C. teaching through Shanti Niketan (Started by Tagore)

D. private school teaching

80. Nowadays, students get education through Internet. This has become a Common practice in the West. Should this practice be adopted in India?

A. No

B. Yes

C. Yes, but must continue to guage their academic performances and guide them from time to time

D. Internet is a new technology. Let us keep our fingers crossed for the time being

81. Nowadays, practical experiments, tours, audio-visual presentations and live examples are used in abundance to teach students. Do you think that these new techniques are useful?

A. No, they waste the time of students and teachers alike

B. Yes, they are useful but must be used according to the need of the students and demands of the subject matter

C. They are partially useful

D. They are very costly

82. The best thing about the teaching profession is that

A. salary is more in comparison to the quantum of work

B. one can take up other profession during the spare time

C. the company of children gives pleasure

D. there are least numbers of risks and responsibilities

83. As a teacher, what is your view about going on strike?

A. Sometimes, going on strikes becomes a necessity

B. Strikes must be banned by the government

C. Going on strike is against the dignity of the teacher

D. Strikes are not solutions to problems

84. A good teacher should show more interest in

A. tuitions

B. enhancement of the knowledge levels of his students

C. self-study

D. in both B and C

85. Text books should be replaced with new ones after some years because

A. students like new text books

B. the teacher gets bored by teaching the same book time and again

C. there is regular upgradation of knowledge levels

D. the government/publishers draw monetary benefits due to this exercise

86. You want to adopt the teaching profession because

A. there is no other method to earn a livelihood

B. there are many others in your family who are teachers

C. you will get an opportunity to handle/train the future citizens of the nation

D. children give more respect and reverance

87. You want to adopt the teaching profession because

A. there is no other profession in your view that is better than this one

B. you love teaching work

C. many members of your clan have been teachers

D. by becoming a teacher, you can do other jobs as well that would help you in earning extra income

88. Nowadays, many small English Montessori Schools have sprung up in cities. In your view, the objective of their creation is

A. spread of education

B. spread of good values in children

C. generation of money

D. imparting education to children in the vicinity of their homes

89. In your opinion, that profession is good one in which, one gets an opportunity for

A. enhancement of status and authority

B. status and additional income

C. comfort and easy type of work

D. honour and self-satisfaction

90. If education is made vocation-oriented, this will lead to

A. efficient utilisation of time and money

B. reduction in unemployment

C. increase of interest of students in studies

D. improvements in the economy of the nation

91. In comparison to other (common) professions, people give less importance to the teaching profession. The major reason for this phenomenon is that

A. in the teaching profession, there are limited opportunities to earn money in comparison to other professions

B. teaching is not good from the viewpoint of a profession

C. in teaching work, there is a compulsion of time

D. in teaching work, there is a compulsion of morality

92. A good textbook is one, which essentially includes, besides other special features, the following

A. Directions to teachers

B. Directions to examiners

C. List of chapters

D. Practice exercises

93. Teachers direct and help students in respect of choice of a profession because

A. they are aware of the tastes/orientations of their students

B. they are aware of all the professions

C. they are subject experts

D. they show their efficiencies by giving such type of help

94. "Teaching is not a profession." You

A. fully agree with this statement

B. partially agree with this statement

C. disagree with this statement

D. think that this statement does not have any meaning in the present times

95. A teacher is like a

A. father of the student

B. mother of the student

C. friend of the student

D. all of these

96. The chief quality of a teacher is

A. finesse in teaching

B. expertise in declamation

C. love for disciplines

D. behavioural efficiency

97. A teacher should have

A. costly clothes

B. a collection of personal books

C. facilities for studying and teaching

D. all of these

98. There are two groups of students in the class

A. You will join either of them

B. You will report the matter to the Principal

C. By taking all the students into confidence, you will advise them to refrain from politics as they are too young to indulge in its intricacies

D. You will use both of them to grind your own axe inside as well as outside the school

99. Students do not want to study a subject under your guidance but prefer another teacher. What will be your strategy?

A. Defame the other teacher through vicious propaganda

B. Let the other teacher teach and introspect the reasons of your failure

C. Forcibly teach students yourself, without listening to their demands/requests

D. Taking notes from the other teacher and teaching the subject yourself

100. A student of your class praises a colleague of yours. You will

A. be green with envy and tell him to keep quiet

B. also praise that colleague and tell your students to follow his conduct

C. speak ill of him and highlight his limitations

D. make a bad face and leave the class immediately

101. You have learned that your students praised you in your absence. You will

A. enquire about the names of those students and meet them; you will also throw a party in their honour

B. teach students in a normal manner without having any impact of the encomium bestowed upon you

C. tell every colleague of yours that you command respect of your students

D. take leave from the school and enjoy the glory

102. You are a Junior teacher and your pay package is poor. Your seniors draw hefty salaries. You will

A. talk to the Principal and make a request for a raise

B. work hard and be a master of your subject

C. wait as your increment will automatically come by with the passage of time
D. not like to meet senior teachers because they enjoy more comforts of life than you do

103. In order to enhance your knowledge levels, you will
A. go abroad for studying
B. seek help of professional teachers who give tuitions on a regular basis
C. surf through Internet and download information
D. both A and B

104. In the context of being present in the school on national days (like August 15 and January 26), your view is that
A. you are obeying the order
B. these days are occasions for entertainment
C. there is no use of going
D. this helps in strengthening unity and integrity of the country

105. In your view, the major objective of co-education is
A. to reduce the expenditure being incurred on education
B. to let the boy and the girl understand each other
C. not to open separate schools for female students
D. to check the feelings of inferiority complex of female students

106. In your view, arrangement for "education on environment" in the school
A. is important for creating an awareness among students about the environment
B. is likely to put more burden on students
C. is a mode of entertainment for students
D. is like giving work to teachers

107. In your opinion, the following is important for the purpose of imparting moral education to students in the school
A. Lectures by teachers on morality on a daily basis
B. Distribution of literature related to morality amongst students
C. Making parents/guardians aware of the concepts of morality from time to time
D. Teachers should control and regulate their moral conduct

108. Nowadays, the chief reason for diminishing reputation of the teacher is
A. materialistic viewpoint of the society
B. disregard for his duties
C. a desire to earn more money
D. indifference towards the teaching work

109. The major objective of education is
A. reforming the society
B. making students discipline
C. developing inherent abilities/powers of students
D. making students followers of teachers

110. You are a lady teacher. If your neighbour (who is a lady) criticises you, then you will
A. reply in the same coin
B. indulge in propaganda against her
C. go to meet her family members and complain about her action
D. meet her personally and enquire about the reason for her action

111. Adult education should be under the authority of the following
A. The government
B. Non-government organisations
C. Educated persons
D. All of these

112. Nowadays, the dignity of lady teachers has diminished in the society. The chief reason for this phenomenon is
A. indifference of lady teachers towards their duties
B. indiscipline of students
C. political interference
D. a tendency to earn more money through tuitions

113. In your opinion, education of female children is important because
A. they should also be able to take up jobs after their studies
B. female and male children are equal

C. illiteracy ought to be removed
D. education of the female child leads to the education of the entire family in future

114. In my view, the progress report card of every student should be handed over to his/her parents/guardians because
A. students remain afraid that way
B. there are chances of teaching such students through tuitions
C. parents/guardians know about the progress of their children/wards
D. our responsibility towards the student ends after we send the report card

115. In order to check the decay that is going on in the field of education, it is important
A. to make arrangements for improving the educational system
B. to create awareness among parents/ guardians towards the homework of their children/wards
C. for teachers to take up regular class teaching work
D. to increase the number of teachers

116. In the context of lack of resources and rising population levels of our nation, your view about the programmes related to "Qualitative Improvement in Education" is the following
A. These programmes are obstructions in classroom teaching work
B. These programmes are impractical
C. These programmes are courageous efforts
D. These programmes are wastage of time

117. In your opinion, those parents are deemed good who give
A. money and facilities to their children according to their needs
B. all the things/materials to their children that are needed by them
C. good food and clothes to their children
D. some of their time and love on a regular basis

118. Nowadays, people demand more salaries in relation to the hard work done by them. In your opinion, this is
A. a result of growing inflation
B. is an indicator of decay in the values of human life
C. is indifference towards labour
D. is an indicator of economic progress

119. Besides teaching, as a teacher, what type of attitude you will display regarding other activities of the school?
A. Positive B. Negative
C. Indifferent D. Passive

120. A student is involved in the incident of eveteasing. What type of behaviour will be meted out to him by you?
A. You will throw him out of the school
B. You will insult him in the presence of girls
C. You will advise him to do away with his bad behaviour
D. You will introduce him to a few girls who are of his age

121. What will you do to inculcate the habit of eating together among students?
A. Give them a lecture on the importance of eating together
B. Make arrangements so that teachers and students eat together
C. Arrange a meeting on the benefits that accrue by eating together
D. Discuss the issue among students

122. In order to develop the spirit of responsibility towards the society in students
A. lectures should be given to them from time to time
B. examples of such (responsible) persons should be quoted in the class
C. the importance of such responsibility should be highlighted
D. students should be kept in touch with such (responsible) persons in the society

123. The school is a
A. miniaturised form of society
B. laboratory of the student
C. psychological laboratory
D. miniaturised form of the family

124. Education not only conserves the culture of a nation, but also it
A. makes the latter rich

B. defines the latter
C. makes the latter spiritual
D. makes the latter mass-oriented and popular

125. In your opinion, parents/guardians of students should
A. not attend meetings organised in the school as they lack time
B. send their representatives to learn about the vital points discussed during meetings organised in the school
C. preferably be present during such meetings to know how their children have been performing
D. None of these

126. If the parents/guardians of a child cannot afford to send him to a highly branded and costly school, you will
A. tell them to admit their child to that school only, if he has been granted admission to the same
B. ask them to find another good school because the school in question is not of your liking
C. tell them to try for admission to a school that has good teaching norms and not high fees
D. All of these

127. A school in the immediate vicinity of your residence is not considered to be a good institute. You are a teacher in a different school. You will
A. tell your students that the school in question is not a good one
B. remain quiet about the issue
C. tell your students that all the schools are good and so is the school in your neighbourhood
D. try to persuade students from that school to join your school

128. In the school, a weekly educational programme is shown to students on television. Some parents/guardians file a complaint that their children/wards already spend enough of time on television entertainment. Hence, they request that this programme should not be shown to students during the school hours. You will
A. advise the parents/guardians to check the television based entertainment of their children/wards at homes
B. stop showing the weekly educational programme on television in the school
C. talk to parents/guardians and take the responsibility of advising students
D. invite parents/guardians to watch the weekly educational programme on television so that they are able to realise that the same is useful for children and enhances their knowledge

129. If a student does not complete his home work on a regular basis, what will you do to rectify him?
A. You will complain to the Principal and get him punished
B. You will call the student in privacy and explain to him that (completion of) home work has many advantages
C. You would like to get the cooperation of the student in question
D. You will clearly tell the student that if he continues to ignore his home work, he would not be allowed to appear in the final examination

130. Which quality of the teacher is liked the most by students?
A. His punctuality
B. His impartiality
C. His love for discipline
D. His dominance

131. In your view, to win the confidence of the Principal, a teacher should:
A. keep on giving gifts to the Principal
B. keep on censuring and backbiting other teachers in collusion with the Principal
C. keep on executing his own teaching work in a satisfactory manner
D. gain popularity among students

132. As a teacher, you would:
A. listen to the personal problems of the students only if they were special

B. always listen to the problems of students
C. never listen to the problems of students
D. listen to the problems of students and moderate them to the Principal

133. As a teacher, where would you like to teach?
A. In the school of your own village
B. In the school of your district in which, children of the rich people study
C. In the school whose Principal is your acquaintance
D. In any school

134. Which method would you like to adopt to teach a new subject in the class?
A. You would tell children a day before the lecture that they should read the subject at their homes
B. You would tell students to write an article on that subject
C. You would discuss the subject with students in the light of their knowledge about it; then you would give new sets of information/data about that subject to students
D. You would give a small lecture to students regarding the importance of that (new) subject

135. As a teacher, what would you like to do for your favourite student?
A. You would give him the maximum marks in the tests
B. You would make him the monitor of the class
C. You would not ask any difficult question from him in the class
D. You would adequately support him in his studies

136. The true objective of education is:
A. making students able so that they can earn a living
B. preparing students for jobs
C. helping students acquire knowledge
D. facilitating the all-round development of students

137. In order to raise the standards of education, which one of the following is vital?
A. High salaries of teachers
B. Continuous evaluation of students
C. Continuous evaluation of text books
D. Amendments in syllabi

138. Suppose that a person does not agree with your viewpoint. In such a situation, you would:
A. present the rationale of your view point before him
B. not like to talk to that person
C. consider him to be your opponent
D. behave with him in a rude manner

139. The job of the teacher is to generate:
A. affinity for studies among students
B. confidence in studies among students
C. a belief towards studies among students
D. affection/affiliation for studies among students

140. With the help of a cumulative records
A. the moral levels of children can be evaluated
B. the pace of educational progress of children can be known
C. children can be disciplined
D. the development of children can be gauged

141. If a student has asked you a question and you are not aware of its answer, then what would you like to do in such a situation?
A. You would tell that student that the question is illogical
B. You would not like to answer any question of that student
C. You would scold that student and discourage him to ask such questions
D. You would tell the student that you would find out the answer of that question and tell him about the same the next day

142. What is your opinion about giving home work to students?
A. Highly intelligent students need not be given home work
B. Weak students should be given simple home work
C. All the students should be given the same home work
D. It would be beneficial to give home work to students according to their abilities and capacities

143. It is important for the teacher to have:
A. complete knowledge of the subject
B. complete knowledge of the teaching methods
C. knowledge about the students
D. All of these

144. Which method would be more effective to generate an interest among students for sports/games?
A. Showing them big-league matches
B. Giving new sports gear to children
C. Telling students that sports and games are as important as studies
D. Playing yourself in the playground along with children

145. Nowadays, the teacher does not enjoy such respect as was given to him during earlier times. The reason for this is that:
A. teachers take up tuition work
B. the character of teachers is not the same as it was during earlier times
C. teachers do not do their duties with dedication
D. All of these

146. Nowadays, students do not have a zeal to study. The reason for this is that:
A. they are unable to get enough of motivation to study
B. they feel that their future would not be right even after they complete their studies
C. they do not get a conducive environment for pursuing their studies
D. they opine that there is no need to study with special dedication (or zeal) to pass the examination

147. The best method to evaluate the achievements of students is the:
A. annual examination
B. bi-annual examination
C. quarterly examination
D. continuous evaluation

148. In your opinion, what would be the ideal seating arrangement for students in a class?
A. They should be made to sit according to their roll numbers
B. Friends should be allowed to sit close to one another
C. Little children should be made to sit in the front while bigger children should be told to sit on the backbenches
D. Intelligent children should be made to sit in the front while weak students should be told to sit on the backbenches

149. It has been mentioned in *Rigveda* that education:
A. is a characteristic of a civilised society
B. a source of knowledge and enlightenment
C. is the ultimate goal of the life
D. is knowledge

150. Education not only preserves the culture, but also it makes the latter:
A. enriched
B. defined
C. spiritual
D. popular among masses

151. Informal education of the child:
A. is carried out in a planned manner
B. starts from his environment
C. is given to him by an institution
D. is effected with efforts

152. The objective of education is all-round development of the child. Which one of the following is not included in this development?
A. Physical development
B. Intelligence development
C. Moral and spiritual development
D. Economic development

153. The objective of basic education of Gandhiji was to:
A. let the child come face-to-face with truth
B. make the child a sea of knowledge
C. to mould the child according to the needs of the society
D. to teach him a lesson of non-violence and truth

154. The basic education system was based on the viewpoint that the child:
A. learns all the good things with the cooperation of the people of the society

B. can get more knowledge by reading books
C. can get better education through a meaningful and creative piece of work
D. is not interested to learn anything without economic motivation

155. Gandhiji has given great importance to purposeful creative activity under the gamut of basic education. Which one of the following can be called purposeful creative activity?
A. Embroidery
B. Dyeing
C. Making toys of clay
D. All of these

156. Educational philosophy tells us what type of education should be imparted and why. On the contrary, the relationship of educational psychology is with the aspect of:
A. "when and how"
B. "whom and till what time"
C. "to whom and why"
D. All of these

157. The study of child psychology:
A. helps the teacher understand the discipline-related to education
B. gives a correct viewpoint about the problems related to education
C. helps him improve his abilities
D. helps him present ideals before the children

158. In order to effect the teaching of students in the most appropriate manner, who helps the teacher?
A. The class monitor
B. The study of child psychology
C. The blackboard
D. The presentation of the lesson plan

159. If a student is insulted by the teacher before the students of the class, then, as a result, the student, in all probability may:
A. become a fighter and arrogant
B. start concentrating more on his studies
C. start respecting the teacher more than ever before
D. Any one of these

160. Normally, students do not ask questions from the teacher during the course of class teaching, even if they may not be understanding the lecture being taught by the teacher. The chief reason for this phenomenon is that
A. they are afraid that the teacher would reprimand them and send them away
B. they think that if they ask questions, they might be counted amongst the dull students of the class
C. they may not be able to comprehend, which question should be asked
D. All of these

161. What is the best method, in your opinion, to help the little children remember a subject?
A. Understanding it from the heart
B. Remembering with care
C. Repeating it time to time and remembering it
D. Storing it in the brain

162. Why is there a need of mid day meal for little children in the school?
A. Children are habitual of eating time and again
B. Due to the greed for lunch, children do not remain absent from school
C. Children get some nutritional diet
D. Laziness of children is removed

163. When should the meeting of Parent-Teachers Association be held?
A. After the declaration of the result of the examination
B. After admission of new students in school
C. From time to time
D. At the occasion of annual function (or any other similar occasion)

164. Herbart has given a five-stage suggestion in the context of classroom teaching. The objective statement stage:
A. comes before the introduction
B. comes between introduction and presentation
C. comes after introduction and presentation
D. comes after generalisation

165. The presentation stage was deemed the most important in the five-stage system of Herbart. Hence, it is clear that this system:
A. gives the major status to the student
B. gives the major status to the subject matter
C. gives the major status to the teacher
D. gives the major status to the ability of student to assimilate knowledge

166. The lesson plan:
A. gives the knowledge of the success or failure of teaching to the teacher
B. is a means of connecting the previous knowledge of the students with their previous knowledge
C. makes the teacher successful in doing his work in a superior manner
D. All of these

167. Under Glover's scheme:
A. students do not take an active part in the teaching process
B. the teacher does not take an active part in teaching
C. questions are not asked
D. students take an active part in teaching process

168. The educational method of Socrates:
A. was a question method
B. did not have the concept of imposition of knowledge on the student from outside
C. had the concept of movement of the student in the direction of auto-education
D. All of these

169. Who, from among the following, had propounded the principle of "pupil activity?"
A. Rousseau B. Handerson
C. Commenius D. Binet

170. Who is known as the pioneer of the principle of "pupil activity" in Europe?
A. John Adams B. Lyndon
C. Glover D. Rousseau

171. Who is deemed the creator of the play-way method of education?
A. Caldwel Cook B. Madam Montessori
C. Froebel D. John Dewey

172. The special feature of the play-way method is that:
A. sports/games take the place of work (studies)
B. there is no importance of work (studies) in it
C. the monotony or boredom of work (studies) is removed by incorporating sports/games
D. education cannot be completed without sports/games

173. The word 'kindergarten' has been drawn from the German language. Its meaning is a
A. small garden
B. beautiful garden
C. flower garden
D. children's garden

174. In the kindergarten system of teaching, the status of the teacher is like that of a:
A. potter B. gardener
C. (earthen) lamp D. referee

175. The Montessori system of education:
A. teaches students the writing and reading skills through the psychological method
B. does not believe in the system of auto-education
C. does not develop self-discipline among students
D. does not give adequate importance to the interests and curiosity of students

176. The Montessori system of teaching is:
A. focused on the teacher
B. focused on the textbook
C. focused on the child
D. focused on the study material

177. Who was the pioneer of the Heuristic method of teaching?
A. Herbert Spencer
B. Professor Armstrong
C. John Adams
D. Monroe

178. In which system of education, was the teaching of senses emphasised upon?
A. Kindergarten System
B. Montessori System
C. Heuristic System
D. None of these

179. "This system trains the student to find the facts, rules and principles through his own efforts, organise the knowledge gained and define the general rules." The aforesaid statement is referred to the–

A. Montessori system of teaching
B. Kindergarten system of teaching
C. Heuristic system of teaching
D. Play-way method of teaching

180. With whom, is the project teaching method associated?

A. Rousseau
B. Froebel
C. Dewey and Kilpatric
D. Armstrong

181. The project method of teaching imparts practical knowledge to the student, because:

A. it accepts the personal diversities (of the students)
B. it develops the latent powers of the student
C. the basis of knowledge of the student is his personal experiences
D. it gives an opportunity to ponder over the logic and for debates

182. The Dalton Plan:

A. is not suitable for children of lower age groups
B. is not child-focused
C. considers the curriculum to be practicable
D. does not accept the personal diversities

183. The chief aim of basic education is to:

A. make the student self-dependent
B. give the knowledge of the basic elements of education
C. make students philosophers
D. All of these

184. Which one of the following statements is correct in the context of objective type questions?

A. It is very easy to construct these questions
B. The power of expression of students is known through these questions
C. The genuine thinking of students is known by these questions
D. A very large portion of the curriculum can be included (in the test/examination) with the help of these questions

185. Those students, who have very small heights, develop an inferiority complex. What would you recommend to such a student?

A. He should do away with his inferiority complex
B. He should take up exercises to increase his height
C. He should achieve excellence in some other field
D. He should wear shoes with high heels

186. If teachers send monthly reports of students to their parents/guardians, then:

A. teachers get the time for gossiping
B. teachers have to do such pieces of work as make them unpopular
C. the relationships are maintained between the teachers and their parents/guardians of his students
D. the responsibility of teachers towards their students is minimised

187. Little children are highly agile and active. You would:

A. stop their activity
B. try to reduce the levels of their activity
C. study their activity
D. give them useful education with the help of their activity

188. Who, from among the following scholars, had stated, "Sport is the innate natural tendency of a child?"

A. Stern
B. Valvetine
C. McDugal
D. Nun

189. All the teaching methods of modern type, like Kindergarten, Montessori, Dalton Basic and project methods:

A. are based on the principle of activity method
B. are based on synthetic method
C. are based on the laboratory method
D. are not based on any one of these methods

190. In order to make the senses of little children capable and active, you would:
A. put materials before them and let them examine the same
B. get the job of lifting and putting objects done from them
C. keep them active
D. tell them to sit quietly in the class

191. Which method, from among the following, would you adopt to evaluate the power of expression and style of students?
A. You would ask questions from them and take answers of the same from them
B. You would give them questions and tell them to write down their answers
C. You would give them objective type question as home work
D. All of these

192. On which one of the following, does the Montessori method lay the maximum emphasis?
A. Personal development of the student
B. Social development of the student
C. Moral development of the student
D. All-round development of the student

193. For whom is the Dalton system of education useful?
A. Infants
B. Little children
C. Grown up children
D. All of these

194. The following three qualities must be present in an examination:
A. validity, reliability and practicality
B. comprehensiveness, evaluation and usability
C. validity, evaluation and practicality
D. comprehensiveness, evaluation and practicality

195. One of the principles of education is—the child should be given new (sets of) knowledge by knowing about his previous sets of knowledge. How can we know about the previous knowledge of the child?
A. By asking his parents/guardians
B. By talking to them
C. By asking questions from them
D. By reading books on psychology

196. The answer booklets of students should be evaluated by other teachers and not by their own teachers. By doing this, students would:
A. get more marks
B. know about the reality of their knowledge levels
C. not be given unjust and partial treatment
D. develop more self-confidence

197. According to Dewey, education is a:
A. social need
B. personal need
C. psychological need
D. theoretical need

198. Quite often, students don't complete their home work on a regular basis. What could be the possible reason for this?
A. Students might not have got the cooperation of their parents/guardians at their homes
B. Students might not have got the time due to other pieces of work (or engagements)
C. Students might not be knowing how to complete home work
D. Some students may have forgotten to complete home work

199. The curriculum should be flexible. If it were not so, then:
A. the development of students with different personalities would not be possible due to it
B. it would become subject-focused
C. it would not be able to encourage societal feelings
D. it would not be able to become popular among students

200. You are in favour of school inspection from time to time because:
A. on this occasions, attention is not given to studies and an artificial atmosphere is created; this leads to cleaning of the school and all pieces of work are updated.

B. due to the fear of inspection, some good tasks are carried out

C. teachers get an opportunity to have discussions with senior officers of the education department

D. All of these

201. Student-centred teaching means:

A. taking care of the need(s) of every student

B. letting students do whatever they like

C. give free education to all the students

D. take complete cooperation of students in teaching

202. Who gave the statement, "In a school, arrangements should be made for the free and natural expressions of a child?"

A. T. Remont B. Rhyburn

C. Montessori D. Lyndon

203. Personal education is most important for:

A. intelligent students

B. students who are slow learners

C. Both of these A and B

D. None of these

204. Which subject can be taught in the best manner through the Heuristic system of teaching?

A. Science

B. Languages

C. Arts

D. Only B and C

205. What suggestion would you give to check the habit of cramming among students?

A. A change in evaluation

B. A change in the examination/test method

C. A change in the teaching method

D. A change in the interests of students

206. If a student uses indecent language, then a possible reason for this behaviour of the student could be that:

A. a similar type of language may be spoken at his home

B. the same language may be spoken in most of the homes in his neighbourhood

C. his colleagues/friends may be speaking this language

D. All of these

207. When the teacher, who has taught the students, evaluates their examination test booklets, then what is the possibility, from among the following?

A. The teacher would give less marks to the students so that they work harder than before in their studies

B. The teacher would give pass marks to all the students

C. It is possible that impartial evaluation is not done

D. All of these

208. The best system of class teaching is the one in which:

A. there is no need for the question-answer session

B. the teacher asks questions from his students

C. the student removes his doubts after consulting his teacher

D. both the teacher and students ask questions

209. What type of questions would you like to ask in the class?

A. The ones whose answers can be given by all the students

B. The ones whose answers cannot be given by all the students

C. The ones whose answers can perhaps be given by none of the students

D. The ones whose answers may be given by students after thinking about them

210. Defence mechanism acts in a subconscious manner (*i.e.*, without the humans being aware of its activity). Which one of the following is correct in the context of this mechanism?

A. Mentally dull students are not able to use it quite often

B. Intelligent students extensively use this method

C. All the students use this method

D. Those students, who are slow learners, are unable to use it

211. The basis of social discipline is:

A. fear and punishment

B. condemnation and praise

C. a desire to become virtuous

D. refinement of good moral values

212. There is a fear of creation of problem related to discipline if:
A. students fall in or have bad company
B. students are dominated or suppressed through artificial methods
C. the school is not located at an appropriate placc
D. All of these

213. Little children are unable to pronounce long and difficult words in the right manner. What type of solution would you like to pursue?
A. You would make them speak such words time and again
B. You would make them speak such words by dividing them into parts first
C. You would take the help of such words as have almost similar pronunciations as those of the difficult words
D. Both B and C

214. The proof of complete expertise in knowledge gained by a student is that he:
A. has acquired that knowledge through toil
B. has fully understood that knowledge
C. can successfully use that knowledge
D. has acquired/gained knowledge theoretically

215. Who played the most significant role in making English as a medium of education during the British rule in India?
A. William Bentick B. Curzon
C. McCaulay D. Dalhousie

216. Who gets the credit of starting the Dalton method of education?
A. Dr. Dalton B. Parkhurst
C. Kilpatrick D. Pinsent

217. While learning a language from the psychological viewpoint, little children:
A. learn sentences first of all
B. learn words first of all
C. learn the alphabet first of all
D. learn the vowels first of all

218. What did pragmatism give birth to?
A. Basic education
B. Project method
C. Play method of education
D. None of these

219. Who was the pioneer of the thought of pragmatism in the field of education?
A. Kilpatrick B. John Dewey
C. William James D. Pestalozzi

220. Who started the movement of naturalism in the field of education?
A. Pestalozzi B. Herbart
C. Spencer D. Dewey

221. Pestalozzi was of the opinion that:
A. education should be in accordance with the development of the child
B. the teacher should respect the personality of the child
C. the objective of education is to develop the mental powers of the child
D. All of these

222. Education would be meaningful only then, when it would be:
A. curriculum-centred
B. teacher-centred
C. society-centred
D. student-centred

223. If a student wears unironed and dirty clothes and comes to the class, then you would:
A. not let him sit in the class
B. make fun of him in the class
C. tell him, through hints/gestures, that it is not a good habit to come to the class in such clothes
D. not pay any attention to this issue

224. Under the Wennetka Plan:
A. there is no room for conventional education
B. there is no room for the lesson method
C. there is no room for classroom teaching
D. there is no room for any one of these

225. The theoretical basis of the Montessori educational system is:
A. complete freedom to the child to play the games of his own choice
B. that the child gets motivation from his teacher
C. complete freedom to the child in expressing his interests
D. that sports/games help in the education of the child

226. One benefit of regularly evaluating the home work given to children is that:

A. children do not forget to bring their completed home work

B. you remain abreast of the progress of students

C. children remain informed about their weaknesses

D. All of these

227. You have been given the responsibility of making the question paper of the final examination of the students of a class. You would

A. put all the easy questions in the question paper

B. put easy questions first in the question paper and then, put difficult questions

C. give the same marks to all the questions—essay type and objective type

D. put fifty per cent questions of a difficult level

228. Under the analytical method of class teaching, the student:

A. moves from the unknown to the known

B. moves from the known to the unknown

C. analyses two known facts

D. compares two known facts

229. The correct meaning of the curriculum is:

A. a collection of all the curricular activities

B. a collection of all those experiences that the school wants children to imbibe

C. a collection of the compulsory and optional subjects

D. a collection of that (study) material by memorising which, students can pass in their (respective) classes

230. The contributions of Rousseau are vital in the field of education. Which one of the following is not his contribution?

A. Child psychology and child-centred education

B. The central role of the teacher in education

C. The importance of sports in education

D. Improvements in the curricula

231. The availability of diaries with students leads to the following chief advantage:

A. their parents/guardians remain abreast with their studies on a regular basis

B. children get support in improving their handwriting

C. children get support in remembering the topics related to studies

D. children get support in completing their curricula

232. The best benefit that can accrue due to the meeting of the parent and the teacher is that

A. both the parent and teacher agree about the goals of achievement of the child

B. the teacher explains on what basis he has given marks to the child (and how many marks have been given in various subjects)

C. The parent/guardian tells the teacher about the previous background (or past) of the child

D. The parent/guardian asks the teacher how and to what extent he can help the child complete his home work

233. In the school, the weekly educational programme is shown on the television in the class. Some parents/guardians meet the teacher and complain that their children are already spending a lot of time watching television at their (respective) homes. The parents/guardians want that children should not be shown to the television programme in the school. What should the teacher do in such a situation?

A. He should advise the parents/guardians that they should control the habit of watching television of their children at homes

B. After receiving the complaint by parents/ guardians, he should stop the weekly television education programme in the school

C. He should talk to parents/guardians and take the responsibility of advising/ convincing students

D. He should invite all the parents guardians to the weekly television education programme in the school so that they are able to find out that this programme is very beneficial for children and also, enhances their knowledge levels

234. On what basis, should the achievement of a student be evaluated?

A. By comparing the achievement of a student with that of the most intelligent student of the class

B. By comparing the achievement of a student with the expectation from an ordinary student of the class

C. By comparing the present achievement of the student with his previous record of achievements

D. By comparing the achievement of the student with all three mentioned in option A, B and C

235. Guidance is given so that the student is able to identify himself and develop his abilities. Which one of the following statements is not correct in this context?

A. Without any guidance with a vision, it is not possible to impart good education

B. In the absence of effective education, guidance cannot be successful

C. Guidance and education are complementary to each other

D. The importance of guidance during the beginning stage of education is much more than it is during the subsequent stages of education

236. How can the ability of experimentation be developed among the students of science?

A. By showing them experiments in the class

B. By telling them about the benefits of carrying out (scientific) experiments

C. By letting them practise their experiments

D. By ordering them to complete the experiments at their homes

237. You plan to organise a small bazaar in the school so that little children of your school get the actual practice and know-how of purchasing goods from the market and paying for them in cash. The Principal of your school does not give you the permission to organise this bazaar. What would you do in such a situation?

A. You would organise the bazaar even if you do not get the permission of your Principal, because the same is being organised to give a new experience to children

B. You would persuade children to go to the Principal and get his permission (to organise the bazaar)

C. You would personally meet the Principal and try to get his permission by explaining him about the importance of organising the bazaar

D. You would take other teachers of the school along with you and meet the officials of the education department; to tell those officials how your Principal creates problems for you

238. What is your opinion about the development of skills?

A. Children of same mental age learn at the same speed

B. It is just possible that children of the same mental age may not be able to learn at the same speed

C. The mental age of those children, who learn at the same speed, is the same

D. All of these

239. The following scholar had stated, "Whosoever has the power to do something, does work; the one who cannot do anything, teaches."

A. Karl Jung

B. Henry Bernard

C. George Bernard Shaw

D. Alexander Pope

240. In which country, were the kindergarten schools inaugurated for the first time?

A. England

B. France

C. Italy

D. Germany

241. Making the students of a primary class cram the multiplication tables:

A. amounts to tyranny on little students

B. is misuse of the memory of children

C. helps children in solving questions in the future

D. is absolutely useless

242. The most important contribution of Froebel in the field of education was:
A. Public Schools
B. Kindergarten
C. Education of the disabled
D. The project method of education

243. Do you feel that the class curriculum should be the same for both the male and female students?
A. Yes, there should be no difference between the curricula of these students
B. No, the curriculum of female students should be in accordance with their physical and emotional needs
C. Yes, education for the purpose of making them capable of jobs should be the same for both of them
D. No, the curricula for both the male and female students should be totally different

244. In primary schools, Operation Blackboard:
A. has been promoted to raise the educational standards
B. is related to giving mid-day meals to students
C. is related to increasing the (physical) facilities in primary schools
D. is related to training of teachers

245. The first ever district, which had achieved full literacy, is:
A. Eranakulam (Kerala)
B. Trivendrum (Kerala)
C. Kottayam (Kerala)
D. Trichur (Kerala)

246. Which one of the following is not true in the context of Navodaya Vidyalayas?
A. Navodaya Vidyalayas are there for giving the best and most modern education (through the latest methods) to the intelligent students
B. These vidyalayas are run by the Navodaya School Committee
C. During the Seventh Five Year Plan, the target of opening at least one Navodaya Vidyalaya in every district was set
D. Female and urban students cannot take admission in these schools

247. Which Institution is responsible for the spread of university education, coordination and maintenance of standards of education in Universities?
A. NCERT
B. UGC
C. Education Advisory Board
D. The Ministry of Education

248. The best argument for group intelligence test is that it:
A. treats all the children equally
B. provides the teacher with diagnostic information
C. is less tension-producing than an individual test
D. is the least expensive method to determine the IQ

249. It is no use making students forcibly sit in the class, if they are not willing to study or learn. What is important for creating an urge in their minds to study or learn?
A. Discipline B. Recreation
C. High ideals D. Motivation

250. Motivation is a:
A. physical state
B. psychological state
C. neural state
D. natural state

251. The greatest advantage of programmed instruction is that student:
A. can gain knowledge here without the help of the teacher through self-study
B. is guided here by reinforcement
C. does not have to think here what he has to do further
D. None of the above

252. Which of the following is an example of oral communication?
A. Vijay recited a poem loudly while standing on terrace
B. Signal became red from green on the crossing
C. Baby was crying for drawing the attention of the mother
D. Sunil read the letter for Anil

253. When does symbolic communication or non-verbal communication become more effective than oral or written communication?
- A. When sender is at such a distance from the receiver that the later can not hear the former
- B. When environment is surcharged with noise pollution
- C. When it is necessary to demonstrate gestures
- D. All of the above

254. How is small group communication different from large group communication?
- A. Small group offers more opportunities to influence the participant than the large group
- B. Interaction is very much limited in small group communication
- C. Small group takes less time to send the message
- D. Communication provides better feed back to participants in large group

255. Discussion method can be very effective in the class if:
- A. topic of discussion is announced just before the discussion starts
- B. topic of discussion is announced well before the discussion
- C. topic of discussion is written on the black board at the time of discussion
- D. None of the above

256. Why are children compared with plants?
- A. The rate of progress is very slow for both of them
- B. Both of them need food to develop
- C. Just as plants maintain their growth if they are cut and cleaned, in the same way, students are also checked by the process of evaluation to keep them moving on the path of progress
- D. All of these

257. Why is intelligence testing necessary?
- A. So that students can be categorised into different groups according to their intellectual abilities and teaching can be arranged according to their specific abilities
- B. So that mentally retarded children be checked to take admission in normal schools
- C. So that talented students can be identified to provide them special teaching according to their potentials
- D. A and C both

258. For lesson planning, which of the following is first required?
- A. Evaluation of entering behaviour of pupils
- B. Analysis of teaching task
- C. Determination of objectives
- D. None of the above

259. What is the advantage of studying reference books and other study material?
- A. They develop comprehensiveness in knowledge
- B. They develop decision power
- C. They entertain the pupil
- D. Good marks are obtained in the examination.

260. Which of the following is necessary in order to maintain the educational standard in private educational institutions?
- A. Transparent examination system
- B. Ensuring good salaries to teachers
- C. Extra-evaluation of the students from time to time
- D. All of these

261. In order to save the students from the disturbance in their studies, the teacher:
- A. should take them on an excursion
- B. should change his tone and pitch during teaching
- C. should use suitable teaching strategies and techniques in order to make his subject interesting
- D. should keep on asking questions from his students

262. What can we know by keeping an eye on the body language of pupils?
- A. Which student in the class is in tension
- B. Which student is not attentive to teaching-learning process
- C. Which student can do what in future
- D. All of the above

263. While preparing the lesson plan for the class, what should be kept by the teacher in view as a major decisive factor?
A. The average student of the class should also be benefited from this lesson plan
B. Objectives of teaching achieved
C. The aims of the curriculum should be achieved
D. All of these

264. A student of your class informs you in a secret manner that three students of your class copy one another's test copies quite often during the tests. He also gives you the names of those students. What would be your reaction upon getting this information?
A. You would not pay heed to the information given by him
B. You would like those three students
C. You would reprimand those three students
D. You would think why that student had given you that information

265. The method of silent reading:
A. increases the comprehension skill
B. helps remember in a better manner
C. does not waste time
D. All of these

266. If during the course of classroom teaching, students do not show positive reactions, then, in your opinion, its reason could be traced in the following:
A. in that subject, which is being taught to students
B. in that issue/topic, which is being taught to students
C. in that style in which, students are being taught/trained
D. All of these

267. In the class, the class monitor beats up a student (who is creating mischief) in your absence. After entering into the class, you would:
A. punish the monitor
B. remove him from the post of monitor
C. tell the monitor to apologise to the student he had thrashed
D. tell the monitor in privacy that he has no right to beat up any of the students

268. Why is adult education necessary:
A. the number of adults is the largest
B. it would be easy for adults to get jobs
C. it is less expensive to educate adults
D. educated adults would also make all possible efforts to educate their children

269. Some students of your class have very high levels of intelligence. They do not find the study material (being taught in the class) to be challenging. What would you like to do in the context of such students?
A. You would tell them that they may or may not come to the class, depending upon their wish
B. You would tell the Principal that such students should be taught in the next academic standard
C. You would allocate them such special tasks as would be more difficult than those allocated to the students of normal intelligence
D. You would tell them that they should spend most of their time in the library

270. The Principal would be able to do his work in a better manner, if he:
A. works with concensus in the school
B. takes decisions in cooperation with and consent of other teachers
C. gives the maximum importance to discipline
D. organises meetings of teachers for solving each and every problem

271. The actual benefit of giving home work would accrue only when the teacher regularly evaluates the home work of his students and:
A. give them marks accordingly
B. keep on telling them about their mistakes
C. keep records of mistakes of his students so that he may be able to present such records before their parents/guardians
D. tell during the parent teacher meetings what type (and quantity) of home work was got done by his students

272. An expert educationist has compared the school with a garden. He states that in a school:
A. the feeling of (appreciation for) beauty should be developed among students
B. students should get an opportunity to have a view of the nature
C. students should be looked after just like delicate plants
D. students should be allowed to roam about freely in the school

273. What type of problem can possibly surface due to the development of the feelings of disgust, disappointment and lack of interest among students?
A. The problem of discipline
B. The problem of frequent absence of students
C. The problem of adoption of corrupt means during the examinations
D. All of these

274. Do you agree with the statement of a scholar that "a little child is immature in terms of intelligence and helpless and should not be given so much freedom that he is completely destroyed."
A. No
B. Yes, partially
C. Yes, fully
D. No, because if he is not given freedom, even then he can be destroyed

275. A little child can identify a cow. You give him the knowledge about the use of the tail of the cow or its habit of lumination. Which one of the following denotes this technique?
A. From direct to indirect
B. From indefinite to definite
C. From experience to logic
D. From general to particular

276. What is your opinion about giving permission to pupils to ask questions in the class?
A. Complete freedom should be given to students to ask questions in the class
B. They should not be given permission to ask questions in the class
C. They should be given freedom to ask questions only when it is very much needed, so that time is not wasted without reason
D. None of the above

277. If a student is using unfair means in the examination by the support of political leaders or gundas, what will you do in such a case?
A. You will ignore the situation
B. You will act according to the rule
C. You would not like to develop enmity with such a student
D. You will conduct the examination by taking the help of the police

278. Which of the following is called the most difficult period of social adjustment?
A. Later childhood stage
B. Pre-adolescence period in the context of boys and girls both
C. Adolescence period
D. Period of adulthood

279. Sex education can be imparted to high school children by/in:
A. co-education
B. religious and moral education
C. the form of a separate subject
D. A and B both

280. The exhibition of sex related activities in boys and girls of pre-primary classes can be explained as:
A. a serious problem whose effect in the long run can be harmful
B. a normal but full of curiosity behaviour which will be rectified automatically when they develop their sense of understanding
C. a behaviour that children have inherited from the gene of their parents
D. All of the above

281. What should a teacher do in order to integrate the child of lonely loving nature to the group?
A. He should nominate him the member of a good group
B. Project method should be used more and more in the class so that they can learn how to work in a group

C. Such social qualities should be developed in the child so that the group may come closer to him and he comes to like the group as well
D. All of the above

282. The parameter of good school discipline is:
A. absence of mismanagement and noise in the school
B. obedience of rules and regulations by students and teachers with pleasure
C. good responsible behaviour
D. All of the above

283. "Give respect and get respect". This proverb is applicable in
A. offices and working places
B. social situations
C. all the places including schools equally
D. only in schools

284. Majority of students in rural areas do not take admission after high school because
A. intermediate colleges are generally not available there and they go long distances to attend colleges
B. education is not providing them employment howsoever high it is in standard
C. they can't bear the expenses of education which is high at this level
D. A and B both

285. Students can go to another school for admission by leaving their school if
A. the treatment of their teacher is very strict and hard
B. teachers insult and condemn their students
C. there is no coordination between teachers and students
D. All of the above

286. Which type of education is beneficial for students and the society both at present?
A. Education giving knowledge of technology
B. Employment oriented professional education
C. Religious education emphasizing moral values
D. Education providing specialization

287. The rate of development of games' interest can be increased in students only when
A. they are given refreshment after games
B. they are given ample opportunities to take part in play activities in schools and these activities are linked with the rules of motivation
C. students should be given marks on games activities also
D. All of these

288. What is your opinion on tuition or any other type of coaching classes?
A. Coaching makes a teacher studious and his knowledge increases
B. It reduces the dignity of a teacher to a great extent
C. Students do not get time for self-study if they are associated with a tuition and they also fail to complete their home work
D. B and C both

289. Why physical health is also necessary along with mental health for a teacher?
A. Teacher has to be very active in the class while teaching
B. Physical and mental both type of activities are required in teaching
C. A teacher is bound to play with his students also which requires strong physical heath
D. A and B both

290. Study of newspapers and magazines helps us
A. to know the current affairs and day to day events
B. improves the good habits of teachers
C. both of the above
D. None of the above

291. What can be the result if women education is made at all levels of education approachable?
A. Education system can be a failure due to this extravagance
B. Women will come to the level of men after some time
C. Due to this encouragement people will stop the practice of female foeticide and sex ratio will improve in few years
D. B and C both

292. Who should really control the education upto middle level in your opinion?
A. Village pradhan, chairman of the municipal board or mayor
B. Community through elected representatives
C. State government
D. Central government

293. Which of the following things is needed to improve whole education system?
A. Change in the attitude of teachers
B. Change in the attitude of principals
C. Change in the curriculum
D. Change in the thinking of the government

294. Teaching profession is more suitable for women than other professions because
A. it can give them more number of holidays
B. it requires working in less number of hours
C. it can help them to earn more money by tuition works
D. this profession gives respect to women on one hand and on the other hand, there is less chance of misbehaviour meted out to women

295. Powerful medium of providing sex education is
A. textbooks
B. education imparted by parents
C. guidance given by the teacher
D. films on sex-related problems

296. In parents' meet if parents do not agree with the viewpoint of teacher, then
A. teacher must try to remove the doubts of parents to the maximum level possible
B. the teacher should leave the meeting
C. teacher should concede to guardians by considering them superior
D. teacher should not express his disagreement before his students

297. If you are included in a jury of debate competition
A. you will feel proud
B. you will give decision according to the performance of the participants
C. you will give decision on the basis of decision given by others
D. you will not give any weightage to the content. You will consider only the expression

298. What is your view-point regarding open schooling system?
A. It is a good source of education extension
B. This gives chance of education to those students also who happen to leave schooling in the middle due to any reason
C. Learning material is obtained here at home
D. A and B both

299. The similarity between teacher and a doctor is that
A. both of them are social workers
B. both of them take remedial measures after proper diagnosis
C. both of them come from the same educational background at least at school level
D. both of them are professionals

300. As a teacher, which type of student would you like most?
A. He who is obedient
B. He who is active and hard working
C. He who is peace loving
D. He who comes to school by completing his home work daily

301. Of the following, the best example of an anecdotal report is
A. "Tom is always fidgeting; he must be hyperactive".
B. "Tom doesn't like reading; he always fidgets during a reading session."
C. "On 12/1, 12/2, 12/4, during the reading group time, Tom fidgeted in his seat."
D. "Tom is fidgeting; his parents must be putting a lot of pressure on him."

302. The informal textbook test is
A. a method of evaluating a pupil's preference for a particular basal reader
B. the same as an open-textbook test
C. a simple procedure for parents to use in checking their child's homework
D. a procedure for determining the reading level of a child

303. The limitation of the inductive method of teaching is that
A. it wastes time and is slow
B. it goes students and opportunity to practise and so, develops their brains
C. it is not a psychological method
D. in this method, the student does participate in the process of learning

304. The deductive method of teaching
A. imparts knowledge at a fast pace
B. does not impart knowledge at a fast pace
C. makes the work of the teacher quite complicated
D. is very useful for children

305. Which one of the following statements is not correct?
A. Inductive and deductive methods of teaching are complements of each other
B. Both the methods are used simultaneously
C. Both the methods are opponents of each other
D. The principle, which is identified/formed with the help of the inductive method, is tested with the help of the deductive method

306. Which one of the following is not true in the context of class teaching or group teaching?
A. It motivates students for group work (collective work)
B. It increases the teaching ability of the teacher
C. It saves money, time and space
D. It is not useful for mentally retarded students

307. Which one of the following does not happen under the personalised teaching system?
A. The student gets complete attention from the teacher
B. The student gets ample opportunities to work according to his tastes/interests
C. The teacher is the centre of education
D. The teacher is able to understand the attitudes of the student

308. In the project education technique, the work load on the teacher is
A. very high
B. comparatively low
C. low
D. nil

309. The main objective of basic education is to
A. make the student self-dependent
B. give the knowledge of basic elements of education to the student
C. make the student a philosopher
D. All of these

310. Basic education is
A. activity based B. student based
C. handicraft based D. All of these

311. Under the Wennetka Plan, which one of the following has a position of major importance?
A. Personalised education
B. Conventional education
C. Group education
D. Class education

312. Who is known as the father of educational psychology?
A. Pestology B. Dewey
C. Herbart D. Spencer

313. "There should be no difference between the words and deeds of a teacher." who gave this statement?
A. Mcckennan B. John Locke
C. Rousseau D. Aristotle

314. In your opinion, a successful teacher is one, who
A. gives home work regularly
B. gives good marks in examinations
C. takes keen interest in the progress of students
D. comes to school on time

315. A teacher should be proud of that student who
A. is dedicated to the profession he is in
B. generating a lot of money in business
C. acting well in movies
D. building in future of students with dedication by becoming a teacher

316. After becoming a teacher, you will like to teach which of the following level?
A. Primary levels B. Middle level
C. Graduate level D. Technical

317. In your class, a student is not able to answer a question due to fear even if he knows it. You will

A. tell him the answer
B. try to find the basic reasons of his fear
C. tell him time and again to answer the question
D. ask for an answer from another student

318. For a good teacher, the item of contentment is

A. high status
B. money
C. respect and prestige
D. support of masses

319. For the students of middle classes, the system of "examination centre in the school itself" is justified because

A. students do not have to go far away from the school
B. students get the facility to copy in their own school
C. students remain disciplined in their own school
D. students feel disappointed at other examination centres

320. You will like that student who is

A. soft spoken
B. respects his elders
C. hard working in academics
D. having all the qualities stated in steps A, B and C

321. What will be your attitude towards those students who are weak in studies?

A. Empathetic : So that they are able to study with more concentration and hard work
B. Harsh : So that they may become afraid and so, study by working hard
C. Liberal : So that they may be able to solve their problems without fears
D. Affectional : So that they may not quit school due to desperation

322. In your school, there are four sections (A, B, C and D) in class 5. The students of section D are weakest in studies. You have been allocated section D for teaching. What will be your attitude?

A. My job is to teach : I shall teach
B. This is a problem : I will have to work harder in order to teach this class
C. I am pleased : I will use all my powers for the development of students of this class
D. Studying is the job of students Whosoever will study, shall pass; whosoever will not study, shall fail

323. You find a student to be intelligent. You will

A. remain pleased with him
B. not give him additional homework
C. motivate him so that he can make more progress
D. inform his parents about the fact that he is intelligent

324. If some students are not in a mood to study in the class, you will

A. force them to study
B. tell those students to leave the class and enjoy
C. warn them that they must study else you will report the matter to the Principal
D. tell them some interesting things related to their interests or your own subject

325. The problem of maintaining discipline in the class is related to which one of the following?

A. Which subject is being taught
B. How interesting is the subject being taught
C. How are students seated in the class
D. All of these

326. If student is too shy to participate in the class, you will

A. not ask questions from him
B. ask only those questions from him whose answers can be given by him
C. not ask those questions from him whose answers are beyond his means and due to which, he may become an object of ridicule in the class
D. ask questions from him only when he is keen to answer them

327. Which of the following functions of education is not related to social change?

A. Education should check undesirable social change

B. Education should accelerate the process of social change
C. Education should also change with the social change
D. All of the above

328. Some students speak ill of their teachers in their absence (and you are one of them). You will
A. punish those students
B. report the matter to the Principal
C. talk to those students with an open heart and advise them to discuss the issue with all those teachers about whom, they nurture any grudge
D. Speak ill of those students in the presence of those students who support you

329. Of the following, the situation that will cause the greatest difficulty for a child in the initial stages of reading instruction is
A. confusion of left and right directionality
B. possessing a value of IQ of 90
C. never having attended kindergarten
D. being an avid television viewer

330. All of the following are true about phobias, except that
A. they are generated by early emotional experiences
B. acrophobia is a fear of open places; agoraphobia is a fear of high places
C. the sufferer cannot control the impulse to avoid them
D. the sufferer

331. Special Education is related to
A. adult education programmes
B. educational programmes for the disabled
C. educational programmes for talented students
D. teachers training programmes

332. Oral reading in the schools of today
A. is of no use
B. is appropriate when it is useful
C. should be used only for reading poetry
D. should not start before the fifth grade

333. The problem of unemployment can be solved by
A. making all the people literate
B. concentrating on character building
C. starting courses of professional education in schools
D. higher education

334. The teacher has to learn about problems prevalent in the field of education because
A. only a teacher can find the remedies of such problems
B. only a teacher can tell about them to the Principal
C. he can tell other teachers
D. he is aware of the structure of the society

335. Which of the following is an important technological factor of social change?
A. Improvement in communication and transport
B. Mechnization of daily life
C. Opening domestic markets of international trade
D. All of the above

336. The chief cause of degradation of education is the conversion of education into a profession. You
A. fully agree with this statement
B. partially agree with this statement
C. disagree with this statement
D. feel that there is no relationship of education with profession

337. Your suggestion for those children, who are weak in studies, is that
A. they should study through tuitions at home
B. they should complete their homework with the help of their parents
C. they should improve upon their studies in remedial classes that are held after the school hours
D. they should remember only important questions for appearing in examinations

338. You have been told to accommodate two mentally retarded children in your class. You will
A. refuse to accept them as your students
B. tell the Principal to accommodate them in another class that is exclusively meant for mentally retarded children

C. learn techniques to teach such students and accept them as a part of your class
D. ignore those children in the class

339. The major reason of growing indiscipline in schools is
A. political interference
B. interference of parents/guardians
C. influence of students' unions
D. lack of proper guidance

340. In order to develop the virtue of compassion in students, you will
A. tell them about its importance
B. give examples in this context
C. show them the behaviour of kind persons
D. arrange academic activities related to compassion in the school

341. In order to develop the spirit of labour in students
A. the teacher himself should indulge in labour
B. the teacher should deliver lectures on the importance of labour
C. students should be given opportunities to do labour from time to time
D. students should be given examples of labouring people

342. The Parents Teachers Association (PTA) has great importance because
A. students meet their teachers along with their parents
B. both parents/guardians and teachers get an opportunity to learn about the problems of one another
C. teachers and parents/guardians sit together and discuss ways and means to solve the problems of students
D. the administration of the school is improved through the work of this association

343. A child has been admitted to your school who belongs to a backward family/background from the cultural viewpoint. You will
A. keep him in a class in which, there are many more students of backward background from the cultural viewpoint
B. send a teacher to know more about the backward cultural background of that child
C. keep him in a normal class but will make special arrangements for teaching him, keeping his special needs in view
D. advise him to take up vocational education

344. In which of the following ways education can promote social mobility?
A. It can make the person liberal in his attitude and thinking
B. It can enable us to get administrative power
C. It can help to change occupation
D. All of the above

345. If a student is not able to answer a question during the course of the lecture, then you will:
A. scold him and hence, insult him
B. tell him the correct answer yourself
C. try to understand why that student was not able to give correct answer
D. advise the student to study more carefully

346. You think that taking surprise tests is justified because:
A. students remain frightened due to these
B. you do not have to get yourself prepared at home for this purpose
C. you can escape the teaching session due to the alibi of taking a surprise test
D. the abilities and knowledge levels of students can be truly judged through such tests

347. In your opinion, what should be the age for sending little children to school?
A. When the child starts speaking
B. When the child develops an interest in studies
C. When the child attains the age of plus five years
D. When the child attains the age of plus three years

348. Some students quietly run away from school. In order to check this habit of such students, you would:
A. try to know why they run away from school
B. inform the Principal about their habit of running away from school

C. inform the parents of such children about their habit of running away from school
D. try to make class-teaching more interesting

349. Suppose that you give tuition to a student and he fails in the annual examination. In such a situation, you would:
A. request the Principal to help him get through
B. request other teachers to increase his marks
C. suggest the parent/guardian of the student that he/she should try to use references to contact other teachers so that they increase the marks of the student
D. teach that student with a renewed vigour and toil in future

350. If a student misbehaves with you, then as a teacher, what would be your reaction?
A. You would file a complaint with the Principal
B. You would punish the student so that he pays evenly for his offense
C. You would pardon the student and forget the incident
D. You would complain to other teachers of the school and initiate a campaign to expel him from the school.

351. A student is very weak in mathematics. What would you like to do to help him?
A. You would get an advice from the Principal in this context
B. You would give proper advice to the parents of the student in this context
C. You would talk to the student and find out what are his problems in mathematics; later you would remove those problems
D. You would order the most intelligent student in mathematics (of the class) to help the weak student

352. Some students of your class have weak eye-sights. They are unable to clearly see whatever is written on the blackboard. What is your opinion about solving this problems?
A. Let these children sit in the front seats in the class
B. Call the parents/guardians of such children and advise them to arrange spectacles for their respective Children/wards
C. Tell these children to get their eye-sights rectified/corrected through suitable methods
D. All of these

353. Which method would you deem suitable for rectifying those students who interrupt the teaching process in the class?
A. They should be sent out of the class
B. They should be given harsh punishment in the class itself
C. They should be ignored
D. A complaint should be filed against them with the Principal

354. More indiscipline usually prevails in the class if:
A. the number of students is more than the specified norm
B. there is not enough work to keep children occupied
C. there are not enough playgrounds and other facilities for the children to play
D. the teacher is not able to make classroom teaching interesting enough

355. Which aspect would you like to emphasise upon while using visual aids during class teaching?
A. You would present such aids in a dramatic manner
B. They should be in accordance with the subject to be taught
C. They should be capable of taking children from the unknown to the known
D. You would tell children about them well in advance

356. The use of audio-visual material/aids in the class is:
A. more useful for those students who are slow learners
B. more useful for those students who are intelligent
C. enhances the curiosity of children
D. takes the concentration of students away from the main subject

357. Mal-adjustment and frustration are developed in the children when:
A. they are not sent to school
B. their needs are ignored
C. their parents give them more love and affection than is due for them
D. they are not able to pass the examinations

358. In order to understand the mal-adjustment and frustration of children and also, to treat them effectively, the teacher gets good support from the:
A. Principal of the school
B. parents/guardians of the children
C. study of child psychology
D. friendly treatment of children

359. Only one teacher teaches little children in school. Do you consider it to be beneficial?
A. It does not make any difference
B. It is a beneficial custom
C. It is a boring custom
D. It harms both the teacher and the students

360. Why do you consider it to be beneficial to call a student to the blackboard and get a question/problem solved by him?
A. Through this method, the student gets the practice of writing neatly
B. Confidence is created in the student through this method
C. You are able to learn whether the student knows how to solve the question or not
D. Both B and C

361. The inductive method of teaching has the following shortcoming:
A. It wastes a lot of time as it is slow
B. It develops the brain of the student by giving him an opportunity to praise
C. It is not psychological
D. The student does not take part in the process of learning under this method

362. The deductive method:
A. provides knowledge at high speed
B. does not provide knowledge at high speed
C. makes the job of the teacher quite complicated
D. is very useful for little children

363. The deductive method of teaching has the following limitation:
A. It develops a habit of cramming (mugging up) the text
B. It fails in the task of verifying the truth
C. It wastes the time of the student
D. All of these

364. Some facts have been appended ahead with respect to the deductive method of teaching. Which one of these facts is incorrect?
A. It is not psychological
B. It lays emphasis on imitation
C. It is useful for higher classes
D. It takes one from "work to reason"

365. Which one of the following statements is not correct?
A. The inductive and deductive methods are complementaries of each other
B. Both the inductive and deductive methods are used simultaneously
C. The inductive and deductive methods are opponents of each other
D. The rule, which is found out (or formulated) with the help of the inductive method, is tested (for its truth and validity) through the deductive method

366. The meaning of drill lessons is:
A. revision of the learned facts in the same format
B. putting the facts in an order before students
C. trying to know whether they are understanding whatever is being taught to them or not
D. keeping students active

367. A new student has been admitted to your school. He belongs to a backward family, environment or surrounding (from a cultural viewpoint). You would:
A. keep him in such a class as already has other children of backward families/environments/surroundings (from the cultural viewpoint)
B. send a teacher to get information about the backward cultural environment or surrounding of that child

C. keep him in a normal class but make special teaching arrangements for his special academic needs
D. advise him to an institute that imparts professional education

368. If poor and talented both types of students are in sizable number in the class, then teacher:
A. should keep his level of teaching high so that weak students may come to the level of average ones by elevation
B. should keep his level of teaching low so that all types of students can be benefited from it
C. should keep his teaching at average level. Besides he should provide some additional remedial measures to weak students
D. All of the above

369. In order to popularise adult education, the most important suggestion is the following:
A. those, who study, should be encouraged
B. those, who study, should be taught by linking their education with their vocations
C. good schools should be opened in villages
D. good teachers of the cities should be sent to teach them

370. If you request to the Principal to give fee concession to a poor student but your request is not responded to by the Principal, what will be your reaction at this?
A. You will again request to the Principal
B. You will take leave from the school for some days in order to hide your insult
C. You will encourage the student to realize the situation and you will try to help him to avail some other facilities
D. None of the above

371. What should a teacher do for very weak students of the class?
A. He should help and coach them in his spare time
B. He banish them from the class lest they should fail in the examination
C. He should suggest them to arrange tuition
D. All of the above

372. How do you feel over the discrimination on the basis of caste, creed or ethnicity as a teacher?
A. This system is rooted into religion and belief, so, it can not be eradicated
B. This is an unscientific attitude which can not be given any weightage in the present day social system
C. This feeling should be nipped out from the society without delay
D. B and C both

373. Which of the following pupils should be shown more sympathy by the teacher?
A. The pupil whose conduct is very fine
B. The pupil who takes tuition from his teacher
C. The pupil whose loss is directly the result of teacher's fault
D. The pupil who gets harm because of his own fault

374. If some students of the school tease a child on his way home, what should a class teacher do when he comes to know this incident?
A. Severe punishment should be given to those teasing the child
B. He should ensure safe and painless return of the child to his home
C. Teasing students should be rusticated from the school
D. All of the above

375. How can you de-addict the bad habits of students?
A. By telling them motivating stories which can clarify the consequences of bad habits
B. By seeking cooperation of their parents
C. By having strict vigil over them
D. All of the above

376. Knowing the religion and caste of a child in the class
A. is very essential because its report is sent to the education department
B. is not necessary at all
C. is essential because it tells us the family background of students

D. is necessary so that education can be given to pupils according to their respective abilities

377. The advantage of including population education in the school curriculum is that
A. students can be informed about the problems arisen out of the population explosion
B. students will be able to make their families happy due to this education
C. students will be able to know the methods of birth control and limit their families in future
D. All of the above

378. Students should be given freedom to ask questions in the class
A. at the end of the lesson
B. whenever the students feel any difficulty in the lesson
C. when they are asked by the teacher to do so
D. All of the above

379. If you teach in a co-educational school, then you will give much attention on
A. the care and learning of girls
B. the care and learning of boys
C. the talented boys and girls of the school
D. all of them equally irrespective of their gender differences

380. Your suggestion for those children, who are weak in studies, is that
A. they should study through tuitions at home
B. they should complete their homework with the help of their parents
C. they should improve upon their studies in remedial classes that are held after the school hours
D. they should remember only important questions for appearing in examinations

381. You have been told to accommodate two mentally retarded children in your class. You will
A. refuse to accept them as your students
B. tell the Principal to accommodate them in another class that is exclusively meant for mentally retarded children
C. learn techniques to teach such students and accept them as a part of your class
D. ignore those children in the class

382. Keeping in view the lack of resources and rising population levels of the nation, (in your opinion), giving more emphasis to adult education programmes is
A. a proposal for entertainment only
B. impractical
C. a courageous and laudable action/ behaviour
D. like giving opportunities for employment to teachers

383. Adult education should be under the authority of the following
A. The government
B. Non-government organisations
C. Educated persons
D. All of these

384. The best teacher in a village school is he who
A. carries community experiences to the class room
B. prepares instructional programmes in the interest of the community
C. carries classrom experiences to the community
D. All of the above

385. A child has been admitted to your school who belongs to a backward family/background from the cultural viewpoint. You will
A. keep him in a class in which, there are many more students of backward background from the cultural viewpoint
B. send a teacher to know more about the backward cultural background of that child
C. keep him in a normal class but will make special arrangements for teaching him, keeping his special needs in view
D. advise him to take up vocational education

386. You are away from your home and studying in another city. Due to an urgent piece of work, your father is not able to send you money in time. Then, you
A. fly into a rage

B. try to understand his handicaps
C. enquire from him by making phone calls
D. arrange money from another source and carry on your work

387. In order to bring the students of backward classes at par with other students, what will you do?
A. Reform in the educational system
B. Reservation for backward classes
C. By giving more aid to the students of backward classes
D. None of these

388. Talented students do not like the teaching profession. You believe that the reason for this phenomenon is that
A. there are little financial rewards in the teaching profession
B. these students do not have any interest in teaching
C. these students want to earn more money
D. there is no status in the teaching profession

389. If some students are unable to buy text books due to their poverty, what will you do for such students?
A. You will collect money for them by taking contributions from your colleagues
B. You will help them to get the books issued from book bank
C. You will arrange books for them by spending money from your pocket
D. All of the above

390. If you come to know after several tests that a particular students is talented, then you
A. will always be pleased with him
B. will give him extra home work
C. will motivate him more for further progress
D. will inform his parent about his achievement at once

391. How can you de-addict the habit of lying in children?
A. By rewarding those who speak the truth
B. By telling them such stories in which bad consequences of telling lies is shown
C. By motivating them to speak the truth
D. All of the above

392. Creative writing should be an activity planned for
A. only those children reading on grade level
B. only those children who can spell and also can write cohesive sentences
C. only those children who want to write for the newspaper of the class
D. all children of the class

393. Special Education is related to
A. adult education programmes
B. educational programmes for the disabled and gifted both
C. educational prorammes for talented students only
D. teachers training programmes

394. Which of the following will foster creativity among learners?
A. Providing opportunities to question and to nurture the innate talents of every learner
B. Emphasizing achievement goals from the beginning of school life
C. Coaching students for good marks in examination
D. Teaching the students the practical value of good education

395. A student of V-grade with 'visual deficiency' should be
A. helped with his/her routine-work by parents and friends
B. treated normally in the classroom and provided support through Audio CDs
C. given special treatment in the classroom
D. excused to do a lower level of work

396. .... is *not* considered a sign of 'being gifted'.
A. Fighting with others
B. Novelty in expression
C. Curiosity
D. Creative ideas

397. Education of children with special needs should be provided
A. by methods developed for special children in special schools
B. in special schools
C. by special teachers in special schools
D. along with other normal children

398. A teacher wants the gifted children of her class to achieve their potential. Which of the following should she ***not*** do to achieve her objective?
A. Segregate them from their peers for special attention
B. Challenge them to enhance their creativity
C. Teach them to enjoy non-academic activities
D. Teach them to manage stress

399. A creative learner refers to one who is
A. capable of scoring consistently good marks in tests
B. good at lateral thinking and problem solving
C. very talented in drawing and painting
D. highly intelligent

400. Every learner is unique means that
A. A common curriculum for all learners is not possible
B. It is impossible to develop the potential of learners in a heterogeneous class
C. No two learners are alike in their abilities, interests and talents
D. Learners do not have any common qualities, nor do they share common goals

401. Centrally sponsored scheme of Integrated Education for disabled children aims at providing educational opportunities to children with disabilities in
A. Open schools
B. Blind Relief Association schools
C. Regular schools
D. Special schools

402. Which of the following behaviours is not a manifestation of emotional disturbance?
A. Delinquency B. Bullying nature
C. Truancy D. Autism

403. A provision for education for the children with disabilities can be done through
A. Inclusive education
B. Mainstreaming
C. Integration
D. None of these

404. 'Child belonging to weaker section' means
A. A child belonging to such parents whose annual income is low
B. A child belonging to such parents who come under the disadvantaged group
C. A child belonging to such parents who come under the category of below poverty line
D. A child belonging to such parents whose annual income is lower than the minimum limit specfied by the appropriate government

405. The National Curriculum Framework, 2005 under the heading 'quality dimension' gives more importance to
A. Physical resources
B. Qualified and Motivated teachers
C. Experiences designed for the child in terms of knowledge
D. Experiences designed for the child and curriculum reform

406. The National Curriculum Framework, 2005 suggests which of the following examination reforms?
A. Class X examination optional
B. State level exams to be conducted at different stages of school education
C. Competitive entrance examinations optional
D. All of these

407. Which of the following is a better strategy for teaching children with special needs?
A. Discussion in the classroom involving maximum number of students
B. Demonstration by teacher involving students
C. Cooperative learning and peer tutoring
D. Ability grouping for teaching

408. Ability of knowing the meaning of problem, weaknesses and gaps related to environment is a characteristic of
A. Gifted children
B. Average children
C. Creative children
D. None of them

409. A cricket player develops the skill of bowling, but it does not affect his skill of batting. It is known as
A. positive transfer of training
B. negative transfer of training
C. zero transfer of training
D. None of these

410. Which of the following will serve as a most satisfying defence mechanism for the physically handicapped individual?
A. Identification
B. Rationalization
C. Fantasy
D. None of these

411. In order to nurture creativity, a teacher should take help of which of the following methods?
A. Brainstorming
B. Lecture method
C. Audio-visual aids
D. All of these

412. National Curriculum Framework, 2005 suggests some activities to promote peace education. Which one of the following is enlisted in the curriculum framework?
A. Organise programmes to promote an attitude of respect and responsiblity towards women
B. Teach moral education
C. Teach peace education as a separate subject
D. Integrate peace education in the curriculum

413. National Curriculum Framework, 2005 talks of major shifts from
A. knowledge as given and fixed as it evolves and is created
B. educational focus to disciplinary focus
C. learner centric to teacher centric
D. None of these

414. In the National Curriculum Framework, 2005 under the heading 'Examination Reforms' which of the following reforms has been suggested?
A. Open book exams
B. Continuous comprehensive evaluation
C. Group work evaluation
D. All of these

415. Gardner formulated a list of seven Intelligencies, which among the following is not one of them:
A. Spatial Intelligence
B. Emotional Intelligence
C. Interpersonal Intelligence
D. Linguistic Intelligence

416. Which of the following is the true statement in reference to intelligence:
A. Intelligence is the ability to adjust
B. Intelligence is the ability to learn
C. Intelligence is the ability of Abstract Reasoning
D. All of these

417. What should be the role of teacher in meeting the individual differences?
A. Try to know the abilities, interest and aptitude of individuals
B. Try to adjust the curriculum as per the needs of individuals
C. Both A and B
D. None of these

418. A few students in your class are exceptionally bright, you will teach them:
A. along with the class
B. along with higher classes
C. by using enriched programmes
D. only when they want

419. The major purpose of diagnostic test is that of identifying:
A. the general area of weakness in class performance
B. specific nature of remedial programme needed
C. the causes underlying academic difficulties
D. the specific nature of pupil difficulties

420. Special education is related to
A. educational for talented students
B. educational programmes for disabled
C. training programmes for Teachers
D. training programme for retarded

421. The educator, who promoted the idea of five formal steps in learning, was
A. Rousseau B. Comenius
C. Pestalozzi D. Herbart

422. Out of the following, in which lesson, a geneal rule is explained first and then, knowledge is accumulated on the basis of that rule?

A. Deductive lesson
B. Inductive lesson
C. Developing lesson
D. knowledge lesson

423. The principles of activity method accept the following viewpoint:

A. The student gets knowledge by getting motivation from natural tendencies
B. The student should be given freedom to gain knowledge
C. The best development of the student is effected by his on actions/activities
D. All of these

424. The basis of the activity method is

A. searching for the unknown
B. making the text book the centre of learning
C. that the student cannot gain knowledge without the instigation of the teacher
D. right type of guidance to the creative power of students

425. The activity technique is

A. Class-centred
B. teacher-centred
C. Subject-centred
D. Student-centred

426. In class room teaching (group teaching) method, students

A. get little opportunities to take part in class work
B. get many opportunities to take part in class work
C. get sufficient opportunities to take part in class work
D. do not get any opportunity to take part is class work

427. If you have been appointed as a judge in a declamation contest, you will

A. give a decision according to the decision taken by another judge
B. give importance to an effecitve speaker
C. give preference to a student of your school
D. give preference to a student leader

428. You have been appointed at a place where the local language is not understood by you. In such a situation, you will

A. try to learn that local language
B. try to get yourself transferred to some other place
C. become perplexed
D. take leave and stay at home

429. If a student comes late to the school on a daily basis, then it will be appropriate to

A. throw him out of the class
B. punish him in the presence of students
C. complain to the Principal that he is always late
D. find out the reasons for his behaviour

430. In your view, in order to check the ongoing decay in the field of education, it is important

A. to arrange the presence of police force in the school
B. to make proper arrangements for sports activities in the school
C. to develop awareness about completing homework among students
D. for teacher to teach in their classes regularly and with dedication

431. An effective and successful female teacher is one who

A. is beautiful in physical terms
B. comes to school regularly
C. is good in terms of knowledge of her subject and its presentation/communication
D. is a favourite of the headmistress

432. I like such types of books as contain

A. enertaining material
B. tips for households
C. material that enhances my knowledge and is entertaining too
D. stories and fables

433. You are teaching in the class. The headmistress calls for you. You will

A. immediately go to meet her
B. bluntly refuse to go
C. send a note and explain the situation you are in
D. go only after the bell rings

434. You will like to spend your spare time by
A. indulging in gossips
B. travelling and enjoying
C. involving yourself in self-study
D. remaining involved in prayers

435. If you are forced to give pass marks to a failed student, you will
A. give pass marks to the student as demanded by circumstances
B. never give pass marks to that student
C. discuss the issue with your colleagues and then, take an action
D. take leave from school

436. A teacher uses the "Comparison Technique" while teaching. He must ensure that while he uses this technique
A. Students should not be completely aware of those two things/objects/clauses that need to be compared
B. students must be fully aware of those two things/objects/clauses that need to be compared
C. he assumes that students must have read something about those two things/objects/clauses
D. there must be no study material available about those two things/objects/clauses

437. The experimental technique of education can be used
A. to teach all types of subjects
B. to teach only a few subjects successfully
C. for gaining knowledge by hearing
D. to take the student from the state of generalisation to the state of specialisation

438. When was "Operation Blackboard" commenced in India?
A. 1990 B. 1988
C. 1986 D. 1984

439. During a conference, the mother of the third grader asks the teacher how she can help improve her child's reading ability. Of the following the poorest recommendation is that she should
A. severely limit the child watching of televistion
B. read to the child
C. take the child on trips to interesting places in the community
D. give the child books as presents for birthdays and special occasions

440. If a student does not understand a point/concept in the class
A. You will tell him to ask you after the class
B. You will explain it to him only twice and then, move to next point/concept in question
C. until and unless the student has fully understood it, you will not move ahead and try to clear the point/concept in question
D. Snub the student and make him sit quietly

441. In order to teach the basic principles of science, you will use the following technique
A. Inductive method B. Deductive method
C. Decroly method D. Wennetka Plan

442. Most of the students of your class have failed to get pass marks in the class test. You will
A. praise those students who have passed
B. teach the students thoroughly about the same topic and take another test
C. identify weak students and tell them to study separately
D. call the parents/guardians of those students who have failed and advise them to pay more attention to their studies

443. If, on a certain day, children are not in a mood to study, then
A. the teacher should sit along with them, laugh along with them and have fun
B. they should be told to conduct an interesting activity on that day
C. they should be ordered to remain seated in the class without talking
D. they should be freed

444. Due to many holidays and strikes, only half of the syllabus has been covered in the class. You will
A. persuade students to complete the syllabus themselves
B. give them notes and hints for important

questions that are likely to be asked in the examination

C. take extra classes and complete the syllabus carefully but according to the pace of understanding of students

D. not show any enthusiasm to complete the syllabus unless students ask you to do so

445. The standards of education are being upgraded on a regular basis. As a result, the level of difficulty is being raised in each subject. You will

A. study for extra hours at home and prepare your subject thoroughly

B. give homework to students that should include difficult questions of the new syllabus

C. persuade students to join such a school as will not have tough syllabi

D. not touch upon the new/difficult topics but teach only old/conventional topics

446. The objective of Principle of Revision is

A. repeating the gained sets of knowledge to make them permanant in the minds of students

B. remembering the sets of information by heart (mugging up)

C. making homework easier

D. making the subject matter easier

447. How will you develop good tastes among students in the class?

A. By wearing high-value clothes and using old jewellery and perfumes

B. By giving them examples of people/ celebrities who have good tastes/values

C. By portraying youself as a man/woman of high tastes

D. By telling students that you meet people only of high tastes

448. The teacher is curious to know more about the abilities, intelligence and behaviour of a new student in the class. He will do well to

A. ask him about his traits in the presence of other students

B. introduce himself to the student and interact with him inside and outside the class

C. get his record of mistakes done in the past or in the previous school

D. ignore him as a newcomer and be strict with him

449. While teaching a lesson, the teacher should ask the maximum number of questions in the following phase

A. Introduction Phase B. Growth Phase

C. Revision Phase D. None of these

450. If you have to take the class of another teacher, who is absent, you will

A. teach according to your own whims and preferences

B. share jokes with students but not teach

C. start from the point where their teacher had finished during the last lecture

D. take attendance and then tell the students to disperse

451. If you are not prepared to teach students because you are not prepared (due to a marriage ceremony that you had to attend the night before), you will

A. take attendance of students and tell them stories

B. apologise to students and tell them that you will not be able to teach on that day

C. apologise to students and tell them to ask questions from the lectures given earlier

D. start teaching them and cover the topic that you were not able to prepare

452. Students should become studious to the maximum extent. For this, it is important

A. to develop interest in them

B. that class work should be more

C. that writing work should be more

D. that home work should be more

453. Whose habits does a little child adopt?

A. Of teachers

B. Of his family members

C. Of the classmates and friends of his school

D. Of his friends

454. The students of first standard are making a noise. In order to calm them down, you will

A. scold them

B. tell them to go to the playground and play

C. tell them a story
D. do nothing

455. All of the following are the characteristic features of an effective teacher except
A. differential treatment meted out to students of his class
B. emphasis upon the quick control of the problematic situation
C. emphasizing group discussion for the purpose of clarifying the objectives
D. emphasis upon standard

456. Of the following statements about slow learners and bright children, the correct one is that
A. bright children are likely to have a higher incidence of emotional problem
B. slow learners are likely to have greater manual dexterity
C. both groups strive for success in school
D. both groups are difficult to identify when their members are very young

457. The trial-and-error method of instruction is best enhanced by
A. role playing
B. independent study
C. an audio-visual lesson
D. a developmental lesson

458. Improvement in comprehension skills is mostly likely to result from
A. guided silent reading
B. listening to tapes of children's stories
C. guided oral reading
D. unstructured silent reading

459. You like that group of students that has the following qualities
A. willing to serve, respecting, hardworking
B. soft spoken, praising others, clever
C. dedicated, studious, respecting and treating with warmth
D. hardworking, sportsman, loquacious

460. The teacher can develop honesty and other good virtues in students by
A. giving lectures
B. giving examples
C. giving an example of an honest student of the class
D. giving his/her own example

461. In order to ensure regular attendance of students in school
A. it should be made a place of pleasure
B. more homework should be given to students
C. students should be given freedom to work according to their tastes and orientations
D. regular meetings of parents/guardians should be arranged

462. The reason why students run from school is
A. lack of interesting class teaching work
B. lack of interest in studies on the part of students
C. not giving punishment to students
D. callous attitude of teachers towards the problem

463. A teacher asks questions from students during classroom teaching sessions. Should he help/guide them so that they may be able to arrive at correct answer?
A. Yes
B. No
C. Yes. Little indirect help
D. Never

464. A student of your class tells you in a secret manner that three students of the class generally copy one another's test copies during tests. He also discloses their names to you. Upon getting this information, what will be your reaction?
A. You will not pay attention to his story
B. You will like to talk to three students named by him
C. You will give a piece of your mind to all the three students
D. You will ponder think why he gave you this information

465. A teacher of your school exploits his students. In such a situation, you will
A. complain about him to the Principal
B. not like to interfere in the affair
C. advise him not to exploit his students
D. lead a peaceful agitation to oppose his actions

466. A teacher should present his lesson plan to the students
A. in a logical manner
B. in a psychological manner
C. by joining it with the previous sets of their knowledge
D. in a planned order

467. If I am required to evaluate test booklets of an examination, I will
A. let all the students get through the examination
B. give them marks quite liberally
C. adopt a tough stance while giving marks
D. give marks according to answers given by students

468. You are watching movie in a theatre along with your friends. During the period of intermission, you come across a few students of your class. You will
A. try to avoid them
B. ask them whether they liked the movie and then slip away with your friends
C. meet them with warmth, introduce them to your friends and offer them tea/cold drinks
D. leave the theatre because you will not like to be seen with your friends

469. Some students want you to take part in a cricket match. Two teams have been formed one from your own class and another from a class not taught by you. You will
A. be a member of the team formed from the class taught by you
B. be a member of the team formed from the class not taught by you
C. like to be a referee in the match
D. not like to join students in the cricket match

470. Which quality of the teacher is liked the most by his students?
A. His punctuality (in terms of time)
B. His impartial attitude
C. His love for discipline
D. His command

471. During an educational tour, what will you expect from those students who are accompanying you?
A. Students should see everything/item/place carefully and ask questions from students regarding the same
B. Students should not ask questions from the teacher; they must see everything quietly
C. Students should jot down the questions to be asked in their notebooks
D. Students should move about freely; they should also allow the teacher to move about with pleasure

472. The teacher must have good moral character and values. This will
A. lead to good impact on his/her students
B. enhance his reputation in the society
C. lead his/her students to make efforts for developing good moral character
D. motivate students not to do wrong deeds

473. A student of your class uses obscene and abusive language/remarks quite often. In order to rectify this flaw of the student, you will
A. punish him
B. advise him
C. talk to his parents/guardians and try to know the root cause of the problem
D. report the matter to the Principal

474. In the context of including moral education in the academic syllabi of students, your opinion is that
A. it is an additional burden on students
B. it is beneficial for developing the character of students
C. this is the demand of the times
D. there is no justification for imparting moral education during such times as are highly immoral

475. According to your opinion, the following is important for bringing improvement in education
A. Creating an atmosphere for teaching and studying
B. Advertising heavily through newspapers
C. Ensuring the maintenance of interest of parents/guardians in education
D. putting preassure on the government

476. If the teacher uses different techniques during the teaching work,
A. students pay more attention
B. teaching becomes easier
C. teaching becomes interesting
D. all of these

477. A teacher must take interest in research. That is because
A. this develops the knowledge base of the teacher
B. the teacher remains busy in his work
C. the teacher always keeps on studying and learning
D. all of the aforesaid tasks are feasible

478. You have been directed to prepare the time table for class eight. In order to give more hours for practical work, what would be the viewpoint/supporting argument that you would put before the headmistress?
A. In the practical class, children get a new environment
B. Through practical work, students get an opportunity to learn all those things (by doing) that they study in the class
C. In a class of practical work, students get enough time to play
D. In a class of practical work, the responsibility of teaching (on the part of teacher) is somewhat reduced

479. Most educators agree that oral reading
A. comes naturally to good readers
B. is so difficult to do well that it is a waste of time to teach it
C. is useful only for appreciation of poetry
D. requires an audience situation

480. What is your opinion about the present educational system?
A. It is a correct system
B. There is a need to effect improvements in it
C. It has more limitations and less advantages
D. It is neither good nor bad

481. Your view about the type of education to be imparted to students is that
A. education should be religious in nature
B. education should be vocation oriented
C. education should be technical
D. military education should be imparted

482. In order to win the trust of students, the teacher should behave with them like a
A. mother
B. friend
C. teacher
D. father

483. In your school, some teachers consider tuition to be their profession. In such a situation, what will you do?
A. You will tell them about the losses accruing due to the same
B. You will also join their group
C. You will report to the Principal about them
D. You will not have any relationship with them

484. Now-a-days Vidyalayas are
A. only for urban children
B. for the intelligent studens of both the rural and urban area
C. for those children who are willing to become soldiers
D. for rural children

485. The curriculum of students should
A. be associated with the realities of life
B. be motivated by religion
C. offer a helping hand in achieving the ideals
D. revolve around the truth

486. The curriculum, to be prepared for children, should be
A. meaningful
B. oriented towards productivity
C. such as should have flexibility
D. All of the above

487. Education philosophy tells us what type of education should be imparted and why. On the contrary, the relationship of educational psychology is with the aspect of
A. to whom and why
B. whom and till what time
C. when and how
D. all of the above

488. As a teacher, what type of behaviour of a student would be deemed serious by you?
A. Slightly slow/weak in studies

B. Taking to other students in the class during the course of a lecture
C. Asking too many questions in the class
D. Incomplete home work

489. If your wife also teaches in the same school, you will
A. exchange notes with her on a regular basis
B. meet her only during the recess hour
C. meet her in the presence of her colleagues
D. avoid meeting her in public

490. All the teachers of your school are on strike. You will
A. teach students in a secret manner
B. go to the office of the Principal and sit there
C. not go to school but remain at home
D. join teachers in strike

491. Your colleague does not teach properly in her class. Instead, she tells her pupils to meet her at her residence for tuitions. What is your opinion about her?
A. She is doing an excellent job
B. She is harming the interests of her students
C. Her action is worth condemnation
D. All of these are correct

492. You are a teacher and do your work quite efficiently. What do you expect in return?
A. An award
B. Cash prize
C. Publishing of your name in newspapers
D. A few words of praise at functions or annual days of the school

493. There is no harm for a teacher to take help, in the context of academic work, from
A. his colleagues B. his students
C. principal D. books

494. In teachers' room (Common room), a teacher comments that your students do not view you as a good teacher. You will
A. have a fight with that teacher
B. go to meet those students who passed such a nasty comment
C. tell that teacher that they may be right and you will try to improve your teaching methods and knowledge levels
D. tell him bluntly that he does not know anything about your subject

495. You are known as the right hand man of the Principal. You should concentrate on
A. personal affairs of the Principal
B. activities of the students' union as they are directed against the Principal
C. your subject, students and teaching methods only
D. making plans to become Vice-Principal

496. You are quite popular among your colleagues. You will use this opportunity to
A. form a teachers' union
B. develop new/novel techniques for education
C. take teachers to picnic spots
D. threaten the administration and the Principal and get some of your trivial demands accepted

497. In a class, two students who sit together occasionally fight each other. As a teacher of that class, what action would you take in this context?
A. You would make them sit separately, at a distance
B. You would call the parents of both these students and apprise them of the situation
C. You would advise them to live together in peace
D. You would file a complain with the Principal

498. Some students of your class have weak eye sights. They are unable to clearly see whatever is written on the blackboard. What is your opinion about solving this problems?
A. Tell these children to get their eye sights rectified through suitable methods
B. Call the parents/guardians of such children and advise them to arrange spectables for their respective children
C. Tell these children to read by going closer to the blackboard
D. Let these children sit in the front seats in the class

499. In order to remain in the good books of your Principal, you should
- A. give him gifts quite frequently
- B. speak ill against other teachers in front of the Principal
- C. keep on doing your teaching work as per your satisfaction and according to the needs of your students
- D. try to become popular among students

500. You sincerely feel that you are not fit for the teaching profession because your command over the subject is poor. You can communicate properly. You are also popular among students. You will
- A. give up the teaching profession
- B. ask your students to give valid suggestions
- C. work hard and prepare your subject throughly
- D. be perplexed and try to take rest, away from your city and family members

501. You will give maximum marks to a student
- A. who pays you visits regularly at your residence
- B. always sits in the front row of the class
- C. works hard and does well in his class tests and examinations
- D. who is a child of your most trusted colleague

502. According to your opinion, Parents' Teachers' Association (PTA) is
- A. of no use as it wastes your time
- B. of great value because you are able to interact with parents of your students
- C. an ideal body for taking care of academic affairs of your school
- D. All of these

503. If you are free during the school hours, the best way to spend time will be
- A. to indulge in gossiping with your colleagues in the canteen
- B. to read books 'magazines' and journals in the library
- C. to play football with students of your class
- D. to go home and again come back when you have to teach

504. Dynamic technologies and teaching methods have forced you to learn new things almost every week. You will
- A. be fed up of this dynamism and take up teaching of an innocuous subject like history
- B. try to persuade the Principal that adoption of new technologies and knowledge sets will be difficult for children of the school
- C. learn new technologies (like computers, multimedia, Internet, testing techniques etc.) and transfer the knowledge so gained to your students
- D. try to get a job in a school that does not give attention to dynamic technologies and new methods of teaching

505. The educational system of today promotes "educated unemployment". The reason is that
- A. education gives theoretical knowledge only
- B. professional education is not a part of education
- C. the objective of education is not vivid
- D. All of these

506. The teacher ought to know about the problems prevalent in the field of education. The reason is that
- A. only a teacher can do something about solving them
- B. he can tell about the same to another teacher
- C. teachers can tell the government about it
- D. with this knowledge, the teacher can have information about education

507. In the wake of serious shortages of resources and rising population of our nation, you have the following views about the programmes for improving the standards of education (under the aegis of national policy of education).
- A. They are impractical
- B. They are courageous and laudable efforts
- C. They are new forms of traditional programmes
- D. They increase the workload of teachers

508. In the present times, the major reason for the poor state of primary education is
- A. Spending more time on Doordarshan

B. poor ratio of teachers and students
C. dependence upon cheap help books (guides)
D. solitary families

509. In the present times, the chief reason of degradation of moral education is
A. lack of national character
B. lack of education on religion
C. solitary families
D. dominance of money in the society

510. Keeping in view the lack of resources and rising population levels of the nation, (in your opinion), giving more emphasis to adult education programmes is
A. a proposal for entertainment only
B. impractical
C. a courageous and laudable action/ behaviour
D. like giving opportunities for employment to teachers

511. It is important to impart education about (moral) values to students because
A. due to this, their mental development would be faster
B. parents of students will be happy
C. students would have more dedication towards and awareness about good virtues/ values
D. this is also a type of education

512. It is very much important to inculcate good habits of the teacher in students. This is the chief responsibility of
A. the teacher
B. guardians of children
C. parents of children
D. All of these

513. The position of a teacher is that of respect in the society because
A. teachers are the symbols of simplicity and knowledge
B. nobody can become a doctor or an engineer without the blessings of teachers
C. teachers are the builders of destiny of a nation
D. teachers are the guides of politicians and bigwigs

514. The reason for the prevalence of dogmas and immoral customs in the society is
A. religious fundamentalism
B. caste system and differences of class
C. poverty
D. lack of awareness and the problem illiteracy

515. The reason for diminishing importance of the teacher in the society is
A. low income of the teacher
B. keen interest being taken by teachers in politics
C. indifference of the teacher towards his/her profession
D. incomplete knowledge of teachers about their subjects

516. A teacher should continue to incorporate new sets of knowledge in his subject matter on a continuous basis so that
A. he may be able to give latest knowledge to his students
B. students may remain calm in the class
C. students may be impressed by the teaching abilities of the teacher
D. knowledge levels of the teacher may be enhanced

517. When you see children fighting on the road, you will
A. pacify them by giving them advice
B. tell them to run away
C. tell people to resolve the issue/problem
D. ignore the situation and go away

518. If one of parents/guardians does not come to meet you, what will you do?
A. You will not pay attention to that student
B. You will write to the parent/guardian
C. Personally go to meet them
D. Start punishing the child

519. In order to please students and their parents/ guardians, teacher should
A. praise the child in the presence of his parent/guardian
B. try to improve the academic record of his students
C. keep his work and actions unbiased
D. work according to the interest of students and their parents/guardians

520. If you are assigned a duty in elections, you will
A. try to get the elections cancelled
B. try to send a colleague of yours in your place
C. like to go because in the event of defiance of the order, you may be punished
D. like to go with pleasure because obeying rules is your prime duty

521. If an inter-school sports meet is organised in your school, you will
A. oppose it as female students of your school may be exploited at such occasions
B. support it as players of your school would learn new techniques of games
C. remain neutral to the idea
D. ask the Principal to take a decision in this context

522. Why do you like teaching work?
A. Children do not remain naughty in the presence of the teacher
B. Your parents had told you that it is a dignified profession
C. You have an interest in teaching
D. The person keeps on reading a lot in this profession

523. One solution to make class teaching more effective/meaningful is the following:
A. give home work in excess
B. stop the students after the school time and have discussions with them
C. immediately after the class lecture, ask questions related to the lecture
D. tell children that if they have not understood the lesson, you will teach the same once again

524. By which trait of the teacher, the students are generally impressed?
A. His knowledge/learning
B. His high moral character
C. His tough discipline
D. His relationship with the Principal

525. If, on a certain day, you are very tired and not in a mood to teach students in the class, then you will
A. Free children and send them home
B. Request your colleague (teacher) to teach children in your place
C. Tell children an ideal story
D. Tell children to go out and play

526. The best way to encourage a teacher, who works with complete dedication, is to:
A. give him a prize
B. give him an advance increment in his salary
C. arrange a felicitation function and felicitate him
D. praise his work from time to time

527. Whose behaviour affects students the most?
A. That of the Principal
B. That of a politician
C. That of a teacher
D. That of a tutor

528. By which method, students learn to the maximum extent and with the utmost speed?
A. By seeing
B. By reading
C. By listening
D. By doing themselves

529. What should the teacher do to maintain the interest of students in class teaching?
A. Extensive use of examples from the practical life
B. Extensive use of teaching materials/aids
C. Giving ample opportunities to students for discussion/deliberations
D. All of these

530. Why would you like to take additional responsibilities as a teacher?
A. In order to gain new experiences
B. In order to please your Principal
C. In order to become popular among students
D. In order to cooperate

531. If a student criticises another teacher in your presence, then you would:
A. punish him
B. inform that teacher about the critical remarks passed by that student
C. ignore his remarks/discussion
D. reprimand that student and spare him

532. A teacher should work according to:
A. his own liking/whims
B. the needs of the time
C. his capacity to work
D. his need

533. You are teaching in the classroom and one student is busy reading a story book (instead of giving attention to the lecture). What would you do in such a situation?
A. You would reprimand that student and show him the way out of the class
B. You would tell the student to leave the story book and concentrate on the subject being taught
C. You would purposely ignore that student
D. You would wait for another student to complain about that student so that you may be able to file a complaint against him with the Principal

534. In order to participate in a conference or seminar, which is related to teaching, you would:
A. take leave from the school
B. get the permission of the Principal
C. not get the permission of the Principal
D. quietly leave the school and attend the conference or seminar

535. Some teachers give tuitions. In your opinion, what is the reason for this?
A. They get ample opportunities to revise the subject matter being studied (when they give tuitions)
B. That is how they are able to keep themselves busy in quite a useful manner
C. They are always involved in earning (more) money
D. They nurture intense feelings of welfare of students

536. A superior teacher is one who:
A. gives his complete time to the school
B. strictly follows the norms of discipline
C. takes an interest in the all-round development of students
D. gives leadership to students

537. As a teacher, what type of behaviour of a student would be deemed serious by you?
A. Incomplete home work
B. Asking too many questions in the class
C. Talking to other students in the class during the course of a lecture
D. Slightly slow/weak in studies

538. Even after telling/explaning time and again in the class, a student is not able to understand a point. In such a situation, you would:
A. reprimand that student and show him the way out of the class
B. deem him incorrigible and stop paying attention to him
C. use another method/solution/material to explain the point/concept to him
D. call his parent/guardian and advise him to look for another arrangement for the study of their child/ward

539. What suggestion would you like to give in order to stop the practice of copying in the examination hall?
A. All the examinees should be allowed to appear in the examination only after they are thoroughly searched
B. Those who are caught copying, should not be admitted to any school; they should also not be allowed to appear in any examination
C. Necessary improvements should be effected in the examination system
D. All the examinees should be given a free hand to copy during examinations

540. Which teacher, in your view, is the best?
A. The one who deals with students only under the gamut of teaching
B. The one who is willing to get the maximum information related to the lives of children
C. The one who is popular among students due to his love for discipline
D. The one who is a well-wisher of students

541. If a student asks an out of context question in your class, then, as a teacher, you would:
A. punish him
B. ignore his question

C. tell him that the question is out-of-context
D. tell the student that you would answer his question after the class

542. If you find that many students take leave on the day of weekly test, then what solution would you like to devise to solve this problem?
A. You would stop taking weekly tests
B. You would inform the parents/guardians of the absent students in this context
C. You would take the test of the absent students the very next day
D. You would take weekly test on any day of the week

543. If you, as a teacher, have complete knowledge of your subject, then only:
A. you would be able to get respect from students
B. your students would pass with good marks
C. other teachers would also be impressed by you
D. you would be able to eliminate the doubts of your students

544. How can the habit of stealing be removed from among students?
A. By giving harsh punishment
B. By giving them the threats of coercion/ punishment
C. By reprimanding them
D. By giving them good advice and keeping a vigilant eye over them

545. Even after repeated instructions from your end, a student comes late to the class. What action would you like to take in such a situation?
A. You would not let him enter into your classroom
B. You would inform his parents/guardians in this context
C. You would inform the Principal of the school in this context
D. You would ignore him

546. In order to win the trust of students, the teacher should behave with them like a:
A. father B. mother
C. teacher D. friend

547. From your viewpoint, whose development is the most important among students?
A. Dedication towards work
B. Self-confidence
C. The importance of labour
D. An affinity for religion

548. Who, from among the following, had stated, "Motivation is the art of generating interest in the mind of the student?"
A. Thomson
B. Kothari
C. McCaulay
D. Rabindra Nath Tagore

549. The special feature of meaningful examination is the following:
A. All the students get through this examination with good marks
B. Students should get more marks than they had hoped for
C. This examination should be able to differentiate capable students from the incapable ones
D. Students should not fear this type of examination

550. The practical method of making students understand the meaning of difficult words is to:
A. give their synonyms
B. give their antonyms
C. teach them the usage of such words in sentences
D. All of these

551. The opinion of the French scholar, Montesque, was that education should:
A. be based on personal experiences
B. be based on the scriptures (*Shastras*)
C. be based on books
D. essentially have an influence (or shade) of philosophy

552. The famous educationist, Bacon, had the opinion that the objective of education is:
A. make the child an ideal citizen
B. make the child useful for the society
C. help the child become capable enough to make a living
D. make the child liberal

ANSWERS

1	2	3	4	5	6	7	8	9	10
A	C	B	B	B	B	D	C	A	A
11	**12**	**13**	**14**	**15**	**16**	**17**	**18**	**19**	**20**
B	B	A	C	C	C	D	D	C	D
21	**22**	**23**	**24**	**25**	**26**	**27**	**28**	**29**	**30**
C	A	C	C	C	A	D	D	C	A
31	**32**	**33**	**34**	**35**	**36**	**37**	**38**	**39**	**40**
D	D	B	*	B	*	*	D	C	D
41	**42**	**43**	**44**	**45**	**46**	**47**	**48**	**49**	**50**
C	D	D	C	C	D	C	A	C	D
51	**52**	**53**	**54**	**55**	**56**	**57**	**58**	**59**	**60**
A	A	D	D	D	B	A	C	C	D
61	**62**	**63**	**64**	**65**	**66**	**67**	**68**	**69**	**70**
C	D	C	B	B	C	A	B	B	C
71	**72**	**73**	**74**	**75**	**76**	**77**	**78**	**79**	**80**
D	D	B	B	D	C	B	D	C	C
81	**82**	**83**	**84**	**85**	**86**	**87**	**88**	**89**	**90**
B	C	D	D	C	C	B	C	D	C
91	**92**	**93**	**94**	**95**	**96**	**97**	**98**	**99**	**100**
D	D	A	C	D	A	C	C	B	B
101	**102**	**103**	**104**	**105**	**106**	**107**	**108**	**109**	**110**
B	B	C	D	D	A	D	A	C	D
111	**112**	**113**	**114**	**115**	**116**	**117**	**118**	**119**	**120**
D	C	D	C	A	C	D	D	A	C
121	**122**	**123**	**124**	**125**	**126**	**127**	**128**	**129**	**130**
B	D	A	D	C	C	C	D	B	B
131	**132**	**133**	**134**	**135**	**136**	**137**	**138**	**139**	**140**
C	B	D	C	D	D	B	A	A	B
141	**142**	**143**	**144**	**145**	**146**	**147**	**148**	**149**	**150**
D	D	D	D	D	A	D	A	B	A
151	**152**	**153**	**154**	**155**	**156**	**157**	**158**	**159**	**160**
B	D	A	C	D	A	C	B	A	D
161	**162**	**163**	**164**	**165**	**166**	**167**	**168**	**169**	**170**
C	C	C	B	B	D	D	D	D	D
171	**172**	**173**	**174**	**175**	**176**	**177**	**178**	**179**	**180**
A	C	D	B	A	C	B	B	C	C

181	182	183	184	185	186	187	188	189	190
C	A	D	D	C	C	D	C	A	A
191	192	193	194	195	196	197	198	199	200
B	A	C	A	C	C	A	B	A	D
201	202	203	204	205	206	207	208	209	210
A	C	C	A	B	D	C	D	D	C
211	212	213	214	215	216	217	218	219	220
D	D	D	C	C	B	B	B	B	A
221	222	223	224	225	226	227	228	229	230
D	D	C	D	C	D	B	A	B	B
231	232	233	234	235	236	237	238	239	240
A	A	D	C	B	C	C	B	C	D
241	242	243	244	245	246	247	248	249	250
C	B	A	C	A	D	B	B	D	B
251	252	253	254	255	256	257	258	259	260
A	A	D	A	B	C	D	C	A	D
261	262	263	264	265	266	267	268	269	270
C	B	D	C	D	D	D	D	C	A
271	272	273	274	275	276	277	278	279	280
B	C	D	B	D	A	B	C	C	B
281	282	283	284	285	286	287	288	289	290
D	D	C	D	D	B	B	D	D	A
291	292	293	294	295	296	297	298	299	300
D	B	D	D	C	A	B	D	B	B
301	302	303	304	305	306	307	308	309	310
C	D	A	A	C	D	C	A	D	D
311	312	313	314	315	316	317	318	319	320
A	C	A	C	D	*	B	C	A	D
321	322	323	324	325	326	327	328	329	330
A	C	C	D	D	B	D	C	A	B
331	332	333	334	335	336	337	338	339	340
B	B	C	A	D	B	C	C	D	D
341	342	343	344	345	346	347	348	349	350
C	C	C	D	C	D	C	A	D	C
351	352	353	354	355	356	357	358	359	360
C	D	C	D	B	C	B	C	B	D
361	362	363	364	365	366	367	368	369	370
A	A	A	A	C	A	C	C	B	C

371	372	373	374	375	376	377	378	379	380
A	D	C	B	D	B	D	D	D	C
381	382	383	384	385	386	387	388	389	390
C	C	D	D	C	B & D	A	A	D	C
391	392	393	394	395	396	397	398	399	400
D	D	B	A	B	A	D	A	B	C
401	402	403	404	405	406	407	408	409	410
C	D	A	D	D	A	C	C	C	C
411	412	413	414	415	416	417	418	419	420
A	D	A	D	B	D	C	C	C	B
421	422	423	424	425	426	427	428	429	430
D	A	D	D	D	B	B	A	D	D
431	432	433	434	435	436	437	438	439	440
C	C	C	C	*	B	A	C	A	C
441	442	443	444	445	446	447	448	449	450
A	B	B	C	A	A	B	B	B	C
451	452	453	454	455	456	457	458	459	460
C	A	B	C	A	C	A	A	C	D
461	462	463	464	465	466	467	468	469	470
A & D	A	C	B	C	A	D	C	C	B
471	472	473	474	475	476	477	478	479	480
A	A	C	B	A	D	A	B	D	B
481	482	483	484	485	486	487	488	489	490
B	B	A	B	A	D	C	B	A	D
491	492	493	494	495	496	497	498	499	500
C	D	*	C	C	B	A	D	C	C
501	502	503	504	505	506	507	508	509	510
C	B	B	C	D	A	B	B	D	C
511	512	513	514	515	516	517	518	519	520
C	D	C	D	C	A	A	B	C	D
521	522	523	524	525	526	527	528	529	530
B	C	C	A	C	D	C	D	D	A
531	532	533	534	535	536	537	538	539	540
D	B	B	B	C	C	C	C	C	D
541	542	543	544	545	546	547	548	549	550
D	B	D	D	B	D	B	D	C	D
551	552								
D	B								

**** These are personal opinion questions. Option choice may vary. Mark according to your preference.***

EXPLANATORY ANSWERS

1. **(A):** High test reliability suggests that a pupil is likely to maintain a similar performance level when taking an equivalent test. Reliability refers to the consistency of test results over time and different instances.

2. **(C):** The scenario described is a measure of the test's reliability. If a student maintains their position relative to others in multiple instances of the test, it indicates consistent performance, a hallmark of a reliable test.

3. **(B):** A sociogram is most useful for studying relationships among pupils. It visually represents the social dynamics and interrelations within a group, which is helpful for understanding social connections and patterns.

4. **(B):** Provides the teacher with diagnostic information: Group intelligence tests can provide valuable information about students' strengths and weaknesses, such as verbal abilities, quantitative skills, and reasoning aptitude. This information can help teachers tailor their instruction to meet the individual needs of their students.

5. **(B):** Using standardized test results for report card marks is the least justifiable use. Standardized tests are designed to measure specific skills or knowledge and may not fully capture a student's overall performance or learning progress in a class.

6. **(B):** The term "identical elements" is closely associated with the transfer of learning. It refers to the concept that the more similar the learning and application contexts are, the more likely it is that learning will transfer.

7. **(D):** The evaluation of personality is best made through the use of a projective test. These tests are designed to let a person respond to ambiguous stimuli, potentially revealing hidden emotions and internal conflicts.

8. **(C):** Group tests with grade-specific norms and administered according to uniform procedures in a manual are known as standardized tests. They provide a consistent, comparative measure of performance across different individuals or groups.

9. **(A):** If the average IQ is low but science test results are high, it might indicate that the science curriculum in this school is particularly effective, exceeding the quality in other parts of the city.

10. **(A):** The limitation of the five-stage system of Herbart is making the students passive. This educational approach, while structured and comprehensive, can sometimes lead to a passive learning experience, where students are more receptive than actively engaged.

11. **(B):** A lesson where examples are given first followed by the derivation of a general rule or principle is known as an inductive lesson. This method starts with specific instances and asks students to derive the general rule.

12. **(B):** For knowledge lessons, Herbart's five-stage system is often used. This system is a structured approach to teaching that involves specific stages designed to build upon each other to facilitate learning.

13. **(A):** Caldwell Cook, an American educator, is credited with developing the play-way method of education in the early 1900s. He proposed that children learn best through play and that education should be a joyful and engaging experience. Cook's ideas were influenced by the work of Friedrich Froebel, a German educator who emphasized the importance of early childhood education and play in child development.

While Caldwell Cook is generally considered to be the creator of the play-way method of education, Friedrich Froebel's work on early childhood education and play was also influential in the development of this method. Froebel's concept of the Kindergarten, a school for young children where play is central to the curriculum, had a significant impact on the development of the play-way method.

14. (C): The special feature of the play-way method is that games are incorporated into studies to remove the boredom and monotony of traditional learning methods. This approach blends play with educational content.

15. (C): The project method of teaching is associated with John Dewey. This method emphasizes learning by doing and encourages students to engage in projects that are relevant to their interests and real-world problems.

16. (C): The statement describes the heuristic method of teaching. This methodology encourages students to discover facts, rules, and principles through their own efforts, promoting active engagement and self-directed learning.

17. (D): In Garry's Plan, work, play, and learning are all given equal importance. This educational approach seeks to balance different aspects of the child's development.

18. (D): Under the Winnetka Plan, the diversity of students' interests, abilities, and needs are all recognized. This approach is designed to cater to the individual differences of each student.

19. (C): The Dalton Plan is well-suited for older children because it provides them with the opportunity to take more ownership of their learning. Students are responsible for managing their time, setting goals, and completing their assignments independently. This helps them to develop important skills such as self-discipline, organization, and time management.

20. (D): The criticisms of Herbart's five-stage method include: a lack of scope for individual diversity of students, difficulty in coordinating various subjects, and a lack of requirement for generalization in teaching subjects like language, history, and geography. These limitations suggest the method may not adequately address the diverse needs and learning styles of all students.

21. (C): Montessori is known for emphasizing the need for free and natural expressions of a child in the school setting. Her educational philosophy focuses on allowing children to explore and learn at their own pace in a prepared environment.

22. (A): According to Dewey, education is a social need. He viewed education as an integral part of the social experience, emphasizing the interaction between the individual and their environment.

23. (C): The incorrect statement regarding Gandhi's views on education is "Literacy is education." Gandhi believed in a broad concept of education that went beyond mere literacy, encompassing moral, ethical, and practical skills.

24. (C): The theoretical basis of the Montessori educational system is the freedom of the child in expressing his tastes/orientations. Montessori education is characterized by giving children the freedom to choose their activities and learn through their own experiences.

25. (C): The Dalton Plan emphasizes student-centered learning, where students take an active role in their education, and learning is tailored to individual needs and interests.

26. (A): Rousseau, an 18th-century French philosopher, educator, and writer, believed that children learn best through active engagement and exploration of their surroundings. He emphasized the importance of self-discovery and experiential learning, advocating for a child-centered approach to education that fostered natural curiosity and hands-on learning experiences.

Rousseau's ideas on pupil activity were influential in the development of educational philosophies such as Montessori and Waldorf, which emphasize individualized instruction, play-based learning, and the creation of a stimulating and prepared environment for children to explore and learn independently.

27. (D): The Personalized System of Education is designed to cater to individual learning needs, allowing students to progress at their own pace. It tends to minimize competition, foster socialization, and aims to make learning more efficient and effective.

28. (C): Froebel's most important contribution to education was his development of the kindergarten. He is recognized for creating this early childhood educational environment that combines play, singing, and practical activities.

29. (B): Arnold Gesell is the one among the listed theorists who is not closely allied with the stimulus-response learning theory. Gesell focused on child development and emphasized the role of maturation.

30. (A): The statement about the significance of early learning is most closely associated with the writings of Benjamin Bloom. Bloom's work in educational psychology highlighted the importance of the early years in laying the foundation for later academic achievement.

31. (D): The least appropriate item in a pupil's cumulative folder is a subjective statement like "Is an emotionally disturbed child." Educational records should focus on objective, factual information rather than subjective judgments.

32. (D): The creation of a students' union in a school is generally viewed positively as it develops the spirit of leadership among students. It provides them with opportunities to practice decision-making, teamwork, and responsibility.

33. (B): Including sex education in the academic curriculum is necessary for the enlightenment of society. It helps in providing accurate information, dispelling myths, and promoting healthy attitudes and behaviours.

34. (*): *These are personal opinion questions. Option choice may vary. Mark according to your preference.*

35. (B): To help a student who is always scared or full of fears, the teacher should talk to the student with love and affection. Building a trusting relationship can help alleviate the student's fears and encourage confidence.

36. (*): *These are personal opinion questions. Option choice may vary. Mark according to your preference.*

37. (*): *These are personal opinion questions. Option choice may vary. Mark according to your preference.*

38. (D): Any teacher can become favorite among his students by behaving with them in a sympathetic manner. Empathy and understanding in a teacher-student relationship can create a positive and conducive learning environment.

39. (C): An easy method to impress students is to keep your conduct ideal. Being a role model through your behaviour and actions can positively influence students and gain their respect.

40. (D): To encourage good students, all of the listed methods can be effective: praising them, allocating tasks of responsibility, and treating them in a friendly manner. Each approach contributes to motivating and supporting students in different ways.

41. (C): If you realize that a student you punished was innocent, the appropriate action is to apologize to the student. Acknowledging the mistake helps maintain respect and trust in the teacher-student relationship.

42. **(D):** If an intelligent student is disrupting class discipline, it's important to understand his problem and make an effort to solve it. Effective discipline involves addressing underlying issues, not just the surface behaviour.

43. **(D):** In current times, a lady teacher may face the maximum number of problems due to a fall in the values of life. Societal changes and shifting values can pose challenges in maintaining discipline and respect in the classroom.

44. **(C):** If a student forgets to bring the fees on the fee day, a compassionate and reasonable approach would be to allow him to bring the fees on the next fee day.

45. **(C):** If a student has been failing for two years, as his class teacher, you should try to identify the reasons for his failure. Understanding the root cause can help in providing the appropriate support and intervention.

46. **(D):** To improve the academic performance of students who are weak in the subject you teach, it's important to give them personalized assistance and support and help elevate their understanding and skills.

47. **(C):** If you are a lady teacher interacting with people of reputed society, you should be proud to inform them that you are a teacher. Teaching is a noble profession, and there's dignity in being an educator.

48. **(A):** An example of verbal illustration is a simile. A simile uses comparison, typically with "like" or "as," to make a description more vivid or understandable.

49. **(C):** If a student gives a wrong answer with mistakes in language, grammar, and facts, the best approach is to ask the student to find out and rectify the mistakes themselves. This encourages active learning and self-correction.

50. **(D):** All the given questions are incorrect as they assume subjective judgments and can be considered leading or biased questions. They do not allow for objective or open-ended responses.

51. **(A):** For students who give wrong answers, a constructive approach is to encourage them to repeat the correct answer multiple times. This can help reinforce the correct information and aid in learning.

52. **(A):** A teacher who is liked by students is often one who listens to their problems. Being attentive to students' concerns fosters a positive and supportive classroom environment.

53. **(D):** Students may not take interest in studies if the academic curriculum is not of the right content or quality. An engaging and relevant curriculum can significantly enhance student interest and motivation.

54. **(D):** A normal child of twelve years of age is most likely to be eager for peer approval. This age is typically characterized by a strong desire to fit in and be accepted by peers.

55. **(D):** Creative writing should be an activity planned for all children. Encouraging creativity in writing is beneficial for students at all levels, not just those who are already proficient in reading and writing.

56. **(B):** The most promising step for a teacher to improve class discipline is to evaluate his/her materials, methods, and approaches to children. Reflecting and adjusting teaching strategies can often lead to better classroom management.

57. **(A):** If a quiet, reserved fourth grader brings road maps to school and looks at them often, the teacher should encourage the pupil to talk about them during a show-and-tell period. This acknowledges the child's interest and encourages sharing and communication.

58. **(C):** Lesson planning should be guided primarily by the consideration of the curriculum goals. Ensuring that lessons align with curriculum objectives is key to effective teaching and learning.

59. (D): In a kindergarten class, it would be unreasonable to expect a child to know when it is time to clean up without guidance. Young children often need reminders and assistance with transitions and time management.

60. (D): If a male eighth-grade student expresses feelings of love for you, the appropriate response would be to involve his parents or guardians and make a combined effort to address the situation. This maintains professional boundaries and addresses the student's behaviour in a responsible manner.

61. (C): If students are not studying their subjects, the teacher should first try to understand why they lack interest. Identifying the root causes can help in addressing the issue more effectively than punitive measures.

62. (D): The statement that is least educationally valid is that overlearning constitutes wastage of time. Overlearning, or practicing beyond just mastering the material, can actually strengthen retention and understanding.

63. (C): For a group of sixth graders reading at a fourth-grade level, the best material would be a high-interest, low-level book of stories. This would be engaging while still accessible to their reading level.

64. (B): A child's natural activity can be channeled into promoting physical development. Encouraging engagement in sports, active play, and physical activities can contribute to the child's overall physical well-being and development. Physical activities are essential for fostering motor skills, coordination, and a healthy lifestyle.

65. (B): If a parent refuses to give permission for a class trip, the teacher should first confer with the parent to discuss the educational purpose of the trip. This dialogue can address concerns and highlight the trip's value.

66. (C): The behavior of a fifteen-year-old student wearing the same type of sweaters as his lady teacher is an example of identification. It's a psychological process where a person emulates or mimics someone they admire or respect.

67. (A): If misbehavior persists despite punishment, the teacher is probably practicing the policy of negative reinforcement. This approach can unintentionally reinforce unwanted behavior by giving it attention.

68. (B): If poor attendance is noticed on test days, the teacher should consider scheduling tests throughout the week. This could help alleviate test-related anxiety or avoidance behaviours.

69. (B): If a student comes to class in dirty and crumpled clothes, a discreet and sensitive approach would be to advise him privately to come to class in clean clothes. Public humiliation or isolation should be avoided.

70. (C): Arranging educational tours for students is important because they provide knowledge through direct contact with new environments, people, and educational institutions. Such experiences can be invaluable for real-world learning.

71. (D): All of the options listed contribute to the factors that make our present system of education less effective in preparing students for the workforce and reducing unemployment rates.

(*a*) **Only knowledge-based education:** Focusing solely on theoretical knowledge and academic rigor without emphasizing practical skills and vocational training limits students' ability to apply their learning to real-world scenarios and secure employment opportunities.

(*b*) **Education based on outdated policies:** Relying on outdated educational policies and philosophies, such as those established by Lord Macaulay, may not adequately address the evolving demands of the modern job market and the skills required for success in the 21st century.

(*c*) **Lack of vocational orientation:** Neglecting vocational education and career guidance hinders students' exploration of career paths, development of job-specific skills, and preparation for transitioning into the workforce.

In combination, these factors contribute to a mismatch between the skills and knowledge imparted in our education system and the competencies demanded by employers. This mismatch leads to a higher percentage of graduates struggling to find suitable employment, increasing the unemployment rate.

72. **(D):** Knowledge of child psychology is essential for a primary teacher because it helps the teacher understand the behaviour of children. Understanding psychological development aids in effective teaching and classroom management.

73. **(B):** Navodaya Vidyalayas were created under the National Education Policy to enable students with good abilities from both cities and villages to study in such schools. These schools aim to provide quality education to talented students from diverse backgrounds.

74. **(B):** Achievement grouping involves organizing students based on their academic performance or achievement levels. It does not necessarily align with the philosophy of allowing students to move at their own pace. In achievement grouping, students are often placed in classes or groups according to their academic abilities, which may not provide the same flexibility for individual pacing as non-graded primary classes, pre-kindergarten classes, or team teaching. The quoted philosophy emphasizes flexibility and individual pacing, which may not be fully realized in achievement grouping scenarios.

75. **(D):** Teachers are likely to play an intelligent role in curriculum improvement when they participate with other staff members in devising the curriculum for the school. Collaboration among educators ensures a well-rounded and effective curriculum.

76. **(C):** This approach ensures that students are not overwhelmed by demanding subjects throughout the day and have a balanced workload that allows them to focus effectively on each subject. Distributing subjects based on difficulty can help prevent fatigue, promote engagement, and optimize learning outcomes.

77. **(B):** The most unreliable predictor of educational achievement is the ethnic origin of parents. Factors like classroom experiences and family background are more significant in influencing educational outcomes.

78. **(D):** The statement that slow children derive more benefit from a lecture than brighter children do is not true. Developmental lessons, with their active participation, often benefit all students more than traditional lectures.

79. **(C):** A non-traditional method of education is teaching through Shanti Niketan, started by Rabindranath Tagore. Shanti Niketan emphasized holistic education and learning in a natural environment.

80. **(C):** Yes, the practice of getting education through the Internet, common in the West, should be adopted in India, but it must include continuous monitoring of academic performances and guidance. Online education can provide access to diverse resources and learning opportunities.

81. **(B):** Yes, new techniques like practical experiments, tours, audio-visual presentations, and live examples are useful, but they must be used according to the needs of the students and the demands of the subject matter. These methods can enhance learning by making it more engaging and relevant.

82. (C): The best thing about the teaching profession is often considered to be the company of children and the pleasure derived from interacting with and shaping young minds.

83. (D): Going on strike is generally viewed as not a solution to problems. It's often seen as contrary to the professional and ethical responsibilities of teachers, whose primary duty is to educate and support their students.

84. (D): A good teacher should show more interest in both the enhancement of the knowledge levels of his students (B) and self-study (C). Continuous learning and focusing on student development are key aspects of effective teaching.

85. (C): Textbooks should be replaced with new ones after some years due to the regular upgradation of knowledge levels. Updating educational materials ensures that students receive the most current and relevant information.

86. (C): Choosing the teaching profession because it offers an opportunity to handle/ train the future citizens of the nation reflects a commitment to shaping and influencing the next generation positively.

87. (B): A good reason to adopt the teaching profession is a love for teaching work. Passion for the profession is crucial for being an effective and dedicated teacher.

88. (C): The proliferation of small English Montessori Schools in cities is often seen as primarily driven by the generation of money. While these schools may provide valuable services, the commercial aspect is a significant factor in their establishment.

89. (D): A good profession is one in which one gets an opportunity for honor and self-satisfaction. Professions that provide a sense of fulfillment and contribute positively to society are often highly regarded.

90. (C): Vocation-oriented education can make learning more relevant and engaging for students. When students see how their studies can be applied to the real world, they are more likely to be interested in learning and to succeed in school.

91. (D): Teachers are expected to be role models for their students and to uphold high moral standards. They are expected to be honest, fair, and compassionate. They are also expected to be knowledgeable and up-to-date on the latest educational practices.

92. (D): A good textbook, besides other special features, essentially includes practice exercises for doing a lot of homework. These exercises help reinforce learning and provide students with the opportunity to apply what they have learned.

93. (A): Teachers direct and help students in the choice of a profession because they are aware of the tastes/orientations of their students. Teachers often understand their students' strengths, interests, and potential, which can guide appropriate career advice.

94. (C): Disagree with the statement "Teaching is not a profession." Teaching is widely recognized as a profession that requires specific skills, training, and a commitment to ongoing learning and ethical standards.

95. (D): A teacher is like all of these: a father, a mother, and a friend of the student. Teachers often play multiple roles in their students' lives, providing guidance, care, support, and mentorship.

96. (A): Finesse in teaching encompasses a broader set of skills and attributes that are essential for effectively conveying information, engaging students, and facilitating learning.

97. (C): A teacher should have facilities for studying and teaching. This includes having access to resources, materials, and an environment conducive to both learning and teaching effectively.

98. (C): If there are two groups of students in the class, the best approach would be to take all the students into confidence and advise them to refrain from politics, as they are too young to indulge in its intricacies. This encourages unity and focuses on education.

99. **(B):** If students prefer another teacher for a subject, the best strategy would be to let the other teacher teach and introspect the reasons for your failure. Self-reflection can lead to improvement and growth as a teacher.

100. **(B):** If a student praises a colleague of yours, the appropriate response would be to also praise that colleague and tell your students to follow his conduct. Acknowledging and supporting colleagues' strengths fosters a positive and collaborative educational environment.

101. **(B):** If you learn that your students praised you in your absence, the most professional response would be to continue teaching them in a normal manner without being overly influenced by the praise. This maintains professionalism and focus on the primary goal of education.

102. **(B):** If you are a junior teacher with a poor pay package, the most constructive approach is to work hard and become a master of your subject. Excelling in your field can lead to recognition and potential career advancement.

103. **(C):** To enhance your knowledge levels, surfing through the Internet and downloading information is a practical and accessible method. It allows you to access a wide range of resources and stay updated with current information in your field.

104. **(D):** Being present in the school on national days like August 15 and January 26 is important as it helps in strengthening unity and integrity of the country. These occasions also provide an opportunity to instill a sense of patriotism and community in students.

105. **(B):** The major objective of co-education is to let boys and girls understand each other. Co-education promotes mutual respect, equality, and prepares students for a world where both genders work and interact together.

106. **(A):** Arrangement for "education on environment" in the school is important for creating awareness among students about the environment. Environmental education is crucial for fostering responsible attitudes and behaviours towards the planet.

107. **(D):** For imparting moral education to students in the school, it's important that teachers control and regulate their moral conduct. Teachers serve as role models, and their behaviour can greatly influence students' understanding and adoption of moral values.

108. **(A):** The chief reason for the diminishing reputation of the teacher is often seen as the materialistic viewpoint of the society. This societal shift can overshadow the intrinsic value of teaching and its impact.

109. **(C):** The major objective of education is developing the inherent abilities/powers of students. Education should aim at fostering the overall development of students, enabling them to realize their full potential.

110. **(D):** If a neighbour criticizes you, the best course of action would be to meet her personally and inquire about the reason for her action. This approach seeks to understand the issue directly and can help in resolving any misunderstandings or conflicts.

111. **(D):** Adult education can be under the authority of various entities, and a collaborative approach is often beneficial. The government can play a role in formulating policies and providing resources. Non-governmental organizations may contribute through initiatives and programs. Educated persons can also play a role in providing education and support. Therefore, a combination of government, non-government organizations, and educated individuals working together is a comprehensive approach to adult education.

112. **(C):** Political interference can affect the functioning of educational institutions, create instability, and impact the professional standing of teachers, including female educators. While other factors such as student indiscipline or teachers seeking additional income through tuitions might also play a role, political interference is often considered a major contributing factor to the decline in the dignity of teachers.

113. **(D):** Education of female children is important because it leads to the education of the entire family in the future. Educated women are more likely to ensure that their children, and thereby their families, are educated as well.

114. **(C):** The progress report card of every student should be handed over to his/her parents/ guardians because it lets them know about the progress of their children/wards. This facilitates parental involvement in their child's education.

115. **(A):** To check the decay in the field of education, it is important to make arrangements for improving the educational system. This includes updating curricula, improving teaching methods, and enhancing teacher training.

116. **(C):** In the context of limited resources and rising population levels, programs related to "Qualitative Improvement in Education" are courageous efforts. They aim to enhance the quality of education despite challenging circumstances.

117. **(D):** Good parents are those who give some of their time and love on a regular basis to their children. Emotional support and parental involvement are crucial for a child's overall well-being and development.

118. **(D):** The demand for higher salaries can be seen as a reflection of economic progress. As societies and economies develop, there is often an expectation that compensation for labour should keep pace with the overall economic growth.

119. **(A):** As a teacher, regarding other activities of the school, a positive attitude should be displayed. Being actively involved and supportive of school activities contributes to a better school environment and student experience.

120. **(C):** If a student is involved in eve-teasing, the appropriate response would be to advise him to do away with his bad behaviour. It's important to address such issues with seriousness and guide students towards understanding the impact of their actions and correcting their behaviour.

121. **(B):** To inculcate the habit of eating together among students, making arrangements so that teachers and students eat together can be effective. This creates a communal atmosphere and sets a practical example.

122. **(D):** To develop the spirit of responsibility towards society in students, keeping them in touch with responsible persons in the society can be impactful. Direct interaction with role models can inspire and teach practical aspects of social responsibility.

123. **(A):** The school is a miniaturized form of society. It mirrors various aspects of societal structure and interactions, providing a context for students to learn about social norms, responsibilities, and relationships.

124. **(D):** Education not only conserves the culture of a nation but also has the potential to make it mass-oriented and popular. Education helps disseminate cultural knowledge, traditions, and values among the masses, contributing to the popularity and widespread understanding of the culture.

125. **(C):** Parents/guardians of students should preferably be present during meetings organized in the school to know how their children have been performing. Active parental involvement is important for a child's educational success.

126. (C): If the parents/guardians of a child cannot afford a highly branded and costly school, advising them to try for admission to a school that has good teaching norms and not high fees is a sensible suggestion. Quality education does not always correlate with high fees.

127. (C): It is a reasonable approach, as it emphasizes a positive and inclusive perspective. This response acknowledges the value of education in general and suggests that every school has its strengths.

128. (D): If some parents/guardians complain about a weekly educational program shown on television during school hours, inviting them to watch the program to realize its educational value can be a constructive approach. This can help them understand the program's benefits.

129. (B): If a student does not complete his homework on a regular basis, calling the student in privacy and explaining the advantages of completing homework can be effective. This approach addresses the issue directly and constructively.

130. (B): The quality of a teacher that is most liked by students is his impartiality. Fairness in treatment and judgment creates a sense of trust and respect among students.

131. (C): To win the confidence of the Principal, a teacher should keep on executing his own teaching work in a satisfactory manner. Professionalism and dedication to one's duties are key to earning respect and trust.

132. (B): As a teacher, you should always listen to the problems of students. Being approachable and empathetic towards students' concerns is an important aspect of the teaching profession.

133. (D): As a teacher, the ideal approach is to be willing to teach in any school. This demonstrates flexibility and a commitment to the profession regardless of the location or student demographic.

134. (C): To teach a new subject in the class, discussing the subject with students in light of their existing knowledge about it, and then providing new sets of information/data about that subject is an effective method. This approach engages students and builds on their prior knowledge.

135. (D): For your favorite student, as a teacher, you should adequately support him in his studies. It's important to maintain fairness and professionalism, supporting all students equally.

136. (D): The true objective of education is facilitating the all-round development of students. Education should aim at holistic growth, including intellectual, emotional, social, and physical development.

137. (B): To raise the standards of education, continuous evaluation of students is vital. Regular assessment helps in tracking student progress, identifying areas needing improvement, and tailoring teaching methods to student needs.

138. (A): If a person does not agree with your viewpoint, you should present the rationale of your viewpoint before him. Open and respectful dialogue is important in discussing differing opinions.

139. (A): The job of the teacher is to generate an affinity for studies among students. Inspiring interest and love for learning is a fundamental role of educators.

140. (B): With the help of cumulative records, the pace of educational progress of children can be known. These records provide a comprehensive view of a student's academic and developmental progress over time.

141. (D): If a student asks a question and you do not know the answer, the best approach is to acknowledge this and tell the student that you will find out the answer and inform them later. This approach shows honesty and a commitment to learning.

142. (D): It would be beneficial to give homework to students according to their abilities and capacities. Differentiating homework can help cater to the individual needs and skill levels of each student.

143. (D): It is important for the teacher to have all of these: complete knowledge of the subject, complete knowledge of teaching methods, and knowledge about the students. A combination of these elements contributes to effective teaching.

144. (D): Playing yourself in the playground along with children can be an effective method to generate interest among students for sports/ games. Active participation and enthusiasm from the teacher can be contagious.

145. (D): The diminished respect for teachers nowadays can be attributed to all of these reasons: teachers taking up tuition work, a change in the character of teachers compared to earlier times, and a lack of dedication in performing their duties.

146. (A): Students are more likely to engage in learning when they feel that it is personally meaningful and relevant to their lives. When they perceive the learning process as disconnected from their interests, goals, and personal development, they lose interest and motivation.

147. (D): The best method to evaluate the achievements of students is continuous evaluation. This approach allows for ongoing assessment of student learning and progress, providing a more comprehensive understanding of their abilities.

148. (A): The ideal seating arrangement for students in a class could be to have them sit according to their roll numbers. This method is impartial and can help in maintaining order and organization in the classroom.

149. (B): In the Rigveda, it is mentioned that education is a source of knowledge and enlightenment. This perspective highlights the role of education in providing wisdom and understanding.

150. (A): Education not only preserves culture, but it also enriches it. Education contributes to the growth and development of cultural values, traditions, and knowledge.

151. (B): Informal education of the child starts from his environment. It is the learning that occurs naturally through the child's daily interactions and experiences within their surroundings, rather than in a structured educational setting.

152. (D): Economic development is not typically included in the all-round development of a child as conceptualized in educational objectives. The focus is generally on physical, intellectual, and moral/spiritual development.

153. (A): The objective of basic education of Gandhiji was to let the child come face-to-face with truth. Gandhiji's philosophy of education emphasized the importance of truth and practical learning through life experiences.

154. (C): The basic education system was based on the viewpoint that the child can get better education through meaningful and creative work. Gandhiji's concept of basic education, or Nai Talim, emphasized learning through productive work.

155. (D): All of these activities - Embroidery, Dyeing, Making toys of clay - can be called purposeful creative activities under the gamut of basic education. Gandhiji emphasized the importance of learning through engaging in productive and creative work.

156. (A): The relationship of educational psychology is with the aspect of "when and how." It focuses on understanding the learning processes and how best to teach, based on the psychological development and needs of learners.

157. (C): Child psychology provides educators with a comprehensive understanding of how children think, feel, and behave, enabling them to tailor their teaching methods and approaches to the specific needs of their students.

158. **(B):** In order to effect the teaching of students in the most appropriate manner, the study of child psychology helps the teacher. It provides insights into how children think, learn, and develop, guiding teachers in their instructional methods.

159. **(A):** If a student is insulted by the teacher before the class, the student may become more defiant and arrogant as a result. Such negative reinforcement can harm the student-teacher relationship and impact the student's self-esteem.

160. **(D):** All of these reasons can contribute to why students might not ask questions during class, even if they do not understand the lecture. Fear of reprimand, fear of being seen as dull, and not knowing what to ask are common barriers to student participation.

161. **(C):** The best method to help little children remember a subject is by repeating it time to time and remembering it. Repetition aids memory, especially in young children, by reinforcing the information.

162. **(C):** The need for a mid-day meal for little children in school primarily revolves around ensuring children get some nutritional diet. This is particularly important in contexts where children might not receive adequate nutrition at home.

163. **(C):** The meetings of Parent-Teachers Associations should be held from time to time, not just on specific occasions. Regular meetings ensure ongoing communication and collaboration between parents and teachers regarding students' educational progress.

164. **(B):** The objective statement stage, also known as the "statement of aims" or "learning objectives stage," typically occurs after the preparation stage and before the presentation stage. It involves explicitly stating the specific learning goals for the lesson, ensuring that both the teacher and students have a clear understanding of what is expected to be learned.

165. **(B):** Since the presentation stage was deemed the most important in Herbart's five-stage system, it indicates that this system gives major status to the subject matter. The presentation stage is central to the delivery of the educational content.

166. **(D):** A lesson plan serves all of these purposes: it informs the teacher about the success or failure of teaching, connects current learning with previous knowledge of the students, and helps the teacher conduct their work more effectively.

167. **(D):** Under Glover's scheme, students take an active part in the teaching process. This approach is student-centered and encourages active learning and participation from the students.

168. **(D):** The educational method of Socrates included all of these aspects: it was a question method, did not impose knowledge on the student from outside, and promoted the concept of the student moving towards auto-education.

169. **(D):** Alfred Binet propounded the principle of pupil activity in education. Binet believed that teaching should focus on developing a child's mental processes, such as memory, perception, and thinking.

170. **(D):** Rousseau is known as the pioneer of the principle of "pupil activity" in Europe. His educational theories greatly emphasized the importance of active and natural learning processes.

171. **(A):** Henry Caldwell Cook, a British educator, is credited with coining the term "play-way method" and advocating for its use in education. His book, "The Play Way," published in 1917, outlined his philosophy and practical strategies for incorporating play into the learning process.

Cook believed that play was a natural and effective way for children to learn. He observed that children learn through exploration, experimentation, and social interaction, all of which are inherent in play. He argued that by incorporating play into the curriculum, teachers could create a more engaging and enjoyable learning environment for children.

172. **(C):** The special feature of the play-way method is that it removes the monotony or boredom of work (studies) by incorporating sports/games into the learning process, making it more engaging and enjoyable for children.

173. **(D):** The word 'kindergarten' is drawn from the German language, and it means a children's garden. The term reflects the nurturing and growth-focused environment of these early childhood education settings.

174. **(B):** In the kindergarten system of teaching, the status of the teacher is like that of a gardener. This metaphor reflects the teacher's role in nurturing and guiding the development of young children, much like a gardener tends to plants.

175. **(A):** The Montessori system of education teaches students writing and reading skills through a psychological method. It emphasizes learning through discovery and manipulation of materials, rather than direct instruction.

176. **(C):** The Montessori system of teaching is focused on the child. It is child-centered, with an emphasis on individual pacing, interests, and the development of a child's independence and potential.

177. **(B):** Professor Armstrong was the pioneer of the Heuristic method of teaching. This method emphasizes self-discovery, encouraging students to learn through their own experiences and investigations.

178. **(B):** In the Montessori System of education, the teaching of senses was emphasized. The Montessori approach involves sensory-based learning materials that encourage children to use their senses to explore and understand their environment.

179. **(C):** The statement refers to the Heuristic system of teaching. This system trains students to discover facts, rules, and principles through their own efforts and to organize and generalize the knowledge they acquire.

180. **(C):** The project teaching method is associated with Dewey and Kilpatrick. This educational approach emphasizes learning by doing and encourages students to engage in projects that are relevant to their interests and real-world problems.

181. **(C):** The project method of teaching imparts practical knowledge to the student because the basis of the student's knowledge is his personal experiences. This method encourages learning through active involvement in meaningful projects that relate to real-world scenarios.

182. **(A):** The Dalton Plan, developed by Helen Parkhurst, is a student-centered approach to education that emphasizes individualized learning and self-directed instruction. The Dalton Plan's emphasis on self-paced learning and independent work may be challenging for younger children who still require more guidance and structure in their learning environment. While the Dalton Plan has its strengths and can be beneficial for older students, its suitability for younger age groups remains a topic of discussion and debate.

183. **(D):** Basic education aims to make the student self-dependent, provide knowledge of the basic elements of education, and encourage philosophical development.

184. **(D):** A very large portion of the curriculum can be included (in the test/examination) with the help of objective-type questions. These questions allow for broad coverage of material in a concise and time-efficient manner.

185. **(C):** For students who develop an inferiority complex due to very small height, it is recommended that they achieve excellence in some other field. This approach focuses on developing strengths and talents in areas unrelated to physical attributes.

186. **(C):** If teachers send monthly reports of students to their parents/guardians, it helps maintain relationships between the teachers and the parents/guardians of the students. Regular communication supports engagement and collaboration in the student's education.

187. **(D):** Given that little children are highly agile and active, the best approach is to give them useful education with the help of their activity. Utilizing their natural energy and curiosity can enhance learning experiences.

188. **(C):** McDougal stated, "Sport is the innate natural tendency of a child." This perspective recognizes the natural inclination of children towards physical activity and play as a crucial aspect of their development.

189. **(A):** All the teaching methods of the modern type, like Kindergarten, Montessori, Dalton, Basic, and project methods, are based on the principle of the activity method. This principle emphasizes active participation and hands-on learning.

190. **(A):** In order to make the senses of little children capable and active, you would put materials before them and let them examine the same. Engaging their senses through direct interaction with various materials is an effective way to stimulate sensory development.

191. **(B):** To evaluate the power of expression and style of students, giving them questions and telling them to write down their answers is an effective method. Written responses allow students to demonstrate their ability to articulate thoughts and express themselves clearly.

192. **(A):** The Montessori method lays the maximum emphasis on the personal development of the student. It focuses on individual progress and learning, encouraging self-directed, hands-on learning experiences.

193. **(C):** The Dalton system of education is particularly useful for grown-up children. This system emphasizes self-directed learning and personal responsibility, which are more suitable for older, more independent learners.

194. **(A):** In an examination, the three essential qualities that must be present are validity, reliability, and practicality. Validity ensures the test measures what it is supposed to measure, reliability ensures consistency in results, and practicality pertains to the feasibility of the examination.

195. **(C):** To know about the previous knowledge of a child, asking questions from them is an effective approach. This allows the teacher to assess the child's existing knowledge base and understanding, which can inform subsequent teaching.

196. **(C):** Having answer booklets evaluated by other teachers and not by their own teachers can help ensure that students are not given unjust and partial treatment. This practice promotes fairness and objectivity in grading.

197. **(A):** According to Dewey, education is a social need. He emphasized the role of education in social and community life and viewed it as an essential aspect of a functioning society.

198. **(B):** In today's busy world, students are often juggling a multitude of commitments, including schoolwork, extracurricular activities, sports, and part-time jobs. When students are overwhelmed with responsibilities, homework can easily fall to the bottom of the priority list.

199. **(A):** The curriculum should be flexible to facilitate the development of students with different personalities. A rigid curriculum might not cater to the varied needs, interests, and abilities of all students.

200. **(D):** School inspections are valuable because they help schools identify areas for improvement, promote accountability, encourage collaboration, and enhance school culture.

201. **(A):** Student-centered teaching means taking care of the needs of every student. This approach focuses on the interests, abilities, and learning styles of students, placing them at the center of the educational process.

202. **(C):** Maria Montessori gave the statement, "In a school, arrangements should be made for the free and natural expressions of a child." Her educational philosophy emphasizes creating learning environments that allow for the natural development and expression of children.

203. **(C):** Personal education is important for both intelligent students and students who are slow learners. Each group has unique educational needs that require personalized attention to ensure effective learning.

204. **(A):** The Heuristic system of teaching is most effectively applied to the teaching of Science. This method encourages students to discover and learn through hands-on experimentation and exploration, which is particularly suited to scientific subjects.

205. **(B):** To check the habit of cramming among students, a change in the examination/test method is recommended. Shifting towards assessments that evaluate understanding and application rather than rote memorization can discourage cramming.

206. **(D):** If a student uses indecent language, it could be due to any of these reasons: exposure to similar language at home, in the neighborhood, or among peers/friends. The behaviour is likely influenced by the environment and social interactions.

207. **(C):** When the teacher who has taught the students evaluates their examination test booklets, there is a possibility that impartial evaluation is not done. Familiarity with students can lead to conscious or unconscious bias in grading.

208. **(D):** The best system of class teaching is one in which both the teacher and students ask questions. This interactive approach encourages engagement, curiosity, and deeper understanding.

209. **(D):** In the class, it is preferable to ask questions whose answers may be given by students after thinking about them. This encourages critical thinking and active participation.

210. **(C):** The defense mechanism acts in a subconscious manner, and it is used by all students, regardless of their mental abilities. This psychological process operates independently of conscious thought and is a universal aspect of human behaviour.

211. **(D):** The basis of social discipline is the refinement of good moral values. Effective social discipline stems from internalized values and understanding rather than external factors like fear or punishment.

212. **(D):** There is a fear of the creation of discipline-related problems if any of these conditions are present: students fall into bad company, students are dominated or suppressed through artificial methods, or the school is not located in an appropriate place.

213. **(D):** For little children who are unable to pronounce long and difficult words, a combination of methods B and C would be effective: making them speak such words by dividing them into parts, and using words with similar pronunciations to ease the learning process.

214. **(C):** The proof of complete expertise in knowledge gained by a student is that he can successfully use that knowledge.

Practical application of knowledge is a key indicator of true understanding.

215. (C): Lord Macaulay played the most significant role in making English the medium of education during British rule in India. His minute on Indian education in **1835** advocated for the promotion of English education.

216. (B): Helen Parkhurst gets the credit for starting the Dalton method of education. This approach emphasizes a flexible, student-centered approach to learning, where students are given independence in managing their work.

217. (B): From a psychological viewpoint, little children learn words first of all when learning a language. This process typically involves acquiring vocabulary before understanding more complex structures like sentences or the alphabet.

218. (B): Pragmatism gave birth to the project method in education. This method emphasizes learning through engaging in real-world projects and practical activities, an approach that aligns with the principles of pragmatism.

219. (B): John Dewey was the pioneer of the thought of pragmatism in the field of education. He advocated for an experiential, student-centered approach, emphasizing the importance of learning through doing.

220. (A): Johann Heinrich Pestalozzi started the movement of naturalism in the field of education. His educational philosophy focused on the natural development of children and the importance of a nurturing environment for learning.

221. (D): Pestalozzi was of the opinion that all of these aspects were important: education should be in accordance with the development of the child, the teacher should respect the personality of the child, and the objective of education is to develop the mental powers of the child.

222. (D): Education would be meaningful only when it is student-centered. This approach emphasizes the needs, interests, and learning styles of students, making education more relevant and effective for them.

223. (C): If a student wears unironed and dirty clothes and comes to class, the appropriate response would be to tell him, through hints/ gestures, that it is not a good habit to come to class in such clothes. This approach addresses the issue without embarrassing the student publicly.

224. (D): The Winnetka Plan, developed by Carleton Washburne in Winnetka, Illinois, was an educational experiment that emphasized individualized instruction, student choice, and self-pace learning. It was designed to break away from traditional methods of classroom teaching and provide students with a more personalized learning experience.

225. (C): The theoretical basis of the Montessori educational system is complete freedom for the child in expressing his interests. Montessori education emphasizes self-directed learning and allowing children to choose activities based on their interests.

226. (D): One benefit of regularly evaluating the homework given to children is all of these: it ensures children do not forget to bring their completed homework, helps teachers stay abreast of students' progress, and informs children about their weaknesses.

227. (B): . Creating an effective and balanced question paper involves considering the difficulty level of questions and their distribution. Starting with relatively easier questions allows students to build confidence and get into the flow of the examination. This can help them manage their time efficiently and approach more challenging questions with a positive mindset.

228. (A): The analytical method of class teaching involves breaking down a complex concept or problem into its smaller, more manageable parts. This approach allows students to gradually build their understanding of the material by moving from the unknown to the known.

229. (B): The correct meaning of the curriculum is a collection of all those experiences that the school wants children to imbibe. It includes the planned interaction of students with instructional content, materials, resources, and processes for evaluating the attainment of educational objectives.

230. (B): The central role of the teacher in education is not a contribution of Rousseau. His contributions were more focused on child psychology, child-centered education, the importance of sports in education, and improvements in curricula. Rousseau emphasized naturalism and the development of the child over the teacher's centrality in education.

231. (A): The chief advantage of students having diaries is that their parents/guardians remain abreast with their studies on a regular basis. Diaries can be used to track homework assignments, upcoming tests, and other important academic information.

232. (A): The best benefit that can accrue due to the meeting of a parent and a teacher is that both the parent and teacher agree about the goals of achievement of the child. This facilitates a shared understanding and collaborative approach towards the child's education.

233. (D): In the situation where parents/guardians are concerned about excessive TV watching, the teacher should invite them to the weekly educational program at school so they can see its educational value and understand how it enhances children's knowledge.

234. (C): The achievement of a student should be evaluated by comparing the present achievement of the student with his previous record of achievements. This approach focuses on individual progress rather than comparison with others.

235. (B): Guidance can still be meaningful and beneficial even in the absence of formal education. Guidance helps individuals discover and develop their abilities, and it can occur in various aspects of life, not just within the confines of a formal education system. Effective guidance can contribute significantly to personal development and self-identification, irrespective of the level of formal education.

236. (C): The ability of experimentation among science students can be developed by letting them practice their experiments. Hands-on experience is crucial in learning scientific concepts and developing experimental skills.

237. (C): If the Principal does not give permission to organize a bazaar, the appropriate action would be to personally meet the Principal and try to get his permission by explaining the educational value and importance of organizing the bazaar.

238. (B): It is just possible that children of the same mental age may not be able to learn at the same speed. Learning speed can vary due to a variety of factors, including individual learning styles, motivation, and environmental influences.

239. (C): The statement "Whosoever has the power to do something, does work; the one who cannot do anything, teaches" is attributed to George Bernard Shaw. This statement is often viewed as a cynical perspective on teaching.

240. (D): Kindergarten schools were inaugurated for the first time in Germany. Friedrich Froebel, a German educator, is credited with starting the first kindergarten in 1837, emphasizing the importance of play and nurturing in early childhood education.

241. (C): Making the students of a primary class memorize multiplication tables helps children in solving questions in the future.

Memorization of basic mathematical facts can aid in quicker calculation skills and foundational understanding for more complex mathematics.

242. (B): The most important contribution of Froebel in the field of education was the Kindergarten. He introduced this concept to provide a nurturing and playful environment for the early educational development of children.

243. (A): Yes, the class curriculum should be the same for both male and female students. There should be no difference between the curricula of these students as both deserve equal educational opportunities and content.

244. (C): Operation Blackboard is related to increasing the physical facilities in primary schools. It was an initiative aimed at improving the infrastructure and learning environment in primary schools.

245. (A): Ernakulam in Kerala was the first district to achieve full literacy. It was recognized as a fully literate district in the early **1990**s, setting a precedent for literacy campaigns in other districts.

246. (D): The statement that is not true about Navodaya Vidyalayas is that female and urban students cannot take admission in these schools. Navodaya Vidyalayas are open to all students, regardless of gender or urban/rural background, based on their performance in the entrance test.

247. (B): The University Grants Commission (UGC) is responsible for the spread of university education, coordination, and maintenance of standards of education in universities in India.

248. (B): While group intelligence tests can be administered to a large group of students simultaneously, making them a more efficient and cost-effective method of assessment, their primary benefit lies in the diagnostic information they provide to teachers.

249. (D): The key to creating an urge in students' minds to study or learn is motivation. Effective teaching involves not only instructing but also motivating students to engage with the material and find personal meaning and interest in it.

250. (B): Motivation is a psychological state. It is an internal process that activates, guides, and maintains behaviour towards achieving a particular goal.

251. (A): Programmed instruction is designed to allow students to learn independently through self-paced study. It provides instructional materials that guide students through a sequence of steps or "programmed" content, allowing them to acquire knowledge without constant supervision from a teacher. The advantage lies in the self-directed learning aspect facilitated by the programmed materials.

252. (A): Vijay reciting a poem loudly while standing on the terrace is an example of oral communication. It involves the use of spoken words to convey a message.

253. (D): Symbolic communication or non-verbal communication becomes more effective than oral or written communication when the sender is at a distance from the receiver, the environment is surcharged with noise pollution, or when it is necessary to demonstrate gestures. These scenarios make non-verbal cues more effective or necessary.

254. (A): Small group communication is different from large group communication in that the small group offers more opportunities to influence the participants. It allows for more interaction and personal engagement among members.

255. (B): The discussion method can be very effective in class if the topic of discussion is announced well before the discussion. This allows students time to prepare and think about the topic, leading to a more informed and engaging discussion.

256. **(C):** Children are compared with plants because just as plants maintain their growth if they are cut and cleaned, similarly, students are also checked by the process of evaluation to keep them moving on the path of progress. Both require nurturing, care, and regular attention for healthy development.

257. **(D):** Intelligence testing is necessary both to categorize students into different groups according to their intellectual abilities (for tailored teaching) and to identify talented students for providing them special teaching according to their potentials.

258. **(C):** For lesson planning, the first requirement is the determination of objectives. Establishing clear objectives is essential to guide the direction and focus of the lesson.

259. **(A):** The advantage of studying reference books and other study materials is that they develop comprehensiveness in knowledge. They provide a broader and deeper understanding of subjects beyond the standard textbooks.

260. **(D):** To maintain the educational standard in private educational institutions, all of these are necessary: a transparent examination system, ensuring good salaries to teachers, and extra-evaluation of the students from time to time. These measures collectively help in upholding quality education standards.

261. **(C):** To save students from disturbance in their studies, the teacher should use suitable teaching strategies and techniques to make the subject interesting. Engaging teaching methods can help maintain students' attention and interest.

262. **(B):** By keeping an eye on the body language of pupils, one can understand which student is not attentive to the teaching-learning process. Body language can reveal a lot about a student's engagement, focus, and emotional state.

263. **(D):** While preparing the lesson plan for the class, the teacher should keep all of these as major decisive factors: the benefit of the average student, achievement of teaching objectives, and the fulfillment of the aims of the curriculum.

264. **(C):** Upon receiving information about cheating during tests, the appropriate response would be to address the issue with those three students discreetly. It's important to investigate the matter and take appropriate action to maintain academic integrity.

265. **(D):** The method of silent reading offers several benefits: it increases comprehension skills, helps in better retention, and does not waste time as students can read at their own pace.

266. **(D):** If students do not show positive reactions during classroom teaching, the reason could be found in any of these: the subject being taught, the specific topic or issue, or the teaching style. It's important to identify and address the underlying cause.

267. **(D):** If a class monitor beats up a student in your absence, the appropriate action would be to tell the monitor in privacy that he has no right to physically discipline any of the students. Physical punishment is not acceptable and should be addressed.

268. **(D):** Adult education is necessary because educated adults would also make all possible efforts to educate their children. Adult education has a ripple effect, improving the educational prospects for future generations.

269. **(C):** For students with very high levels of intelligence who do not find the standard study material challenging, allocating them special tasks that are more difficult than those given to students of normal intelligence is a good approach. This can help keep them engaged and challenged.

270. **(A):** Working with consensus in a school means making decisions and addressing issues through general agreement and shared understanding among the members of the school community, including teachers, staff, and administrators. This collaborative approach fosters a sense of unity, teamwork, and mutual respect among the school's stakeholders.

271. **(B):** The actual benefit of giving homework accrues only when the teacher regularly evaluates the homework of students and keeps on telling them about their mistakes. This feedback is crucial for students to understand their errors and learn from them.

272. **(C):** An expert educationist comparing the school with a garden implies that students should be looked after just like delicate plants. This metaphor suggests that children, like plants, need careful nurturing and a supportive environment to grow and develop.

273. **(D):** The development of feelings of disgust, disappointment, and lack of interest among students can possibly lead to all of these problems: discipline issues, frequent absences, and the adoption of corrupt means during examinations.

274. **(B):** While it is true that young children are still developing their cognitive abilities and are more vulnerable to harm than adults, this does not mean that they should be completely deprived of freedom. Giving children some freedom to explore, experiment, and make their own decisions is essential for their development. This helps them to learn about the world, develop their independence, and build self-confidence.

275. **(D):** The technique of moving from a general concept (a cow) to more specific details (the use of the cow's tail or its habit of rumination) is denoted as moving from general to particular. This teaching method starts with familiar, broader concepts and gradually introduces more detailed and specific information.

276. **(A):** Complete freedom should be given to students to ask questions in the class. Encouraging questions fosters a more interactive and engaging learning environment and helps clarify students' understanding.

277. **(B):** If a student is using unfair means in the examination with the support of political leaders or others, the appropriate action is to act according to the rule. Maintaining the integrity of the examination process is crucial, and rules should be enforced irrespective of outside influences.

278. **(C):** The adolescence period is called the most difficult period of social adjustment. Adolescence is marked by significant physical, emotional, and social changes, making it a challenging time for adjustment.

279. **(C):** Sex education is a crucial aspect of comprehensive education, particularly for high school students who are undergoing significant physical, emotional, and social changes. Integrating sex education into the school curriculum through a separate subject allows for a dedicated space to address various topics related to sexuality, healthy relationships, and sexual health, ensuring that students receive comprehensive and accurate information.

280. **(B):** The exhibition of sex-related activities in boys and girls of pre-primary classes is typically a normal behaviour full of curiosity, which will likely be rectified automatically as they develop their sense of understanding. Such behaviours are part of natural developmental curiosity at that age.

281. **(D):** To integrate a child of a lonely loving nature into a group, the teacher should employ a combination of strategies: nominating them as a member of a good group, using project methods to foster group work skills, and developing social qualities in the child to facilitate group acceptance and interaction.

282. (D): The parameter of good school discipline includes all of the above: absence of mismanagement and noise, obedience of rules and regulations by students and teachers with pleasure, and good responsible behaviour.

283. (C): The proverb "Give respect and get respect" is applicable in all places, including schools equally. Respect is a universal value that enhances relationships and interactions in any setting.

284. (D): The majority of students in rural areas do not take admission after high school for both reasons: intermediate colleges are generally not available nearby, and education does not guarantee employment regardless of its standard.

285. (D): Students may consider transferring to another school if they face any of these issues: strict and hard treatment by teachers, teachers insulting and condemning students, or lack of coordination between teachers and students.

286. (B): Employment-oriented professional education is beneficial for both students and society at present. Such education equips students with skills directly applicable to the workforce, addressing both individual career needs and societal employment demands.

287. (B): The rate of development of games' interest in students can be increased if they are given ample opportunities to take part in play activities in schools and these activities are linked with the rules of motivation. Encouraging participation and linking activities to motivational factors can enhance engagement in games.

288. (D): The opinion on tuition or any other type of coaching classes includes both: it reduces the dignity of a teacher to a great extent, and students may not get time for self-study, failing to complete their homework.

289. (D): Physical health is necessary for a teacher along with mental health because the teacher has to be very active in class while teaching, and both physical and mental activities are required in teaching.

290. (A): The study of newspapers and magazines helps us to know current affairs and day-to-day events. It's an important source for staying informed about the world and can also enhance general knowledge and literacy.

291. (D): Making women's education approachable at all levels can lead to women coming to the level of men over time, and due to this encouragement, people may stop the practice of female foeticide, leading to an improvement in the sex ratio.

292. (B): Education up to the middle level should ideally be controlled by the community through elected representatives. This approach allows for more localized and relevant educational decisions that reflect the needs and values of the community.

293. (D): To improve the entire education system, a change in the thinking of the government is needed. Government policies and priorities have a significant impact on the structure, resources, and overall quality of the education system.

294. (D): The teaching profession is more suitable for women than other professions because it offers respect to women and has a lower chance of misbehaviour towards them. Teaching also aligns well with nurturing skills often associated with women.

295. (C): A powerful medium for providing sex education is the guidance given by the teacher. Educators can offer structured, informed, and sensitive teaching about sexual health and relationships, which is crucial for young people.

296. (A): If parents do not agree with the viewpoint of a teacher during a parents' meeting, the teacher should try to remove the doubts of parents to the maximum level possible. Open communication and addressing concerns are important for building trust and understanding.

297. (B): If included in a jury of a debate competition, the appropriate approach is to give a decision according to the performance of the participants. Decisions should be based on objective criteria related to the debate.

298. (D): The open schooling system is a good source of education extension and provides an opportunity for education to those students who had to leave schooling in the middle due to various reasons. It offers a flexible learning path for diverse needs.

299. (B): The similarity between a teacher and a doctor is that both take remedial measures after proper diagnosis. In their respective fields, they assess the situation or problem and then apply their knowledge and skills to provide solutions.

300. (B): As a teacher, the most likable type of student would be one who is active and hardworking. Such students show a strong commitment to learning and are often more engaged and participatory in the educational process.

301. (C): The best example of an anecdotal report is "On **12/1**, **12/2**, **12/4**, during the reading group time, Tom fidgeted in his seat." This statement provides specific observations on particular dates, which is characteristic of anecdotal records.

302. (D): The informal textbook test is a procedure for determining the reading level of a child. It is typically used to assess a student's reading ability and to match them with appropriate reading materials.

303. (A): The limitation of the inductive method of teaching is that it wastes time and is slow. This method involves moving from specific instances to broader generalizations, which can be a time-consuming process.

304. (A): The deductive method of teaching imparts knowledge at a fast pace. It begins with a general principle and moves towards specific examples, allowing for quicker coverage of material.

305. (C): The statement that is not correct is that both the inductive and deductive methods are opponents of each other. In reality, these methods are complementary, often used together in teaching to enhance understanding.

306. (D): The statement that is not true about class teaching or group teaching is that it is not useful for mentally retarded students. Group teaching can be beneficial for all students, including those with special needs, provided that appropriate accommodations and support are in place.

307. (C): Under the personalized teaching system, the teacher is not the center of education. Rather, the student is at the center, with teaching tailored to their individual needs, interests, and pace of learning.

308. (A): In the project education technique, the workload on the teacher is very high. Teachers need to plan, organize, supervise, and assess complex projects, which requires significant effort and involvement.

309. (D): Basic education aims to provide students with a foundation of knowledge and skills, make them self-dependent, and equip them with a fundamental understanding of key elements of education. It encompasses not only the transmission of essential knowledge but also the development of critical thinking, problem-solving abilities, and life skills that contribute to a student's overall development. Therefore, all the options-making the student self-dependent, giving knowledge of basic elements of education, and fostering a broader understanding-are integral aspects of the objectives of basic education.

310. (D): Basic education is all of these: activity-based, student-based, and handicraft-based.

It combines hands-on learning activities, focuses on the student's interests and abilities, and often includes elements of handicraft or practical skills.

311. **(A):** Under the Winnetka Plan, personalized education has a position of major importance. This educational approach emphasizes individualized learning, allowing students to progress at their own pace and according to their abilities.

312. **(C):** Herbart is known as the father of educational psychology. Johann Friedrich Herbart made significant contributions to educational theory, including the development of pedagogical methods based on psychological principles.

313. **(A):** McKennan was an educationalist who emphasized the importance of teachers being role models for their students. He believed that teachers should live by the same principles that they teach, and that they should be consistent in their words and actions. This quote reflects his belief that teachers have a responsibility to uphold high standards of behaviour and to set a good example for their students.

314. **(C):** In the opinion of many, a successful teacher is one who takes a keen interest in the progress of students. This involves being dedicated to students' learning, understanding their needs, and actively supporting their academic and personal development.

315. **(D):** A teacher should be proud of a student who is building the future of students with dedication by becoming a teacher. This reflects the student's commitment to education and the continuation of positive educational values.

316. **(*):** *These are personal opinion questions. Option choice may vary. Mark according to your preference.*

317. **(B):** If a student is not able to answer a question due to fear even if he knows it, the teacher should try to find the basic reasons for his fear. Understanding and addressing the underlying causes of the student's anxiety can help him become more confident and participative.

318. **(C):** For a good teacher, the item of contentment is respect and prestige. Recognition of their work and the positive impact they have on students' lives often brings greater satisfaction than monetary rewards or status.

319. **(A):** For students of middle classes, the system of "examination center in the school itself" is justified because it ensures that students do not have to go far away from their school. This can reduce stress and logistical issues associated with exams.

320. **(D):** The ideal student would possess all the qualities stated in steps A, B, and C: being soft-spoken, respecting elders, and being hardworking in academics. These qualities together represent a well-rounded and admirable student.

321. **(A):** An empathetic attitude towards students who are weak in studies is appropriate. This approach helps create a supportive environment where students feel encouraged to study with more concentration and hard work.

322. **(C):** If allocated to teach the weakest section (section D) in class **5**, a positive and proactive attitude is ideal. Being pleased and using all your abilities for the development of students in this class reflects a commitment to improving their academic performance.

323. **(C):** If you find a student to be intelligent, the best approach is to motivate him so that he can make more progress. Encouraging and challenging intelligent students helps them to reach their full potential.

324. **(D):** If some students are not in the mood to study in the class, telling them some interesting things related to their interests or your subject can be an effective way to re-engage them. This approach can reignite their interest and focus on the class.

325. (D): The problem of maintaining discipline in the class is related to all of these factors: the subject being taught, how interesting the subject is, and how students are seated in the class. Each aspect can influence the overall discipline and engagement in the classroom.

326. (B): For a student who is too shy to participate in the class, a good approach is to ask only those questions whose answers can be given by him. This can help build the student's confidence and encourage more participation.

327. (D): All of the options provided relate to the role of education in social change: Education should check undesirable social change, accelerate the process of social change, and also change with social change.

328. (C): If some students speak ill of their teachers in their absence, the best approach is to talk to those students with an open heart and advise them to discuss the issue directly with the teachers about whom they have grievances. This encourages open communication and resolution of issues.

329. (A): The situation that will cause the greatest difficulty for a child in the initial stages of reading instruction is confusion of left and right directionality. This difficulty can impact the child's ability to understand and follow the flow of written text.

330. (B): The statement about phobias that is not true is that acrophobia is a fear of open places; agoraphobia is a fear of high places. In reality, acrophobia is the fear of heights, and agoraphobia is the fear of open or crowded spaces.

331. (B): Special Education is related to educational programmes for the disabled. It focuses on meeting the educational needs of children with disabilities, ensuring they receive appropriate instruction tailored to their individual requirements.

332. (B): Oral reading in schools today is appropriate when it is useful. It can be a valuable tool for developing reading fluency, comprehension, and expression, especially in younger grades.

333. (C): The problem of unemployment can be solved by starting courses of professional education in schools. These courses provide practical skills and vocational training, which can help students become job-ready and reduce unemployment.

334. (A): The teacher has to learn about problems prevalent in the field of education because only a teacher can find the remedies for such problems. Teachers, being directly involved in the educational process, are well-placed to identify and address these issues.

335. (D): All of the options listed are important technological factors of social change: Improvement in communication and transport, mechanization of daily life, and opening domestic markets to international trade.

336. (B): Partially agreeing with the statement that the degradation of education is due to its conversion into a profession acknowledges that while professionalization has certain drawbacks, it is not the sole reason for educational challenges.

337. (C): For children who are weak in studies, the suggestion would be that they should improve their studies in remedial classes held after school hours. Remedial classes provide additional support and focused teaching to help students catch up.

338. (C): If asked to accommodate two mentally retarded children in your class, the appropriate response would be to learn techniques to teach such students and accept them as a part of your class. This inclusive approach ensures all students receive the education they deserve.

339. (D): The major reason for growing indiscipline in schools is often the lack of proper guidance. When students are not adequately guided or supervised, it can lead to disciplinary issues.

340. **(D):** To develop the virtue of compassion in students, arranging academic activities related to compassion in the school would be most effective. This experiential approach allows students to engage with the concept of compassion actively and meaningfully.

341. **(C):** To develop the spirit of labor in students, they should be given opportunities to do labor from time to time. This hands-on approach allows students to experience the value and dignity of labor directly.

342. **(C):** The Parents Teachers Association (PTA) is important because it enables teachers and parents/guardians to sit together and discuss ways and means to solve the problems of students. This collaboration fosters a better understanding and more effective solutions.

343. **(C):** For a child from a culturally backward family/background, the best approach is to keep him in a normal class but make special arrangements for teaching him, keeping his special needs in view. This ensures the child receives the necessary support while being integrated with other students.

344. **(D):** Education can promote social mobility in all the listed ways: by making a person liberal in attitude and thinking, enabling administrative power acquisition, and helping to change occupation. Education opens up opportunities and can be a catalyst for social and economic advancement.

345. **(C):** If a student is unable to answer a question during a lecture, the appropriate action is to try to understand why the student was not able to give the correct answer. This approach is more constructive and can help in addressing the student's learning needs.

346. **(D):** Taking surprise tests is justified because they can truly judge the abilities and knowledge levels of students. Surprise tests evaluate students' understanding and retention without prior preparation, providing a more accurate assessment of their learning.

347. **(C):** The appropriate age for sending little children to school is generally when the child attains the age of plus five years. This age is typically considered suitable for starting formal education.

348. **(A):** To address the issue of students quietly running away from school, it's important to try to understand why they run away. Identifying the underlying reasons can help in taking appropriate measures to address their concerns or problems.

349. **(D):** If a student you tutor fails in the annual examination, the appropriate response is to teach that student with renewed vigor and effort in the future. This approach focuses on improvement and learning from past shortcomings.

350. **(C):** If a student misbehaves with you, as a teacher, a suitable reaction would be to pardon the student and forget the incident, especially if it's a one-time occurrence or minor issue. Understanding and forgiveness can be effective in teaching students about consequences and responsibility.

351. **(C):** To help a student who is weak in mathematics, the best approach would be to talk to the student and find out what his problems are in mathematics; later, you would work to remove those problems. Understanding the specific difficulties the student faces allows for targeted and effective support.

352. **(D):** For students with weak eyesight who are unable to see the blackboard clearly, all these measures are appropriate: letting them sit in the front seats, advising their parents to arrange for spectacles, and encouraging the students to get their eyesight corrected.

353. **(C):** For students who interrupt the teaching process in the class, ignoring them can sometimes be an effective method, especially if the interruptions are minor or seeking attention. It's important to understand the reason for the interruptions to decide the best approach.

354. **(D):** More indiscipline usually prevails in the class if the teacher is not able to make classroom teaching interesting enough. Engaging and dynamic teaching methods can significantly improve classroom discipline by capturing students' attention.

355. **(B):** When using visual aids during class teaching, the most important aspect to emphasize is that they should be in accordance with the subject being taught. Relevance to the topic ensures that the aids enhance understanding and learning.

356. **(C):** The use of audio-visual materials/aids in the class enhances the curiosity of children. These tools can make learning more interactive and engaging for students of all learning styles.

357. **(B):** Mal-adjustment and frustration are developed in children when their needs are ignored. Children need to feel understood, cared for, and supported; ignoring their needs can lead to emotional and behavioral issues.

358. **(C):** In understanding and effectively treating the mal-adjustment and frustration of children, the study of child psychology provides good support to the teacher. Knowledge of child psychology helps teachers understand the underlying issues and appropriate strategies for intervention.

359. **(B):** Having only one teacher for little children in school can be beneficial, as it provides consistency and stability in the learning environment. Young children often benefit from a single primary caregiver or teacher who understands their needs and development.

360. **(D):** Calling a student to the blackboard to solve a question/problem is beneficial because it builds confidence in the student and allows the teacher to assess whether the student knows how to solve the question. This method actively involves the student in the learning process and provides immediate feedback.

361. **(A):** The inductive method of teaching has the shortcoming that it can be time-consuming and slow. This method involves moving from specific instances to broader generalizations, which requires time to gather and analyze examples.

362. **(A):** The deductive method provides knowledge at a high speed. It starts with a general principle or rule and then applies it to specific cases, allowing for quicker knowledge transfer compared to the inductive method.

363. **(A):** The limitation of the deductive method of teaching is that it can develop a habit of cramming (mugging up) the text. Because this method often involves starting with general rules or principles, students might focus on memorizing these rather than understanding underlying concepts.

364. **(A):** The statement that the deductive method is not psychological is incorrect. The deductive method can be aligned with psychological principles, especially when it is used to apply general rules to specific instances in a way that engages critical thinking.

365. **(C):** The statement that inductive and deductive methods are opponents of each other is not correct. In fact, these methods are complementary and often used together in teaching to enhance the overall learning experience.

366. **(A):** Drill lessons refer to the revision of learned facts in the same format. These are repetitive exercises aimed at reinforcing knowledge and skills through practice.

367. **(C):** For a new student from a culturally backward background, the most appropriate action would be to keep him in a normal class but make special teaching arrangements for his special academic needs. This approach ensures the student receives the necessary support while integrating with the rest of the class.

368. (C): If there are both poor and talented students in sizable numbers in a class, the teacher should keep the teaching at an average level and provide additional remedial measures for weak students. This approach helps cater to the needs of all students, ensuring no one is left behind.

369. (B): To popularize adult education, the most important suggestion is to link education with their vocations. This practical approach makes learning relevant and valuable to their lives and work.

370. (C): If a request for fee concession for a poor student is not responded to by the Principal, a suitable reaction would be to encourage the student to understand the situation and try to help him avail other facilities or support systems. This proactive approach focuses on finding alternative solutions.

371. (A): For very weak students of the class, a teacher should help and coach them in his spare time. This extra support can assist these students in understanding the material better and improving their academic performance.

372. (D): As a teacher, the feeling towards discrimination based on caste, creed, or ethnicity should be that it is an unscientific attitude which cannot be given any weightage in the present-day social system and that this feeling should be eradicated from society without delay.

373. (C): Among the given options, more sympathy should be shown by the teacher to the pupil whose loss is directly the result of the teacher's fault. It is important for teachers to acknowledge their own mistakes and provide additional support to students who may have been adversely affected by these errors.

374. (B): If a teacher comes to know that some students of the school tease a child on his way home, he should ensure the safe and painless return of the child to his home. Additionally, the teacher should address the behaviour of the teasing students appropriately.

375. (D): To de-addict students from bad habits, a combination of approaches is effective: telling them motivating stories to clarify the consequences of bad habits, seeking cooperation from their parents, and having strict vigilance over them.

376. (B): Knowing the religion and caste of a child in the class is not necessary at all. Education should be imparted impartially and without discrimination based on these factors.

377. (D): The advantage of including population education in the school curriculum is that students can be informed about the problems arisen out of the population explosion, they will be able to make their families happy due to this education, and they will know the methods of birth control to limit their families in the future.

378. (D): Students should be given freedom to ask questions in the class at all the given times: at the end of the lesson, whenever they feel any difficulty in the lesson, and when they are asked by the teacher to do so.

379. (D): If teaching in a co-educational school, equal attention should be given to all students irrespective of their gender differences. This approach ensures fair and inclusive education for both boys and girls.

380. (C): For children who are weak in studies, the suggestion would be that they should improve upon their studies in remedial classes that are held after school hours. Remedial classes provide focused support and additional learning opportunities.

381. (C): If instructed to accommodate two mentally retarded children in your class, the most appropriate action would be to learn techniques to teach such students and accept them as a part of your class. This inclusive approach ensures all students receive appropriate education and support.

382. **(C):** In the context of limited resources and a rising population, giving more emphasis to adult education programs is a courageous and laudable action/behaviour. Adult education plays a crucial role in improving literacy and providing skills for better employment and quality of life.

383. **(D):** Adult education should be under the authority of all of these entities: the government, non-government organizations, and educated persons. A collaborative approach involving multiple stakeholders can enhance the effectiveness and reach of adult education programs.

384. **(D):** The best teacher in a village school is one who carries community experiences to the classroom, prepares instructional programs in the interest of the community, and carries classroom experiences to the community. This approach helps in making education relevant and beneficial for both students and the community.

385. **(C):** For a child from a culturally backward background, the most suitable approach is to keep him in a normal class but make special arrangements for teaching him, keeping his special needs in view. This ensures the child is included in the regular classroom while receiving the necessary support.

386. **(B & D):**

(B): If you are away from home and your father is unable to send you money on time, the most understanding response would be to try to understand his handicaps. This shows empathy and maturity in handling the situation.

(D): In a situation where your father is unable to send you money due to an urgent piece of work, the most appropriate response can be arranging money from another source and carry on your work. This option demonstrates understanding, responsibility, and resourcefulness in addressing the situation.

387. **(A):** To bring students of backward classes at par with other students, reform in the educational system is essential. Such reforms could include enhanced support, better access to resources, and inclusive teaching practices.

388. **(A):** The belief that talented students do not like the teaching profession due to little financial rewards is a common perspective. The perception of limited financial incentives in teaching compared to other professions can deter talented students from pursuing a career in education.

389. **(D):** For students who are unable to buy textbooks due to poverty, all of these actions would be helpful: collecting money from colleagues, helping them get books from a book bank, and arranging books by spending money from your pocket.

390. **(C):** If you identify a student as talented after several tests, the most constructive action is to motivate him more for further progress. Encouraging and nurturing talent is crucial in helping talented students reach their full potential.

391. **(D):** To de-addict the habit of lying in children, all of the above methods can be effective: rewarding those who speak the truth, telling them stories where the bad consequences of lying are shown, and motivating them to speak the truth. Each of these approaches addresses the issue from different angles, providing a comprehensive strategy.

392. **(D):** Creative writing should be an activity planned for all children of the class. Creative expression is important for every child, regardless of their reading level or writing skills, as it fosters imagination, creativity, and personal expression.

393. (B): Special Education is related to educational programs for the disabled and gifted students. These programs are designed to cater to the unique learning needs of these children, providing them with the appropriate resources and teaching methods.

394. (A): Fostering creativity among learners can be achieved by providing opportunities to question and nurturing the innate talents of every learner. Encouraging inquiry and creativity helps in the development of innovative and critical thinking skills.

395. (B): A student of V-grade with 'visual deficiency' should be treated normally in the classroom and provided support through Audio CDs. This approach helps in including the student in regular educational activities while providing the necessary resources to cater to their visual impairment.

396. (A): Fighting with others is not considered a sign of 'being gifted'. Giftedness typically involves positive traits like novelty in expression, curiosity, and creative ideas, rather than aggressive or disruptive behaviours.

397. (D): Education of children with special needs should be provided along with other normal children. This inclusive education approach ensures that children with special needs can learn in a mainstream environment, which is beneficial for their social and academic development.

398. (A): To help gifted children achieve their potential, a teacher should not segregate them from their peers for special attention. Instead, providing challenging material, teaching them to enjoy non-academic activities, and helping them manage stress are more beneficial strategies.

399. (B): A creative learner refers to one who is good at lateral thinking and problem-solving. Creativity in learning often involves the ability to think outside the box and come up with innovative solutions to problems.

400. (C): "Every learner is unique" means that no two learners are alike in their abilities, interests, and talents. While learners may share some common qualities and goals, each individual has their own unique learning style and pace.

401. (C): The Centrally sponsored scheme of Integrated Education for Disabled Children focuses on providing educational opportunities for children with disabilities in regular schools. This approach is part of the inclusive education philosophy, aiming to integrate students with disabilities into the general education classrooms, allowing them to study alongside their peers without disabilities.

402. (D): Autism is not a manifestation of emotional disturbance, but rather a developmental disorder that affects communication and behaviour. Emotional disturbances are typically characterized by issues such as delinquency, bullying, and truancy, which involve difficulties in emotional regulation and social behaviour.

403. (A): A provision for education for children with disabilities can be most effectively done through inclusive education. This approach involves educating children with disabilities in regular classrooms alongside their non-disabled peers, promoting diversity, and providing equal opportunities for all students to learn and participate in school life.

404. (D): 'Child belonging to a weaker section' refers to a child whose parents' annual income is lower than the minimum limit specified by the appropriate government. This definition focuses on economic criteria to determine eligibility for certain educational benefits or programs.

405. (D): The National Curriculum Framework, 2005, under the heading 'quality dimension', gives more importance to experiences designed for the child and curriculum reform.

This approach emphasizes a child-centric and holistic view of education, focusing on the quality of learning experiences and the overall design of the curriculum to meet the diverse needs of students.

406. **(A):** The National Curriculum Framework, 2005, suggests making the Class X examination optional as part of the examination reforms. This recommendation is aimed at reducing the stress and pressure associated with board examinations and encouraging a more comprehensive and holistic approach to education.

407. **(C):** For teaching children with special needs, a better strategy is cooperative learning and peer tutoring. This approach involves students working in groups to help each other learn, which can be especially beneficial for children with special needs, providing them with support and opportunities to interact with peers.

408. **(C):** The ability to understand the meaning of a problem, and to identify weaknesses and gaps related to the environment, is a characteristic of creative children. Creative individuals are often adept at thinking outside the box, identifying novel solutions, and seeing connections that others might miss.

409. **(C):** When a cricket player develops the skill of bowling, but it does not affect his skill of batting, it is known as zero transfer of training. This means that learning or improvement in one area (bowling) does not have a positive or negative effect on a related but distinct area (batting).

410. **(C):** The most satisfying defense mechanism for a physically handicapped individual depends on the individual's specific personality and coping style. However, in general, Fantasy can be a particularly satisfying defense mechanism for these individuals. Fantasy can provide a temporary escape from the harsh realities of physical limitations and allow individuals to imagine themselves overcoming their challenges and achieving their goals. It can also offer a sense of hope and inspiration, which can be especially valuable for those who are struggling with their disability.

411. **(A):** To nurture creativity in students, a teacher should make use of brainstorming methods. Brainstorming encourages creative thinking and idea generation, allowing students to explore multiple solutions and perspectives without immediate judgement or criticism.

412. **(D):** The National Curriculum Framework, **2005** suggests integrating peace education in the curriculum to promote peace education. This approach involves incorporating peace-related themes and values into various subjects and classroom activities, rather than teaching it as a separate subject.

413. **(A):** The National Curriculum Framework, **2005** talks of major shifts from viewing knowledge as given and fixed to seeing it as something that evolves and is created. This perspective encourages a more dynamic and constructive approach to learning, where students are seen as active participants in the creation and understanding of knowledge.

414. **(D):** In the National Curriculum Framework, 2005, under the heading 'Examination Reforms', the suggested reforms include open book exams, continuous comprehensive evaluation (CCE), and group work evaluation. These reforms aim to move away from traditional examination methods, promoting more holistic and varied assessment approaches that better reflect the students' understanding and skills.

415. **(B):** Emotional Intelligence is not one of the seven intelligences formulated by Howard Gardner. Gardner's theory of multiple intelligences includes Spatial, Interpersonal, and Linguistic Intelligence, among others, but does not include Emotional Intelligence as a distinct category.

416. (D): The true statement in reference to intelligence is that it encompasses the ability to adjust, the ability to learn, and the ability of abstract reasoning. Intelligence is a complex and multi-dimensional concept that includes various cognitive abilities and processes.

417. (C): In meeting the individual differences of students, the role of the teacher should include both trying to know the abilities, interest, and aptitude of individuals and adjusting the curriculum as per the needs of individuals. Personalized attention and adaptation of teaching methods are key to addressing diverse learning needs.

418. (C): For exceptionally bright students in a class, the teacher should teach them by using enriched programmes. These programmes provide additional challenges and opportunities for deeper exploration of subjects, catering to the advanced learning needs of these students.

419. (D): The major purpose of diagnostic tests is to identify the specific nature of pupil difficulties. Diagnostic tests help in understanding the particular areas where a student may be struggling, enabling targeted intervention and support.

420. (B): Special education is related to educational programmes for disabled students. It involves tailoring teaching methods, resources, and learning environments to meet the unique needs of students with disabilities, ensuring they receive a quality education.

421. (D): The educator who promoted the idea of five formal steps in learning was Johann Friedrich Herbart. These steps are known as Herbartian steps and include preparation, presentation, association, generalization, and application. This model focuses on systematic instruction and the interrelation of subjects.

422. (A): In a deductive lesson, a general rule is explained first, and then knowledge is accumulated based on that rule. This approach involves starting with a broad concept or principle and then applying it to specific examples or situations.

423. (D): The principles of the activity method accept the viewpoint that the student gets knowledge by getting motivation from natural tendencies, should be given freedom to gain knowledge, and the best development of the student is effected by his own actions/activities. It is a holistic approach that emphasizes learning through doing.

424. (D): The basis of the activity method is the right type of guidance to the creative power of students. This method focuses on facilitating learning by engaging students in meaningful activities and guiding them to explore, inquire, and construct knowledge.

425. (D): The activity technique is student-centred. It emphasizes the active participation of students in their learning process, encouraging them to engage in activities that promote critical thinking, creativity, and practical application of knowledge.

426. (B): In classroom teaching (group teaching) method, students get many opportunities to take part in class work. This approach promotes interaction, collaboration, and active participation among students.

427. (B): If appointed as a judge in a declamation contest, it's important to give importance to an effective speaker, basing the decision on the quality of speech and delivery, rather than external factors like affiliation with a particular school or student leadership.

428. (A): If appointed in a place where the local language is not understood, the best approach would be to try to learn that local language. This effort shows respect for the local culture and facilitates better communication and integration.

429. (D): If a student comes late to school on a daily basis, it would be appropriate to find out the reasons for his behaviour.

Understanding the underlying issues can lead to more effective and empathetic solutions than punitive measures.

430. **(D):** To check the ongoing decay in the field of education, it is important for teachers to teach in their classes regularly and with dedication. Committed and consistent teaching is crucial for maintaining educational standards and fostering a positive learning environment.

431. **(C):** An effective and successful female teacher is one who is good in terms of knowledge of her subject and its presentation/communication. The effectiveness of a teacher is determined by her ability to convey knowledge and engage students, regardless of her physical appearance or favor with the administration.

432. **(C):** Preferring books that enhance knowledge and are entertaining too indicates a balanced approach to reading. Such books not only provide valuable information but also keep the reader engaged and interested.

433. **(C):** If the headmistress calls while teaching, the appropriate action would be to send a note explaining the situation. This respects the importance of both the ongoing class and the headmistress's request, showing professionalism and responsibility.

434. **(C):** Choosing to spend spare time involving oneself in self-study reflects a commitment to personal growth and education. This choice indicates a desire to continuously learn and improve one's knowledge and skills.

435. **(*):** *These are personal opinion questions. Option choice may vary. Mark according to your preference.*

436. **(B):** When using the "Comparison Technique" in teaching, it is important that students must be fully aware of those two things/objects/clauses that need to be compared. This awareness ensures that the comparison is meaningful and understandable to the students.

437. **(A):** The experimental technique of education can be used to teach a wide variety of subjects, from science and mathematics to language arts and social studies. This technique is particularly effective for teaching subjects that involve hands-on activities and experimentation.

438. **(C):** "Operation Blackboard" was commenced in India in **1986**. This program aimed at improving the basic educational infrastructure and resources in the country's primary schools.

439. **(A):** The poorest recommendation for a mother looking to improve her child's reading ability is to severely limit the child's watching of television. While moderation in watching TV is advisable, it's more effective to actively engage the child in reading activities and to foster a love for reading through interactive and enjoyable methods.

440. **(C):** If a student does not understand a point/concept in the class, the best approach is to ensure that the student has fully understood it before moving ahead, trying to clear the point/concept in question. This approach shows commitment to each student's learning and understanding.

441. **(A):** To teach the basic principles of science, the inductive method is often the most effective. This approach involves observing specific instances or experiments and then deriving general principles from these observations, which is a foundational approach in scientific learning.

442. **(B):** If most students have failed to get pass marks in a class test, the appropriate action would be to re-teach the topic thoroughly and then conduct another test. This approach ensures that students have another opportunity to learn and understand the material better.

443. **(B):** If children are not in a mood to study on a certain day, they should be engaged in an interesting activity related to the subject.

This can make learning more enjoyable and effective, even when students are not in a conventional learning mood.

444. (C): If only half of the syllabus has been covered due to holidays and strikes, the best course of action would be to take extra classes and complete the syllabus carefully, keeping in mind the pace of understanding of the students. This shows commitment to their education and ensures that they are well-prepared.

445. (A): In response to the upgrading of education standards and increased difficulty in subjects, a teacher should study extra hours at home and prepare the subject thoroughly. This dedication will enable the teacher to effectively teach the new and more challenging material.

446. (A): The objective of the Principle of Revision is repeating the gained sets of knowledge to make them permanent in the minds of students. Regular revision helps in reinforcing learning and ensuring long-term retention of information.

447. (B): To develop good tastes among students in the class, a teacher can give them examples of people or celebrities who have good tastes/ values. Modeling and discussing admirable qualities and tastes can inspire students to adopt similar values.

448. (B): To know more about the abilities, intelligence, and behaviour of a new student in the class, the teacher should introduce himself to the student and interact with him inside and outside the class. This approach helps in building a rapport and understanding the student better.

449. (B): The Growth Phase is typically the phase of a lesson where new concepts, ideas, or skills are introduced and developed. During this phase, the teacher may ask questions to assess understanding, stimulate critical thinking, and encourage active participation in the learning process. Asking questions in the Growth Phase helps students engage with the material and deepen their understanding as they explore new concepts.

450. (C): If required to take the class of another teacher who is absent, the best approach is to start from the point where their teacher had finished during the last lecture. This ensures continuity in learning and respects the curriculum plan of the absent teacher.

451. (C): If unprepared to teach due to a personal commitment the previous night, a respectful approach would be to apologize to students and encourage them to ask questions from previous lectures. This maintains a learning environment and encourages student engagement.

452. (A): To make students more studious, it is crucial to develop interest in them. When students are interested in the subject matter, they are more likely to engage deeply with the material and study effectively.

453. (B): A little child primarily adopts habits from his family members. The family environment plays a crucial role in the early developmental stages of a child, influencing their behaviours, attitudes, and habits.

454. (C): To calm down noisy first standard students, telling them a story can be an effective approach. Stories can capture their attention and interest, bringing calm and focus to the classroom.

455. (A): Differential treatment meted out to students of a class is not a characteristic feature of an effective teacher. Effective teaching involves treating all students fairly and equitably, providing equal opportunities for learning and participation.

456. (C): The correct statement about slow learners and bright children is that both groups strive for success in school. Despite their differing learning paces and abilities, both groups generally share a common goal of achieving success in their educational pursuits.

457. **(A):** The trial-and-error method of instruction is best enhanced by role playing. Role playing allows students to experiment with different scenarios and learn from the outcomes, which aligns well with the trial-and-error learning process.

458. **(A):** Improvement in comprehension skills is most likely to result from guided silent reading. This method allows students to process and understand the material at their own pace, with guidance from the teacher to develop comprehension skills.

459. **(C):** A group of students that is dedicated, studious, respecting, and treating with warmth would be most appreciated. These qualities reflect a positive learning attitude, respect for others, and a dedication to academic and personal growth.

460. **(D):** A teacher can develop honesty and other good virtues in students most effectively by giving his/her own example. Modeling positive behavior and virtues is a powerful way to influence students and promote the development of good character.

461. **(A & D):**

(A): To ensure regular attendance of students in school, it should be made a place of pleasure. This involves creating an engaging, supportive, and enjoyable learning environment where students feel motivated and happy to attend.

(D): The effective approach to ensure regular attendance of students in school is regular meetings of parents/guardians should be arranged. This is because parental involvement plays a crucial role in shaping a child's attitude towards education and their commitment to attending school regularly.

462. **(A):** One reason why students may run from school is the lack of interesting class teaching work. If the classroom activities are engaging, relevant, and interactive, students are more likely to be interested in attending school and participating in the learning process.

463. **(C):** When a teacher asks questions during classroom sessions, providing a little indirect help or guidance to students can be beneficial. This approach encourages students to think critically and arrive at the correct answer, while still offering some support.

464. **(B):** Upon receiving information that three students are copying during tests, it would be appropriate to talk to the students named. This allows for a direct and discreet approach to address the issue and understand the situation better.

465. **(C):** If a teacher is exploiting his students, a suitable course of action would be to advise him not to exploit his students. It's important to address the issue directly with the teacher, encouraging them to change their behaviour.

466. **(A):** A teacher should present his lesson plan to the students in a logical manner. This ensures that the content is structured, coherent, and understandable, facilitating effective learning.

467. **(D):** When evaluating test booklets, it's important to give marks according to the answers given by students. This ensures a fair and objective assessment based on the students' performance.

468. **(C):** If you encounter your students while watching a movie in a theatre, meeting them with warmth, introducing them to your friends, and offering them tea/cold drinks is a friendly and appropriate response. This demonstrates a positive and approachable attitude.

469. **(C):** In a situation where students invite you to participate in a cricket match, opting to be a referee in the match is a neutral and fair choice. This allows you to be involved without showing favoritism to any one team.

470. **(B):** The quality most liked by students in a teacher is his impartial attitude. Fairness in treatment, grading, and interaction is crucial in building trust and respect in the classroom.

471. **(A):** During an educational tour, it's expected that students should observe everything carefully and ask questions regarding what they see. This active engagement enhances their learning experience and makes the tour more educational and interactive.

472. **(A):** A teacher having good moral character and values leads to a positive impact on his/her students. By modeling ethical behaviour and strong values, a teacher can influence students to develop similar qualities.

473. **(C):** To rectify the use of obscene and abusive language by a student, it would be effective to talk to the student's parents/guardians and try to understand the root cause of the problem. Addressing the underlying issues can lead to more effective and long-term solutions.

474. **(B):** Including moral education in the academic syllabi of students is beneficial for developing the character of students. It helps in instilling values and ethical principles that are important for their personal development and social behaviour.

475. **(A):** An important factor for bringing improvement in education is creating an atmosphere conducive to teaching and studying. A supportive and engaging learning environment is key to effective education.

476. **(D):** If a teacher uses different techniques during the teaching process, it can lead to increased student attention, make teaching easier, and make the learning process more interesting. Variety in teaching methods can cater to different learning styles and keep students engaged.

477. **(A):** A teacher must take interest in research because this develops the knowledge base of the teacher. Engaging in research keeps teachers updated on the latest developments in their field and enhances their expertise.

478. **(B):** To support giving more hours for practical work in the timetable for class eight, a convincing argument is that through practical work, students get an opportunity to learn by doing what they study in class. This hands-on experience is crucial for understanding and applying theoretical knowledge.

479. **(D):** Most educators agree that oral reading requires an audience situation. This context provides a purpose for the reading and can help improve fluency, expression, and comprehension skills.

480. **(B):** The current educational system, while having strengths, also needs improvements. Continuous evaluation and adaptation are necessary to address the evolving needs of students and the changing demands of society.

481. **(B):** Education should be vocation-oriented. This approach ensures that students are equipped with the skills and knowledge necessary to excel in their chosen careers and contribute effectively to society.

482. **(B):** To win the trust of students, a teacher should behave with them like a friend. This approach fosters a friendly and supportive environment in the classroom, encouraging open communication and a strong teacher-student relationship.

483. **(A):** If some teachers consider tuition to be their profession, it would be advisable to inform them about the potential negative impacts of this approach on their teaching responsibilities and student learning. Highlighting the drawbacks can encourage a re-evaluation of their priorities.

484. **(B):** Kendriya Vidyalayas (KVs) are a system of central government schools in India that were primarily established for the education of the children of employees of the Central

Government, but they are not exclusively for urban or rural children. Kendriya Vidyalayas aim to provide quality education to the children of transferable central government employees, including defense personnel, by accommodating students from various backgrounds, irrespective of their rural or urban residence.

485. **(A):** The curriculum of students should be associated with the realities of life. This relevance ensures that the education they receive is practical and applicable to real-world situations, preparing them for life beyond the classroom.

486. **(D):** The curriculum prepared for children should be meaningful, oriented towards productivity, and have flexibility. Such a curriculum addresses the diverse needs of learners and prepares them effectively for various aspects of life.

487. **(C):** The relationship of educational psychology is with the aspect of when and how education should be imparted. It focuses on understanding the learning processes and developing effective teaching strategies based on psychological principles.

488. **(B):** As a teacher, a student's behaviour of talking to other students in the class during the course of a lecture would be deemed serious. This behaviour is disruptive and can hinder the learning process for both the student and their peers.

489. **(A):** If your wife also teaches in the same school, exchanging notes with her on a regular basis would be a professional and productive way to collaborate and enhance teaching practices.

490. **(D):** If all the teachers of your school are on strike, joining them in the strike is a solidarity choice, assuming the strike is for a justifiable cause. It's important to be united with your colleagues in professional matters, especially when advocating for common interests or improvements.

491. **(C):** Her action of not teaching properly in class and instead telling her pupils to meet her at her residence for tuitions is worth condemnation. This behaviour undermines the integrity of the teaching profession and the educational system, and it may not be in the best interests of her students.

492. **(D):** As a teacher who does your work efficiently, a reasonable expectation in return would be a few words of praise at functions or annual days of the school. Recognition and appreciation for your efforts can be motivating and fulfilling.

493. **(*):** *These are personal opinion questions. Option choice may vary. Mark according to your preference.*

494. **(C):** If a teacher in the teachers' room comments that your students do not view you as a good teacher, a constructive response would be to acknowledge the possibility and express a willingness to improve your teaching methods and knowledge levels.

495. **(C):** Being known as the right-hand man of the Principal, you should concentrate on your subject, students, and teaching methods only. Focusing on these core responsibilities is crucial for your professional integrity and effectiveness as an educator.

496. **(B):** If you are quite popular among your colleagues, you should use this opportunity to develop new/novel techniques for education. Leveraging your influence for the betterment of teaching methods can have a positive impact on the learning environment.

497. **(A):** If two students who sit together in a class occasionally fight each other, a practical action would be to make them sit separately, at a distance. This can help prevent further conflicts and maintain a conducive learning environment.

498. **(D):** For students with weak eyesight who are unable to clearly see the blackboard, letting these children sit in the front seats in the class is a considerate and practical solution. It enables them to see better without needing to move closer to the blackboard.

499. **(C):** To remain in the good books of your Principal, you should keep on doing your teaching work as per your satisfaction and according to the needs of your students. Performing your duties diligently and effectively is the best way to earn respect and recognition.

500. **(C):** If you feel that your command over the subject is poor, the best course of action is to work hard and prepare your subject thoroughly. Enhancing your subject knowledge and teaching skills can improve your effectiveness as a teacher and increase your confidence in the profession.

501. **(C):** Maximum marks should be given to a student who works hard and does well in his class tests and examinations. Marks should reflect the student's academic performance and effort, not personal relationships or other non-academic factors.

502. **(B):** The Parents' Teachers' Association (PTA) is of great value because it provides a platform for teachers to interact with the parents of their students. This interaction can foster a collaborative approach to students' education and well-being.

503. **(B):** If you are free during school hours, the best way to spend time would be to read books, magazines, and journals in the library. This not only enhances your knowledge but also sets a good example for students about the importance of continuous learning.

504. **(C):** With the advent of dynamic technologies and teaching methods, the appropriate response is to learn new technologies (like computers, multimedia, Internet, testing techniques, etc.) and transfer the knowledge so gained to your students. Adapting to technological advancements is crucial in modern education.

505. **(D):** The issue of "educated unemployment" is attributed to all of these factors: education providing mostly theoretical knowledge, lack of integration of professional education, and unclear objectives of education. These aspects contribute to the gap between education and employability.

506. **(A):** A teacher ought to know about the problems prevalent in the field of education primarily because only a teacher can actively contribute to solving them. Understanding these issues is crucial for effective teaching and for advocating improvements in the education system.

507. **(B):** The programmes for improving the standards of education, under the aegis of the national policy of education, are courageous and laudable efforts. Despite the challenges of resource shortages and rising population, striving to improve educational standards is commendable.

508. **(B):** In the present times, the poor state of primary education is majorly due to the poor ratio of teachers to students. Overcrowded classrooms and insufficient teacher attention can significantly hinder the quality of education.

509. **(D):** The chief reason for the degradation of moral education in the present times is the dominance of money in society. Materialistic values often overshadow moral and ethical considerations, impacting the effectiveness of moral education.

510. **(C):** Giving more emphasis to adult education programmes, despite the lack of resources and rising population levels, is a courageous and laudable action/behaviour. Adult education is vital for empowering individuals and improving societal welfare.

511. **(C):** It is important to impart education about moral values to students because this would lead to more dedication towards and awareness about good virtues/values. Moral education plays a crucial role in shaping a student's character and ethical framework.

512. **(D):** Inculcating good habits of the teacher in students is the chief responsibility of the teacher, guardians, and parents. All these stakeholders in a child's education contribute to shaping their habits and values.

513. **(C):** The position of a teacher is respected in society because teachers are considered the builders of the destiny of a nation. They play a pivotal role in educating and shaping future generations, contributing significantly to the development of a society.

514. **(D):** The prevalence of dogmas and immoral customs in society is largely due to lack of awareness and the problem of illiteracy. Education and awareness can help overcome these issues by promoting critical thinking and informed decision-making.

515. **(C):** The diminishing importance of the teacher in society can be attributed to the indifference of the teacher towards his/her profession. A lack of commitment and enthusiasm in teaching can undermine the respect and value placed on the profession.

516. **(A):** A teacher should continuously incorporate new sets of knowledge into his subject matter so that he may be able to give the latest knowledge to his students. Staying updated with current information and trends is essential for providing a relevant and comprehensive education.

517. **(A):** If you see children fighting on the road, the appropriate action would be to pacify them by giving them advice. Intervening to resolve conflicts peacefully demonstrates responsible and caring behaviour.

518. **(B):** If one of the parents/guardians does not come to meet you, a suitable approach would be to write to the parent/guardian. This shows initiative in maintaining communication and addressing any potential issues or concerns.

519. **(C):** Teachers should aim for fairness and impartiality in their interactions with students and their parents/guardians. Being unbiased contributes to a positive and respectful learning environment. It's important for teachers to treat all students equally, recognizing and appreciating their individual strengths and achievements without favoritism. This approach fosters trust and credibility in the teacher-student-parent relationship.

520. **(D):** If you are assigned a duty in elections, the appropriate response is to go with pleasure because obeying rules is your prime duty. Fulfilling assigned duties, especially in the context of a democratic process like elections, is an important civic responsibility.

521. **(B):** Supporting the organization of an inter-school sports meet is beneficial as players from your school would learn new techniques of games and gain valuable experience. Such events also promote sportsmanship, teamwork, and interaction with peers from other schools.

522. **(C):** A genuine interest in teaching is a compelling reason to like the profession. Passion for educating and shaping young minds is fundamental to being an effective and motivated teacher.

523. **(C):** To make class teaching more effective and meaningful, immediately asking questions related to the lecture after it concludes can be highly effective. This strategy helps reinforce learning, ensures student engagement, and assesses understanding.

524. **(A):** Students are generally impressed by a teacher's knowledge and learning. Demonstrating a strong command of the subject matter and the ability to convey it effectively garners respect and admiration from students.

525. **(C):** If you are very tired and not in a mood to teach, telling children an ideal story can be a good alternative. Stories can be educational and engaging, and they offer a way to connect with students while providing a lighter teaching approach.

526. (D): The best way to encourage a teacher who works with complete dedication is to praise his work from time to time. Recognition and appreciation of efforts can be a great motivator and reinforces positive behaviour.

527. (C): The behaviour of a teacher affects students the most. Teachers are role models and authority figures in the classroom, and their behaviour can significantly influence students' attitudes, behaviour, and learning.

528. (D): Students learn to the maximum extent and with the utmost speed by doing things themselves. Hands-on, experiential learning enables students to apply concepts practically, enhancing understanding and retention.

529. (D): To maintain the interest of students in class teaching, employing all of these strategies is effective: extensive use of examples from practical life, extensive use of teaching materials/aids, and giving ample opportunities for discussion and deliberation.

530. (A): Taking additional responsibilities as a teacher to gain new experiences is a valid reason. Such responsibilities can provide opportunities for personal and professional growth, allowing teachers to acquire new skills and perspectives.

531. (D): If a student criticizes another teacher in your presence, the appropriate action would be to reprimand that student for disrespect and explain the importance of respecting all teachers, while sparing him from severe punishment. It's important to address the behaviour without escalating the situation.

532. (B): A teacher should work according to the needs of the time. This approach ensures that teaching methods and content are relevant, effective, and cater to the current educational requirements and challenges.

533. (B): If a student is reading a storybook instead of paying attention to the lecture, you should ask the student to put the book away and concentrate on the subject being taught. This maintains classroom discipline and focus on the lesson.

534. (B): To participate in a conference or seminar related to teaching, you should get permission from the Principal. This maintains professionalism and ensures that your responsibilities at school are managed appropriately.

535. (C): A common reason why some teachers give tuitions is that they are always involved in earning more money. While there may be various motivations for giving tuitions, additional income is often a significant factor.

536. (C): A superior teacher is one who takes an interest in the all-round development of students. This includes not only academic growth but also personal, social, and emotional development.

537. (C): Talking to other students in the class during the course of a lecture would be deemed serious behaviour by a teacher. This disrupts the learning environment and shows a lack of respect for the teacher and fellow students.

538. (C): If a student is not able to understand a point even after repeated explanations, you should use another method or material to explain the concept to them. Adapting your teaching approach to meet the needs of individual students is a mark of a good teacher.

539. (C): To stop the practice of copying in the examination hall, necessary improvements should be effected in the examination system. This could include better invigilation, more effective assessment methods, and fostering a culture of academic integrity.

540. (D): The best teacher is the one who is a well-wisher of students. A teacher who genuinely cares for and supports the overall well-being and success of their students is likely to be effective and respected.

541. **(D):** If a student asks an out-of-context question in class, a considerate approach is to tell the student that you would answer his question after the class. This ensures that the flow of the lesson isn't disrupted while still acknowledging and respecting the student's curiosity.

542. **(B):** If a significant number of students are consistently taking leave on the day of the weekly test, it would be beneficial to communicate this concern to their parents/ guardians. By informing them about the issue, you involve them in the process and seek their support in ensuring regular attendance, especially on test days. This approach encourages parental involvement and cooperation in addressing the problem.

543. **(D):** Having complete knowledge of your subject as a teacher enables you to eliminate the doubts of your students effectively. Thorough subject knowledge is crucial for clarifying students' questions and enhancing their understanding.

544. **(D):** To address the habit of stealing among students, giving them good advice and keeping a vigilant eye over them can be effective. This approach combines guidance with monitoring and can help in correcting the behaviour more constructively than punishment alone.

545. **(B):** If a student consistently comes late to class even after repeated instructions, informing his parents/guardians about the issue is a proactive step. This can help in understanding the reasons behind the lateness and in finding a solution.

546. **(D):** To win the trust of students, a teacher should behave with them like a friend. A friendly approach fosters an open, supportive, and trusting classroom environment.

547. **(B):** From a developmental perspective, fostering self-confidence among students is of great importance. Self-confidence is key to students' academic success, personal development, and ability to face challenges.

548. **(D):** The quote "Motivation is the art of generating interest in the mind of the student" is attributed to Rabindra Nath Tagore. Tagore was a Bengali polymath who reshaped Bengali literature and music, as well as Indian art with Contextual Modernism in the late 19th and early 20th centuries.

549. **(C):** A meaningful examination should be able to differentiate capable students from the incapable ones. This means that the examination must be fair and challenging enough to accurately assess students' understanding and abilities.

550. **(D):** The practical method of making students understand the meaning of difficult words is to use all of these techniques: giving their synonyms, giving their antonyms, and teaching them the usage of such words in sentences. This comprehensive approach helps students grasp the full meaning and usage of the words.

551. **(D):** The French scholar, Montesquieu, believed that education should essentially have an influence (or shade) of philosophy. He advocated for an education that is critical thinking, moral reasoning, and an understanding of the principles of government and society. He also emphasized the importance of adapting education to the needs of the individual and the society in which they live.

552. **(C):** Francis Bacon, the famous educationist, opined that the objective of education is to help the child become capable enough to make a living. Bacon's view of education was pragmatic, focusing on the practical aspects of learning that would enable individuals to be self-sufficient and economically independent.

❑ ❑ ❑

KNOWLEDGE OF COMPUTER

A BRIEF HISTORY OF COMPUTERS

INTRODUCTION OF COMPUTER

Computer is the most amazing machine man has ever created. Today computers are used in almost all walks of life: bank, hospitals, schools, publishing, manufacturing, entertainment, shops, libraries, factories, games, elections, security services etc. A computer is basically a programmable computing machine. In this chapter we will discuss the various parts of the computer which make the fast and better computation. We will provide a better solution to the problems related to the organization of computer.

GENERATIONS OF COMPUTERS

The first Generation: Vacuum Tubes

ENIAC

The ENIAC (Electronic Numerical Integrator And Computer), designed by and constructed under the supervision of John Mauchly and John Presper Eckert at the University of Pennsylvania, was the world's first general-purpose electronic digital computer. The project was a response to U.S. wartime needs. Mauchly, a professor of electrical engineering at the University of Pennsylvania and Eckert, one of his graduate students, proposed to build a general-purpose computer using vacuum tubes. In 1943, this proposal was accepted by the Army, and work began on the ENIAC. The resulting machine was enormous, weighing 30 tons, occupying 15,000 square feet of floor space, and containing more than 18,000 vacuum tubes. When operating, it consumed 140 kilowatts of power. It was also substantially faster than any electronic-mechanical computer, being capable of 5000 additions per second.

The ENIAC was decimal rather than a binary machine. That is, numbers were represented in decimal form and arithmetic was performed in the decimal system. Its memory consisted of 20 "accumulators", each capable of holding a 10-digit decimal number. Each digit was represented by a ring of 10 vacuum tubes. At any time, only one vacuum tube was in the ON state, representing one of the 10 digits. The major drawback of the ENIAC was that it had to be programmed manually by setting switches and plugging and unplugging cables.

The ENIAC was completed in 1946, too late to be used in the war effort. Instead, its first task was to perform a series of complex calculations that were used to help determine the feasibility of the H-bomb. The ENIAC continued to be used until 1955.

The Von Neumann Machine

The programming process could be facilitated if the program could be represented in a form suitable for storing in memory alongside the data. Then, a computer could get its instructions by reading them from memory, and a program could be set of altered by setting the values of a portion of memory.

This idea, known as the Stored-program concept, is usually attributed to the ENIAC designers, most notably the mathematician John Von Neumann, who was a consultant on the ENIAC project. The idea was also developed at about the same time by Turing. The first publication of the idea was in a 1945 proposal by Von Neumann for a new computer, the EDVAC (Electronic Discrete Variable Computer).

In 1946, von Neumann and his colleagues began the design of a new stored-program computer, referred to as the IAS computer, at the Princeton

Institute for Advanced Studies. The IAS computer, although not completed until 1952, is the prototype of all subsequent general-purpose computers. Figure below shows the general structure of the IAS computer. It consists of:

- A main memory, which stores both data and instructions.
- An arithmetic-logical unit (ALU) capable of operating on binary data.
- A control unit, which interprets the instructions in memory and causes them to be executed.
- Input and output (I/O) equipment operated by the control unit.

Commercial Computers

The 1950's saw the birth of the computer industry with two companies, Sperry and IBM, dominating the marketplace.

In 1947, Eckert and Mauchly formed the Eckert-Mauchly Computer Corporation to manufacture computers commercially. Their first successful machine was the UNIVAC I (Universal Automatic Computer), which was commissioned by the Bureau of the Census for the 1950 calculations. The Eckert-Mauchly Computer Corporation became part of the UNIVAC division of Sperry-Rand Corporation, which went on to build a series of successor machines.

The UNIVAC II, which had greater memory capacity and higher performance than the UNIVAC I, was delivered in the late 1950's and illustrates several trends that have remained characteristic of the computer industry. First, advances in technology allow companies to continue to build larger, more powerful computers. Second, each company tries to make its new machines upward compatible with the older machines. This means that the programs written for the older machines can be executed on the new machine. This strategy is adopted in the hopes of retaining the customer base; that is, when a customer decides to buy a newer machine, he is likely to get it from the same company to avoid losing the investment in programs.

The UNIVAC division also began development of the 1100 series of computers, which was to be its bread and butter. This series illustrates a distinction that existed at one time. The first model, the UNIVAC 1103, and its successors for many years were primarily intended for scientific applications, involving long and complex calculations. Other companies concentrated on business applications, which involved processing large amounts of text data. This split has largely disappeared but it was evident for a number of years.

IBM, which was then the major manufacturer of punched-card processing equipment, delivered its first electronic stored-program computer, the 701, in 1953. The 701 was intended primarily for scientific applications. In 1955, IBM introduced the companion 702 product, which had a number of hardware features that suited it to business applications. These were the first of a long series of 700/7000 computers that established IBM as the overwhelmingly dominant computer manufacturer.

The Second Generation: Transistors

The first major change in the electronic computer came with the replacement of the vacuum tube by the transistor. The transistor is smaller, cheaper, and dissipates less heal than a vacuum tube but can be used in the same way as a vacuum tube to construct computers. Unlike the vacuum tube, which requires wires, metal plates, a glass capsule, and a vacuum, the transistor is a solid-state device, made from silicon. The transistor was invented at Bell Labs in 1947 and by the 1950's had launched an electronic revolution. It was not until the late 1950s, however, that fully transistorized computers were commercially available. IBM again was not the first company to deliver the new technology. NCR and more successfully RCA were the front-runners with some small transistor machines. IBM followed shortly with the 7000 series.

The use of the transistor defines the second generation of computers. It has become widely accepted to classify computers into generations based on the fundamental hardware technology employed. Each new generation is characterized by greater processing performance, larger memory capacity, and smaller size than the previous one.

The Third Generation: Integrated Circuits

A single, self-contained transistor is called a discrete component. Throughout the 1950s and early 1960s, electronic equipment was composed largely of discrete components—transistors, resistors, capacitors, and so on. Discrete components were manufactured separately, packaged in their own containers, and soldered or wired together onto circuit boards, which were then installed in computers, oscilloscopes, and other electronic equipment. Whenever an electronic device called for a transistor, a little tube of metal containing a pinhead-sized piece of silicon had to be soldered to a circuit board. The entire manufacturing process, from transistor to circuit board, was expensive and cumbersome.

These facts of life were beginning to create problems in the computer industry. Early second-generation computers contained about 10,000 transistors. This figure grew to the hundreds of thousands, making the manufacture of newer, more powerful machines increasingly difficult. In 1958 came the achievement that revolutionized electronics and started the era of microelectronics: the invention of the integrated circuit. It is the integrated circuit that defines the third generation of computers. Perhaps the two most important members of the third generation are the IBM System/360 and the DEC PDP-8.

Later Generations

Beyond the third generation there is less general agreement on defining generations of computers. There have been a fourth and a fifth generation, based on advances in integrated circuit technology. With the introduction of large-scale integration (LSI), more than 1000,000 components can be placed on a single integrated circuit chip.

The Summary of Generations of Computer

- Vacuum tube - 1946-1957
- Transistor - 1958-1964
- Small scale integration: 1965

Up to 100 devices on a chip

- **Medium scale integration: -1971**

100-3,000 devices on a chip

- **Large scale integration :1971-1977**

3,000 - 100,000 devices on a chip

- **Very large scale integration: 1978 -1991**

100,000 - 100,000,000 devices on a chip

- **Ultra large scale integration : 1991**

Over 100,000,000 devices on a chip

FUNCTIONAL UNITS OF COMPUTER

Computer allocates the task between its various functional units. The computer system is divided into three separate functional units for its operation. They are:

- Central Processing Unit (CPU)
- Arithmetic Logical Unit (ALU)
- Control Unit (CU)

Central Processing Unit (CPU)

The ALU and the CU of a computer system are jointly known as the Central Processing Unit. You may call CPU as the brain of any computer system. It is just like brain that takes all major decisions, makes all sorts of calculations and directs different parts of the computer functions by activating and controlling the operations.

Arithmetic Logical Unit (ALU)

After you enter data through the input device it is stored in the Primary storage unit. The actual processing of the data and instruction are performed by Arithmetic Logical Unit. The major operations performed by the ALU are addition, subtraction, multiplication, division, logic and comparison. Data is transferred to ALU from storage unit when required. After processing the output is returned back to storage unit for further processing or getting stored.

Control Unit (CU)

The next component of computer is the Control Unit, which acts like the supervisor seeing that things are done in proper fashion. The control unit determines the sequence in which computer programs and instructions are executed. Things like processing of programs stored in the main memory, interpretation of the instructions and issuing of signals for other units of the computer to execute them. It also acts as a switch board operator when several users access the computer simultaneously. Thereby it coordinates the activities of computer's peripheral as they perform the input and output.

PARTS OF THE COMPUTER

There is basically two parts of the computer:

(a) Hardware

(b) Software

(a) Hardware

Hardware is best described as a device that is physically connected to your computer or something that can be physically touched. A CD-ROM, Monitor, Printer, and video card are all examples of computer hardware. Without any hardware your computer would not exist and software would have nothing to run on. The image to the right is of a web cam, an example of an external hardware peripheral that allows users to make basic videos, transmit videos of themselves over the Internet, and take pictures.

Computer hardwares are:

- **Central Processing Unit (CPU):** The "microprocessor" brain of the computer system is called the central processing unit. Everything that a computer does is overseen by the CPU.
- **Memory:** This is very fast storage used to hold data. It has to be fast because it connects directly to the microprocessor. There are several specific types of memory in a computer.
- **RAM (Random Access Memory):**It is used to temporarily store information that the computer is currently working with.
- **ROM (Read Only Memory):** A permanent type of memory storage used by the computer for important data that does not change.
- **Keyboard:** Generally used to type or select an option on the screen. It is an input device.
- **Mouse:** It is an input device which is used to point and select some option on VDU.
- **VDU (Visual Display Unit):** It is an output device where the output of any command is displayed *i.e.*, The screen.
- **Printer:** It is the output device. Different types of printer are:
  1. Dot matrix printer
  2. Inkjet Printer
  3. Laser Printer etc.
- **Floppy Disk Drives:** It is a common form of removable storage. Floppy disk are extremely inexpensive and easy to save information.
- **Scanner:** It is an input device. A scanner scans an image and transform the image to ASCII Graphics. These codes can be edited, manipulated & then printed.
- **CD-ROM Drive:** It is an input device. To read a CD-ROM disk a CD-ROM drive is required. One can only read from it and cannot write on it.
- **DVD-ROM:** DVD-ROM is similar to Cd-Rom but is capable of holding much more information.
- **CD-Writer:** It is input device. To write from other CD to your CD, writer is used.

(b) Software

Software is a collection of commands that help users to communicate with the computer or help the computer perform specific tasks for them. Without any type of software the computer would be of no use.

Examples of software **programs** or **applications** would be the **Operating System** (DOS, Windows, UNIX, MacOS and various others), **Wordprocessor** (typing letters), **Spreadsheet** (financial info), **Database** (inventory control and address book), **Graphics program**, **Internet Browser**, **Email** and many others.

Software is capable of performing specific tasks, as opposed to hardware which only perform mechanical tasks that they are mechanically designed for. Practical computer systems divide software systems into three major groups:

System Software

System software is a program that manages and supports the computer resources and operations of a computer system while it executes various tasks such as processing data and information, controlling hardware components, and allowing users to use application software. That is, systems software functions as a *bridge* between computer system hardware and the application software. System software is made up of many control programs, including the operating system, communications software and database manager. Computer software includes operating systems, device drivers, diagnostic tools and more.

Systems software consists of three kinds of programs. The system management programs, system support programs, and system development programs. These are explained briefly.

System Management Programs

These are programs that manage the application software, computer hardware, and data resources of the computer system. These programs include operating systems, operating environment programs, database management programs, and telecommunications monitor programs. Among these, the most important system management programs are operating systems. The operating systems are needed to study more details. There are two reasons. First, users need to know their functions first. For the second, there are many kinds of operating systems available today.

Telecommunications monitor programs are additions of the operating systems of microcomputers. These programs provide the extra logic for the computer system to control a class of communications devices.

System Support Programs

These are the programs that help the operations and management of a computer system. They provide a variety of support services to let the computer hardware and other system programs run efficiently. The major system support programs are system utility programs, system performance monitor programs, and system security monitor programs (virus checking programs).

System Development Programs

These are programs that help users develop information system programs and prepare user programs for computer processing. These programs may analyze and design systems and program itself. The main system development programs are programming language translators, programming environment programs, computer-aided software engineering packages.

Programming Software

Software that assists a programmer in writing computer programs.

Application Software

Allows users to accomplish one or more tasks. Application software utilizes the capacities of a computer directly for a dedicated task. Application software is able to manipulate text, numbers and graphics. It can be in the form of software focused on a certain single task like word processing, spreadsheet or playing of audio and video files. Here, we look at the application software types along with some examples of application software of each type.

Different Types of Application Software

- **Word Processing Software:** This software enables users to create and edit documents. The most popular examples of this type of software are MS-Word, WordPad and Notepad among other text editors.
- **Database Software:** Database is a structured collection of data. A computer database relies on database software to organize data and enable database users to perform database operations. Database software allows users to store and retrieve data from databases. Examples are Oracle, MSAccess, etc.

- **Spreadsheet Software:** Excel, Lotus 1-2-3 and Apple Numbers are some examples of spreadsheet software. Spreadsheet software allows users to perform calculations using spreadsheets. They simulate paper worksheets by displaying multiple cells that make up a grid.
- **Multimedia Software:** They allow users to create and play audio and video files. They are capable of playing media files. Audio converters, audio players, burners, video encoders and decoders are some forms of multimedia software. Examples of this type of software include Real Player and Media Player.
- **Presentation Software:** The software that is used to display information in the form of a slide show is known as presentation software. This type of software includes three functions, namely, editing that allows insertion and formatting of text, methods to include graphics in the text and a functionality of executing slide shows. Microsoft PowerPoint is the best example of presentation software.
- **Enterprise Software:** It deals with the needs of organization processes and data flow. Customer relationship management or the financial processes in an organization are carried out with the help of enterprise software.
- **Information Worker Software:** Individual projects within a department and individual needs of creation and management of information are handled by information worker software. Documentation tools, resource management tools and personal management systems fall under the category of this type of application software.
- **Educational Software:** It has the capabilities of running tests and tracking progress. It also has the capabilities of a collaborative software. It is often used in teaching and self-learning. Dictionaries like Britannica and Encarta, mathematical software like Matlab and others like Google Earth and NASA World Wind are some of the well-known names in this category.
- **Simulation Software:** It is used to simulate physical or abstract systems. Simulation software finds applications in both, research and entertainment. Flight simulators and scientific simulators are examples of simulation software.
- **Content Access Software:** It is used to access content without editing. Common examples of content access software are web browsers and media players.
- **Application Suites:** An application suite is an important type of application software. It consists of a group of applications combined to perform related functions. OpenOffice.org and Microsoft Office are the best examples of this type of application software. These application suites, as you know, come as bundles of applications like word processors, spreadsheets, presentation software, etc. Applications in the suite can work together or operate on each other's files.

Utility Software

Utility software is system software designed to help analyze, configure, optimize or maintain a computer. A single piece of utility software is usually called a utility or tool.

Utility software usually focuses on how the computer infrastructure (including the computer hardware, operating system, application software and data storage) operates. Due to this focus, utilities are often rather technical and targeted at people with an advanced level of computer knowledge - in contrast to application software, which allows users to do things like creating text documents, playing games, listening to music or viewing websites.

Utility Software Examples

- **Anti-virus** utilities scan for computer viruses.
- **Backup** utilities can make a copy of all information stored on a disk, and restore either the entire disk (e.g. in an event of

disk failure) or selected files (e.g. in an event of accidental deletion).

- **Data compression** utilities output a shorter stream or a smaller file when provided with a stream or file.
- **Disk cleaners** can find files that are unnecessary to computer operation, or take up considerable amounts of space. Disk cleaner helps the user to decide what to delete when their hard disk is full.
- **Disk compression** utilities can transparently compress/uncompress the contents of a disk, increasing the capacity of the disk.
- **Disk defragmenters** can detect computer files whose contents are broken across several locations on the hard disk, and move the fragments to one location to increase efficiency.
- **Disk partitions** can divide an individual drive into multiple logical drives, each with its own file system which can be mounted by the operating system and treated as an individual drive.
- **Disk space analyzers** for the visualization of disk space usage by getting the size for each folder (including sub folders) & files in folder or drive, showing the distribution of the used space.
- **Archive** utilities output a stream or a single file when provided with a directory or a set of files. Archive utilities, unlike archive suites, usually do not include compression or encryption capabilities. Some archive utilities may even have a separate un-archive utility for the reverse operation.
- **File managers** provide a convenient method of performing routine data management tasks, such as deleting, renaming, cataloging, uncataloging, moving, copying, merging, generating and modifying data sets.
- **Memory testers** check for memory failures.
- **Network utilities** analyze the computer's network connectivity, configure network settings, check data transfer or log events.
- **Registry cleaners** clean and optimize the Windows registry by removing old registry keys that are no longer in use.
- **Screensavers** were desired to prevent phosphor burn-in on CRT and plasma computer monitors by blanking the screen or filling it with moving images or patterns when the computer is not in use. Contemporary screensavers are used primarily for entertainment or security.

Firmware

Firmware is a program for the hardware. It is an embedded coded (program) for the hardware. So, it can perform its function specifically for which device is made. Every device has inbuilt firmware that gives the device ability to perform its work. There are lots of devices that use a screen and buttons. The device consists of firmware that instruct the device to perform certain functions on given command. Examples are a video card and sound card.

COMPUTER FUNDAMENTAL

COMPUTER

Computer is an advanced electronic device that takes raw data as input from the user and processes these data under the control of set of instructions (called program) and gives the result (output) and saves output for the future use. It can process both numerical and non-numerical (arithmetic and logical) calculations.

A computer has four functions:

(*a*) accepts data **Input**
(*b*) processes data **Processing**
(*c*) produces output **Output**
(*d*) stores results **Storage**

Input (Data)

Input is the raw information entered into a computer from the input devices. It is the collection of letters, numbers, images etc.

Process

Process is the operation of data as per given instruction. It is totally internal process of the computer system.

Output

Output is the processed data given by computer after data processing. Output is also called as Result. We can save these results in the storage devices for the future use.

COMPUTER SYSTEM

All of the components of a computer system can be summarized with the simple equations.

COMPUTER SYSTEM = HARDWARE + SOFTWARE + USER

Hardware = Internal Devices + Peripheral Devices

All physical parts of the computer (or everything that we can touch) are known as Hardware.

Software = Programs

Software gives "intelligence" to the computer.

USER = Person, who operates computer.

PROCESSOR

The main unit inside the computer is the CPU. This unit is responsible for all events inside the computer. It controls all internal and external devices, performs arithmetic and logic operations. The CPU (Central Processing Unit) is the device that interprets and executes instructions.

SOFTWARE

Software, simply are the computer programs. The instructions given to the computer in the form of a program is called Software. Software is the set of programs, which are used for different purposes. All the programs used in computer to perform specific task is called Software.

Types of Software

1. System software

(a) Operating System Software: Operating system is an example of system software, which provide the platform to the application softwares.

DOS, Windows XP, Windows Vista, Unix/Linux, MAC/OS X etc.

(b) Utility Software: Windows Explorer (File/Folder Management), Windows Media Player, Anti-Virus Utilities, Disk Defragmentation, Disk Clean, BackUp, WinZip, WinRAR etc...

2. Application software

(a) Package Software: MS Office 2003, MS Office 2007, Macromedia (Dreamweaver, Flash, Freehand), Adobe (PageMaker, PhotoShop)

(b) Tailored or Custom Software: SAGE (Accounting), Galileo/Worldspan (Travel) etc.

COMPUTER LANGUAGES & SCRIPTING

Low Level Language

(*i*) Machine Level Language

(*ii*) Assembly Language

Machine language

These language instructions are directly executed by CPU. It is in the form of '0' and '1' means in binary language.

Assembly language

The endeavor of giving machine language instructions a name structure that means bit strings of instructions of machine language are given name here.

- **High Level Language:** The user friendly language ...more natural language than assembly language. Like C++, Java etc.
- **Assembler:** It is a program written in a computer language which convert assembly language into machine language.
- **Compiler:** It is also a program written in a computer language, which convert high level language to machine language.

High Level Language

COBOL (Common Business Oriented Language), FORTRAN (Formula Translation), BASIC (Beginner's All-purpose Symbolic Instruction Code), C, C++ etc. are the examples of High Level Language.

TYPES OF COMPUTER

On the Basis of Working Principle

(a) **Analog Computer:** An analog computer (spelt analogue in British English) is a form of computer that uses *continuous* physical phenomena such as electrical, mechanical, or hydraulic quantities to model the problem being solved.

(b) **Digital Computer:** A computer that performs calculations and logical operations with quantities represented as digits, usually in the binary number system.

(c) **Hybrid Computer (Analog + Digital):** A combination of computers those are capable of inputting and outputting in both digital and analog signals. A hybrid computer system setup offers a cost effective method of performing complex simulations.

COMPUTER TYPES ON THE BASIS OF SIZE

(a) Super Computer

The fastest type of computer. Supercomputers are very expensive and are employed for specialized applications that require immense amounts of mathematical calculations. For example, weather forecasting requires a supercomputer. Other uses of supercomputers include animated graphics, fluid dynamic calculations, nuclear energy research, and petroleum exploration.

The chief difference between a supercomputer and a mainframe is that a supercomputer channels all its power into executing a few programs as fast as possible, whereas a mainframe uses its power to execute many programs concurrently.

(b) Mainframe Computer

A very large and expensive computer capable of supporting hundreds, or even thousands, of users simultaneously. In the hierarchy that starts with a simple microprocessor (in watches, for example) at the bottom and moves to supercomputers at the top, mainframes are just below supercomputers. In some ways, mainframes are more powerful than supercomputers because they support more simultaneous programs. But supercomputers can execute a single program faster than a mainframe.

(c) Mini Computer

A midsized computer. In size and power, minicomputers lie between *workstations* and *mainframes*. In the past decade, the distinction between large minicomputers and small mainframes has blurred, however, as has the distinction between small minicomputers and workstations. But in general, a minicomputer is a multiprocessing system capable of supporting from 4 to about 200 users simultaneously.

(d) Micro Computer

(*i*) **Desktop Computer:** A personal or micro-mini computer sufficient to fit on a desk.

(*ii*) **Laptop Computer:** A portable computer complete with an integrated screen and keyboard. It is generally smaller in size than a desktop computer and larger than a notebook computer.

(*iii*) **Palmtop Computer/Digital Diary/ Notebook/PDAs:** A hand-sized computer. Palmtops have no keyboard but the screen serves both as an input and output device.

(e) Workstations

A terminal or desktop computer in a network. In this context, workstation is just a generic term for a user's machine (client machine) in contrast to a "server" or "mainframe."

BOOTING

The process of loading the system files of the operating system from the disk into the computer memory to complete the circuitry requirement of the computer system is called booting.

Types of Booting

There are two types of booting:

- **Cold Booting:** If the computer is in off state and we boot the computer by pressing the power switch 'ON' from the CPU box then it is called as cold booting.
- **Warm Booting:** If the computer is already 'ON' and we restart it by pressing the 'RESET' button from the CPU box or CTRL, ALT and DEL key simultaneously from the keyboard then it is called warm booting.

COMPUTER HARDWARE

HARDWARE

The **hardware** are the parts of the computer itself including the Central Processing Unit (CPU) and related **microchips** and **micro-circuitry**, keyboards, monitors, case and drives (hard, CD, DVD, floppy, optical, tape, etc...). Other extra parts called **peripheral components** or **devices** include mouse, printers, modems, scanners, digital cameras and cards (sound, colour, video) etc... Together they are often referred to as a **personal computer**.

Central Processing Unit

Though the term relates to a specific chip or the **processor** a CPU's performance is determined by the rest of the computer's **circuitry** and **chips**.

Currently the Pentium chip or processor, made by Intel, is the most common CPU though there are many other companies that produce processors for personal computers. Examples are the CPU made by Motorola and AMD.

With faster processors the **clock speed** becomes more important. Compared to some of the first computers which operated at below 30 **megahertz** (MHz) the Pentium chips began at 75 MHz in the late 1990's. Speeds now exceed 3000+ MHz or 3 **gigahertz** (GHz) and different chip manufacturers use different measuring standards (check your local computer store for the latest speed). It depends on the **circuit board** that the chip is housed in, or the **motherboard**, as to whether you are able to upgrade to a faster chip. The motherboard contains the circuitry and connections that allow the various components to communicate with each other.

Though there were many computers using many different processors previous to this I call the 80286 processor the advent of home computers as these were the processors that made computers available for the average person. Using a processor before the 286 involved learning a proprietary system and software. Most new software are being developed for the newest and fastest processors so it can be difficult to use an older computer system.

Keyboard

The keyboard is used to type information into the computer or **input** information. There are many different keyboard layouts and sizes with the most common for Latin based languages being the QWERTY layout (named for the first 6 keys). The standard keyboard has 101 keys. Notebooks have embedded keys accessible by special keys or by pressing key combinations (CTRL or Command and P for example). **Ergonomically** designed keyboards are designed to make typing easier. Hand held devices have various and different keyboard configurations and **touch screens**.

Some of the keys have a special use. They are referred to as command keys. The 3 most common are the Control (CTRL), Alternate (Alt) and the Shift keys though there can be more (the Windows key for example or the Command key). Each key on a standard keyboard has one or two characters. Press the key to get the lower character and hold Shift to get the upper.

Removable Storage and/or Disk Drives

All disks need a **drive** to get information off - or **read** - and put information on the disk - or **write**. Each drive is designed for a specific type of disk whether it is a CD, DVD, hard disk or floppy. Often the term 'disk' and 'drive' are used to describe the same thing but it helps to understand that the disk is the **storage device** which contains computer files - or software - and the drive is the mechanism that runs the disk.

Digital flash drives work slightly differently as they use **memory cards** to store information so there are no moving parts. Digital cameras also use Flash memory cards to store information, in this case photographs. **Hand held devices** use digital drives and many also use removable or built in memory cards.

Mouse

Most modern computers today are run using a mouse controlled pointer. Generally if the mouse has two buttons the left one is used to **select** objects and text and the right one is used to **access menus**. If the mouse has one button (Mac for instance) it controls all the activity and a mouse with a third button can be used by specific software programs.

One type of mouse has a round ball under the bottom of the mouse that rolls and turns two wheels which control the direction of the pointer on the screen. Another type of mouse uses an optical system to track the movement of the mouse. **Laptop** computers use touch pads, buttons and other devices to control the pointer. Hand helds use a combination of devices to control the pointer, including touch screens.

Note: It is important to clean the mouse periodically, particularly if it becomes sluggish. A ball type mouse has a small circular panel that can be opened, allowing you to remove the ball. Lint can be removed carefully with a tooth pick or tweezers and the ball can be washed with mild detergent. A build up will accumulate on the small wheels in the mouse. Use a small instrument or finger nail to scrape it off taking care not to scratch the wheels. Track balls can be cleaned much like a mouse and touch-pad can be wiped with a clean, damp cloth. An optical mouse can accumulate material from the surface that it is in contact with which can be removed with a finger nail or small instrument.

Monitors

The monitor shows information on the screen when you type. This is called **outputting** information. When the computer needs more information it will display a message on the screen, usually through a **dialog box**. Monitors come in many types and sizes. The resolution of the monitor determines the sharpness of the screen. The resolution can be adjusted to control the screen's display..

Most desktop computers use a monitor with a **cathode tube** or **liquid crystal display**. Most notebooks use a liquid crystal display monitor.

To get the full benefit of today's software with full colour graphics and animation, computers need a colour monitor with a display or **graphics** card.

Printers

The printer takes the information on your screen and transfers it to paper or a **hard copy**. There are many different types of printers with various levels of quality. The three basic types of printer are; **dot matrix**, **inkjet**, and **laser**.

- Dot matrix printers work like a typewriter transferring ink from a ribbon to paper with a series or 'matrix' of tiny pins.
- Ink jet printers work like dot matrix printers but fire a stream of ink from a cartridge directly onto the paper.

- Laser printers use the same technology as a photocopier using heat to transfer toner onto paper.

Modem

A modem is used to translate information transferred through telephone lines, cable, satellite or line-of-sight wireless.

The term stands for **modulate and demodulate** which changes the signal from **digital**, which computers use, to **analog**, which telephones use and then back again. **Digital modems** transfer digital information directly without changing to analog.

Modems are measured by the speed that the information is transferred. The measuring tool is called the **baud rate**. Originally modems worked at speeds below 2400 baud but today analog speeds of 56,000 baud are standard. Cable, wireless or digital subscriber lines can transfer information much faster with rates of 300,000 baud and up.

Modems also use **Error Correction** which corrects for transmission errors by constantly checking whether the information was received properly or not and Compression which allows for faster data transfer rates. Information is transferred in **packets**. Each packet is checked for errors and is re-sent if there is an error.

Anyone who has used the Internet has noticed that at times the information travels at different speeds. Depending on the amount of information that is being transferred, the information will arrive at it's destination at different times. The amount of information that can travel through a line is limited. This limit is called **bandwidth**.

There are many more variables involved in communication technology using computers, much of which is covered in the section on the Internet.

Scanners

Scanners allow you to transfer pictures and photographs to your computer. A scanner 'scans' the image from the top to the bottom, one line at a time and transfers it to the computer as a series of bits or a bitmap. You can then take that image and use it in a paint program, send it out as a fax or print it. With optional **Optical Character Recognition** (OCR) software you can convert printed documents such as newspaper articles to text that can be used in your word processor. Most scanners use **TWAIN** software that makes the scanner accessable by other software applications.

Digital cameras allow you to take digital photographs. The images are stored on a memory chip or disk that can be transferred to your computer. Some cameras can also capture sound and video.

Case

The case houses the microchips and circuitry that run the computer. Desktop models usually sit under the monitor and tower models beside. They come in many sizes, including desktop, mini, midi, and full tower. There is usually room inside to expand or add components at a later time. By removing the cover off the case you may find plate covered, empty slots that allow you to add cards. There are various types of slots including IDE, ASI, USB, PCI and Firewire slots.

Depending on the type notebook computers may have room to expand. Most Notebooks also have connections or ports that allows expansion or connection to exterior, peripheral devices such as monitor, portable hard-drives or other devices.

Cards

Cards are components added to computers to increase their capability. When adding a peripheral device make sure that your computer has a slot of the type needed by the device.

Sound cards allow computers to produce sound like music and voice. The older sound cards were 8 bit then 16 bit then 32 bit. Though the human ear can't distinguish the fine difference between sounds produced by the more powerful sound card they allow for more complex music and music production.

Colour cards allow computers to produce colour (with a colour monitor of course). The first colour cards were 2 bit which produced 4 colours [CGA]. It was amazing what could be done with those 4 colours. Next came 4 bit allowing for 16

[EGA and VGA] colours. Then came 16 bit allowing for 1064 colours and then 24 bit which allows for almost 17 million colours and now 32 bit and higher allow monitors to display almost a billion separate colours.

Video cards allow computers to display video and animation. Some video cards allow computers to display television as well as capture frames from video. A video card with a digital video camera allows computers users to produce live video. A high speed connection is required for effective video transmission.

Network cards allow computers to connect together to communicate with each other. Network cards have connections for cable, thin wire or wireless networks for more information.

Cables connect internal components to the **Motherboard**, which is a board with series of electronic path ways and connections allowing the CPU to communicate with the other components of the computer.

Memory

Memory can be very confusing but is usually one of the easiest pieces of hardware to add to your computer. It is common to confuse **chip memory** with disk storage. An example of the difference between memory and storage would be the difference between a table where the actual work is done (memory) and a filing cabinet where the finished product is stored (disk). To add a bit more confusion, the computer's hard disk can be used as **temporary memory** when the program needs more than the chips can provide.

Random Access Memory or **RAM** is the memory that the computer uses to temporarily store the information as it is being processed. The more information being processed the more RAM the computer needs.

One of the first home computers used 64 kilobytes of RAM memory (Commodore 64). Today's modern computers need a minimum of 64 Mb (recommended 128 Mb or more) to run Windows or OS 10 with modern software. RAM memory chips come in many different sizes and speeds and can usually be **expanded**. Older computers came with 512 Kb of memory which could be expanded to a maximum of 640 Kb. In most modern computers the memory can be expanded by adding or replacing the memory chips depending on the processor you have and the type of memory your computer uses. Memory chips range in size from 1 Mb to 4 Gb. As computer technology changes the type of memory changes as well making old memory chips obsolete. Check your computer manual to find out what kind of memory your computer uses before purchasing new memory chips

MULTIPLE CHOICE QUESTIONS

1. Android is a mobile operating system designed primarily for touchscreen mobile devices such as smartphones and tablets. Which among the following was the first Android Operating System?

A. Cupcake B. Alpha
C. Gingerbread D. Doughnut
E. Eclair

2. Which among the following key combinations can be used to search in Windows Explorer?

A. Ctrl + F B. Ctrl + S
C. Ctrl + G D. Alt + S
E. None of the above

3. A router is a networking device that forwards data packets and is connected to two or more data lines from different networks. Which among the following was the earliest device which had almost the same functionality as that of a router?

A. Interface Delay Device
B. Interface Traffic Manager
C. Interface Routing Processor
D. Interface Message Processor
E. Interface Data Manager

4. A vacuum tube (also called a VT, electron tube or, in the UK, a valve) is a device sometimes used to amplify electronic signals. Vacuum Tubes were used in which generation of Computers?

A. 1st Generation B. 2nd Generation
C. 3rd Generation D. 4th Generation
D. 5th Generation

5. In Computer programming API is a set of subroutine definitions, protocols, and tools for building software and applications. Which among the following is an application programming interface for the programm-ing language Java, which defines how a client may access a database?

A. J2EE B. JDK
C. JAVA SE D. JDBC
E. JSX

6. Which of the following errors occurs when software tries to access protected memory?

A. Segmentation Fault
B. Displaytime Error
C. IO Error
D. Runtime Error
E. Zero Division Error

7. Which among the following is a term representing unit of data storage in computer memory?

A. Pixel B. Decimal
C. Octet D. Point
E. Fragment

8. Microsoft PowerPoint is a slide show presentation program for use on both Microsoft and Apple Macintosh operating systems. In MS PowerPoint Broadcast is a feature available in which tab?

A. File B. View
C. Slide Show D. Transitions
E. Review

9. Which among the following carries signals that control the actions of the computer?

A. Control Bus B. Data Bus
C. Memory Unit D. NIC
E. Address Bus

10. Which among the following is not a secondary memory?

A. Cache B. Pen Drive
C. Hard Disk D. Memory Card
E. Memory Stick

11. Which among the following is a cloud computing platform and infrastructure created by Microsoft?

A. Simple Storage Service
B. Atmos
C. Openstack Swift
D. OceanStore
E. Azure

12. After a credit card transaction has been authorized by the issuing bank by sending an authorization code to the merchant, the settlement stage of the process begins. Which of the following is a system type used to process such statements?

A. Multi-tasking B. Memory Processing
C. Level Processing D. Batch Processing
E. Online Processing

13. Assembly is a ______ based low-level language replacing binary machine-code instructions, which are very hard to remember, it is the classic and uncontroversial example of a low level language.

A. Memory B. High Level
C. Key D. Mnemonic
E. FORTRAN

14. China now has more of the world's fastest supercomputers than other countries. Which among the following is a Chinese super-computer?

A. BlueGene/Q system
B. Cray XC30
C. Shaheen II
D. Fujitsu's K
E. Tianhe-2

15. Which among the following is an important circuitry in a computer system that does the arithmetic and logical processing?

A. Memory B. ALU
C. Flag Register D. CU
E. Calculator

16. Which among the following is not a mobile Operating System?

A. Bada
B. Safari
C. Symbian
D. MeeGo
E. WebOS

17. Which among the following key can be used as a shortcut to rename a folder in Microsoft Windows 8 and higher versions?

A. F2
B. F4
C. F6
D. F9
E. F11

18. AT & T designed its first commercial modem, specifically for converting digital computer data to analog for transmission across its long distance network. What is the name of the modem?

A. Telex
B. Memex
C. CompuServe
D. Bell 103 dataset
E. Dataphone

19. Integrated Chips or IC's were started to be in use from which generation of computers?

A. 1st Generation
B. 2nd Generation
C. 3rd Generation
D. 4th Generation
E. 5th Generation

20. In Computer programming there is a set of subroutine definitions, protocols, and tools for building software and applications. Which among the following is a term for sets of requirements that govern how one application can talk to another?

A. UPS
B. API
C. CGI
D. J2EE
E. OLE

21. When you first turn on a computer, the COU is preset to execute instructions stored in ....

A. RAM
B. Flash memory
C. ROM
D. The CD-ROM
E. The ALU

22. Which of the following is **not** a function of the control unit?

A. Read instructions
B. Interpret instructions
C. Execute instructions
D. Direct operations
E. Provide control signals

23. What are .bas, .doc, .htm examples of in computing?

A. Extensions
B. Protocols
C. Databases
D. Other than those given as options
E. Domains

24. Documents converted to .... can be published to the web.

A. a doc file
B. http
C. Other than those given as options
D. machine language
E. HTML

25. What kind of software would you most likely use to keep track of a billing account?

A. Web authoring
B. electronic publishing
C. spreadsheet
D. word processing
E. Power point

26. A computer virus normally attaches itself to another computer program known as a ....

A. host program
B. target program
C. backdoor program
D. Bluetooth
E. Trojan horse

27. When a file contains instructions that can be carried out by the computer. It is often called a(n) .... file.

A. Other than those given as options
B. information
C. application
D. executable
E. data

28. Data duplication wastes the space, but also promotes a more serious problem called ....

A. Isolated data
B. Data inconsistency
C. Other than those given as options
D. Program dependency
E. Separated data

29. Which of the following is **not** a version of the Windows operating system software for the PC?

A. ME B. 98
C. XP D. 10
E. 95

30. The main directory of a disk is called the .... directory.

A. network B. folder
C. root D. File
E. Other than those given as options

31. Which of the following is **not** an example of application software?

A. Word processing software
B. Spreadsheet software
C. Operating system software
D. Database software
E. Graphics software

32. Which of the following is **not** true about RAM?

A. RAM is the same as hard disk storage
B. RAM is a temporary storage area
C. RAM is volatile
D. RAM is a primary memory
E. All are true

33. The data storage hierarchy consists of ....

A. Bits, Bytes, Records, Fields, files and databases
B. Characters, fields, records, files and databases
C. Bytes, bits, fields, records, files and databases
D. Bits, bytes, fields, records, files and databases
E. Other than those given as options

34. = Sum (B1 B0) is an example of a ....

A. function B. cell address
C. formula D. value
E. Other than those given as options

35. .... are often delivered to a PC through an email attachment and are often designed to do harm.

A. Portals
B. Spam
C. Viruses
D. Other than those given as options
E. E-mail messages

36. Decreasing the amount of space required to store data and programs is accomplished by ....

A. Crashing B. Disk caching
C. RAID D. file compression
E. Other than those given as options

37. What is the difference between a CD-ROM and CD-RW?

A. They are the same –just two different terms used by different manufacturers
B. A CD-Rom can be written to and a CD-RW cannot
C. Other than those given as options
D. A CD-ROM holds more information than a CD-RW
E. A CD-RW can be written to but a CD-ROM can only be read from

38. Computer program are written in a high-level programming language, however, the human readable version of a program is called ....

A. word size B. source code
C. instruction set D. Read & Write code
E. None of these

39. The clock rate of a processor is measured in ....

A. megabytes or gigabytes
B. milliseconds
C. megahertz or gigahertz
D. nanoseconds
E. micro hertz

40. When cutting and pasting, the item cut is temporarily stored in the ....

A. dashboard B. ROM
C. hard drive D. Diskette
E. clipboard

41. Copying the Excel 2007 formula = SUM (A1:A5) from cell A6 to cell B6 will result in what formula for cell B6?

A. = SUM (B6:A6)
B. < SUM (A1:B6)
C. = SUM (B1:A5)

D. > SUM (B1:B5)
E. Other than those given as options

42. RAM is used as a short memory because it—
A. has small capacity B. is very expensive
C. is programmable D. volatile
E. not very useful

43. The Num Lock Key and Caps Lock Key are considered .... because their function changes each time you press them.
A. toggle B. dual
C. function D. cursor control
E. control

44. OLE stands for—
A. Offline Linking and Embedding
B. Online Link Emulation
C. Object Link Export
D. Object Linking and Embedding
E. Online Link Embedding

45. Microsoft Word is an example of—
A. Application software
B. An input device
C. System software
D. A processing system
E. An operating system

46. Which of the following is not an example of an output device?
A. Speaker B. Plotter
C. Microphone D. Printer
E. Monitor

47. The digital telecommunications, termed as ISDN is an abbreviation for—
A. Interactive Standard Dynamic Networks
B. Integrated Standard Digital Networks
C. Internet Services Data Network
D. International Services Data Network
E. Integrated Services Digital Network

48. Which of the following places the common data elements in order to the smallest from the largest?
A. Character, file, field, record, database
B. Character, field, record, file, database
C. Character, record, field, database, file
D. Character, file, record, field, database
E. Character, field, record, database, file

49. Software made freely available to the public by the publisher is called—
A. Fair use
B. Compact disc
C. Freeware
D. Process ware
E. Copyright

50. A web site's own unique Internet address that no other web site can use is its—
A. Search Engine B. FTP
C. URL D. WWW
E. IP v 6

51. The windows shortcut to delete an item permanently is—
A. Shift + Delete B. Shift + F1
C. Ctrl + F1 D. Ctrl + F2
E. Shift + F2

52. WAN is a type of computer network. It stands for—
A. Wireless Array Network
B. Wild Area Network
C. Wide Access Network
D. Wide Area Network
E. Wireless Area Network

53. Which of the following is a type for intercepting computer communications?
A. Hacking B. Sniffing
C. Pretexting D. Spoofing
E. Phishing

54. Which key allows movement from one cell of a table to the next?
A. Shift B. CTRL
C. Esc D. Tab
E. ALT

55. Pressing the .... key will make the number pad act as directional arrows.
A. Caps lock B. Arrow lock
C. Shift D. Esc
E. Num lock

56. The most widely used device in communication is a —
A. Coprocessor B. Channel
C. Bus D. Modem
E. Scanner

57. Codes consisting of light and dark marks which may be optically read is known as—
A. Mnemonics B. Stripe-code
C. Decoder D. Special-code
E. Bar code

58. Which of the following is not a type of data storage media?
A. Magnetic Tape B. A Database
C. Hard Disc D. Optical Disc
E. Magnetic Disc

59. Compiler means—
A. A program which translates source code into object program
B. Keypunch Operator
C. A person who compiles source programs
D. The same thing as a programmer
E. Computer data operator

60. Which of the following is operating system software?
A. Microsoft Access
B. Microsoft Windows
C. Microsoft Power Point
D. Microsoft Excel
E. Microsoft Word

61. Reusable optical storage will typically have the acronym ....
A. CD B. DVD
C. ROM D. RW
E. None of these

62. .... is processed by the computer into information.
A. Data B. Numbers
C. Alphabets D. Pictures
E. None of these

63. A .... is an electronic device that process data, converting it into information.
A. computer B. processor
C. case D. stylus
E. None of these

64. File extensions are used in order to
A. name the file
B. ensure the filename is not lost
C. identify the file
D. identify the file type
E. None of these

65. The most common type of storage devices are ....
A. persistent B. optical
C. magnetic D. flash
E. None of these

66. "GUI" stands for ....
A. Gnutella Universal Interface
B. Graphical User Interface
C. Graphic Uninstall/Install
D. General Utility Interface
E. None of these

67. A .... is a design tool that graphically shows the logic in a solution algorithm.
A. flowchart B. hierarchy chart
C. structure chart D. context diagram
E. None of these

68. A file that contains definitions of the paragraph and character styles for your document and all things you customised toolbars and menus is called a ....
A. guide B. pattern
C. base document D. template
E. None of these

69. Programs designed specifically to address general-purpose applications and special-purpose applications are called ....
A. operating system
B. system software
C. application software
D. Management information systems
E. None of these

70. A.......... contains buttons and menus that provide quick access to commonly used commands.
A. toolbar B. menu bar
C. window D. find
E. None of these

71. .... has invented the mechanical calculator for adding numbers
A. Charles Babbage B. Newton
C. Pascal D. Peano
E. E.F. Codd

72. A unit of hardware used to monitor the computer processing
A. Terminal B. Console

C. CPU D. Server
E. Client

73. Which of these is not a feature of a reentrant procedure
A. multiple users can share a single copy of a program during the same period
B. The program code can modify itself
C. The local data for each user process must be stored separately
D. the permanent part is the code
E. the temporary part is the pointer back to the calling program and local variables used by that program

74. What is the split-MAC architecture
A. The split-MAC architecture uses MAC addresses to create a forward/filter table and break up broadcast domains
B. The split-MAC architecture uses MAC addresses on the wireless network and IP addresses on the wired network
C. The split-MAC architecture allows the splitting of 802.11 protocol packets between the AP and the controller to allow processing by both devices
D. The split-MAC architecture uses MAC addresses to create a forward/filter table and break up collision domains
E. All of these

75. In .... normal form, all non-key fields of data structure are dependent on the whole key
A. First B. Second
C. Third D. Fourth
E. Fifth

76. For selecting or highlighting, which of the following is generally used?
A. Icon B. Keyboard
C. Mouse D. Floppy Disk
E. None of these

77. What does storage unit provide?
A. Place for typing data
B. Storage for information and instruction
C. Place for printing information
D. All of the above
E. None of these

78. Which type of memory is closely related to processor?
A. Main Memory
B. Secondary Memory
C. Disk Memory
D. Tape Memory
E. None of these

79. Which device is used to access your computer by other computer or for talk over phone?
A. RAM B. CD ROM Drive
C. Modem D. Hard Drive
E. None of these

80. Permanent Memory in computer is called
A. RAM B. ROM
C. CPU D. CD ROM
E. None of these

81. .... allows users to upload files to an online site so they can be viewed and edited from another location.
A. General-purpose application
B. Microsoft Outlook
C. Web-hosted technology
D. Office Live
E. None of these

82. What feature adjusts the top and bottom margins so that the text is centered vertically on the printed page?
A. Vertical justifying
B. Vertical adjusting
C. Dual centering
D. Horizontal centering
E. Vertical centering

83. Which of these is **not** a means of personal communication on the internet?
A. chat B. instant messaging
C. instanotes D. electronic mail
E. None of these

84. What is the overall term for creating, editing, formating, storing, retrieving, and printing a text document?
A. Word processing
B. Spreadsheet design
C. Web design
D. Database management
E. Presentation generation

85. Fourth-generation mobile technology provides enhanced capabilities allowing the transfer of both .... data, including full-motion video, high-speed internet access, and video-conferencing.
A. video data and information
B. voice and nonvoice
C. music and video
D. video and audio
E. None of these

86. .... is a form of denial of service attack in which a hostile client repeatedly sends SYN packets to every port on the server using fake IP addresses.
A. Cybergaming crime
B. Memory shaving
C. Syn flooding
D. Software piracy
E. None of these

87. Which of these is a point-and-draw device?
A. mouse B. scanner
C. printer D. CD-ROM
E. keyboard

88. The letter and number of the intersecting column and row is the—
A. cell location
B. cell position
C. cell address
D. cell coordinates
E. cell contents

89. A set of rules for telling the computer what operations to perform is called a—
A. procedural language
B. structures
C. natural language
D. command language
E. programming language

90. A detailed written description of the programming cycle and the program, along with the test results and a printout of the program is called—
A. documentation B. output
C. reporting D. spec sheets
E. Directory

91. Forms that are used to organize business data into rows and columns are called—
A. transaction sheets B. registers
C. business forms D. sheet-spreads
E. spreadsheets

92. In Power Point, the Header & Footer button can be found on the Insert tab in what group?
A. Illustrations group B. Object group
C. Text group D. Tables group
E. None of these

93. A(n) .... is a set of programs designed to manage the resources of a computer, including starting the computer, managing programs, managing memory and coordinating tasks between input and output devices.
A. application suite
B. compiler
C. input/output system
D. interface
E. operating system (OS)

94. A typical slide in a slide presentation would **not** include—
A. photo images charts and graphs
B. graphs and clip art
C. clip art and audio clips
D. full-motion video
E. content templates

95. The PC productivity tool that manipulates data organized in rows and columns is called a—
A. spreadsheet
B. word processing document
C. presentation mechanism
D. database record manager
E. EDI creator

96. In the absence of parentheses, the order of operation is—
A. Exponentiation, addition or subtraction, multiplication or division
B. Addition or subtraction, multiplication or division, exponentiation
C. Multiplication or division, exponentiation, addition or subtraction
D. Exponentiation, multiplication or division, addition or subtraction
E. Addition or subtraction, exponentiation, Multiplication or division

97. To find the Paste Special option, you use the Clipboard group on the ...... tab of PowerPoint.
A. Design B. Slide Show
C. Page Layout D. Insert
E. Home

98. Which view display miniature images of photographs within a folder?
A. Tiles view and Icons view
B. Thumbnails view and Filmstrip view
C. Details view and List view
D. All views display a miniature image
E. None of these

99. Usually downloaded into folders that hold temporary internet files, ... are written to your computer's hard disk by some of the Web sites you visit.
A. anonymous files B. behaviour files
C. banner ads D. large files
E. cookies

100. What is the easiest way to change the phrase, revenues, profits, gross margin, to read revenues, profit and gross margin?
A. Use the insert mode, position the cursor before the g in gross, then type the word and followed by a space
B. Use the insert mode, position the cursor after the g in gross, then type the word and followed by a space
C. Use the overtype mode, position the cursor before the g in gross, then type the word and followed by a space
D. Use the overtype mode, position the cursor after the g in gross, then type the word and followed by a space
E. None of these

101. A program, either talk or music, that is made available in digital format for automatic download over the internet is called a —
A. wiki B. broadcast
C. vodcast D. blog
E. podcast

102. Which PowerPoint view displays each slide of the presentation as a thumbnail and is useful for rearranging slides?
A. Slide Sorter B. Slide Show
C. Slide Master D. Notes Page
E. Slide Design

103. Different components on the motherboard of a PC unit are linked together by sets of parallel electrical conducting lines. What are these lines called?
A. Conductors B. Buses
C. Connectors D. Consecutives
E. None of these

104. What is the name given to those applications that combine text, sound, graphics, motion video, and/or animation?
A. motionware B. anigraphics
C. videoscapes D. multimedia
E. maxomedia

105. A USB communication device that supports data encryption for secure wireless communication for notebook users is called a—
A. USB wireless network adapter
B. wireless switch
C. wireless hub
D. router
E. None of these

106. A(n) .... language reflects the way people think mathematically.
A. cross-platform programming
B. 3GL business programming
C. event-driven programming
D. functional
E. None of these

107. When entering text within a document, the Enter key is normally pressed at the end of every—
A. Line B. Sentence
C. Paragraph D. Word
E. File

108. When a real-time telephone call between people is made over the Internet using computers, it is called—
A. a chat session
B. an e-mail
C. an instant message
D. Internet telephony
E. None of these

109. Which of the following is the first step in sizing a window?
A. Point to the title bar
B. Pull down the View menu to display the toolbar
C. Point to any corner or border
D. Pull down the View menu and change to large icons
E. None of these

110. Which of the following software could assist someone who **cannot** use their hands for computer input?
A. Video conferencing
B. Speech recognition
C. Audio digitizer
D. Synthesizer
E. None of these

111. .... a document means the file is transferred from another computer to your computer.
A. Uploading
B. Really Simple Syndication (RSS)
C. Accessing
D. Downloading
E. Upgrading

112. Which computer memory is used for storing programs and data currently being processed by the CPU?
A. Mass memory
B. Internal memory
C. Non-volatile memory
D. PROM
E. None of these

113. Computers that control processes accept data in a continuous—
A. data traffic pattern
B. data highway
C. infinite loop
D. feedback loop
E. slot

114. What refers to a set of characters of a particular design?
A. keyface B. formation
C. calligraph D. stencil
E. typeface

115. .... is used by public and private enterprises to publish and share financial information with each other and industry analysts across all computer platforms and the Internet.
A. Extensible Markup Language (EML)
B. Extensible Business Reporting Language (XBRL)
C. Enterprise Application Integration (EAI)
D. Sales Force Automation (SFA) software
E. None of these

116. Which part of the computer is used for calculating and comparing?
A. ALU B. Control unit
C. Disk unit D. Modem
E. None of these

117. The method of Internet access that requires a phone line, but offers faster access speeds than dial-up is the .... connection.
A. cable access
B. satellite access
C. fibre-optic service
D. Digital Subscriber Line (DSL)
E. modem

118. .... software creats a mirror image of the entire hard disk, including the operating system, application, files and data.
A. Operating system B. Backup software
C. Utility programs D. Driver imaging
E. None of these

119. What is a URL?
A. a computer software program
B. a type of programming object
C. the address of a document or "page" on the World Wide Web
D. an acronym for Unlimited Resources for Learning
E. a piece of hardware

120. What is the significance of a faded (dimmed) command in a pull-down menu?
A. The command is not currently accessible
B. A dialog box appears if the command is selected
C. A Help window appears if the command is selected

D. There are no equivalent keystrokes for the particular command
E. None of these

121. Your business has contracted with another company to have them host and run an application for your company over the Internet. The company providing this service to your business is called an —
A. Internet service provider
B. Internet access provider
C. Application service provider
D. Application access provider
E. Outsource agency

122. A(n) .... allows you to access you e-mail from anywhere.
A. Forum
B. Webmail interface
C. Message Board
D. Weblog
E. None of these

123. Which of the following would you find on LinkedIn?
A. Games B. Connections
C. Chat D. Applications
E. None of these

124. .... is a technique that is used to send more than one call over a single line.
A. Digital transmission
B. Infrared transmission
C. Digitizing
D. Streaming
E. Multiplexing

125. The Search Companion can —
A. Locate all files containing a specified phrase
B. Restrict its search to a specified set of folders
C. Locate all files containing a specified phrase and restrict its search to a specified set of folders
D. Cannot locate all files containing a specified phrase or restrict its search to a specified set of folders
E. None of these

126. Which of the following **cannot** be part of an e-mail address?
A. Period (.) B. At sign (@)
C. Space ( ) D. Underscore (_)
E. None of these

127. Which of the following must be contained in a URL?
A. a protocol identifier
B. the letters, www.
C. the unique registered domain name
D. www. and the unique registered domain name
E. a protocol identifier, www. and the unique registered domain name

128. Which of the following information systems focuses on making manufacturing processes more efficient and of higher quality?
A. Computer-aided manufacturing
B. Computer-integrated manufacturing
C. Computer-aided software engineering
D. Computer-aided system engineering
E. None of these

129. A mistake in an algorithm that causes **incorrect** results is called a—
A. logical error B. syntax error
C. procedural error D. compiler error
E. machine error

130. Unsolicited e-mail is known as—
A. spam B. bologna
C. RAMJAM D. ham
E. None of these

131. To change selected text to all capital letters, click the change case button, then click ....
A. UPPERCASE B. UPPER ALL
C. CAPS LOCK D. Lock Upper
E. Large Size

132. A person who used his or her expertise to gain access to other people's computers to get information illegally or do damage is a ......
A. hacker
B. analyst
C. instant messenger
D. programmer
E. spammer

133. A device that connects to a network without the use of cables is said to be ......
A. distributed B. free
C. centralized D. open source
E. None of these

134. Non-physical components of the computer are referred to as
A. CPU B. software
C. hardware D. program
E. None of these

135. The most common type of storage devices are ....
A. persistent B. optical
C. magnetic D. flash
E. steel

136. Codes consisting of lines of varying widths or lengths that are computer-readable are known as–
A. an ASCII code
B. a magnetic tape
C. an OCR scanner
D. a bar code
E. None of these

137. A Web site's main page is called its–
A. Home Page
B. Browser Page
C. Search Page
D. Bookmark
E. None of these

138. Part number, part description, and number of parts ordered are examples of–
A. control B. output
C. processing D. feedback
E. input

139. To access properties of an object, the mouse technique to use is–
A. dragging B. dropping
C. right-clicking D. shift-clicking
E. None of these

140. Computers use the .... number system to store data and perform calculations.
A. binary B. octal
C. decimal D. hexadecimal
E. None of these

141. .... are attempts by individuals to obtain confidential information from you by falsifying their identity.
A. Phishing trips B. Computer viruses
C. Spyware scams D. Viruses
E. Phishing scams

142. Why is it unethical to share copyrighted files with your friends?
A. It is not unethical, because it is legal.
B. It is unethical because the files are being given for free.
C. Sharing copyrighted files without permission breaks copyright laws.
D. It is not unethical because the files are being given for free.
E. It is not unethical—anyone can access a computer.

143. Which of the following can be used to select the entire document?
A. CTRL + A B. ALT + F5
C. SHIFT + A D. CTRL + K
E. CTRL + H

144. To instruct Word to fit the width of a column to the contents of a table automatically, click the .... button and then point to AutoFit Contents.
A. Fit to Form B. Format
C. Autosize D. Contents
E. AutoFit

145. The simultaneous processing of two or more programs by multiple processors is–
A. multiprogramming B. multitasking
C. time-sharing D. multiprocessing
E. None of these

146. A disk's content that is recorded at the time of manufacture and that cannot be changed or erased by the user is–
A. memory-only B. write-only
C. once-only D. run-only
E. read-only

147. What is the permanent memory built into your computer called?
A. RAM B. Floppy
C. CPU D. CD-ROM
E. ROM

148. The default view in Excel is .... view.
A. Work B. Auto
C. Normal D. Roman
E. None of these

149. What displays the contents of the active cell in Excel?
A. Namebox B. RowHeadings
C. Formulabar D. Taskpane
E. None of these

150. In Word you can force a page break–
A. By positioning your cursor at the appropriate place and pressing the F1 key
B. By positioning your cursor at the appropriate place and pressing Ctrl+Enter
C. By using the Insert/Section Break
D. By changing the font size of your document
E. None of these

151. Grouping and processing all of a firm's transactions at one time is called–
A. a database management system
B. batch processing
C. a real-time system
D. an on-line system
E. None of these

152. Help Menu is available at which button?
A. End B. Start
C. Turn off D. Restart
E. Reboot

153. You can keep your personal files/folders in–
A. My Folder B. My Documents
C. My Files D. My Text
E. None of these

154. A central computer that holds collections of data and programs for many PCs, workstations, and other computers is a(n) –
A. supercomputer B. minicomputer
C. laptop D. server
E. None of these

155. When you save to this, your data will remain intact even when the computer is turned off–
A. RAM
B. motherboard
C. secondary storage device
D. primary storage device
E. None of these

156. The .... folder retains copies of messages that you have started but are not yet ready to send.
A. Drafts B. Outbox
C. Address Book D. Sent Items
E. Inbox

157. You can.........a search by providing more information the search engine can use to select a smaller, more useful set of results.
A. refine B. expand
C. load D. query
E. slowdown

158. The contents of .... are lost when the computer turns off.
A. storage B. input
C. output D. memory
E. None of these

159. The .... enables you to simultaneously keep multiple Web pages open in one browser window.
A. tab box B. pop-up helper
C. tab row D. address bar
E. Esc key

160. A DVD is an example of a(n) –
A. hard disk
B. optical disc
C. output device
D. solid-state storage device
E. None of these

161. The basic unit of a worksheet into which you enter data in Excel is called a ....
A. tab B. cell
C. box D. range
E. None of these

162. .... is the process of dividing the disk into tracks and sectors.
A. Tracking
B. Formatting
C. Crashing
D. Allotting
E. None of these

163. Which ports connect special types of music instruments to sound cards?
A. BUS B. CPU
C. USB D. MIDI
E. MINI

164. The process of transferring files from a computer on the Internet to your computer is called ....
A. downloading B. uploading
C. FTP D. JPEG
E. downsizing

165. In Excel, ... allows users to bring together copies of work books that other users have worked on independently.
A. Copying B. Merging
C. Pasting D. Compiling
E. None of these

166. If you want to connect to your own computer through the Internet from another location, you can use–
A. e-mail B. FTP
C. instant message D. Telnet
E. None of these

167. To reload a Web page, press the .... button.
A. Redo B. Reload
C. Restore D. Ctrl
E. Refresh

168. Mobile Commerce is best described as–
A. The use of Kiosks in marketing
B. Transporting products
C. Buying and selling goods/services through wireless handheld devices
D. Using notebook PC's in marketing
E. None of the above

169. Video processors consist of .... and ...., which store and process images.
A. CPU and VGA B. CPU and memory
C. VGA and memory D. VGI and DVI
E. None of these

170. .... are words that a programming language has set aside for its own use.
A. Control words B. Control structures
C. Reserved words D. Reserved keys
E. None of these

171. What is the process of copying software programs from secondary storage media to the hard disk called?
A. configuration B. download
C. storage D. upload
E. installation

172. This first step in the transaction processing cycle captures business data through various modes such as optical scanning or at an electronic commerce website–
A. Document and report generation
B. Database maintenance
C. Transaction processing start-up
D. Data Entry
E. None of these

173. When the pointer is positioned on a ...., it is shaped like a hand.
A. Grammar error B. Formatting error
C. ScreenTip D. Spelling error
E. Hyperlink

174. The computer abbreviation KB usually means–
A. Key Block B. Kernel Boot
C. Key Byte D. Kit Bit
E. Kilo Byte

175. Which of the following are advantages of CD-ROM as a storage media?
A. CD-ROM is an inexpensive way to store large amount of data and information
B. CD-ROM disks retrieve data and information more quickly than magnetic disks do
C. CD-ROMs make less errors than magnetic media
D. All of the above
E. None of the above

176. A(n) ....is a special visual and audio effect applied in PowerPoint to text or content.
A. animation B. flash
C. wipe D. dissolve
E. None of these

177. Which of the following is a storage device that uses rigid, permanently installed magnetic disks to store data/information–
A. floppy diskette B. hard disk

C. permanent disk D. optical disk
E. None of these

178. The piece of hardware that converts your computer's digital signal to an analog signal that can travel over telephone lines is called a–
A. red wire B. blue cord
C. tower D. modem
E. None of these

179. Personal computers can be connected together to form a–
A. server B. supercomputer
C. network D. enterprise
E. None of these

180. A .... is the term used when a search engine returns a Web page that matches the search criteria.
A. blog B. hit
C. link D. view
E. success

181. What type of resource is most likely to be a shared common resource in a computer network?
A. Printers
B. Speaker
C. Floppy disk drives
D. Keyboards
E. None of these

182. Example of non-numeric data is ....
A. Employee address B. Examination score
C. Bank balance D. All of these
E. None of these

183. ....represents raw facts, whereas .... is data made meaningful.
A. Information, reporting
B. Data, information
C. Information, bits
D. Records, bytes
E. Bits, bytes

184. A word in a web page that, when clicked, opens another document ....
A. Anchor B. URL
C. Hyperlink D. Reference
E. None of these

185. A computer cannot "boot" if it does not have the ....
A. Compiler B. Loader
C. Operating System D. Assembler
E. None of these

186. What characteristic of read-only memory (ROM) makes it useful?
A. ROM information can be easily updated
B. Data in ROM is nonvolatile, that is, it remains there even without electrical power
C. ROM provides very large amounts of inexpensive data storage
D. ROM chips are easily swapped between different brands of computers
E. None of these

187. Which of the following refers to a small, single-site network?
A. LAN B. DSL
C. RAM D. USB
E. CPU

188. Which keystroke will take you at the beginning or the end of a long document?
A. Ctrl + PageUp and Ctrl + PageDown
B. Shift + Home and Shift + End
C. Ctrl + Home and Ctrl + End
D. The only way is by using the right scroll bar
E. None of these

189. Coded entries which are used to gain access to a computer system are called ....
A. Entry codes B. Passwords
C. Security commands D. Code words
E. None of these

190. In Word you can force a page break ....
A. By positioning your cursor at the appropriate place and pressing the F1 key
B. By using the Insert/Section Break
C. By positioning your cursor at the appropriate place and pressing Ctrl+Enter
D. By changing the font size of your document
E. None of these

ANSWERS

1	2	3	4	5	6	7	8	9	10
B	A	D	A	D	A	C	C	A	A
11	**12**	**13**	**14**	**15**	**16**	**17**	**18**	**19**	**20**
E	D	D	E	B	B	A	E	C	B
21	**22**	**23**	**24**	**25**	**26**	**27**	**28**	**29**	**30**
C	D	A	E	C	E	D	B	A	C
31	**32**	**33**	**34**	**35**	**36**	**37**	**38**	**39**	**40**
C	A	D	C	C	D	E	B	C	E
41	**42**	**43**	**44**	**45**	**46**	**47**	**48**	**49**	**50**
A	D	A	D	A	C	E	B	C	C
51	**52**	**53**	**54**	**55**	**56**	**57**	**58**	**59**	**60**
A	D	B	D	B	D	E	B	A	B
61	**62**	**63**	**64**	**65**	**66**	**67**	**68**	**69**	**70**
D	A	A	D	B	B	A	D	C	A
71	**72**	**73**	**74**	**75**	**76**	**77**	**78**	**79**	**80**
C	B	B	D	D	C	B	A	C	B
81	**82**	**83**	**84**	**85**	**86**	**87**	**88**	**89**	**90**
C	E	C	A	B	C	A	C	E	A
91	**92**	**93**	**94**	**95**	**96**	**97**	**98**	**99**	**100**
E	C	E	E	A	D	E	B	E	A
101	**102**	**103**	**104**	**105**	**106**	**107**	**108**	**109**	**110**
E	A	B	D	A	D	C	D	C	B
111	**112**	**113**	**114**	**115**	**116**	**117**	**118**	**119**	**120**
D	B	D	E	B	A	D	B	C	A
121	**122**	**123**	**124**	**125**	**126**	**127**	**128**	**129**	**130**
E	B	B	E	C	C	C	B	A	A
131	**132**	**133**	**134**	**135**	**136**	**137**	**138**	**139**	**140**
A	A	E	B	C	D	A	E	C	A
141	**142**	**143**	**144**	**145**	**146**	**147**	**148**	**149**	**150**
A	C	A	A	D	E	E	C	C	B
151	**152**	**153**	**154**	**155**	**156**	**157**	**158**	**159**	**160**
C	B	B	D	D	A	A	B	C	B
161	**162**	**163**	**164**	**165**	**166**	**167**	**168**	**169**	**170**
B	B	C	A	B	D	E	C	C	C
171	**172**	**173**	**174**	**175**	**176**	**177**	**178**	**179**	**180**
E	D	C	E	D	A	B	D	C	C
181	**182**	**183**	**184**	**185**	**186**	**187**	**188**	**189**	**190**
A	A	B	C	C	B	A	A	B	C

●●●

ENGLISH LANGUAGE

1. Comprehension Passages

ENGLISH LANGUAGE COMPREHENSION

The objective of language comprehension test is to ascertain the ability of the candidates to understand the passage properly. Therefore candidates are required to take notice of the following points:

1. Read the full passage very attentively and intelligently.
2. Try to comprehend the gist of it.
3. Make a mental note of all the important details and points given in the passage.
4. Read the passage for the second time in case you have not been able to understand it satisfactorily.
5. Divide the time proportionately for all the passages.
6. Answer the questions on the basis of facts, as given in the paragraph.
7. Don't waste much time in answering the questions of any one passage.
8. Check all the answers once again, very carefully, to see whether any question is left unanswered by mistake.

MODEL QUESTIONS (FOR PRACTICE)

Directions: *Each of the following passages is followed by five questions. Read the passage carefully and then answer the questions that follow each. For each question, four probable answers A, B, C and D are given. Only one out of these is correct. Choose the correct answer.*

PASSAGE-1

The use of words like 'welcome', 'thank you', 'please', etc., at the right moment reflects a polite nature. The civic sense also lies within the scope of good manners. We should not shout or talk loudly in public places like hospitals and libraries and create disturbance. We should not cheat people or make fun of them. Cleanliness is also necessary. We must not throw the waste on roads and make use of dustbins. We should not harm the public property as it belongs to all of us. While in a queue, discipline should be maintained. We must give fair chance to others.

1. Expressions like 'welcome' 'thank you' and 'please' reflect
   A. happiness B. discipline
   C. civic sense D. polite nature
2. While in a library, we should
   A. respect others B. avoid arguments
   C. talk in low tone D. be courteous
3. A public property belongs to
   A. nobody
   B. all of us
   C. government
   D. one who maintains it

4. Discipline is
   A. the rule of proper conduct or action
   B. the rule of road sense
   C. making use of dustbins
   D. forming a queue
5. The most appropriate title for this passage would be
   A. Polite Nature
   B. Courtesy
   C. Good Manners
   D. Civic Sense

PASSAGE-2

There is an old proverb 'Early to bed and early to rise makes a man healthy and wise.' I am in the habit of getting up early in the morning and have formed the habit of taking long morning walks in the past two years. It is a light exercise and best for physical fitness. The morning air which is fresh and pure is beneficial for the lungs. The early rays of the rising sun are good for healthy skin. 'Health is wealth' and doctors also recommend morning walk to their patients for gaining sound health and freshness of energy.

1. What is good for lungs?
   A. Sunrays B. Fresh air
   C. Sound sleep D. Light exercise
2. What is a light exercise?
   A. Early to bed
   B. Early to rise
   C. Morning walk
   D. Gaining sound health
3. What is good for skin?
   A. Fresh air
   B. Morning air
   C. Morning walk
   D. Rising sun's rays
4. What is best for physical fitness?
   A. Light exercise
   B. Long morning walk
   C. Early to rise
   D. Fresh and pure air
5. Long morning walk
   A. bring sound sleep
   B. ensures physical fitness
   C. ensures healthy skin
   D. keeps healthy, wealthy and wise

PASSAGE-3

Mahatma Gandhi lived a splendid long life and has set great moral standards before us. He showed to the world the true way to peace. He wished to see India prosper but he became a martyr for the noble cause of Hindu-Muslim unity at the time of partition when a religious fanatic, Nathuram Godse, shot him dead on January 30, 1948. His last words were 'Hey Ram'. He lived and died for his country and countryman.

1. Mahatma Gandhi showed the world the true way to
   A. prosperity B. love
   C. truth D. peace
2. Mahatma Gandhi became a martyr for the noble cause of
   A. truth
   B. non-violence
   C. freedom of India
   D. Hindu-Muslim unity
3. Mahatma Gandhi was shot dead
   A. before India achieved independence
   B. by a mad man
   C. by an intolerant religious person
   D. by a non-religious person
4. Mahatma Gandhi set great moral standards. It means
   A. he was a great religious teacher
   B. he was a great moralist
   C. he made India morally stronger
   D. moral was everything to him
5. Gandhiji lived and died for his country and countryman. It means
   A. he was born in India and died in India
   B. he was a patriot
   C. he was a great moralist
   D. he sacrified his life for India and her people

PASSAGE-4

On one hot day a crow felt very thirsty. He flew from one place to another in search of water. After long hours of labour he found a pitcher. Eagerly, he perched on the mouth of the pitcher. He found that the water was at the bottom of the vessel. He tried his best to dip his beak but did not succeed. He did not know what to do. Suddenly some pebbles lying nearby gave him an idea. One by one he dropped the pebbles with his beak into the pitcher. The level of water slowly came up to the mouth of the pitcher. The crow then drank the water and quenched his thirst.

1. The crow found a pitcher
A. as it flew
B. after many hours of labour
C. full of water
D. which was empty

2. What is the moral of the passage?
A. No pains, no gains
B. God helps those who help themselves
C. Necessity is the mother of invention
D. Try and try again, you will succeed at last

3. The crow flew from place to place
A. in search of pitcher
B. in search of pebbles
C. in search of water
D. in search of a vessel

4. The pitcher, the crow found
A. was full of water
B. was dry
C. had little water in the bottom
D. had water up to its mouth

5. As the crow dropped pebbles into the pitcher, what happend?
A. The pitcher broke down
B. The water leaked one of the pitcher
C. The level of water into the pitcher rose up slowly
D. Water level immediately rose to the mouth of the pitcher

PASSAGE-5

Once upon a time a crane and a fox lived in a forest. They were good friend. One day the fox invited the crane to a feast. He made a tasty food and served it before the crane on a plate. The crane could not eat anything because of the long beak. But the fox licked all his food. The crane felt insulted. He decided to teach the fox a lesson. Next day he invited the fox. He prepared the same tasty food and placed it in front of the fox inside a narrow glass. The crane ate easily while the fox looked on. Now, it was the fox's turn to remain hungry.

1. What is the moral of the passage?
A. Beware of the wicked
B. One good turn deserves another
C. Be contented with what you have
D. Tit for tat

2. The crane could not eat tasty food because the
A. food was served in a shallow plate
B. food was very hot
C. food was served in a long jar
D. crane was not hungry

3. The fox had to remain hungry because
A. the food served was not enough in quantity
B. the food was served inside a narrow glass
C. the food served was not tasty
D. the food was all liquid

4. Why did the crane feel insulted?
A. Because he was invited to feast but he could not eat anything
B. Because the food was served in a shallow plate and he could not eat
C. Because the food was too hot
D. Because the fox gulped all the food quickly

5. The crane successfully taught a lesson to the fox when he invited the fox to a feast and served the food
A. in a narrow glass
B. in a large plate
C. in a broken plate
D. in a long jar

PASSAGE-6

The family set down at the table and began to talk about the summer holidays. They had to decide a place to visit during the vacation. Should they go to their village or to a hill station? The parents preferred the village while the children wished to go the hill station. After few moments of discussion the elders decided to visit both the places. First they shall go to the village for a week and then stay at the hill station for the remaining days. For the first time the family shall be together during the holidays. The children were happy with the holiday plan.

1. The purpose for which the family set down at the table was
   A. to decide a place to visit during the vacation
   B. to educate the children how to carry articles during a visit to a hill station
   C. to decide the date when they should start their journey
   D. to tell the children that they will visit a hill station during this vacation
2. The final plan was to visit
   A. their village
   B. a hill station
   C. their village as well as a hill station
   D. their home town
3. The final decision was made by
   A. the boys B. the girls
   C. the women D. the elders
4. They decided first to go to their village and stay there for
   A. a day B. a week
   C. ten days D. a fortnight
5. Why were children happy?
   A. Because a hill station was included in their holiday plan
   B. Because a visit to their village was excluded from their holiday plan
   C. Because their choice prevailed
   D. Because they were going all alone to the hill station

PASSAGE-7

Once Govind intended to go on pilgrimage with his family. He asked Mirind to accompany. But for his trade's reason, he did not go with him. So Govind thought it safe to leave the box of his jewellery with him, as it was dangerous to leave it in a lone house or take it on the journey. So he went to him with the box. He took him to a lonely place under a tree and handed it over to him. He told Mirind, "Keep it safe with you. I shall return from the journey after six month then I shall take it back from you." Mirind said, "Don't worry, I shall keep it as safe as own."

1. Govind intended to go
   A. for a business trip
   B. to a hill station
   C. on a long journey to a sacred place
   D. to his home town for a long period
2. Why did Govind leave his box of jewellery with Mirind?
   A. Because it was not safe to take the box with him on a long journey
   B. Because Mirind was his fast friend
   C. Because the box was very heavy
   D. Because his house was unsafe
3. Why did Govind take Mirind to a lonely place?
   A. To tell him that the box contained valuable jewellery
   B. So that no third person could see box
   C. To show him what was within the box
   D. To tell him that the box will remain with him
4. Where did Govind hand over the box of jewellery to Mirind?
   A. At Mirind's house
   B. At his own house
   C. In a lonely place
   D. In a lonely place under a tree
5. It was not safe to leave the box in a lone house. Here the word 'lone house' means
   A. a house in a deserted place
   B. a house where none lives
   C. a house without door and lcck
   D. a house near the forest

PASSAGE-8

Zahir-ud-din Babar was the first Mughal emperor of India. A descendent of Timur on father's side and Changez Khan on his mother's side, Babar was a brave warrior. After defeating Ibrahim Lodhi in the First Battle of Panipat in 1526 he entered Delhi and soon gained control over Agra. After many more battles with Rajputs he extended his empire over Punjab, Uttar Pradesh and north Bihar. He died at a young age of 48 years in 1530 at his capital Agra without getting much time to consolidate his victories.

1. Zahir-ud-din Babar was the first
   A. Muslim ruler of India
   B. Mughal ruler of India
   C. Afghan ruler of India
   D. Turk ruler of India
2. Babar was born in the years
   A. 1480 B. 1482
   C. 1492 D. 1962
3. Babar first occupied
   A. Punjab B. Agra
   C. Delhi D. Panipat
4. Babar was a brave warrior. Here brave warrior means
   A. courageous soldier
   B. a kind hearted soldier
   C. a clever fighter
   D. a victorious general
5. Babar extended his empire over Punjab and Uttar Pradesh after many more battles with the
   A. Afghans B. Rajputs
   C. Mughals D. Lodhies

PASSAGE-9

Our National Flag is tricolour. It has three equal horizontal strips. The strip at the top is saffron, in the middle is white and at the bottom is green. The ratio of width to length of the flag is 2 : 3. In the centre of the white strip is a wheel in navy blue. The wheel represents the *chakra*. Its design is similar to the wheel which appears on the abacus of the Sarnath Lion Capital of Ashoka. Its diameter approximates to the width of the white strip. The wheel has 24 spokes. It was adopted by Constituent Assembly on July 22, 1947. We love our national flag. We respect it. We are ready to sacrifice our life to protect its honour. It represents the nation. So it is a symbol of national honour.

1. In our national flag the wheel is located in the centre of
   A. saffron strip B. white strip
   C. green strip D. blue strip
2. In our national flag which of the strips is at the bottom in our national flag
   A. blue C. saffron
   B. white D. green
3. Why do we love our national flag?
   A. Because it is tricolour
   B. Because it has three strips
   C. Because it has a wheel at the centre
   D. Because it is a symbol of national honour
4. Our national flag was approved by
   A. President
   B. Lok Sabha
   C. Parliament
   D. Constituent Assembly
5. The diameter approximates to the width of the white strip. Here the word 'approximates' means
   A. is more or less equal
   B. is exactly equal
   C. is not equal
   D. is related

PASSAGE-10

Distance in large cities are long. All the people do not have their own means of transport. They have to depend upon the state or private buses. The number of bus users is very large. Every bus stop is, therefore, crowded. The number of buses is not adequate. Thus people suffer the torture of long wait at the bus stop. Some bus stops are quite orderly. People form queues and get into the buses turn by turn. However, often this order is forgotten and confusion spreads when the bus comes and the law of jungle prevails.

1. Why are the bus stops crowded?
   A. Because they are small is size
   B. Because the number of passengers is very large
   C. Because they are situated at some busy centre
   D. Because people do not form queues
2. Long wait at the bus stop is the result of
   A. over-crowding in the buses
   B. late running of buses
   C. shortage of buses
   D. slow speed of buses
3. Some bus stops are quite orderly where
   A. there is no crowd
   B. the number of buses is adequate

C. people do not have to wait for long
D. people form queues and enter the buses one by one

4. Most of the people who travel by buses are
A. non-working
B. do not have their own vehicles
C. have to go a long distance
D. live in large cities

5. What happens when people do not have their own transport?
A. They have to wait for a bus at a bus stop
B. They have to depend upon the state or private buses
C. They have to travel long distances
D. They form queues and get into buses one by one

PASSAGE-11

A certain king once fell ill and doctors said that only a sudden fright would restore his health but the king was not a man for anyone to play tricks on, except his fool. One day, when the fool was with him in his boat he cleverly pushed the king into water but he was rescued and put to bed. The fright, the bath and bed cured the diseased king, but he was so angry with the fool that he turned him out of the country.

1. What did the doctor say about the king?
A. Only a sudden fright would restore the king's health
B. Only fool would cure the king
C. Only a boat trick could cure the king
D. The king had suffered a sudden fright

2. He cleverly pushed the king into water but *he* was rescued and put to bed. In this sentence *he* refers to
A. the king B. the fool
C. the doctor D. the river

3. When the fool pushed the king into water they were
A. in the palace B. in the bed
C. in the garden D. in a boat

4. Who played the trick on the king?
A. The doctor B. The boatman
C. The fool D. The fright

5. The fool who cured the king was
A. rewarded
B. thrown into water
C. turned out of the country
D. put into jail

ANSWERS

	1	2	3	4	5
Passage 1.	D	C	B	A	C
Passage 2.	B	C	D	B	B
Passage 3.	D	D	C	B	D
Passage 4.	B	C	C	C	C
Passage 5.	D	A	B	B	A
Passage 6.	A	C	D	B	A
Passage 7.	C	A	B	D	B
Passage 8.	B	B	C	A	B
Passage 9.	B	D	D	D	A
Passage 10.	B	C	D	B	B
Passage 11.	A	A	D	C	C

2. English Grammar

PARTS OF SPEECH

Part of speech	Definition or Function	Examples
Noun	Name of a person, place, animal, quality or thing	Ram, boy, dog pen, sun, Delhi, truth, honesty
Pronoun	Used in place of a noun	I, you, he she, they
Articles & Determiners	Points out indefinite and definite nouns	a, an, the, few, some
Adjective	Describes a noun or pronoun	big, honest, wooden valuable, quiet, deep, soft, narrow
Adverb	Describes a verb, an adjective or another adverb	silently, widely, softly, quietly, very, carefully
Verb	Tells about action or state of something or someone	is, am, was, have, do, like, walk, work, make, throw, tell
Conjuction	Joins words, clauses or sentences	and, but, when, yet, while, else
Preposition	Links a noun or pronoun to another word	at, to, after, on for, under, over, with
Interjection	Expresses sudden feelings or emotions	Ah!, Alas!, oh!, ouch!, hi!, well!, Hurrah!

NOUNS

A word which denotes a person, a thing, an animal or a place is said to be a noun.

There are two noun numbers in English — the *Singular* and the *Plural.*

Singular Numbers : A noun that denotes one person or one thing, is said to be in the Singular number. For example — book, pencil, bird, dog, hen etc. are in singular number.

Plural Number : A noun that denotes more than one person or one thing is said to be in plural number. For example — boys, pens, lions, girls, men etc. are in plural number.

REMEMBER

Singular	*Plural*
Cat	Cats
Book	Books
Pen	Pens
Room	Rooms
Tree	Trees
Bus	Buses
Bush	Bushes
Box	Boxes
Glass	Glasses
Dish	Dishes
Judge	Judges
Tax	Taxes
Watch	Watches
Calf	Calves
Thief	Thieves
Knife	Knives

Singular	Plural
Scarf	Scarves
Wife	Wives
Leaf	Leaves
Wolf	Wolves
Half	Halves
Monarch	Monarchs
Roof	Roofs
Hoof	Hoofs
Gulf	Gulfs
Staff	Staffs
Radio	Radios
Bamboo	Bamboos
Folio	Folios
Hero	Heroes
Volcano	Volcanoes
Mango	Mangoes
Potato	Potatoes
Photo	Photos
Piano	Pianos
Baby	Babies
Fly	Flies
Country	Countries
Lady	Ladies
Boy	Boys
Monkey	Monkeys
Ox	Oxen
Child	Children
Man	Men
Woman	Women
Tooth	Teeth
Axis	Axes
Basis	Bases
Foot	Feet
Goose	Geese
Englishman	Englishmen
Radius	Radii
Vertex	Vertices
Stimulus	Stimuli

1. Note the plurals of the following nouns:

Singular	*Plural*	*Singular*	*Plural*
copy	copies	cry	cries
baby	babies	duty	duties
body	bodies	country	countries
family	families	diary	diaries
fly	flies	fairy	fairies
city	cities	spy	spies
army	armies	storey	storeys
bay	bays	monkey	monkeys

2. The following nouns do not undergo any change in plural form, in general.

Singular	*Plural*	*Singular*	*Plural*
deer	deer	sheep	sheep
thousand	thousand	pair	pair
hundred	hundred	score	score
dozen	dozen	gross	gross

Note: We can write—

(*a*) thousands of men; (*b*) two pairs of shoes; (*c*) dozens of mangoes; (*d*) scores of people etc.

But—

(*a*) two thousand rupees; (*b*) three hundred men; (*c*) five dozen eggs, etc.

3. The following nouns are usually used in plural forms. They take a plural verb after them—

eatables	fetters	surroundings
riches	alms	spectacles
trousers	pants	scissors
premises	thanks	annals
congratulations	goods	shorts
tongs	pains	arms
breeches	(for troubles)	

4. The following are the nouns which are plural in appearance but are usually used in singular number. They are followed by a singular verb—

news	politics	physics
mathematics	economics	ethics
politics	classics	gallows
statistics	athletics	innings
mechanics	summons	mumps

5. Collective nouns often used as plurals—

public	police	cattle
audience	clergy	folk
people	poultry	nation
elite	gentry	glitterati

6. The nouns that are usually used in singular forms—

advice	hair	rice
fuel	alphabet	machinery
offspring	issue	furniture
mischief	stationery	luggage
bedding	information	abuse

7. Material nouns are always used in singular number—

gold	copper	milk
water	silk	wool

Note: They may be used in plural with a different meaning.

copper coins (coppers), chains or fetters (irons), cans made of tin (tins).

GENDERS

The difference in sex is denoted by Gender in grammar. The various genders are as follows :

1. **Masculine Gender :** A noun that denotes a male is said to be of the masculine gender, as man, uncle, ox, boy etc.
2. **Feminine Gender :** A noun that denotes a female is said to be of feminine gender, as woman, aunt, princess, cow etc.
3. **Common Gender :** Nouns which denote both males and females are said to be of the common gender, as friend, cousin, person, parent, baby etc.
4. **Neuter Gender :** A noun that denotes the name of object without life is said to be of neuter gender, as file, table, pencil.

REMEMBER

Masculine	*Feminine*
Boy	Girl
Son	Daughter
Brother	Sister
Murderer	Murderess
Sorcerer	Sorceress
Son-in-law	Daughter-in-law
Father-in-law	Mother-in-law
Man-servant	Maid-servant
Land-lord	Land-lady
Bachelor	Maid
Gentleman	Lady
Monk	Nun
Earl	Countess
Lad	Lass
Sir	Madam
Duke	Dutchess
Emperor	Empress
Milk-man	Milk-maid
Pea-cock	Pea-hen

Masculine	*Feminine*
Step-father	Step-mother
Hero	Heroine
Viceroy	Vicerine
Mr.	Mrs.
Governor	Governess
Master	Mistress
Wizard	Witch
Heir	Heiress
Host	Hostess
Lion	Lioness
Mayor	Mayoress
Actor	Actress
Buck	Doe
Colt	Filly
Dog	Bitch
Horse	Mare
Count	Countess
Hunter	Huntress
Prince	Princess
Abbot	Abbess
God	Goddess
Author	Authoress
Ox	Cow
Widower	Widow
Grand-father	Grand-mother
He-goat	She-goat
Milk-man	Milk-woman
Bridegroom	Bride
Tiger	Tigress
Priest	Priestess
Poet	Poetess
Shepherd	Shepherdess
Nephew	Niece
Stag	Hind

PRONOUNS

The repetition of a noun in a sentence or a set of sentences is really boring. So, instead of repeating the noun, we can use a word (for that noun) called the pronoun.

"A pronoun is a word that we use instead of a noun".

Example:

This is *Sachin. He* plays cricket.

Note: *He* is the pronoun used in place of *Sachin.*

Kinds of Pronouns

1. **Personal pronouns :** A pronoun which is used instead of the name of a person is known as a 'Personal Pronoun'. A list of the 'Personal pronouns' is listed below :

I, my, mine, me, we (First Person)
You, your, yours (Second Person)
He, his, him, she, her, hers, it,
its, they, their, theirs, them (Third Person)

2. **Demonstrative, Indefinite and Distributive Pronouns :**

(a) Demonstrative Pronouns : Pronouns used to point out the objects to which they refer are called Demonstrative Pronouns.

Examples :

(i) *This* is a present from my uncle.
(ii) *These* are merely excuses.
(iii) Bembay mangoes are better than *those* of Bangaluru.

(b) Indefinite Pronouns : All pronouns which refer to persons or things in a general way and do not refer to any particular person or thing are called Indefinite Pronouns.

Examples :

(i) *Somebody* has stolen my watch.
(ii) *Few* escaped unhurt.
(iii) Did you ask *anybody* to come?

(c) Distributive Pronouns : Each, either, neither are called distributive pronouns because they refer to persons or things one at a time. For this reason they are always singular and followed by the verb in singular.

Examples :

(i) *Each* of the men received a reward.
(ii) *These* men received *each* a reward.
(iii) *Either* of you can go.

3. **Relative Pronouns :** A relative pronoun refers or relates to some noun going before, which is called its Antecedent.

Examples :

(i) I met Hari *who* used to live here.
(ii) I have found the pen *which* I had lost.
(iii) Here is the book *that* you lent me.

4. **Interrogative Pronouns :** These pronouns, are used for asking questions.

Examples :

(i) *Whose* book is this?
(ii) *What* will all the neighbours say?
(iii) *Which* do you prefer, tea or coffee?

Note : Interrogative pronouns can also be used in asking indirect questions. Consider the following examples :

(i) I asked *who* was speaking.
(ii) Tell me *what* you have done.
(iii) Say *which* you would like best.

Behaviour of the Pronouns

1. If three pronouns are used together in the same sentence they are arranged in the following order :

2	+	3	+	1
↓		↓		↓
Second Person		Third Person		First Person

Examples :

I, you and he must help *that* poor man. (Incorrect)

You, he and I must help *that* poor man. (Correct)

2. When two or more singular nouns are joined by and, the pronoun used for them should be plural.

Examples :

Mohan and Sohan are friends. *They* play football. *They* live at Lajpat Nagar.

3. But if these nouns joined by and refer to the same person or thing, the pronoun used should be singular.

Examples :

(i) Delhi, the beautiful city and the capital of India, is famous for *its* historical monuments.
(ii) The manager and owner of the firm expressed *his* views on the demands of the workers.

4. When two nouns are used with as well as, the pronoun agrees with the first subject.
   Examples :
   (a) Mohan as well as his friends is doing *his* work.
   (b) The students as well as their teachers are doing *their* work.
5. When two singular nouns joined by 'and' are preceded by *each* or *every,* the pronoun used must be singular and should agree in gender with the second noun.
   Examples :
   (a) Every man and every woman will do *her* best for the nation.
   (b) Each boy and each girl went to *her* house.
6. When two nouns are joined by using 'with', the pronoun agrees with the noun coming before 'with'.
   Examples :
   (a) The boy with *his* parents has gone to see a movie.
   (b) The children with *their* parents have gone to picnic.
7. When two different nouns are joined by either.......... or; neither .... nor, the pronoun is used according to the number and gender of the second noun.
   Examples :
   (a) Either your sister or you have done *your* work.
   (b) Neither the students nor the teacher was in *his* class.
8. The pronoun coming after '*than*' must be in the same case as that coming before '*than*'.
   Examples :
   (a) She plays better than *me.* (Incorrect)
   She plays better than *I.* (Correct)
   (b) His elder brother is more intelligent than *him.* (Incorrect)
   His elder brother is more intelligent than *he*. (Correct)
9. 'Many a' always takes a singular pronoun and singular verb.
   Example :
   Many a soldier has met *his* death in the battle field.
10. 'Who', 'Whose', 'Whom' are used only for persons.
   Examples :
   (a) *Who* is knocking at the door?
   (b) *Whose* pen is this?
   (c) *What* do you want?
11. 'Which' is used for things.
   Example :
   Which game do you like?

MULTIPLE CHOICE QUESTIONS

Directions: *In the following questions choose the correct options to fill the blanks.*

1. The place was so dirty that ..... wished to run away from there.
A. everybody B. anybody
C. few D. some

2. ..... was there to help me.
A. Somebody B. Anything
C. Anybody D. Nobody

3. Is there .... to eat?
A. some B. something
C. any D. few

4. ..... of the students were making a great noise.
A. Anyone B. Somebody
C. Many D. Nobody

5. ..... of the students can solve this sum.
A. Someone B. Anybody
C. Somebody D. None

6. ...... of us should try our best to make India a heaven.
A. Any B. Somebody
C. Anybody D. All

7. ...... of us do not know the real meaning of our lives.
A. Any B. Something
C. Several D. Many

8. My .... black.
A. hairs are B. hair is
C. hairs shall D. hair will

9. She saw two .... on the last Sunday.
A. thiefs B. theifs
C. thieves D. theives

10. My sister is a ....
A. bacheloress B. bachelor
C. unmaried D. spinster

11. One is supposed to do ....
A. our duty B. their duty
C. one's duty D. his duty

12. Take anything .... you want.
A. that B. which
C. than D. then

13. I cannot tolerate ....
A. separated you
B. your separation
C. separation from you
D. you separated

14. He is .... faithful partner.
A. Yours B. You
C. Your D. Your's

15. Ajay is more smart than ....
A. her B. hers
C. herself D. she

16. Vivek works harder than ....
A. me B. I
C. her D. his

17. They should help ....
A. the poor people B. the poor
C. the poor persons D. the poor peoples

18. .... are mad.
A. All his sons B. His all sons
C. Sons all his D. All sons his

19. The poor fellow .... to fate.
A. resigned
B. resigned himself
C. resigned itself
D. resigned themselves

20. Nobody will help you but ....
A. I B. me
C. ours D. his

21. It is a good chance, You must avail .... this opportunity.
A. of B. yourself of
C. for D. from

22. The person who is elected .... my relative.
A. is B. he is
C. his D. him

23. He made ....
A. yours mention B. mention of you
C. mention for you D. mention about you

24. .... I know, he is quite faithful.
A. As far as B. So far as
C. So far this D. So far so

25. It is a duty of a person to take .... for his family.
A. pain B. pains
C. pain-killers D. pained

26. She does not love .... husband.
A. his B. her
C. its D. their

27. Let .... work together.
A. him and me B. he and I
C. he and him D. I and me

28. Copper, Silver and Gold ....
A. each will do B. either will do
C. any one will do D. any will do

29. Jessica and Roma are very irregular .... habits.
A. in her B. in their
C. in its D. in every

30. One likes to enjoy .... who was a great poet.
A. The sonnets of Shakespeare
B. Shakespeare's sonnets
C. Sonnets
D. Shakespeare

31. That is the boy .... everybody loves.
A. whom B. who
C. that D. whose

32. That is the girl .... won the first prize.
A. whom B. who
C. whose D. which

33. That is the man .... purse was lost.
A. who B. whom
C. whose D. their

ANSWERS

1	2	3	4	5	6	7	8	9	10
A	D	B	C	D	D	D	B	C	D
11	**12**	**13**	**14**	**15**	**16**	**17**	**18**	**19**	**20**
C	A	C	C	D	B	B	A	B	B
21	**22**	**23**	**24**	**25**	**26**	**27**	**28**	**29**	**30**
B	A	B	A	B	B	A	C	B	A
31	**32**	**33**							
A	B	C							

ARTICLES

The family of the articles has only three members. They are : A, An and The. However, they fall under two groups :

(a) Definite Article *(b)* Indefinite Article

'The' is known as definite article whereas 'a' and 'an' are known as indefinite articles.

Use of the Definite Article 'The'

'The' is used before

1. The superlative degree :
   He is the ablest man of the town.
   (ablest is a superlative degree)
2. The name of states, countries etc. having a descriptive name :
   (i) The J & K is a small state. (J & K is a descriptive name)
   (ii) He lives in the U.S.A. (U.S.A. is a descriptive name)
   (But the Delhi and the America are wrong because neither Delhi nor America is a descriptive name)
3. The names of the scriptures :
   The Gita is a holy book. (Gita is a scripture)
4. Name of newspapers :
   The Tribune is published from Chandigarh.
5. Name of rivers, canals, seas, oceans, bays, gulfs, groups of islands etc. :
   (i) The Ganga is a holy river.
   (ii) The Indian Ocean is the deepest ocean.
   (iii) The Persian Gulf is a narrow gulf.
6. The name of famous buildings :
   The Taj is one of the best buildings in India.
7. The names of nationals, sects and communities:
   (i) The English defeated the Germans in the World War.
   (ii) The rich should help the poor.
   (iii) The Hindus believe in the caste system.
8. Proper nouns used as common nouns :
   (i) Kalidas is the Shakespeare of India.
   (ii) Delhi is the London of India.
9. Famous historical events :
   The Industrial Revolution changed the face of England.
10. The directions and the celestial bodies:
    The sun rises in the east.
11. Titles :
    Akbar, the Great was loved by his subjects.

Do not use 'the'

1. Before languages :
   The English is an international language. (Incorrect)
   English is an international language. (Correct)
2. Before the names of games :
   The hockey is a popular game. (Incorrect)
   Hockey is a popular game. (Correct)

Use of the Indefinite Articles 'A' and 'An'

'A' is used before :

1. All singular common nouns beginning with a consonant :
   (i) A boy sings a song.

(ii) A black and a white cow were grazing in the field.

2. If a word begins with a vowel but gives the sound of a consonant, 'a' should be used before it :
   (i) He was helped in his work by a European.
   (ii) He is a one-eyed man.
   (iii) It is a useful work.

'An' is used as follows :

1. All singular common nouns beginning with a vowel (*i.e.*, a, e, i, o, u) :
   (i) He is an artist.
   (ii) He is an old man.
   (iii) I intend to buy an umbrella.
2. If a word starts with a consonant but gives the sound of a vowel, "an" should be used before it :
   (i) Brutus is an honourable man.
   (ii) He is an honour to his profession.
   (iii) He is an L.L.B.
   (iv) He is an M.A.
   (v) You will reach there in an hour.

Demonstratives, that, these and those

1. The demonstrative adjectives and pronouns are for objects nearby the speaker:
   this (singular) those (plural)
   and for objects far away from the speaker.
   That (singular) those (plural)
2. Demonstratives are the only adjectives that agree in number with their nouns.
   That hat is nice.
   Those hats are nice.
3. When there is the idea of selection, the pronoun "one" (or "ones") often follows the demonstrative.
   I want a book. I'll get this (one).
   If the demonstrative is followed by an adjective, "one"(or "ones") must be used.
   I want a book. I'll get this big one.

MULTIPLE CHOICE QUESTIONS

Directions: *In the following questions choose the correct options to fill the blanks.*

1. .... will have to be paid for this material.
A. Half rupee B. Half a rupee
C. A half rupee D. An half rupee

2. .... is taking keen interest in India.
A. The USA B. USA
C. An USA D. A USA

3. Only .... can save our country.
A. the Hitler B. a Hitler
C. Hitler D. an Hitler

4. I can run for ....
A. hundred miles B. the hundred miles
C. a hundred miles D. an hundred miles.

5. .... man-eater has been killed.
A. The B. A
C. An D. Either A or B

6. What .... fine idea!
A. the B. an
C. a D. No article

7. .... earth is moving around the sun.
A. An B. A
C. The D. No article

8. This is .... first example while I got.
A. the B. a
C. an D. No article

9. This is .... house which was built during earthquake.
A. a B. an
C. the D. No article

10. .... America is a rich country.
A. The B. An
C. A D. No article

11. .... U.S.A. is a developed country.
A. A B. An
C. The D. No article

12. .... Bible is a holy book.
A. A B. The
C. An D. No article

13. .... rich should help the poor.
A. The B. A
C. An D. No article

14. .... Gold is a costly metal.
A. The B. A
C. An D. No article

15. Kalidas is .... Shakespeare of India.
A. a B. an
C. the D. No article

16. I cannot do .... difficult work.
A. a such B. the such
C. such the D. such a

17. How foolish .... plan it is!
A. a B. an
C. the D. No article

18. An ink is .... useful article.
A. an B. a
C. the D. No article

19. There are .... husband and wife.
A. a B. an
C. the D. No article

20. He is learning .... French
A. the B. a
C. an D. No article

ANSWERS

1	2	3	4	5	6	7	8	9	10
B	A	B	C	D	C	C	A	C	D
11	**12**	**13**	**14**	**15**	**16**	**17**	**18**	**19**	**20**
C	B	A	D	C	D	A	B	D	D

ADJECTIVES & ADVERBS

An Adjective is a word which adds something to the meaning of a noun or a pronoun.

Mridula is an *intelligent* girl.
He has a *black* goat.
He is a *brilliant* student.
She is a *clever* girl.
It is a *beautiful* picture.

In the sentences given above, the words in italics are adjectives.

An Adverb is a word which qualifies the meaning of a Verb, an Adjective or another Adverb.

(*i*) He talks *slowly*.
(*ii*) He is a *very* good student.
(*iii*) He talks *very* slowly.

In sentence (*i*), *slowly* qualifies the verb *talks*.

In sentence (*ii*), *very* qualifies the adjective *good*.

In sentence (*iii*), *very* qualifies the adverb *slowly*.

Adjectives have three degrees of comparison :

1. **Positive Degree :** It expresses the common form of an adjective.
   Example :
   Ram is a *tall* boy.
   In the above sentence *tall* is an adjective and expresses the common form.
2. **Comparative Degree :** It expresses the more of the same form.
   Example :
   Ram is *taller* than Mahesh.
   In the above sentence *taller* is an adjective that expresses the more of the common form of the adjective *tall*.

"When and How to Use" Comparative Degree?

(a) Comparative Degree is used when two persons or two groups of persons or things are compared.
Examples :
(a) He is *wiser* than his younger brother.
(b) This glass is *cleaner* than the other.

(b) When two different qualities in the same person are compared, more is used instead of 'er' to form the comparative. The formula used in this case should be :
More + Positive Degree
She is *fairer* than polite. (Incorrect)
She is *more fair* than polite. (Correct)

(c) When selection of one out of two persons or things is meant, the degree of comparison is followed by of and *the* is used before it.
Example :
Zia is abler of *the* two sisters.

(d) If two comparatives are used in the same sentence to impress upon an idea, both should be preceded by the definite article.

Examples :

(i) The higher you go, the cooler it is.

(ii) The more we get, the more we desire.

(e) When one person or thing is compared with another of the same kind, other is used after the comparative degree. In such sentences other is normally preceded by any or all.

Examples :

(i) Kalidas is greater than any dramatist. (Incorrect)

Kalidas is greater than any other dramatist. (Correct)

(ii) Lead is heavier than all metals. (Incorrect)

Lead is heavier than all other metals. (Correct)

(f) Senior, junior, superior, inferior, prior, anterior (earlier than) and posterior (later than) are always followed by 'to'.

Examples :

(i) Ram is senior *to* Mohan by three years.

(ii) That pen is inferior *to* that.

(iii) He is junior *to* me in rank.

(iv) This event was posterior *to* that.

Note: Never use *than* after the above mentioned adjectives.

Important Information

(a) 'Preferable' is also used as an adjective of the comparative degree. As such, it is always followed by *to* and not *a*.

Death is preferable than dishonour. (Incorrect)

Death is preferable *to* dishonour. (Correct)

(b) To intensify the Degree of comparison, we use *far* or *much* before the comparative.

Examples :

(i) This book is *far* better than that.

(ii) His performance was *much* better than Mohan's.

Warning : Always avoid the use of double comparatives.

Don't say : Ram is more cleverer than his younger brother.

Say: Ram is cleverer than his younger brother.

3. **Superlative Degree :** It expresses the most of the common form of an adjective.

Example :

He is the ablest man of the town.

How and when to use the Superlative Degree?

(a) The Superlative Degree is used when more than two persons or things are compared.

(b) The Superlative Degree is generally preceded by 'the' and followed by 'of' in most of the cases or otherwise.

(c) When an adjective of the superlative degree is preceded by a Possessive Adjective or a Noun in the Possessive case, 'the' should not be used before it.

Example :

Which is Kalidas' best play?

It will be a blunder to use 'the' before the Superlative Degree in such cases.

Don't say : Which is Kalidas' the best play.

(d) To intensify the degree of comparison, *by far* is used before the superlative degree.

Example :

India is *by far* the most beautiful country of the world.

Note: Always avoid the use of double superlatives.

Don't say : He is the most strongest boy in the class.

Say : He is the strongest boy in the class.

Use of some Important Adjectives

1. (a) '**Some**' is used as follows :

(i) With countable nouns where it means—a little, a small quantity.

(ii) In a question which shows some request.

Examples :

(i) There is some water in the bottle.

(ii) Some of the students were absent yesterday.

(iii) Will you have some milk?

(iv) Will you buy some fruit for me?

(b) '**Any**' is used as follows :

(i) In negative sentences.

(ii) In interrogative sentences.

(iii) After 'Hardly', 'Scarcely' and 'Barely'.
(iv) After 'If'.

Examples :

(i) There is not any sugar in the pot.
(ii) We haven't any rice in the house.
(iii) I have hardly any money.
(iv) There are scarcely any plants in this field.
(v) If there is any danger, blow the whistle.

2. (a) **Older :** Older (and oldest) are used for persons animals and things. But 'Older' and 'Oldest' refer to the persons who do not belong to the same family.

Examples :

(i) Radha is older than Shyama.
(ii) John is the oldest member of the staff. 'Older' and 'Oldest' refer to the persons who do not belong to the same family.

(b) **Elder** (and **eldest**) are used in respect of the members of the same family like sons, daughters, brothers, sisters.

Examples :

(i) My elder sister is a lecturer.
(ii) Meenakshi is the eldest of the three sisters.

Note :

(i) 'Elder' is not followed by 'than'.
(ii) 'Elder' and 'Eldest' cannot be used for things.

3. (a) **'Few'** is negative and is the opposite of 'Many'. It means 'not many'.

(b) **'A few'** is positive and means 'some at least'. It is the opposite of 'None'.

(c) **'The few'** means 'minority' and suggests 'whether there is'.

Examples :

(i) We have few holidays in school.
(ii) Only a few boys will fail in the examination.
(iii) The few poems that he wrote are very popular.

4. (a) **Further** means 'something additional'.

(b) **Farther** means 'a greater distance'.

Examples :

(i) Further discussion will be held in the office of the principal.
(ii) Amritsar is farther from Delhi than Ambala.

5. (a) **Little** is negative. It means, 'not much', or 'hardly any'.

(b) **A little** is positive. It means 'some quantity'.

(c) **The little** denotes quantity. It means, 'not much but all that is, or whatever quantity there is'.

Examples :

(i) There is little hope of his success.
(ii) He knows a little of everything.
(iii) I have spent the little money I had.
(iv) The little knowledge of shoe-making proved very useful to me.

6. (a) **'Much'** expresses 'quantity'.

(b) **'Many'** expresses 'number'.

(c) **'Many a'**—'Singular noun' and 'Singular verb' are used with 'many a'.

Examples :

(i) There is not *much* water in the jug.
(ii) *Many* boys are absent today.
(iii) *Many* a battle has been fought on the soil of India.

7. (a) **'Less'** denotes 'in a small degree'.

(b) **'Fewer'** denotes 'number'.

Examples :

(i) He devotes less time to his studies.
(ii) There are no fewer than ten chairs in this room.

8. (a) **'Each'** is used for a single number of 'two persons' or 'things'.

(b) **'Every'** is used for a single number of 'many persons' or 'things'.

Examples :

(i) Each boy must take part in games.
(ii) There are only two poets. Each poet recited his poem.
(iii) Every man dies in this world.
(iv) Every man is expected to do his duty.

9. (a) **'Either'** means one of the two or both.

(b) **'Neither'** is negative of the either.

Examples :

(i) You may buy either of these two chairs.
(ii) Neither of them could speak on the stage.

10. (a) '**Later**' expresses 'late in time'.
(b) '**Latter**' means 'second in position or order'.

Examples :

(i) My father reached later than I expected.

(ii) The latter position was better than the former.

Use of some Important Adverbs

1. (a) Also, too, enough:

(i) He taught English. Also, he edited the school magazine

(ii) He is a writer and also he is a painter.

(iii) He is too obstinate to listen to any reason.

(iv) This is too difficult a piece for the junior students.

(v) Sarla was kind enough to help the poor.

(vi) He is brave enough to help the truth.

Note: 'Too' is used in a negative sense, but enough is used in a positive sense.

(b) Fairly and rather: Both suggest the meaning 'moderately'. But, mainly 'fairly' is used with the words that denote a positive meaning and rather is used with the words that denote a negative meaning:

(i) Rita did fairly well in that competition, but her performance was rather poor in sports.

(ii) Mona is fairly rich, but she is rather stingy.

Note: 'Rather' can also be used in a positive sense.

(i) This is a rather interesting job.

(ii) That boy is rather smart.

(c) Hardly, barely, scarcely: These words mostly convey the negative suggestions and are almost similar.

(i) I have hardly any strength now.

(ii) There was barely any supply to the township,

(iii) There were scarcely a hundred guests present.

Note: With slight variance in the meaning, the words given above convey the idea of 'very little', 'not enough', 'lack of quantity and number'.

(d) Yet, Still: These adverbs can often be used to connect the sentence units:

(i) He has been defeated many times in the contest; still he wants to be a competitor.

(ii) Mona was sick; yet she went on doing her work.

(e) Alone:

(i) He alone (none else) is capable of handling that fire,

(ii) He hunted all alone in the forest. (not in any company)

Special Note:

(a) Apart from their conventional positions the adverbs might be used in different positions with different meanings and angles.

(i) He had only four books.

(ii) John only contacted his friend in need.

(iii) He greeted me only.

(iv) Only he greeted me there.

(b) Inversion: Some adverbs can be inverted *i.e.* placed in the beginning of the sentence and then be followed by an interrogative form. The most common of these adverb are: so, seldom, never, nowhere, under no circumstances, hardly, scarcely etc.

(i) So big was the bus that it could not enter the narrow lane.

(ii) Hardly had he reached the station when he received the message.

MULTIPLE CHOICE QUESTIONS

Directions: *In the following questions choose the correct options to fill the blanks.*

1. The girl whom you met is the .... sister of Ravi.

A. eldest B. elder
C. older D. oldest

2. The historical place is ....

A. seeing worth

B. worthy of seeing
C. worth seeing
D. worthy seeing

3. These flowers smell ....
A. sweet B. sweetly
C. more sweetly D. sweetest

4. .... aspirant cannot pass the entrance examination.
A. Each B. Every
C. All D. No

5. Harivansh Rai .... second Shakespeare.
A. is a B. is
C. is the D. is an

6. .... student in the class got prizes.
A. Each and every B. Every and each
C. Every D. Never

7. It is .... picture than the one we saw last Monday.
A. interesting B. much interesting
C. more interesting D. most interesting

8. She is clever ....
A. that her mother is
B. as her mother is
C. to her mother is
D. than her mother is

9. They will get ....
A. Red, green and black paper
B. Red, green black paper
C. Red and green and black paper
D. Red green black paper

10. Health is .... wealth.
A. preferable to
B. more preferable than
C. more preferable to
D. most preferable then

11. .... water that was in the jug evaporated.
A. Little B. The little
C. Small D. A small

12. He has not sung .... songs.
A. much B. most
C. more D. many

13. Srishti has searched .... office.
A. whole the B. the whole
C. a whole D. some whole

14. Premchand was .... best and .... famous writer.
A. a, the most B. the, a most
C. the, more D. the, the most

15. William Shakespeare is famous as ....
A. a poet and a dramatist
B. a poet and dramatist
C. the poet and the dramatist
D. a poet and the dramatist

16. What does .... leader suggest?
A. other B. another
C. others D. anothers

17. He .... money.
A. has few B. have few
C. has little D. have little

18. The .... boys are rewarded.
A. first two B. two first
C. firsts two D. two's first

19. He is .... brave.
A. stronger than
B. stronger then
C. more strong then
D. more strong than

20. No sooner said ....
A. so done B. and done
C. then done D. but done

21. She returned .... than I had thought.
A. quickly B. more quicker
C. more quickly D. quicker

22. He is .... foolish person.
A. rather the B. a rather
C. rather a D. rather

23. This pen .... rupees.
A. costs twenty
B. twenty costs only
C. costs only twenty
D. only costs twenty

24. It is .... pride.
A. nothing else but
B. nothing else than
C. else nothing than
D. but

25. This tea is .... to drink.
A. too hot B. very hot
C. enough hot D. much hot

ANSWERS

1	2	3	4	5	6	7	8	9	10
A	C	A	B	A	C	C	C	A	A
11	12	13	14	15	16	17	18	19	20
B	D	B	D	B	B	C	A	D	C
21	22	23	24	25					
C	C	C	A	A					

DETERMINERS

Determiners are actually Adjectives. They are always followed by nouns.

Determiners are of the following kinds:

1. Demonstrative Determiners

this, that, these, those

2. Possessive Determiners

my, our, your, his, her, its, their

3. Quantitative Determiners

some, any, much, enough, sufficient, whole, a little, the little, little, all, both

4. Numerical Determiners

a few, some, few, the few, any, several, many, no, etc.

One, two, three ... (Cardinals)

First, second, third ... (Ordinals)

5. Distributive Determiners

either, neither

6. Articles

Indefinite: a, an

Definite: the

MULTIPLE CHOICE QUESTIONS

Directions: *In the following questions choose the correct options to fill the blanks.*

1. Give me .... rice.
A. some B. few
C. a few D. any

2. .... sheep grazing on the slope of the hill had gone away.
A. Any B. The few
C. This D. Much

3. Have you got .... magazines to read?
A. all B. much
C. some D. little

4. I have .... money that I want to spend on shares.
A. any B. much
C. less D. some

5. There is .... owl on the branch of the tree.
A. a B. the
C. an D. some

6. My brother is .... MBA.
A. a B. an
C. the D. any

7. Have you got .... cheese?
A. some B. many
C. a few D. few

8. No, I have not got .... cheese.
A. many B. few
C. any D. some

9. There is only .... milk left in the bottle.
A. enough B. few
C. much D. a little

10. There is .... hope of his recovery.
A. any B. little
C. many D. few

11. .... dogs were barking at the strangers.
A. Some B. Any
C. Much D. Less

12. The girl bought her father .... juice.
A. few B. some
C. any D. many

13. You should take .... honey everyday.
A. any B. many
C. a little D. a few

14. .... boy was punished by the teacher.
A. Either B. All
C. Any D. Many

15. .... girl was asked to join the army.
A. None B. Neither
C. All D. Any

16. .... water in the jug has been drunk by Mohan.
A. The little B. The few
C. A few D. Few

17. I shall play .... piano at the party.
A. some B. any
C. the D. few

18. .... labourers were found dead in the mine.
A. Any B. Fewer
C. Many D. Less

19. Could I borrow .... umbrella?
A. our B. your
C. yours D. my

20. My brother is standing in the .... row.
A. any B. many
C. some D. first

ANSWERS

1	2	3	4	5	6	7	8	9	10
A	B	C	D	C	B	A	C	D	B
11	**12**	**13**	**14**	**15**	**16**	**17**	**18**	**19**	**20**
A	B	C	A	B	A	C	C	B	D

THE VERB

A Verb is a word that tells something about the action or state of or happenning to a person or thing.

A Verb tells the following:

1. What a person or thing does.
Sachin goes to school daily.
The bell *rang* loudly.
Many birds fly in the sky.
She *sang* a song.

2. What a person or thing is.
India *is* the biggest democracy in the world.
Ram Mehar *is* very rich.
They *are* happy.

3. What is done to a person or thing.
You *are liked* by all.
Two thieves *were arrested.*
Four students *were punished* by the teacher.

4. What happens to a person or thing.
His maternal uncle *died* last week.
Two ships *sank* yesterday.
Leaves *turn* yellow in autumn.

5. What a person or thing has, had, and so on.
I *have* a new car.
He *had* a scooter last year.
He *has* several cows and goats.

It goes without saying that a verb is the most important part of a sentence. No sentence is complete without a Verb.

Important Information

1. If two or more singular nouns are joined by 'and' the verb used will be plural.

Example:
(i) He and I were going to the market.
(ii) Ram and Mohan are friends.

2. If two singular nouns joined by 'and' points out to the same thing or person, the verb used must be singular.

Example:
(i) Rice and curry is the favourite food of the Punjabis.
(ii) The Collector and District Magistrate is away.

3. In case two subjects are joined by 'as well as' the verb agrees with the first subject.

Example :
(i) Kanta as well as her children is playing.
(ii) Children as well as their mother are playing.

In the case of first sentence the verb (is) agrees with Kanta and in the case of second sentence the verb (are) agrees with the children.

4. 'Neither', 'Either', 'Every', 'Each', 'Everyone', and 'Many a' are followed by a singular verb.
   Example :
   (i) Either of the plans is to be adopted.
   (ii) Neither of the two brothers is sure to pass.
   (iii) Every student is expected to be obedient.
   (iv) Everyone of them desires this.
   (v) Many a person is drowned in the sea.
5. If two subjects are joined by 'Either .... or' / 'Neither .... nor', the verb agrees with the subject near to it.
   Example :
   (i) Either my brother or I am to do this work.
   (ii) Neither he nor they are prepared to do this work.
6. 'A great many' is always followed by a 'plural noun' and a 'plural verb'. For example :
   A great many students have been declared successful.
7. Similarly if two subjects are joined by 'with', 'together with', 'no less than', in addition to 'and not', etc. the verb agrees with the first subject.
   Example :
   (i) The boy with his parents has arrived.
   (ii) He, no less than I, is to blame.
8. Nouns, plural in form, but singular in meaning, take a singular verb.
   Example :
   This news was broadcast from television yesterday.

MULTIPLE CHOICE QUESTIONS

Directions: *In the following questions choose the correct options to fill the blanks.*

1. The bus with all its passengers .... lost.
A. were B. was
C. are D. would

2. You as well as I .... responsible for this work.
A. am B. are
C. was D. is

3. Raghava like all his companions .... a spoiled child.
A. are B. were
C. is D. will be

4. Pen and ink .... required for me.
A. are B. were
C. is D. has required

5. Every girl and every boy .... attended the seminar.
A. have B. has
C. is D. are

6. Not only she but all her sisters ...... been married.
A. has B. have
C. is D. are

7. There .... nothing but miseries in life.
A. is B. are
C. were D. will be

8. Neither prose nor poem .... given.
A. were B. was
C. has D. have

9. Either he or I .... wrong.
A. is B. are
C. am D. were

10. Either Sulekha or Rekha .... coming here.
A. are B. is
C. were D. have

11. .... the child or his parents to blame?
A. Is B. Are
C. Were D. Has

12. You and I .... neighbours.
A. am B. are
C. was D. has

13. The house with all its belongings ..... sold away.
A. were B. are
C. was D. must

14. Either water or juice .... required.
A. is B. are
C. were D. has

15. There were not as many tables as .... required.
A. was B. were
C. is D. are

16. They each .... a book.
A. have B. are
C. has D. is

17. He and I .... class friends.
A. is B. am
C. was D. are

18. She as well as I .... guilty.
A. is B. are
C. am D. must be

19. Purushottam .... not read more on this chapter.
A. needs B. has been need
C. need D. had been need

20. He came .... to his aunt.
A. run B. running
C. to run D. in run

21. She dislikes .... meat.
A. eat to B. to eat
C. eating D. to eating

22. He likes ....
A. sing to B. singing
C. to sing D. to singing

23. We are ready .... the match.
A. play to B. to playing
C. playing D. to play

24. .... is injurious to health.
A. Smoking B. To smoke
C. To smoking D. Smoke to

25. He loves .... raw vegetables.
A. eaten B. eating
C. to eating D. eat to

26. He seemed .... finished his homework.
A. have to B. to have
C. having D. to having

ANSWERS

1	2	3	4	5	6	7	8	9	10
B	B	C	C	B	B	A	B	C	B
11	**12**	**13**	**14**	**15**	**16**	**17**	**18**	**19**	**20**
A	B	C	A	B	A	D	A	C	B
21	**22**	**23**	**24**	**25**	**26**				
C	B	D	A	B	B				

CONJUNCTIONS

A conjunction is a word which connects words, clauses or sentences.

Look at the following sentences.

(i) He bought apples *and* mangoes.

(ii) God made the country *and* man made the town.

(iii) The door was open *but* there was no one in the house.

(iv) He knows that I am here *and* that I want to see him.

In the sentence (i), *and* connects two words—*apples* and *mangoes.*

In the sentence (ii), *and* connects two sentences—*God made the country* and *man made the town.*

In the sentence (iii), *but* connects two sentences—*The door was open* and *there was no one in the house.*

In the sentence (iv), *and* connects two clauses—*that I am here* and *that I want to see him.*

The main coordinating conjunctions are: and, but, for, or, nor, also, either ..... or, neither ..... nor.

There are some conjunctions which are used in pairs. They are:

either .... or, ... neither .... nor, both .... and, though .... yet, whether .... or, not only .... but also.

Example: *Either* take it *or* leave it.

It is *neither* useful *nor* ornamental.

They *both* like *and* respect me.

Though he is suffering from high fever, *yet* he does not cry.

He does not care *whether* you go *or* stay.

He is *not only* doltish, *but also* obstinate.

The conjunctions which are used in pairs in this way, are called correlative conjunctions, or merely correlatives.

Use of Important Conjunctions

1. **As soon as :** As soon as denotes simultaneous time.

   Example : As soon as he saw his enemy, he took to his heels.

2. **No sooner .... than :**

   (a) 'No sooner' is always followed by 'than'.

   (b) Please remember that 'No sooner' is always followed by do/does/did. As such only first form of the verb should be used after the subject.

   Example :

   No sooner did he see his enemy than he took to his heels.

3. **Hardly :** Hardly is followed by when.

   Examples :

   (i) Hardly had I left the house when it started raining.

   (ii) We had hardly come into the room when his father began chastising him.

   Note :

   A. Hardly is never followed by than.

   B. 'Scarcely' can also be used in the sense and manner of 'Hardly'.

4. **Lest :** Lest is used in the sense of so that .... not. It is always followed by should. Lest is negative in sense. Hence 'not' should never be used with it.

   Example :

   Work hard lest you should fail.

   Note : 'Lest' is always followed by 'should' and not 'may'.

5. **Unless :** Unless expresses condition. It is also used in the negative sense. Use of 'not' is not allowed with unless because unless is already in the negative sense.

   Example :

   Unless you labour hard you will not pass.

6. **Until :** 'Until' expresses time. It means 'till not'.

   Example :

   Wait here until I return.

   Note : Until is in the negative sense. So 'not' should not be used with it. Example :

   Wait here until I do not return. (Incorrect)

   Wait here until I return. (Correct)

7. **As well as :** When two subjects are joined by 'as well as', the verb always agrees with the first subject.

   Examples : –

   (i) The teacher as well as students is playing.

   (ii) Students as well as the teacher are playing.

   Note : 'Both' and 'as well as' cannot be used together in the same sentence.

   Examples :

   Both Sita as well as Kanta are beautiful. (Incorrect)

   Sita as well as Kanta is beautiful. (Correct)

   Both Sita and Kanta are beautiful. (Correct)

8. **As if :** 'As if' is used in the sense of pretension. While using 'as if' in a sentence, we should see that even the third person singular subject gets 'were'.

   Example :

   He talks as if he were mad.

9. **Till :** Till expresses time. Till is always used in the affirmative.

   Example :

   We did not come back till sunset.

10. **Rather than :** 'Rather than' is used in the sense of 'preference'. 'Rather' is always followed by 'than'.

    Example :

    I would rather die than submit.

11. **As long as/so long as :** Both express time during which an action or event takes place.

    Example :

    As long as there is life, there is hope.

12. **However :** It is both a subordinate and co-ordinate clause.

    Examples :

    (a) Mala worked hard, she however, failed.

    (b) However hard he may work, he cannot pass.

13. **Such as :** 'Such as' gives us the sense of 'like'. Such is always followed by 'as'.

    Example :

    Life is such a puzzle as cannot be solved.

MULTIPLE CHOICE QUESTIONS

Directions: *In the following questions choose the correct options to fill the blanks.*

1. Neither he .... his friend is good.
   A. or B. and
   C. but D. nor

2. The officer asked the peon .... why he was late.
   A. that B. if
   C. but D. No word needed

3. Both Ajay .... Vijay are intelligent.
   A. or B. nor
   C. and D. No word needed

4. No Sooner did the thief see the public .... he ran away.
   A. then B. and
   C. but D. than

5. Abhinav .... his brothers was going to Mumbai.
   A. but B. yet
   C. No word needed D. together with

6. He behaves .... he were the captain of the team.
   A. as if B. as
   C. No word needed D. that

7. Either Rupali .... Sonali is going to attend the meeting.
   A. and B. but
   C. nor D. or

8. Neither Nirmal .... Ashwinee is going to listen the speech.
   A. and B. but
   C. nor D. or

9. Ravi .... Prakash are going to Kolkata.
   A. or B. nor
   C. but D. and

10. Rice .... curry is my usual breakfast.
    A. and B. but
    C. then D. than

11. Hardly had he left .... his brother came.
    A. then B. than
    C. when D. that

12. I would rather have a copy .... a book.
    A. then B. than
    C. when D. that

13. He is no other .... my friend.
    A. then B. than
    C. when D. but

14. He saw a snake ....he awoke.
    A. then B. when
    C. than D. No word needed

15. Ten years have passed .... my grandmother died.
    A. since B. when
    C. then D. than

16. She is .... good .... bad.
    A. either, not B. neither, or
    C. neither, nor D. neither, than

17. The cellphone is both cheap .... best.
    A. than B. and
    C. then D. or

18. No sooner did the rogue see the police .... he disappeared.
    A. then B. than
    C. so D. because

19. Srishti will go .... Sanju goes.
    A. if B. than
    C. then D. although

20. She is wise .... timid.
    A. and B. yet
    C. but D. however

21. Make hay .... the sun shines.
    A. though B. while
    C. after D. before

22. He is so weak .... he cannot walk.
    A. but B. that
    C. then D. so

23. Although he is rich, ... he is unhappy.
    A. but B. yet
    C. so D. still

24. Wait here .... I come back.
    A. till B. until
    C. before D. after

25. He is my friend .... I shall help him.
A. so
B. hence
C. that is why
D. therefore

26. He must go away .... he will be beaten.
A. otherwise B. and
C. or D. else

27. God loves good men .... good men love God.
A. and B. or
C. that D. those

28. He was late .... he was not punished.
A. but B. yet
C. still D. therefore

29. Walk slowly ...., you may fall.
A. and B. or
C. so D. otherwise

30. Work hard, ... you will fail.
A. and B. or
C. otherwise D. else

ANSWERS

1	2	3	4	5	6	7	8	9	10
D	D	C	D	D	A	D	C	D	A
11	**12**	**13**	**14**	**15**	**16**	**17**	**18**	**19**	**20**
C	B	B	B	A	C	B	B	A	C
21	**22**	**23**	**24**	**25**	**26**	**27**	**28**	**29**	**30**
B	B	B	A	B	C	A	C	D	D

PREPOSITIONS

A *Preposition* is a word which is placed before a noun or a pronoun to show its relation to some other word in the sentence.

1. I saw a goat *in* the field.
2. I am fond *of* hot coffee.

In sentence 1, the word *in* shows the relation between two things—*goat* and *field.*

In sentence 2, the word *of* shows the relation between the attribute expressed by the adjective *found* and *tea.*

The words *in* and *of* are here used as prepositions.

The noun or pronoun which is used with a preposition is called its object. The noun or pronoun is in the objective case. It is governed by the preposition. Now it is absolutely clear that in sentence 1, the noun *field* is in the objective case. The word *field* is governed by the preposition *in.*

A preposition may have two or more objects.

The road runs over *hill* and *plain.*

Here, the words *hill* and *plain* are used as objects.

Use of Important Prepositions

1. Among, Between

'**Among**' is used for more than two persons or things; '**Between**' is used only for two.

Examples :

(i) Distribute these sweets *among* the poor students of the class.

(ii) Distribute these books *between* Ram and Shyam.

2. Among, In

'**Among**' is used before collective plural nouns. '**In**' is used before collective singular nouns.

Examples :

(i) I found him standing *among* the crowd.

(ii) I saw him in the crowd.

3. Beside, Besides

'**Beside**' means 'by the side of'. '**Besides**' means 'in addition to'.

Examples :

(i) The daughter was sitting *beside* her mother.

(ii) *Besides* his relatives, he invited his friends also.

4. In, Within

'**In**' means at the expiry of a period of time in future, '**Within**' means before the expiry of a period of time in any tense.

Examples :

(i) She will return *in* a week.

(ii) I shall finish my work *within* a weak.

5. On, Upon

'**On**' is used for things at rest; '**Upon**' is used for things in motion.

Examples :

(i) He is sitting *on* the floor.

(ii) The dog sprang *upon* the table.

6. By, With

'**By**' denotes the agent or doer, '**With**' denotes the instrument with which anything is done.

Examples :

(i) The bird was killed *by* the hunter with an arrow.

(ii) He beat the dog *with* a stick.

(iii) I shall reach here *by* five o'clock.

7. After, In

'**After**' means at the end of a period of time in the past. '**In**' means at the end of a period of time in future.

Examples :

(i) I shall return your book *in* a week.

(ii) He returned the book *after* a week.

8. For, From, Since

'**For**' is used before a noun denoting a period of time with all the tenses. '**From**' is used before a noun or phrase denoting a point of time, it is used in all the tenses. '**Since**' is used before a noun or phrase denoting some point of time and is always produced by a verb in the perfect continuous tense or third form of a verb.

Examples :

(i) We have been playing cards *for* two hours.

(ii) She stayed with her uncle *from* the 15th of March to the 15th of May.

(iii) I have been reading this book *since* morning.

9. Above, Over

'Above' means 'higher from', **Over** is used in the following four senses :

(i) In the sense of 'above' :
At noon, the sun is *over* our heads.

(ii) In the sense of 'beyond' :
I cannot get *over* my disappointment.

(iii) In the sense of 'Superiority' :
God *over* all blesses for ever more.

(iv) In the sense of 'Conclusion' :
It is all *over* with me.

10. At, Towards

'At' denotes the idea of aim, **'Towards'** denotes the idea of destination.

Examples :

(i) He threw the stone *at* the cat.

(ii) He went *towards* the house.

11. At, In, On

'At' is used as follows :

(i) **'At'** is used with small towns and villages.

Examples :

(a) He was born *at* Sonepat.

(b) He lives *at* village Bangra. (Bangra is a village)

(ii) **'At'** is used before a noun denoting a definite point of time.

Example :

He called on me *at* 9 p.m. yesterday.

'In' is used as follows :

(iii) **'In'** is used with the names of big cities, provinces and countries.

Examples :

(a) His father lives *in* England.

(b) His younger brother lives *in* Calcutta.

(iv) **'In'** is used before the names of months and years.

Example :

His elder sister was born *in* 1972 *in* the month of May.

'On' is used with dates and names of days.

Examples :

(a) I joined college *on* the 26th April.

(b) He will leave for Kolkata *on* Wednesday next.

Important Information

1. **'In'** is also used in the following phrases :
In the morning; In the evening, In winter, In summer.

2. '**In**' also denotes a place inside anything. He travelled *in* a crowded bus.
3. '**At**' is used in the following phrases : *At* home, *At* the station, *At* work, *At* play.

12. Below, Beneath

Below means 'of lower level in position, dignity and expectation' etc. *Beneath* means 'under'.

Examples :

(i) It is *below* my dignity to talk to her.
(ii) They rested *beneath* the shade of a tree.

13. In, Into, To

'**In**' expresses Rest or Motion inside anything. '**Into**' expresses Motion towards the inside of anything or change from one medium to another. '**To**' denotes motion from one place to another.

Examples :

(i) The boys are *in* the room.
(ii) Translate this passage from English *into* Hindi.
(iii) Every morning he goes *to* the temple.

14. Till, By, Of, Off

- 'Till' means upto or not earlier than.
- 'By' means not later than.
- 'Of' shows cause, source, separation, quality, contents, possession, apposition, point of reference, space in time etc.
- 'Off' shows separation at a near distance, and detached condition.

Consider the following examples:

(i) I shall work *till* 5 a.m.
(ii) Madhu died *of* cancer.
(iii) The nib *of* the pen is made *of* gold.
(iv) He presented me a bottle *of* perfume.
(v) Our principal is a man *of* principle.
(vi) He lived in the house *of* his friend.
(vii) *By* this time tomorrow, I'll have finished my job.
(viii) My house is *off* the road.
(ix) The book fell *off* the table.

MULTIPLE CHOICE QUESTIONS

Directions: *Tick the correct preposition for the blank in each of the following sentences.*

1. He applied ...... the manager.
A. for B. to
C. with D. by

2. Trust ...... God and do the right.
A. in B. for
C. to D. with

3. She is worthy ...... a prize.
A. with B. for
C. to D. of

4. Mr. Gomes has no taste ...... music.
A. of B. for
C. with D. to

5. You are hard ...... hearing.
A. at B. of
C. with D. for

6. He is sure ...... his success
A. for B. with
C. on D. of

7. Preeti was warned ...... the danger ahead.
A. for B. at
C. of D. about

8. I am thankful ...... you for a good advice.
A. for B. with
C. to D. of

9. Deepak would not surrender ...... the police.
A. with B. to
C. for D. on

10. The small plant in your lawn is very sensitive ...... touch.
A. on B. with
C. to D. about

11. Divya was sure to succeed ...... the examination.
A. for B. in
C. to D. with

12. Geeta was jealous ...... Ravina's beauty.
A. to B. with
C. for D. of

13. He was ignorant ..... what was happening there.
A. for B. of
C. to D. with

14. Your pen is inferior ...... mine.
A. than B. with
C. from D. to

15. Reenu is no match ...... Meenu.
A. to B. for
C. with D. upon

16. It is necessary ...... you to apply for this job.
A. on B. with
C. for D. to

17. Be loyal ...... your country.
A. for B. to
C. on D. with

18. Mukesh is junior ...... me.
A. than B. to
C. from D. of

19. Deepika was innocent ...... the crime.
A. of B. with
C. from D. to

20. I am desirous.... joining the Indian cricket team.
A. for B. of
C. to D. on

ANSWERS

1	2	3	4	5	6	7	8	9	10
B	A	D	B	B	D	D	D	B	D
11	**12**	**13**	**14**	**15**	**16**	**17**	**18**	**19**	**20**
B	D	B	D	B	D	B	B	A	B

SYNONYMS

A synonym is a word which conveys a meaning similar to the given word.

REMEMBER

Words	*Synonyms*
Add	Increase
Adequate	Enough
Adjust	Adapt
All	Aggregate
Allow	Permit
Abode	Dwelling
Apt	Proper
Assess	Appraise
Accuse	Calumniate
Abashed	Timid
Annoy	Displease
Ample	Enough, Sufficient
Amplify	Increase
Apathetic	Unenthusiastic
Accost	Address
Authentic	True

Words	*Synonyms*
Adjust	Fit
Approve	Assent, Allow, Accept
Adapt	Conform
Adversary	Opponent, Rival, Competitor
Beat	Whack
Benign	Kind
Breeze	Zephyr
Baffle	Puzzle
Booty	Spoil
Beauty	Charm
Beast	Animal
Bandit	Robber
Blaze	Shine
Bond	Tie
Bend	Twist
Bate	Diminish
Beg	Plead
Barbaric	Wild, Savage
Bashful	Shy, Reserved

Words	*Synonyms*
Begin	Start
Blend	Mix, Mingle
Bizarre	Funny
Below	Under
Bedevil	Confuse
Bemoan	Lament
Babble	Nonsense
Blame	Fault
Behaviour	Demeanour
Call	Accost
Copy	Imitate
Close	Shut
Caress	Love
Camp	Stay
Connect	Attach
Cut	Injure, Curtail
Cling	Stick
Conical	Funny
Convey	Carry
Conspicuous	Prominent
Cheerful	Happy, Pleasant
Curtail	Decrease
Cheerless	Sad, Dejected
Curious	Strange
Circumstance	Factor, Situation, Condition
Competent	Capable
Congruent	Overlapping
Cope	Deal, Endure
Confident	Sure
Complex	Intricate
Cajole	Coax, Flatter
Cunning	Crafty
Delectable	Joyful, Delightful
Devilish	Diabolical
Delicate	Soft
Devil	Fiend
Delay	Postpone
Dislike	Repugnance
Destroy	Ruin

Words	*Synonyms*
Dwell	Live, Dilate
Declare	Pronounce
Drunk	Flushed
Deficient	Lacking
Damn	Condemn, Curse
Decrease	Diminish
Destruction	Devastation
Efficient	Competent
Ethnic	Racial
Enthral	Enslave
Earnest	Serious
Envious	Jealous
Ending	Final
Egg	Incite
Extempore	At once
Extensive	Far-ranging
Extra	Surplus
Existence	Life
Exceed	Overstep
Enormous	Vast
Excessive	Superfluous
Free	Unhindered
Frigid	Cold
Feed	Cater
Fame	Reputation
Frame	Make
First	Initial
Frighten	Terrorise, Intimidate
Fervent	Fervid
Fall	Decline
Feeble	Frail
Fickle	Changeable
Finish	Conclude
Fraud	Deception
Forgiving	Placable
Grow	Develop
Greed	Avidity
Greet	Welcome
Grave	Serious
Group	Constellation

Words	*Synonyms*
Given	Bestowed
Gratitude	Thankfulness
Have	Possess
Hire	Rent
Hit	Strike
Handsome	Beautiful
Hinder	Prevent
Heap	Pile
Hope	Expect
Hard	Harsh
Help	Aid
Hymn	Song
Henpecked	Enslaved
Hoodwink	Mystify, Cheat
Humble	Polite, Urbane, Modest
Harass	Vex, Trouble
Impart	Instil
Intact	Untouched
Instal	Establish
Indict	Impeach
Imitate	Ape
Instigate	Incite
Initiate	Start, Introduce
Inimical	Unfriendly
Insufferable	Intolerable
Impartiality	Justice
Jolly	Merry
Joyful	Delectable
Join	Conjoin
Kind	Benign
Kill	Murder
Kindred	Similar
Kinship	Relationship
Keen	Sharp
Knowledge	Scholarship
Lazy	Slothful
Large	Substantial, Gargantuan
Listless	Careless, Lackadaisical
Lax	Loose
Little	Small
Lifelike	Realistic

Words	*Synonyms*
Lofty	High
Lenient	Soft, Gentle
Lacking	Deficient, Wanting
Lessen	Decrease
Middleclass	Bourgeois
Mitigate	Lessen, Abate
Modesty	Humility, Lowliness
Mix	Mingle, Blend
Mixture	Mingling
Mixed	Assorted
Modify	Decrease
Mean	Imply
Multifarious	Varied
Miscarry	Abort
Note	Notice
Noble	Stately
Native	Indigenous
Needful	Necessary
Notify	Declare
Nervous	Shaky, Tremulous, Timid
Natural	Spontaneous
Near	Close
Normal	Natural
Offend	Displease
Oppress	Persecute, Tyrannize
Opponent	Adversary
Obstruct	Hinder, Check
Offence	Fault
Offender	Villain
Overstep	Exceed
Overlapping	Congruent
Occult	Mystic
Profane	Unholy
Patience	Forbearance
Pornographic	Obscene
Plenitude	Abundance
Prominent	Important
Prodigal	Spender
Procrastinate	Postpone
Promote	Develop, Honour
Persecute	Tyrannise

Words	*Synonyms*
Profess	Claim
Pliant	Flexible
Plebian	Common
Polished	Sophisticated
Quake	Shake
Quit	Leave
Queer	Eccentric
Quell	Suppress
Quantify	Allot
Reply	Answer
Relinquish	Retire
Read	Peruse
Relation	Reference
Render	Do
Remainder	Residuals
Repeat	Reiterate
Repentant	Contrite
Retaliative	Retaliatory
Rumour	Hearsay
Reveal	Divulge
Ritualistic	Ceremonious
Soft	Delicate
Sort	Kind, Choose, Select
Selfish	Egoistic
Sensual	Earthly
Suppress	Quell, Check
Stimulate	Provoke
Tasteless	Insipid
Travel	Journey
True	Authentic, Faithful, Truthful
Turbulence	Turmoil
Tragedy	Calamity
Tasteful	Tasty, Delicious
Touching	Painful
Thankful	Grateful
Tremendous	Great, Huge
Tough	Strong
Terminate	Conclude, End
Theory	Doctrine
Tell	Relate
Tremble	Shake, Shiver
Urge	Spur

Words	*Synonyms*
Unbeaten	Unsubdued
Use	Utilize, Practise
Underhand	Unfair, Undue
Unfair	Unjust
Unravel	Reveal, Divulge
Unimportant	Common
Unconcerned	Apathetic
Unimitated	Inimitable
Unfortunate	Unlucky
Understand	Perceive, Comprehend
Vain	Proud, Haughty, Conceited, Shameless
Vale	Valley, Dale, Dell
Vice	Fault
Virtue	Quality
Veracity	Reality
Value	Price, Prize
Vex	Tease
Vibrate	Quiver, Shake
Violent	Excessive
Vivid	Clear, Lucid
Victory	Triumph
Vulgar	Indecent
Virtuous	Honest
Variegated	Varied, Multifarious
Well	Good
Yell	Cry, Shout
Yonder	There
Yearn	Wish, Desire
Yoke	Slavery
Zest	Earnestness, Enthusiasm
Zealous	Earnest

ANTONYMS

A antonym is a word which conveys a meaning opposite to the given word.

REMEMBER

Words	*Antonyms*
Abhor	Love
Abnormal	Normal
Able	Unable
Acceptable	Unacceptable
Adequate	Inadequate
Amusing	Boring

Words	Antonyms
Angry	Calm
Apex	Bottom
Attract	Repel
Bad	Good
Barren	Fertile
Beautiful	Ugly
Bitter	Sweet
Brave	Cowardly
Brief	Lengthy
Bright	Dull
Calm	Violent
Careful	Careless
Clear	Vague, Cloudy
Cold	Hot
Cruel	Kind
Dear	Cheap
Deep	Shallow
Difficult	Easy
Direct	Indirect
Dishonest	Honest
Disobey	Obey
Encourage	Discourage
Enormous	Tiny
Excellent	Bad
Expensive	Cheap
Eat	Fast
Fair	Unfair
Fake	Authentic
False	True
Famous	Notorious
Fool	Genius
Generous	Miserly
Genius	Fool
Genuine	Unauthentic
Gigantic	Tiny
Glad	Depressed
Good	Bad
Great	Little
Happy	Sad

Words	Antonyms
Hard	Soft
Hate	Love
Honest	Dishonest
Idle	Busy
Immoral	Moral
Include	Exclude
Incorrect	Correct
Intelligent	Unintelligent
Kind	Cruel
Like	Dislike
Long	Short
Lucid	Vague
Major	Minor
Naive	Experienced
Nadir	Apex
Neat	Clumsy
Obedient	Disobedient
Obscure	Clear
Oppose	Support
Optimistic	Pessimistic
Out	In
Patience	Impatience
Peaceful	Belligerent
Pious	Impious
Polite	Impolite
Potent	Impotent
Prominent	Unimportant
Proper	Improper
Pure	Impure
Quick	Slow
Quiet	Disturbance
Real	False, Unreal
Reject	Select, Choose
Reliable	Unreliable
Respect	Disrespect
Right	Wrong
Robust	Feeble, Weak
Sad	Happy

Words	Antonyms
Secret	Open
Sensible	Insensible
Severe	Mild
Sharp	Blunt
Simple	Complex
Sociable	Unsociable
Tall	Short
Tidy	Untidy
Uncanny	Canny
Violent	Calm
Vivid	Vague

Words	Antonyms
Strong	Weak
Big	Small
Easy	Difficult
Fast	Slow
High	Low
Catchy	Unattractive
Ugly	Handsome, Beautiful, Tidy
Tasty	Insipid
Sonorous	Harsh

MULTIPLE CHOICE QUESTIONS

Directions (Qs. 1 to 20): *In the following questions choose the word which best expresses the meaning of the given word.*

1. ABSURD
   A. Foolish B. Simple
   C. Courageous D. Silly

2. ABANDON
   A. Lose B. Profit
   C. Vacate D. Foil

3. CAJOLE
   A. Pause B. Lenient
   C. Blast D. Lure

4. COMBAT
   A. Fight B. Conflict
   C. Shoot D. Quarrel

5. LAMENT
   A. Condone B. Console
   C. Complain D. Contribution

6. DEBACLE
   A. Disgrace B. Defeat
   C. Collapse D. Decline

7. SHIVER
   A. Fear B. Tremble
   C. Shake D. Ache

8. TORTURE
   A. Terror B. Harassment
   C. Torment D. Tranquility

9. LAUDABLE
   A. Lovable B. Commendable
   C. Profitable D. Oblivious

10. FIXED
    A. Sterile B. Static
    C. Stubborn D. Parennial

11. QUEER
    A. Unfamiliar B. Cute
    C. Curious D. Strange

12. SUFFICIENT
    A. Fit B. Proper
    C. Adequate D. Vast

13. GLOSS
    A. Brightness B. Soothing
    C. Rubbing D. Miracle

14. LONGING
    A. Prune B. Apathy
    C. Curtail D. Craving

15. JEER
    A. Applaud B. Magnanimity
    C. Avoid D. Scoff

16. ZENITH
    A. Minimum B. Nadir
    C. Plant D. Peak

17. GARB
    A. Distort B. Dress
    C. Trivial D. Rage

18. ABHOR
A. Rude B. Reconcile
C. Crave D. Detest

19. YIELD
A. Shum B. Incisive
C. Retain D. Surrender

20. YOKE
A. Twist B. Release
C. Link D. Extra

Directions (Qs. 21 to 38): *In the following questions choose the word which best expresses the opposite of the given word.*

21. TRAGIC
A. Dramatic B. Strong
C. Gentle D. Comic

22. ORAL
A. Verbal B. Sane
C. Minor D. Written

23. ADMIRE
A. Hate B. Unlike
C. Dislike D. Enough

24. VIOLENT
A. Gentle B. Savage
C. Haughty D. Decline

25. ADVERSITY
A. Windfall B. Inprosperity
C. Prosperity D. Slave

26. GENUINE
A. Spurious B. Obscure
C. Countless D. Apathetic

27. GRUDGE
A. Essence B. Guile
C. Goodwill D. Ill-will

28. STIFF
A. Soft B. Courteous
C. Lively D. Flexible

29. VANITY
A. Conceit B. Pride
C. Ostentious D. Humility

30. FRONT
A. Upper B. Unusual
C. Back D. Rear

31. ATTRACT
A. Lured B. Longing
C. Repel D. Disguise

32. COMFORT
A. Discomfort B. Discontent
C. Uncomfort D. Miscomfort

33. WELCOME
A. Repel B. Accept
C. Resist D. Fight

34. TACTFUL
A. Naive B. Loose
C. Strict D. Uncivilized

35. DUTIFUL
A. Harmful B. Watchful
C. Forgetful D. Remiss

36. RIGID
A. Flux B. Adoptable
C. Yielding D. Adaptable

37. RARE
A. Petty B. Poor
C. Small D. Common

38. ZEAL
A. Despair B. Calmness
C. Passiveness D. Indifference

ANSWERS

1	2	3	4	5	6	7	8	9	10
D	C	D	A	C	C	B	C	B	B
11	12	13	14	15	16	17	18	19	20
D	C	A	D	D	D	B	D	D	C
21	22	23	24	25	26	27	28	29	30
D	D	C	A	C	A	C	D	D	D
31	32	33	34	35	36	37	38		
C	A	C	A	D	D	D	D		

3. Sentence Completion

It is such an exercise which starts with the primary schools and continues in the highest level of competitive examinations. One must practise it regularly to score well.

Directions (Qs. 1 to 15): *Pick out the most effective word(s) from the given words to fill in the blanks to make the sentence meaningfully complete.*

1. The student ...... that book from the library to study at home.

A. issued B. borrowed
C. hired D. lent

2. I wish I ...... a king.

A. was B. am
C. should be D. were

3. He ...... to listen to my arguments and walked away.

A. denied B. disliked
C. objected D. refused

4. The flow of blood was so ...... that the patient died.

A. intense B. adequate
C. profuse D. extensive

5. When I met her yesterday, it was the first time I ...... her since Christmas.

A. saw B. have seen
C. had seen D. have been seing

6. Can you pay ...... all these articles?

A. for B. of
C. off D. out

7. I ...... you to be at the party this evening.

A. expect B. hope
C. look forward to D. desire

8. ...... being a handicapped person, he is very cooperative and self-reliant.

A. Because B. Although
C. Since D. Despite

9. The child broke ...... from his mother and ran towards the painting.

A. away B. after
C. down D. with

10. With his ...... income, he finds it difficult to live a comfortable life.

A. brief B. sufficient
C. meagre D. huge

11. He could ...... a lot of money in such a short time by using his intelligence and working hard.

A. spend B. spoil
C. exchange D. accumulate

12. Though the brothers are twins, they look ......

A. alike B. handsome
C. indifferent D. different

13. Unfavourable weather conditions can ...... illness.

A. cure B. detect
C. treat D. enhance

14. No sooner did the bell ring, ... the actor started singing.

A. when B. than
C. after D. before

15. If I ...... realised it, I would not have acted on his advice.

A. was B. had
C. were D. have

Directions (Qs. 16 to 25): *In each question, an incomplete statement (Stem) followed by four fillers* *is given. Pick out the best one which can complete the incomplete stem correctly and meaningfully.*

16. Unless you work harder you will fail, means .....
A. if you fail you will work harder.
B. you must at least plan well than you will not fail.
C. hardly you will fail if you do not desire so.
D. if you do not put more efforts, then you will fail.

17. Even if it rains I shall come, means .....
A. if I come it will not rain.
B. if it rains I shall not come.
C. I will certainly come whether it rains or not.
D. whenever there is rain I shall come.

18. Dinesh is as stupid as he is lazy means .....
A. Dinesh is stupid because he is lazy.
B. Dinesh is lazy because he is stupid.
C. Dinesh is either stupid or lazy.
D. Dinesh is equally stupid and lazy.

19. He is so lazy that he .....
A. cannot depend on others for getting his work done.
B. cannot delay the schedule of completing the work.
C. can seldom complete his work on time.
D. dislike to postpone the work that he undertakes to do.

20. He always stammers in public meetings, but his today's speech .....
A. was fairly audible to everyone present in the hall.
B. was not received satisfactorily.
C. could not be understood properly.
D. was free from that defect.

21. In order to raise the company's profit, the employees .....
A. demanded two additional increments.
B. decided to go on paid holidays.
C. requested the management to implement new welfare schemes.
D. offered to work overtime without any compensation.

22. Although, he is reputed for making very candid statements, ...
A. his today's speech was not fairly audible.
B. his promises had always been realistic.
C. his speech was very interesting.
D. his today's statements were very ambiguous.

23. I felt somewhat more relaxed .....
A. but tense as compared to earlier.
B. and tense as compared to earlier.
C. as there was already no tension at all.
D. and tension-free as compared to earlier.

24. With great efforts his son succeeded in convincing him not to donate his entire wealth to an orphanage .....
A. and lead the life of a wealthy merchant.
B. but to a home for the forsaken children.
C. and make an orphan of himself.
D. as the orphanage needed a lot of donations.

25. Even though it is a very large house, ...
A. there is a lot of space available in it for children.
B. there is hardly any space available for children.
C. there is no dearth of space for children.
D. the servants take a long time to clean it.

ANSWERS

1	2	3	4	5	6	7	8	9	10
B	D	D	C	C	A	A	D	A	C
11	**12**	**13**	**14**	**15**	**16**	**17**	**18**	**19**	**20**
D	D	D	B	B	D	C	D	C	D
21	**22**	**23**	**24**	**25**					
D	D	D	C	B					

4. Spotting Errors

The most common errors in English are of spellings, grammar and usage of words. By regular practice, the errors can be easily spotted and minimised.

MULTIPLE CHOICE QUESTIONS

Directions: *In the following questions some of the sentences have errors and some are correct. Find out which part of a sentence has an error, the number of that part is your answer. If a sentence is free from errors, then your answer is D i.e., No error.*

1. (A) Either Ram or/(B) you is responsible/(C) for this action./(D) No error.

2. (A) The student flatly denied/(B) that he had copied/(C) in the examination hall./(D) No error.

3. (A) By the time you arrive tomorrow/(B) I have finished/(C) my work./(D) No error.

4. (A) The captain with the members of his team/ (B) are returning/(C) after a fortnight./(D) No error.

5. (A) After returning from/(B) an all-India tour/ (C) I had to describe about it./(D) No error.

6. (A) The teacher asked his students/(B) if they had gone through/(C) either of the three chapters included in the prescribed text./(D) No error.

7. (A) Do you know/(B) how old were you/(C) when you came here?/(D) No error.

8. (A) Beware of/(B) a fair-weather friend/(C) who is neither a friend in need nor a friend indeed./ (D) No error.

9. (A) Copernicus proved/(B) that Earth/(C) moves round the Sun./(D) No error.

10. (A) The property/(B) was divided/(C) among the two brothers./(D) No error.

11. (A) I am quite certain/(B) that the lady is not only greedy/(C) but miserly./(D) No error.

12. (A) The brilliant success in the examination/ (B) as well as his record in sports/(C) deserves high praise./(D) No error.

13. (A) I cannot find/(B) where has he gone/(C) though I have tried may best./(D) No error.

14. (A) If I was/(B) the Prime Minister of India/(C) I would work wonders/(D) No error.

15. (A) If it weren't/(B) for you,/(C) I wouldn't be alive today./(D) No error.

16. (A) He looked like a lion/(B) baulked from/ (C) its prey./(D) No error.

17. (A) Widespread flooding/(B) is affecting/(C) large areas of the villages./(D) No error.

18. (A) If we really set to/(B) we can get the whole house/(C) cleaned in an afternoon./(D) No error.

19. (A) It's arrogant for you/(B) to assume you'll/ (C)win every time./(D) No error.

20. (A) The two books are the same/(B) except for the fact that this/(C) has an answer in the back./(D) No error.

21. (A) Your husband doesn't/(B) believe that you are older/(C) than I./(D) No error.

22. (A) I could not/(B) answer to/(C) the question./(D) No error.

23. (A) Two years passed/(B) since/(C) my cousin died./(D) No error.

24. (A) I am learning English/(B) for ten years/(C) without much effect./(D) No error.

25. (A) Ramesh has agreed/(B) to marry with the girl/(C) of his parent's choice./ (D) No error.

26. (A) When he was arriving./(B) the party was/(C) in full swing./(D) No error.

27. (A) The most studious boy/(B) in the class/(C) was made as the captain./(D) No error.

28. (A) I am participating/(B) in the two-miles race/(C) tomorrow morning./(D) No error.

29. (A) When the boy committed a mistake/(B) the teacher made him to do/(C) the sum again./(D) No error.

30. (A) Whenever a person lost anything/(B) the poor folk around/(C) are suspected./(D) No error.

ANSWERS

1	2	3	4	5	6	7	8	9	10
B	D	B	B	C	C	D	D	B	C
11	12	13	14	15	16	17	18	19	20
C	D	B	A	C	C	C	A	A	C
21	22	23	24	25	26	27	28	29	30
C	B	A	A	B	A	C	B	B	A

EXPLANATORY ANSWERS

1. Replace 'is' by 'are'.

2. No error.

3. Replace 'have' by 'would have'.

4. Replace 'are' by 'is'.

5. Replace 'had to describe' by 'described'.

6. Replace 'either' by 'any'.

7. No error.

8. No error.

9. Omit 'that'.

10. Replace 'among' by 'between'.

11. Add 'also'.

12. No error.

13. Replace 'has he' by 'he has'.

14. Replace 'was' by 'were'.

15. Replace 'wouldn't be' by 'would not have been'.

16. Replace 'its' by 'his'.

17. Replace 'areas' by 'area'.

18. Replace 'set to' by 'set on'.

19. Replace 'for' by 'of'.

20. Replace 'in' by 'on'.

21. Replace 'I' by 'me'.

22. Omit 'to'.

23. Replace 'passed' by 'have passed'.

24. Replace 'am' by 'have been'.

25. Omit 'with'.

26. Replace 'was arriving' by 'arrived'.

27. Omit 'as'.

28. Replace 'in' by 'at'.

29. Omit 'to'.

30. Replace 'lost' by 'loses'.

5. One Word Substitution

There are many single words in English language which can be perfectly used for a number of words. These words help in expressing ideas in a short and correct manner for the right occasion. Such words not only increase the vocabulary but also enable you to economise in the use of words to a great extent.

Multiple Word Expression	***Substitution***
One who always looks towards the bright side of things	Optimist
One who always looks towards the dark side of things	Pessimist
The time when one develops from a child into an adult	Adolescence
The process of growing more plants in order to form a forest.	Afforestation
The science which deals with farming	Agriculture
From some other country or place etc.	Alien
A term, etc. giving more than one meaning	Ambiguous
A vehicle which is used to carry sick persons	Ambulance
An animal which can live both in water and on land	Amphibian
A lawless situation when there is no government	Anarchy
Belonging to the history of thousands of years old	Ancient
Once a year	Annual
A very old object but still valuable	Antique
Words of opposite meanings	Antonyms
Words of similar meanings	Synonyms
Signatures of a famous person	Autograph
A government led by one person with absolute authority	Autocracy
A written work of one's own life history	Autobiography
A person who has never been married	Bachelor
A person usually having no hair on his head	Bald
A place where one can deposit money and get interest	Bank
A person who cuts our hair	Barber
A building/group of buildings where soldiers live	Barracks
A person who makes buns and biscuits	Baker
A person who lives by asking people for food and money without doing any useful job	Beggar
The crime of having married to two persons at the same time	Bigamy
The branch of science which deals with the study of plants	Botany
Able to speak two languages	Bilingual

Multiple Word Expression	*Substitution*
Able to speak more than two languages	Polyglot
The branch of science which deals with the living organisms	Biology
A powerful snow storm	Blizzard
A great successful book or movie	Blockbuster
A short news on the radio or TV	Bulletin
A system in which the most important works are organised by the government officials	Bureaucracy
A person who has no vision in his eyes	Blind
A page or a series of pages on which the information of days, weeks, months, etc. is given	Calendar
A person who eats human flesh	Cannibal
A complete list of items often arranged alphabetically	Catalogue
A sudden disaster	Catastrophe
A period of 100 years	Century
A branch of science which deals with chemicals	Chemistry
A printed leaf usually issued by banks that we sign to carry certain financial deal	Cheque
A person who makes or mends shoes	Cobbler
A group of people who has been chosen by others to make decisions on their own	Committee
A building in which nuns live	Convent
An animal which feeds on other animals	Carnivorous
A person who does criticism	Critic
A person who cannot hear	Deaf
A condition in which one loses a lot of water from one's body because of vomiting, etc.	Dehydration
A system of government in which the people cast their votes to elect their leaders	Democracy
The study of skin problems	Dermatology
A long piece of land covered with sand	Desert
The art of managing relationships between countries	Diplomacy
A piece of information about the words in a book form	Dictionary
A piece of information about the telephone numbers of the people in a book from	Directory
A person in charge of a newspapers, magazine etc.	Editor
A person who thinks he is better than the others	Egoist
To leave your country and settle in some other country	Emigrate
A book or series of books giving almost all knowledge about an area or some persons etc.	Encyclopaedia
Study of insects	Entomology
Time when day and night are of the same duration	Equinox
To sell things out of the country	Export
To purchase things from some other country	Import
A plant or animal no longer in existence	Extinct
A situation when there is a shortage of food for a long period of time	Famine
An amount of money that we pay for some action or services	Fee
Related to women	Feminine
An animal strong and aggressive	Ferocious

Multiple Word Expression	*Substitution*
A piece of land where plants grow easily from the soil that is favourable to them	Fertile
A work of literature having some imaginary events	Fiction
A large amount of water covering certain area	Flood
A person who sells flowers	Florist
A religious ceremony for burying or cremating a dead person	Funeral
A substance which kills fungus	Fungicide
A person studying or having studied the diseases and the related things of female reproductory system	Gynaecologist
The murder of the person of the same group race or country	Genocide
A substance which kills germs	Germicide
A situation in which many people die because of fire during war	Holocaust
The act of killing a person deliberately	Homicide
A word having the pronunciation as the other one does but it differs in meaning	Homophone
A word having the same spelling as the other one does but it is pronounced in some other way	Homonym
A person who is attracted towards the person of the same sex	Homosexual
Go across and parallel to the ground	Horizontal
A substance which kills the insects	Insecticide
That cannot be corrected	Incorrigible
That cannot be defeated	Invincible
That cannot be eaten	Inedible
That cannot be seen	Invisible
A place in a school or college where books are kept for the benefit of students, teachers etc.	Library
A place in a school or college where scientific experiments are performed	Laboratory
An official who is a judge in the lowest court	Magistrate
A piece of music or a book before it is printed	Manuscript
Related to men	Masculine
One who believes in the existence of God	A theist
One who does not believe in the existence of good	An atheist
That can be believed	Credible
That cannot be believed	Incredible
That which dissolves in a solvent	Soluble
That which does not dissolves in a solvent	Insoluble
Hard writing that can be read	Legible
Hard writing that cannot be read	Illegible
A person who does jobs beneficial to mankind	Philanthropist
A person who goes on foot	Pedestrian
A person who fights for his own country	Patriot
An act of killing oneself	Suicide
A woman whose husband is dead	Widow
A man whose wife is dead	Widower
A person who eats vegetarian and non-vegetarian diets	Omnivorous

Multiple Word Expression	*Substitution*
Something which is everywhere at the same time	Omnipresent
One who knows everything	Omniscient
A child who does not have parents	Orphan
An award etc. given after the death of the person	Posthumous
The place where animals are kept for amusement and to increase the knowledge of the public	Zoo
The science which deals with the study of animals	Zoology

MULTIPLE CHOICE QUESTIONS

Directions: *In questions given below, out of the four alternatives, choose the one which can be substituted for the given words/sentences.*

1. Something that relates to everyone in the world
A. General B. Common
C. Usual D. Universal

2. An expression of mild disapproval
A. Warning B. Denigration
C. Impertinence D. Reproof

3. One who is not easily pleased by anything
A. Maiden B. Medieval
C. Precarious D. Fastidious

4. Murder of a king
A. Infanticide B. Matricide
C. Genocide D. Regicide

5. A remedy for all diseases
A. Stoic B. Marvei
C. Panacea D. Recompense

6. A dramatic performance
A. Mask B. Mosque
C. Masque D. Mascot

7. Study of birds
A. Orology B. Optology
C. Ophthalmology D. Ornithology

8. Ready to believe
A. Credulous B. Credible
C. Creditable D. Incredible

9. Incapable of being seen through
A. Ductile B. Opaque
C. Obsolete D. Potable

10. One who eats everything
A. Omnivorous B. Omniscient
C. Irresistible D. Insolvent

11. A place where bees are kept is called
A. An apiary B. A mole
C. A hive D. A sanctuary

12. One who cannot be corrected
A. Incurable B. Incorrigible
C. Hardened D. Invulnerable

13. One who is in charge of a museum
A. Curator B. Supervisor
C. Caretaker D. Warden

14. Continuing fight between parties, families, clans, etc.
A. Enmity B. Feud
C. Quarrel D. Skirmish

15. A voice loud enough to be heard
A. Audible B. Applaudable
C. Laudable D. Oral

16. A paper written by hand
A. Handicraft B. Manuscript
C. Handiwork D. Thesis

17. Habitually silent or talking little
A. Serville B. Unequivocal
C. Taciturn D. Synoptic

18. To slap with a flat object
A. Chop B. Hew
C. Gnaw D. Swat

19. A person who speaks many languages
A. Linguist B. Monolingual
C. Polyglot D. Bilingual

20. A light sailing-boat built specially for racing
A. Canoe B. Yacht
C. Frigate D. Dinghy

21. A fixed orbit in space in relation to earth
A. Geological B. Geo-synchronous
C. Geo-centric D. Geo-stationary

22. A style in which a writer makes a display of his knowledge
A. Pedantic B. Verbose
C. Pompous D. Ornate

23. A religious discourse
A. Preach B. Stanza
C. Sanctorum D. Sermon

24. A place that provides refuge
A. Asylum B. Sanatorium
C. Shelter D. Orphanage

25. Detailed plan of a journey
A. Travelogue B. Travelkit
C. Schedule D. Itinerary

26. A person who insists on something
A. Disciplinarian B. Stickler
C. Instantaneous D. Boaster

27. A drawing on transparent paper
A. Red print B. Blue print
C. Negative D. Transparency

28. One who believes that all things and events in life are predetermined is a
A. Fatalist B. Puritan
C. Egoist D. Tyrant

29. A school boy who cuts classes frequently is a
A. Defeatist B. Sycophant
C. Truant D. Martinet

30. The act of violating the sanctity of the church is
A. Blasphemy B. Heresy
C. Sacrilege D. Desecration

31. A place where monks live as a secluded community
A. Cathedral B. Diocese
C. Convent D. Monastery

32. One who is fond of fighting
A. Bellicose B. Aggressive
C. Belligerent D. Militant

33. Tending to move away from the centre or axis
A. Centrifugal B. Centripetal
C. Axiomatic D. Awry

34. Words inscribed on tomb
A. Epitome B. Epistle
C. Epilogue D. Epitaph

35. Leave or remove from a place considered dangerous
A. Evade B. Evacuate
C. Avoid D. Exterminate

36. Original inhabitants of a country
A. Abroge B. Aborger
C. Aborgory D. Aborigins

37. Government by the officials
A. Theocracy B. Plutocracy
C. Bureaucracy D. Democracy

38. Incapable of being exhausted
A. Inexhaustible B. Inaexhaustible
C. Exhaustable D. Non-tired

39. A person of good understanding, knowledge and reasoning power
A. Expert B. Intellectual
C. Snob D. Literate

40. One absorbed in his own thoughts and feelings rather than in things outside
A. Scholar B. Recluse
C. Introvert D. Intellectual

ANSWERS

1	2	3	4	5	6	7	8	9	10
D	D	D	D	C	C	D	A	B	A
11	**12**	**13**	**14**	**15**	**16**	**17**	**18**	**19**	**20**
A	B	A	B	A	B	C	D	A	B
21	**22**	**23**	**24**	**25**	**26**	**27**	**28**	**29**	**30**
D	A	D	A	D	B	D	A	C	C
31	**32**	**33**	**34**	**35**	**36**	**37**	**38**	**39**	**40**
D	A	A	D	B	B	C	A	B	C

6. Spelling Errors

There are thousands of words in English language. It is difficult to remember the spellings and meanings of all at once. Try to learn as many as you can. Use a dictionary regularly.

Directions: *Find the correctly spelt words.*

1. A. Damage B. Dammage
C. Damaige D. Dammege

2. A. Efficiant B. Effecient
C. Efficient D. Eficient

3. A. Schedule B. Schdule
C. Schedale D. Schedeule

4. A. Occurad B. Occurred
C. Ocurred D. Occured

5. A. Grieff B. Grief
C. Grieef D. Grrief

6. A. Guarantee B. Garuntee
C. Guaruntee D. Gaurantee

7. A. Meddicine B. Medicine
C. Medicene D. Medicinne

8. A. Benefeted B. Benefitted
C. Benifited D. Benefited

9. A. Acommodation B. Acomodation
C. Accomodation D. Accommodation

10. A. Querrelsome B. Quarrelsame
C. Quarrelsome D. Querralsome

11. A. Sympathetic B. Smypathetic
C. Sympothetic D. Sympethetic

12. A. Prograssive B. Progressive
C. Progresive D. Prograsive

13. A. Uncivilized B. Uncevilized
C. Uncivillized D. Uncevelized

14. A. Extravagant B. Extreragent
C. Extreregant D. Extravegent

15. A. Missunderstood B. Miesunderstood
C. Misunderstood D. Misunderstod

16. A. Belligerent B. Beligirent
C. Belligarant D. Belligerrent

17. A. Astonished B. Astronished
C. Astoneshed D. Asstonished

18. A. Sincerely B. Sencerely
C. Sincerelly D. Sincerrely

19. A. Rigourous B. Rigerous
C. Rigorous D. Regerous

20. A. Satellite B. Sattellite
C. Satelite D. Sattelite

21. A. Pesanger B. Passenger
C. Pessenger D. Pasanger

22. A. Humurous B. Humorous
C. Humoreus D. Humorrous

23. A. Exeggerate B. Exaggerate
C. Exadgerate D. Exagerate

24. A. Fariegn B. Forein
C. Foriegn D. Foreign

25. A. Excesive B. Excessive
C. Exccessive D. Exccesive

26. A. Forcaust B. Forcast
C. Forecast D. Forecaste

27. A. Paralleted B. Paralelled
C. Parralleled D. Parallelled

28. A. Ocasion B. Occassion
C. Occasion D. Ocassion

29. A. Boquet B. Bouquet
C. Bouquete D. Bouquette

30. A. Chettering B. Chaterring
C. Chattering D. Chatcring

31. A. Discourage B. Disscourage
C. Discourege D. Discaurage

32. A. Curageous B. Courageous
C. Courrageous D. Couregeous

33. A. Abandon B. Abanddon
C. Abendon D. Abbandon

34. A. Embarassment
B. Emberrassement
C. Embarrassment
D. Embbaresment

35. A. Eccintric B. Eccentrie
C. Eccentric D. Eccintrie

36. A. Occasional B. Occassional
C. Occesional D. Occessional

37. A. Querrel B. Querral
C. Quarrel D. Quarel

38. A. Contrebution B. Contribution
C. Contributtion D. Conterbution

39. A. Desgrace B. Disgrece
C. Disgrice D. Disgrace

40. A. Harassment B. Herassment
C. Harasment D. Harassmient

41. A. Imaginative B. Imeginative
C. Imagenative D. Imaginetive

42. A. Suficient B. Suficiant
C. Sufficient D. Sufficiant

43. A. Adequate B. Edequate
C. Adaquete D. Edaquete

44. A. Exparienced B. Experianced
C. Experienced D. Experrienced

45. A. Flatering B. Fletering
C. Flattering D. Fletaring

46. A. Cuttiveted B. Culltrivated
C. Cultivated D. Caltivated

47. A. Praiceworthy B. Peiseworthy
C. Praiseworthy D. Praisaworthy

48. A. Profesional B. Professionel
C. Professional D. Profissional

49. A. Ameteur B. Amateur
C. Amataur D. Amateor

50. A. Unfevourable B. Unfevaurable
C. Unfavourable D. Unfivourable

ANSWERS

1	2	3	4	5	6	7	8	9	10
A	C	A	B	B	A	B	B	D	C
11	**12**	**13**	**14**	**15**	**16**	**17**	**18**	**19**	**20**
A	B	A	A	C	A	A	A	C	A
21	**22**	**23**	**24**	**25**	**26**	**27**	**28**	**29**	**30**
B	B	B	D	B	C	A	C	B	C
31	**32**	**33**	**34**	**35**	**36**	**37**	**38**	**39**	**40**
A	B	A	C	C	A	C	B	D	A
41	**42**	**43**	**44**	**45**	**46**	**47**	**48**	**49**	**50**
A	C	A	C	A	C	C	C	B	C

सामान्य हिंदी

व्याकरण

व्याकरण वह शास्त्र है जिसके द्वारा किसी भी भाषा के शब्दों और वाक्यों के शुद्ध स्वरूपों एवं शुद्ध प्रयोगों का ज्ञान कराया जाता है।

व्याकरण के चार अंग हैं : (i) वर्ण विचार (ii) शब्द विचार (iii) पद विचार और (iv) वाक्य विचार

भाषा : भाषा अभिव्यक्ति का एक ऐसा साधन है जिसके द्वारा मनुष्य अपने विचारों को दूसरों पर प्रकट कर सकता है और दूसरों के विचार जान सकता है। भाषा के दो रूप हैं–(i) मौखिक और (ii) लिखित।

बोली : भाषा का क्षेत्रीय रूप बोली कहलाता है।

लिपि : किसी भी भाषा के लिखने की विधि को लिपि कहते हैं।

वर्ण : हिन्दी भाषा में प्रयुक्त सबसे छोटी ध्वनि वर्ण कहलाती है। जैसे–अ, आ, ई, क्, ख्, आदि

वर्णमाला : वर्णों के समुदाय को वर्णमाला कहते हैं। हिन्दी वर्णमाला में 44 वर्ण हैं। जिनमें 11 स्वर तथा 33 व्यंजन हैं।

स्वरवर्ण : उन वर्णों को कहते हैं, जिनका उच्चारण बिना किसी दूसरे वर्ण की सहायता से होता है। हिन्दी में 11 स्वर हैं–अ, आ, इ, ई, उ, ऊ, ए, ऐ, ओ, औ, ऋ।

व्यंजन वर्ण : उन वर्णों को कहते हैं, जिनका उच्चारण स्वर वर्णों की सहायता के बिना नहीं हो सकता है। इनकी संख्या 33 है–

क ख ग घ ड़ च

छ ज झ ञ ट् ठ

ड ढ़ ण त थ द

ध न प फ ब भ

म य र ल व श

ष स ह।

वर्ण : एक या अधिक वर्णों से बनी हुई स्वतन्त्र सार्थक ध्वनि शब्द कहलाती है।

शब्दों को तत्सम, तद्भव, देशज और विदेशी भागों में बाँटा जाता है।

तत्सम : जो शब्द संस्कृत भाषा से हिन्दी में बिना किसी परिवर्तन के लिए जाते हैं वे तत्सम कहलाते हैं, जैसे– अग्नि, क्षेत्र, मित्र, नासिका आदि।

तद्भव : उन शब्दों को कहते हैं, जो संस्कृत से ही लिए गए हैं, परन्तु हिन्दी में आने पर जिनका रूप बदल गया है। जैसे–आग, खेत, रात आदि।

देशज : उन शब्दों को कहते हैं, जो बोलचाल तथा देश की अन्य भाषाओं से लिए गए हैं। जैसे–कटोरा, झंझत, डिबिया, लोटा आदि।

विदेशज या विदेशी : उन शब्दों को कहते हैं, जो किसी विदेशी भाषा से आए हैं।

जैसे–स्कूल, कार, कमरा, खुदा, जोश, सरकार आदि।

शब्द सम्पदा

तत्सम शब्दों के तद्भव रूप

तत्सम	तद्भव	तत्सम	तद्भव
अग्नि	आग	अद्य	आज
अष्ट	आठ	अक्षि	आँख
अर्ध	आधा	अस्थि	हड्डी
अश्रु	आँसू	आम्र	आम

तत्सम	तद्भव	तत्सम	तद्भव
ग्राम	गाँव	गर्दभ	गधा
गृध्र	गीध	गौर	गोरा
गृह	घर	घट	घड़ा
धातु	धात	धृत	घी

तत्सम	तद्भव	तत्सम	तद्भव
लक्ष	लाख	सप्त	सात
त्वम्	तुम	दुग्ध	दूध
रत्न	रतन	वर्ष	बरस
भक्त	भगत	मर्कट	बन्दर
रात्रि	रात	उलूक	उल्लू
अन्धकार	अन्धेरा	क्षीर	खीर
निद्रा	नींद	पृष्ठ	पीठ
ज्येष्ठ	जेठ	स्वर्ण	सोना
श्वास	साँस	काक	काग
कार्य	काज	कर्ण	कान
पाद	पाँव	हस्त	हाथ
नासिका	नाक	कंटक	काँटा
दश	दस	दधि	दही
दीप	दीया	निद्रा	नींद
नव	नौ	पत्र	पत्ता

तत्सम	तद्भव	तत्सम	तद्भव
प्रस्तर	पत्थर	जिह्वा	जीभ
हस्ती	हाथी	दन्त	दाँत
क्षेत्र	खेत	नृत्य	नाच
सूचिका	सूई	स्वर्णकार	सुनार
लोक	लोग	पर्यङ्क	पलंग
स्वप्न	सपना	कातर	कायर
पुत्र	पूत	मानव	मनुष्य
शत	सौ	पुष्प	फूल
पक्व	पक्का	कृषक	किसान
कर्म	कार्य	आम्र	आम
कर्ण	कान	अष्ट	आठ
घंटिका	घंटी	चन्द्र	चन्द
यव	जौ	धूम्र	धुआँ
भ्रमर	भँवर		

विराम चिह्न

विराम का अर्थ रुकना। अपने विचारों को ठीक ढंग से प्रकट करने के पढ़ते अथवा लिखते समय हमें कुछ रुकना पड़ता है। इस प्रकार के रुकने को विराम कहते हैं। प्रत्येक-विराम के लिए अलग-अलग चिह्न हैं–

पूर्ण विराम	[।]
अल्प विराम	[,]
अर्ध विराम	[;]
प्रश्न बोधक	[?]
विस्मयादि बोधक	[!]
योजक	[–]
उद्धरण	[" "]

कारक

कारक शब्द उस रूप को कहते हैं, जिससे संज्ञा या सर्वनाम वाक्य के साथ सम्बन्ध जाना जाता है।

जैसे–शीला कलम **से** लिखती है।

यह सीमा **की** पुस्तक है।

कारक के भेद विभक्ति चिह्नों सहित

कारक	विभक्ति
कर्त्ता	ने
कर्म	को
करण	से
सम्प्रदान	के लिए
अपादान	से
सम्बन्ध	का, के, की
अधिकरण	में, पर
सम्बोधन	हे, अरे!

पर्यायवाची शब्द

जिन शब्दों से एक समान अर्थ का बोध होता है, उन्हें पर्यायवाची या समानार्थी शब्द कहते हैं।

कुछ पर्यायवाची शब्दों के उदाहरण निम्नलिखित हैं–

आग – अग्नि, अनल, पावक, हुताशन, ज्वाला।

आकाश – नभ, आसमान, गगन, लोभ।

असुर – राक्षस, दानव, निशाचर, दैत्य।

अमृत – अभिय, पीयूष, सुधा, सोम।

अन्धकार – अन्धेरा, तिमिर, तम, तमिस्त्र।

आँख – नेत्र, नयन, लोचन, चक्षु, दृग।

कमल – जलज, पंकज, नीरज, राजीव।

इन्द्र – सुरपति, देवेन्द्र, सुरेन्द्र, देवेश।
ईश्वर – प्रभु, भगवान, जगदीश, दीनबन्धु।
पक्षी – खग, विहग, चिड़िया, नभचर।
बादल – घन, जलधर, वारिद, नीरद।
गंगा – सुरसरि, जाह्नवी, त्रिपथगा, देवनदी, विष्णुपदी।
चन्द्रमा – शशि, मयंक, निशाकर, सुधाकर, सुधांशु, सोम हिमांशु, राकेश।
जल – पानी, नीर, लोभ, अम्बु, सलिल, क्षीर, वारि।
फूल – पुष्प, कुसुम, सुमन, प्रसून, सारंग।
पृथ्वी – भू, भूमि, धरा, वसुन्धरा, वसुधा, धरती क्षमा, लोक।
कपड़ा – पट, वस्त्र, चीर, अम्बर, दुकूल।
घर – गृह, गेह, निकेतन, आलय, निलय, भवन, शाला, धाम, सदन।
जंगल – वन, कानन, अरण्य, विपिन।
तालाब – सरोवर, ताल, जलाशय, तड़ाग।
दिन – दिवस, वासर, वार।
पहाड़ – गिरि, पर्वत, गूधर, नग, महीधर, मेरू।
पत्थर – पहाड़, प्रस्तर, पाहन।
पवन – वायु, समीर, हवा, मारुत, अनिल।
पुत्र – सुत, तनय, पूत, आत्मज।
बिजली – तड़ित, चपला, दामिनी।
वृक्ष – तरू, रूख, विटप, पेड़।
मनुष्य – नर, मानव, मनुज, आदमी।
हाथी – करि, हस्ती, गज।
मित्र – सखा, मीत, सहचर, दोस्त।
राजा – नरेश, नृप, महीप, भूप।
समुद्र – सागर, सिन्धु, जलधि, नीरधि।
सरस्वती – शारदा, वागेश्वरी, भारती, महाश्वेता।
साँप – पन्नग, सर्प, विषधर, अहि, व्याल।
सूर्य – दिनकर, दिवाकर, रवि, भानु, भास्कर।
स्त्री – नारी, महिला, दारा, वामा।
शरीर – देह, तन, काया, गात, बदन।
गणेश – गजानन, गणपति, विनायक, एकदन्त, गजवदन लम्बोदर, विघ्न नाशक।
घोड़ा – तुरंग, बाजि, हय, अश्व, घोटक।
युद्ध – समर, रण, संग्राम।
सिंह – केसरी, मृगराज, केहरी।
शत्रु – अरि, रिपु, बैरी।
विष्णु – हरि, कमलेश, रमापति, चक्रपाणि, केशव, माधव, पीताम्बर।
कोष – खजाना, भण्डार, निधि।
धन – दौलत, द्रव्य, मुद्रा।
तलवार – कृपाण, असि, खड्ग।
अंग – भाग, हिस्सा, अवयव।
चोर – तस्कर, दस्यु, रजनीचर।
पत्नी – भार्या, दारा, गृहिणी।
पुत्र – तनय, सुत, लड़का, बेटा।
पुत्री – तनया, सुता, लड़की, बेटी।
माता – जननी, अम्बा, अम्बिका, अम्मा, माँ, धात्री।
मोर – शिखी, नीलकण्ठ, मयूर।
मृत्यु – मौत, काल, देहान्त।
रक्त – रुधिर, शोणित, खून, लहू।
विष – जहर, हलाहल, गरल।
सोना – कंचन, स्वर्ण, कनक।
हृदय – उर, छाती, वक्ष, वक्षस्थल, हिय, हिया।
सभा – अधिवेशन, परिषद्, बैठक, महासभा, समागम, समिति, सम्मेलन।
यमुना – कालिन्दी, कृष्णा, जमुना, रविसुता तरणि-तनुजा।

विलोम-शब्द

शब्दों के अपने निश्चित अर्थ होते हैं। उन अर्थों के विपरीत अर्थ देने वाले शब्द को विलोम-शब्द कहते हैं।

शब्द	विलोम	शब्द	विलोम	शब्द	विलोम	शब्द	विलोम
अमृत	विष	उदार	संकीर्ण	आदि	अन्त	उत्थान	पतन
अनुकूल	प्रतिकूल	अनुराग	विराग	इच्छा	अनिच्छा	उचित	अनुचित

शब्द	विलोम	शब्द	विलोम
अल्पायु	दीर्घायु	अनुज	अग्रज
उन्नति	अवनति	आकाश	पाताल
अधिक	न्यून	आयात	निर्यात
एक	अनेक	अन्धकार	प्रकाश
अर्थ	अनर्थ	उदय	अस्त
परकीया	स्वकीया	जड़	चेतन
जय	पराजय	अनिवार्य	वैकल्पिक
नकद	उधार	अपेक्षा	उपेक्षा
उपस्थित	अनुपस्थित	आदर	अनादर
अन्धेरा	उजाला	अपना	पराया
उत्तम	अधम	आय	व्यय
सुपुत्र	कुपुत्र	स्वाधीन	पराधीन
आहार	निराहार	कठोर	कोमल
दाता	याचक	दोषी	निर्दोषि
खेद	प्रसन्नता	धनी	निर्धन
निकट	दूर	चर	अचर
देव	दानव	खरा	खोटा
गरीब	अमीर	प्रेम	घृणा
जीवन	मृत्यु	बुरा	भला
सजीव	निर्जीव	मित्र	शत्रु
सुगन्ध	दुर्गन्ध	मौखिक	लिखित
संक्षेप	विस्तार	कटु	मधुर
आरम्भ	अन्त	कड़वा	मीठा
कृतज्ञ	कृतघ्न	दिन	रात
साक्षर	निरक्षर	पवित्र	अपवित्र
पाप	पुण्य	जल	थल
धीर	अधीर	निर्मल	मलिन
गुण	अवगुण	नश्वर	अनश्वर
निन्दा	स्तुति	भारी	हल्का
मनुष्यता	पशुता	सरस	नीरस
मान	अपमान	क्रय	विक्रय

शब्द	विलोम	शब्द	विलोम
धर्म	अधर्म	गहरा	उथला
गुरु	शिष्य	पक्ष	विपक्ष
जन्म	मृत्यु	बन्धन	मुक्ति
यश	अपयश	ज्ञान	अज्ञान
आदर	अनादर	पूर्ण	अपूर्ण
सफल	असफल	शान्त	अशान्त
कीर्ति	अपकीर्ति	वादी	प्रतिवादी
आस्तिक	नास्तिक	स्वदेश	परदेश
सज्जन	दुर्जन	राग	द्वेष
ऊसर	उर्वर	उदार	कृपण
अगला	पिछला	अगम	सुगम
अग्नि	जल	अति	अल्प
अर्थ	अनर्थ	अतल	वितल
अत्यधिक	स्वल्प	अद्यः	उपरि
अधिकतम	न्यूनतम	अतिवृष्टि	अनावृष्टि
अनाथ	सनाथ	ईश्वर	जीव
अनुलोम	विलोम	अर्पण	ग्रहण
अवनि	अम्बर	अस्त	उदय
आकर्षण	विकर्षण	आगे	पीछे
आजाद	गुलाम	आदान	प्रदान
आधुनिक	प्राचीन	आना	जाना
आय	व्यय	आयात	निर्यात
आवश्यक	अनावश्यक	आशा	निराशा
आस्था	अनास्था	इहलोक	परलोक
उच्च	निम्न	उत्थान	पतन
उपकार	अपकार	उपयोग	दुरुपयोग
एकता	अनेकता	कल	आज
कृत्रिम	प्राकृत	कृष्ण	शुक्ल
कपूत	सपूत	कोमल	कठोर
गगन	धरा	ज्ञान	अज्ञान
झूठ	सच		

लिंग

लिंग का अर्थ है 'चिह्न'। लिंग शब्द उस चिह्न को कहते हैं जिससे वस्तु के पुरुष या स्त्री होने की कल्पना हो। लिंग दो प्रकार के होते हैं—(1) पुल्लिंग (2) स्त्रीलिंग

पुल्लिंग–पुल्लिंग संज्ञा के उस रूप को कहते हैं जिससे उसके पुरुष होने का ज्ञान होता है। जैसे–राम, श्याम, घोड़ा, हाथी, कुत्ता आदि। **स्त्रीलिंग**–स्त्रीलिंग संज्ञा के उस रूप को

कहते हैं जिससे उसके स्त्री होने का ज्ञान हो। जैसे–भैंस, गाय, बकरी, सीता, रमा इत्यादि।

पुल्लिंग	स्त्रीलिंग	पुल्लिंग	स्त्रीलिंग
इन्द्र	इन्द्राणी	मेहतर	मेहतरानी
नौकर	नौकरानी	जेठ	जेठानी
देवर	देवरानी	सेठ	सेठानी
पण्डित	पण्डिताइन	ओझा	ओझाइन
बनिया	बनियाइन	दुबे	दुबाइन
हलवाई	हलवाइन	चौबे	चौबाइन
गुरु	गुरुआइन	लड़का	लड़की
दास	दासी	कबूतर	कबूतरी
हिरण	हिरणी	क्षत्रिय	क्षत्राणी
मुगल	मुगलानी	हिन्दू	हिन्दुआनी
चौधरी	चौधरानी	भव	भवानी
लाला	ललाइन	पण्डा	पण्डाइन
ठाकुर	ठकुराइन	बाबू	बबुआइन
घोड़ा	घोड़ी	गूँगा	गूँगी
बच्चा	बच्ची	चाचा	चाची
बकरा	बकरी	मामा	मामी
मुर्गा	मुर्गी	साला	साली
चींटा	चींटी	रस्सा	रस्सी
देव	देवी	ब्राह्मण	ब्राह्मणी
बेटा	बेटी	बूढ़ा	बुढ़िया
चूहा	चुहिया	डिब्बा	डिबिया
गुड्डा	गुड़िया	कुम्हार	कुम्हारिन
सुनार	सुनारिन	नाती	नातिन
जुलाहा	जुलाहिन	दर्जी	दर्जिन
पापी	पापिन	हाथी	हथिनी
पिता	माता	बैल	गाय
कवि	कवयित्री	विधुर	विधवा
बाप	माँ	बादशाह	बेगम

पुल्लिंग	स्त्रीलिंग	पुल्लिंग	स्त्रीलिंग
नर	मादा	मर्द	औरत
युवक	युवती	वर	वधू
सम्राट्	सम्राज्ञी	साढू	साली
फूफा	बुआ	पुत्र	पुत्री
पहाड़	पहाड़ी	गोप	गोपी
गधा	गधी	तरुण	तरुणी
नर्तक	नर्तकी	बेटा	बिटिया
बछड़ा	बछिया	चिड़ा	चिड़िया
बन्दर	बन्दरिया	कुत्ता	कुतिया
नाई	नाइन	धोबी	धोबिन
ग्वाला	ग्वालिन	भंगी	भंगिन
स्वामी	स्वामिनी	विद्वान्	विदुषी
साधु	साध्वी	पुरुष	स्त्री
पति	पत्नी	वीर	वीरांगना
साहब	मेम	सास	ससुर
मियाँ	बीबी	राजा	रानी
बिलाड़	बिल्ली	अनुज	अनुजा
छात्र	छात्रा	महोदय	महोदया
प्रिय	प्रिया	मामा	मामी
लोटा	लुटिया	मोर	मोरनी
शेर	शेरनी	जाट	जाटिन
डाक्टर	डाक्टरनी	मालिक	मालकिन
माली	मालिन	बाघ	बाघिन
हाथी	हथिनी	स्वामी	स्वामिनी
बालक	बालिका	धनवान	धनवती
धावक	धाविका	नेता	नेत्री
गुणवान	गुणवती	नर	मादा
अभिनेता	अभिनेत्री	प्राचार्य	प्राचार्या
प्रबन्धकर्ता	प्रबन्धकर्ती	दाता	दात्री
ननदोई	ननद	अध्यापक	अध्यापिका

वचन

शब्द के जिस रूप से उसके एक अथवा अनेक होने का बोध हो, उसे वचन कहते हैं।

हिन्दी में दो वचन होते हैं–

(1) एकवचन और (2) बहुवचन

एकवचन–शब्द के जिस रूप से एक ही वस्तु का बोध हो, उसे एकवचन कहते हैं। जैसे–लड़का, गाय, बकरी, घोड़ा, राम, सीता आदि।

बहुवचन–शब्द के जिस रूप से अनेकता का बोध हो उसे बहुवचन कहते हैं। जैसे–लड़के, कपड़े, गायें आदि।

एकवचन	बहुवचन	एकवचन	बहुवचन
लड़का	लड़के	कौवा	कौवे
बेटा	बेटे	कमरा	कमरे
कपड़ा	कपड़े	बहन	बहनें
चीज	चीजें	गधा	गधे
रुपया	रुपये	घोड़ा	घोड़े
नहर	नहरें	रात	रातें
बात	बातें	सड़क	सड़कें
दाना	दाने	लोटा	लोटे
पैसा	पैसे	पुस्तक	पुस्तकें
कन्या	कन्याएँ	वधू	वधुएँ
नारी	नारियाँ	लड़की	लड़कियाँ
मुर्गा	मुर्गे	घण्टा	घण्टे
गद्दा	गद्दे	हीरा	हीरे
बच्चा	बच्चे	प्याला	प्याले
छाता	छाते	गाय	गायें
कथा	कथाएँ	कविता	कविताएँ
बहू	बहुएँ	टोपी	टोपियाँ
नाली	नालियाँ	बेटा	बेटे
ताला	ताले	जूता	जूते

एकवचन	बहुवचन	एकवचन	बहुवचन
डिबिया	डिबियाँ	नाक	नाकें
पूँछ	पूँछें	मूँछ	मूँछें
चिड़िया	चिड़ियाँ	सरिता	सरिताएँ
बालिका	बालिकाएँ	चाभी	चाभियाँ
कहानी	कहानियाँ	दरवाजा	दरवाजे
कलम	कलमें	कुटिया	कुटियाँ
रानी	रानियाँ	नाई	नाइयों
माता	माताएँ	बाल	बालों
हाथ	हाथों	मुख	मुख
कोट	कोट	दाँत	दाँतों
नाखून	नाखूनों	पैर	पैरों
बैल	बैलों	माली	मालियों
राजा	राजाओं	पिता	पिता
चन्द्रमा	चन्द्रमा	कवि	कवियों
मुनि	मुनियों	कौआ	कौए
छात्रा	छात्राएँ	सेना	सेनाएँ
दिशा	दिशाएँ	गुड़िया	गुड़ियाँ
मेज	मेजें	भैंस	भैंसें
अंगूर	अंगूरों	समुद्र	समुद्र
केला	केले	पत्ता	पत्ते

अनेक शब्दों के लिए एक शब्द

जिसकी कोई उपमा न हो : **अनुपम**
तेज बुद्धि वाला : **कुशाग्रबुद्धि**
कल्पना से परे हो : **कल्पनातीत**
जो उपकार नहीं मानता है : **कृतघ्न**
जो उपकार मानता है : **कृतज्ञ**
किसी की हँसी उड़ाना : **उपहास**
ऊपर कहा हुआ : **उपर्युक्त**
ऊपर लिखा हुआ : **उपरलिखित**
जिस पर उपकार किया गया हो : **उपकृत**
इतिहास का ज्ञाता : **इतिहासज्ञ**
आलोचना करने वाला : **आलोचक**
ईश्वर में आस्था रखने वाला : **आस्तिक**
बिना वेतन का : **अवैतनिक**
जो कहा न जा सके : **अकथनीय**
जो गिना न जा सके : **अगणित**

जिसका कोई शत्रु ही न जन्मा हो : **अजातशत्रु**
जिसके समान कोई दूसरा न हो : **अद्वितीय**
जो परिचित न हो : **अपरिचित**
आकाश में उड़ने वाला : **नभचर**
जो टुकड़े-टुकड़े हो गया हो : **खण्डित**
मछली की तरह आँखों वाली : **मीनाक्षी**
मयूर की तरह आँखों वाली : **मयूराक्षी**
बच्चों के लिए काम की वस्तु : **बालोपयोगी**
जिसकी बहुत अधिक चर्चा हो : **बहुचर्चित**
जिस स्त्री को कभी सन्तान न हुई हो : **बन्ध्या (बाँझ)**
फेन से भरा हुआ : **फेनिल**
प्रिय बोलने वाली स्त्री : **प्रियम्वदा**
जिसकी उपमा न हो : **निरुपम**
जो थोड़ी देर पहले पैदा हुआ हो : **नवजात**
जिसका कोई आधार न हो : **निराधार**

नगर में वास करने वाला : **नागरिक**
रात में घूमने वाला : **निशाचर**
ईश्वर में विश्वास न रखने वाला : **नास्तिक**
माँस न खाने वाला : **निरामिष**
बिल्कुल बर्बाद हो गया : **ध्वस्त**
जिसकी धर्म में निष्ठा हो : **धर्मनिष्ठ**
देखने योग्य : **दर्शनीय**
बहुत तेज चलने वाला : **द्रुतगामी**
जो किसी पक्ष में न रहे : **तटस्थ**
तत्त्व को जानने वाला : **तत्त्वज्ञ**
तप करने वाला : **तपस्वी**
जिसे देखकर डर लगे : **डरावना**
जो जन्म से अन्ध हो : **जन्मान्ध**
जीने की प्रबल इच्छा : **जिजीविषा**
जिसने इन्द्रियों को जीत लिया हो : **जितेन्द्रिय**
चिन्ता में डूबा हुआ : **चिन्तित**
जो बहुत समय तक ठहरे : **चिरस्थायी**
जिसकी चार भुजाएँ हों : **चतुर्भुज**
जिसके हाथ में चक्र हों : **चक्रपाणि**
जिससे घृणा की जाए : **घृणित**
जिसे गुप्त रखा जाए : **गोपनीय**
गणित ज्ञाता : **गणितज्ञ**
आकाश को चूमने वाला : **गगनचुम्बी**
जिसका आदि न हो : **अनादि**
जो कुछ न जानता हो : **अज्ञ**
जो अनुकरण करने योग्य हो : **अनुकरणीय**
जिसका अन्त न हो : **अनन्त**
जो कभी न मरे : **अमर**
जो कम बोलता हो : **अल्पभाषी**
जिसका इलाज न हो : **लाइलाज**
जिसका कोई नाथ न हो : **अनाथ**
कम जानने वाला : **अल्पज्ञ**
जहाँ जाना सम्भव न हो : **अगम**
बड़ा भाई : **अग्रज**
कम खाने वाला : **अल्पाहारी**
जो बात पहले कभी न हुई हो : **अभूतपूर्व**
दूसरों के पीछे चलने वाला : **अनुचर**
जो पहले न पढ़ा हो : **अपठित**

जिसके आर-पार दिखाई देता हो : **पारदर्शी**
आज्ञा पालन करने वाला : **आज्ञाकारी**
काम से जी चुराने वाला : **कामचोर**
प्रतिदिन होने वाला : **दैनिक**
जिसका कोई अर्थ न हो : **निरर्थक**
हाथ से लिखा हुआ : **हस्तलिखित**
आँखों के सामने होने वाला : **प्रत्यक्ष**
जिसका आचरण अच्छा हो : **सदाचारी**
वह पुरुष जिसकी पत्नी मर गई हो : **विधुर**
वह स्त्री जिसका पति मर गया हो : **विधवा**
जिसका रूप अच्छा न हो : **कुरूप**
सदा सत्य बोलने वाला : **सत्यवादी**
बड़ी इमारत के टूटे-फूटे भाग : **खण्डहर**
प्रशंसा के योग्य : **प्रशंसनीय**
जहाँ अनाथ रहते हों : **अनाथालय**
प्रत्येक मास होने वाला : **मासिक**
जहाँ पानी के जहाज आकर रुकते हैं : **बन्दरगाह**
प्रत्येक सप्ताह होने वाला : **साप्ताहिक**
प्रत्येक वर्ष होने वाला : **वार्षिक**
जो कठिनाई से मिले : **दुर्लभ**
जिसका आकार हो : **साकार**
जिसका आकार न हो : **निराकार**
जो कभी बूढ़ा न हो : **अजर**
बहुत बोलने वाला : **वाचाल**
पृथ्वी पर रहने वाला : **थलचर**
जल में रहने वाला : **जलचर**
नभ में विचरण करने वाला : **नभचर**
जल-थल दोनों में रहने वाला : **उभयचर**
जिसमें रस न हो : **नीरस**
पढ़ने वाला : **पाठक**
जो भाषण देता हो : **वक्ता**
जो साथ में पढ़ता हो : **सहपाठी**
जिसके नीचे रेखा खींची हो : **रेखांकित**
जानने की इच्छा रखने वाला : **जिज्ञासु**
जिसकी कोई सन्तान न हो : **निःसन्तान**
जिसका कोई मूल्य न हो : **अमूल्य**
जो वन में घूमता हो : **वनचर**
जो इस लोक के बाहर की बात हो : **अलौकिक**

जो इस लोक की बात हो	: **लौकिक**
जिसका सम्बन्ध पश्चिम से हो	: **पाश्चात्य**
जो स्थिर रहे	: **स्थावर**
दुःखान्त नाटक	: **त्रासदी**
ज्ञान देने वाली	: **ज्ञानदा**
भूत, वर्तमान भविष्य को देखने वाला	: **त्रिकालदर्शी**
जो क्षमा के योग्य हो	: **क्षम्य**
हिंसा करने वाला	: **हिंसक**
हित चाहने वाला	: **हितैषी**
सब कुछ जानने वाला	: **सर्वज्ञ**
जो स्वयं पैदा हुआ हो	: **स्वयंभू**
जो शरण में आया हो	: **शरणागत**
जिसका वर्णन न किया जा सके	: **वर्णनातीत**
व्याकरण जानने वाला	: **वैयाकरण**
रचना करने वाला	: **रचयिता**
खून से रंगा हुआ	: **रक्तरंजित**
अत्यन्त सुन्दर स्त्री	: **रूपसी**
कीर्तिमान पुरुष	: **यशस्वी**

महत्त्वपूर्ण शब्दों की भाववाचक संज्ञा

शब्द	भाववाचक संज्ञा	शब्द	भाववाचक संज्ञा	शब्द	भाववाचक संज्ञा	शब्द	भाववाचक संज्ञा
दास	दासता	क्षत्रिय	क्षत्रियत्व	अहं	अहंकार	अपना	अपनापन
पशु	पशुता	बालक	बालकपन	व्यक्ति	व्यक्तित्व	मीठा	मिठास
बन्धु	बन्धुत्व	मित्र	मित्रता	गरीब	गरीबी	सफल	सफलता
बूढ़ा	बुढ़ापा	सती	सतीत्व	बुरा	बुराई	स्वस्थ	स्वास्थ्य
सेवक	सेवा	शिशु	शैशव	सरल	सरलता	कंजुस	कंजुसी
अपना	अपनत्व	पराया	परायापन	कमजोर	कमजोरी	हरा	हरियाली
सर्व	सर्वस्व	मम	ममत्व	गर्म	गर्मी	मोटा	मोटाई
पण्डित	पाण्डित्य	पुरुष	पुरुषत्व	चालाक	चालाकी	गम्भीर	गम्भीरता
ब्राह्मण	ब्राह्मणत्व	बच्चा	बचपन	पढ़ना	पढ़ाई	लिखना	लिखाई
प्रभु	प्रभुता	नारी	नारीत्व	थकना	थकावट	लिखना	लिखावट
देव	देवत्व	लड़का	लड़कपन	लूटना	लूट	लड़ना	लड़ाई
मनुष्य	मनुष्यता	दानव	दानवता	हँसना	हँसी	आप	अपनत्व
निज	निजता	स्व	स्वत्व				

महत्त्वपूर्ण शब्दों के विशेषण

शब्द	विशेषण	शब्द	विशेषण	शब्द	विशेषण	शब्द	विशेषण
अंक	अंकित	अर्थ	आर्थिक	तीन	तीसरा	झगड़ा	झगड़ालू
इतिहास	ऐतिहासिक	उदासी	उदास	ठण्ड	ठण्डा	जाति	जातीय
कलंक	कलंकित	कुसुम	कुसुमित	काँटा	कँटीला	विदेश	विदेशी
जटा	जटिल	भार	भारी	रोज	रोजाना	भूगोल	भौगोलिक
बनारस	बनारसी	बाजार	बाजारू	पीड़ा	पीड़ित	पुत्र	पुत्रवान
प्यास	प्यासा	पुराण	पौराणिक	आलस्य	आलसी	अंतर	आंतरिक
पंक	पंकित	पक्ष	पाक्षिक	ईर्ष्या	ईर्ष्यालु	कर्म	कर्मठ
धन	धनी	दो	दूसरा	करुणा	कारुणिक	कृपा	कृपालु

शब्द	विशेषण	शब्द	विशेषण	शब्द	विशेषण	शब्द	विशेषण
गुण	गुणी	जल	जलमय	फ्रांस	फ्रांसीसी	बाहर	बाहरी
जीव	जैविक	तट	तटस्थ	भय	भयभीत	मधु	मधुर
तर्क	तार्किक	धर्म	धार्मिक	मौन	मौनी	मन	मानसिक
नमक	नमकीन	पत्थर	पथरीला	मानव	मानवीय	रक्षा	रक्षक
पल्लव	पल्लवित	पान	पनवाड़ी	रघु	राघव	रोग	रोगी
मुख	मुखर	मिठास	मीठा	वर्ष	वार्षिक	शक्ति	शक्तिशाली
मास	मासिक	मद	मादक	श्रम	श्रमिक	अंत	अंतिम
रक्त	रक्तिम	रस	रसीला	कागज	कागजी	मर्म	मार्मिक
वन	वन्य	विष्णु	वैष्णव	शब्द	शाब्दिक	अज्ञान	अज्ञानी
शहर	शहरी	तप	तपस्वी	गुलाब	गुलाबी	प्रकृति	प्राकृतिक
जापान	जापानी	तेज	तेजस्वी	परिचय	परिचित	पूजा	पुजारी
तत्त्व	तात्त्विक	दया	दयालु	रोग	रोगी	ग्राम	ग्रामीण
देव	दैविक	निंदा	निंदक	सुगंध	सुगंधित	मैं	मेरा
नव	नवीन	पोषण	पोषक	जो	जैसा	आप	आप-सा
पेट	पेटू	पाप	पापी	तुम	तुम्हारा	कौन	कैसा
पूजा	पूज्य	भूख	भूखा	वह	वैसा	पढ़ना	पढ़ाकू
फेन	फेनिल	भारत	भारतीय	गाना	गायक	बेचना	बिकाऊ
माया	मायावी	रंग	रंगीन	भागना	भगोड़ा	वन्द	वन्दनीय
विष	विषैला	श्री	श्रीमान	चलना	चलती	घूमना	घुमक्कड़
सुर	सुरीला	विवाह	वैवाहिक	चलना	चालू	मरना	मरियल
आदर	आदरणीय	ऋण	ऋणी	भूलना	भुलक्कड़	पीछे	पिछला
किताब	किताबी	क्रम	क्रमिक	भीतर	भीतरी	नीचे	निम्न
ग्राम	ग्रामीण	घर	घरेलू	अणु	आणविक	अधिकार	आधिकारिक
चतुर	चतुरता	जहर	जहरीला	अनुभव	अनुभवी	अन्याय	अन्यायी
सप्ताह	साप्ताहिक	अनुभव	अनुभवी	अपमान	अपमानित	अभ्यास	अभ्यासी
ओज	ओजस्वी	कल्पना	काल्पनिक	अवश्य	आवश्यक	आदि	आदिम
कुल	कुलीन	गाँव	गँवार	आयु	आयुष्मान्	उदय	उदित
चमक	चमकीला	चाचा	चचेरा	उपज	उपजाऊ	एकता	एक
दीन	दीनता	नगर	नागरिक	अंत	अंतिम	कुल	कुलीन
नागपुर	नागपुरी	परिवार	पारिवारिक	खर्च	खर्चीला	खून	खूनी
पुष्प	पुष्पित	पिता	पैतृक	गुण	गुणी		

श्रुतिसम भिन्नार्थक शब्द

शब्द	अर्थ	शब्द	अर्थ	शब्द	अर्थ	शब्द	अर्थ
आदि	आरम्भ	आदी	अभ्यस्त	अरि	शत्रु	अरी	सम्बोधन
कुल	वंश	कूल	किनारा	अगम	दुर्गम	आगम	शास्त्र

शब्द	अर्थ	शब्द	अर्थ	शब्द	अर्थ	शब्द	अर्थ
अयश	अपकीर्ति	अयस्क	लोहा	पुर	नगर	पूर	बाढ़
अपेक्षा	चाहना, तुलना में	उपेक्षा	निरादर	भवन	महल	भुवन	संसार
अनिल	हवा	अनल	आग	लक्ष्य	उद्देश्य	लक्ष	लाख
अवधि	काल, समय	अवधी	अवध की भाषा	सर	तालाब	शर	बाण
आयात	बाहर से आना	आयत	एक आकृति	सर्ग	अध्याय	स्वर्ग	एक लोक
चिर	पुराना	चीर	कपड़ा	कर्म	कार्य	क्रम	सिलसिला
तनु	पतला	तनू	पुत्र, गाय	चिता	शव जलाने के लिए लकड़ियों का ढेर	चीता	बाघ
तरंग	लहर	तुरंग	घोड़ा	शव	लाश	शब	रात
दारा	स्त्री	द्वार	दरवाजा	शस्त्र	हथियार	शास्त्र	ग्रन्थ
दूत	संदेशवाहक	द्यूत	जुआ	श्रवण	सुनना	श्रमण	बौद्ध संन्यासी
जलद	बादल	जलज	कमल	मत	विचार	मत्त	मस्त
प्रदीप	दीपक	प्रतीप	उल्टा	शोक	दुःख	शौक	चाव
प्रसाद	कृपा	प्रासाद	महल	ग्रह	नक्षत्र	गृह	घर
पास	निकट	पाश	बन्धन	कपट	धोखा	कपाट	दरवाजा
द्विप	हाथी	द्वीप	टापू	उपयुक्त	ठीक	उपर्युक्त	ऊपर कहा गया
देव	देवता	दैव	भाग्य	सुत	बेटा	सूत	धागा
नीर	जल	नीड़	घोंसला	शूर	वीर	सूर	अंधा
पवन	वायु	पावन	पवित्र	श्याम	कृष्ण	शाम	संध्या
बन्द	खुला नहीं	बद	बुरा	दिन	वार	दीन	गरीब
पथ	रास्ता	पथ्य	रोगी का भोजन	कटिबद्ध	तैयार रहना	करबद्ध	हाथ जोड़ना

अनेकार्थक शब्द

शब्द	विभिन्न अर्थ	शब्द	विभिन्न अर्थ
अंक	संख्या, गोद	जड़	मूर्ख, मूल
अक्षर	वर्ण, ईश्वर	कल	मशीन, आनेवाला कल, चैन
पानी	जल, प्रतिष्ठा	सुर	देवता, स्वर
अचल	पर्वत, स्थिर	द्विज	पक्षी, ब्राह्मण
आम	फल, सामान्य	तीर	किनारा, बाण
अंबर	वस्त्र, आकाश	प्रकृति	स्वभाव, कुदरत
अवस्था	आयु, दशा	पत्र	चिट्ठी, पत्र
उत्तर	दिशा, जबाव	पद	पैर, उपाधि
विधि	तरीका, भाग्य	फल	परिणाम, फल
कर	हाथ, टैक्स	तनु	पतला, कोमल
कनक	सोना, धतुरा	वर्ण	रंग, जाति
गुरु	श्रेष्ठ, शिक्षक	हल	समाधान, खेत जोतने का साधन
हान	भारी हथौड़ा, बादल	अशोक	राजा, वृक्ष

शब्द	विभिन्न अर्थ	शब्द	विभिन्न अर्थ
आभीर	अहीर, एक राग	घट	घड़ा, हृदय
एकाक्ष	काना, कौआ	जलज	कमल, मछली
खल	दुष्ट, खलिहान	हेम	सोना, जल

सामान्य अशुद्धियाँ

अशुद्ध	शुद्ध	अशुद्ध	शुद्ध	अशुद्ध	शुद्ध	अशुद्ध	शुद्ध
दुनियां	दुनिया	श्रीमति	श्रीमती	शताब्दि	शताब्दी	लड़ायी	लड़ाई
सामिग्री	सामग्री	वापिस	वापस	स्थाई	स्थायी	लिखायी	लिखाई
प्रदर्शिनी	प्रदर्शनी	द्वारिका	द्वारका	अलोकिक	अलौकिक	कृप्या	कृपया
ऊत्थान	उत्थान	दुसरा	दूसरा	गंवार	गँवार	असोक	अशोक
प्रशाद	प्रसाद	अमावश्या	अमावस्या	दुस्कर	दुष्कर	मूल्यावान	मूल्यवान्
बसंत	वसंत	बर्ष	वर्ष	नवम्	नवम	क्षात्र	छात्र
विना	बिना	बन	वन	छमा	क्षमा	प्रन्तु	परन्तु
दाइत्व	दायित्व	सम्वाद	संवाद	प्रीक्षा	परीक्षा	मरयादा	मर्यादा
कुन्डली	कुण्डली	मॉसिक	मानसिक	दुदर्शा	दुर्दशा	विषेश	विशेष
कन्ठ	कण्ठ	अगामी	आगामी	उज्वल	उज्ज्वल	आल्हाद	आहलाद्
सप्ताहिक	साप्ताहिक	संसारिक	सांसारिक	महत्व	महत्त्व	उपलक्ष	उपलक्ष्य
आधीन	अधीन	हस्ताक्षेप	हस्तक्षेप	लीये	लिये	पिओ	पियो
बरात	बारात	क्षत्रीय	क्षत्रिय	हुये	हुए	कवित्री	कवयित्री
तिथी	तिथि	कालीदास	कालिदास	प्रमात्मा	परमात्मा	घनिष्ट	घनिष्ठ
पुर्ती	पूर्ति	अतिथी	अतिथि	यथेष्ठ	यथेष्ट	पियास	प्यास
नीती	नीति	ग्रहणी	गृहिणी	व्यस्क	वयस्क	त्यौहार	त्योहार
क्यूँ	क्यों	साधू	साधु	मुसलिम	मुस्लिम	ऐैनक	ऐनक
वधु	वधू	रेणू	रेणु	नोकरी	नौकरी	कल्यान	कल्याण
नुपुर	नूपुर	निर्वान	निर्वाण	पाणी	पानी	आसा	आशा
जादु	जादू	द्रश्य	दृश्य	हुदय	हृदय	घ्रणा	घृणा
अनुग्रहीत	अनुगृहीत	बृज	ब्रज	श्रंगार	शृंगार	हिन्दुस्थान	हिन्दुस्तान
बनस्पति	वनस्पति	श्राप	शाप	प्रशन	प्रश्न	ग्यान	ज्ञान
सैना	सेना	सेनिक	सैनिक	अन्धेरा	अँधेरा	पेड	पेड़
इतिहासिक	ऐतिहासिक	प्रथक	पृथक	महयान्हन	मध्यान्ह	मेंहदी	मेहंदी
सम्पति	सम्पत्ति	कृतघन	कृतघ्न	शमशान	श्मशान	चिन्ह	चिह्न
बिमारी	बीमारी	व्यक्तिक	वैयक्तिक	कुंज	कुब्ज	ग्रहस्थ	गृहस्थ
वितीत	व्यतीत	निस्वार्थ	निःस्वार्थ	अजोध्या	अयोध्या	अनधिकार	अनाधिकार
परिस्थित	परिस्थिति	रचियता	रचयिता	अनिष्ठा	अनिष्ट	अनुकुल	अनुकूल
मैथिलिशरण	मैथिलीशरण	आर्शिवाद	आशीर्वाद	अनुसंगिक	आनुषंगिक	अनुशरण	अनुसरण
निरिक्षण	निरीक्षण	पत्नि	पत्नी	अभिसेक	अभिषेक	अरमाण	अरमान

अशुद्ध	शुद्ध	अशुद्ध	शुद्ध	अशुद्ध	शुद्ध	अशुद्ध	शुद्ध
अहिल्या	अहल्या	आदरनीय	आदरणीय	सम्राज	साम्राज्य	सविनयपूर्वक	सविनय
आविस्कार	आविष्कार	उँचाई	ऊँचाई	सिंदुर	सिंदूर	स्त्रवण	श्रवण
उत्तरदाई	उत्तरदायी	उपर	ऊपर	हरीश्चन्द्र	हरिश्चन्द्र	हिन्दु	हिन्दू
उपरोक्त	उपर्युक्त	उश्रृंखल	उच्छृंखल	हिन्दूस्तान	हिन्दुस्तान	बुद्धिवान	बुद्धिमान्
कलस	कलश	कल्यान	कल्याण	भाग्यमान	भाग्यवान	विद्वान	विद्वान्
गनित	गणित	जबाब	जवाब	श्रीमान	श्रीमान्	आंख	आँख
तत्व	तत्त्व	तलाब	तालाब	ऊंट	ऊँट	कंगना	कँगना
तिरष्कार	तिरस्कार	त्रिवार्षिक	त्रैवार्षिक	गँगा	गंगा	गांधी	गाँधी
दिपिका	दीपिका	देहिक	दैहिक	जांच	जाँच	तांगा	ताँगा
द्वन्द	द्वन्द्व	नरायन	नारायण	दांत	दाँत	मंहगा	महँगा
निरव	नीरव	निरोग	नीरोग	मांस	माँस	मुंह	मुँह
पुष्टी	पुष्टि	पुस्प	पुष्प	सांप	साँप	सांस	साँस
पेत्रिक	पैतृक	प्रनय	प्रणय	हुँकार	हुंकार	निर्पेक्ष	निरपेक्ष
प्रनाम	प्रणाम	प्रयाप्त	पर्याप्त	भाष्कर	भास्कर	सन्मुख	सम्मुख
प्रसंशा	प्रशंसा	प्रांगन	प्रांगण	माताहीन	मातृहीन	विद्यार्थि	विद्यार्थी
प्रान	प्राण	पृष्ट	पृष्ठ	गुणि	गुणी	द्वैवाषिक	द्विवार्षिक
ब्रत	व्रत	भगीरथी	भागीरथी	पूज्यनीय	पूजनीय	अकाश	आकाश
भरथ	भरत	भष्म	भस्म	इद	ईद	इसलाम	इस्लाम
मंत्रीमंडल	मंत्रिमण्डल	रसायण	रसायन	ऐसा	ऐसा	दोसरा	दूसरा
राज्यमहल	राजमहल	रामायन	रामायण	पुत्रि	पुत्री	प्रस्तूत	प्रस्तुत
वनोवास	वनवास	वानी	वाणी	हरयाली	हरियाली	दिवाली	दीवाली
वाल्मीकी	वाल्मीकि	वास्प	वाष्प	राष्ट्रिय	राष्ट्रीय	एकहरा	इकहरा
व्योहार	व्यवहार	सन्यासी	संन्यासी	एतबार	इतबार		

वाक्यगत अशुद्धियाँ

अशुद्ध	शुद्ध
हम अच्छी भाषण दिए थे।	हमने अच्छा भाषण दिया था।
आप खाए कि नहीं?	आपने खाया कि नहीं?
वह मुझे देखा तो घबरा गया।	उसने मुझे देखा तो घबरा गया।
मैं किताब पढ़ा हूँ।	मैंने किताब पढ़ी है।
मैं सारी पुस्तक पढ़ डाली।	मैंने सारी पुस्तक पढ़ डाली।
सीता भात खायी।	सीता ने भात खाया।
राम रोटी खाया।	राम ने रोटी खायी।
लड़की ने दही गिरा दी।	लड़की ने दही गिरा दिया।
शुद्ध गाय की घी दो।	गाय का शुद्ध घी दो।
तुम, मैं और वह चलेगा।	तुम, वह और मैं चलूँगा।
राम और सीता आयी थी।	राम और सीता आए थे।
भाई-बहन जा रही हैं।	भाई-बहन जा रहे हैं।
वह लड़की को बुलाओ।	उस लड़की को बुलाओ।
मेरे लिए पढ़ता हूँ।	अपने लिए पढ़ता हूँ।
सीता राम की आज्ञाकारी पत्नी थी।	सीता राम की आज्ञाकारिणी पत्नी थीं।
देरी न करना।	देर न करना।
उसे मृत्युदण्ड की सजा मिली।	उसे मृत्युदण्ड मिला।
हमारे शिक्षक प्रश्न पूछते हैं।	हमारे शिक्षक प्रश्न करते हैं।
कै बजे? तीन बजा।	कितना बजा? तीन बजे।

अशुद्ध	शुद्ध
उसका प्राण उड़ गया।	उसके प्राण उड़ गये।
मैंने आँख से देखा।	मैंने आँखों से देखा।
अपन को पढ़ना है।	मुझे पढ़ना है।
पुस्तक फट गया।	पुस्तक फट गई है।
घोड़ी तेज दौड़ता है।	घोड़ी तेज दौड़ती है।
मेरा प्रणम स्वीकार करो।	मेरा प्रणाम स्वीकार करो।
दो बालक खेलता है।	दो बालक खेलते हैं।
ये सब मेरा पुस्तक है।	ये सब मेरी पुस्तकें हैं।
सूरज पूरब में उगते हैं।	सूरज पूर्व में उगता है।
वह लौट आए।	वे लौट आए।
वहाँ अनेकों लोग थे।	वहाँ अनेक लोग थे।

अशुद्ध	शुद्ध
मेरे को मत मारो।	मुझे मत मारो।
मोहन ने पत्र को पढ़ा।	मोहन ने पत्र पढ़ा।
पुस्तक पर नहीं लिखो।	पुस्तक पर मत लिखो।
वह सज्जन पुरुष है।	वह सज्जन है।
आप हमारे घर आओ।	आप हमारे घर आइए।
हम आपसे कुछ कहे थे।	हमने आपसे कुछ कहा था।
मकान की दायीं ओर सड़क है।	मकान के दायीं ओर सड़क है।
पिताजी घर नहीं हैं।	पिताजी घर पर नहीं हैं।
घर पर सब कुशल हैं।	घर में सब कुशल हैं।
उसे भारी दुःख हुआ।	उसे बहुत दुःख हुआ।
सड़क में मत खेलो।	सड़क पर मत खेलो।

मुहावरे तथा लोकोक्तियाँ

- अँगूठी का नगीना–अत्यन्त महत्त्वपूर्ण।
- अंधा दरबार–न्यायहीन स्थान।
- अंधेर नगरी–न्याय का अभाव।
- अक्ल का दुश्मन–मूर्ख।
- अक्ल का दुम–मूर्ख।
- आँख का तारा–अतिप्रिय।
- ईद का चाँद–बहुत दिनों के बाद दिखाई देना।
- कछुआ चाल–धीमी गति।
- काला नाग–दुष्ट आदमी।
- किताबी कीड़ा–सदैव कुछ-न-कुछ पढ़ना।
- किस्मत का मारा–भाग्य का मन्द।
- कोल्हू का बैल–बहुत कठिन परिश्रम करनेवाला।
- कोड़ी का तीन–तुच्छ।
- खाली हाथ–पैसे का अभाव।
- गाजर-मूली–अशक्त।
- गुलर का फूल–दुर्लभ वस्तु।
- गोबर-गणेश–निरामूर्ख।
- घर का उजाला–कुल-दीपक।
- घड़ियाली आँसू–बनावटी शोक।
- चलता-पुरजा–चालाक।
- चाँद का टुकड़ा–परम सुन्दर वस्तु या व्यक्ति।
- चाँदी का जूता–रिश्वत।
- चार दिन की चाँदनी–थोड़े समय का सुख।
- जलती आँख–क्रोधाभिभूत।
- जीभ का पतला–लालची।
- टेढ़ी खीर–विकट काम।
- ठिकाने की बात–न्यायसंगत बात।
- अढ़ाई दिन की हुकूमत–थोड़े समय का ऐश्वर्य।
- तकदीर का सिकन्दर–भाग्य का बलवान्।
- थाली का बैंगन–मत बदलते रहना।
- दाँत कटी रोटी–घनिष्ठता।
- दाहिना हाथ–सहायक।
- दिल का बादशाह–बहुत बड़ा उदार।
- दूध का दूध और पानी का पानी–उचित न्याय।
- दूध का धोआ–निर्दोष।
- दो दिन का मेहमान–बहुत थोड़े समय ठहरने वाला।
- धरती का फूल–ऐसा व्यक्ति जो हाल में अमीर हुआ है।
- धोबी का कुत्ता–निकम्मा।
- नसीब का मारा–बुरे दिन देखनेवाला।
- निन्यानबे का फेरा–धन बढ़ाने की चिन्ता।
- पत्थर का कलेजा–हर दुःख सहने की शक्ति।
- पत्थर की लकीर–चिरस्थायी सदा सत्य।
- फूलों की सेज–आनन्ददायक कार्य।
- बगुला-भगत–कपटी व्यक्ति।
- बच्चों का खेल–साधारण काम।
- बलि का बकरा–निःसहाय व्यक्ति।

- बरसाती बादल–अस्थायी।
- बात का पक्का–सत्यवादी।
- बायें हाथ का खेल–सरल काम।
- बिन बादल बरसात–असमय लाभ।
- बे-पेंदी का लोटा–बे ठिकाने का आदमी।
- भागीरथ प्रयत्न–अत्यधिक परिश्रम।
- भीष्म प्रतिज्ञा–दृढ़ संकल्प।
- मक्खी चूस–कंजूस।
- मिट्टी के मोल–बहुत सस्ता।
- मोटा असामी–मूर्ख मालदार।
- राम कहानी–आत्मवृतान्त।
- लँगोटिया यार– बचपन का मित्र।
- हवाई महल–कोरी कल्पना।
- आँख लगना–नींद आना।
- आँख खुलना–होश में आना।
- आँखें दिखाना–क्रोध से घूरना।
- आँसू पोंछना–धैर्य बँधाना।
- अन्धे की लकड़ी–एकमात्र सहारा।
- कान भरना–चुगली करना।
- कान पर जूँ न रेंगना–कोई असर न होना।
- नाक कटना–प्रतिष्ठा खत्म होना।
- नाक रगड़ना–दीनता दिखाना।
- नाकों चने चबवाना–खूब सताना।
- मुँह की खाना–बुरी तरह हारना।
- आस्तीन का साँप–विश्वासघाती मित्र।
- कन्धे से कन्धा मिलाना–पूरा सहयोग करना।
- ईंट से ईंट बजाना–पूरी तरह नष्ट कर देना।
- नौ दो ग्यारह होना–भाग जाना।
- दाँत खट्टे करना–बुरी तरह हराना।
- हाथ मलना–पछताना।
- खून का प्यासा–जानी दुश्मन।
- घी के दिए जलाना–खुशी मनाना।
- चार चाँद लगाना–प्रतिष्ठा बढ़ाना।
- तीन तेरह होना–अलग-अलग होना।
- पानी फेर देना–नाश कर देना।
- गाल बजाना–डींगे मारना।
- जान से हाथ धो बैठना–मारा जाना।
- पानी-पानी होना–बहुत लज्जित होना।
- फूला न समाना–बहुत प्रसन्न होना।
- अपना उल्लू सीधा करना–अपना मतलब निकालना।
- आँखें चुरा लेना–अनदेखा कर देना।
- अन्धे की लाठी–एकमात्र सहारा।
- आसमान पर चढ़ना–बहुत अभिमान करना।
- आँखें खुलना–होश आना।
- चोरी और सीना जोरी–दोषी होकर धमकाना।
- आग में घी डालना–क्रोध को भड़काना।
- अँगुली पर नचाना– अच्छी तरह वश में करना।
- एक आँख से देखना–समान दृष्टि से देखना।
- एक ही थैले के चट्टे-बट्टे–एक जैसे।
- ओखली में सिर देना–जान-बूझकर आपत्ति मोल लेना।
- कलेजा मुँह को आना–बहुत दुःखी होना।
- कफन बाँधकर चलना–मौत से न घबराना।
- काँटे बिछाना–बाधा डालना।
- कलेजा ठण्डा होना–सन्तोष होना।
- कमर कसना–तैयार होना।
- खून खौलना–जोश में आना।
- खाक छानना–मारे-मारे फिरना।
- गागर में सागर भरना–थोड़े शब्दों में बहुत कुछ कह देना।
- घाव पर नमक छिड़कना–दुखी को अधिक दुखी करना।
- घी के दिए जलाना–खुशी मनाना।
- घोड़े बेचकर सोना–गहरी नींद में सोना।
- चल बसना–परलोक सिधारना।
- छठी का दूध याद आना–भारी संकट में पड़ना।
- छाती पर साँप लोटना–बहुत ईर्ष्या होना।
- जमीन पर पैर न रखना–अधिक घमण्ड होना।
- झक मारना–व्यर्थ समय खोना।
- टेढ़ी खीर–कठिन काम।
- डींग मारना–अपनी झूठी प्रशंसा करना।
- डूब मरना–बहुत लज्जित होना।
- तलवे चाटना–चापलूसी करना।
- ताक में रहना–मौका ढूँढ़ते रहना।
- दंग रह जाना–आश्चर्य में पड़ जाना।
- दाल न गलना–वश न चलना।
- दाल में काला होना–संदेह होना।
- पीठ दिखाना–हारकर भागना।
- मुँह तोड़ उत्तर देना–खरा उत्तर देना।

वस्तुनिष्ठ प्रश्न

अभ्यास-1

निर्देशः *नीचे प्रत्येक शुद्ध शब्द की वर्तनी के लिए चार विकल्प दिए गए हैं। आपको सही विकल्प का चयन करना है।*

1. A. ऋषि B. ऋषी C. रिषी D. ऋसि

2. A. विषेसन B. विशेषण C. विसेशन D. विशेशन

3. A. दुशासन B. दुसाशन C. दूशाषण D. दुःशासन

4. A. संस्कृति B. संसकृति C. संष्कृति D. संस्कृती

5. A. दूनियां B. दुनियां C. दुनिया D. दूनिआ

6. A. टिपनी B. टिप्पणि C. टिप्पणी D. टिप्पनी

7. A. शाषण B. साशन C. शासन D. शाशन

8. A. किसमस B. किरसमस C. क्रिसमूस D. कृसमस

9. A. अनुग्रहित B. अनुग्रहीत C. अनुगृहीत D. अनुग्रहित

10. A. पराकम B. प्राक्रम C. पराक्रम D. प्राकर्म

11. A. नायका B. नाइका C. नाइक D. नायिका

12. A. समरिधी B. समद्धी C. समृद्धि D. समरिद्धि

13. A. युधिष्ठर B. यूधिष्ठर C. युधिष्ठिर D. युधिष्टर

14. A. वाल्मीकि B. बाल्मीकि C. बालमीकि D. बाल्मिक

15. A. परलोकिक B. प्रलौकिक C. पारलौकिक D. परलौकिक

16. A. त्रितीय B. तर्तीय C. तृतीय D. तिरतीय

17. A. व्योहार B. व्यौहार C. व्यवहार D. ब्यवहार

18. A. अहिल्या B. अहल्या C. अहिलया D. अहीलया

19. A. आदरनीय B. आदरणीय C. आदरनीया D. आदरणीया

20. A. आर्द B. आद्र C. आर्द्र D. आर्दृ

21. A. आधीन B. अधिन C. अधीन D. अधीम

22. A. आविस्कार B. आविष्कार C. आवीस्कार D. आविश्कार

23. A. आसा B. आषा C. आशा D. अशा

24. A. उज्वल B. उजज्ज्वल C. उजज्वल D. उज्ज्वल

25. A. उन्नती B. उन्नित C. उन्नति D. उन्नती

26. A. कलस B. कलष C. कलश D. कलशा

27. A. गनीत B. गनित C. गणीत D. गणित

28. A. तलाव B. तालाव C. तलाब D. तालाब

29. A. दुष्ट B. दूष्ट C. दुस्त D. दुश्त

30. A. निरोग B. निररोग C. नीरोग D. नीरोगी

उत्तरमाला

1. A	**2.** B	**3.** D	**4.** A	**5.** C
6. C	**7.** C	**8.** C	**9.** C	**10.** C
11. D	**12.** C	**13.** C	**14.** A	**15.** C
16. C	**17.** C	**18.** B	**19.** B	**20.** C
21. C	**22.** B	**23.** C	**24.** D	**25.** C
26. C	**27.** D	**28.** D	**29.** A	**30.** C

अभ्यास-2

निर्देशः *नीचे कुछ शब्द दिए गए हैं। प्रत्येक के पर्यायवाची के चार विकल्प दिएं गए हैं। इनमें से एक विकल्प सही पर्यायवाची है, उसका चयन कीजिए :*

1. अग्नि
A. अनिल B. अनल
C. गर्म D. ताप

2. अमृत
A. पीयूष B. गरल
C. सरस D. जीवनदायनी

3. आँख
A. लोचन B. आस्थि
C. वदन D. जलज

4. आकाश
A. अनन्त B. पाताल
C. वितल D. तल

5. कपड़ा
A. परिधान B. पटिका
C. पीताम्बर D. लँहगा

6. कमल
A. सरोज B. सरोवर
C. पंक D. पुष्प

7. गंगा
A. पाताल नदी B. हिमनदी
C. भागीरथ D. त्रिपथगा

8. चाँद
A. मयंक B. भानु
C. दिनकर D. रवि

9. नदी
A. सरिता B. प्रवाह
C. धारा D. जलधर

10. पर्वत
A. पत्थर B. चट्टान
C. शिखर D. मेरू

11. पवन
A. अनिल B. अनल
C. अग D. विहग

12. पति
A. साजन B. प्रिया
C. भार्या D. दारा

13. पानी
A. मही B. मेदिनी
C. अम्बु D. तरणी

14. पुत्र
A. आत्मज B. तनया
C. सुता D. आत्मजा

15. पुत्री
A. सुता B. सुत
C. आत्मज D. नन्दन

16. फूल
A. बहार B. मधु
C. माधव D. सुमन

17. वृक्ष
A. विटप B. अम्र
C. प्रसून D. रसा

18. बादल
A. अज B. व्यामोह
C. नीरद D. मधुप

19. बिजली
A. चंचला B. खटका
C. त्रास D. संत्रास

20. माता
A. धात्री B. धरणी
C. धरित्री D. श्यामा

21. घोषणा
A. आवाज B. पुकारना
C. ऐलान D. ललकारना

22. उत्कर्ष
A. आकर्षण B. विकर्षण
C. उन्नति D. निष्कर्ष

23. उदय
A. अन्त B. विकास
C. प्रगट D. व्यस्त

24. दक्ष
A. निपुण B. समर्थ
C. कर्मठ D. मेहनती

25. संवाद
A. विवाद B. झगड़ा
C. सम्बोधन D. वार्तालाप

उत्तरमाला

1. B	**2.** A	**3.** A	**4.** A	**5.** A
6. A	**7.** D	**8.** A	**9.** A	**10.** D
11. A	**12.** A	**13.** C	**14.** A	**15.** A
16. D	**17.** A	**18.** C	**19.** A	**20.** A
21. C	**22.** C	**23.** C	**24.** A	**25.** D

अभ्यास-3

निर्देशः *नीचे चार-चार शब्दों के समूह दिए गए हैं। प्रत्येक समूह में एक शब्द बेमेल है तथा शेष तीन शब्द पर्यायवाची हैं, आपको उस शब्द का चयन करना है, जो बेमेल है :*

1. A. तम B. अंधकार
C. तिमिर D. अंश

2. A. अनल B. आग
C. दहन D. तमिस्रा

3. A. अतुल B. अद्वितीय
C. अनुपम D. शुष्मा

4. A. अहं B. अहंकार
C. दर्प D. निराला

5. A. पता B. खोज
C. जाँच D. शोध

6. A. गरल B. पीयूष
C. सुधा D. सोम

7. A. कानन B. जंगल
C. पादप D. वन

8. A. अश्व B. गज
C. घोड़ा D. तुरंग

9. A. दानव B. मानव
C. दैत्य D. राक्षस

10. A. आँख B. चक्षु
C. नयन D. मुख

11. A. अन्तरिक्ष B. वसुन्धरा
C. आसमान D. गगन

12. A. इच्छा B. अभिलाषा
C. कामना D. प्रयोजन

13. A. कपड़ा B. चीर
C. वसन D. पोशाक

14. A. अब्ज B. कमल
C. राजीव D. आम्र

15. A. कोयल B. पिक
C. काग D. वनप्रिय

16. A. गंगा B. देवनदी
C. गोदावरी D. भागीरथी

17. A. गणेश B. एकदन्त
C. देवराज D. गणपति

18. A. घर B. निलय
C. निकेतन D. झोपड़ी

19. A. चाँद B. हिमांशु
C. विनायक D. सुधांशु

20. A. नदी B. तरणी
C. तटिनी D. सरिता

21. A. पक्षी B. चिड़िया
C. सुमन D. विहग

22. A. पवन B. अचला
C. वात D. वायु

23. A. समीर B. पृथ्वी
C. भू D. भूमि

24. A. पानी B. समीर
C. अम्बु D. जल

25. A. पुत्र B. तनया
C. तनय D. सुत

26. A. पुत्र B. तनया
C. सुता D. कन्या

27. A. गृहिणी B. आदमी
C. पुरुष D. नर

28. A. मधु B. फूल
C. पुष्प D. सुमन

29. A. माधव B. तरु
C. पेड़ D. वृक्ष

30. A. माता B. अम्बु
C. अम्मा D. जननी

उत्तरमाला

1. D	**2.** D	**3.** D	**4.** D	**5.** A
6. A	**7.** C	**8.** B	**9.** B	**10.** D
11. B	**12.** D	**13.** D	**14.** D	**15.** C
16. C	**17.** C	**18.** D	**19.** C	**20.** B
21. C	**22.** B	**23.** A	**24.** B	**25.** B
26. A	**27.** A	**28.** A	**29.** A	**30.** B

अभ्यास-4

निर्देशः ***गहरे काले शब्द*** *के विलोम शब्द का चयन कीजिए:*

1. उसे हर काम में **सफलता** मिल रही है।
A. असफलता B. सफल
C. कुशलता D. निपुणता

2. कभी किसी की **निन्दा** नहीं करनी चाहिए।
A. गुणगान B. स्तुति
C. प्रशंसा D. यशोगान

3. आलस्य व्यक्ति का सबसे बड़ा **दुश्मन** है।
A. शत्रु B. घातक
C. मित्र D. सहायक

4. वे बुढ़ापे से **दुखी** हैं।
A. अप्रसन्न B. सुखी
C. खुश D. नाराज

5. यहाँ उसकी **चतुराई** नहीं चली।
A. चालाकी B. बहादुरी
C. निपुणता D. मूर्खता

6. शहद की **मिठास** कम नहीं होती।
A. मीठा B. तीखा
C. कडुवा D. खट्टा

7. साहसी के **साहस** को देखकर मैं चकित रह गया।
A. हिम्मत B. बहादुरी
C. निडर D. भय

8. फिल्मोत्सव में सर्वश्रेष्ठ **अभिनेता** को पुरस्कार प्रदान किया गया।
A. हीरोइन B. नेत्री
C. मीनाक्षी D. अभिनेत्री

9. नाटक में नायक और **नायिका** की भूमिका महत्वपूर्ण होती है:
A. हीरो B. नायक
C. नेत्र D. नेता

10. कवि-सम्मेलन में एक कवि और एक **कवयित्री** को आमंत्रित किया गया था।
A. लेखक B. सम्पादक
C. नेता D. कवि

11. विद्यालय के वार्षिकोत्सव के लिए नेता और एक **नेत्री** को आमंत्रित किया गया।
A. अभिनेता B. विद्वान्
C. विदुषी D. नेता

12. मोहन बहुत **चतुर** है।
A. निपुण B. तेज
C. सुस्त D. मूर्ख

13. सोहन अब पूर्ण **स्वस्थ** है।
A. प्रसन्न B. खुश
C. अस्वस्थ D. अप्रसन्न

14. पक्षी **आकाश** में उड़ते हैं :
A. गगन B. नभ
C. धरती D. पाताल

15. वह विद्यालय में देर से आया और **अनुपस्थित** हो गया।
A. पूर्व B. उपस्थित
C. प्रवेश D. समयपूर्व

16. **बालक** चाँद की ओर देख रहा है।
A. बालिका B. लड़का
C. बच्चा D. बच्ची

17. मैं उसके विचार से बिल्कुल **सहमत** नहीं हूँ।
A. समर्थन B. सहमति
C. असहमत D. प्रशंसक

18. उसकी हालत **अधिक** खराब है।
A. बहुत B. कम
C. ठीक D. कुशल

19. **धर्म** की सर्वत्र विजय होती है:
A. अधर्म B. ज्ञान
C. भक्ति D. ईमानदारी

20. अच्छे चरित्र के बिना जीवन **निरर्थक** है:
A. व्यर्थ B. अर्थपूर्ण
C. सार्थक D. कुशल

21. **ईमानदारी** बड़ी दुर्लभ वस्तु है:
A. सच्चाई B. भलाई
C. बेइमानी D. परोपकारी

22. एवरेस्ट संसार का सबसे **ऊँचा** पर्वत है:
A. नीचा B. वितल
C. पाताल D. मध्यम

23. वह विश्वास के **योग्य** नहीं है:
A. काबिल B. विश्वासी
C. अयोग्य D. बेकार

24. क्या वह इतना **मूर्ख** है?
A. चालाक B. विद्वान्
C. बुद्धिमान D. धूर्त

25. कितना सुहावना **दृश्य** है!
A. अदृश्य B. दर्शनीय
C. सुन्दर D. व्यर्थ

उत्तरमाला

1. A	**2.** C	**3.** C	**4.** B	**5.** D
6. C	**7.** D	**8.** D	**9.** B	**10.** D
11. D	**12.** D	**13.** C	**14.** D	**15.** B
16. A	**17.** C	**18.** B	**19.** A	**20.** C
21. C	**22.** A	**23.** C	**24.** C	**25.** A

अभ्यास-5

निर्देशः नीचे प्रत्येक **काले गहरे शब्द** के चार विलोम दिए गए हैं। इनमें सही विलोम का चयन कीजिए :

1. अग्नि
A. आग B. अनल
C. दहन D. जल

2. अग्रज
A. अनुज B. भ्राता
C. भाई D. अम्बा

3. अच्छा
A. बुरा B. खराब
C. गंदा D. भ्रष्ट

4. अंत
A. प्रारम्भ B. समाप्त
C. शेष D. अल्प

5. अचल
A. विचल B. वितल
C. सजल D. चल

6. अति
A. अधिक B. बहुत
C. अल्प D. कम

7. अत्यधिक
A. अल्प B. अधिक
C. स्वल्प D. न्यूनतम

8. अंधकार
A. अंधेरा B. प्रकाश
C. रात्रि D. दिन

9. अतिवृष्टि
A. अनावृष्टि B. वृष्टि
C. वर्षा D. वर्षण

10. अनाथ
A. नाथ B. स्वामी
C. मासिक D. सनाथ

11. अनुकूल
A. मनोकूल B. प्रतिकूल
C. अनुकरण D. मनस्वी

12. अनुराग
A. राग B. विराग
C. विग्रह D. स्नेह

13. अन्त
A. श्री गणेश B. आदि
C. शुरुआत D. समाप्त

14. अपना
A. अपनत्व B. पराया
C. मित्र D. शत्रु

15. अपमान
A. मान B. सम्मान
C. वर्तमान D. स्वाभिमान

16. अपेक्षा
A. इच्छा B. स्वेच्छा
C. प्रविच्छा D. उपेक्षा

17. अमर
A. मर्त्य B. मृत्यु
C. सुधा D. गरल

18. अल्पायु

A. चिरायु B. उमरदराज
C. नश्वर D. सनातन

19. अस्त

A. उदय B. विकास
C. निर्माण D. सृष्टि

20. आकर्षण

A. प्रतिकर्षण B. विकर्षण
C. सम्मोहन D. विरत

21. आकाश

A. गगन B. नभ
C. वसुन्धरा D. पाताल

22. आगे

A. पीछे B. पूर्व
C. पृष्ट D. पृष्ठ

23. आजाद

A. स्वतंत्र B. स्वतंत्रतता
C. परतंत्र D. गुलाम

24. आदान

A. आयात B. निर्यात
C. प्रदान D. निदान

25. आधुनिक

A. अर्वाचीन B. नूतन
C. प्राचीन D. वर्तमान

उत्तरमाला

1. D	**2.** A	**3.** A	**4.** A	**5.** D
6. D	**7.** C	**8.** B	**9.** A	**10.** D
11. B	**12.** B	**13.** A	**14.** B	**15.** B
16. D	**17.** A	**18.** A	**19.** A	**20.** B
21. D	**22.** A	**23.** D	**24.** C	**25.** C

अभ्यास-6

निर्देशः *नीचे कुछ शब्द दिए गए हैं प्रत्येक शब्द के चार वैकल्पिक अर्थ दिए गए हैं। सही अर्थ का चयन कीजिए :*

1. सुरक्षित

A. कुशल B. घटना
C. दुर्घटना D. बचाव

2. प्रतिभाशाली

A. सज्जन B. कुशाग्र
C. विद्वान् D. वैभवशाली

3. आत्मसमर्पण

A. अपने आप को सौंपना B. समर्पण
C. अर्पण D. त्यागज

4. सिद्धहस्त

A. निपुण B. कर्मठ
C. मेहनती D. परिश्रमी

5. सुशोभित

A. मजेदार B. सुस्वागतम्
C. अच्छा D. शोभा पाना

6. स्वादिष्ट

A. मजेदार B. बेकार
C. मीठा D. तीखा

7. स्वावलम्बी

A. निर्भर B. परालंबी
C. आत्मनिर्भर D. अतिथि

8. उपकरण

A. साधन B. युक्ति
C. यंत्र D. मशीन

9. कीमत

A. क्रय B. विक्रय
C. मूल्य D. बिक्री

10. संगठन

A. एकता B. अनेकता
C. समूह D. संस्था

11. विपत्ति

A. दुख B. विपदा
C. मुसीबत D. सुख

12. तृण

A. तिनका B. धूल
C. धूप D. लकड़ी

13. आश्चर्य

A. निरीक्षण B. दृष्टिगोचर
C. हैरानी D. थकावट

14. हार्दिक

A. हृदय से B. शरीर से
C. मन से D. मस्तिष्क से

15. नियति
A. भाग्य B. किनारा
C. समय D. पवित्र

16. सुगन्धित
A. दुर्गन्ध B. खुशबू वाला
C. फूल D. कमल

17. उत्साह
A. होश B. हवास
C. जोश D. हिम्मत

18. सहयोग
A. मिलन सार B. मेहनती
C. परोपकारी D. आपसी सहायता

19. मुसीबत
A. विपत्ति B. सुशोभित
C. सहायता D. मदद

20. निरक्षर
A. साक्षर B. दर्शनीय
C. पठनीय D. अनपढ़

21. उपवन
A. वन B. तीर
C. जंगल D. बाग

22. मेघ
A. बादल B. पंकज
C. राजीव D. मेघनाद

23. आधुनिक
A. प्राचीन B. पुरातन
C. भूतकाल D. आज का

24. तीर
A. वाण B. धनुष
C. किनारा D. नदी

25. परीक्षण
A. जाँच B. पड़ताल
C. परीक्षा D. इम्तहान

26. अभिवादन
A. नमस्ते B. प्रणाम
C. बधाई D. शुभकामना

27. सर्वत्र
A. नश्वर B. सजीव
C. ईश्वर D. सभी जगह

28. हलवाहा
A. चरवाहा B. किसान
C. मजदूर D. हल चलाने वाला

29. शिखर
A. पर्वत B. पहाड़
C. टीला D. चोटी

30. भयानक
A. डरावना B. भयभीत
C. डरना D. खूँखार

उत्तरमाला

1. D	**2.** B	**3.** A	**4.** A	**5.** D
6. A	**7.** C	**8.** C	**9.** C	**10.** A
11. C	**12.** A	**13.** C	**14.** A	**15.** A
16. B	**17.** C	**18.** D	**19.** A	**20.** D
21. D	**22.** A	**23.** D	**24.** A	**25.** A
26. B	**27.** D	**28.** D	**29.** D	**30.** A

अभ्यास-7

निर्देशः *नीचे कुछ शब्द दिए जा रहे हैं। प्रत्येक शब्द के* **उपसर्ग** *के सन्दर्भ में चार विकल्प दिए गए हैं। आपको सही विकल्प का चयन करना है :*

1. अलबत्ता
A. अ B. अल
C. लब D. त्ता

2. अलगरज
A. अल B. लग
C. गर D. रज

3. कमसिन
A. क B. कम
C. सि D. सिन

4. अनमोल
A. अ B. अन
C. मो D. मोल

5. अनजान
A. अ B. अन
C. जा D. जान

6. अनपढ़
A. अ B. पढ़
C. प D. अन

7. अधखिला
A. अ B. अध
C. ला D. खिला

8. अधजला
A. अ B. ज
C. अध D. ला

9. अधपका
A. अ B. अध
C. पका D. का

10. अघखिला
A. अ B. अघ
C. खिला D. ला

11. उन्नीस
A. उन B. उन्
C. नीस D. स

12. उनसठ
A. उ B. उन
C. सठ D. ठ

13. दुकाल
A. द B. दुक
C. दु D. काल

14. दुबला
A. दब B. दुब
C. ला D. दु

15. निकम्मा
A. नि B. निक
C. कम्मा D. मा

16. निर्लज्ज
A. निर B. निल
C. नि D. लज्ज

17. बिनब्याहा
A. बि B. बिन
C. ब्याहा D. हा

18. भरपेट
A. भर B. पेट
C. पे D. ट

19. भरपाई
A. भ B. र
C. पा D. भर

20. कुपात्र
A. कु B. कुप
C. पा D. पात्र

21. सुजान
A. सु B. सुज
C. सुजा D. जान

22. गैर कानूनी
A. गै B. गैर
C. कानु D. नुनी

23. गैरसरकारी
A. गैर B. सर
C. का D. कारी

24. अपमान
A. अ B. अप
C. मा D. मान

25. अनुशासन
A. अ B. शासन
C. सन D. अनु

26. अविनीत
A. अवि B. अ
C. नी D. नीत

27. अभिमान
A. अभि B. अ
C. मा D. मान

28. अभियान
A. अ B. मान
C. यान D. अभि

29. अध्ययन
A. अध् B. अधि
C. यन D. न

30. निश्चल
A. नि B. निर
C. निस D. चल

उत्तरमाला

1. B	**2.** A	**3.** B	**4.** B	**5.** B
6. D	**7.** B	**8.** C	**9.** B	**10.** B
11. A	**12.** B	**13.** C	**14.** D	**15.** B
16. A	**17.** B	**18.** A	**19.** D	**20.** A

21. A **22.** B **23.** A **24.** B **25.** D
26. B **27.** A **28.** D **29.** B **30.** A

अभ्यास-8

निर्देशः *निम्नलिखित शब्दों में प्रयुक्त प्रत्यय सम्बन्धी चार विकल्प दिए गए हैं, सही विकल्प का चयन कीजिए :*

1. भलाई
A. ई B. लाई
C. आई D. भला

2. चतुराई
A. चतु B. रा
C. ई D. आई

3. भूखा
A. भू B. भूख
C. खा D. आ

4. भिड़न्त
A. भिड़ B. भि
C. न्त D. अन्त

5. प्यासा
A. आस B. सा
C. आसा D. सा

6. बिकाऊ
A. बिक B. काऊ
C. आऊ D. ऊ

7. तैराक
A. तै B. तैर
C. राक D. आक

8. सन्नाटा
A. सन् B. सन्ना
C. नाटा D. आटा

9. लोहार
A. लोह B. आरा
C. आरी D. आर

10. मिलान
A. आना B. आने
C. आनी D. आन

11. चढ़ाव
A. चढ़ B. चढ़ा
C. आव D. व

12. लगाव
A. लग B. अव
C. आव D. गाव

13. लिखावट
A. लिख B. लिखा
C. वट D. आवट

14. मिलावट
A. मिल B. वट
C. आवट D. ट

15. मिठास
A. मिठ B. ठास
C. आस D. स

16. चिकनाहट
A. चिक B. नाह्ट
C. हट D. आहट

17. सड़ियल
A. सड़ B. यल
C. ड़ियल D. इयल

18. मरियल
A. मर B. यल
C. मरि D. इयल

19. गड़रिया
A. गड़ B. इया
C. रिया D. या

20. सजीला
A. ईला B. इला
C. ला D. स

21. लुटेरा
A. लुट B. एरा
C. ऐरा D. रा

22. लठैत
A. ए B. ऐ
C. ऐत D. त

23. भगोड़ा
A. ओ B. ओड़ा
C. ड़ा D. भगो

24. खपत
A. ख B. प
C. त D. पत

25. जीवट
A. व B. अट
C. जीव D. जी

उत्तरमाला

1. C	**2.** D	**3.** D	**4.** D	**5.** D
6. C	**7.** D	**8.** D	**9.** D	**10.** D
11. C	**12.** C	**13.** D	**14.** C	**15.** C
16. D	**17.** D	**18.** D	**19.** B	**20.** A
21. B	**22.** C	**23.** B	**24.** C	**25.** B

अभ्यास-9

निर्देशः *नीचे कुछ मुहावरे दिए गए हैं। प्रत्येक के अर्थ के लिए चार विकल्प दिए गए हैं। आपको सही विकल्प का चयन करना है :*

1. अक्ल पर पत्थर पड़ना
A. बुद्धि काम न करना B. दुविधा होना
C. संकट में होना D. परेशान होना

2. अपना उल्लू सीधा करना
A. अवसर देखना B. काम निकालना
C. मतलब साधना D. मूर्ख बनाना

3. अपने मुँह मियाँ-मिट्ठू बनना
A. मिठाई खाना
B. प्रशंसा करना
C. निंदा करना
D. अपनी प्रशंसा स्वयं करना

4. अपने पाँव पर आप कुल्हाड़ी मारना
A. हानि पहुँचाना B. खेद होना
C. अपना पैर काटना D. अपनी हानि स्वयं करना

5. आँखें चुरा लेना
A. भाग जाना B. छिप जाना
C. अनदेखा करना D. मिल जाना

6. अक्ल का दुश्मन
A. मित्र होना B. शत्रु होना
C. महामूर्ख D. महाविद्वान्

7. अंधे की लाठी
A. एक मात्र सहारा B. मित्र होना
C. शत्रु होना D. दुख पहुँचाना

8. आकाश-पाताल एक करना
A. भाग-दौड़ करना B. परेशान होना
C. थक जाना D. कठिन परिश्रम करना

9. घड़ों पानी पड़ना
A. लज्जित होना B. तुच्छ समझना
C. लाभ होना D. थकावट

10. अगर-मगर करना
A. नुकसान करना B. बहाने बनाना
C. बदनाम करना D. कपट करना

11. मुँह की खाना
A. गिर जाना B. हार जाना
C. भाग जाना D. व्यर्थ होना

12. आस्तीन का साँप होना
A. शत्रु B. मित्र
C. कपटी मित्र D. दयालु

13. एक आँख से देखना
A. बुरा व्यवहार B. समान व्यवहार
C. कपट करन D. लज्जित होना

14. बाल-बाँका न होना
A. घायल होना B. साफ बच जाना
C. क्रोधित होना D. स्वस्थ होना

15. दाँतों तले उँगली दबाना
A. उँगली काटना B. चिंतित हो जाना
C. चकित रह जाना D. प्रसन्न हो जाना

16. जान के लाले पड़ना
A. मरने का खतरा होना B. भाग जाना
C. हार जाना D. मुश्किल में पड़ना

17. बोली मारना
A. ताना देना B. सताना
C. मजाक करना D. याद दिलाना

18. अंधों में काना राजा
A. मूर्खों में अल्पज्ञ को विद्वान् माना जाना
B. सबको मूर्ख समझना
C. अत्यधिक महत्त्वपूर्ण
D. काना राजा

19. अक्ल के घोड़े दौड़ाना
A. बुद्धि लड़ाना
B. कल्पना करना
C. तरह-तरह के उपाय सोचना
D. ज्ञान-प्राप्त करना

20. पानी उतर जाना
A. शर्म करना B. लज्जित न होना
C. भाग जाना D. इज्जत करना

21. तीन-पाँच करना
A. तितर-बितर करना
B. वचन देकर फिर जाना
C. घुमा-फिरा कर बातें करना
D. परेशान करना

22. हथियार डाल देना
A. हार जाना B. जीत जाना
C. धोखा देना D. विजय होना

23. आँख खुलना
A. होश में आना B. अत्यन्त प्यार होना
C. उल्टा काम करना D. क्रोध करना

24. कमर सीधी करना
A. थक जाना B. थकावट दूर करना
C. काम करना D. परिश्रम करना

25. पगड़ी रखना
A. चैन की सांस लेना
B. अपमान करना
C. दया की भीख माँगना
D. अपमान होना

26. लोहा मानना
A. संघर्ष करना
B. विजय होना
C. श्रेष्ठता स्वीकार करना
D. खुशामद करना

27. काठ मार जाना
A. दुःखी होना B. चुप होना
C. सफल होना D. मर जाना

28. चाँद पर थूकना
A. अपमान करना
B. बढ़कर बातें करना
C. महान पुरुष पर लांछन लगाना
D. महत्त्वाकांक्षी होना

29. उगल देना
A. अपराध स्वीकार कर लेना
B. सच बोलना
C. उल्टी करना
D. अनपच होना

30. हाथ मलना
A. पश्चाताप करना B. सर्दी मिटाना
C. दुख करना D. तैयार होना

उत्तरमाला

1. A	2. C	3. D	4. D	5. C
6. C	7. A	8. D	9. A	10. B
11. B	12. C	13. B	14. B	15. C
16. D	17. A	18. A	19. A	20. B
21. C	22. A	23. A	24. B	25. C
26. C	27. B	28. C	29. A	30. A

अभ्यास-10

निर्देशः *नीचे कुछ वाक्य खण्ड दिए गए हैं, पूरे वाक्य खण्ड के लिए एक शब्द का चयन कीजिए।*

1. जिसका आदि न हो
A. अनंत B. अमर
C. शाश्वत D. अनादि

2. जो कुछ न जानता हो
A. मूर्ख B. महामूर्ख
C. ज्ञानी D. अज्ञ

3. जो अनुकरण करने योग्य हो
A. अनुकरणीय B. अद्वितीय
C. आदरणीय D. अगम

4. जिसका अंत न हो
A. अनंत B. अनादि
C. आदि D. परलोक

5. जो कभी न मरे
A. मर्त्य B. मुर्त्त
C. अर्मुत्त D. अमर

6. जिसके समान दूसरा न हो
A. अनुकूल B. प्रतिकूल
C. कृतज्ञ D. अद्वितीय

7. जो कम बोलता हो
A. मृदुभाषी B. वाचाल
C. अल्पभाषी D. अल्पज्ञ

8. जिसका इलाज न हो
A. मरणशील B. अमरत्व
C. बिमारी D. लाइलाज

9. जिस का विश्वास न किया जा सके
A. विश्वसनीय B. अविश्वसनीय
C. विश्वासी D. धूर्त्त

10. जिसका कोई नाथ न हो
A. सनाथ B. स्वामी
C. नाथ D. अनाथ

11. कम जानने वाला
A. अल्पज्ञ B. अज्ञ
C. विद् D. विद्वान

12. जहाँ जाना संभव न हो
A. दुर्गम B. अगम
C. तल D. वितल

13. कम खाने वाला
A. बहुभोजी B. पेटु
C. कंजूस D. अल्पाहारी

14. जो बात पहले कभी न हुई हो
A. भूतपूर्व B. अभूतपूर्व
C. प्राचीन D. अर्वाचीन

15. जिस स्त्री के सन्तान न हों
A. बाँझ B. कुलटा
C. पतिता D. विधवा

16. जो कहा न जा सके
A. अकथनीय B. अकथ्य
C. करणीय D. सम्भव

17. एहसान न मानने वाला
A. कृतज्ञ B. कृतघ्न
C. आस्तिक D. विश्वासी

18. जिसने देश के साथ विश्वासघात किया हो
A. विश्वासघाती B. द्रोही
C. आतंकवादी D. देश द्रोही

19. जिसने राष्ट्र के हित में अपना जीवन बलिदान कर दिया हो
A. देशभक्त B. शहीद
C. राष्ट्रभूत D. भारतपुत्र

20. वह जमीन जिसमें कुछ भी पैदा न हो
A. ऊसर B. बंजर
C. उर्वर D. पथरीला

21. वह वस्तु जिसकी चाह हो
A. श्रेष्ठ B. आवश्यक
C. इच्छित D. अभीष्ट

22. दूसरों के पीछे चलने वाला
A. अनुयायी B. अनुज
C. अनुचर D. अनुकरणीय

23. जो पहले न पढ़ा हो
A. पठित B. अपठित
C. पठनीय D. अपठनीय

24. जिसके आर-पार दिखाई देता हो
A. अपारदर्शी B. गम्य
C. अगम्य D. पारदर्शी

25. आज्ञा पालन करने वाला
A. शिष्य B. शिष्या
C. अनुचर D. आज्ञाकारी

26. काम से जी चुराने वाला
A. कामचोर B. आलसी
C. कर्मठ D. परिश्रमी

27. प्रतिदिन होने वाला
A. दैनिक B. शाश्वत
C. सनातन D. अमर

28. जिसका कोई अर्थ न हो
A. सार्थक B. निरर्थक
C. आर्थिक D. अनार्थिक

29. उपकार मानने वाला
A. कृतज्ञ B. कृतघ्न
C. विश्वासी D. अनुयायी

30. हाथ से लिखा हुआ
A. पठनीय B. अपठनीय
C. स्पष्ट D. हस्तलिखित

उत्तरमाला

1. D	**2.** D	**3.** A	**4.** A	**5.** D
6. D	**7.** C	**8.** D	**9.** B	**10.** D
11. A	**12.** A	**13.** D	**14.** B	**15.** A
16. A	**17.** B	**18.** D	**19.** B	**20.** A
21. C	**22.** C	**23.** B	**24.** D	**25.** D
26. A	**27.** A	**28.** B	**29.** A	**30.** D

अभ्यास-11

निर्देशः *नीचे कुछ संज्ञा शब्द दिए जा रहे हैं। प्रत्येक के संज्ञा-भेद के लिए चार विकल्प दिए गये है। सही विकल्प का चयन कीजिए :*

1. तुलसीदास
A. जातिवाचक B. भाववाचक
C. व्यक्तिवाचक D. समूहवाचक

2. यमुना
A. व्यक्तिवाचक B. जातिवाचक
C. समूहवाचक D. भाववाचक

3. बच्चा
A. जातिवाचक B. समूहवाचक
C. भाववाचक D. व्यक्तिवाचक

4. मानवता
A. भाववाचक B. जातिवाचक
C. द्रव्यवाचक D. समूहवाचक

5. हिमालय
A. व्यक्तिवाचक B. जातिवाचक
C. भाववाचक D. समूहवाचक

6. भारत
A. जातिवाचक B. भाववाचक
C. व्यक्तिवाचक D. समूहवाचक

7. एशिया
A. व्यक्तिवाचक B. भाववाचक
C. द्रव्यवाचक D. समूहवाचक

8. महाराष्ट्र
A. जातिवाचक B. व्यक्तिवाचक
C. समूहवाचक D. द्रव्यवाचक

9. सूर सागर
A. व्यक्तिवाचक B. भाववाचक
C. द्रव्यवाचक D. समूहवाचक

10. सोमवार
A. जातिवाचक B. व्यक्तिवाचक
C. द्रव्यवाचक D. समूहवाचक

11. खटमल
A. जातिवाचक B. व्यक्तिवाचक
C. द्रव्यवाचक D. समूहवाचक

12. मैना
A. जातिवाचक B. व्यक्तिवाचक
C. द्रव्यवाचक D. समूहवाचक

13. चाँदी
A. द्रव्यवाचक B. समूहवाचक
C. भाववाचक D. व्यक्तिवाचक

14. अच्छाई
A. भाववाचक B. समूहवाचक
C. जातिवाचक D. व्यक्तिवाचक

15. पीतल
A. द्रव्यवाचक B. भाववाचक
C. व्यक्तिवाचक D. जातिवाचक

16. वीरता
A. भाववाचक B. जातिवाचक
C. द्रव्यवाचक D. समूहवाचक

17. रूस
A. जातिवाचक B. व्यक्तिवाचक
C. भाववाचक D. द्रव्यवाचक

18. लम्बाई
A. भाववाचक B. समूहवाचक
C. द्रव्यवाचक D. व्यक्तिवाचक

19. दल
A. जातिवाचक B. व्यक्तिवाचक
C. समूहवाचक D. द्रव्यवाचक

20. मार्च
A. समूहवाचक B. व्यक्तिवाचक
C. द्रव्यवाचक D. जातिवाचक

21. झुण्ड
A. समूहवाचक B. जातिवाचक
C. व्यक्तिवाचक D. द्रव्यवाचक

22. टोली
A. जातिवाचक B. व्यक्तिवाचक
C. समूहवाचक D. द्रव्यवाचक

23. सुभाष चौक
A. जातिवाचक B. समूहवाचक
C. व्यक्तिवाचक D. भाववाचक

24. संघ
A. जातिवाचक B. द्रव्यवाचक
C. समूहवाचक D. भाववाचक

25. गिरोह
A. समूहवाचक B. द्रव्यवाचक
C. जातिवाचक D. भाववाचक

उत्तरमाला

1. C	**2.** A	**3.** A	**4.** A	**5.** A
6. C	**7.** A	**8.** B	**9.** A	**10.** B
11. A	**12.** A	**13.** A	**14.** A	**15.** A
16. A	**17.** B	**18.** A	**19.** C	**20.** B
21. A	**22.** C	**23.** C	**24.** C	**25.** A

अभ्यास-12

निर्देशः *नीचे दिए गए वाक्य में रिक्त स्थान है। प्रत्येक वाक्य के नीचे कारक चिह्न दिए गए हैं। रिक्त स्थान की पूर्ति के लिए उपयुक्त कारक चिह्न का चयन कीजिए :*

1. निम्नलिखित शब्दों........अर्थ बताइए
A. का B. के
C. से D. पर

2. सरकार मुझे नौकरी........मत निकालिए
A. पर B. में
C. से D. को

3. इस कथन........पुष्टि कीजिए
A. को B. से
C. की D. ने

4. छात्र-छात्राएँ राष्ट्र........सम्पत्ति और उसके भावी कर्णधार होते हैं
A. के B. की
C. को D. में

5. प्रत्येक प्रश्न........चार सम्भावित उत्तर दिए गए हैं
A. के लिए B. में
C. के D. से

6. माता बच्चे........पढ़ाती है
A. को B. के
C. की D. से

7. गुरुजी........सबसे छोटे लड़के को एक नारंगी दी
A. ने B. को
C. से D. के लिए

8. मोहन सोहन से मिलने........गया है
A. से B. के
C. को D. के लिए

9. उसने कलम........लिखा
A. के B. में
C. पर D. से

10. मैं ड्राइवर........गाड़ी चलवाता हूँ
A. के B. पर
C. में D. से

11. शिक्षक छात्रों........पुस्तक पढ़वाते हैं
A. के लिए B. मैं
C. पर D. से

12. मैंने दाढ़ी........उसे मुसलमान समझ लिया
A. से B. के
C. को D. के लिए

13. श्याम अपने भाई हरि........आम लाया है
A. के B. के लिए
C. का D. पर

14. मोहन घर........आता है
A. में B. पर
C. से D. का

15. उसे पाँच दिनों........मूर्च्छा आया करती है
A. पर B. से
C. के D. को

16. मेधावी छात्र परीक्षा........चोरी नहीं करते
A. में B. पर
C. से D. के लिए

17. अच्छे आदमी........पहचान क्या है?
A. के B. का
C. की D. के लिए

18. परिश्रम........सफलता निश्चित है
A. से B. के
C. को D. के लिए

19. शूर्पणखा........नाक और कान काटे गए
A. का B. की
C. के D. से

20. युद ने राधा........तीन संतरे दिए
A. से B. के
C. के लिए D. को

उत्तरमाला

1. A	**2.** C	**3.** C	**4.** B	**5.** C
6. A	**7.** A	**8.** D	**9.** D	**10.** D
11. D	**12.** A	**13.** B	**14.** C	**15.** B
16. D	**17.** C	**18.** A	**19.** B	**20.** D

गद्यांश (अपठित-बोध)

गद्यांश 1

यदि हम निरन्तर प्रयत्न करेंगे तो निश्चय ही अपने सभी लक्ष्यों को प्राप्त कर लेंगे, किन्तु प्रायः देखा जाता है कि अधिक आशावादी लोग थोड़ा सा प्रयत्न करके अधिक फल की कामना करने लगते हैं और मनोवांछित फल प्राप्त न होने पर निराश हो जाते हैं। अतः जीवन में सफलता प्राप्त करने के लिए परिस्थितियों के समक्ष घुटने न टेकें, बल्कि दृढ़ता से उनका मुकाबला करें। याद रखें, जितना कठोर हमारा परिश्रम होगा उसका फल भी उतना ही मीठा होगा।

उपर्युक्त गद्यांश को ध्यानपूर्वक पढ़ें और निम्न प्रश्नों के उत्तर के लिए सही विकल्प को चुनें:

1. फल न मिलने पर कौन निराश हो जाते हैं?
A. आशावादी लोग B. कम आशावादी लोग
C. अधिक आशावादी लोग D. निराशावादी लोग

2. लक्ष्य प्राप्ति के लिए क्या किया जाना चाहिए?
A. फल की कामना
B. हिम्मत से मुकाबला
C. निरन्तर प्रयत्न
D. परिस्थितियों से मुकाबला

3. आशावादी शब्द का विलोम शब्द है:
A. निराश B. निराशावादी
B. दुखी D. अप्रसन्न

4. मनोवांछित शब्द का क्या अर्थ है?
A. इच्छित B. परीक्षित
C. लाभदायक D. मन को खुश करने वाले

5. परिश्रम शब्द का अर्थ है:
A. साहस B. हिम्मत
C. काम D. कठिन मेहनत

गद्यांश 2

पन्द्रह अगस्त 1947 को हमारा देश स्वतंत्र हुआ। स्वतन्त्रता प्राप्ति के बाद विश्व के दूसरे देशों के साथ भारत के राजनयिक एवं सांस्कृतिक सम्बन्ध जुड़े। पर्यटकों के साथ-साथ राजनीतिज्ञों और साहित्यकारों को भी विदेश यात्रा के पर्याप्त अवसर मिले। विभिन्न प्रकार की छात्रवृत्तियों के माध्यम से बहुत से लोग विदेशों में पढ़ने गए। बहुत से लोगों ने विदेशों में उपलब्ध आजीविका के अवसरों का लाभ उठाया। इन सबके परिणामस्वरूप प्रचुर मात्रा में यात्रावृत्तांत लिखे गए। विदेश-विषयक यात्रावृतांत्तों में रूस और स्वदेश-विषयक यात्रावृतांत्तों में लेखकों की दृष्टि कश्मीर से कन्याकुमारी तक व्याप्त हुई।

उपर्युक्त गद्यांश को ध्यानपूर्वक पढ़ें और निम्नलिखित प्रश्नों के उत्तर के लिए सही विकल्प को चुनें:

1. भारत कब स्वतंत्र हुआ?
A. 15 अगस्त 1947
B. 15 अगस्त 1946
C. 15 अगस्त 1948
D. 15 अगस्त 1949

2. स्वतंत्र भारत के अन्य देशों के साथ किस प्रकार के संबंध जुड़े?
A. राजनीतिक
B. राजनयिक
C. धार्मिक
D. राजनयिक एवं सांस्कृतिक

3. आजीविका का क्या अर्थ है?
A. उपार्जन B. वेतन
C. मेहनत D. रोजगार

4. यात्रा-वृत्तांत का क्या अर्थ है?
A. भ्रमण B. पर्यटन
C. सफरनामा D. विदेशभ्रमण

5. स्वतंत्र का विलोम शब्द है:
A. परतंत्र B. आजाद
C. गुलामी D. मुक्ति

गद्यांश 3

युवा वर्ग का मस्तिष्क नई-नई बातों की ओर ज्यादा तेज दौड़ता है। उसमें अन्य वर्ग के व्यक्तियों से अधिक आवेश और शक्ति होती है। इस अवस्था में यदि सही शिक्षा और

उचित मार्ग-दर्शन न मिले तो यही शक्ति प्रेरणा और निर्माण के स्थान पर विनाश की ओर ले जाती है। बिगड़ने और बनने की यही आयु होती है। दुर्भाग्य से हमारे देश में शिक्षा पद्धति केवल उपाधि बाँटने का काम ही करती है। एक सम्पूर्ण व्यक्तित्वपूर्ण मनुष्य बनाना आज की शिक्षा पद्धति के लिए मुश्किल है।

उपर्युक्त गद्यांश को ध्यानपूर्वक पढ़ें और निम्नलिखित प्रश्नों के उत्तर के लिए सही विकल्प को चुनें।

1. निर्माण का विलोम शब्द क्या हैं?
A. रचना B. बनावट
C. विनाश D. सृजन

2. मार्ग-दर्शन का क्या अर्थ है?
A. उपाधि B. रास्ता
C. उद्देश्य D. रास्ता दिखलाना

3. शक्ति विनाश की ओर कब अग्रसर होती है?
A. अधिक आवेश और शक्ति के अभाव में
B. सही शिक्षा और उचित मार्ग दर्शन के अभाव में
C. दुर्भाग्यपूर्ण शिक्षा पद्धति के कारण
D. इनमें से कोई नहीं

4. हमारे देश की शिक्षा पद्धति क्या कार्य करती है?
A. मार्ग-दर्शन B. शक्ति प्रेरणा
C. उपाधि देना D. उपर्युक्त सभी

5. दुर्भाग्य का विपरीत शब्द है:
A. भाग्य B. सौभाग्य
C. भाग्यशाली D. भाग्यवान

गद्यांश 4

भिखारी की भाँति गिड़गिड़ाना प्रेम की भाषा नहीं है। यहाँ तक कि मुक्ति के लिए भगवान् की उपासना करना भी अधम उपासना में गिना जाता है। प्रेम कोई पुरस्कार नहीं चाहता। प्रेम सर्वथा प्रेम के लिए ही होता है। भक्त इसलिए प्रेम करता है कि बिना प्रेम किए वह रह ही नहीं सकता। जब तुम किसी मनोहर प्राकृतिक दृश्य को देखकर उस पर मोहित हो जाते हो तो तुम किसी फल की याचना नहीं करते और न वह दृश्य ही तुमसे कुछ माँगता है। फिर भी उस दृश्य का दर्शन तुम्हारे मन को आनंद से भर देता है।

उपर्युक्त गद्यांश को ध्यानपूर्वक पढ़ें और निम्नलिखित प्रश्नों के उत्तर के लिए सही विकल्प का चयन करें:

1. प्रेम का उद्देश्य क्या होता है?
A. मुक्ति B. उपासना
C. भक्ति D. प्रेम

2. मुक्ति का अर्थ है:
A. आजादी B. स्वतंत्रता
C. परतंत्र D. निर्वाण

3. कैसी उपासना अधम मानी गई है?
A. प्रेम की उपासना
B. भगवान की उपासना
C. मुक्ति की उपासना
D. भक्ति की उपासना

4. मनोहर शब्द हैं:
A. विशेषण B. संज्ञा
C. सर्वनाम D. अव्यय

5. प्राकृतिक शब्द का अर्थ है:
A. ईश्वरीय B. मानव संबंधी
C. प्रकृति संबंधी D. प्रेम संबंधी

गद्यांश 5

कुछ लोग भाग्यवादी होते हैं और सब-कुछ भाग्य के सहारे छोड़कर कर्म से विरत हो जाते हैं। ऐसे लोग समाज के लिए बोझ हैं। वे कभी कोई बड़ा काम नहीं कर पाते। बड़ी-बड़ी खोज, बड़े-बड़े आविष्कार और बड़े-बड़े निर्माण कार्य कर्मशील लोगों के द्वारा ही संभव हो सके हैं। हम अपनी बुद्धि और प्रतिभा तथा कार्य-क्षमता के बल पर सही मार्ग पर चल सकते हैं, किन्तु बिना कठिन श्रम के अपने लक्ष्य तक नहीं पहुँच सकते। कठिन परिश्रम करने के बाद पाई गई सफलता हमारे मन को अलौकिक आनंद से भर देती है। यदि हम अपने कार्य में अपेक्षित श्रम नहीं करते तो हमारा मन ग्लानि का अनुभव करता है।

उपर्युक्त गद्यांश को ध्यानपूर्वक पढ़ें और निम्नलिखित प्रश्नों के उत्तर के लिए सही विकल्प चुनें:

1. "आविष्कार" शब्द का अर्थ है :
A. अनुसंधान B. खोज
C. निर्माण D. विनाश

2. **अलौकिक** शब्द का क्या अर्थ है?
A. संसारिक B. भौतिक
C. अमानुषी D. प्राकृतिक

3. सफलता का विलोम क्या है?
A. सफल B. असफल
C. सफलतापूर्वक D. असफलता

4. परिश्रम करने और न करने से हमारे जीवन पर क्या प्रभाव पड़ता है?
A. लोग भाग्यवादी बन जाते हैं
B. कर्म से विरत हो जाते हैं
C. मन में ग्लानि का अनुभव होता है
D. इनमें से कोई नहीं

5. किस प्रकार के लोग समाज के लिए बोझ हैं?
A. भाग्यवादी B. कर्मठ
C. परिश्रमी D. प्रतिभाशाली

गद्यांश 6

वैदिक काल से हिमालय के पहाड़ बहुत पवित्र माने जाते हैं। इसमें कोई सन्देह नहीं कि हिमालय के पहाड़ों का दृश्य अति सुन्दर है। उसकी विशालता को देखकर मन में आनन्द और कृतज्ञता की लहर उठती है। ऐसा लगता है कि यह विशाल सृष्टि प्रभु की अनुपम देन है। सारी सृष्टि के प्रति समभाव जाग्रत होता है। वस्तुतः यह दृष्टि कोरी कल्पनात्मक या आध्यात्मिक नहीं है। देखा जाए तो सारे भारत की जलवायु का समतोल करने वाले यह हिमालय के पहाड़ हैं, विशेषकर उत्तरी भारत को वर्षा और पानी देने वाले ये ही हैं। गंगोत्री, यमुनोत्री, बद्री, केदार को तीर्थ माना जाता है, जो व्यर्थ कल्पना नहीं है। उन स्थानों से निकलने वाली पवित्र नदियाँ ही वास्तव में हमारी प्राणदात्री रही हैं।

उपर्युक्त गद्यांश को ध्यानपूर्वक पढ़ें और निम्नलिखित प्रश्नों के उत्तर के लिए सही विकल्प चुनें :

1. हिमालय के पर्वत बहुत पवित्र कब से माने जाते हैं?
A. पाषाण काल से B. वैदिक काल से
C. प्राचीन काल से D. आधुनिक काल से

2. विशालता शब्द है :
A. जातिवाचक B. भाववाचक
C. विशेषण D. सर्वनाम

3. भारत की जलवायु को समतोल कौन करता है?
A. गंगोत्री B. यमुनोत्री
C. केदार D. हिमालय

4. सृष्टि का समानार्थक शब्द है :
A. सृजन B. रचना
C. प्रकृति D. संसार

5. प्राणदात्री का क्या अर्थ है?
A. गंगोत्री
B. यमुनोत्री
C. प्राणसंचार करने वाली
D. समभाव जाग्रत करने वाली

गद्यांश 7

सच्चा मित्र एक शिक्षक की भाँति होता है। जिस प्रकार शिक्षक अपने छात्र को सन्मार्ग की ही ओर अग्रसर करता है, उसी प्रकार एक सच्चा मित्र अपने मित्र को पाप के गर्त में गिरने से बचाता है। मानव-जीवन अधिक रहस्यपूर्ण है। कभी-कभी जीवन में ऐसे अवसर उपस्थित हो जाते हैं, जब मनुष्य की धर्मबुद्धि नष्ट हो जाती है और उसका मन द्रुत गति से पाप की ओर दौड़ता है। ऐसे समय में मित्र का ही उपदेश अधिक कल्याणकारी सिद्ध होता है। मित्र के उपदेश का जितना प्रभाव हृदय पर पड़ता है, उतना और किसी का नहीं पड़ता है।

उपर्युक्त गद्यांश को ध्यानपूर्वक पढ़ें और निम्नलिखित प्रश्नों के उत्तर के लिए सही विकल्प चुनें :

1. सच्चा मित्र किस प्रकार का होता है?
A. विपत्ति में सहायता देने वाला
B. गलत मार्ग पर चलने से रोकने वाला
C. शिक्षक के भाँति
D. धार्मिक गुरु की तरह

2. सन्मार्ग शब्द का विपरीत शब्द है :
A. अग्रसर B. कुमार्ग
C. सुमार्ग D. मार्गदर्शक

3. व्यक्ति को पाप के गर्त्त में गिरने से कौन बचाता है?
A. शिक्षक B. भाई
C. पिता D. सच्चा मित्र

4. मानव पाप की ओर कब दौड़ता है?
   A. जब स्वार्थी बन जाता है
   B. जब धर्म-बुद्धि नष्ट हो जाती है
   C. जब सच्चामित्र साथ छोड़ देता है
   D. जब धनवान बन जाता है

5. उपदेश में कौन-सा उपसर्ग है?
   A. उ B. उप
   C. दे D. देश

गद्यांश 8

सब तरह के भावों को प्रकट करने की योग्यता रखने वाली और निर्दोष होने पर भी यदि कोई भाषा अपना निज का साहित्य नहीं रखती, तो वह रूपवती भिखारिन की तरह कदापि आदरणीय नहीं हो सकती। उनकी शोभा, उसकी बड़ी सम्पन्नता, उसकी मान-मर्यादा उसके साहित्य पर ही अवलम्बित रहती है। उसके विचारों और राजनैतिक स्थितियों का प्रतिबिम्ब देखने को यदि कहीं मिल सकता है, तो उसके ग्रन्थ साहित्य में मिल सकता है। सामाजिक शक्ति या सजीवता, सामाजिक अशक्ति या निर्जीवता और सामाजिक सभ्यता तथा असभ्यता का निर्णायक एकमात्र साहित्य है।

उपर्युक्त गद्यांश को ध्यानपूर्वक पढ़ें और निम्नलिखित प्रश्नों के उत्तर के लिए सही विकल्प चुनें :

1. साहित्य विहीन भाषा किस प्रकार की होती है?
   A. आदरणीय B. भिखारिन
   C. रूपवती D. रूपवती भिखारिन

2. रूपवती का पुल्लिंग रूप है:
   A. रूपवान B. सुन्दर
   C. सुन्दरी D. रूपवत

3. भाषा की मान मर्यादा किस पर निर्भर करती है?
   A. लिपि पर B. साहित्यकार पर
   C. भक्ति पर D. साहित्य पर

4. "सम्पन्नता" शब्द का विपरीत शब्द है:
   A. गरीबी B. विपन्न
   C. अमीर D. विपन्नता

5. राजनैतिक, सामाजिक शक्ति का दर्शन हमें किसमें मिलता है?
   A. समाज B. राज्य
   C. नेता D. साहित्य

गद्यांश 9

स्वतंत्र भारत का सम्पूर्ण दायित्व आज विद्यार्थियों के ही ऊपर है, क्योंकि आज जो विद्यार्थी हैं, वे ही कल स्वतंत्र भारत के नागरिक होंगे। भारत की उन्नति, उसका उत्थान उन्हीं की उन्नति और उत्थान पर निर्भर करता है। अतः विद्यार्थियों को चाहिए कि वे अपने भावी जीवन का निर्माण बड़ी सतर्कता और सावधानी के साथ करें। उन्हें प्रत्येक क्षण अपने राष्ट्र, अपने समाज, अपने धर्म, अपनी संस्कृति को अपनी आँखों के सामने रखना चाहिए, जिससे उनके जीवन से राष्ट्र को कुछ बल प्राप्त हो सके। जो विद्यार्थी राष्ट्रीय दृष्टिकोण से अपने जीवन का निर्माण नहीं करते, वे राष्ट्र और समाज के लिए भार-स्वरूप हैं।

उपर्युक्त गद्यांश को ध्यानपूर्वक पढ़ें और निम्नलिखित प्रश्नों के उत्तर के लिए सही विकल्प चुनें :

1. भारत की उन्नति किस पर निर्भर करती है?
   A. युवाओं पर B. नेताओं पर
   C. साहित्यकारों पर D. विद्यार्थियों पर

2. **उन्नति** का समानार्थक शब्द है :
   A. पतन B. उत्थान
   C. विकास D. उदय

3. **उत्थान** का विपरीत शब्द है :
   A. उदय B. पतन
   C. पराजय D. हार

4. किसे अपने जीवन का निर्माण सतर्कता और सावधानी से करना चाहिए?
   A. युवाओं को B. नेताओं को
   C. बच्चों को D. विद्यार्थियों को

5. धर्म, संस्कृति तथा समाज का रक्षक कौन है?
   A. नागरिक B. ग्रामीण
   C. विद्यार्थी D. युवा

गद्यांश 10

हास्य एक ऐसा माध्यम है, जो नीरस-जीवन को भी सुखद बना देता है। हास्य का जादू इतना प्रभावशाली होता है कि वह छूत के रोग की तरह चारों ओर फैल जाता है। जिसने कभी हँसना नहीं सीखा, सचमुच उसने जीना नहीं सीखा। सामान्यतः मनुष्य को जीवन में इतनी मुसीबतें झेलनी

पड़ती हैं कि वह अपने जीवन को पहाड़ समझने लगता है। ऐसे दूभर जीवन को यदि जीने योग्य बनाना हो तो उसके लिए आवश्यक है कि जीवन में हँसने की गुंजाइश हो। हँसी के सहारे मनुष्य अपने कष्टों को भुलाने का प्रयत्न करता है। संघर्ष, तनाव, व्यस्तता, घुटन यदि आज के जीवन की सहज देन हैं, तो इनसे बचने के लिए यह आवश्यक है कि हम हँसना सीखें।

उपर्युक्त गद्यांश को ध्यानपूर्वक पढ़ें और निम्नलिखित प्रश्नों के उत्तर के लिए सही विकल्प चुनें :

1. नीरस जीवन को कौन सुखद बना देता है?
A. संगीत B. गीत
C. आमोद प्रमोद D. हास्य

2. **नीरस** का संधि विच्छेद है :
A. नी + रस B. नि + रस
C. निः + रस D. नीः + रस

3. किसका जीवन व्यर्थ है?
A. जिसने रोना नहीं सीखा
B. जिसने हँसना नहीं सीखा
C. जिसने गाना नहीं सीखा
D. इनमें से कोई नहीं

4. **हँसना** शब्द है :
A. संज्ञा B. विशेषण
C. क्रिया विशेषण D. क्रिया

5. तनाव और घुटन से बचने के लिए क्या करना चाहिए?
A. रोना चाहिए B. गाना चाहिए
C. हँसना चाहिए D. काम करना चाहिए

गद्यांश 11

किसी पुस्तक को पढ़ने में जल्दी नहीं करनी चाहिए, जो कुछ लेखक कहता है, उसे समझने की चेष्टा करनी चाहिए। प्रत्येक शब्द का अर्थ समझने की चेष्टा करनी चाहिए। यदि लेखक योग्य है, तो दूसरी बार वह पुस्तक और अधिक आनन्द देगी और तीसरी बार और अधिक। प्रत्येक बार अध्ययन करने पर आपको नवीन सुन्दर और नए विचार मिलेंगे और उसे आप जितना ही पढ़ेंगे, उतना ही स्नेह करने लगेंगे। सहस्रों व्यक्तियों ने गीता और रामायण तथा कुरान और बाइबिल को बार-बार पढ़ा है। उनका अनुभव है कि प्रत्येक बार उन्हें नई सूझ और नए विचार मिलते गए। कुछ लोग तो इस बात पर गर्व करते हैं कि उन्होंने अमुक पुस्तक को अनेक बार पढ़ा है, उन्हें कंठस्थ हो गई है।

उपर्युक्त गद्यांश को ध्यानपूर्वक पढ़ें और निम्नलिखित प्रश्नों के उत्तर के लिए सही विकल्प चुनें :

1. किसे समझने की चेष्टा करनी चाहिए?
A. पुस्तक B. रामायण
C. महाभारत D. गीता

2. पुस्तक की सजीवता किस पर निर्भर करती है?
A. लेखक B. प्रकाशक
C. पाठक D. चिन्तक

3. **आनन्द** का विपरीत शब्द है :
A. शोक B. दुख
C. संताप D. खुशी

4. नवीन, सुन्दर और नए विचार हमें कहाँ से प्राप्त होता हैं?
A. पुस्तक को बार-बार पढ़कर
B. सुनकर
C. भाषण से
D. अच्छे व्यक्तियों से मिलने पर

5. **कंठस्थ** शब्द का शब्दार्थ है :
A. कंठ में स्थित B. सुंदर कंठ
C. जबानी याद D. पंडित जी

गद्यांश 12

अहिंसा परम धर्म है और हिंसा आपद् धर्म। मनुष्य बराबर अहिंसा की ओर चलना चाहता है, किन्तु परिस्थितियाँ उससे हिंसा कराती है, अर्थात् परमधर्म की रक्षा के लिए आदमी बराबर आपद्धर्म से काम लेता रहा है। भारत अपनी सेनाओं को विघटित कर दे, तब भी उसका अपमान उससे अधिक होने वाला नहीं, जितना नेफा में हुआ। किन्तु परमधर्म पर टिकने की सामर्थ्य अगर भारत में नहीं है, तो आपद्धर्म पर उसे आना चाहिए। व्यवहारतः आपद्धर्म परमधर्म का विरोधी नहीं, उसका रक्षक है।

उपर्युक्त गद्यांश को ध्यानपूर्वक पढ़ें और निम्नलिखित प्रश्नों के उत्तर के लिए सही विकल्प चुनें :

1. **परमधर्म** का विपरीत शब्द है :
   A. महान धर्म　B. आपद्धर्म
   C. सच्चाधर्म　D. इनमें से कोई नहीं
2. आपद्धर्म किसे कहा जाता है?
   A. अहिंसा　B. सत्याग्रह
   C. विपत्ति　D. हिंसा
3. मानव से हिंसा कौन करवाती है?
   A. लोभ　B. स्वार्थ
   C. द्वेष　D. परिस्थितियाँ
4. **सामर्थ्य** का शब्दार्थ है :
   A. संघर्ष　B. परिश्रम
   C. शक्ति　D. पराक्रम
5. **परमधर्म** की रक्षा कौन करता है?
   A. अहिंसा　B. हिंसा
   C. आपदधर्म　D. युद्ध

गद्यांश 13

वर्तमान काल विज्ञापन का युग माना जाता है। समाचार-पत्रों के अतिरिक्त रेडियो और टेलीविजन भी विज्ञापन के सफल साधन हैं। विज्ञापन का मूल उद्देश्य उत्पादक और भोक्ता में सीधा सम्पर्क स्थापित करना होता है। जितना अधिक विज्ञापन किसी पदार्थ का होगा, उतनी ही उसकी लोकप्रियता बढ़ेगी। इन विज्ञापनों पर धन तो अधिक व्यय होता है, पर इनसे बिक्री बढ़ जाती है। ग्राहक जब इन आकर्षक विज्ञापनों को देखता है तो वह उस वस्तु-विशेष के प्रति आकृष्ट होकर उसे खरीदने को बाध्य हो जाता है।

उपर्युक्त गद्यांश को ध्यानपूर्वक पढ़ें और निम्नलिखित प्रश्नों के उत्तर के लिए सही विकल्प चुनें :

1. वर्तमान को किसका युग माना जाता है?
   A. फैशन　B. विज्ञापन
   C. संगीत　D. धन
2. उत्पादक तथा भोक्ता के बीच कौन संबंध स्थापित करता है?
   A. टेलीविजन　B. समाचार-पत्र
   C. रेडियो　D. विज्ञापन
3. **वर्तमान** शब्द का विपरीत शब्द है :
   A. अर्वाचीन　B. आधुनिक
   C. आजकल　D. प्राचीन
4. **आकर्षक** का शब्दार्थ है :
   A. विकर्षक　B. सुन्दर
   C. मनमोहक　D. आश्चर्यजनक
5. भोक्ता किस कारण वस्तुओं को खरीदने के लिए बाध्य हो जाता है?
   A. विज्ञापन
   B. आकर्षक विज्ञापन
   C. लोकप्रियता के कारण
   D. आसानी से उपलब्ध होना

गद्यांश 14

लगभग दो सौ वर्ष की गुलामी ने भारत के राष्ट्रीय स्वाभिमान को पैरों से रौंद डाला, हमारी संस्कृति को समाप्त कर दिया, हमारे विश्वासों को हिला दिया और हमारे आत्मविश्वास को चकनाचूर कर दिया, किन्तु अपने इस बूढ़े देश से प्यार करने वाले, इसके एक सामान्य संकेत पर प्राण न्यौछावर करने वाले दीवानों का अभाव न था। एक आवाज उठी और देखते ही देखते राष्ट्र का दबा हुआ आत्माभिमान उन्मत्त हो उठा। इतिहास साक्षी है जाने और अनजाने सहस्त्रों देशभक्त स्वतंत्रता की अनमोल निधि को पाने के लिए शहीद हो गए।

उपर्युक्त गद्यांश को ध्यानपूर्वक पढ़ें और निम्नलिखित प्रश्नों के उत्तर के लिए सही विकल्प चुनें :

1. **स्वाभिमान** का संधि विच्छेद है:
   A. स्वा + भिमान　B. स्वः + अभिमान
   C. स्व + अभिमान　D. स्वा + अभिमान
2. भारत का राष्ट्रीय स्वाभिमान किस कारण समाप्त हो गया था?
   A. लम्बे गुलामी से　B. निरंकुश शासक से
   C. स्वार्थी मानव से　D. धर्म के विनाश से
3. **आत्मविश्वास** का शब्दार्थ है
   A. घमण्ड　B. गर्व
   C. अपने पर विश्वास　D. अभिमान
4. भारत की अनमोल निधि को पाने के लिए कौन शहीद हो गए?
   A. देशभक्त　B. नेता
   C. युवा　D. युवती

5. अनमोल निधि का शब्दार्थ है:

A. अनन्त खजाना B. अमूल्य खजाना

C. बहुमूल्य D. स्वतंत्रता

गद्यांश 15

दुनिया के विभिन्न देशों के विकास पर विहंगम दृष्टि डालने से यह स्पष्ट हो जाता है कि आज जिस देश ने वैज्ञानिक उपलब्धियों के सहारे अपना औद्योगीकरण कर लिया, उसी को उन्नत देश कहा जाता है। जिस देश में औद्योगीकरण का स्तर नीचा है, वह पिछड़ा हुआ देश कहा जाता है। वैज्ञानिक आविष्कारों और औद्योगीकरण के आधार पर ही किसी देश की प्रगति को आँका जाता रहा है। विज्ञान ने मानव को पूरी तरह बदल दिया है।

उपर्युक्त गद्यांश को ध्यानपूर्वक पढ़ें और निम्नलिखित प्रश्नों के उत्तर के लिए सही विकल्प चुनें :

1. विहंगम दृष्टि का क्या अर्थ है?

A. एक झलक B. गहन दृष्टि

C. गहन चिन्तन D. इनमें से कोई नहीं

2. विकास का विपरीत शब्द है :

A. उत्थान B. उदय

C. पतन D. विनाश

3. वैज्ञानिक शब्द में कौन-सा प्रत्यय हैं?

A. निक B. वै

C. ईक D. इक

4. मानव जीवन को किसने बदल दिया है :

A. विकास B. वैज्ञानिक

C. विज्ञान D. उद्योग

5. किसी भी देश की स्तर को किससे नापा जाता है?

A. उपलब्धियों पर

B. औद्योगीकरण से

C. वैज्ञानिकों से

D. आविष्कारों से

गद्यांश 16

विश्व का वर्तमान उन्नत रूप मानव-श्रम की ही कहानी कह रहा है। गगन चुंबी अट्टालिकाएँ, लंबी-चौड़ी सड़कें, बड़े-बड़े विशाल नगर आकाश में उड़ते वायुयान तथा मानव-जीवन को सुखी और समृद्ध बनाने में योगदान करने वाले ज्ञान-विज्ञान के अनन्त रूप-ये सभी मनुष्य के श्रम का जयघोष करते हैं। स्पष्ट है कि मनुष्य और उसका शरीर विधाता की अनुपम रचना है जो निश्चय ही महान उद्देश्यों की संपूर्ति के लिए दिया गया है। इस दुर्लभ तन को यदि हम आलस्य, प्रसाद अथवा घटिया कामों में गँवा देते हैं तो उस विधाता के प्रति अन्याय करते हैं।

उपर्युक्त गद्यांश को ध्यानपूर्वक पढ़ें और निम्नलिखित प्रश्नों के उत्तर के लिए सही विकल्प चुनें :

1. विश्व का वर्तमान रूप किसका उद्‌योतक है?

A. चिन्तक का B. नेता का

C. वैज्ञानिक का D. मानव श्रम

2. गगन चुंबी अट्टालिकाएँ का अर्थ है :

A. आकाश में उड़ने वाला

B. आकाश को छूने वाला

C. बहुमंजिली इमारत

D. इनमें से कोई नहीं

3. आकाश का समानार्थक शब्द है :

A. वसुन्धरा B. धरा

C. पयोद D. गगन

4. सुखी का विपरीत शब्द है :

A. प्रसन्न B. अप्रसन्न

C. दुखी D. उदासी

5. विधाता की अनुपम रचना क्या है?

A. मानव शरीर B. समुद्र

C. वन D. पृथ्वी

गद्यांश 17

हमारे देश में एक ऐसा भी युग था जब नैतिक और आध्यात्मिक विकास ही जीवन का वास्तविक लक्ष्य माना जाता था। अहिंसा की भावना सर्वोपरि थी। आज पूरा जीवन दर्शन ही बदल गया है। सर्वत्र पैसे की हाय-हाय तथा धन का उपार्जन ही मुख्य ध्येय हो गया है, भले ही धन-उपार्जन के तरीके गलत ही क्यों न हों? इन सबका असर मनुष्य के प्रतिदिन के जीवन पर पड़ रहा है। समाज का वातावरण दूषित हो गया है-

बाह्य वातावरण तो दूषित है ही, आज सब जानते हैं पर्यावरण की समस्याएँ कितनी चिन्तनीय हो उठी है। इन

सबके कारण मानसिक और शारीरिक तनाव-खिंचाव और व्याधियाँ पैदा हो रही हैं।

उपर्युक्त गद्यांश को ध्यानपूर्वक पढ़ें और निम्नलिखित प्रश्नों के उत्तर के लिए सही विकल्प चुनें :

1. भारत का प्राचीन आदर्श था :

A. सत्य और अहिंसा

B. नैतिक और आध्यात्मिक विकास

C. धन उपार्जन

D. इनमें से कोई नहीं

2. **अहिंसा** का विपरीत शब्द है :

A. हिंसा B. सत्याग्रह

C. विनम्रता D. नैतिकता

3. जीवन दर्शन क्यों बदल गया है?

A. हिंसा के कारण

B. अहिंसा के कारण

C. धन लिप्सा के कारण

D. आध्यात्मिक विकास के कारण

4. समाज का वातावरण दूषित क्यों हो गया है?

A. शारीरिक तनाव

B. मानसिक व्याधियाँ

C. पर्यावरण की समस्याएँ

D. धन उपार्जन के गलत तरीके

5. **पर्यावरण** का शब्दार्थ हैः

A. जलमंडल B. स्थलमंडल

C. वायुमंडल D. वातावरण

गद्यांश 18

राजा राम मोहन राय में "होनहार बिरवान के होत चीकने पांत" वाली कहावत पूरी तरह चरितार्थ हुई। बाल्यकाल में उनकी बुद्धि कितनी कुशाग्र थी, इसकी अनेक कहानियाँ सुनी जाती हैं। उनके पिता ने उनकी पढ़ाई का समुचित प्रबन्ध किया। गाँव की पाठशाला में उन्होंने बंगला सीखी। उन दिनों कचहरियों में फारसी का बोलबाला था। अतः उन्होंने घर पर ही मौलवी से फारसी पढ़ी। नौ वर्ष की उम्र में वे अरबी की उच्च शिक्षा के लिए पटना भेजे गये। पटना उस समय भारतवर्ष में इस्लामी संस्कृति का केन्द्र था। पटना में वे तीन वर्ष तक रहे। उन्होंने कुरान का मूल अरबी में अध्ययन किया। चार वर्ष तक काशी में संस्कृत का अध्ययन किया। उपनिषदों के अद्वैतवाद का उनपर पूरा प्रभाव पड़ा। फलतः उन्हें निराकार ईश्वर पर विश्वास हुआ।

उपर्युक्त गद्यांश को ध्यानपूर्वक पढ़ें और निम्नलिखित प्रश्नों के उत्तर के लिए सही विकल्प चुनें :

1. राजा राममोहन राय ने बंगला कहाँ सीखी?

A. पटना B. काशी

C. कलकत्ता D. गाँव की पाठशाला

2. अरबी की शिक्षा उन्होंने कहाँ पाई?

A. काशी B. पटना

C. ईरान D. ईराक

3. संस्कृत साहित्य का अध्ययन उन्होंने कहाँ किया?

A. पटना B. काशी

C. इलाहाबाद D. कलकत्ता

4. **कुशाग्र** शब्द का अर्थ है :

A. तेज B. बुद्धिमान

C. होनहार D. विद्वान्

5. निराकार शब्द का विलोम है :

A. साकार B. आकार

C. विशाल D. मूर्ति

गद्यांश 19

मोती राजा साहब की सवारी का खास हाथी था। यों तो वह बहुत सीधा और समझदार था, पर कभी-कभी उसका मिजाज गर्म हो जाता था। एक बार पागलपन में उसने अपने महावत को मार डाला। राजा साहब ने यह खबर सुनी, तो उन्हें बहुत क्रोध आया, मोती की पदवी छिन गई। उसे राजा साहब की सवारी से निकाल दिया गया। कुलियों की तरह उसे लकड़ियाँ ढ़ोनी पड़ती, पत्थर लादने पड़ते और शाम को वह पीपल के नीचे मोटी जंजीरों से बाँध दिया जाता।

उपर्युक्त गद्यांश को ध्यानपूर्वक पढ़ें और निम्नलिखित प्रश्नों के उत्तर के लिए सही विकल्प चुनें :

1. राजा साहब की सवारी के हाथी का क्या नाम था?

A. सोना B. मोती

C. हीरा D. ऐरावत

2. किसने महावत को मार डाला था?

A. राजा B. हाथी

C. मोती D. दरबारी

3. **मिजाज** शब्द का शब्दार्थ है :

A. विचार B. ध्यान
C. मन D. दिल

4. किसकी पदवी छिन गई थी?

A. महावत की B. राजा की
C. मोती की D. हाथी की

5. समझदार और सीधा कौन था?

A. राजा साहब B. महावत
C. मोती D. इनमें से कोई नहीं

गद्यांश 20

मनुष्य का यह दावा है कि वह सक्षम है, समर्थ है। हिमालय की तराई में घने जंगलों के बीच में बना एक छोटा-सा स्टेशन, जो दोपहर के बाद वाली ढ़लती धूप में भी बुरी तरह जल रहा था, मानो मनुष्य के इस दावे का प्रमाण था। प्रकृति इस मनुष्य के वश में है, वह इस प्रकृति को मनचाहा नवीन रूप देता है। वह इस प्रकृति के साथ न जाने कितने खिलवाड़ करता है। तराई का वह जंगल भी तो उसी प्रकृति का एक भाग था।

उपर्युक्त गद्यांश को ध्यानपूर्वक पढ़ें और निम्नलिखित प्रश्नों के उत्तर के लिए सही विकल्प चुनें :

1. **सक्षम** शब्द समानार्थक शब्द है :

A. समर्थ B. शक्तिशाली
C. कायर D. निर्माता

2. सक्षम और समर्थ होने का दावा कौन करता है?

A. प्रकृति B. मानव
C. दानव D. पशु

3. छोटा-सा स्टेशन कहाँ स्थित है?

A. घने जंगलों में B. हिमालय की तराई में
C. नदी के किनारे D. नगर में

4. प्रकृति के साथ कौन खिलवाड़ करता है?

A. मानव B. वैज्ञानिक
C. नेता D. युवा

5. **नवीन** का विपरीत शब्द है :

A. पुराना B. नूतन
C. नवनीत D. अतीत

गद्यांश 21

पता नहीं जंगल में भी प्राण होते हैं या नहीं। वैसे जन्म लेना, मरना, शैशव, युवावस्था और वृद्धावस्था, जीवन के सब चिह्न जंगल में होते हैं। न जाने कितने पशु-पक्षी इन जंगलों की गोद में आश्रय लिए हुए हैं। कभी भयानक रूप से क्रुद्ध और उबलते हुए और कभी निष्प्राण से सुखे हुए नदी-नाले। ये सब जंगल के भाग हैं और जंगल के अन्दर इन अनगिनत प्राणियों में जीवन-मरण का संघर्ष चला करता है। रोज ही जन्म होते हैं, रोज ही मृत्यु के फेरे लगते हैं। जीवन-मरण की सीमाओं में बद्ध जो प्रकृति का क्रम है। वह तो चलता ही रहता है।

उपर्युक्त गद्यांश को ध्यानपूर्वक पढ़ें और निम्नलिखित प्रश्नों के उत्तर के लिए सही विकल्प चुनें :

1. जीवन के सब चिह्न किसमें होते है?

A. जंगल में
B. मानव में
C. पशु में
D. पादप में

2. **शैशव** का शब्दार्थ है :

A. युवा B. बुढ़ापा
C. बचपन D. नश्वर

3. जंगलों में कौन आश्रय लेता है :

A. पशु-पक्षी B. जन्तु
C. पादप D. मानव

4. **निष्प्राण** का समानार्थक शब्द है :

A. सजीव B. निर्जीव
C. शाश्वत D. नश्वर

5. **जीवन** का विपरीत शब्द है :

A. मरण B. अमर
C. प्राण D. नश्वर

गद्यांश 22

यह आदान-प्रदान ही मानव-सभ्यता का मूल स्रोत है; इस आदान-प्रदान के लिए ही मुनष्य ने पहाड़ों को लाँघकर और सागरों को पार करके दुनिया के हर-एक कोने का पता लगाया। इस आदान-प्रदान की क्रिया-प्रतिक्रिया के रूप में न जाने कितने युद्ध लड़े गए, न जाने कितने देश बरबाद किए गए, न जाने कितनी सभ्यताएँ नष्ट की गई और यह आदान-प्रदान चल रहा है।

उपर्युक्त गद्यांश को ध्यानपूर्वक पढ़ें और निम्नलिखित प्रश्नों के उत्तर के लिए सही विकल्प चुनें :

1. मानव-सभ्यता का मूल स्रोत क्या है?
   A. आदान　　B. प्रदान
   C. आदान-प्रदान　　D. इनमें से कोई नहीं
2. **मानव** का विपरीत शब्द है :
   A. नर　　B. मनुष्य
   C. दानव　　D. दुष्ट
3. दुनिया के हर एक भाग का पता किसने किया है?
   A. मानव　　B. खोजकर्ता
   C. आविष्कारक　　D. दानव
4. युद्ध क्यों लड़े गए थे :
   A. क्रिया-प्रतिक्रिया के कारण
   B. आदान-प्रदान के कारण
   C. स्वार्थ के कारण
   D. धन उपार्जन के कारण
5. **आदान-प्रदान** शब्द है :
   A. विपरीत शब्द
   B. क्रिया विशेषण
   C. पर्यायवाची शब्द
   D. सहचर-शब्द

उत्तरमाला

गद्यांश	1	2	3	4	5
गद्यांश 1	C	D	B	A	D
गद्यांश 2	A	D	D	C	A
गद्यांश 3	C	D	B	C	B
गद्यांश 4	D	D	C	A	C
गद्यांश 5	B	D	D	C	A
गद्यांश 6	B	B	D	A	C
गद्यांश 7	C	B	D	B	B
गद्यांश 8	D	A	D	D	D
गद्यांश 9	D	B	B	D	C
गद्यांश 10	D	C	B	D	C
गद्यांश 11	A	A	A	A	C
गद्यांश 12	B	D	D	C	C
गद्यांश 13	B	D	D	C	B
गद्यांश 14	C	A	C	A	B
गद्यांश 15	A	D	C	C	B
गद्यांश 16	D	C	D	C	A
गद्यांश 17	B	A	C	D	D
गद्यांश 18	D	B	B	A	A
गद्यांश 19	B	C	C	C	C
गद्यांश 20	A	B	B	A	A
गद्यांश 21	C	C	A	B	A
गद्यांश 22	C	C	A	B	D

❑❑❑

GENERAL INTELLIGENCE AND REASONING

SERIES

Directions : *In each of the following series determine the order of the letters. Then from the given options select the one which will complete the given series.*

1. BMK, DLM, FKO, HJQ, ?

A. JIR B. JIT
C. JHS D. JIS

2. A, CD, FGH, ?

A. IJKL B. KLMN
C. JKLM D. LMNO

3. BXJ, ETL, HPN, KLP, ?

A. PHR B. NIR
C. NHR D. MHR

4. PUF, QVG, RWH, ?

A. SXI B. SYZ
C. SXJ D. SVI

5. DEF, HIJ, MNO, ?

A. RTV B. STU
C. PTU D. SRU

Directions : *Which of the following groups of letters will complete the given series?*

6. ab---b-bbaa-

A. babba B. abaab
C. abbab D. baaab

7. aa-ab--aaa-a

A. baaa B. abab
C. aaab D. aabb

8. -baa-aab-a-a

A. baab B. abab
C. aaba D. aabb

9. -a cca-ccca-acccc-aaa

A. ccaa B. acca
C. caac D. caaa

10. c-bbb--abbbb-abbb-

A. abccb B. bacbb
C. aabcb D. abacb

Directions : *In the following questions, select the number(s) from the given options for completing the given series.*

11. 3, 9, 27, 81, 243, ?

A. 486 B. 729
C. 972 D. 359

12. 1, 6, 12, 19, 27, ?

A. 38 B. 35
C. 36 D. 54

13. 2, 6, 14, 30, 62, ?

A. 126 B. 128
C. 120 D. 130

14. 8, 48, 16, 96, 32, ?

A. 192 B. 150
C. 64 D. 288

15. 2, 8, 14, 24, 34, 48, ?

A. 66 B. 62
C. 58 D. 64

Directions : *In the given series find the number which is wrong.*

16. 5, 25, 120, 625, 3125, 15625

A. 15625 B. 625
C. 120 D. 5

17. 4, 8, 11, 22, 18, 36, 24, 50

A. 8 B. 22
C. 36 D. 24

18. 2, 4, 12, 24, 72, 142, 432

A. 432 B. 12
C. 142 D. 72

19. 2, 3, 4, 4, 6, 8, 9, 12, 16

A. 3 B. 9
C. 6 D. 12

20. 97, 91, 86, 83, 79, 77, 76, 76

A. 86 B. 76
C. 91 D. 83

ANSWERS

1	2	3	4	5	6	7	8	9	10
D	C	C	A	B	D	C	B	D	A
11	**12**	**13**	**14**	**15**	**16**	**17**	**18**	**19**	**20**
B	C	A	A	B	C	D	C	B	D

SOME SELECTED EXPLANATORY ANSWERS

1. The letters in one group correspond to the letters in the next group in the manner +2, –1, +2 respectively.

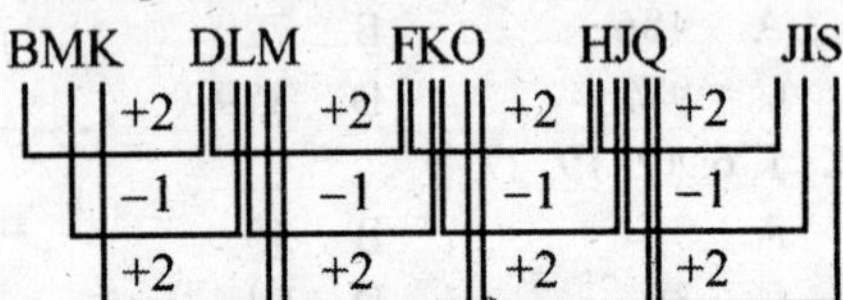

2. The letters are in natural sequence and from one group to the next one letter is dropped. Also the number of letters in groups is increased by one.

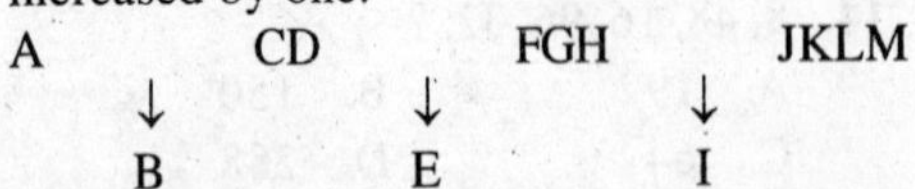

3. The letters in one group correspond to the letters in the next group in the manner +3, – 4, +2 respectively, *i.e.*,

BXJ ETL HPN KLP NHR

+3 +3 +3 +3

–4 –4 –4 –4

+2 +2 +2 +2

4. The three letters in each group are moved one step forward.

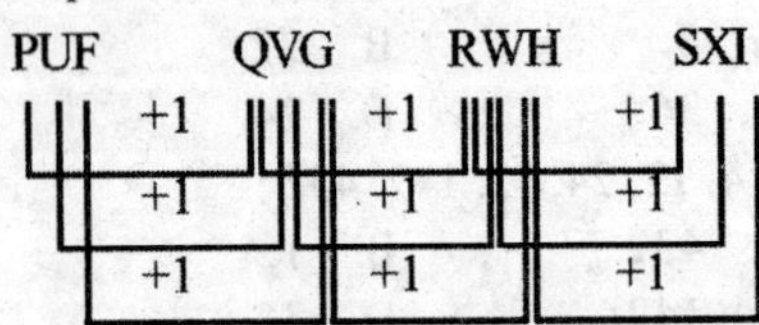

5. The letters are in natural order. The number of letters dropped in between the groups is increased by one at each step.

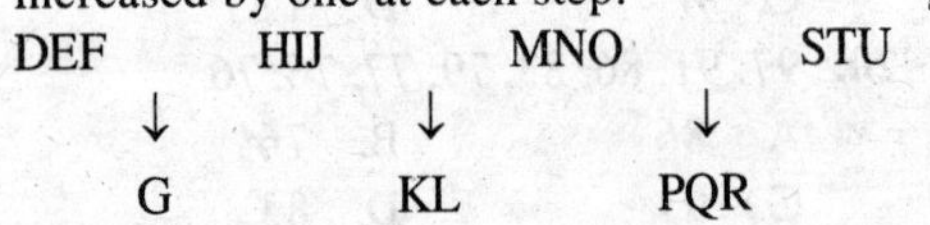

6. The series is abbaab, abbaab

7. The series is aaaaba, aaaaba

8. The series is aba, aba, aba, aba

9. The series is c,a,cc,aa, ccc, aaa, cccc, aaaa

10. The series is cabbbb, cabbbb, cabbbb

11. The numbers in the series are multiplied by 3 to get the next numbers.

12. The difference between the numbers in the series increases by 1, after beginning from 5, *i.e.*,

1 6 12 19 27 36

+5 +6 +7 +8 +9

13. The difference between the numbers in the series doubles each time, after beginning from 4, *i.e.*,

2 6 14 30 62 126

+4 +8 +16 +32 +64

14. *Explanation I* : The sequence in the series is × 6, ÷ 3 which is repeated.

8 48 16 96 32 192

× 6 ÷ 3 × 6 ÷ 3 × 6

Explanation II : There are two alternate series and the numbers are multiplied by 2.

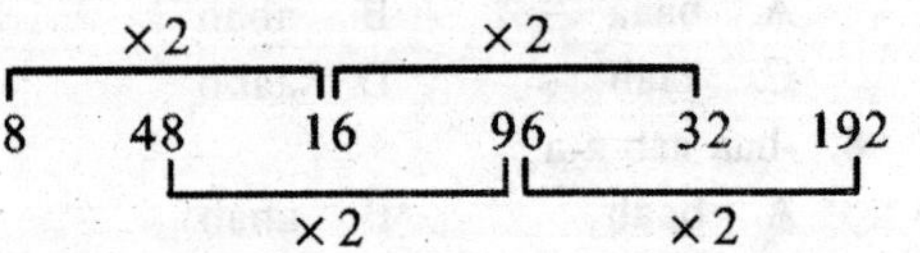

Series I : 8, 16, 32

Series II : 48, 96, 192

15. The sequence in the series is :

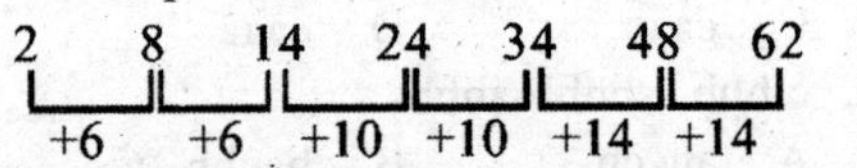

The difference increases by 4 at alternate step.

16. The numbers in the series are multiplied by 5 to get the next number.
∴ 125 should be in place of 120.

17. Two numbers form a pair. The first number increases by 7 for the next pair and the second number is the double of first number.

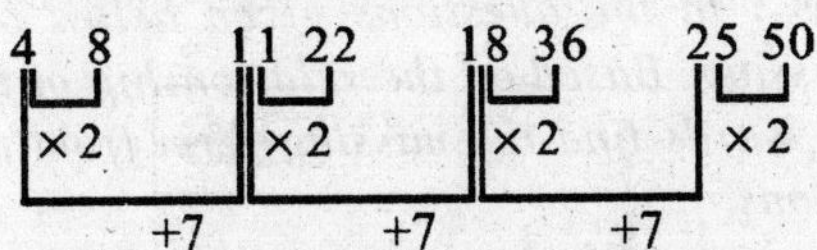

∴ 25 should be in place of 24.

18. There are two alternate series and in each series, the numbers are multiplied by 6 to get the next number.

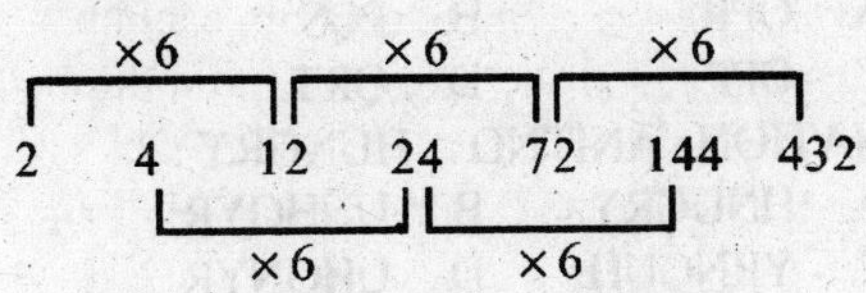

∴ 144 should be in place of 142.

19. There are three alternate series and in each series, the numbers are multiplied by 2 to get the next number.

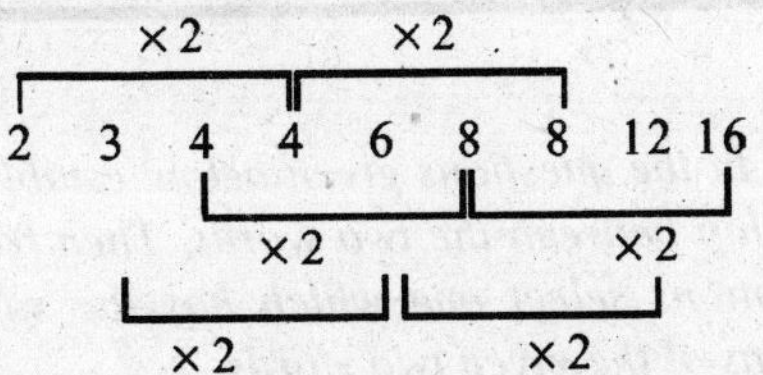

Series I : 2, 4, 8
Series II : 3, 6, 12
Series III : 4, 8, 16
∴ 8 should be in place of 9.

20. The difference between the consecutive numbers in the series decreases by 1 at each step.

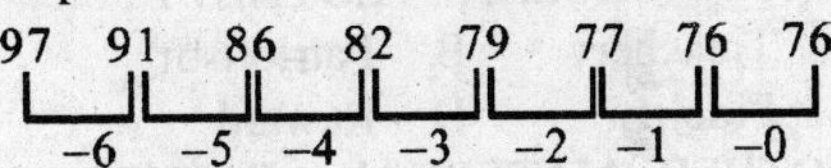

∴ 82 should be in place of 83.

ANALOGIES OR RELATIONSHIPS

Directions : *In the questions given below establish the relationship between the two words. Then from the given options select one which has the same relationship as of the given two words.*

1. ADULT : BABY : : FLOWER : ?
   A. Seed B. Bud
   C. Fruit D. Butterfly
2. WRITER : READER : : PRODUCER : ?
   A. Creator B. Contractor
   C. Creature D. Consumer
3. ENTRANCE : EXIT : : LOYALTY : ?
   A. Treachery B. Patriotism
   C. Fidelity D. Reward
4. MOTHER : MATERNAL : : FATHER : ?
   A. Eternal B. Detrimental
   C. Paternal D. Formidable

Directions : *In the questions given below one term is missing. Based on the relationship of the two given words find the missing term from the given options.*

5. GFC : CFG : : RPJ : ?
   A. JRP B. JPR
   C. PJR D. RJP
6. BCF : DEG : : MNQ : ?
   A. OPR B. PQS
   C. OPP D. QRT
7. NATION : ANITNO : : HUNGRY : ?
   A. HNUGRY B. UNHGYR
   C. YRNGUH D. UHGNYR
8. SSTU : MMNO : : AABC : ?
   A. GGHH B. IJKK
   C. XXYZ D. NOOP

ANSWERS

1	2	3	4	5	6	7	8
B	D	A	C	B	A	D	C

SOME SELECTED EXPLANATORY ANSWERS

1. The youngone of an adult is a baby and that of a flower is a bud.
2. A writer aims to please the readers by his writings, a producer aims to please the consumers by his products.
3. The related words are opposites.
4. Relations on the mother's side are maternal and on the father's side paternal.
5. The letters of the first group are reversed.

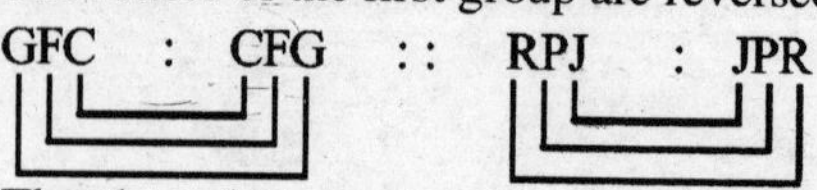

6. The three letters are moved 2, 2 and 1 steps forward respectively.

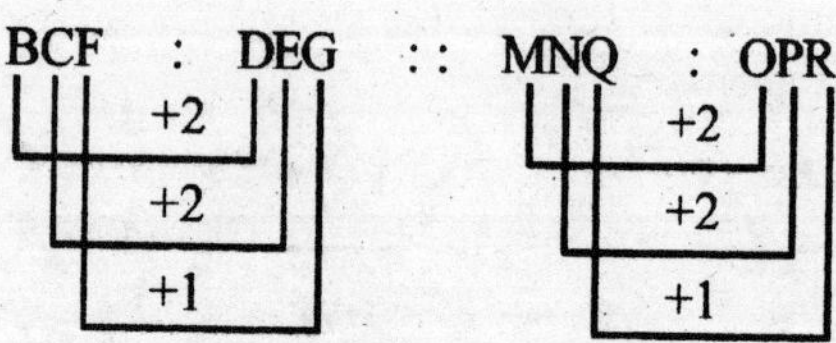

7. The word is divided in sections of two letters and the letters are reversed.

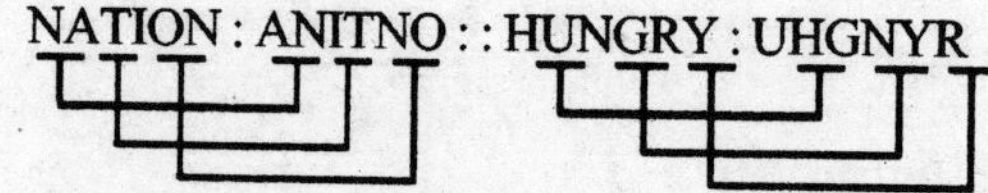

8. The first letter in each group is repeated and followed by two consecutive letters.

ODD ONE OUT

Directions : *Three of the following four in each question are alike in a certain way and so form a group. Select the group of letters that does not belong to that group.*

1. A. ACE B. LOR
C. GIK D. VXZ

2. A. TSR B. LKJ
C. PQO D. HGF

3. A. EF LM B. KJ SR
C. XW HG D. ED YX

4. A. JOPK B. BOPC
C. QOPR D. TOPS

5. A. DfH B. MoQ
C. UwY D. InO

6. A. JKkL B. OPpQ
C. DEEf D. VWwX

7. A. BdfH B. FHJL
C. RTvX D. uVwX

8. A. DFHEG B. TWXUV
C. OQSPR D. JLNKM

9. A. FEUV B. DCXW
C. BAZY D. HGTS

10. A. UTSR B. XYZW
C. ONML D. IHGF

ANSWERS

1	2	3	4	5	6	7	8	9	10
B	C	A	D	D	C	D	B	A	B

SOME SELECTED EXPLANATORY ANSWERS

1. The sequence in each group is +2. Only option B has sequence in +3, *i.e.,*

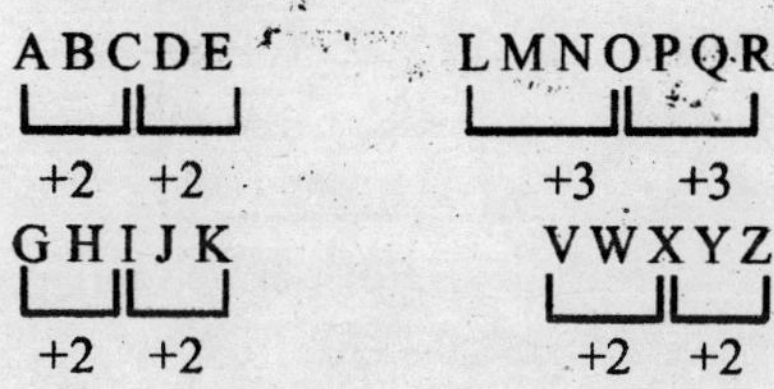

2. The sequence of alphabet in each group is in reverse order. Only option C has sequence in disturbed order.

3. Two consecutive alphabet in each group are in reverse sequence (–1), *i.e.,*

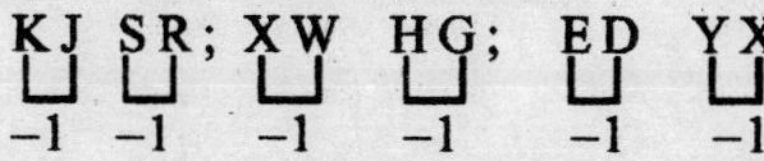

Only in option (A) the sequence is in natural order (+1), *i.e.,*

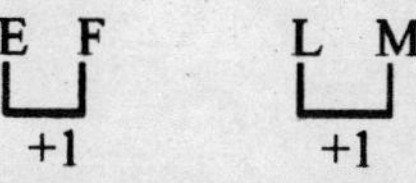

4. In each group, letters 'OP' are common. The two corner alphabet are in natural order (+1); *i.e.,*

JOPK ; BOPC ; QOPR
+1 +1 +1

Only in option (D) they are in reverse order (–1); *i.e.,*

TOPS
–1

5. In other groups, only the alphabet in the centre is of lower case. In this option letter 'L' on the left is also in lower case.
6. In other groups, the third letter which is a repeat of the second alphabet is in lower case.
7. In each group, the sequence of the alphabet, irrespective of the case, is +2; *i.e.*,

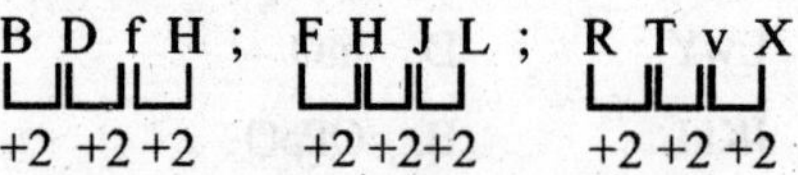

Only in option (D) the sequence is in natural order (+1), *i.e.*,

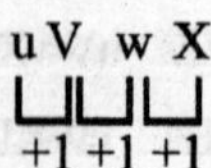

8. In each group; the alphabet at positions-first, fourth, second, fifth and third, form a natural sequence.
In option (B), the alphabet at positions first, fourth, fifth, second and third, form the natural sequence.
9. In each group, two alphabets in the corner and two alphabets in the centre correspond to their reverse order positioned alphabet. *i.e.*,

natural order → A B C D E F G H I J K L M
reverse order → Z Y X W V U T S R Q P O N
natural order → N O P Q R S T U V W X Y Z
reverse order → M L K J I H G F E D C B A

As such—
D corresponds with W and
C corresponds with X.
B corresponds with Y and
A corresponds with Z.
H corresponds with S and
G corresponds with T.
Similarly,
F should correspond with U and
E should correspond with V;
i.e. letters 'UV' should be written as 'VU'
10. In each group, the alphabet are in reverse order. In option (B), the order is disturbed.

CODING AND DECODING

Directions : *In the following questions select the right option which indicates the correct code for the word or letter given in the question.*

1. If CHAIR is coded as FKDLU then RAID is coded as :

A. ULGD B. ULKG
C. ULDG D. UDLG

2. If CONDEMN is coded as CNODMEN, then TEACHER is coded as :

A. TEACHER B. TAEECHR
C. TCAEEHR D. TAECEHR

3. In a code language COME is written as XLNV and ABLE as ZYOV. How will MOLLY be written in that code?

A. NLOBO B. NLBOO
C. LNOOB D. NLOOB

4. In a certain code PROFESSION is written as EFORPNOISS. In the same code DICTIONARY will be written as :

A. YRANOITCID
B. ITCIDYRANO
C. ITCIDYRNAO
D. ITCDIYARNO

5. JUNE is coded as NXPF, how will STAY be coded in the same manner?

A. WWCZ B. WVCZ
C. WWDB D. VWZC

Directions : *In the following questions study the coded patterns and then select the right option from the given alternatives.*

6. In a certain language, (a) 'go ju mi' stands for 'plenty of money'; (b) pao ju go nei vu' for 'money creates lots of problems'; (c) 'kol vu nei' for 'problems create tension'; and (d) 'sol tun ju haw' for 'still money is needed'. Which of the following words stand for 'money'?

A. nei B. ju
C. haw D. go

7. In a certain language, (a) 'FOR' stands for 'old is gold'; (b) 'ROT' stands for 'gold is pure'; (c) 'ROM' stands for 'gold is costly'. How will 'pure old gold is costly' be written?

A. TFROM B. FOTRM
C. FTORM D. TOMRF

8. In a certain code '415' means 'milk is hot'; '18' means 'hot soup'; and '895' means 'soup is tasty'. What number will indicate the word 'tasty'?

A. 9 B. 8
C. 5 D. 4

9. In a certain code '643' means 'she is beautiful', '593' means 'he is handsome', and '567' means 'handsome meets beautiful'. What number will indicate the word 'meets'?

A. 5 B. 3
C. 7 D. 6

10. In a certain code language, (a) 'dugo hui mul zo' stands for 'work is very hard'; (b) 'hui dugo ba ki' for 'Bingo is very smart'; (c) 'nano mul dugo' for 'cake is hard', and (d) 'mul ki qu' for 'smart and hard'. Which of the following words stand for 'Bingo'?

A. jalu B. dugo
C. ki D. ba

ANSWERS

1	2	3	4	5	6	7	8	9	10
D	D	D	B	A	B	A	A	C	D

SOME SELECTED EXPLANATORY ANSWERS

2. In this word, the second and third letters interchange their places and the fifth and sixth letters do the same. Other letters retain their position.

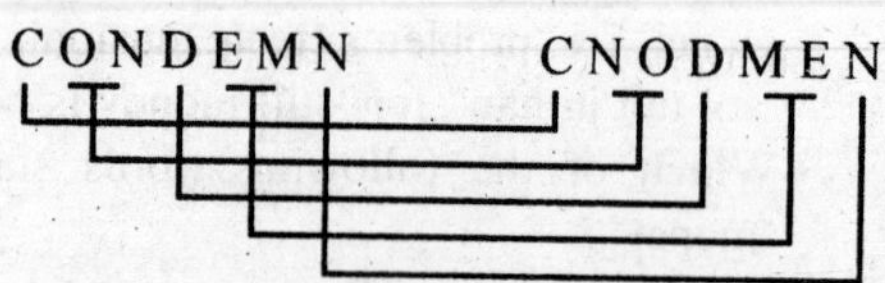

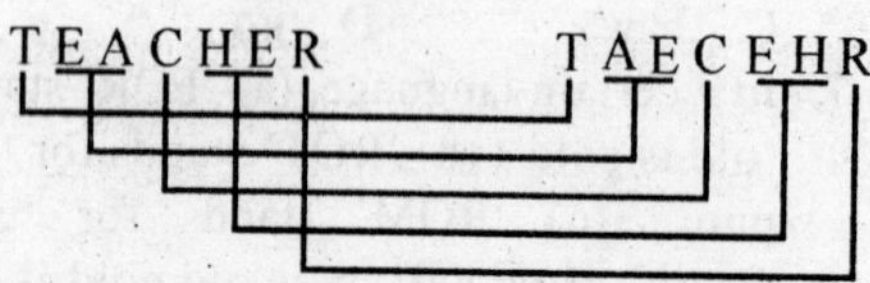

3. The letters of the word are coded by their represented letters in the reverse series.

C O M E → letters in natural series
X L N V → letters in reverse series
↓ ↓ ↓ ↓
3rd 15th 13th 5th → position of letters
A B L E → letters in natural series
Z Y O V → letters in reverse series
↓ ↓ ↓ ↓
1st 2nd 12th 5th → position of letters

Similarly,

M O L L Y → letters in natural series
N L O O B → letters in reverse series
↓ ↓ ↓ ↓ ↓
13th 15th 12th 12th 25th → position of letters

4. The word is divided into two equal parts and the letters of each part are written backwards.

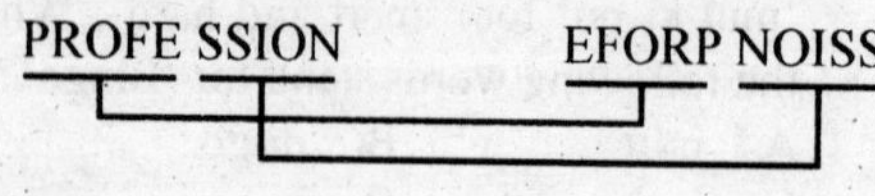

Similarly,

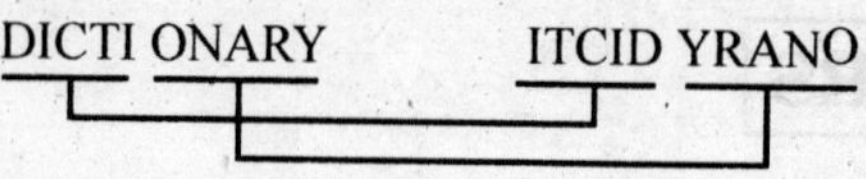

5. The word is coded by moving the letters +4, +3, +2, and +1 steps respectively.

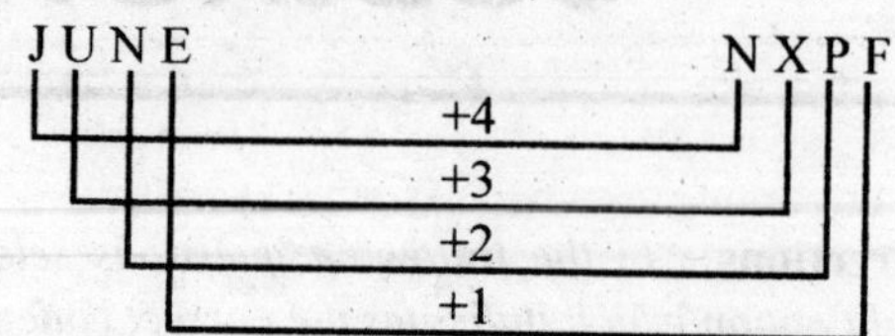

Similarly,

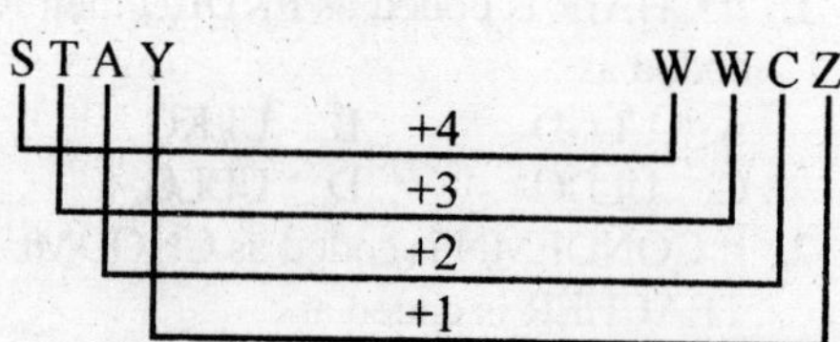

6.

	Code	Sentence
1.	go *ju* mi	plenty of *money*
2.	pao *ju* go nei vu	*money* creates lots of problems
3.	kol vu nei	problems create tension
4.	sol tun *ju* haw	still *money* is needed

In 1st, 2nd and 4th codes and their sentences the word 'ju' is repeated and so is 'money'.

8.

	Code	Sentence
1.	415	milk is hot
2.	18	hot soup
3.	895	soup is *tasty*

From 3rd code and its sentence neither number '9' is repeated nor the word 'tasty'.

9.

	Code	Sentence
1.	643	she is beautiful
2.	593	he is handsome
3.	567	handsome *meets* beautiful

From 3rd code and its sentence, neither number '7' nor the word 'meets' is repeated.

10.

	Code	Sentence
1.	*dugo hui* mul zo	work *is very* hard
2.	*hui dugo* **ba** *ki*	**Bingo** *is very smart*
3.	nano mul *dugo*	cake is *hard*
4.	mul *ki* qu	*smart* and hard

From 2nd code and its sentence, neither 'ba' nor 'Bingo' is repeated.
(Words repeated are in italics)

STATEMENT ANALYSIS

1. Among five friends, A is heavier than B; C is lighter than D; B is lighter than D but heavier than E. Who among them is the heaviest?
   A. B B. C
   C. A D. Can't say
2. Pune is bigger than Jhansi, Sitapur is bigger than Chittor. Raigarh is not as big as Jhansi, but is bigger than Sitapur. Chittor is not as big as Sitapur. Which is the smallest?
   A. Jhansi B. Pune
   C. Chittor D. Sitapur
3. Ajay works more than Ram. Alok works as much as Raju. Pankaj works less than Alok. Ram works more than Alok. Who works the most of all?
   A. Ajay B. Ram
   C. Alok D. Raju
4. Vipul is taller than Hans. Hans is taller than Anand. Alok is taller than Ashok. Ashok is taller than Hans. Who among them is the tallest?
   A. Vipul
   B. Alok
   C. Ashok
   D. Cannot be determined
5. Pramod is taller than Gopal. Gopal is shorter than Madhu. To find out who among them is the tallest, which of the following further informations is necessary?
   A. Madhu is taller than Gopal.
   B. Madhu is shorter than Pramod's brother
   C. Pramod is taller than Madhu.
   D. Pramod is taller than Madhu's brother.
6. Among five friends P, Q, R, S and T, who is the youngest? To arrive at the answer which of the following information given in the statements (*a*) and (*b*) is sufficient?
   (*a*) R is younger than P and T.
   (*b*) S is younger than Q.
   A. Only (*a*) alone is sufficient
   B. Either (*a*) or (*b*) is sufficient
   C. Both (*a*) and (*b*) together are needed
   D. Both (*a*) and (*b*) together are not sufficient
7. Sushma is richer than Rashmi whereas Anand is richer than Priya. Arun is as rich as Rashmi. Shoba is richer than Sushma. Which of the following statements is correct according to the above propositions?
   A. Rashmi is poorer than Priya.
   B. Priya is richer than Arun
   C. Arun is poorer than Sushma.
   D. Anand is richer than Rashmi
8. A is elder to B while C and D are elder to E who lies between A and B. If C be elder to B, which one of the following statements is necessarily true?
   A. E is elder to B
   B. A is elder to C
   C. C is elder to D
   D. D is elder to C
9. Vikram is taller than Rajan but shorter than Annie. Jamal is taller than Annie. Sita is taller than Vikram. Rajan is shorter than Sita. Who is the shortest of all in the group?
   A. Sita
   B. Rajan
   C. Vikram
   D. Cannot be determined
10. Suresh is as much older than Kamal as he is younger than Prabodh. Navin is as old as Kamal. Which of the following statements is wrong?
    A. Suresh is older than Navin
    B. Kamal is younger than Suresh
    C. Prabodh is not the oldest
    D. Navin is younger than Prabodh

ANSWERS

1	2	3	4	5	6	7	8	9	10
D	C	A	D	C	D	C	A	B	C

SOME SELECTED EXPLANATORY ANSWERS

1. The five friends in descending order of weight are : A/D, B/C, E or A/D, B, C/E. Either A or D is the heaviest.

2. The order of cities in descending order of size is : Pune, Jhansi, Raigarh, Sitapur, Chittor.

3. On the basis of doing work, the descending order will be : Ajay, Ram, Alok/Raju, Pankaj.

4. On the basis of height, the descending order will be Vipul/Alok, Ashok, Hans, Anand. Either Vipul or Alok is the tallest.

5. According to the information both Pramod and Madhu are taller than Gopal. Option (c) decides who is the tallest.

6. Statements are not inter-related.

7. On the basis of wealth, the descending order will be :

1. Shobha, Sushma, Rashmi/Arun
2. Anand, *and* Priya

(The two statements are not inter-related.)

8. The order in descending seniority will be : A/C/D, E, B.

9. On the basis of height the descending order will be :

Jamal/Sita, Annie, Vikram, Rajan.

or

Jamal, Sita/Annie, Vikram, Rajan.

10. On the basis of age the descending order will be : Prabodh, Suresh, Kamal/Navin.

PLACE ARRANGEMENT

Directions : *In the following questions, understand the arrangement pattern and then select the right answer from the given options :*

1. Five boys are sitting in a row. Raghu is not adjacent to Shyam or Amit. Ajay is not adjacent to Shyam. Raghu is adjacent to Mayank. If Mayank is at the middle in the row, then Ajay is adjacent to whom out of the following?

A. Amit B. Raghu
C. Mayank D. Shyam

2. Mini is to the right of Rajni but to the left of Ananta. Saya is to the right of Mini but to the left of Jaya. Who is on the extreme left if all the girls are facing North?

A. Jaya B. Mini
C. Rajni D. Saya

3. Kittu is in-between Mohan and Sohan. Raju is to the left of Sohan and Shyam is to the right of Mohan. If all of the friends are sitting facing South, then who is on their extreme right?

A. Mohan B. Sohan
C. Kittu D. Shyam

4. A, B, C, D and E are running one behind the other. C is not near E and A is not near D. B is next to A and E is not near D. Who is in the middle?

A. B B. E
C. A D. Cannot be said

5. O, P, Q, R, S and T are standing on a bench according to their height. P is taller than O but shorter than S. Only S is taller than T. R is shorter than P but taller than Q. Who is the shortest?

A. O B. Q
C. P D. Cannot be said

ANSWERS

1	2	3	4	5
B	C	D	A	D

SOME SELECTED EXPLANATORY ANSWERS

1. The order of sitting is :
Amit, Shyam, Mayank, Ajay, Raghu
or
Ajay, Raghu, Mayank, Amit, Shyam

2. The order in which the girls are positioned is :
Rajni, Mini, Ananta, Saya, Jaya
or
Saya, Jaya, Ananta
or
Saya, Ananta, Jaya

3. The order of sitting while facing South is:
Shyam, Mohan, Kittu, Sohan, Raju.

4. The positions while running behind the other is :

E		E
A		A
B	*or*	B
C		D
D		C

5. In descending order of height, the standing positions are :

S		S
T		T
P	*or*	P
R		R
O		Q
Q		O

Either O or Q is the shortest. The information given is not enough to clarify the answer.

DIRECTION SENSE

Directions : *In the following questions, select the right answer from the given options to depict the correct direction/distance.*

1. Kittu walks towards East and then towards South. After walking some distance he turns towards West and then turns to his left. In which direction is he walking now?
   A. North B. South
   C. East D. West
2. A person is driving towards West. What sequence of directions should he follow so that he is driving towards South?
   A. left, right, right B. right, right, left
   C. left, left, left D. right, right, right
3. Richa drives 8 km to the South, turns left and drives 5 km. Again, she turns left and drives 8 km. How far is she from her starting point?
   A. 3 km B. 5 km
   C. 8 km D. 13 km
4. Dingi runs 40 km towards North then turns right and runs 50 km. He turns right and runs 30 km, and once again turns right and runs 50 km. How far is he from his starting point?
   A. 90 km B. 50 km
   C. 10 km D. 5 km
5. Debu walks towards East then towards North and turning 45° right walks for a while and lastly turns towards left. In which direction is he walking now?
   A. North B. East
   C. South-East D. North-West

ANSWERS

1	2	3	4	5
B	D	B	C	D

SOME SELECTED EXPLANATORY ANSWERS

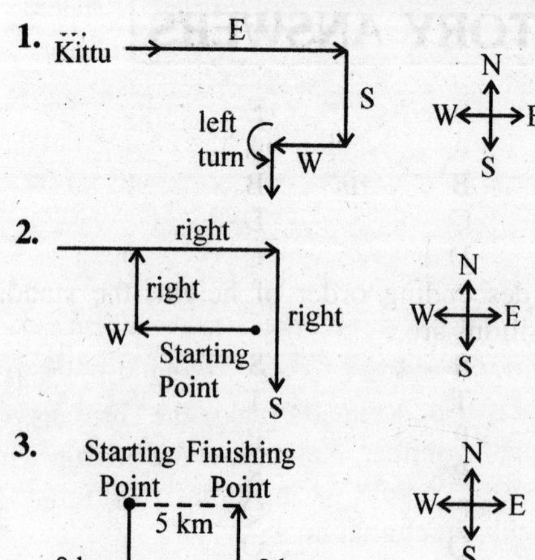

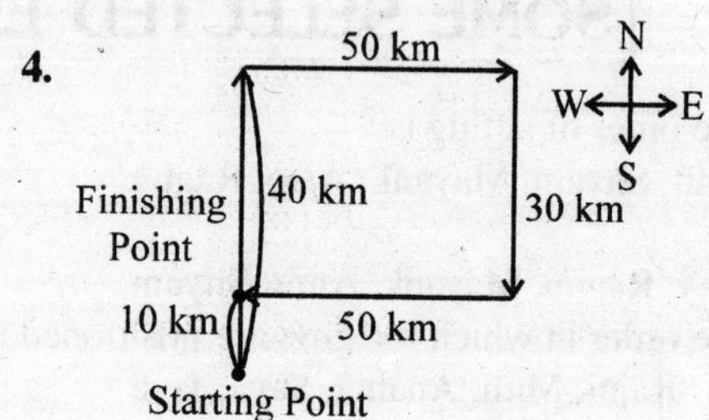

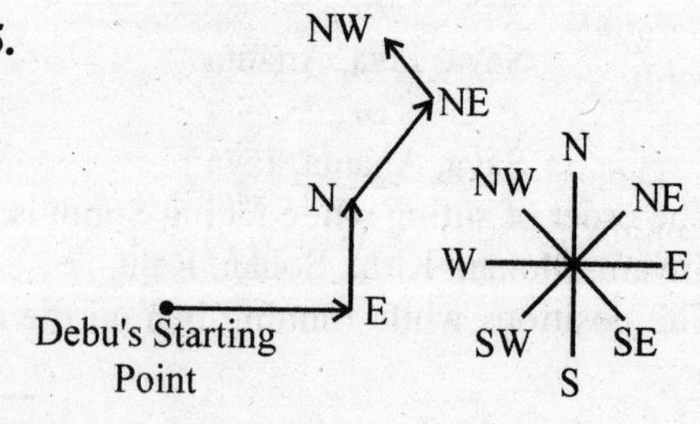

BLOOD RELATIONSHIPS

Directions : *In each of the following questions keenly study the relationship mentioned between the persons, and then from the given options select the right relationship as the answer.*

1. 'A' is the father of 'B' and 'C'. 'B' is the son of 'A' but 'C' is not the son of 'A'. What is 'C's' relation with 'A'?
   A. Daughter B. Son
   C. Niece D. Nephew
2. A lady said, "The person standing there is my grandfather's only son's daughter". How is the lady related to the standing person?
   A. Sister B. Mother
   C. Aunt D. Cousin
3. Ravi is the brother of Amit's son's son. What is Amit's relation to Ravi?
   A. Cousin B. Father
   C. Grandfather D. Son
4. Mayank said, "My mother is the sister of Rajat's brother." What is Rajat's relation with Mayank?
   A. Cousin B. Maternal uncle
   C. Uncle D. Brother-in-law
5. Introducing Lily, Raghav said, "Her father is my mother's only son". How is Lily related to Raghav?
   A. Aunt B. Daughter
   C. Mother D. Sister

ANSWERS

1	2	3	4	5
A	A	C	B	B

SOME SELECTED EXPLANATORY ANSWERS

1.

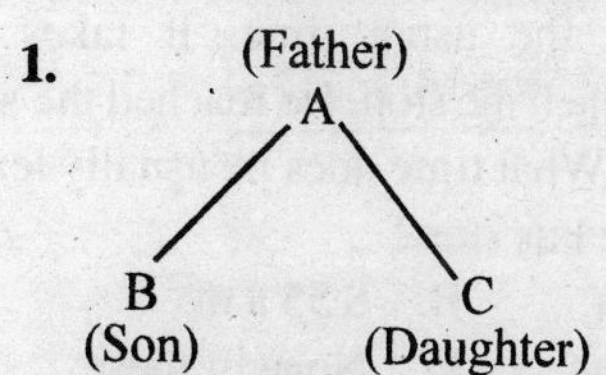

'C' is not the son of 'A', but 'A' is the father of 'C'. So, 'C' is the daughter of 'A'.

2. Grand father

Father
(only son)

Daughter
(standing person)

Lady
(sister)

Lady's grandfather's son is lady's father and father's daughter will only be lady's sister.

4.

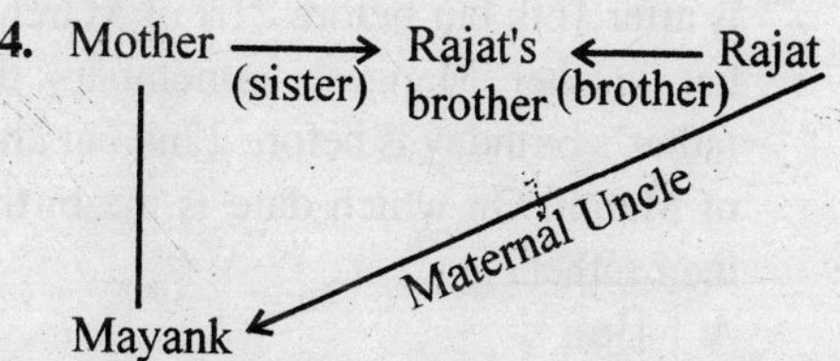

Mayank's mother is the sister of Rajat's brother. So Rajat is also the brother of Mayank's mother. Relation of the brother with his sister's child is maternal. So Rajat is Mayank's maternal uncle.

CALENDAR, CLOCK, TIME, DISTANCE

1. If the day before yesterday was Thursday, when will Sunday be?
   A. Tomorrow B. Day after tomorrow
   C. Today D. Two days after today
2. There are twenty people working in an office. The first group of five works between 8:00 A.M. and 2:00 PM. The second group of ten works between 10:00 AM to 4:00 PM. And the third group of five works between 12 noon to 6:00 PM. There are three computers in the office which all the employees frequently use. During which of the following hours the computers are likely to be used most?
   A. 1:00 PM - 3:00 PM
   B. 12 noon - 2:00 PM
   C. 2:00 PM - 4:00 PM
   D. 10:00 AM - 12 noon
3. If the seventh day of a month is three (3) days earlier than Friday, what day will it be on the nineteenth day of the month?
   A. Sunday B. Monday
   C. Wednesday D. Friday
4. Radha remembers that her father's birthday is after 16th but before 21st of March, while her brother Mangesh remembers that his father's birthday is before 22nd but after 19th of March. On which date is the birthday of their father?
   A. 19th
   B. 20th
   C. 21st
   D. Cannot be determined
5. A man is three (3) years older than his wife and four (4) times as old as his son. If the son attains an age of fifteen (15) years after three (3) years, what is the present age of the mother?
   A. 60 years B. 51 years
   C. 48 years D. 45 years
6. A clock is so placed that at 12 noon its minute hand points towards north-east. In which direction does its hour hand point at 1.30 P.M.?
   A. East B. West
   C. North D. South
7. If in the above question clock is turned through an angle of 135° in an anticlockwise direction, in which direction will its minute hand point at 8.45 P.M.?
   A. East B. West
   C. North D. South
8. A couple married in 1980 had two children, one in 1982 and the other in 1984. Their combined ages will equal the years of the marriage in?
   A. 1986 B. 1985
   C. 1987 D. 1988
9. Manoj left home for the bus stop 15 minutes earlier than the usual time. It takes 10 minutes to reach the stop. He reached the stop at 8.40 a.m. What time does he usually leave home for the bus stop?
   A. 8.30 a.m. B. 8.55 a.m.
   C. 8.45 p.m. D. None of these
10. Mamuni went to the movies nine days ago. She goes to the movies only on Thursday. What day of the week is today?
    A. Sunday B. Tuesday
    C. Thursday D. Saturday
11. If Thursday was the day after the day before yesterday five days ago, what is the least number of days ago when Sunday was three days before the day after tomorrow?
    A. Two days ago
    B. Three days ago

C. Four days ago
D. Five days ago

12. 1.12.91 is the first Sunday. Which is the fourth Tuesday of December 91?

A. 31.12.91 B. 24.12.91
C. 17.12.91 D. 26.12.91

13. If the third day of a month is Monday, which of the following will be the fifth day from 21st of that month?

A. Tuesday B. Monday
C. Wednesday D. Thursday

14. Keshav runs a factory in three shifts of eight hours each with 210 employees. In each shift minimum of 80 employees are required to run the factory effectively. No employee can be allowed to work for more than 16 hours a day. At least how many employees will be required to work for 16 hours every day?

A. 30
B. 60
C. Data inadequate
D. None of these

15. If 15 horses eat 15 bags of gram in 15 days, in how many days will one horse eat one bag of grain?

A. 15 days B. 1/15 days
C. 1 day D. 30 days

16. A century leap year is divisible by :

A. 4 B. 16
C. 40 D. 400

17. If the fifth day of a month is Friday, which of the following will be the Seventh day from 10th of that month?

A. Tuesday B. Monday
C. Wednesday D. Thursday

18. Day after tomorrow is my birthday. On the same day next week falls 'Holi'. Today is Monday. What will be the day after 'Holi'?

A. Wednesday B. Thursday
C. Friday D. Saturday

19. A clock shows the time as 3 : 30 p.m. If the minute hand gains 2 minutes every hour, how many minutes will the clock gain by 4 a.m.?

A. 23 Minutes B. 24 Minutes
C. 25 Minutes D. 26 Minutes

20. Two brothers were expected to return home on the same day. Rajat returned 3 days earlier but Rohit returned 4 days later. If Rajat returned on Thursday, what was the expected day when both the brothers were to return home and when did Rohit Return?

A. Wednesday, Sunday
B. Thursday, Monday
C. Sunday, Thursday
D. Monday, Friday

ANSWERS

1	2	3	4	5	6	7	8	9	10
A	B	A	B	A	A	D	A	D	D
11	**12**	**13**	**14**	**15**	**16**	**17**	**18**	**19**	**20**
A	B	C	D	A	D	C	B	C	C

SOME SELECTED EXPLANATORY ANSWERS

1. Thursday —Day-before-yesterday
Friday —Yesterday
Saturday —Today
Sunday — Tomorrow

2. 1. 5 people work between 8 a.m. to 2 p.m.
2. 10 people work between 10 a.m. to 4 p.m.
3. 5 people work between 12 noon to 6 p.m.

So, computers are used most between 12 noon to 2 p.m.

3. 7th day is 3 days earlier than Friday so, 10th day is Friday, so also is 17th.

∴ 19th day will be 2nd day ahead of Friday, *i.e.*, Sunday.

4. Father's birthday

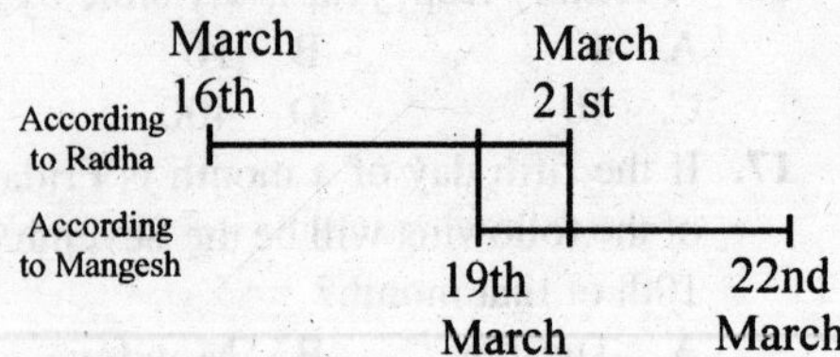

∴ Their father's birthday is on 20th March.

5. Present age of son is 15 – 3 = 12 years. Age of the man is 4 times the age of son, *i.e.*,

12 × 4 = 48 years

Man is 3 years elder to his wife/son's mother.

So Age of the mother is 48 – 3 = 45 years

6.

At 12 noon

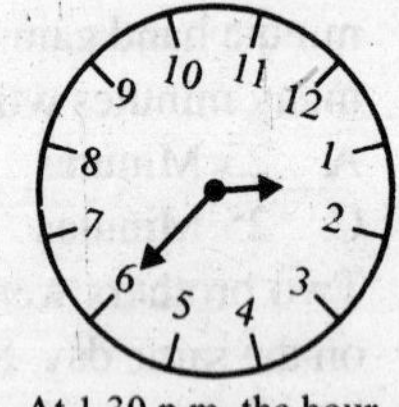

At 1.30 p.m. the hour hand will point towards East.

7.

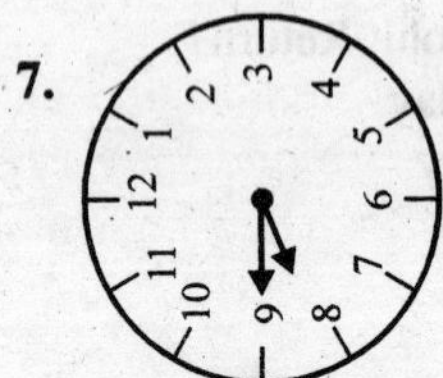

After rotating the clock in earlier question, its minute hand will point towards South at 8:45 p.m.

8. 1982 — 2 years later — 1st child

1984 — 4 years later — 2nd child

Total age of children — 2 years.

1985 — 5 years later — Total age of children: 4 years.

1986 — 6 years later — Total age of children : 6 years.

9. Manoj reached the bus stop at 8.40 a.m. He left his home at 8:40 – 10 minutes = 8:30 a.m. He left 15 minutes earlier than usual, so his actual time of leaving home is 8:30 am + 15 minutes = 8:45 a.m.

10. Mamuni goes to the movies on Thursday, so nine days ago was Thursday.

∴ Two days ago was also Thursday. So, today is Saturday.

11. Day after the day-before-yesterday five days ago is the 6th day which is Thursday. And so, the 3rd day will be Sunday. Three days before the day-after-tomorrow is Yesterday which is the 1st day of the five days. So, two days ago was Sunday.

12. First Sunday is on 1st December

First Tuesday is on 3rd December

3 weeks later, Fourth Tuesday will be on 3 + (7 × 3) = 24th December.

13. 3rd day of the month is Monday

5th day from 21st is 26th

26 – 3 = 23 days

23 days later, 23/7 leaves 2 days.

So, two days ahead of Monday will be Wednesday.

14. 80 employees are required for double shift.

15. 15 horses eat 15 bags of grain in 15 days

15 horses eat 1 bag of grain in 1 day

1 horse eats 1 bag of grain in 15 days

16. A leap year is divisible by 4 and a century leap year is divisible by 400.

17. Seventh day from 10th is 17th.

5th day is Friday. Next Friday is on 12th, 17 – 12 = 5, 5 days ahead of Friday will be Wednesday. So, 17th is Wednesday.

18. Today is Monday

Day-after-tomorrow is Wednesday

Next week 'Holi' is also on Wednesday

So, Day after Holi is Thursday.

19. Hours between 3:30 p.m. and 4 a.m. are — 12½ hours. Number of minutes gained will be 12½ × 2 = 25 minutes.

20. Rajat returned on Thursday. 3 days later was the day of expected return, *i.e.*, Sunday. Rohit returned 4 days after Sunday, *i.e.*, Thursday.

ROWS AND RANKS

1. In a row of trees, one tree is fifth from either end of the row. How many trees are in the row?

A. 11 B. 8
C. 10 D. 9

2. Jaya ranks 5th in a class of 53. What is her rank from the bottom in the class?

A. 49th B. 48th
C. 47th D. 50th

3. Mohan ranks twenty-first in a class of sixty-five students. What will be his (Mohan's) rank if the lowest candidate is assigned rank 1?

A. 44th B. 45th
C. 46th D. Data inadequate

4. If Rahul finds that he is 12th from the right in a line of boys and 4th from the left, how many boys should be added to the line such that there are 28 boys in the line?

A. 12 B. 14
C. 20 D. 13

5. In a row of boys, Rajan is tenth from the right and Suraj is tenth from the left. When Rajan and Suraj interchange their positions, Suraj will be twenty-seventh from the left. Which of the following will be Rajan's position from the right?

A. Tenth
B. Twenty-sixth
C. Twenty-ninth
D. None of these

6. Mahesh and Suresh are ranked 11th and 12th respectively from the top in a class of 41 students. What will be their respective ranks from the bottom?

A. 32nd and 33rd
B. 29th and 30th
C. 30th and 31st
D. 31st and 30th

7. Uma ranked 8th from the top and 37th from bottom in a class. How many students are there in the class?

A. 47 B. 46
C. 45 D. None of these

8. In a queue, Sadiq is 14th from the front and Joseph is 17th from the end, while Jane is in between Sadiq and Joseph. If Sadiq be ahead of Joseph and there be 48 persons in the queue, how many persons are there between Sadiq and Jane?

A. 5 B. 6
C. 7 D. 8

9. Rohan ranked eleventh from the top and twenty-seventh from the bottom among the students who passed the annual examination in a class. If the number of students who failed in the examination was 12, how many students appeared for the examination?

A. 48
B. 49
C. 50
D. Cannot be determined

10. Some boys are sitting in a row. P is sitting fourteenth from the left and Q is seventh from the right. If there are four boys between P and Q, how many boys are there in the row?

A. 19 B. 21
C. 25 D. 23

ANSWERS

1	2	3	4	5	6	7	8	9	10
D	A	B	D	D	D	D	C	B	C

SOME SELECTED EXPLANATORY ANSWERS

1. 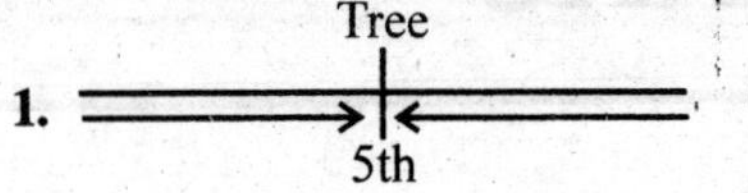

Total number of trees in the row are :
(5 + 5) –1 = 9

2. 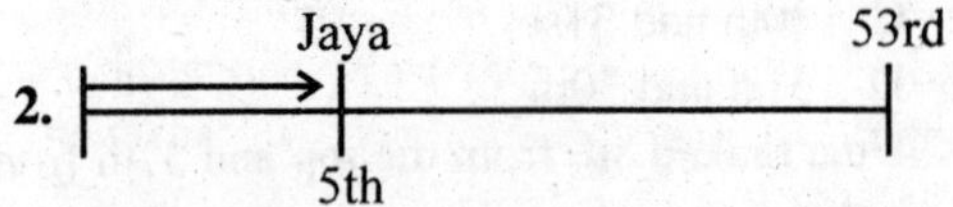

Jaya's rank from the bottom is :
(53 – 5) +1 = 49th.

3. 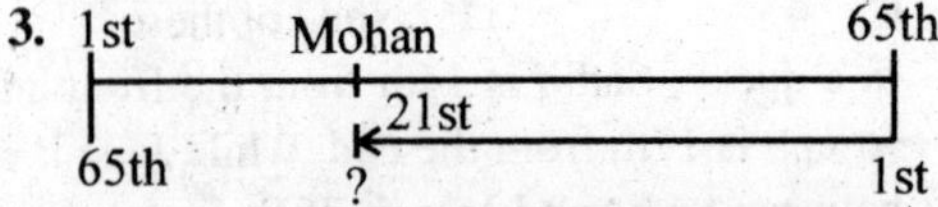

Note : Mohan's rank from the last or the question asked means the same.
Mohan's rank is (65 – 21) +1 = 45th

4. 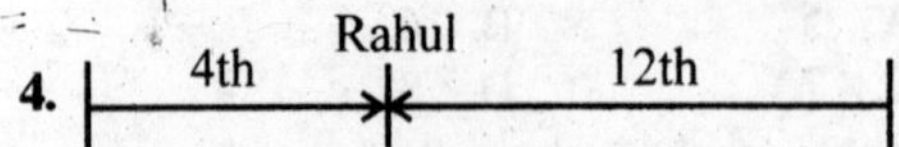

The number of boys in the line are :
(4 + 12) – 1 = 15
To make a line of 28 boys, (28 –15) *i.e.* 13 more boys are needed.

5. 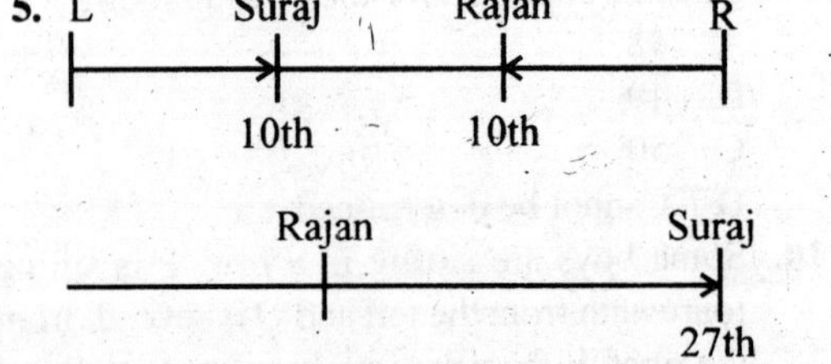

As the position of boys is equal from both ends, Rajan will also be 27th from the right after changing positions.

6. 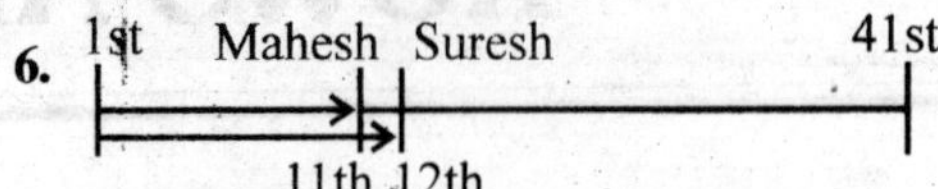

Mahesh's position from bottom is :
(41 – 11) + 1 = 31st
Suresh's position from bottom is :
(41 – 12) +1 = 30th

7. 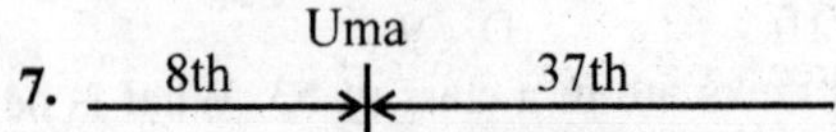

Total number of students in the class are :
(8 + 37) – 1 = 44

8. 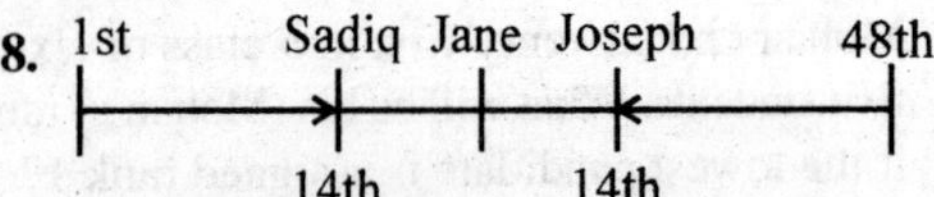

Sadiq's position from last is :
(48 – 14) + 1 = 35th
Number of persons between Sadiq and Joseph are (35 – 17) – 1 = 17
Jane is in-between Sadiq and Joseph *i.e.,* she's at 9th position from both the boys.
∴ there are 8 persons between Sadiq and Jane.
Note : (8 + 8) – 1 = 17

9. 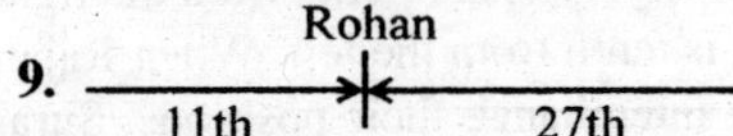

Number of students who passed the examination (11+ 27) – 1 = 37
Those who failed = 12
Total number of students who appeared in the examination = 37 + 12 = 49.

10. 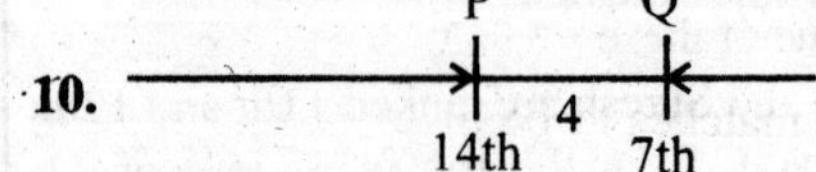

The number of boys in the row are :
(14 + 4 + 7) = 25

NUMBER PROBLEMS

1. How many 6's are there in the following series of numbers which are preceded by 7 but not immediately followed by 9?
   6 7 9 5 6 9 7 6 8 7 6 7 8 6 9 4 6 7 7 6 9 5 7 6 3
   A. One B. Two
   C. Three D. Four
2. In a chess tournament each of six players will play every other player exactly once. How many matches will be played during the tournament?
   A. 12 B. 15
   C. 30 D. 36
3. How many 4's are there in the following series which are preceded by 7, but are not preceded by 8?
   3 4 5 7 4 3 7 4 8 5 4 3 7 4 9 8 4 7 2 7 4 1 3 6
   A. 1 B. 2
   C. 3 D. 4
4. How many even numbers are there in the following series of numbers, each of which is immediately preceded by an odd number, but not immediately followed by an even number?
   5 3 4 8 9 7 1 6 5 3 2 9 8 4 3 5
   A. Nil B. 1
   C. 2 D. 3
5. If all the numbers from 1 to 51 which are exactly divisible by 3 are arranged in descending order, which of the following numbers will come at the seventh and tenth places from the top?
   A. 33 & 27 B. 33 & 21
   C. 21 & 30 D. 33 & 24

ANSWERS

1	2	3	4	5
C	B	D	C	D

SOME SELECTED EXPLANATORY ANSWERS

1. 6 7 9 5 6 9 7 6 8 7 6 7 8 6 9 4 6 7 7 6 9 5 7 6 3
   (7 6 8 = 1, 7 6 7 = 2, 7 6 3 = 3)
2. When all the players have to play with each other then the method of calculating the number of matches to be played is $\frac{n(n-1)}{2}$ where 'n' is the number of players playing the match. So, the number of matches played will be :
   $(6 \times 5) \div 2 = 30 \div 2 = 15$
3. 3 4 5 7 4 3 7 4 8 5 4 3 7 4 9 8 4 7 2 7 4 1 3 6
   (7 4 = 1, 7 4 = 2, 7 4 = 3, 7 4 = 4)
4. 5 3 4 8 9 7 1 6 5 3 2 9 8 4 3 5
   (1 6 5 = 1, 3 2 9 = 2)
5. The numbers divisible by 3 in descending order are :
   51, 48, 45, 42, 39, 36, 33, 30 (7th), 27, 24 (10th), 21, 18, 15, 12, 9, 6, 3.

SYMBOL SUBSTITUTION

1. If "+" means "–"; "–" means "×"; "×" means "÷" and "÷" means "+", then
$15 \times 5 \div 10 + 5 - 3 = ?$

A. 9.5 B. 0
C. – 2 D. 24

2. If "+" means "–"; "–" means "×"; "×" means "÷" and "÷" means "+", then
$15 \times 3 \div 15 + 5 - 2 = ?$

A. 0 B. 10
C. 20 D. 6

3. If "+" means "÷"; "×" means "–"; "÷" means "+" and "–" means "×", then
$16 \div 8 \times 6 - 2 + 12 = ?$

A. 22 B. 24
C. 23 D. 20

4. If "+" means "×"; "–" means "÷"; "÷" means "+" and "×" means "–", then what will be the value of $20 \div 40 - 4 \times 5 + 6 = ?$

A. 60 B. 1.67
C. 150 D. 0

5. If "+" means "×"; "–" means "÷"; "×" means "–" and "÷" means "+", then
$5 + 8 - 4 \times 2 \div 9 = ?$

A. 15 B. 13
C. 17 D. 11

ANSWERS

1	2	3	4	5
C	B	C	D	C

SOME SELECTED EXPLANATORY ANSWERS

1. $15 \div 5 + 10 - 5 \times 3$
$3 + 10 - 15 = -2$

2. $15 \div 3 + 15 - 5 \times 2$
$5 + 15 - 10 = 10$

3. $16 + 8 - 6 \times 2 \div 12$
$16 + 8 - 1 = 23$

4. $20 + 40 \div 4 - 5 \times 6$
$20 + 10 - 30 = 0$

5. $5 \times 8 \div 4 - 2 + 9$
$10 - 2 + 9 = 17$

MISSING NUMBERS

Directions : *In each question given below which one number can be placed at the sign of interrogation?*

1.

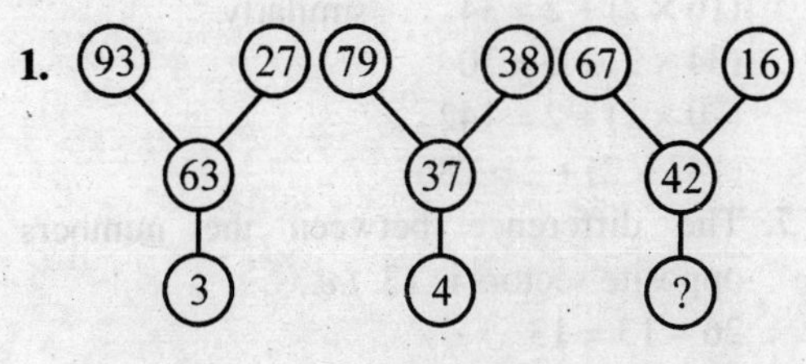

A. 5 B. 6
C. 8 D. 9

2.

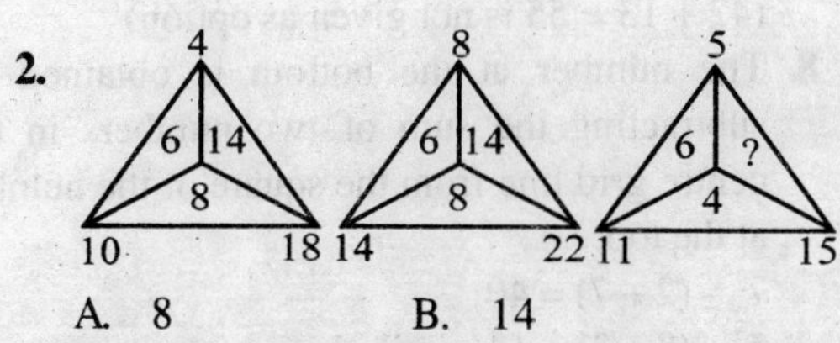

A. 8 B. 14
C. 10 D. 6

3.

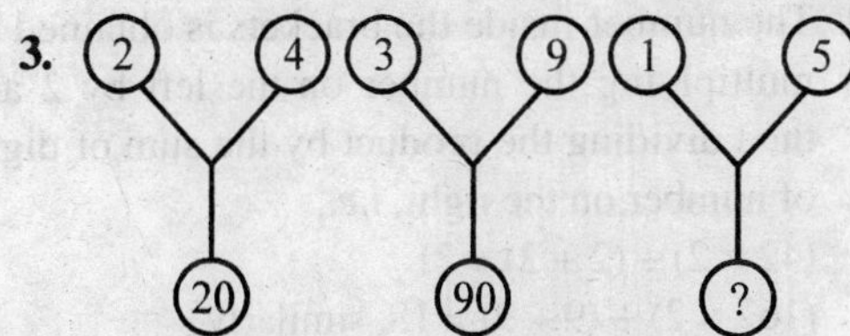

A. 20 B. 25
C. 26 D. 75

4.

27	22	50
13	12	26
9	2	?

A. 12 B. 39
C. 18 D. 24

5.

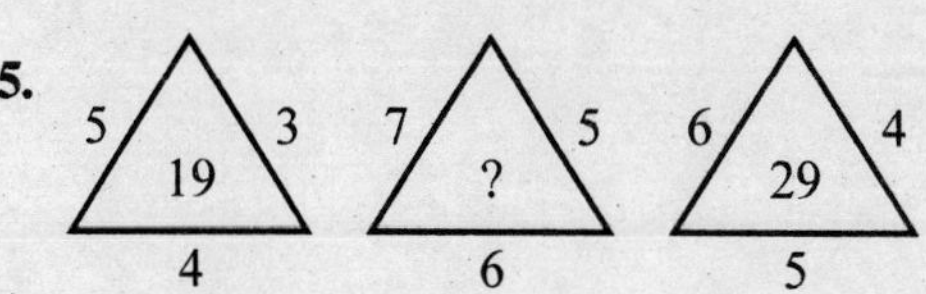

A. 25 B. 47
C. 37 D. 41

6.

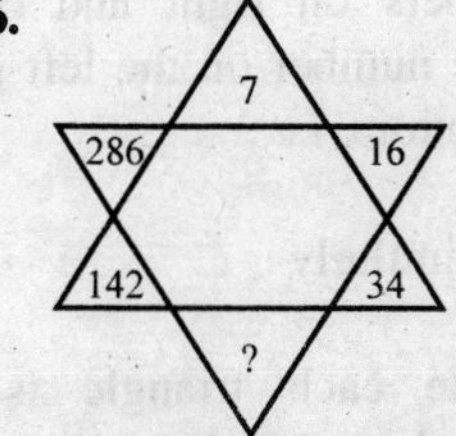

A. 70 B. 68
C. 56 D. 92

7.

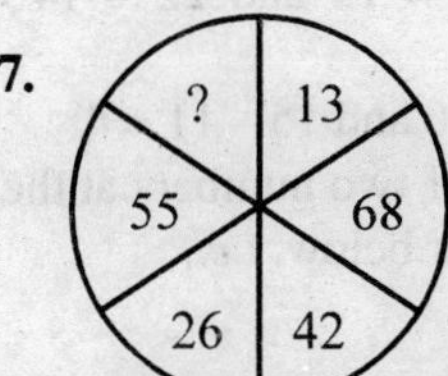

A. 41 B. 37
C. 29 D. 25

8.

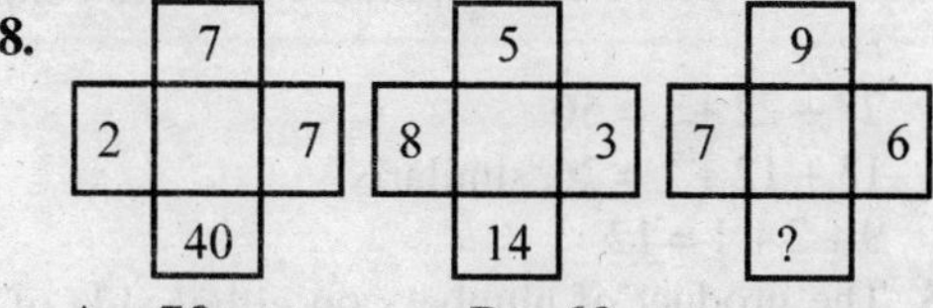

A. 72 B. 68
C. 82 D. 96

9.

42	(21)	22
78	(?)	84
162	(18)	99

A. 12 B. 13
C. 60 D. 72

10.

16 25 19

107 209 ?

7 10 20 4 2 17

A. 68 B. 93
C. 175 D. 217

ANSWERS

1	2	3	4	5	6	7	8	9	10
D	C	C	A	D	A	C	B	B	A

SOME SELECTED EXPLANATORY ANSWERS

1. The sum of numbers on right and centre subtracted from the number on the left gives the number at the bottom, *i.e.,*
$93 - (27 + 63) = 3$
$79 - (38 + 37) = 4$, similarly
$67 - (16 + 42) = 9$

2. The number inside each triangle is the difference of the numbers at its base *i.e.*
$10 - 4 = 6$, $18 - 4 = 14$ and $18 - 10 = 8$
$14 - 8 = 6$, $22 - 8 = 14$ and $22 - 14 = 8$, similarly
$11 - 5 = 6$, $15 - 5 = 10$ and $15 - 11 = 4$.

3. The sum of squares of two numbers at the top gives the third number below, *i.e.,*
$2^2 + 4^2 = 20$
$3^2 + 9^2 = 90$, similarly
$1^2 + 5^2 = 26$

4. The sum of numbers in 1st and 2nd column plus 1 is the number in the 3rd column, *i.e.,*
$27 + 22 + 1 = 50$
$13 + 12 + 1 = 26$, similarly
$9 + 2 + 1 = 12$

5. The product of numbers on either side of the triangle plus the number at the base is the number inside the triangle, *i.e.,*
$(5 \times 3) + 4 = 19$
$(6 \times 4) + 5 = 29$, similarly
$(7 \times 5) + 6 = 41$

6. Clockwise starting from number 7, the next number is obtained by doubling the number and adding 2, *i.e.,*
$(7 \times 2) + 2 = 16$
$(16 \times 2) + 2 = 34 \ldots$, similarly
$(34 \times 2) + 2 = 70$
$(70 \times 2) + 2 = 142$
$(142 \times 2) + 2 = 286$

7. The difference between the numbers in opposite sectors is 13, *i.e.,*
$26 - 13 = 13$
$68 - 55 = 13$, similarly
The missing number is $42 - 13 = 29$
($42 + 13 = 55$ is not given as option)

8. The number at the bottom is obtained by subtracting the sum of two numbers in the centre grid line from the square of the number at the top, *i.e.,*
$7^2 - (2 + 7) = 40$
$5^2 - (8 + 3) = 14$, similarly
$9^2 - (7 + 6) = 68$

9. The number inside the brackets is obtained by multiplying the number on the left by 2 and then dividing the product by the sum of digits of number on the right, *i.e.,*
$(42 \times 2) \div (2 + 2) = 21$
$(162 \times 2) \div (9 + 9) = 18$, similarly
$(78 \times 2) \div (8 + 4) = 13$

10. Subtracting the sum of squares of two numbers at the base from the square of number at the apex gives the number inside the triangle, *i.e.,*
$16^2 - (7^2 + 10^2) = 107$
$25^2 - (20^2 + 4^2) = 209$, similarly
$19^2 - (2^2 + 17^2) = 68$

ALPHABET PROBLEMS

Directions : *The following questions are based on alphabet series in natural or reverse order and the combinations that can be made by changing the position of alphabet in given words.*

1. Which alphabet comes immediately before the sixth alphabet from the left extreme in alphabetical series?

A. U B. E
C. F D. V

2. Which letter is midway between G and S?

A. L B. N
C. M D. No letter

3. Which letter should be ninth letter to the left of ninth letter from the right if the first half of the alphabet is reversed?

A. I B. D
C. F D. E

4. If the alphabet is in reverse order, which letter will be eighth letter to the left of the seventh letter counting from the right end?

A. O B. P
C. N D. Q

5. What will be the fifth letter to the right of the thirteenth letter from the right?

A. R B. S
C. I D. O

ANSWERS

1	2	3	4	5
B	C	D	A	B

SOME SELECTED EXPLANATORY ANSWERS

1.

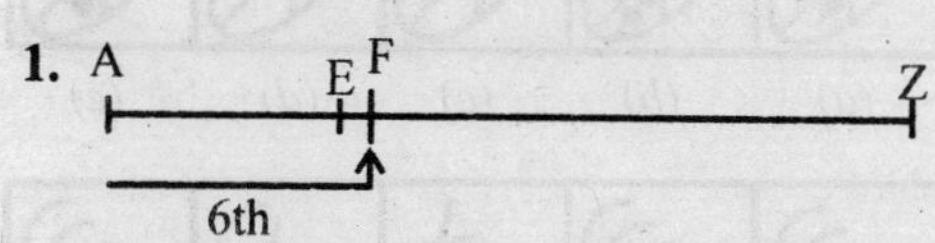

Sixth letter from left is 'F' and letter immediately before 'F' is 'E'.

2.

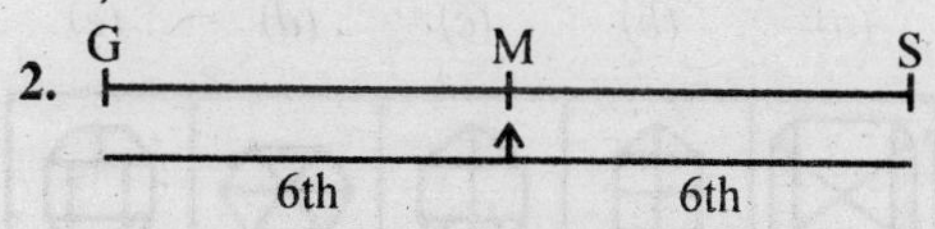

'M' is midway between G and S.

3. MLKJIHGFEDCBANOPQRSTUVWXYZ

9th 9th

4. ZYXWVUTSRQPONMLKJIHGFEDCBA

8th 7th

5.

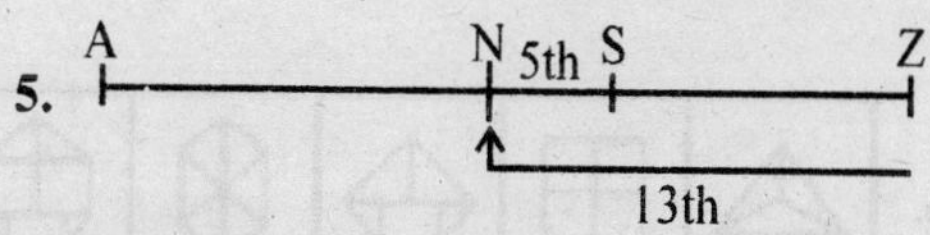

13th letter from right is 'N' and 5th letter to the right of 'N' is 'S'.

NON-VERBAL SERIES

Directions (Q. 1–10) : *In each of the following questions which one of the five answer figures given below should come after the problem figures if the sequence are continued?*

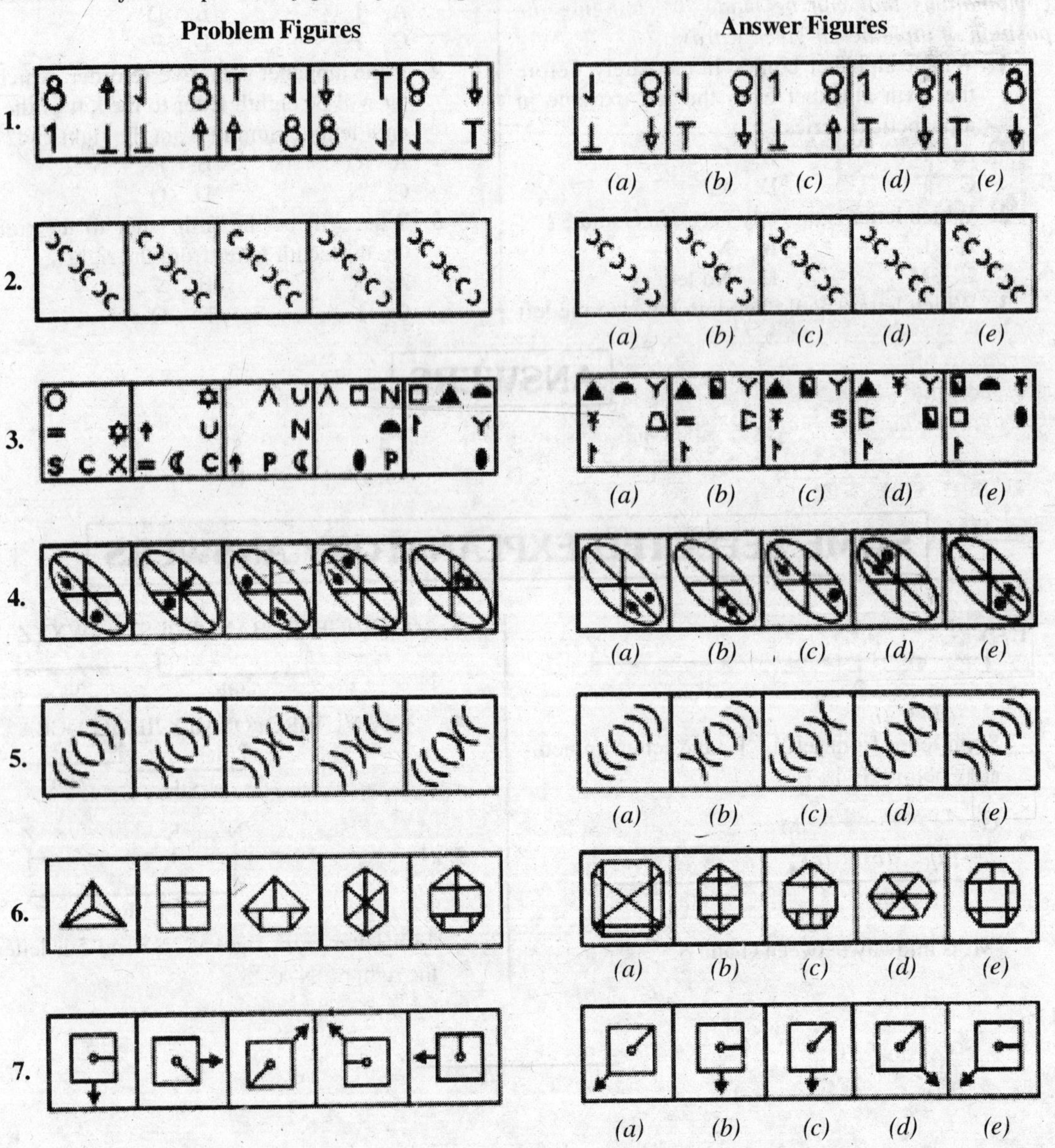

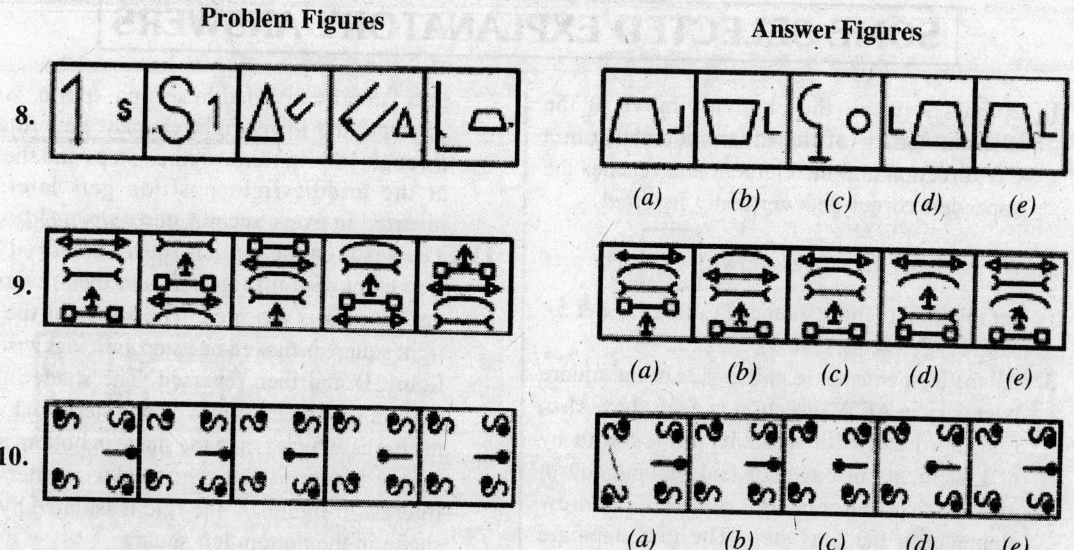

Directions (Q. 11-20) : *In each of these questions, a series begins with an unmarked figure on the extreme left in the row of figures. One and only one of the five lettered figures in the series does not fit into the series. The two unmarked figures, one on the extreme left and the other on the extreme right fit into the series. Take as many aspects into account as possible of the figures in the series and find out the one and only of the five marked figures which does not fit into the series. The letter of that figure is the answer.*

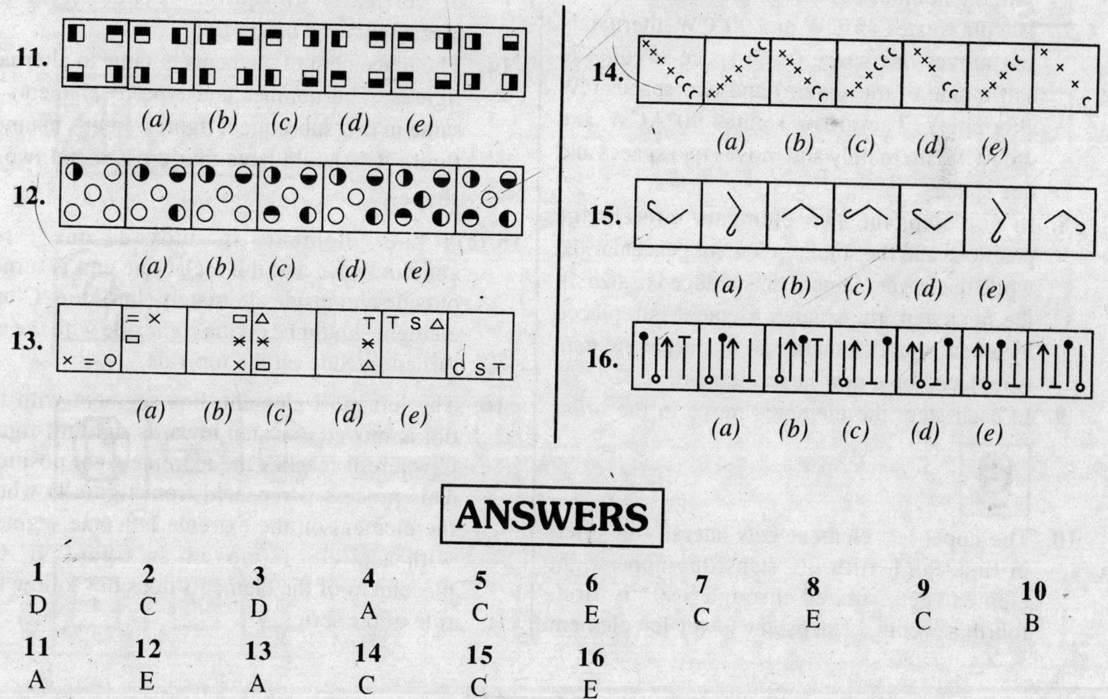

ANSWERS

1	2	3	4	5	6	7	8	9	10
D	C	D	A	C	E	C	E	C	B
11	**12**	**13**	**14**	**15**	**16**				
A	E	A	C	C	E				

SOME SELECTED EXPLANATORY ANSWERS

1. In each step, all the elements move to the adjacent corner (of the square boundary) in a CW direction and the element that reaches the upper-left corner gets vertically inverted.

2. We can label the arcs as shown [figure]. The arcs get inverted in the sequence (1 & 2), (3, 4 & 5), (6 & 1), (2, 3 & 4), (5 & 6), ...

3. All the elements move half-a-side of the square boundary in ACW direction in each step. Also, first, third and fifth elements are replaced by new elements in one step and second, fourth and sixth elements are replaced by new elements in the next step. The two steps are repeated alternately.

4. In each step, the dot moves one space CW and the arrow moves two spaces CW.

5. One arc and four arcs get inverted alternately.

6. The number of parts increases by one along with the number of sides in the figure.

7. The pin rotates 45°CW and 90°CW alternately and moves one space (each space is equal to half-a-side of the square) and two spaces CW alternately. The arrow rotates 90°ACW and 45°ACW alternately and moves two spaces and one space.

8. In one step, the two elements interchange positions and the smaller element gets enlarged while the larger element gets reduced in size. In the next step, the smaller element is replaced by a new small element and the larger element is replaced by a new large element.

9. In each step, the elements move in the order

.

10. The upper-left element gets laterally inverted in first, third, fifth. .... steps; the upper-right element gets rotated through 180° is first, fourth, seventh,.... steps; the lower-left element gets laterally inverted in second, fourth, sixth, ... steps; the lower-right element gets rotated through 180^c in third, sixth,... steps and the pin at the middle-right position gets laterally inverted in every second step.

11. The shade in the top left square is moved one step clockwise till figure B and then reversed, the process is repeated. The shade in the top right square is moved one step anticlockwise till figure D and then reversed. The shade in the bottom left square is moved one step clockwise in alternate figures and the shade in bottom right square is moved one step clockwise after two figures. In figure 'A' the rule is isolated by the shade in the bottom left square.

12. In alternate figures a new circle is shaded clockwise. The pattern of the shade is also moved clockwise. In figure 'E' right half of the circle in the centre should have been shaded.

13. The three elements are placed either horizontally or vertically. In option 'A' neither of the placements can be applied.

14. The placement of elements is same in alternate figures. The number and type of elements is same in two subsequent figures. In this manner, figure 'C' should have four crosses and two C shapes.

15. *(c)*: The element is moved one step anticlockwise and the arc at one end is turned outside and inside alternately. In figure 'C' the element should be on the right side with the arc turned outside on the top side.

16. The left most element, line segment with the dot is moved one step towards right till figure C where it reaches the extreme right position. This process is repeated from figure D where the element on the extreme left, line segment with a circle, is moved. In figure 'E' the placement of the elements does not follow the rule of the series.

GENERAL KNOWLEDGE

INDIAN HISTORY

☛ *Famous Sites of Indus Valley Civilization*

Name of Site	*Year of Excavation*	*River/ Sea coast*	*Discoverer*
Harappa (Montgomery–Pakistan)	1921	Ravi River	Dayaram Sahney
Mohanjodaro (Larkana–Pakistan)	1922	Indus River	Rakhal Das Banerjee
Chanhudaro (Sindh–Pakistan)	1931	Indus River	N.G. Mazumdar
Alamgir pur (Meerut – U.P.)	1952-55	Hindan River	Yagyadatta Sharma
Ropar (Punjab)	1953	Sutlej River	Yagyadatta Sharma
Rangpur (Kathiabar–Gujarat)	1953	Bhabar River	Madho Swaroop Vatsa, Rang Nath Rao
Kotdigi (Sindh–Pakistan)	1953	Indus River	Fazal Ahmed Khan
Lothal (Ahmedabad-Gujarat)	1954	Bhogwa River	Rang Nath Rao
Kalibanga (Ganganagar–Rajasthan)	1961	Ghaggar River	Brajwasi Lal
Surkotara (Kutch–Gujarat)	1967	Ghaggar River	Ravindra Singh Vishta
Banawali (Hissar Haryana)	1973	Ghaggar River	Ravindra Singh Vishta
Balakote	1979	Arabian Sea	George F. Dales
Dhaulavira (Gujarat)	1963-68	—	J.P. Joshi
	1990-91	—	Dr. R.S. Vishta

☛ *Wellknown Quotations*

"Swarajya is My Birthright" — Bal Gangadhar Tilak
"Give me blood, I shall give you freedom" — Netajee Subhash Chandra Bose
"Inqalab Zindabad" — Bhagat Singh
"Saare Jahan Se Achcha, Hindustan Hamara" — Dr. Mohammed Iqbal
"Dilli Chalo" — Subhash Chandra Bose
"Sarfaroshi ki tamanna, Ab Hamare Dil Mein Hai" — Ram Prasad Bismil
"I am socialist by nature" — Jawahar Lal Nehru
"Go to Vedas" — Swami Dayanand
"Aaram Haram Hai" — Jawahar Lal Nehru
"Jai Jawan, Jai Kisan" — Lal Bahadur Shastri
"Jai Jawan, Jai Kisan, Jai Vigyan" — Atal Bihari Vajpayee
"Speak less, work more" — Sanjay Gandhi
"Vijayee Vishwa Tiranga Pyara" — Shyam Lal Gupta
"Quit India" — Mahatma Gandhi
"Hindi, Hindu, Hindustan" — Bhartendu Harishchandra

"Purna Swarajya"	— Jawahar Lal Nehru
"Every lathi blow inflicted on my body will prove a nail in British coffin"	— Lala Lajpat Rai
"Jai Hind"	— Subhash Chandra Bose
"Do or die"	— Mahatma Gandhi
"Who lives if India dies"	— Jawahar Lal Nehru
"Vande Mataram"	— Bankim Chandra Chatterjee
"Jana Gana Mana Adhinayaka Jai Hai"	—Rabindranath Tagore
"Hate sin, not the sinner"	— Mahatma Gandhi
"Service of the people is the service of God"	— Swami Vivekananda
"Truth and non-violence are my God"	— Mahatma Gandhi

☛ Battles and Wars In India

War	Year	Result
Battle of Kalinga	(261 B.C.)	Ashoka defeated the king of Kalinga
Second battle of Tarain	(1192 A.D.)	Muhammad Gori defeated Prithviraj Chauhan
First battle of Panipat	(1526 A.D.)	Babar defeated Ibrahim Lodi
Battle of Khanwa	(1527 A.D.)	Babar defeated Rana Sanga
Battle of Chausa	(1539 A.D.)	Shershah Suri defeated Humayun and became ruler of Delhi
Second Battle of Panipat	(1556 A.D.)	Akbar defeated Hemu
Battle of Talikota	(1565 A.D.)	Allied forces of Bijapur, Bidar, Golkunda and Ahamadnagar defeated the King of Vijay Nagar
Battle of Haldighati	(1576 A.D.)	Some historian say that this battle was indecisive but some say that Rana Pratap was defeated by Akbar
Battle of Palasey	(1757 A.D.)	British forces defeated Nawab of Bengal Sirajudoulla
Battle of Wandiwash	(1760 A.D.)	British forces defeated the French
Third battle of Panipat	(1761 A.D.)	Maratha were defeated by Ahmad Shah Abadali
Battle of Buxar	(1764 A.D.)	British forces defeated the combined forces of Mir Quasim, Shah Alam Mughal empire and Awadh's Nawab
Third Anglo-Maratha War	(1792 A.D.)	Maratha were conclusively defeated
Fourth Anglo-Mysore War	(1799 A.D.)	Tipu Sultan died fighting the British forces
Second Anglo-Sikh War	(1848 A.D.)	British forces annexed Punjab from Sikh rulers
Indo-China War	(1962 A.D.)	China attacked India unilaterally and annexed some area
Indo-Pak War	(1965 A.D.)	Pakistan attacked India but had to suffer severe setbacks
Indo-Pak War	(1971 A.D.)	Pak declare war against India.

☛ Socio-Religious Movements and Organisation

Year	Place	Name of the Organisation	Founder
1815	Calcutta	Atmiya Sabha	Ram Mohan Roy
1828	Calcutta	Brahmo Samaj	Ram Mohan Roy
1829	Calcutta	Dharma Sabha	Radhakanta Dev
1839	Calcutta	Tattvabodhini Sabha	Debendranath Tagore
1840	Punjab	Nirankaris	Dayal Das, Darbara Singh, Rattan Chand etc.

Year	Place	Name of the Organisation	Founder
1844	Surat	Manav Dharma Sabha	Durgaram Manchharam
1849	Bombay	Paramhansa Mandli	Dadoba Pandurung
1857	Punjab	Namdharis	Ram Singh
1861	Agra	Radha Swami Satsang	Tulsi Ram
1866	Calcutta	Brahmo Samaj of India	Keshab Chandra Sen
1866	Deoband	Dar-ul-Ulum	Maulana Hussain Ahmed
1867	Bombay	Prarthna Samaj	Atmaram Pandurung
1875	Bombay	Arya Samaj	Swami Dayanand Saraswati
1875	New York (USA)	Theosophical Society	Madam H.P. Blavatsky and Col. H.S. Olcott
1878	Calcutta	Sadharan Brahmo Samaj	Anand Mohan Bose
1884	Pune (Poona)	Deccan Education Society	G.G. Agarkar
1886	Aligarh	Muhammadan Educational Conference	Syed Ahmad Khan
1887	Bombay	Indian National Conference	M.G. Ranade
1887	Lahore	Deva Samaj	Shivnarayan Agnihotri
1894	Lucknow	Nadwah-ul-Ulama	Maulana Shibli Numani
1897	Belur	Ramakrishna Mission	Swami Vivekananda
1905	Bombay	Servents of Indian Society	Gopal Krishna Gokhale
1909	Pune (Poona)	Poona Seva Sadan	Mrs. Ramabai Ranade and G.K. Devadhar
1911	Bombay	Social Service League	N.M. Joshi
1914	Allahabad	Seva Samiti	H.N. Kunzru

☛ *Newspapers and Journals*

- Bengal Gazette (1780) (India's first newspaper) — James Angustus Hikky
- Kesari — B.G. Tilak
- Maratha — B.G. Tilak
- Sudharak — G.K. Gokhale
- Amrit Bazar Patrika — Shishir Kumar Ghosh and Motilal Ghosh
- Yugantar — Bhupendranath Datta and Birender Kumar Ghosh
- Bombay Chronicle — Firoze Shah Mehta
- New India (Daily) — Annie Besant

☛ *Books and Authors*

- Causes of the Indian Mutiny — Sir Syed Ahmed Khan
- Ghulam Giri — Jyotiba Phule
- Anandmath — Bankim Chand Chatterjee
- Satyarth Prakash — Swami Dayanand
- Unhappy India — Lala Lajpat Rai
- India Divided — Dr. Rajendra Prasad
- The Discovery of India — J.L. Nehru
- Neel Darpan — Dinbandhu Mitra
- Hind Swaraj — M.K. Gandhi
- What Congress and Gandhi have done to the untouchables — Dr. B.R. Ambedkar

WORLD HISTORY

- **Ice Age :** Period, beginning from 10,00,000 years ago in which a series of ice caps covered most of the northern parts of the earth.
- **Stone Age :** Period, in which men used tools and weapons made of stone. It began about 1,00,000 years ago.
- **Bronze Age :** Period, when people used bronze tools; period from 3,000 to 1,000 B.C.
- **Iron Age :** Period, when people first used iron tools and weapons. It began at about 1,200 BC and lasted for 1,000 years.
- **Augustine Age :** It refers to the reign of the Emperor Augustus; 27 BC to 14 BC in Latin History.
- **Dark Age :** Period, from the fall of Rome in 476 AD till 1000 AD.
- **Middle Age :** Period, between ancient times and the modern period often given as between the fall of Roman Empire in the 5th century and the Renaissance in the 15th.
- **Elizabethan Age :** Period of the feudal system in Europe from 700 to 1400 AD.
- **Machine Age :** Name given to the period of industrialisation in Britain, began in 1750.
- **Age of Reason :** The 18th century, when philosophy was gaining ground in Europe.
- **Victorian Age :** Period, when Queen Victoria reigned, *i.e.,* 1837-1901. It was an age of technological progress and public morality.
- **Atomic Age :** Period since the explosion of the first atom bomb at Almogordo, New Mexico on July 16, 1945.

Development of Civilisation

- **The first phase :** The first phase of the beginning of the civilisation called Neolithic Revolution, began when man settled in the villages and became a farmer.
- **The second phase :** The second phase was when writing started. This happened in early Bronze Age (3200 to 2000 B.C.). Writing first developed in Egypt, southern Mesopotamia and in southwest Iran.
- **The third phase:** The third phase began when Summerian city states developed. It happened between 3100 to 2570 B.C.
- **The fourth phase :** The fourth phase was that of the setting up of empires. The Summerian city states were incorporated into a powerful empire in about 2370 B.C. by Sargon of Agade. The climax of this phase was when the Persian empire, the largest known empire, came into being.
- **The fifth phase :** In the fifth phase, civilisation shifted from Asia to Mediterranean where it remained for the next 1000 years. There were city states in Greece. During this phase, there were two other important influences on civilisation *(i)* that of Confucius *(ii)* that of Buddha. Confucius, the Chinese philosopher, gave theories which shaped the political organisation of China for many centuries. Similarly, the teachings of Buddha exercised a powerful influence on the civilisation of the Indian subcontinent.
- The Indian empire declined after the death of King Ashoka (232 B.C.). the Chinese Empire declined after the death of the emperor Wu Ti. Then appeared the famous Roman empire when King Rumulus founded Rome. It came to an end in 476 A.D.
- Passing through the Middle Age civilisation entered the modern era. Many movements helped the development of civilisation.

INDIAN CONSTITUTION

- Indian Constitution is a comprehensive document and it is the lengthiest written Constitution in the World.
- **The Preamble of the Constitution:** "We the people of India, having solemnly resolved to Constitute India into a Sovereign, Socialist,

Secular Democratic Republic and to secure to all its citizen."

- **Justice:** Social, economic and political.
- **Liberty:** Of thought, expression, belief, faith and worship.
- **Equality:** Of status and of opportunity, and to promote among them all.
- **Fraternity:** Assuring the dignity of the individual and the unity and integrity of the nation. In our constituent Assembly, this twenty-sixth day of November, 1949, do hereby adopt, enact and give to ourselves this constitution.
- The Constituent Assembly adopted the Constitution of India on November 26, 1949. It came into force on January 26, 1950.
- **Salient Features of the Constitution:** (1) Sovereign, Democratic, Secular, Socialist Republic. (2) Universal Adult Franchise. (3) Federal Structure. (4) Written. (5) Flexible. (6) Provision of Fundamental Rights and Fundamental Duties. (7) Parliamentary Foım of Government. (8) Emergency Provisions. (9) Independent Judiciary.
- **Fundamental Rights:** (1) Right to Equality; (2) Right to Freedom; (3) Right to Freedom of Religion; (4) Cultural and Educational Rights; (5) Right against Exploitation; (6) Right to Constitutional Remedies.
- **Fundamental Duties:** Ten fundamental duties were incorporated in the Constitution through Constitution (42nd) Amendment Act, 1976. The 11th Fundamental Duty [Article 51A (K)] was added through the 86th Constitutional Amendment Act, 2002.
- **Directive Principles of State Policy:** They are not enforceable by any Court but it shall be duty of the State to apply these principles in making laws. These principles include organisation of Village Panchayats, provision for just and human conditions of work, equal pay for equal work, unemployment benefits, assistance in old age and sickness, maternity relief, a uniform civil code for the citizens, provision for compulsory and free education of children, separation of judiciary from executive, organisation of agricultural and animal husbandry on modern scientific lines, prohibition of intoxicating drinks and drugs; protection of national monuments, promotion of international peace and security and settlement of international disputes by arbitration.

☛ Foreign Sources of Indian Constitution

Foreign Sources	*Subject*
Britain	Parliamentary system, collective responsibilities of Cabinet
America	Fundamental right, Citizenship, Independent Judiciary, Judicial review
Canada	Division of powers
Ireland	Directive principles
Germany	Emergency provisions
Russia	Fundamental duties
Australia	Concurrent list

☛ The Supreme Court

- Supreme Court of India, the highest Court of the country, consists of a Chief Justice and not more than 33 Judges appointed by the President. The Judges hold office till the age of 65. For appointment as a Judge of the Supreme Court, a person must be a citizen of India and must have been for at least five years as Judge of a High Court or Advocate of a High Court for at least ten years or he must be, in the opinion of the President, a distinguished jurist. The Supreme Court normally sits in New Delhi.

☛ Parliament

- Parliament is the national legislature of the Indian Union. It consists of two Houses known as the Council of States or the Rajya Sabha and the House of People or Lok Sabha. The President is an integral part of Parliament.
- **Rajya Sabha:** The Rajya Sabha is the Upper House of the Parliament and it is constituted of representatives from the States or the Constituent units of the Indian Union. It is a permanent

body, one-third of its members retiring after every two years. Its maximum strength is 250. Out of these, twelve members are nominated by the President from well-known personalities in the realm of Science, Art, Literature and Social Service. Rest of 238 representatives of the States and Union Territories are elected.

- **Lok Sabha:** The Lok Sabha whose life is five years, is the Lower House of Parliament and comprises of members directly elected by the people. The House of the people (Lok Sabha) at present consists of 543 members directly elected from the states and Union Territories. By the 104th amendment of the Constitution, 2019 the reservation for two members of Anglo Indian Community nominated by President have been abolished. The House of the People shall continue for five years (unless sooner dissolved) from the date of its meeting and no longer and the expiry of the said period of 5 years shall operate as dissolution of the House.
- **Speaker of Lok Sabha:** Speaker is elected by the Lok Sabha from among its members. The Speaker will have the final power to maintain order within the House of the People and to interpret its rules of procedure. Speaker decides whether a bill is a money bill or a non-money bill.

☛ *President*

- The President is the Constitutional head of the Republic of India. He is more or less the titular head of the executive. Really speaking, he is the constitutional head but not the real executive.The real power is vested in the hands of the Council of Ministers.
- **Qualifications:** (i) Indian citizen, (ii) age not less than 35 years, (iii) should have qualification for election to Lok Sabha, (iv) should not hold any office of profit, (v) should not be a Member of Parliament or State Legislature.
- **Powers:** He makes appointments to all the constitutional posts. He can address either House of Parliament and dissolve Lok Sabha. All Bills passed by Parliament must receive his assent to become an Act. He issues ordinances when Parliament is not in session. No Money Bill can be introduced in Lok Sabha without his recommendation. He can grant pardon, reprieve or remit punishment and he can commute death sentences, can declare national emergency, state emergency and financial emergency.

☛ *Vice-President*

- The Vice-President acts as the ex-officio Chairman of the Council of States (Rajya Sabha). He is elected by an electoral college consisting of the members of both Houses of Parliament in accordance with the system of proportional representation by means of the single transferable vote. He must be a citizen of India, not less than 35 years of age, and should be eligible for election as a member of the Council of States. Disputes in connection with election of a president or a vice-president are to be a dealt with in accordance with Article-71. Such disputes shall be decided by the Supreme Court.

☛ *Prime Minister*

- The Constitution lays down that there shall be a Council of Ministers headed by the Prime Minister to aid and advise the President in the exercise of his functions.
- The Prime Minister is the head of the Cabinet. Other Ministers are appointed by the President on his advice. He is the leader of the majority party in the Lok Sabha.
- **Voting Age:** The voting age in the election to the Lok Sabha and State Legislative Assemblies has been reduced from 21 to 18 years by the Constitution (61st) Amendment Act, 1989.

☛ *Governor*

- The Governor is appointed by the President and holds office during the pleasure of the President. Apart from the power to appoint the council of ministers, if the governor finds that the government of state cannot be carried on in accordance with the provisions of the constitution (Art. 356), he may send his report to the President who may assume to himself the functions of the government of the state. (This is popularly known as 'President's Rule').

☛ *High Courts (Article 214-232)*

- The High Court stands at the apex of the State Judiciary.
- As per the Constitution, there shall be a High Court in each State. But there may be a common High Court for two or more States and Union Territory, if it is provided by a law of the Parliament. For example, the Chennai High Court has its Jurisdiction over the State of Tamil Nadu and the Union Territory of Puducherry.
- The State Government has no control over it.
- There are 25 High Courts in India.
- The Calcutta High Court, established in 1862, is the oldest High Court in India.

☛ *Jurisdiction and Seat of High Courts*

Name	Year	Territorial Jurisdiction	Seat
Allahabad	1866	Uttar Pradesh	Prayagraj (Bench at Lucknow)
Andhra Pradesh	2019	Andhra Pradesh	Amaravati
Bombay	1862	Maharashtra, Goa, Dadar and Nagar Haveli and Daman and Diu	Mumbai (Benches at Nagpur, Panaji and Aurangabad)
Calcutta	1862	West Bengal and Andaman & Nicobar	Kolkata (Circuit Bench at Shri Vijaya Puram)
Chhattisgarh	2000	Chhattisgarh	Bilaspur
Delhi	1966	Delhi	Delhi
Gauhati	1948	Assam, Nagaland, Mizoram and Arunachal Pradesh	Guwahati (Benches at Kohima, Aizawl and Itanagar)
Gujarat	1960	Gujarat	Ahmedabad
Himachal Pradesh	1971	Himachal Pradesh	Shimla
Jammu & Kashmir and Ladakh	1928	Jammu & Kashmir, Ladakh	Srinagar and Jammu
Jharkhand	2000	Jharkhand	Ranchi
Karnataka	1884	Karnataka	Bengaluru (Circuit Benches at Dharwar and Gulbarga)
Kerala	1958	Kerala & Lakshadweep	Ernakulam
Madhya Pradesh	1956	Madhya Pradesh	Jabalpur (Benches at Gwalior and Indore)
Madras	1862	Tamil Nadu & Puducherry	Chennai (Bench at Madurai)
Orissa	1948	Odisha	Cuttack
Patna	1916	Bihar	Patna
Punjab and Haryana	1966	Punjab, Haryana and Chandigarh	Chandigarh
Rajasthan	1949	Rajasthan	Jodhpur (Bench at Jaipur)
Sikkim	1975	Sikkim	Gangtok
Uttarakhand	2000	Uttarakhand	Nainital
Telangana	2019	Telangana	Hyderabad
Tripura	2013	Tripura	Agartala
Meghalaya	2013	Meghalaya	Shillong
Manipur	2013	Manipur	Imphal

OUR INDIA

☛ *India : At a Glance*

Population (2011)	: 1,21,08,54,977 (Male: 62,32,70,258; Female: 58,75,84,719)
Decadal Growth (2001-2011)	: 17.7 per cent (Males: 17.1%; Females: 18.3%)
Most populous State	: Uttar Pradesh (16.17% of National Population)
Density of population	: 382 persons per sq. km.
Most densly populated State	: Bihar : 1106 per sq. km
Sex Ratio	: 943 females per 1000 males
Total Literacy Rate	: 73% (Males – 80.9%; Females – 64.06%)
Capital	: New Delhi
Area	: 32,87,263 sq km
Geographic Location	: Between 8°4' and 37°6' north latitudes
	: Between 68°7' and 97°25' east longitudes
Coastline Length	: 7,516.6 km including the coastline of Lakshadweep, Andaman & Nicobar Islands.
Major Languages	: 22
National Anthem	: Jana Gana Mana
National Currency	: Rupee (₹)
National Animal	: Tiger
National Aquatic Animal	: Dolphin
National Bird	: Peacock
National River	: Ganga
Legislature	: Bicameral Legislature at the Centre; Uni/Bicameral Legislatures in States
Executive	: President, Vice-President and Council of Ministers at the Centre; Governor and Council of Ministers in States
Judiciary	: Independent from Executive with Supreme Court at the apex of the hierarchy

☛ *India: States & Union Territories*

States/Union Territories	*Capital*	*Area in (Sq. Km.)*	*Languages*
Andhra Pradesh	Amaravati	160,229	Telugu, Urdu
Arunachal Pradesh	Itanagar	83,743	Nyishi, Miji, Wancho Adi etc.
Assam	Dispur	78,438	Assamese
Bihar	Patna	94,163	Hindi, Maithili, Bhojpuri
Chhattisgarh	Raipur	137,898	Hindi
Goa	Panji	3,702	Marathi and Konkani
Gujarat	Gandhinagar	1,96,024	Gujarati

States/Union Territories	Capital	Area in (Sq. Km.)	Languages
Haryana	Chandigarh	44,212	Hindi, Haryanvi
Himachal Pradesh	Shimla	55,673	Hindi and Pahari
Jharkhand	Ranchi	79,714	Hindi, Santhali
Karnataka	Bengaluru	1,91,791	Kannada
Kerala	Thiruvananthapuram	38,863	Malayalam
Madhya Pradesh	Bhopal	308,000	Hindi, Urdu
Maharashtra	Mumbai	307,713	Marathi
Manipur	Imphal	22,327	Manipuri
Meghalaya	Shillong	22,429	Khasi, Garo and English
Mizoram	Aizawl	21,081	Mizo and English
Nagaland	Kohima	16,579	Sema, English
Odisha	Bhubaneswar	155,707	Odiya
Punjab	Chandigarh	50,362	Punjabi
Rajasthan	Jaipur	3,42,239	Hindi and Rajasthani
Sikkim	Gangtok	7,096	Bhutia, Nepali, Lepcha and Limbu
Tamil Nadu	Chennai	1,30,058	Tamil
Telangana	Hyderabad	1,14,840	Telugu
Tripura	Agartala	10,491	Bengali, Kakborak
Uttar Pradesh	Lucknow	2,40,928	Hindi and Urdu
Uttarakhand	Dehradun	53,483	Hindi
West Bengal	Kolkata	88,752	Bengali
Jammu & Kashmir	Srinagar (Summer) Jammu (Winter)	2,22,236*	Kashmiri, Urdu, Dogri
Andaman & Nicobar Island	Shri Vijaya Puram	8,249	Bengali, Hindi, Nicobarese, Tamil, Telugu, and Malayalam
Chandigarh	Chandigarh	114	Hindi, Punjabi
Dadara & Nagar Haveli and Daman & Diu	Daman	603	Gujarati and Hindi
Delhi	Delhi	1483	Hindi, Punjabi and Urdu
Lakshadweep	Kavaratti	32	Malayalam
Puducherry	Puducherry	479	Tamil, Telugu, Malayalam, English and French
Ladakh	Leh	—	Ladakhi

* Including areas of Ladakh and illegally occupied by China and Pakistan.

☛ Population

Second Largest Nation : In terms of the size of population, India is the second largest country in the world, next only to China. China tops the list with 1341.0 million people. India's population constitutes nearly 17.5 per cent of the total world population while her geographical area is only 2.42 per cent of the world area. With such a huge population to support on so small an area, the country finds herself in great difficulty in making any significant dent on its poverty and economic backwardness. India's national income, which is barely 2 per cent of the total global income, clearly shows the tremendous strain of population on her economy.

☛ *2011 Census of India : Population distribution, Density and Literacy rate*

S. No.	State/ Union Territories*	Population 2011			Population Density (per sq. km.)	Literacy Rate 2011		
		Persons	Males	Females	2011	Persons	Males	Females
	INDIA	**1,21,08,54,977**	**62,32,70,258**	**58,75,84,719**	**382**	**73.0**	**80.9**	**64.6**
1.	Jammu and Kashmir	1,25,41,302	66,40,662	59,00,640	124	67.2	76.8	56.4
2.	Himachal Pradesh	68,64,602	34,81,873	33,82,729	123	82.8	89.5	75.9
3.	Punjab	2,77,43,338	1,46,39,465	1,31,03,873	551	75.8	80.4	70.7
4.	Chandigarh*	10,55,450	5,80,663	4,74,787	9,258	86.0	90.0	81.2
5.	Uttarakhand	1,00,86,292	51,37,773	49,48,519	189	78.8	87.4	70.0
6.	Haryana	2,53,51,462	1,34,94,734	1,18,56,728	573	75.6	84.1	65.9
7.	Delhi*	1,67,87,941	89,87,326	78,00,615	11,320	86.2	90.9	80.8
8.	Rajasthan	6,85,48,437	3,55,50,997	3,29,97,440	200	66.1	79.2	52.1
9.	Uttar Pradesh	19,98,12,341	10,44,80,510	9,53,31,831	829	67.7	77.3	57.2
10.	Bihar	10,40,99,452	5,42,78,157	4,98,21,295	1,106	61.8	71.2	51.5
11.	Sikkim	6,10,577	3,23,070	2,87,507	86	81.4	86.6	75.6
12.	Arunachal Pradesh	13,83,727	7,13,912	6,69,815	17	65.4	72.6	57.7
13.	Nagaland	19,78,502	10,24,649	9,53,853	119	79.6	82.8	76.1
14.	Manipur	28,55,794	14,38,586	14,17,208	128	76.94	83.58	70.26
15.	Mizoram	10,97,206	5,55,339	5,41,867	52	91.3	93.3	89.3
16.	Tripura	36,73,917	18,74,376	17,99,541	350	87.2	91.5	82.7
17.	Meghalya	29,66,889	14,91,832	14,75,057	132	74.4	76.0	72.9
18.	Assam	3,12,05,576	1,59,39,443	1,52,66,133	398	72.2	77.8	66.3
19.	West Bengal	9,12,76,115	4,68,09,027	4,44,67,088	1,028	76.3	81.7	70.5
20.	Jharkhand	3,29,88,134	1,69,30,315	1,60,57,819	414	66.4	76.8	55.4
21.	Odisha	4,19,74,218	2,12,12,136	2,07,62,082	270	72.9	81.6	64.0
22.	Chhattisgarh	2,55,45,198	1,28,32,895	1,27,12,303	189	70.3	80.3	60.2
23.	Madhya Pradesh	7,26,26,809	3,76,12,306	3,50,14,503	236	69.3	78.7	59.2
24.	Gujarat	6,04,39,692	3,14,91,260	2,89,48,432	308	78.0	85.8	69.7
25.	Daman and Diu*	2,43,247	1,50,301	92,946	2,191	87.1	91.5	79.5
26.	Dadra & Nagar Haweli*	3,43,709	1,93,760	1,49,949	700	76.2	85.2	64.3
27.	Maharashtra	11,23,74,333	5,82,43,056	5,41,31,277	365	82.3	88.4	75.9
28.	Andhra Pradesh	4,93,86,799	2,47,38,068	2,46,48,731	308	67.4	74.8	60.0
29.	Karnataka	6,10,95,297	3,09,66,657	3,01,28,640	319	75.4	82.5	68.1
30.	Goa	14,58,545	7,39,140	7,19,405	394	88.7	92.6	84.7
31.	Lakshadweep*	64,473	33,123	31,350	2,149	91.8	95.6	87.9
32.	Kerala	3,34,06,061	1,60,27,412	1,73,78,649	860	94.0	96.1	92.1
33.	Tamil Nadu	7,21,47,030	3,61,37,975	3,60,09,055	555	80.1	86.8	73.4
34.	Puducherry*	12,47,953	6,12,511	6,35,442	2,547	85.8	91.3	80.7
35.	Andaman & Nicobar Island*	3,80,581	2,02,871	1,77,710	46	86.6	90.3	82.4
36.	Telangana	3,51,93,978	17,704,078	17,489,900	308	66.5	75.0	57.9

☛ Other Details

(a) Population of India

1951	36,10,88,090	**1961**	43,92,34,771
1971	54,81,59,652	**1981**	68,33,29,097
1991	84,64,21,039	**2001**	102,87,37,436
2011	1,21,08,54,977		

(b) Density of Population (Persons per square kilometre)

1951	113	**1961**	138
1971	177	**1981**	216
1991	267	**2001**	324
2011	382		

(c) Annual Compound Rate of Growth

1941-1951	1.25 per cent
1951-1961	1.96 per cent
1961-1971	2.22 per cent
1971-1981	2.20 per cent
1981-1991	2.14 per cent
1991-2001	1.95 per cent
2001-2011	1.64 per cent

☛ Introductory Facts

- India is world's second largest country next only to China in terms of population (according to 2011 census the population of India is over 121.08 crore).
- India is the largest democracy in the world with the largest number of electors (over 90 crore).
- India is the seventh largest country in the world in terms of size, covering 32,87,263 sq. km, approximately 2.4% of world land area.
- India's mainland extends between latitudes 8°4' and 37°6' north and longitudes 68°7' and 97°25' east. India has a land frontier of about 15,200 km.
- The total length of the coastline of mainland and groups of islands is 7516.6 km approximately.
- Self-sufficient in agricultural production, India is the tenth industrialised country in the world and sixth nation to have gone into outer space.
- India is a nuclear power and has nuclear fission devices for her missile systems and atomic power plants.
- Political Boundary—In the north, the Himalayas separate India from China. Situated between the two countries is Nepal, and to its east lies Bhutan, closely connected to India by special treaty. The two lie along the chain of the Himalayas, and a series of mountain ranges separate India from Myanmar (Burma) on former's eastern border. Also in the east lies Bangladesh wedged in between India's north-eastern States and West Bengal. In the north-west, Pakistan and a very small hook of Afghanistan border India and separate it from Tazikistan, a breakaway republic of former USSR.
- The foreign policy of India is based on Panch Sheela which was adopted by several nations of the world as the cornerstone of their foreign policy. It is this policy round which the non-aligned movement has evolved.

States:

(*i*) Largest population – Uttar Pradesh
(*ii*) Highest density of population – Bihar
(*iii*) Largest in area – Rajasthan
(*iv*) First state to achieve total literacy – Kerala
(*v*) Minimum population (State) – Sikkim
(*vi*) Minimum area (State) – Goa
(*vii*) 1st state to achieve 100% rural electrification – Haryana

☛ Famous Places and Towns in India

- **Ajanta Caves:** Rock cut shrines and monastries at Ajanta in Maharashtra. These Buddhist cave temples, constructed between 100 BC and 7th century AD contain astonishing wall paintings.
- **Elephanta Caves:** Situated on an island 15 miles away from Mumbai; famous for a number of large and remarkable well-executed images of Brahmanical gods.

- **Ellora:** These are 34 cave-temples situated near Aurangabad in Maharashtra. Famous for its rock-cut Kailash Temple.
- **Gomateswara (Karnataka):** The statue (57 feet high) of Jain sage Gomateswara; it is 2000 years old and made out of a single rock.
- **Jagannath Temple:** Famous Hindu Temple situated at Puri in Odisha; annual Rath Yatra Festival is celebrated with great enthusiasm.
- **Khajuraho:** Situated in Bundelkhand (M.P.). It is famous for Mahadeva Temple, built in 10-11th century.
- **Konark Temple:** Famous for the Sun Temple built in the 13th century, 85 kilometers from Puri in Odisha.
- **Nalanda:** A famous university of Buddhist learning in Bihar (near Patna) founded in the 5th Century but now in ruins.
- **Sanchi (Bhopal, M.P.):** Known for Buddhist stupas.
- **Taj Mahal (Agra, U.P.):** A white marble mausoleum built by Shahjahan, the Mughal Emperor, in 1653, in memory of his beloved queen Mumtaz Mahal.
- **Sarnath:** A place near Varanasi where Lord Buddha preached his first sermon.
- **Karwar:** In Karnataka, INS Sea Bird, the biggest and most sophisticated naval base in South Asia.
- **Shakti Sthal:** The cremation spot in New Delhi of late Prime Minister Indira Gandhi.
- **National Theatre, Mumbai:** The 1040-seat Tata Theatre is India's first national theatre which is as beautiful as any of its size in the world.
- **National Science Centre:** Built at a cost of Rs. 15 crores and is situated at Pragati Maidan in New Delhi.
- **Pokhran:** The first Indian nuclear test was carried out in the Pokhran (May 18, 1974) in Rajasthan desert. Again on May 11 & 13, 1998 India conducted 5 tests to attain status of nuclear power state.
- **Koradi:** It is near Nagpur. India's biggest super thermal power station is situated here.
- **Bombay High:** It is a point 120 km. north-west of Mumbai where vast oil deposits have been found.
- **Dilwara Temple:** Near Mount Abu (Rajasthan) where Hindu and Jain Temples built in 11-13 century exist.
- **Buland Darwaja:** A high gate in Fatehpur Sikri near Agra, built by Akbar.
- **Anand Bhawan (Prayagraj):** Ancestral home of the Nehrus.
- **Gaya (Bihar):** Famous Pilgrimage Centre.
- **Darjeeling (West Bengal):** Beautiful hill station and tea gardens.
- **Teen Murti (New Delhi):** Nehru Museum.
- **Sambhar:** A salt lake in Rajasthan.
- **Neyvelli (Tamil Nadu):** Largest Power Station.
- **Victoria Memorial (Kolkata):** An Art Gallery building.
- **Rajghat (Delhi):** Mahatma Gandhi's Samadhi.
- **Gateway of India:** A memorial gate at Mumbai, built in 1911.
- **Sabarmati (Ahmedabad):** Ashram of Gandhiji.
- **Shantivana (Delhi):** Pt. Nehru's Samadhi near Rajghat.
- **Vijayghat (Delhi):** Shri Lal Bahadur Shastri's Samadhi.
- **Brindaban Gardens:** Karnataka.
- **Hanging Garden:** Mumbai.
- **Eden Garden (Kolkata):** Famous Cricket Stadium.
- **Rishikesh (Uttarakhand):** Famous Hindu place of pilgrimage; Antibiotic Factory.
- **Porbunder (Gujarat):** Birth place of Mahatma Gandhi.
- **Sevagram:** Famous Ashram of Gandhiji at Wardha.
- **Shantiniketan:** Varsity near Kolkata founded by Rabindranath Tagore.
- **Rameshwaram:** Sacred place of Hindus.
- **Tower of Victory (Raj.):** A famous monument of marble in Chittor build by Rana Kumbha.
- **Golden Temple (Amritsar):** Famous Sikh Gurdwara.
- **Ankleshwar (Gujarat):** Famous for Petroleum.
- **Nishat Bagh (Kashmir):** Famous Garden.

- **Birla Planetarium, Kolkata:** India's first and world's second biggest planetarium.
- **Triveni (U.P.):** Confluence of the Ganges, Jamuna and mythological Saraswati; a place of pilgrimage for the Hindus.
- **Amarnath:** A place of pilgrimage for the Hindus, situated at a height of about 13,000 ft. in Kashmir.
- **Badrinath:** A place of pilgrimage for the Hindus, near the Gangotry Glacier in the Himalayas.
- **Jalianwala Bagh:** A garden in Amritsar; scene of massacre of innocent Indians by the British on April 13, 1919.
- **India Gate:** A memorial in New Delhi.
- **National Rail Museum:** Established in New Delhi (Chanakyapuri), the museum provides the history of railways in India.
- **National Museum of Natural History:** First of its kind in India, has been established in New Delhi on June 5, 1978.
- **Swatantrata Sangram Sangrahalya and Swatantrata Senani Smarak:** At Red Fort, Delhi. Inaugurated on Oct 2, 1995 by Prime Minister.

☛ Important Hill Stations in India

Station	State/UT
Almora	Uttarakhand
Gulmarg	J & K
Cherrapunji	Meghalaya
Kasauli	Himachal Pradesh
Coonoor	Tamil Nadu
Mahabaleshwar	Maharashtra
Dalhousie	H.P.
Mount Abu	Rajasthan
Darjeeling	West Bengal
Mussoorie	Uttarakhand
Nainital	Uttarakhand
Ranikhet	Uttarakhand
Ootacamund	Tamil Nadu
Shillong	Meghalaya
Panchmarhi	Madhya Pradesh
Shimla	Himachal Pradesh

☛ Famous Newspapers in India

- **English Newspapers:** Amrit Bazar Patrika; The Telegraph; The Statesman; The Times of India; The Hindustan Times; The Tribune; The National Herald; The Financial Express; The Indian Express; The Economic Times; The Hindu; The Patriot; The Pioneer, The Deccan Herald, The Asian Age.
- **Hindi Newspapers:** Vishvamitra; Nai Duniya; Navbharat Times; Hindustan; Aaj; Punjab Kesari; Janasatta; Dainik Jagran; Tribune; Rajasthan Patrika; Amar Ujala; Rashtriya Sahara, Dainik Bhaskar.
- **Other Newspapers & their Languages:** Anand Bazar Patrika & Jugantar (Bengali); Nutan Assamiya (Assamese); Matribhoomi (Odiya); Pratap (Urdu); Gujrati Samachar (Gujarati); Eenadu (Telugu); Kannada Prabha (Kannada); Navkal (Marathi); Dinamani (Tamil); Mathrubhoomi (Malayalam); Loksatta (Marathi); Malayala Manorama (Malayalam).
- **Employment News:** It is a weekly newspaper published by the Government of India in English, Hindi and Urdu. It carries complete information on employment opportunities. It is published from Delhi.

☛ Important Places : In a Nutshell

Place	City/State
Ajanta	Maharashtra
Mausoleum of Akbar	Agra
Amarnath Cave	J&K
Anand Bhawan	Prayagraj
Bhakra Dam	Punjab
Jagannath Temple	Puri (Odisha)
Jama Masjid	Delhi
Black Pagoda	Konark (Odisha)
Vrindavan Garden	Karnataka
Buland Darwaja	Fatehpur Sikri
Charminar	Hyderabad
Chilka Lake	Near Bhubaneswar
Dal Lake	Srinagar
Dilwara Temple	Mount Abu
Elephanta Caves	Mumbai

Place	City/State
Ellora Caves	Aurangabad
Gateway of India	Mumbai
Golden Temple	Amritsar
Gol Gumbaz	Bijapur
Hanging Garden	Mumbai
Hawa Mahal	Jaipur
Howrah Bridge	Kolkata
Kanyakumari Temple	Tamil Nadu
Sun Temple	Konark
Red Tiger Garden	Bengaloru
Qutub Minar	Delhi
Rajghat	Delhi
Shalimar Bagh	Srinagar
Taj Mahal	Agra
Victoria Memorial	Kolkata
Victoria Garden	Mumbai
Victory Tower	Chittorgarh

☛ Important Places and Related Personalities

Place	Personality
Sabarmati Ashram	Mahatma Gandhi
Sadakat Ashram	Dr. Rajdenra Prasad
Pavanar Ashram	Acharya Vinoba Bhave
Jerusalem	Jesus Christ
Shanti Niketan	Rabindranath Tagore
Talawandi	Guru Nanak
Auroville	Mother Anandamai, Maharshi Arbindo Ghosh
Mecca/Madina	Prophet Mohammed Sahib
Waterloo	Napolean Bonaparte
Kapilvastu, Bodh Gaya, Lumbini, Kushi Nagar	Gautama Buddha
Nirmal Hriday	Mother Teresa
Anand Van	Baba Amte
Jallianwala Bagh	General Dyer
Champaran	Gandhiji
Macedonia/Alexandria	Alexander, the Great
Belur	Swami RamKrishna Paramahansa
Corsica, St. Helena	Napolean
Bardoli	Sardar Vallabhabhai Patel
Trafalgar	Nelson
Shantivan, Trimurti Bhawan	Pandit Jawahar Lal Nehru
Vijay Ghat	Lal Bahadur Shastri
Shaktisthal	Indira Gandhi
Samatasthal	Babu Jagjiwan Ram
Kisan Ghat	Chaudhary Charan Singh
Chittorgarh/ Haldighati	Maharana Pratap

☛ First in India

- The first Indian to get the Nobel Prize for Literature: *Rabindra Nath Tagore*
- The first Indian to get the Nobel Prize for Physics: *C.V. Raman*
- The first Indian to get the Nobel Prize for Peace: *Mother Teresa*
- The first Indian to get the Nobel Prize for Economics: *Amartya Sen*
- The first Indian to get Special Oscar award (1992): *Satyajit Ray*
- The first and the last Indian Governor-General of free India: *C. Rajagopalachari*
- The first woman to become the Governor of a State: *Smt. Sarojini Naidu*
- The first Indian Commander-In-Chief: *General K.M. Cariappa*
- The first ever woman to become the Chief Minister of a State: *Smt. Sucheta Kripalani*
- The first Indian woman President of UN General Assembly: *Smt. Vijaylakshmi Pandit*
- The first Indian to become the President of Inter. Court of Justice: *Dr. Nagendra Singh*
- The first Indian woman to swim across the English Channel: *Ms. Aarti Saha*
- The first Indian girl to become Miss Universe: *Miss Sushmita Sen*
- The first Indian girl to become Miss World: *Rita Faria*
- The first Indian to swim across the English Channel: *Mihir Sen*
- The first Field Marshal: *S.H.F.J. Manekshaw*
- The first Indian recipient of Victoria Cross: *Khudadad Khan*

- The first Indian to conquer Mt. Everest: *Sherpa Tenzing (May 29, 1953)*
- The first Indian Cosmonaut (man): *Rakesh Sharma (April 3, 1984)*
- The first Indian Cosmonaut (woman): *Kalpana Chawla (Nov. 19, 1997)*
- The first woman to climb Mt. Everest: *Miss Bachendri Pal (May 23, 1984)*
- The first ICS: *Satyendranath Tagore*
- The first to address the UN General Assembly in Hindi: *Atal Bihari Vajpai*
- The first Newspaper: *Bengal Gazette (Jan 27, 1780)*
- The first Postage Stamp issued: *In 1852*
- The first Telegraph line laid: *In 1851 (Calcutta-Diamond Harbour)*
- The first Railways run: *April 16, 1853 (Mumbai-Thane)*
- The first Electric Train run: *1925 (Mumbai-Kurla)*
- The first Atomic Power Station: *Tarapore (Maharashtra)*
- The first passenger-cum-cargoship made in India: *Harshavardhan*
- The first Satellite: *Aryabhatta (1975)*
- The first President of the Indian National Congress: *W.C. Banerjee*
- The first President of Indian Republic: *Dr. Rajendra Prasad*
- The first woman judge of the Supreme Court: *Ms Fatima Bibi*
- The first to climb Everest without oxygen: *Phu Dorjee (1987)*
- The first film (movie): *Raja Harishchandra*
- The first film (talkie): *Alam Ara*
- The first Metro Railway: *Kolkata Metro Railway*
- The first Test-tube baby, scientifically documented: *Born on August 6, 1986 at K.E.M. Hospital, Mumbai*
- The first TV Centre: *At Delhi*
- The first Indian to get an Oscar: *Bhanu Athaiya*
- The first woman pilot in IAF: *Ms Harita Kaur Deol*
- The first woman to get Olympic Medal: *Karnam Malleswari*
- The first woman Foreign Secretary: *Chokila Iyer*

☛ Superlatives (India)

Highest, Biggest, Largest and Longest in India

- Award for Gallantry, highest: *Param Vir Chakra*
- Award, highest civilian: *Bharat Ratna*
- Bank, with largest number of branches: *State Bank of India*
- Road Bridge, Longest: *Bhupen Hazarika Setu Across Lohit River, Assam (9.15 km.)*
- Cattle Fair, Largest: *Sonepur (Bihar)*
- City, Most Populous: *Mumbai metropolis*
- Corridor, Longest: *Rameshwaram Temple corridor (4,000 ft.)*
- Desert, Largest: *Thar (Rajasthan)*
- Dam, Longest: *Hirakud Dam (Odisha)*
- Delta, Largest: *Sunderban's Delta*
- Dome, Largest: *Gol Gumbaj (Bijapur)*
- Dam, Highest: *Tehri Dam (855 ft.)*
- Gateway, Highest: *Buland Darwaja at Fatehpur Sikri (176 ft.)*
- Lake, Largest (Fresh water): *Wular Lake (Kashmir)*
- Literacy, Highest: *Kerala*
- Museum, Largest: *Indian Museum (Kolkata)*
- Mosque, Biggest: *Jama Masjid (Delhi)*
- Peak, Highest: *K-2 (Pak-Occupied Kashmir)*
- Railway Platform, Longest: *Shree Siddharoodha Swamiji Railway Station Hubballi, Karnataka (1507 mtrs)*
- Railway Bridge, longest: *Vembanad Bridge, Kerala (4.6 km)*
- Railway route, longest: *Passenger train-Dibrugarh to Kanyakumari (4,286 km).*
- River, Longest: *The Ganges (2525 Km)*
- Rainfall, Highest (annual mean): *Mowsynram near Cherrapunji (1178 cm)*
- Road Longest: *NH-44*
- State, with maximum forest cover: *Madhya Pradesh*
- State, with maximum density of population: *Bihar*

- Tunnel, Longest (Road): *Dr. Shyama Prasad Mukherjee Tunnel (J&K 9.28 kms)*
- Tunnel, Longest (Railway): *T-50 Tunnel, between the Khari-Sumber section in J&K (12.77 km)*
- Minar, Highest: *Qutub Minar (Delhi 72.5 m.)*
- Waterfall, Highest: *Kunchikal Waterfall (Karnataka: 455 m)*
- Zoo, Largest: *Arignar Anna Zoological Park (Chennai)*

☛ Famous Indian Rivers

Name of River	*Length (km)*	*Source*	*Joins into*
Betwa	480	Vindhyachal (M.P.)	Yamuna
Brahmaputra	2,900	Mansarovar Lake (Tibet)	Bay of Bengal
Banas	270	Aravalli Hills	Chambal
Cauvery	805	Brahmagiri Hills (Karnataka)	Bay of Bengal
Chambal	965	Janapawa Hills (M.P.)	Yamuna (Etawa)
Indrawati	513	Kalihandi (Odisha)	Godavari
Ganga	2,525	Gangotri	Bay of Bengal
Gandak	425	Nepal	Ganga (Patna)
Godavari	2465	Nasik (Maharashtra)	Bay of Bengal
Hoogly	—	Navadweep (W.B.)	Bay of Bengal
Kshipra	—	Indore	Chambal
Krishna	1,400	Western Ghat	Bay of Bengal
Kosi	730	Gosaithan peak	Ganga
Black Indus (Kali Sindhu)	416	Devas district	Yamuna
Luni	330	Ajmer (Aravalli hills)	Bay of Cutch
Mahanadi	828	Raipur (Chhattisgarh)	Bay of Bengal
Narmada	1,312	Amarkantak Mountain Range (M.P.)	Bay of Khambat
Ravi	720	Rohtang Dale	Chenab
Ramganga	602	Himalaya (Nainital)	Ganga (Near Kannauj)
Sabarmati	416	Udaipur	Rann of Cutch
Sindhu (Indus)	2,880	Near Mansarovar Lake	Arabian Sea
Sutlej	1,500	Near Mansarovar Lake	Chenab
Sone	780	Amarkantak Mountain Range (M.P.)	Ganga (Patna)
Tapti	724	Baitul (M.P.)	Bay of Khambhat
Vyas	625	Rohtang dale	Sutlej
Yamuna	1,375	Yamunotri	Ganga

☛ Important Indian Peaks (Height in Metres)

K-2 : 8611 (Pak-Occupied Kashmir);
Nanga Parbat : 8126;
Broad Peak : 8047 (Pak-Occupied Territory);
Masher Brum E : 7821;
Masher Brum W : 7806 (Pak Occupied Territory);
Kamet : 7756;
Chaukhamba : 7138; (Badrinath Peak)

Kanchenjunga : 8598;
Gasher Brum : 8068 (Pak-Occupied Territory);
Disteghil Sar : 7885 (Pak-Occupied Territory);
Nanda Devi : 7817;
Rakaposhi : 7788 (Pak-Occupied Territory);
Saser Kangri : 7672;
Trisul : 7138.

☛ *Some Major Irrigational and Multipurpose Projects*

S.No.	Name of Project	Related State/UT	River
1.	Bargi Project	Madhya Pradesh	Bargi
2.	Beas	Joint Venture of Haryana, Punjab and Rajasthan	Beas
3.	Bhadra	Karnakata	Bhadra
4.	Bhakra Nangal	Haryana, Punjab and Rajasthan	Sutluj
5.	Bhima I	Maharashtra	Pawana
6.	Bhima II	Maharashtra	Krishna
7.	Chambal	Joint Project of M.P. and Rajasthan	Chambal
8.	Damodar Valley Project	West Bengal and Bihar	Damodar
9.	Dulhasti Power Project	Jammu and Kashmir	Chenab
10.	Farakka	West Bengal	Hooghly
11.	Gandak	Bihar and U.P.	Gandak
12.	Ghataprabha	Karnataka	Ghataprabha
13.	Hasdeo Bango Project	Madhya Pradesh, Chhattisgarh	Hasdeo
14.	Hirakud	Odisha	Mahanadi
15.	Jayakwadi	Maharashtra	Godavari
16.	Kakrapara	Gujarat	Tapti
17.	Kangsbati	West Bengal	Kangsbati and Kumari
18.	Karjan	Gujarat	Karjan
19.	Kosi	Bihar	Kosi
20.	Koyana	Maharashtra	Koyana
21.	Krishna Project	Maharashtra	Krishna
22.	Kukadi	Maharashtra	Kukadi
23.	Left Bank Ghagra Canal	Uttar Pradesh	Ghagra
24.	Madhya Ganga Canal	Uttar Pradesh	Ganga
25.	Mahanadi Delta Scheme	Odisha	(The irrigation scheme will utilise releases from Hirakund Reservoir)
26.	Mahi	Gujarat	Mahi
27.	Malaprabha	Karnataka	Malaprabha
28.	Mayurakshi	West Bengal	Mayurakshi
29.	Nagarjunasagar	Telangana	Krishna
30.	Panam	Gujarat	Panam
31.	Pochampad	Andhra Pradesh	Godavari
32.	Parambikulam Aliyar	Tamil Nadu and Kerala	Perimbikulam
33.	Pong Dam	Punjab	Beas
34.	Ramganga	Uttarakhand	Ramganga
35.	Ranjit Sagar Dam (Thein Dam)	Punjab	Ravi
36.	Rihand	Uttar Pradesh	Rihand
37.	Sabarmati	Gujarat	Sabarmati
38.	Sharda Sahayak	U.P.	Ghagra

S.No.	Name of Project	Related State/UT	River
39.	Sone High Level Canal	Bihar	Sone
40.	Tawa	Madhya Pradesh	Tawa
41.	Tehri Dam	Uttarakhand	Bhagirathi
42.	Tungabhadra	Andhra Pradesh and Karnataka	Tungabhadra
43.	Ukai	Gujarat	Tapti
44.	Upper Krishna	Karnataka	Krishna
45.	Upper Penganga	Maharashtra	Penganga
46.	Uri Power Project	Jammu and Kashmir	Jhelum

☛ Agriculture

Agriculture and Allied sector provides livelihood to 65% to 70% population in India. Three types of crops are cultivated in India.

Crop	Month	Product
Rabi	October-April	Wheat, Barley, Gram, Mustard
Kharif	July-October	Rice, Jowar, Maize, Bajra, Cotton, Jute
Jayad	March-June	Melon, Cucumber

☛ Soils of India

Indian soil has been divided into four categories, viz., Alluvial soil, Black soil, Red soil and Laterite soil. The Indian soil when compared with soil of any other country, is comparatively dry and requires an adquate supply of water for the purpose of cultivation.

☛ Major Indian Crops

Crops	Temp(°c)	Water(cm)	States where Produced
Wheat	15°-25°	60-90	Uttar Pradesh, Madhya Pradesh, Punjab, Haryana.
Rice	24°-26°	80-200	West Bengal, Uttar Pradesh, Telangana, Bihar, Punjab
Maize	18°-21°	50-60	Karnataka, Bihar, Madhya Pradesh, Andhra Pradesh
Jawar	20°-35°	40-60	Maharashtra, Madhya Pradesh, Karnataka
Soyabean	25°-27°	50-120	Madhya Pradesh, Maharashtra, Rajasthan
Cotton	20°-30°	80-150	Maharashtra, Gujarat, Telangana, Karnataka, Madhya Pradesh
Tobacco	20°-25°	75-80	Andhra Pradesh, Gujarat, Karnataka, Maharashtra, Tamil Nadu, Bihar
Tea	24°-30°	100-200	Assam, West Bengal, Kerala, Tamil Nadu, Uttar Pradesh
Ground Nut	15°-25°	60-130	Gujarat, Rajasthan, Madhya Pradesh, Maharashtra

☛ India's wellknown Sanctuaries and National Parks

National Park/Sanctuary	State/UT	Animals
Bandhwgarh National Park	Madhya Pradesh	Tiger, Panther, Cheetah, Sambhar
Bandipur National Park	Karnataka	Elephant, Leopard, Panther, Deer
Carbett National Park	Uttarakhand	Elephant, Panther, Nilgai
Dachigam Sanctuary	Jammu and Kashmir	Leopard, Black Bear, Kasmiri Stag

National Park/Sanctuary	State/UT	Animals
Dalma Sanctuary	Jharkhand	Elephant, Leopard, Pigs
Dudhawa National Park	Uttar Pradesh	Panther, Leopard, Sambhar, Chital
Kewaladev Bird Sanctuary	Bharatpur (Rajasthan)	Siberian Crane, Spoonhill, Stork, Black Deer
Gir National Park	Gujarat	Tiger, Lion, Leopard, Sambhar
Kaziranga National Park	Assam	One-horned Rhinoceros, Buffalo
Manas Sanctuary	Assam	Elephant, Panther, Bear, Sambhar
Betala Tiger Project	Palamu (Jharkhand)	Elephant, Tiger, Buffalo, Deer
Periyar Sanctuary	Kerala	Elephant, Panther, Leopard, Nilgai
Ranthambhor Tiger Project	Rajasthan	Tiger, Deer, Panther, Lion
Sundarban Tiger Reserve	W. Bengal	Leopard, Tiger, Pig, Deer
Shivpuri National Park	Madhya Pradesh	Panther, Chital, Sambhar
Sariska Sanctuary	Rajasthan	Panther, Leopard, Sambhar
Kanha-Kislai National Park	Madhya Pradesh	Tiger, Leopard, Sambhar, Deer
Panchmarhi National Park	Madhya Pradesh	Tiger, Leopard, Buffalo
Hazaribagh National Park	Jharkhand	Panther, Leopard, Deer

☛ Popular Beach Resorts

1. Kovalam	Kerala
2. Juhu	Mumbai
3. Mamallapuram	Tamil Nadu
4. Marina	Chennai, Tamil Nadu
5. Konark	Odisha
6. Puri	Odisha
7. Waltair	Andhra Pradesh
8. Goa	Goa

☛ Major Tribes in India

Tribe	State/UT
Abors	Assam, Arunachal Pradesh
Apatamis	Arunachal Pradesh
Badagas	Nilgiri (Tamil Nadu)
Balga	Madhya Pradesh, Rajasthan, Gujarat
Bhotias	Garhwal and Kumaon regions of Uttarakhand
Birhor	Hazaribagh (Jharkhand)
Chenchus	Andhra Pradesh, Telangana, Odisha
Chhutia	Assam
Gaddis	Himachal Pradesh
Gallong	North East Himalayan Region
Garos	Meghalaya
Gonds	Madhya Pradesh, Chhattisgarh, Bihar, Jharkhand, Odisha, Andhra Pradesh, Telangana
Jarawas	Little Andamans
Khas	Jaunsar-Bawar area in Uttarakhand
Khasis	Assam, Meghalya
Khonds	Odisha
Kol	Madhya Pradesh
Kolam	Andhra Pradesh, Telangana, Chhattisgarh
Kotas	Nilgiri (Tamil Nadu)
Kuki	Manipur
Lepchas	Sikkim
Lushais	Tripura
Mina	Rajasthan
Murias	Bastar region in Chhattisgarh
Mikirs	Assam
Monpa	Arunachal Pradesh
Mundas	Jharkhand
Nagas (Angami, Semi, Ao, Tangkul, Lahora)	Nagaland, Assam
Oarons (also called Kurukh)	Bihar, Jharkhand and Odisha
Onges	Andaman and Nicobar Islands
Santhals	Birbhum region in West Bengal, Hazaribagh, Ranchi and Palamu in Jharkhand
Sentinelese	Andaman and Nicobar
Shompens	Andaman and Nicobar
Todas	Nilgiri (Tamil Nadu)
Uralis	Kerala
Warlis	Maharashtra

☛ Planning in India

The need for planning was felt in India even before independence. A National Planning Committee was set up by the Indian National Congress as early as 1938. The Planning Commission was set up in 1950. It was an advisory body engaged in the task of meaningful national planning.

The main objectives of India's Economic Planning are as follows:

(*i*) securing an increase in National Income;

(*ii*) achieving a planned rate of investment within a given period to bring the actual investment as a proportion of national income to a higher level;

(*iii*) reducing inequality in the distribution of income and wealth;

(*iv*) providing additional employment;

(*v*) adopting measures to increase agricultural production, manufacturing capacity for producers and a favourable balance of payments.

☛ Five Year Plans in India

Plans	*Period*	*Investment (Rs. Crore)*	*Objectives*
First Plan	April 1, 1951-March 31, 1956	1,960	Priority to agriculture, electricity and irrigation.
Second Plan	April 1, 1956—March 31, 1961	4,672	Development of basic and heavy industries.
Third Plan	April 1, 1961—March 31, 1966	8,577	Long term development of India's economy.
Annual Plan	April 1, 1966—March 31, 1967	2,137	
Annual Plan	April 1, 1967—March 31, 1968	2,205	
Annual Plan	April 1,1968—March 31, 1969	2,283	
Fourth Plan	April 1, 1969—March 31, 1974	15,779	Enlarge the income of rural population and supply of goods of mass consumption.
Fifth Plan	April 1,1974—March 31, 1979	39,426	Attain increased self reliance and employment avenues.
Annual Plan	April 1, 1979—March 31, 1980	12,176	
Sixth Plan	April 1, 1980—March 31, 1985	1,09,292	Removal of unemployment
Seventh Plan	April 1, 1985—March 31, 1990	2,18,730	Food work and productivity were the basic priorities.
Eighth Plan	April, 1992—March 31, 1997	4,95,670	Raising employment
Ninth Plan	April 1, 1997—March 31, 2002	9,41,041	Agriculture and rural development
Tenth Plan	April 1, 2002—March 31, 2007	14,91,610	Growth rate 7.8 percent per annum.
Eleventh Plan	April 1, 2007—March 31, 2012	36,44,718	Literacy, Employment, Rural development & Transport development.
Twelfth Plan	April 1, 2012–March 31, 2017	76,69,807	Longterm development of India's economy.

☛ 15-Year Vision Plan

With the end of the Twelfth Plan in March 2017 the era of five year plans came to an end. NITI Aayog has come forward with a draft 15-year vision plan to catapult the country's economy to more than three times as compared to the present day. The new plan is set to replace the centralised five-year plans the country has been following for decades. The new plan is accompanied by shorter sub-plans—a seven-year strategy for 2017-24, and a three-year 'Action Agenda' from 2017-18 to 2019-20. No less than 300 specific action points covering a wide range of sectors have been drawn up as part of the 15-year vision. The 15-year vision document has a seven-year strategy document for 2017-24 as the 'National Development Agenda'. Separately, a three-year 'Action Agenda' from 2017-18 to 2019-20 is also under works to assess funding requirements. The three-year agenda is further divided into seven parts, with a number of specific action points for each part to boost economic growth. India's urban population is expected to increase by 22 crores by 2031. The plan is likely to lay emphasis on urban development, taking a note from China's elaborate long-term development agenda.

☛ NITI Aayog

65-year-old Planning Commission was dissolved and a new institution named NITI Aayog was constituted w.e.f. January 1, 2015. It provides governments at the central and state levels with strategic and technical advice across the spectrum of policy making. As per official declaration, this institution includes matters of national and international import on the economic front, dissemination of best practices from within the country as well as from other nations, the infusion of new policy ideas and specific issue-based support. NITI Aayog is headed by the Prime Minister, who is its chairperson. The Prime Minister appoints a vice-chairperson and a chief executive officer (CEO). The CEO is appointed for a fixed tenure; who has a secretary-level position. The organization have full-time members and up to two part-time members from leading universities, research organizations and other relevant institutions. It also has up to four ex-officio members from the Union council of ministers who are nominated by the Prime Minister. While this is the full-time organizational structure, the new institution comprises a governing council which includes state chief ministers and lieutenant governors of Union Territories.

☛ Finance Commission

Article 280 of the Constitution provides for the appointment of a finance commission every five year. President appoints chairman and members of this commission. Finance commission are to recommend to President the basis for the distribution of the net proceeds of taxes between the centre and the states and the principles which should govern the grants-in-aid to be given to the states out of the consolidated funds of India.

☛ Reserve Bank of India

- It is the Central Bank of the country.
- It was established on April 1, 1935 with a capital of ₹ 5 crore. This capital of ₹ 5 crore was divided into 5 lakh equity shares of ₹ 100 each. In the beginning, the ownership of almost all the share capital was with the non-government share-holders.
- It was nationalized on Jan 1, 1949 as govt. acquired the private share-holdings.
- **Governors:** Ist Governor - Sir Smith (1935-37)
  Ist Indian Governor - C.D. Deshmukh (1948-49)

☛ National Symbols

- **State Emblem:** State Emblem of India is an adaptation from the Sarnath Lion Capital of Ashoka. It was adopted by the Government of India on January 26, 1950. In the adapted form, only three lions are visible, the fourth being hidden from the view. The wheel (Dharma Chakra) appears in relief in the centre of the abacus with a bull on the right and a horse on the left. The bell-shaped lotus has been omitted. The words "Satyameva Jayate" meaning "Truth alone triumphs" are inscribed below the Emblem in Devanagari script.

- **National Flag:** The National Flag of India is a horizontal tricolour of deep saffron (Kesari), white and dark green in equal proportion. In the centre of the white band there is a wheel in navy blue colour. It has 24 spokes. The ratio of the length and the breadth of the flag is 3 : 2. Its design was adopted by the Constituent Assembly of India on July 22, 1947.

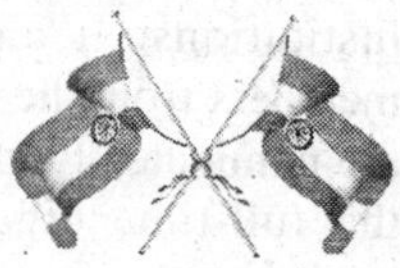

- **National Anthem:** Rabindranath Tagore's song 'Jana-gana-mana' was adopted by the Constituent Assembly as the National Anthem of India on January 24, 1950.

Jana-gan-mana-adhinayaka jaya he,
Bharata-bhagya-vidhata
Punjab-Sindh-Gujarat-Maratha-
Dravida-Utkala-Banga
Vindhya-Himachala-Yamuna-Ganga
Uchhala-jaladhi-taranga.
Tava subha name jage,
Tava subha asisa mange,
Gahe tava jaya gatha,
Jana-gana-mangala-dayak, jaya he
Bharata bhagya vidhata,
Jaya he, jaya he, jaya he,
Jaya jaya jaya, jaya he.

- **National Song:** Bankim Chandra Chatterji's 'Vande Mataram' which was a source of inspiration to the people in their struggle for freedom, has been adopted as National Song. It has an equal status with the National Anthem.

Vande Mataram
Sujalam, suphalam, malayaja-shitalam,
Shasya shyamalam, Mataram
Shubhrajyotsna, pulkita yaminim,
Phulla kusumita drumadalashobhinim,
Subhasinim sumadhura—bhashinim,
Sukhadam, Varadam, Mataram.

- **National Bird and Animal of India:** Peacock and Tiger; **National Aquatic Animal:** Dolphin; **National Flower:** Lotus; **National Calendar:** It was adopted on March 22, 1957. It has 365 days in the year and the first month of the year is Chaitra.
- **Months of the National Calendar:**

1. Chaitra,	2. Vaishakha,
3. Jaishtha,	4. Ashadha,
5. Shravan,	6. Bhadra,
7. Ashvina,	8. Kartika,
9. Marga-Shirsha,	10. Pausha,
11. Magha,	12. Phalguna.

WORLD GEOGRAPHY

- **Earth:** The earth constitutes land, water and air. Land is made up of rocks and soil. It is distributed in continents and islands. The water found in oceans, seas, lakes, etc. occupies about 2/3 of the earth's surface. The earth is surrounded by a cover of air, called atmosphere, which extends up to several hundred kilometres above its surface.
- **Shape:** In ancient times people believed that the earth was flat in shape. Greek philosopher Pythagoras (6th century BC) was the first person to declare that the earth was round. After careful measurement, the scientists have found that the earth is slightly oblate (flattened at poles) and not exactly round.
- **Motions:** The earth has two motions: *(i) Rotation:* Earth makes a complete round on its axis once each 24 hours (more exactly 23 hours, 56 minutes and 4.09 seconds). It causes days and night on the earth. *(ii) Revolution:* The earth makes a complete round of the Sun in one year. This revolution of earth produces alternate seasons.
- ***Some Facts:*** **(1)** Equal Day and Night ---- March 21 and September 23. **(2)** Longest Day ---- June 21. **(3)** Shortest Day ---- December 22. **(4)** The

sunlight takes eight minutes in travelling from the Sun to the Earth. **(5)** Average speed of the earth in orbit ---- 66,600 miles (107,220 km) per hour. **(6)** Earth's equatorial diameter is about 7926 miles (12,756 km). **(7)** Water (oceans, seas, lakes and rivers) occupies nearly 75 per cent of the surface of the earth. **(8)** Earth's average distance from the Moon ---- 2,38,857 miles (3,84,400 km). **(9)** Earth's average distance from the Sun ---- 93 million miles (149.4 million km).

- **Greenwich Time:** It is the local time of the Greenwich observatory in London on 0° meridian. Greenwich time is international standard time.
- **International Date Line:** Half way round the earth from the Greenwich is International Date Line on 180° longitude. It runs down mid-Pacific. It is one day earlier on the east of this line than it is on the west of the line. When it is Monday east of the line, it is Tuesday west of the line.
- **Zones:** On the basis of tem perature and distribution of solar heat on the surface of the earth, the earth has been divided into five zones: (1) Torrid Zone, (2) North Temperate Zone, (3) South Temperate Zone, (4) Arctic Zone, and (5) Antarctic Zone.
- **Continents:** Large land masses forming large geographical divisions are called continents. There are seven continents: (1) Asia (30.0%), (2) Africa (20.3%), (3) North America (16.3%), (4) South America (12.0%), (5) Antarctica (8.9%), (6) Europe (6.7%) and (7) Australia (5.2%).
- **Highest Mountain Peaks:** (1) Everest (Asia-8848 metres), (2) Aconcagua (South America-6960 metres), (3) Mckinley (North America-6194 metres), (4) Kilimanjaro (Africa-5895 metres), (5) Elbrus (Europe-5642 metres), (6) Vinson Massif (Antarctica-5140 metres), (7) Kosciusko (Australia-2228 metres).
- **Largest Oceans:** (1) Pacific Ocean (The largest, covers almost 1/3 of the earth's total area, and the deepest about 6.8 miles at Mariana Trench in western Pacific); (2) Atlantic Ocean, and (3) Indian Ocean. Other seas and gulfs are ---- the Mediterranean Sea, South China Sea, Bering Sea, Caribbean Sea, East China Sea, Sea of Japan, North Sea, Baltic Sea, Hudson Bay and Gulf of Mexico.
- **Longest Rivers:** (1) Nile (6650 km-Africa), (2) Amazon (6437 km-South America), (3) Mississippi-Missouri (6020 km-North America), (4) Yangtze Kiang (5494 km-Asia), (5) Ob Irtysh (5410 km-Europe), (6) Congo (4666 km-Africa).
- **Great Deserts:** (1) Sahara (94 lakh sq km-North Africa), (2) Libyan (11.65 lakh sq km-North Africa), (3) Australian (16 lakh sq km-Australia), (4) Gobi (13 lakh sq km-Mongolia), (5) Great Victoria (6,47,000 sq km-Australia), (6) Syrian (5,20,000 sq km-Arabia), (7) Arabian (23,30,000 sq km Arabia).
- **Largest Islands:** (1) Greenland (21,75,600 sq km) (2) New Guinea (7,77,000 sq km), (3) Borneo (7,25,545 sq km), (4) Malagasy (5,90,000 sq km), (5) Baffin Island (4,76,070 sq km).
- **Highest Waterfalls:** (1) Angel (807 m-Venezuela), (2) Mongefossen (774 m-Norway), (3) Kukenaam (610 m-Venezuela), (4) Ribbon (491 m-USA), (5) King George VI (487 m-Guyana), (6) Upper Yosemite (435 m-USA).

☛ *Major Producers of Crops, Minerals and Industrial goods*

- Coal : China, USA, UK, Germany, Russia, Australia and India
- Cocoa : Ivory Coast, Ghana, South Africa
- Coffee : Brazil, Columbia
- Copper : Chile, USA, Peru, Indonesia
- Cotton : China, India, USA, Russia, Egypt, Brazil, Argentina, Pakistan
- Gold : China, South Africa, Australia, Canada, South America, India
- Grapes : France, Italy, Portugal, California (USA).
- Iron : China, Brazil, Australia, India
- Jute : India, Bangladesh
- Manganese : China, South Africa, Brazil
- Petroleum : USA, Saudi Arabia, Venezuela, Russia

- Rice : China, India, Japan, Myanmar (Burma)
- Rubber : Thailand, Malaysia, Indonesia, Sri Lanka
- Silk : Japan, China, India
- Silver : Mexico, USA, Russia, Peru, India
- Steel : China, USA, Russia, UK
- Tea : China, India, Sri Lanka, Kenya
- Wheat : China, India, Russia, USA, Canada
- Wool : Australia, Argentina, New Zealand, South Africa
- Tobacco : China, USA, India, Brazil, Russia.

☛ Oceans of the World

Pacific	166,241,000 sq km
Atlantic	86,557,000 sq km
Indian	73,427,000 sq km
Arctic	9,485,000 sq km

☛ Major Gulfs of the World

Names	*Areas (Sq. Km.)*
Gulf of Mexico	15,44,000
Gulf of Hudson	12,33,000
Arabian Gulf	2,38,000
Gulf of St. Lawrence	2,37,000
Gulf of California	1,62,000
English Channel	89,900

☛ Largest Deserts of the World

Subtropical	
Sahara, North Africa	94,00,000 sq. km.
Kalahari, Southern Africa	582,727 sq. km.
Thar, India/Pakistan	2,00,000 sq. km.
Great Sandy, Australia	4,00,000 sq. km.
Cool Coastal	
Atacama, Chile S.A.	1,40,000 sq. km
Cool Winter	
Gobi, China	13,00,000 sq. km.
Colorado, Western USA (also called the painted desert)	3,37,000 sq. km.

☛ Longest Rivers

Name	*Country/ Continent*	*Length in Kilometres*
Nile	Africa	6690
Amazon	S. America	6437
Mississippi-Missouri	USA	6020
Yangtze-Kiang	China	5494
Ob-Irtysh	Russia	5410
Lena	Russia	4400
Hwang Ho	China	4344
Niger	Africa	4180
St. Lawrence	Canada (USA)	4023
Murray-Darling	Australia	3780
Volga	Russia	3690
Indus	Asia	2900
Danube	Europe	2850
Orinoco	S. America	2575

☛ Major Riverside Cities

City	*River*	*Country*
Alexandria	Nile	Egypt
Amsterdam	Amsel	Netherland
Ankara	Kizil	Turkey
Baghdad	Tigris	Iraq
Bangkok	Menam	Thailand
Belgrade	Danube	Yugoslavia
Berlin	Spree	Germany
Budapest	Danube	Hungary
Cairo	Nile	Egypt
Chittagong	Karnaphuli	Bangladesh
Karachi	Indus	Pakistan
Khartoum	Blue & White Nile	Sudan
Lahore	Ravi	Pakistan
Lisbon	Tagus	Portugal
Liverpool	Mersey	England
London	Thames	England
Moscow New	Moskva	Russia
Orleans	Mississipi	USA
New York	Hudson	USA
Paris	Seine	France
Rangoon (Yangon)	Irawadi	Myanmar
Rome	Tiber	Italy

☛ Principal Mountain Peaks of the World

	Mountains	Height in Metres	Range	Date of First Ascent
1.	Mount Everest	8,848	Himalayas	May 29, 1953
2.	K-2 (Godwin Austen)	8,611	Karakoram	July 31, 1954
3.	Kanchenjunga	8,598	Himalayas	May 25, 1955
4.	Lhotse	8,511	Himalayas	May 18, 1956
5.	Makalu I	8,481	Himalayas	May 15, 1955
6.	Dhaulagiri I	8,167	Himalayas	May 13, 1960
7.	Mansalu I	8,156	Himalayas	May 9, 1956
8.	Chollyo	8,153	Himalayas	Oct. 19, 1954
9.	Nanga Parbat	8,124	Himalayas	July 3, 1953
10.	Annapurna I	8,091	Himalayas	June 3, 1950
11.	Gasherbrum I	8,068	Karakoram	July 5, 1958
12.	Broad Peak I	8,047	Karakoram	June 9, 1957
13.	Gasherbrum II	8,034	Karakoram	July 7, 1956
14.	Shisha Pangma (Gosainthan)	8,018	Himalayas	May 2, 1964
15.	Gasherbrum III	7,952	Karakoram	Aug. 11, 1975

☛ Famous Straits of the World

Strait	*Between*	*Country*
Malacca Strait	Andaman Sea and South China Sea	Indonesia
Palk Strait	Mannar and Bay of Bengal	India-Sri Lanka
Magellan Strait	Pacific and South Atlantic Ocean	Chile
Dover Strait	English Channel and North Sea	England-France
Berring Strait	Berring Sea and Chukasi Sea	Alaska-Russia
Sugaroo Strait	Japan Sea and Pacific Ocean	Japan
Sunda Strait	Java and Indian Ocean	Indonesia
Gibralter Strait	Mediterranean Sea and Atlantic Ocean	Spain
Harmuj Strait	Persia and Bay of Oman	Oman-Iran
Hudson Strait	Bay of Hudson and Atlantic Ocean	Canada

☛ Signals/Signs and Meaning

Signal/Sign	*Meaning*
Red Triangle	Family Planning
Red Cross	Medical Help
Red Light	Danger, 'Stop' for the movement of vehicles
Green Light	Go

Signal/Sign	*Meaning*
Olive Branch	Peace
White Pigeon or Dove	Peace
Black Strip on Arm	(*i*) Opposition (*ii*) Sorrow
Black Flag	Opposition
Red Flag	(*i*) Danger (*ii*) Revolution

Signal/Sign	Meaning
White Flag	Treaty or Surrender
Yellow Flag	Vehicles with patients of contagious diseases
Two Bones across with a Skull	Danger of electricity
Half mast flown Flag	National mourning
Lotus	Sign of civilization and culture
Wheel (Chakra)	Sign of Progress
A blind folded woman with scale in hand	Sign of Justice
Reversed flown	National calamity flag

☛ National Emblems of Important Countries

Country	National Emblem
America	Golden Rod
Australia	Kangaroo
Ireland	Shamrock
Italy	White Lily
Israel	Candelabrum
Iran	Rose
Canada	White Lily
Great Britain	Rose
Chile	Candor and Huemul
Germany	Corn Flower
Japan	Chrysanthemum
Zimbabwe	Zimbabwe Bird
Denmark	Beach
Turkey	Crescent and Star
The Netherlands	Lion
New Zealand	Kiwi, Fern Southern Cross
Norway	Lion
Nepal	Kukri
Pakistan	Crescent
Poland	Eagle
France	Lily
Belgium	Lion
Bangladesh	Water Lily
Mongolia	The Soyombo
Russia	Double headed eagle
Lebanon	Cedar Tree
Sudan	Secretary Bird
Syria	Eagle
India	Lioned Capital

☛ First in the World

- First Chinese visitor to India: **Fahien**
- First foreign invader of India: **Alexander, the Great (Greek)**
- First person to climb Mt. Everest: **Tenzing Norgay (India) and Edmund Hillary (New Zealand) (1953)**
- First atom bomb dropped at: **Hiroshima (Japan)**
- First man in the space: **Yuri Gagarin (former USSR)**
- First woman in the space: **Valentina Tereshkova (former USSR)**
- First person to walk in the space: **Alexei Leonov (former USSR)**
- First person to land on the moon: **Neil Armstrong (USA)**
- First and the only woman to have climbed Mt. Everest twice: **Santosh Yadav (Indian; May, 1992; May, 1993)**
- First person on Mt. Everest without oxygen: **Phu Dorjee (Indian; 1984)**
- First person to climb Mt. Everest twice: **Nawang Gombu**
- First President of the USA: **George Washington**
- First woman Prime Minister: **Sirimavo Bandaranaike (Sri Lanka)**
- First person to swim across English Channel: **Mathew Webb**
- First woman to swim across English Channel: **Gertrude Caroline Ederle**
- First woman to climb Mt. Everest: **Junko Tabei (Japan)**
- First woman to climb Mt. Everest alone and without oxygen supplies: **Alison Hargreaves (Briton: May 13, 1995)**
- First Aeroplane to fly around the world without refuelling: **Voyager (Dec. 1986)**
- First test-tube Baby: **Louise Brown (UK; 1978)**
- First all-talking Film: **Jaz Singer (1927)**
- First Secretary-General of the UN: **Trygve Lie (Norway: 1946-53)**
- First woman President of the UN General Assembly: **Vijayalakshmi Pandit (India: 1953)**

- First woman to reach North Pole: **Ann Bancroft (1986)**
- First person to reach North Pole: **Robert Peary**
- First person to reach South Pole: **Amundsen (1911)**
- First woman to command Spacecraft in space: **Ellin Collins**

☛ Popular Names

Popular Name	*Real Name*
Badshah Khan	Abdul Ghaffar Khan
Bapu, Father of Nation	M.K. Gandhi
Bard of Avon	William Shakespeare
Chachaji *or* Panditji	Jawaharlal Nehru
Desert Fox	Gen. Rommel (Germany)
Desh Bandhu	C.R. Das
Father of English Poetry	Geoffrey Chaucer
Fuhrer	Adolf Hitler
Grand Old Man of India	Dadabhai Naoroji
Grand Old Man of Britain	W.E. Gladstone
Gurudev	Rabindra Nath Tagore
Guruji	M.S. Golwalkar
Grand Commoner	Pitt, the younger
Iron Man of India	Sardar Patel
Lady with the Lamp	Florence Nightingale
Lal, Bal, Pal	Lala Lajpat Rai, Bal Gangadhar Tilak, Bipin Chandra Pal
Li-Kwan	Pearl Buck
Little Corporal *or* Man of Destiny	Napoleon Bonaparte
Lokmanya	Bal Gangadhar Tilak
Lok Nayak	Jayaprakash Narain
Mahamana	Pt. Madan Mohan Malaviya
Maid of Orleans	Joan of Arc
Maiden Queen	Queen Elizabeth I
Man of Blood and Iron	Prince Bismark
Netaji	Subhash Chandra Bose
Nightingale of India	Sarojini Naidu
Priyadarshini	Indira Gandhi
Punjab Kesari	Lala Lajpat Rai
Wizard of the North	Walter Scott

☛ Geographical Surnames

Geographical Surname	*Real Name*
Bengal's Sorrow	Damodar River
Blue Mountains	Nilgiri Hills
China's Sorrow	Hwang-Ho
City of Palaces	Kolkata
City of Skyscrapers *or* Empire City	New York
City of Dreaming Spires	Oxford
Cockpit of Europe	Belgium
Dark Continent	Africa
Emerald Isle	Ireland
Eternal City	Rome
Forbidden City	Lhasa (Tibet)
Gateway of India	Mumbai
Gate of Tears	Strait of Bab-el-mandab
Gift of the Nile	Egypt
Granite City	Aberdeen (Scotland)
Hermit Kingdom	Korea
Holy Land	Jerusalem (Israel)
Island of Pearls	Bahrain (Persian Gulf)
Island of Cloves	Zanzibar
Key to the Mediterranean	Gibraltar
Land of Five Rivers	Punjab
Land of Golden Pagoda	Myanmar
Land of Kangaroo	Australia
Land of Maple Leaf/Lillies	Canada
Land of Midnight Sun	Norway
Land of Morning Calm	Korea
Land of the Rising Sun	Japan
Land of Thousand Lakes	Finland
Land of Thunderbolt	Bhutan
Land of the White Elephants	Thailand
Manchester of the Orient	Osaka (Japan)
Pearl of the Antilles *or* Sugar Bowl of the World	Cuba
Pink City	Jaipur
Playground of Europe	Switzerland
Queen of the Adriatic	Venice (Italy)
Roof of the World	Pamirs
Sick Man of Europe	Turkiye
Venice of the North	Stockholm (Sweden)
Windy City	Chicago
Whiteman's Grave	Guinea Coast of Africa
World's Loneliest Island	Tristan de Cunha

☛ Countries'/Cities' Names—Old and New

Old Name	New Name
Abyssinia	Ethiopia
Basutoland	Lesotho
Bechuanaland	Botswana
British Honduras	Belize
Burma	Myanmar
Ceylon	Sri Lanka
Zaire	Congo
Constantinople	Istanbul
Dahomey	Benin
Dutch East Indies	Indonesia
East Pakistan	Bangladesh
Formosa	Taiwan
Gold Coast	Ghana
Leningrad	St. Petersburg
Leopoldville	Kinshasa
Mesopotamia	Iraq
North Rhodesia	Zambia
Nyasaland	Malawi
Peking	Beijing
Persia	Iran
Rangoon	Yangon
Salisbury	Harare
Siam	Thailand
South West Africa	Namibia
Southern Rhodesia	Zimbabwe
Turkey	Turkiye

☛ Important towns situated on the River Banks

Town	River
Agra	Yamuna
Ahmedabad	Sabarmati
Prayagraj	Confluence of the Ganga and the Yamuna
Ayodhya	Saryu
Baghdad	Tigris
Berlin	Spree
Cairo	Nile
Kolkata	Hooghly
Cuttack	Mahanadi
Delhi	Yamuna
Dibrugarh	Brahmaputra
Dublin	Liffey
Hardwar	Ganga
Hyderabad	Musi
Jabalpur	Narbada
Kanpur	Ganga
Karachi	Indus
Lahore	Ravi
Leh	Indus
London	Thames
Lucknow	Gomati
Nasik	Godavari
New York	Hudson
Paris	Seine
Patna	Ganga
Rome	Tiber
Srinagar	Jhelum
Surat	Tapti
Sydney	Murray-Darling
Varanasi	Ganga
Vienna	Danube
Washington	Potamac
Yangon	Irawadi

☛ Capital & Currencies

Country	Capital	Currency
• Afghanistan	Kabul	Afghani
• Albania	Tirana	Lek
• Algeria	Algiers	Dinar
• Angola	Luanda	New Kwanza
• Argentina	Buenos Aires	Peso
• Armenia	Yeravan	Dram
• Australia	Canberra	Dollar
• Austria	Vienna	Euro
• Azerbaijan	Baku	Manat
• Bahrain	Manama	Dinar
• Bangladesh	Dhaka	Taka
• Barbados	Bridgetown	Dollar
• Belarus	Minsk	Ruble
• Belgium	Brussels	Euro
• Benin	Porto Novo	Franc
• Bhutan	Thimphu	Ngultrum[1]
• Bolivia	La paz	Dollar
• Botswana	Gaborone	Pula
• Brazil	Brasilia	Real

Country	Capital	Currency
• Bosnia	Sarajevo Herzegovina	Dinar
• Bulgaria	Sofia	Lev
• Cambodia	Phnom-Penh	Riel
• Canada	Ottawa	Dollar
• Chile	Santiago	Peso
• China	Beijing	Yuan
• Colombia	Bogota	Peso
• Congo	Brazzaville	Franc
• Croatia	Zagreb	Kuna
• Cuba	Havana	Peso
• Cyprus	Nicosia	Pound
• Czech Republic	Prague	Koruna
• Denmark	Copenhagen	Krone
• Ecuador	Quito	Sucre
• Egypt	Cairo	Pound
• Estonia	Tallinn	Kroon
• Ethiopia	Addis Ababa	Birr
• Fiji	Suva	Dollar
• Finland	Helsinki	Euro
• France	Paris	Euro
• Georgia	Tbilisi	Lari
• Germany	Berlin	Euro
• Ghana	Accra	Cedi
• Greece	Athens	Euro
• Guatemala	Guatemala City	Quetzal
• Guyana	George Town	Dollar
• Hungary	Budapest	Forint
• Iceland	Reykjavik	Krona
• India	New Delhi	Rupee
• Indonesia	Jakarta	Rupiah
• Iran	Teheran	Rial
• Iraq	Baghdad	Dinar
• Ireland	Dublin	Euro
• Israel	Jerusalem	Shekel
• Italy	Rome	Euro
• Jamaica	Kingston	Dollar
• Japan	Tokyo	Yen
• Jordan	Amman	Dinar
• Kazakhstan	Akmola	Tenge
• Kenya	Nairobi	Shilling
• Korea (S)	Seoul	Won
• Korea (N)	Pyongyang	Won
• Kyrgyzstan	Bishkek	Som
• Kuwait	Kuwait City	Dinar

Country	Capital	Currency
• Laos	Vientiane	Kip
• Latvia	Riga	Lats
• Lebanon	Beirut	Pound
• Liberia	Monrovia	Dollar
• Libya	Tripoli	Dinar
• Lithuania	Vilnius	Litas
• Luxembourg	Luxembourg	Euro
• Macedonia	Skopje	Dinar
• Malawi	Lilongwe	Kwacha
• Malaysia	Kuala Lumpur	Ringgit
• Maldives	Male	Rufiyaa
• Mali	Bamako	Franc
• Mauritius	Port Louis	Rupee
• Mexico	Mexico City	Peso
• Moldavia	Chisinau	Leu
• Mongolia	Ulan Bator	Tugrik
• Morocco	Rabat	Dirham
• Mozambique	Maputo	Metical
• Myanmar	Nay Pyi Taw	Kyat
• Namibia	Winohoek	Dollar
• Nepal	Kathmandu	Rupee
• Netherlands	Amsterdam	Euro
• New Zealand	Wellington	Dollar
• Nigeria	Abuja	Naira
• Norway	Oslo	Krone
• Oman	Muscat	Rial
• Pakistan	Islamabad	Rupee
• Panama	Panama City	Balboa
• Peru	Lima	New Sole
• Philippines	Manila	Peso
• Poland	Warsaw	Zloty
• Portugal	Lisbon	Euro
• Qatar	Doha	Riyal
• Romania	Bucharest	Leu
• Russia	Moscow	Ruble
• Saudi Arabia	Riyadh	Rial
• Senegal	Dakar	Franc
• Slovakia	Bratislava	Koruna (Crown)
• Spain	Madrid	Euro
• Sri Lanka	Colombo	Rupee
• Sudan	Khartoum	Dinar
• Suriname	Paramaribo	Guilder
• Sweden	Stockholm	Krona

Country	Capital	Currency
• Switzerland	Berne	Swiss Francs
• Syria	Damascus	Pound
• South Africa	Capetown (Legislative) Pretoria *(Administrative)*	Rand
• Tadzhikistan	Dushanbe	Ruble
• Taiwan	Taipei	Dollar
• Tanzania	Dodoma	Shilling
• Thailand	Bangkok	Baht
• Tunisia	Tunis	Dinar
• Turkiye	Ankara	Lira
• Turkmania	Ashikabad	Manat
• Uganda	Kampala	Shilling
• Ukraine	Kiev	Hyrvnia
• United Arab Emirates	Abu Dhabi	Dirham
• U.K.	London	Pound Sterling
• U.S.A.	Washington	Dollar
• Uruguay	Montevideo	Peso
• Uzbekistan	Tashkent	Som
• Venezuela	Caracas	Bolivar
• Vietnam	Hanoi	Dong
• Yemen	Sana'a	Rial
• Zimbabwe	Harare	Dollar
• Congo (Democratic Republic)	Kinshasa	Franc
• Zambia	Lusaka	Kwacha

☛ Geographical Explorations/Discoveries

Place	Explorer/Discoverer	Nationality	Year
America	Christopher Columbus	Italy	1492
Hawaii Islands (Sandwich Islands)	Captain James Cook	England	1778
Newfoundland	John Cabot	England	1497
New Zealand	Abel Janszoon Tasman	Holland	1642
North Pole	Robert Peary	USA	1909
Sea Route to India (via Cape of Good Hope)	Vasco da Gama	Portugal	1498
South Pole	Roald Amundsen	Norway	1911

☛ World Famous Official Documents

- **White Paper:** India
- **Orange Book:** Netherlands
- **Yellow Book:** France
- **Green Book:** Italy and Iran
- **White Book:** Portugal, China and Germany
- **Grey Book:** Japan and Belgium.

☛ Animals (Largest and Biggest)

- Fastest animal at short run: *Cheetah*
- Largest existing land animal: *Elephant*
- Largest bird of prey: *Condor, length of the bird is 4 ft.*
- Largest neck (animal): *Giraffe*
- Largest quadruped of the dog family: *Wolf*
- Largest animal of the cat family: *Lion*
- Largest ape or anthropoid: *Goerilla*
- Largest sea animal (mammal): *Blue whale*
- Smallest bird: *Humming bird*
- Longest lived creature: *Blue whale (500 years)*
- Most intelligent animal: *Chimpanzee*
- Tallest animal: *Giraffe*
- Largest bird: *Ostrich*
- The bird that never makes its nest: *Cuckoo*
- Largest sea-bird: *Albatross*
- Fastest bird: *Swift*
- The tree that weeps: *Laurel tree, in the Canary Islands*
- The bird that hides itself in sand, when attacked: *Ostrich*
- The wingless bird or flightless bird: *Kiwi (New Zealand)*
- The animal that can shakes off its tail: *Whale*
- The reptile which changes its colour: *Chameleon*
- The tree from which cricket bat is obtained: *Willow*

☛ National Monuments of Some Famous Countries

Monument	Country	Monument	Country
Great Wall of China	China	Pyramid (Giza)	Egypt
Taj Mahal (Agra)	India	Kinder Disk	Denmark
Emperial Palace (Tokyo)	Japan	Leaning Tower of Pisa	Italy
Opera House (Sydney)	Australia	Statue of Liberty (New York)	USA
Eiffel Tower (Paris)	France	Kremlin (Moscow)	Russia

☛ The Seven Wonders of the World

Ancient World	Modern World	The 'New' Wonder
• The Great Pyramid of Giza	Panama Canal	The Taj Mahal, India
• The Temple of Artemis at Ephesus	Channel Tunnel	Chichen Itza, Mexico
• The Lighthouse of Alexandria	CN Tower	Machu Picchu, Peru
• The Mausoleum at Halicarnassus	Itaipu Dam	Christ Redeemer, Brazil
• The Colossus	Empire State Building	Petra, Jordan
• The Hanging Gardens of Babylon	Golden Gate Bridge	Colosseum, Italy
• The Statue of Zeus of Olympia	Delta Works	The Great Wall, China

☛ Intelligence Agencies of Some Prominent Countries

Country	Intelligence Agency
• India	*Research & Analysis Wing (RAW), Intelligence Bureau (I.B.), Central Bureau of Investigation (C.B.I.)*
• Pakistan	*Inter Service Intelligence (I.S.I.)*
• U.S.A.	*Central Intelligence Agency, Federal Bureau of Investigation*
• Britain	*Military Intelligence (M.I.)-5 and 6, Special Branch, Ultra, Joint Intelligence Organisation*
• Israel	*Mosad*
• Egypt	*Mukhabarat*
• Japan	*Nicho*
• Russia	*K.G.B. (Komitel Gosudarstvennoy Bezopasnosty) (Committee for State Security)*
• Canada	*Security Intelligence Service*
• S. Africa	*Bureau of State Security*
• Iran	*Sabak*
• Iraq	*Al-Mukhabarat*
• Australia	*Australian Security and Intelligence Organisation*
• France	*S.D.E.C.E.*
• Spain	*C.E.S.I.D.*

☛ Important News Agencies of the World

Agency	Country	Agency	Country
PTI, UNI, UNIVARTA	India	Antara	Indonesia
Tanjug	Serbia	Associated Press (AP)	America
Reuters, NAFEN	United Kingdom	Angence France Press (AFP)	France
TASS	Russia		

☛ Famous Newspapers of the World

Newspaper	Place of Publishing	Language	Newspaper	Place of Publishing	Language
• Daily News	New York (America)	*English*	• Guardian	London (Britain)	*English*
• Pravada	Moscow (Russia)	*Russian*	• Al-Ahram	Cairo (Egypt)	*Arabic*
• Merdeca	Jakarta (Indonesia)	*Indonesian*	• Times	London (Britain)	*English*
• People's Daily	Beijing (China)	*Chinese*	• New Statesman	Britain	*English*
• Daily Mirror	Britain	*English*			
• Hindu, Hindustan, Times of India, Tribune, Statesman, Indian Express, Economic Times	India	*English*	• Hindustan, Nav Bharat Times, Rashtriya Sahara, Dainik Jagaran, Punjab Kesari	India	*Hindi*

☛ Name of Parliaments of Some Countries

Country	Name of Parliament	Country	Name of Parliament
Afghanistan	Shora	Norway	Storting
Argentina	National Congress	Poland	Sejm
Australia	Federal Parliament	Russia	Federal Assembly (Council of the Federation and State Duma
Austria	National Assembly	South Africa	National Assembly and Senate
Bangladesh	Jatiya Sangsad	Spain	Cortes Generales
India	Lok Sabha and Rajya Sabha	Sweden	Riksdag
Bhutan	Tshogdu (National Assembly)	Switzerland	Federal Assembly (Nationalrat and Standerat)
Britain	House of Commons and House of Lords	North Korea	Supreme People's Assembly
Canada	House of Commons and Senate	South Korea	National Assembly
China	National People Congress	U.S.A.	Congress (Senate and House of Representatives)
Denmark	Folketing	Ethiopia	Federal Council and House of Representatives
Iran	Majlis (Islamic Consultative Assembly)	Iceland	Alpingi
Israel	Knesset	Bulgaria	National Assembly
Japan	Diet	Cuba	National Assembly of People's Power
Myanmar	Pyithu Hluttaw (People's Assembly)		
Nepal	Rashtriya Panchayat		
The Netherlands	States-General		

☛ Important Cities, Places, Buildings of the World

- **Angkor Vat:** It is a large group of old Hindu temples in Cambodia; a remnant of the Khmer civilisation. The temples were constructed in the first half of the 12th century.
- **Big Ben:** A clock on the tower of the British Parliament building, installed in 1856.
- **Bethlehem:** A town in Jordan; birth place of Christ; a place of pilgrimage.
- **Cape Canaveral:** Situated in Florida (U.S.A.), it is America's spaceship launching centre. Formerly it was known as *Cape Kennedy.*
- **Eiffel Tower:** A tower in Paris (985 ft high); the principal landmark of the city; designed by a French Engineer for the Paris Exposition 1889.
- **Fleet Street:** A street in London, where offices of newspapers are situated.
- **Golden Gate Bridge (U.S.A.):** One of the world's longest suspension bridges, built in 1933-37 across the entrance (Golden Gate) of San Francisco Bay in California. It has a length of 9266 ft.
- **Harappa:** Situated near Montgomery (Pakistan). The famous ruins throw light on 5000-year-old Indus Valley Civilisation.
- **Hiroshima:** A city in Japan; it was the target of the first atom bomb ever dropped on a city (by U.S.A. on August 6, 1945); casualities numbered nearly 1,30,000 and ninety per cent of the city was levelled.
- **India Office Library (London):** A museum of Indian historical works, collected by the British. The library consists of about 3,00,000 books, a large number of manuscripts in Sanskrit, Urdu, Persian and Arabic.
- **Kaaba:** The inner shrine of the great Mosque at Mecca in Saudi Arabia. It is the most sacred place. Muslims face the Kaaba when praying.
- **Karakoram Highway:** It is a 800-km all weather road linking border of China's Sinkiang province with Pakistan.
- **Leaning Tower of Pisa:** A white marble monument (179 feet high) built in the 14th Century in Italy. It is inclined to one side.
- **Mohenjodaro:** Situated in the Larkana District of Sind (Pakistan); ancient ruins throw light on 5,000-year-old Indus Valley Civilisation.
- **Oval, Leeds and Lords (England):** Famous for cricket matches.
- **Panama Canal:** Canal connecting the Atlantic and Pacific Oceans. The canal is 50 miles long and has 12 locks. It was opened to traffic in August, 1914. The canal is administered by the U.S.A.
- **Pentagon (Washington, USA):** It is a five-sided building housing the US Defence Department offices.
- **Burj Khalifa:** It is a 162 storeyed structure built in Dubai having a height of 818 meter. It is now the highest structure of the world. Taipei 101 (508 meter) is now the second highest structure of the world.
- **Pyramids:** Gigantic stone buildings built by the ancient Egyptians in 2700 B.C.; among the seven wonders of the world. The great pyramid at Giza is the largest. These pyramids were tombs for the pharaohs and other important people.
- **Scotland Yard:** Headquarters of the Criminal Investigation Department in London. It is known all over world for its efficient working.
- **Sandhurst (England):** Famous military training institution.
- **Sphinx:** Mythical beast of ancient Egypt; usually represented in art as having a human head and the body of a lion. The most famous one is the great Sphinx, a colossal stone figure at Gizah built in the 26th Century BC.
- **Stonehenge:** Prehistoric monument near Salisbury, England built in between 1800 B.C. and 1500 B.C.
- **Suez Canal:** This canal is an important link between the Mediterranean Sea and the Red Sea. It is about 160 km long and was constructed in 1869 by a French Engineer. It has shortened

the distance between Southampton (England) and Bombay (now Mumbai) by about 4,000 miles. The canal was nationalised by Col. Nasser on July 26, 1956. Port Said is the famous port at the entry from Mediterranean Sea.

- **Vatican:** Official residence of the Pope (in Rome). The smallest country. It enjoys a separate entity in the world. (Area 109 acres).
- **Wall Street (New York):** Famous stock exchange market.

☛ *Some Prominent Races of the World*

Races	*Country*	*Races*	*Country*
Veddas	Sri Lanka	Somaid	West Siberia
Masai	East Africa	Muree	New Zealand
Yakoot	Russian Tundra	Papuans	New Guyana
Pygmy	Congo Basin	Bantu	Central and South Africa
Tartars	Siberia	Baddu	Arab's Desert
Semang	Malaysia	Eskimo	Canada, Tundra Region
Lapps	European Tundra	Hausa	Nigeria
Kirghiz	Steppes (Russia)	Bushman	Kalahari Desert
Red Indian	North America		

☛ *Famous Religions, Founders, Holy Books & Places of Worship*

Religion	*Founder*	*Holy Books*	*Place of Worship*
Hinduism	Hinduism has no one Founder. (This religion is based upon the religion of original Aryan Settlers)	Ramayan, Vedas, Puranas and Geeta	Temple
Sikh	Guru Nanak Dev	Guru Granth Sahib	Gurdwara
Christianity	Jesus Christ	Bible	Church
Islam	Prophet Mohammed	Koran (Quran)	Mosque
Parsi	Zoroaster	Zend Avesta	Fire Temple
Jainism	Adinath Rishavdev	Jain Granth	Jain Temple
Buddhism	Gautam Buddha	Tripitaka	Buddha Temple
Jew	Moosa	Torah	Synagogue

☛ *Principal Ten Language of the World*

Language	*Speaker of the Language (In Millions)*	*Language*	*Speaker of the Language (In Millions)*
Chinese	1,322.8	Arabic	349.3
English	369.9	Bengali	228.7
Hindi	342.2	Portuguese	232.4
Spanish	471.4	Japanese	126.3
Russian	153.7	Lahnda	99.6

Source: The World Almanac 2022.

UNITED NATIONS ORGANISATION

- **Origin:** UN Charter was signed by 50 members on June 26, 1945. It officially came into existence on October 24, 1945.
- **UN Charter:** The Charter is the Constitution of the UNO and contains its aims and objectives and rules and regulations for its functioning.
- **Aims and Objectives:** They are security, welfare and human rights.
- **Headquarters:** New York.
- **Flag:** The flag is light blue in colour, and emblazoned in white, in its centre is the UN symbol—a polar map of world embraced by twin olive branches open at the top.
- **Official Languages:** The official languages of the UN are: English, French, Chinese, Russian, Arabic and Spanish. However, working languages are English & French only.
- **Main Organs of the UNO:** There are six main organs:
  1. General Assembly
  2. Security Council
  3. Economic and Social Council
  4. Trusteeship Council
  5. International Court of Justice, and
  6. Secretariat.

☛ *Famous International Organisations and their Headquarters*

International Organisations	*Headquarters*
• United Nations Organisations (U.N.O.)	New York
• International Monetary Fund (I.M.F.)	Washington
• World Health Organisation (W.H.O.)	Geneva
• Food & Agricultural Organisation (FAO)	Rome
• International Labour Organisation (ILO)	Geneva
• UNESCO	Paris
• International Court of Justice	The Hague
• Universal Postal Union (UPU)	Berne
• International Civil Aviation Organisation (ICAO)	Montreal
• UNIDO	Vienna
• International Atomic Energy Agency (IAEA)	Vienna
• International Finance Corporation (IFC)	Washington
• United Nations Development Programme (UNDP)	New York
• UNICEF	New York
• International Maritime Organisation (IMO)	London
• World Meteorological Organisation (WMO)	Geneva
• International Telecommunication Union (ITU)	Geneva
• Arab League	Cairo
• Commonwealth of Nations	London
• World Trade Organisation (WTO)	Geneva
• International Development Association (IDA)	Washington D.C.
• International Bank for Reconstruction and Development (IBRD)	Washington D.C.
• World Intellectual Property Organisation (WIPO)	Geneva
• Organisation of Islamic Cooperation (OIC)	Jeddah (Saudi Arabia)

Organisation	Headquarters
• Red Cross	Geneva
• Interpol	Lyons
• Asian Development Bank (ADB)	Manila
• North Atlantic Treaty Organisation (NATO)	Brussels
• Association of South East Asian Nations (ASEAN)	Jakarta
• South Asian Association for Regional Cooperation (SAARC)	Kathmandu
• Asia-Pacific Economic Cooperation (APEC)	–
• Organisation for Economic Cooperation and Development (OECD)	Paris
• Organisation of Petroleum Exporting Countries (OPEC)	Vienna
• Common Wealth of Independent States (CIS)	Minsk
• International Olympic Committee (IOC)	Switzerland
• European Union (EU)	Brussels
• Amnesty International (AI)	London
• Shanghai Cooperation Organisation (SCO)	—

DEFENCE

India's Armed Forces

- President of India is the Supreme Commander of the Armed Forces of India.
- Union Cabinet is responsible for national defence.
- Operational control of the armed forces is exercised by the Ministry of Defence.
- The armed forces consist of three services namely:
  (*i*) Army, (*ii*) Navy and (*iii*) Air Force.
- The three services function under their respective Chiefs of Staff namely:
  (*i*) Chief of the Army Staff,
  (*ii*) Chief of the Naval Staff and
  (*iii*) Chief of the Air Staff.
- The post of the Chief of Defence Staff (CDS) was created in 2019. General Bipin Rawat was the first CDS of India.

Army

- Army Headquarters is in New Delhi.
- Army is organised into 7 Commands, *viz.* (*i*) Southern, (*ii*) Eastern, (*iii*) Western, (*iv*) Central, (*v*) Northern (*vi*) South Western and (*vii*) Army Training Command.
- Each Command is under a General Officer Commanding-in-Chief.
- Army consists of a number of arms and services such as: (*i*) Armoured Corps, (*ii*) Regiment of Artillery, (*iii*) Corps of Air Defence, (*iv*) Army Aviation Corps, (*v*) Corps of Engineers/Signals, (*vi*) Infantry, (*vii*) Army Medical/ Nursing Corps, (*viii*) Army Education Corps, (*ix*) Corps of Military Police etc.

Navy

- Navy Headquarters is in New Delhi.
- The Navy has 3 commands—(*i*) Western, (*ii*) Eastern and (*iii*) Southern.
- Each Command is headed by a Flag Officer Commanding-in-Chief.
- The Western and the Eastern Commands are operational commands with their fleets while the Southern Command is responsible for all training activities of Indian Navy.
- Fleets of Indian Navy comprise warships, submarines, aircraft carriers, etc.
- There are two major naval bases at Mumbai and Visakhapatnam.
- Coast Guard was constituted in 1978 with its headquarters at New Delhi. It is responsible for defence and security of India's marine interests and assets.

Air Force

- Air Force Headquarters is in New Delhi.
- Air Force is organised into 5 operational Commands—(*i*) Western Air Command, (*ii*) South-Western Air Command, (*iii*) Central Air Command, (*iv*) Eastern Air Command, and (*v*) Southern Air Command.
- There are two functional commands—(*i*) Maintenance Command, and (*ii*) Training Command.
- Air Force fleet consists of fighter bombers, fighters, Transport, Interceptors and logistic aircrafts and helicopters. Strike aircrafts are: MIG-21, MIG-23, MIG-25, MIG-27, Rafale and Jaguar, Air Defence Aircrafts are: MIG 29, Mirage-2000. Transport fleet consists of AN-32, Boeing-737, HS-748. Helicopters are: MI-8, MI-17, Chetak/Cheetah.
- Chetak/Cheetah helicopters are manufactured by Hindustan Aeronautics Limited (HAL).

☛ Commissioned Ranks in Defence Services

Army	*Navy*	*Air Force*
• General	Admiral	Air Chief Marshal
• Lieutenant-General	Vice-Admiral	Air Marshal
• Major-General	Rear-Admiral	Air Vice-Marshal
• Brigadier	Commodor	Air Commodor
• Colonel	Captain	Group Captain
• Lieutenant-Colonel	Commander	Wing Commander
• Major	Lt.Commander	Squadron Leader
• Captain	Lieutenant	Flight Lieutenant
• Lieutenant	Sub-Lieutenant	Flying Officer

☛ Commanders-in-Chiefs

1. General Sir Rob Lockhart	Aug. 15, 1947 — Dec. 31, 1947
2. General Roy Bucher	Jan. 1, 1948 — Jan. 14, 1949
3. General K. M. Kariappa	Jan. 15, 1949 — Jan. 14, 1953
4. General Maharaj Rajendra Sinhji	Jan. 15, 1953 — March 31, 1955

☛ First Indian Chiefs of Staff of Indian Forces

1. General Maharaj Rajendra Sinhji (Army Staff)	April 1, 1955 — May 14, 1955
2. Vice Admiral R D. Katari (Naval Staff)	April 22, 1958 — June 4, 1962
3. Air Marshal S. Mukherjee (Air Staff)	April 1, 1954 — Nov. 08, 1960

☛ Army Institutes

1. Sainik Schools upto +2 Level	33 places in India
2. Rashtriya Indian Military College (prepare for entrance to N.D.A)	Dehradun
3. National Defence Academy (three services)	Khadakwasla, Pune
4. Indian Military Academy (Army)	Dehradun
5. Officers Training Academy (3 services) Short Courses	Chennai
6. National Defence College	New Delhi
7. The College of Combat	Mhow
8. The College of Military Engineering	Kirkee
9. Military College of Telecommunication Engineering	Mhow
10. The armoured Corps Centre and School	Ahmed Nagar
11. The School Artillery	Deolali
12. The Infantry School	Mhow and Belgaum
13. College of Material Management	Jabalpur

CULTURAL ACTIVITIES

Dance

India has a very rich tradition of tribal, folk and classical dances.

Classical Dance

Dance	State	Famous Artists
• Bharat Natyam	Tamil Nadu	Yamini Krishnamurthy, Rukmini Devi Arundale, Swapna Sundari, Sonal Mansingh, Vaijanti Mala, Mrinalini Sarabhai, Chandralekha, Indrani, Ram Gopal, Bal Saraswati
• Kathakali	Kerala	Gopinath, K.K. Nayar, Kunju-Kurup, T.K. Chandu
• Kuchipudi	Andhra Pradesh	Sapna Sundari, Raja Reddy, Radha Reddy, Vedantam Satyanarayan, Vimpanti Chinna Satyam.
• Kathak	North India	Birju Maharaj, Gopi Krishna, Shambhu Maharaj, Sitara Devi, Vishnu Sharma, Durga Lal, Shobhana Narayan
• Odissi	Odisha	Kelucharan Mahapatra, Indrani Rehman, Madhavi Mudgal, Pratima Bedi, Samyukta Panigrahi, Sonal Mansingh, Debudas
• Manipuri	Manipur	Uday Shankar, Bipin Singh, Suryamukhi, Darohra Jhaveri

Famous Folk-Dance

- Andhra Pradesh: *Dandari, Banjara*
- Asom: *Bihu, Keli Gopal, Sataria*
- Bihar: *Chhau, Magahi, Durga dance*
- W. Bengal: *Kirtan, Kalatri, Asweabadh, Brita, Kalidance*
- Chhattisgarh: *Saila, Karama, Bhagoria*
- Gujarat: *Garba, Rasalila, Tippani, Dandia,*
- Haryana: *Damyal, Lahoor*
- Himachal Pradesh: *Dussehra dance, Hikat, Notio*
- Jammu & Kashmir: *Dumhal*
- Jharkhand: *Jhau, Ghumakudia, Jadur, Sarhul, Soharai, Karama, Vaima, Loojhari, Jat-Jatin, Vidayat*
- Karnataka: *Yakshagan, Dolu Kunitha*
- Kerala: *Mohini Attam, Padayuni*
- Madhya Pradesh: *Lota Nritya, Jawara*
- Maharashtra: *Tamasha, Dahi Handi, Gof, Deepak Dindi*
- Manipur: *Dhol Cholam*
- Meghalaya: *Nongakarem*
- Nagaland: *Bamboo dance*
- Odisha: *Chhau, Maya Shabari, Dalachai*
- Punjab: *Gidda, Bhangra, Panihari*
- Rajasthan: *Ghumar, Kathaputali, Tera Tali*
- Tamil Nadu: *Terukalathu, Kabalatam, Kargam, Pulivesham*
- Tripura: *Hazagiri*
- Uttar Pradesh: *Rasalila, Nautanki, Thali, Huraka, Dhurang, Jhumela, Bol.*
- Uttarakhand: *Kajari, Karan*
- Goa: *Dhode Modini*

Musical Instruments and Artists

- **Flute:** Hari Prasad Chaurasia, Panna Lal Ghosh, T.R. Mahalingam, N. Ramani, Vijaya Raghava Rao
- **Tabla:** Allah Rakha, Gudai Maharaj, Latif Khan, Zakir Hussain
- **Violin:** Lalgudi Jayaraman, L. Subramaniam, M.S. Gopal Krishnan, S. Subrahmaniam, V.G. Jog, N. Rajan
- **Shehnai:** Bismilla Khan, Imrat Khan

- **Sarod:** Ali Akbar Khan, Amjad Ali Khan, Alauddin Khan, Saren Rani, Brij Narayan
- **Sitar:** Pandit Ravishankar, Vilayat Khan
- **Santur:** Shiv Kumar Sharma
- **Rudraveena:** Zia Mohiuddin Dagar
- **Pakhawaj:** Govind Rao, Anokhe Lal, Kanthi Maharaj
- **Mridanga:** Palghat R. Raghu, U.S. Burman
- **Harmonium:** Purushottam Walawakar, M. Dhaulpuri
- **Guitar:** Pt. Vishnu Mohan Bhatt, Brij Bhushan Kalra
- **Ghatam:** T.H. Vinayakaram
- **Janjira:** V. Nagarajan
- **Symphony:** Jubin Mehta

☛ Major Parks & Wild Life Sanctuaries in India

India is rich in flora and fauna. However, due to increasing population and industrial and commercial activities, there has been acute pressure on forests. The Government has taken several steps to check the sharp fall in the number of these species. Among the measures are declaration of certain habitats as national parks and sanctuaries. 106 national parks and 573 sanctuaries have been esta-blished till March 2025, important ones being given below:

- **Assam:** Kaziranga National Park (known for one-horn Rhinoceroses); Manas Sanctuary.
- **Jharkhand:** Hazaribagh National Park; Betla Tiger Reserve Palamau.
- **Gujarat:** Valvadar National Park, Bhavnagar; Marine National Park, Gir Forests.
- **Himachal Pradesh:** Rohla National Park; Motichur Sanctuary.
- **Jammu & Kashmir:** Dachigam Sanctuary.
- **Karnataka:** Bandipur National Park; Bannargheta National Park, Bengaluru; Nagorhole National Park, Coorg; Ranganthitto Bird Sanctuary.
- **Kerala:** Eravikulam Rajmallay National Park. Idduki; Periyar Game Sanctuary.
- **Madhya Pradesh:** Kanha National Park; Bandhavgarh National Park, Shahdol; Shivpuri National Park.
- **Maharashtra:** Taloba National Park, Chandrapur; Pench National Park, Nagpur; Borivali National Park, Mumbai; Nawagaon National Park, Bandara; Melghat National Park.
- **Manipur:** Reibul Lamjao National Park.
- **Odisha:** Simlipal Tiger Sanctuary.
- **Rajasthan:** Sariska Sanctuary; Ghana Bird Sanctuary, Ranthambhor Sanctuary.
- **Sikkim:** Khangchandzenda National Park, Gangtok.
- **Tamil Nadu:** Vedanthangal Bird Sanctuary; Guindy National Park, Chennai; Mudumalai Sanctuary; Kalakad-Munden Thurai Reserve.
- **Uttar Pradesh:** Chandraprabha Sanctuary; Dudhwa National Park, Lakhimpur.
- **West Bengal:** Jaldapara Sanctuary; Sunderbans.
- **Uttarakhand:** Corbett National Park, Nainital.

BOOKS AND AUTHORS

☛ Foreign

Book	Author
Aesop's Fables	Aesop
Adventure of Robinson Crusoe	Daniel Defoe
Adventures of Sherlok Holmes	Arthur Conan Doyle
Alice in Wonderland	Lewis Carrol
Apple Cart	G.B.Shaw
Arabian Nights	Sir Richard Burton
Around the World in Eighty Days	Jules Verne
As You Like It	William Shakespeare
A Tale of Two Cities	Charles Dickens
A Tale of Two Gardens	Octavio Paz
A Thousand Suns	Dominique Lapierre

Book	Author
August Coup	Mikhail S. Gorbachev
Ben Hur	Lewis Wallace
Candida	G.B. Shaw
Das Kapital	Karl Marx
David Copperfield	Charles Dickens
Divine Comedy	A. Dante
Doctor's Dilemma	G.B. Shaw
Famished Road	Ben Okri
Freedom From Fear	Aung San Suu Kyi
Gulistan Bostan	Sheikh Saadi
Gulliver's Travels	Jonathan Swift
Hamlet	William Shakespeare
Iliad	Homer
Inferno	A. Dante
In Memoriam	Lord Tennyson
Ivanhoe	Walter Scott
Julius Caesar	William Shakespeare
Lady Chatterley's Lover	D.H. Lawrence
Lajja	Taslima Nasreen
Les Miserable	Victor Hugo
Leviathan	Thomas Hobbes
Lolita	V. Nobokov
Lycidas	John Milton
Mein Kampf	Adolf Hitler
Merchant of Venice	William Shakespeare
Midnight's Children	Salman Rushdie
Moor's Last Sigh	Salman Rushdie
Mother	Maxim Gorky
Mother India	Katherine Mayo
Nana	Emile Zola

Book	Author
Ninteen Eighty Four	George Orwell
Odyssey	Homer
Origin of Species	Charles Darwin
Othello	William Shakespeare
Paradise Lost	John Milton
Paradise Regained	John Milton
Path to Power	Margaret Thatcher
Pickwick Papers	Charles Dickens
Pride and Prejudice	Jane Austen
Razor's Edge	Somerset Maugham
Republic	Plato
Romeo and Juliet	William Shakespeare
Rubaiyat-i-Omar Khayyam	Edward Fitzgerald (Translator)
Shape of Things to Come	H.G. Wells
The Satanic Verses	Salman Rushdie
The Social Contract	Rousseau
The Tempest	William Shakespeare
Time Machine	H.G. Wells
Tom Sawyer	Mark Twain
Treasure Island	R.L. Stevenson
Twelfth Night	William Shakespeare
Uncle Tom's Cabin	H.B.Stowe
Utopia	Thomas More
Universe Around Us	James Jeans
Vicar of Wakefield	Oliver Goldsmith
War and Peace	Leo Tolstoy
Wealth of Nations	Adam Smith
Wonder That was India	A.L. Basham
Wuthering Heights	Emily Bronte

☛ Indian

Book	Author
Abhigyan Shakuntalam	Kalidas
Ain-i-Akbari	Abul Fazal
Anand Math	Bankim Chandra Chatterjee
Arthashastra	Kautilya
A Suitable Boy	Vikram Seth
Bhagwat Gita	Ved Vyas
Chidambara	Sumitranandan Pant
Devdas	Sarat Chandra Chatterjee
Diwan-i-Ghalib	Mirza Ghalib

Book	Author
Discovery of India	Jawaharlal Nehru
Essays on Gita	Aurobindo Ghosh
Eternal India	Indira Gandhi
Faces of Everest	Major H.P.S. Ahluwalia
Ganadevata	Tarashankar Bandopadhyaya
Geet Govind	Jaya Dev
Geetanjali	R. N. Tagore
Glimpses of World History	Jawaharlal Nehru
Godaan	Prem Chand

Book	Author
Gul-e-Nagma	Firaq Gorakhpuri
Gunahon ka Devta	Dharmveer Bharti
Harsh Charita	Bana Bhatta
Hindu View of Life	S. Radhakrishnan
Idols	Sunil Gavaskar
India Divided	Dr. Rajendra Prasad
The Judgement	Kuldip Nayyar
Juhi ki Kali	Surya Kant Tripathi 'Nirala'
Justice of Peace ke Aansu	Janardan Prasad Singh
Chand ka Munh Terha Hai	Muktibodh
Kapalkundala	Bankim Chandra Chatterjee
Kadambari	Bana Bhatta
Kagaz Te Kanwas	Amrita Pritam
Kamayani	Jai Shankar Prasad
Kitni Nawon Main	S. H. Vatsyayan
Kitni Bar	
Kumar Sambhav	Kalidas
Mahabharata	Ved Vyas
Malgudi Days	R.K. Narayan
Manvini Bhavai	Pannalal Patel
Mati Matal	Gopi Nath Mohanty
Meghdoot	Kalidas
Meena Kumari	Vinod Mehta
Meri Sansadiya Yatra	Atal Behari Vajpayee
Mritunjaya	B.K. Bhattacharya
Mudrarakshasa	Vishakhadatta

Book	Author
My Experiments with Truth	M.K. Gandhi
My Own Boswell	M. Hidayatullah
My Presidential Years	R. Venkataraman
Nisheeth	Uma Shankar Joshi
'No, Sir'	P.G. Mavlankar
One Day Wonders	Sunil Gavaskar
Panchtantra	Vishnu Sharma
Passage to England	Nirad C. Chaudhuri
Prison Diary	Jaya Prakash Narayan
Raghuvansha	Kalidas
Rajtarangini	Kalhana
Ramayana	Balmiki
Ramcharit Manas	Tulsidas
Rukh Te Rishi	Harbhajan Singh
Satyarth Prakash	Swami Dayanand
Sur Sagar	Surdas
The Guide	R.K. Narayan
The Insider	P.V. Narasimharao
The Post Office — (Dak Ghar)	Rabindra Nath Tagore
The God of Small Things	Arundhati Roy
Urvashi	Ram Dhari Singh 'Dinkar'
Yama	Mahadevi Verma
My Country : My Life (Autobiography)	L.K. Advani
The Test of My Life	Yuvraj Singh
Twenty Years in a Decade	Shah Rukh Khan

COMPUTER

- The computer is the system of that electronic device through which various informations are processed on the basis of a definite set of instructions called program and mathematical (numerical) and non-mathematical both types of informations are processed.
- The first mechanical computer was composed or fabricated by Blaise Pascal in 1642 and it is called Pascalene.
- But in 1833, Charles Babbage first time conceived an automatic calculator or computer.
- Charles Babbage is called the father of modern computer.
- Herman made an electronic tabulating machine based on punch cards which operates automatically.
- In 1937, first mechanical computer mark-I was fabricated by Howard Akeen.
- The most outstanding contribution in the development of modern computer goes to John Wan Newmaan who brought the 2nd revolution in the area of computer in 1951.
- He discovered EDVAC (Electronic Discrete Variable Automatic Computer) and utilised the stored program and the binary number system in the computer.

☛ Functions of Computer

- 1. Collection and composition (input) of datas;
  2. Storage of datas.
  3. Processing of datas.
  4. Retrieval or output of the proccessed informations and datas.

☛ Units of Computer

1. Input unit.
2. Central processing unit–CPU.
3. External Memory unit.
4. Output unit.

- The CPU of the computer is called brain of the computer and sometimes CPU is also called Micro Processor of the computer.
- The data is entered through the input unit in the computer and through the central processing unit with the help of External Memory Unit datas are arranged and processed.
- Ultimately by the output unit these datas or informations are issued or released.

☛ Parts of Computer

- **Monitor :** The monitor of the computer is like a television in which the picture appears in the form of doted points on the screen and these are called pixcels.
- **Hard Disc and Floppy Disc :** The Hard Disc is the permanent disc in the computers while the Floppy Disc is the disc utilised when datas or informations are to be transferred from one computer to another.
- **Mouse :** The mouse of the computer is like the remote control of TV through which computer is directly regulated or controlled without utilising the key-board.
- **Printer :** The printer is a device which prints any documents or processed informations of the computer.

☛ Some high level languages

1. **Fortran :** This language was developed for solving the mathematical formulae very quickly and conveniently.
2. **Cobol :** This language was developed for the commerical purposes. For the processing of this language a group of sentences is selected called paragraph and all paragraphs composed are called a section, while all sections composed are called a division.
3. **Basic :** In basic a definite part of the prescribed instruction is only inserted in the computer.
4. **Algol :** This was basically fabricated and designed for the complex algebraic calculations.
5. **PASCAL :** It is an amplified and modified form of ALGOL.
6. **Comal :** This computer language is used for the students of secondary level.
7. **LOGO :** This language is used for children and kids for drawing Graphic line diagrams.
8. **Prolog :** This language is developed in 1973 in France and this language is used for Artificial Intelligence which is capable and equivalent to the logical program.
9. **Forth :** This language was invented by Charles Mure which is frequently used in all types of the works in the computer.

☛ Computer Virus

- The computer virus is an electronic code which is used to abolish or erradicate the inclusive informations or programs of the computer.
- Some important computer viruses are Micheleanjalo, Dork Avangor, kilo, filip, Macmug, Scores, Casecade, Jeruslem, Date crime, Coloumbs crime, Internet virus, Pachcom, Pach EXE, COM-EXE, Marizuana, C-brain, bloody, Chenge Mungu and Desi etc.

☛ Computer Networking

- There are two types of networkings which are usually occur—Local Area Networking (LAN) and Wide Area Networking (WAN).

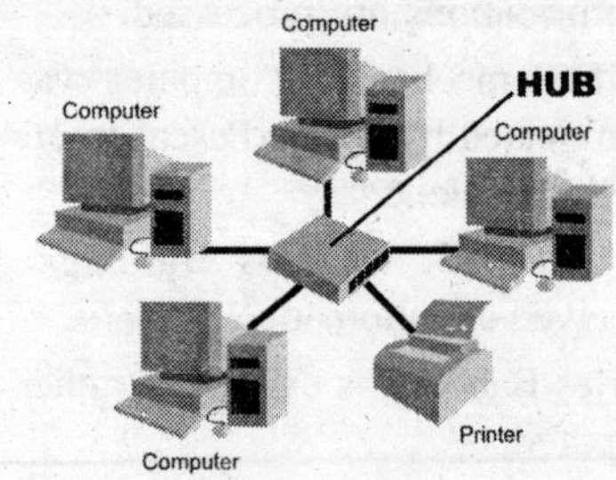

- By Lan all the computers of the same buildings are connected like the computers of university premises, computers of offices etc.
- By WAN all the comptuers of a large area are connected like the computers of all the offices of a city or town etc.
- In India a very large computer network namely INDONET has been installing through which all the main towns and cities has to be interlinked.

☛ *Computer Terminology*

- **Bit :** The bit is a unit of measurement of the electronic data. One bit is either 0 or 1 but not both. On composing 8 bits, 1 byte is formed.
- **Bug :** The Bug is the error in the computer program or system and its eradication is called Debug.
- **Byte :** Total eight bits compose a byte. Thus 8 bits = 1 byte.
- **CD-ROM :** A CD like of music CD in which data can be stored substantially called CD-ROM. In a CD with comparison to floppy extremely more datas can be stored but one problem in it is that one time recorded data can not be deleted or modified.
- **Chip :** It is a thin slice on which by a special mechanism a circuit is designed which is normally made from Silicon.
- **Memory System :** The place where computer data and program are temporarily kept is called Memory system. Usually memory is implied from RAM.
- **Modem :** The device which converts digital signals into analogue signals and vice-versa is called Modem.
- **RAM :** It is Random Access Memory (a place) where datas to be processed are kept temporarily and it is unstable memory.
- **ROM :** It is Read Only Memory and it is stable or Non-valatile memory which doesn't ended after power off.
- **Scanner :** It is a device through which graphic image is transformed to digital image and the scanners are of usually two types one desktop and another hand operating.

☛ *Programing*

- Computers perform phenomenal feats of calculation, but they do not do so in a complicated way.
- They actually carry out very simple operations, such as addition and subtraction.
- They achieve their fantastic computing power by carrying out these operations at incredible speed.
- The programme, or set of instructions for operating the computer, is therefore written as a sequence of very simple steps. (See box below) Several computer languages have been developed for different applications, including BASIC, COBOL, FORTRAN and PASCAL. Writing programmes is very skilled and time-consuming work.
- But for most typical computer applications ready-written programmes are available, called "packages".

☛ *How A Programme Works*

- Without a programme to tell it what to do and how to do it, a computer is unable to function. If, for example, you wanted to know how many times the word 'the' appears in this paragraph, or in the whole book, it would not be enough merely to put the text into a computer and then ask it how many times the word appears. For the computer to accomplish the calculations it has to be told what to do in simple steps. The instructions might be:

1. Scan the text until a space followed by 'T' or 't' is found.
2. If the next letter is not 'h', go back to step 1.
3. If the letter is 'h', is the next letter 'e'?
4. If not, go back to step 1. If it is, go to step 5.
5. If 'e' is followed by a space, add 1 to the total.
6. Go back to step 1.

- A full computer programme for this operation would need to be broken down into even more simple steps, but a series of such programmes could enable a computer to analyse any amount of text in great detail.

SPACE RESEARCH

☛ First in Space

First creator of rules regarding space research	—	Isaac Newton
First artificial satellite launched in space	—	Sputnik-1 (1957)
First living being sent in space	—	Louika (a dog)
Firstever manned spacecraft	—	Vostok-I
First man in space	—	Yuri Gagarin U.S.S.R. (1961)
First woman in space	—	Valentina Tereshkova U.S.S.R. (June 1963)
First man who moved in space out of the spacecraft	—	Alexi Livonov U.S.S.R. (June 1965)
First person to land on moon	—	Neil Armstrong, America (21st July, 1969)
First fourwheeled carriage without human being on moon	—	Leunokhev-I U.S.S.R. (1970)
First space lab in orbit	—	Skylab (America, 1973)
First space shuttle	—	Columbia (America, 1981)
First Indian (man) in space	—	Squadron leader—Rakesh Sharma (13th April, 1984)
First Indian (Woman) in space	—	Kalpana Chawla (19th Nov., 1997)
First American woman in space	—	Sailyride (1983)
First spacecraft on Mars	—	Pathfinder (6 July, 1997)
First woman who lead spacecraft	—	Allin Collis (America)
First spacecraft without man	—	Shenzoo, China (20th Nov. 1999)

☛ Indian Space Programme : At a Glance

Satellite	*Date*	*Type*	*Launch Vehicle*	*Result*
Aryabhatta	19-04-75	Scientific	Cosmos	successful
Bhaskara I	07-06-79	Geosurvey	Cosmos	successful
Rohini	10-08-79	Geosurvey	S.L.V.3	unsuccessful
Rohini D-1	18-07-80	Geosurvey	S.L.V.3	successful
Rohini	31-05-81	Scientific	S.L.V.3	successful
Apple	19-06-81	Communication	Ariane	successful
Bhaskara II	20-11-81	Geosurvey	Cosonos	successful
INSAT-1A	10-04-82	Multipurpose	Delta	unsuccessful
Rohini	17-04-83	Scientific	S.L.V.3	successful
INSAT-1B	30-08-83	Multipurpose	Space Shuttle	successful
SROSS I	24-03-87	Technical	ASLV-D1	unsuccessful
IRS-1A	17-03-88	Remote sensing	Vostok	successful
INSAT-1D	12-06-90	Multipurpose	Delta	successful
IRS-1B	29-08-91	Remote sensing	Vostok	successful
INSAT-2A	10-07-92	Multipurpose	Ariane	successful
SROSS-4	04-05-94	Scientific	ASLV-D3	successful
IRS-P2	15-10-94	Remote sensing	PSLV-D2	successful
INSAT-2C	07-12-95	Telecom	Ariane-4	successful
IRS-1C	28-12-95	Remote sensing	PSLV-D3	successful

Satellite	Date	Type	Launch Vehicle	Result
IRS-P3	20-03-96	Remote sensing	PSLV-D3	successful
IRS-ID	29-09-97	Remote sensing	PSLV	successful
INSAT-3B	22-03-2000	Multipurpose	Ariane	successful
G-SAT-1	18-04-2001	Multipurpose	GSLV-D	successful
INSAT-3C	24-01-2002	Communication	Ariane-4	successful
MAT SAT	12-09-2002	Meteorology	PSLVC-4	successful
CARTOSAT-2	10-01-2007	Communication	PSLV-C7	successful
Chandrayaan-I	22-10-2008	Mapping and Scientific	PSLV-C11	successful
Oceansat-2	24-09-2009	Remote Sensing	PSLV-C14	successful
GSAT-8	21-05-2011	Communication	Ariane-5	successful
Spot-6	09-09-2012	Remote Sensing	PSLV-C21	successful
Saral	25-02-2013	Scientific	PSLV-C20	successful
Mangalyan	05-11-2013	Mapping and Scientific	PSLV-C25	successful
GSAT-14	05-01-2014	Communication	GSLV-D5	successful
IRNSS-1C	16-10-2014	Mapping and Scientific	PSLV-C26	successful
GSAT-6	27-08-2015	Communication	GSLV-D6	successful
Astrosat	28-09-2015	Mapping and Scientific	PSLV-C30	successful
TELEOS-1	16-12-2015	Mapping and Scientific	PSLV-C29	successful
IRNSS-1E	20-01-2016	Mapping and Scientific	PSLV-C31	successful
INSAT-3DR	08-09-2016	Meteorology	GSLV-F05	successful
Cartosat-2 & 103 others	15-02-2017	Multipurpose	PSLV-C37	successful
GSAT-19	05-06-2017	Communication	GSLV-Mark-3D1	successful
Cartosat-2F & others	12-01-2018	Multipurpose	PSLV-C40	successful
IRNSS-1I	12-04-2018	Mapping and Scientific	PSLV-C41	successful
Nova-Sar & S1-04	16-09-2018	Mapping	PSLV-C42	successful
GSAT 31	06-02-2019	Telecommunication	Ariane 5-VCA	successful
Chandrayaan-2	22-07-2019	Mapping and Scientific	GSLV-MK-III	successful
Cartosat-3	27-11-2019	Earth Imaging Satellite	PSLV-C47	successful
RISAT-2 BR1& others	11-12-2019	Earth Imaging Satellite	PSLV-C48	successful
GSAT-30	17-01-2020	Communication	Ariane-5	successful
EOS-01	07-11-2020	Earth Observation	PSLV-C49	successful
Amezonia & 19 others	28-02-2021	Communication	PSLV-C51	successful
EOS-04	14-02-2022	Earth Observation	PSLV-C52	successful
GSAT-24	23-06-2022	Communication	Ariane-5	successful
DS-E0 and others	30-06-2022	Mapping	PSLV-C53	successful
Oceansat-3 & 8 others	26-11-2022	Earth Observation	PSLV-C54	successful
EOS-07	10-02-2023	Earth Observation	SSLV-02	successful
TeLEOS-2 and LUMILITE-4	22-04-2023	Earth Observation	PSLV-C55	successful
Chandrayaan-3	14-07-2023	Lunar observation	LVM-3M4	successful
DS-SAR	30-07-2023	Earth Observation	PSLV-C56	successful
'Aditya-L1'	02-09-2023	Solar Mission	PSLV-C57	successful
XPoSat.	01-01-2024	Earth Observation	PSLV-C58	successful
NVS-02	29-01-2025	Navigation	GSLV-F15	successful
NISAR	30-07-2025	Earth Observation	GSLV-F16	successful

IMPORTANT DATES AND DAYS OF THE YEAR

January

5-11 Road Safety Week
12 National Youth Day
15 Army Day
15-21 Pin Code Week
23 National Day of Patriotism
26 Republic Day
30 Martyr's Day

February

1-14 Oil Conservation Fortnight
14 Valentine's Day

March

4 National Safety Day
8 International Women's Day
15 Consumers' Day
21 World Forest Day
22 World Day for Water
24 World Meteorological Day
1-7 Preservation of Blindness Week

April

7 World Health Day
7-13 Handloom Week
14-20 Fire Service Week
18 World Heritage Day
22 World Earth Day

May

1 May Day
5 National Labour Day
8 World Red Cross Day
11 National Technology Day
15 International Day of the Family
17 World Telecommunication Day
24 Commonwealth Day
31 World No-Tobacco Day

June

5 World Environment Day
21 International Day of Yoga
26 International Day against Drug Abuse and Illicit Trafficking

July

11 World Population Day

August

1-7 World Breast feeding Week
10 Sanskrit Divas
15 Independence Day
20 Sadbhavana Divas

September

1-7 National Nutrition Week
5 Teachers' Day
8 International Literary Day
14 Hindi Diwas
23 World Deaf Day
27 World Tourism Day

October

2 * Gandhi Jayanti
* International Day of Non Violence
* Anti-Leprosy Day
4 World Animal Day
6 World Habitat Day *(Ist Monday)*
8 Indian Air Force Day
14 World Standard Day
15 International Day of Rural Women
16 World Food Day
24 United Nations Day
27 Infantry Day
28 World Thrift Day
31 Anti-Terrorism Day

November

2 All Saints Day
14 Children's Day
15-21 National Cooperative Week
19-25 Quami Ekta Week
20 Child Rights Day
26 Constitution Day

December

1 World AIDS Day
3 World Day for the Disabled
4 Naval Day
7 Flag Day
8 SMRC Day
10 Human Rights Day
14 National Energy Conservation Day

ABBREVIATIONS

A.A.F.	Auxiliary Air Force
A.D.B.	Asian Development Bank
A.I.E.E.E.	All India Engineering Entrance Examination
A.I.C.C.	All-India Congress Committee
A.I.R.	All India Radio
A.M.	Ante meridiem (before noon)
B.B.C.	British Broadcasting Corporation
B.C.C.I.	Board of Control for Cricket in India
BHEL	Bharat Heavy Electricals Ltd.
B.S.F.	Border Security Force
C.A.G.	Comptroller and Auditor-General
C.B.I.	Central Bureau of Investigation
C.I.A.	Central Intelligence Bureau (U.S.A.)
C.I.D.	Criminal Investigation Department
D.D.T.	Dichloro Diphenyl Trichloroethane
E.S.R.O.	European Space Research Organization
E.C.G.	Electro-Cardio Gram
E.V.M.	Electronic Voting Machine
F.D.I.	Foreign Direct Investment
F.C.I.	Food Corporation of India
G.D.P.	Gross Domestic Product
G.P.O.	General Post Office
G.S.T.	Goods and Services Tax
H.M.T.	Hindustan Machine Tools
H.P.	Horse Power
I.A.F.	Indian Air Force
I.A.S.	Indian Administrative Service
INSAT	Indian National Satellite
J.C.O.	Junior Commissioned Officer
L.B.W.	Leg Before Wicket (in cricket)
LL.B.	Bachelor of Law
L.P.G.	Liquefied Petroleum Gas
M.D.	Doctor of Medicine
M.S.	Master of Surgery
M.B.B.S.	Bachelor of Medicine and Bachelor of Surgery
N.A.C.O.	National Aids Control Organisation
NATO	North Atlantic Treaty Organisation
N.C.E.R.T.	National Council of Educational Research and Training
P.I.N.	Postal Index Number
P.N.R.	Passenger Numerical Record
R.A.F.	Rapid Action Force
R.B.I.	Reserve Bank of India
SEBI	Securities Exchange Board of India
U.P.S.C.	Union Public Service Commission
V.I.P.	Very Important Person
V.P.P.	Value Payable Post
W.T.O.	World Trade Organisation
W.H.O.	World Health Organisation (UN)
W.W.W.	World Wide Web
Y.M.C.A.	Young Men's Christian Association
Z.S.	Zoological Society

SPORTS

☛ *Important Cups & Trophies*

International

- *American Cup* : Yacht Racing
- *Ashes* : Cricket
- *Benson and Hedges* : Cricket
- *Colombo Cup* : Football
- *Corbitton Cup* : Table Tennis (Women)
- *Davis Cup* : Lawn Tennis
- *Derby* : Horse Race
- *Grand National* : Horse Streple Chase Race
- *Jules Rimet Trophy* : World Soccer Cup
- *King's Cup* : Air Races
- *Merdeka Cup* : Football
- *Ryder Cup* : Golf
- *Swaythling Cup* : Table Tennis (Men)
- *Thomas Cup* : Badminton
- *Uber Cup* : Badminton (Women)
- *U. Thant Cup* : Tennis
- *Walker Cup* : Golf
- *Wightman Cup* : Lawn Tennis
- *World Cup* : Cricket
- *World Cup* : Hockey
- *Rothman's Trophy* : Cricket
- *William's Cup* : Basketball

- *European Champions Cup* : Football
- *Eisenhower Cup* : Golf
- *Rene Frank Trophy* : Hockey
- *Grand Prix* : Table Tennis
- *Edgbaston Cup* : Lawn Tennis
- *Grand Prix* : Lawn Tennis
- *World Cup* : Weightlifting

National

- *Agha Khan Cup* : Hockey
- *All India Women's Guru Nanak Championship* : Hockey
- *Bangalore Blues Challenge Cup* : Basketball
- *Barna-Bellack Cup* : Table Tennis
- *Beighton Cup* : Hockey
- *Bombay Gold Cup* : Hockey
- *Burdwan Trophy* : Weightlifting
- *Charminar Trophy* : Athletics
- *Chadha Cup* : Badminton
- *C.K. Naydu Trophy* : Cricket
- *Divan Cup* : Badminton
- *Deodhar Trophy* : Cricket
- *Duleep Trophy* : Cricket
- *D.C.M. Cup* : Football
- *Durand Cup* : Football
- *Dhyan Chand Trophy* : Hockey
- *Dr. B.C. Roy Trophy* : Football (Junior)
- *Ezra Cup* : Polo
- *F.A. Cup* : Football
- *G.D. Birla Trophy* : Cricket
- *Guru Nanak Cup* : Hockey
- *Gyanvati Devi Trophy* : Hockey
- *Holkar Trophy* : Bridge
- *Irani Trophy* : Cricket
- *Indira Gold Cup* : Hockey
- *Jawaharlal Challenge* : Air Racing
- *Kuppuswamy Naidu Trophy* : Hockey
- *Jaswant Singh Trophy* : Best Services Sportsman
- *Lady Rattan Tata Trophy* : Hockey
- *MCC Trophy* : Hockey
- *Moinuddaula Gold Cup* : Cricket
- *Murugappa Gold Cup* : Hockey
- *Modi Gold Cup* : Hockey
- *Nehru Trophy* : Hockey
- *Obaidullah Gold Cup* : Hockey
- *Prithi Singh Cup* : Polo
- *Ranji Trophy* : Cricket
- *Rangaswami Cup* : Hockey
- *Ranjit Singh Gold Cup* : Hockey
- *Rene Frank Trophy* : Hockey
- *Radha Mohan Cup* : Polo
- *Rohinton Baria Trophy* : Cricket
- *Rovers Cup* : Football
- *Santosh Trophy* : Football
- *Sir Ashutosh Mukherjee* : Football
- *Subroto Cup* : Football
- *Scindia Gold Cup* : Hockey
- *Sheesh Mahal Trophy* : Cricket
- *Todd Memorial Trophy* : Football
- *Tommy Eman Gold Cup* : Hockey
- *Vittal Trophy* : Football
- *Vizzy Trophy* : Cricket
- *Vijay Merchant Trophy* : Cricket
- *Wellington Trophy* : Rowing

☛ *Sports Terms*

- **Badminton:** Mixed doubles; Deuce; Drop; Smash; Let; Foot work; Setting.
- **Base Ball:** Pitcher; Put out, Strike; Home; Bunt.
- **Billiards:** Cue; Jigger; Pot; Break; In Baulk; In Off; Cannons.
- **Boxing:** Upper cut; Round; Punch; Bout; Knock down; Hitting below the belt; Ring.
- **Bridge:** Finesse; Dummy; Revoke; Grand Slam; Little Slam; No Trump; Rubber.
- **Chess:** Bishop, Gambit; Checkmate; Stalemate.
- **Cricket:** L.B.W. *(leg before wicket)*; Creases, Popping-creases; Stumped; Bye; Leg-Bye; Googly; Hattrick; Maiden over; Drive; Bowling; Duck; Follow-on; No ball; Leg Break; Silly point; Cover point; Hit-wicket; Late-cut; Slip; Off-spinner; In-swing.
- **Football:** Off Side; Block; Drop-kick; Penalty-kick (or *goal kick*); Corner-kick; Free-kick; Dribble; Thrown-in; Foul.

- **Golf:** Boggy; Foursome; Stymic; Tee; Put; Hole; Niblic; Caddie; Links; The green; Bunker.
- **Hockey:** Carried; Short Corner; Bully; Sticks; Off side; Roll in; Striking Circle; Under-cutting; Dribble.
- **Horse racing:** Jockey; Punter.
- **Polo:** Bunker; Chukker; Mallet.
- **Tennis:** Back hand drive; Volley; Smash; Half-volley; Deuce; Service; Let; Grand Slam.

☛ Name of Playing Compound of Different Games

Name of Compound	*Related Sports*
Court	Lawn Tennis, Badminton, Netball, Hand ball, Volleyball, Squash, Kho-Kho, Kabaddi
Diamond	Baseball
Ring	Boxing, Skating, Wrestling, Circus, Riding display
Course	Golf
Board	Table Tennis
Pool	Swimming
Alley	Bowling
Mat	Judo, Karate II
Arena	Horse Riding
Vellodrum	Cycling
Field	Polo, Football, Hockey
Track	Athletics
Pitch	Cricket, Rugby
Rink	Ice Hockey

☛ National Sports and Games of Some Countries

Australia	Cricket
Canada	Ice Hockey
England	Cricket and Rugby Football
Russia	Chess
Scotland	Rugby Football
Spain	Bull Fighting
USA	Baseball
China	Table Tennis
Malaysia	Badminton
Pakistan	Hockey

☛ Stadiums & Places Associated with Sports

Name of Stadium	*Sports*	*Place*
Narendra Modi Stadium	Cricket	Ahmedabad
Jawaharlal Nehru Stadium	Athletics	Delhi
Shivajee Stadium	Hockey	Delhi
National Stadium	Hockey etc.	Delhi
Ambedkar Stadium	Football	Delhi
Indraprastha Stadium	Indoor Games	Delhi
Brabourne Stadium	Cricket	Mumbai
Wankhede Stadium	Cricket	Mumbai
Arun Jaitley Stadium	Cricket	Delhi
Wimbledon	Lawn Tennis	London
Eden Garden	Cricket	Kolkata
Ranjeet Stadium	Football	Kolkata
Green Park Stadium	Cricket	Kanpur
Keenan Stadium	Cricket	Jamshedpur
Nehru (Chepauk) Stadium	Cricket	Chennai
Barabati Stadium	Cricket	Cuttack
Epsum	Derby race	Britain
Lords, Oval, Leeds	Cricket	Britain
Hedingle Manchester	Cricket	Britain
Black Heath	Rugby Football	London
Henley	Boat race	England
Wembley Stadium	Football	London
Hurlingham	Polo	England
White City	Dog-race	England
Aintree	Horse-race	England
Tentbridge	Cricket	England
Patnee Martlake	Boat-race	England
Tibankham	Rugby Football	England
Brookland	Football	England
Sandy Lodge	Golf	Scotland
Forest Hill	Tennis	New York
Brooklyn	Baseball	New York
Yankee Stadium Perth, Brisbane,	Boxing	New York
Melbourne	Cricket	Australia

Number of Players in Some Games/Sports

Sports	No. of Players
Badminton	1 or 2
Baseball	9
Basketball	5
Billiards (Snooker)	1
Boxing	1
Chess	1
Cricket	11
Croquest	13 or 15
Football (Soccer)	11
Hockey	11
Lacrosse	12
Netball	7
Polo Rugby	4
Football (Rugby)	15
Table Tennis	1 or 2
Lawn Tennis	1 or 2
Volleyball	6
Water Polo	7

Olympic Games

First of all these games were held by the Greeks in 776 B.C. on Mount Olympus in honour of the Greek God Zeus. In this way, the history of Olympic Games is about twenty eight hundred years old. These games continued to be held every four years until 394 A.D. When these games were stopped by a royal order of the emperor of Rome. The modern Olympic Games which started in Athens in 1896, are the result of the devotion and dedication of a French educator Baron Pierre de Coubertin and the first Olympic meet in the modern series was held in 1896 in Athens, the Capital of Greece. Since then, they are being held every four years except for breaks during world wars. The Olympic flag is white in colour with five coloured rings, each ring symbolic of a continent. Summer as well as winter Olympics are held in the same year.

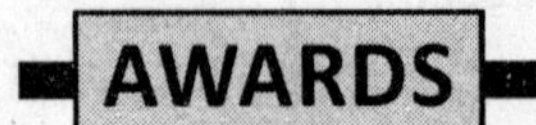

National Awards

I. Civilian Awards

1. **Bharat Ratna:** This is India's highest civilian award. It is given for exceptional work on art, literature, science, sports and recognition of public service of the highest order. Government servants are not eligible for it.
2. **Padma Vibhushan:** This award is given for exceptional and distinguished service in any field, including service rendered by Govt. servants.
3. **Padma Bhushan:** This award is given for distinguished service of a high order in any field, including service rendered by Govt. servants.
4. **Padma Shri:** This award is given for distinguished service in any field, including service rendered by Government servants.

II. Gallantry Awards

1. **Param Vir Chakra:** The highest award for bravery or some daring and pre-eminent act of valour or self-sacrifice in the presence of the enemy, whether on land, at sea or in the air.
2. **Mahavir Chakra:** It is the second highest decoration and is awarded for acts of conspicuous gallantry in the presence of the enemy, whether on land, at sea or in the air.
3. **Vir Chakra:** It is the third in order of awards given for acts of gallantry in the presence of enemy, whether on land, at sea or in the air.
4. **Ashok Chakra:** This medal is awarded for the most conspicuous bravery or some daring or pre-eminent act of valour or self-sacrifice on land, at sea or in the air but not in the presence of enemy.

5. **Vishishta Sewa Medal:** It is awarded to personnel of all the three Services in class I, II and III in recognition of distinguished service of the "most exceptional" and "exceptional" and a "high" order respectively. Prefixes *Parma* and *Ati* are added before first two categories of medals respectively.
6. **Jeewan Raksha Padak:** Awarded for meritorious acts or a series of acts of a human nature displayed in saving life from drowning, fire and rescue operations in mines etc.

III. Other Awards

Awards	*Related to*
• Jnanpith Award	Outstanding contribution to Indian Literature.
• Dada Saheb Phalke Award	Outstanding contribution to Indian cinema (films).
• Arjuna Awards	Given to sportspersons who distinguish themselves in different sports disciplines.
• Dronacharya Awards	Given to outstanding Indian Sports Coaches.
• Bhatnagar Awards	Given for important contribution to any field of science.
• Krishi Pandit Award	It is given to agriculturist showing maximum per acre production.

☛ International Awards

1. **Nobel Prizes:** These Prizes were instituted in 1901 by a Swedish scientist, Dr. Alfred Nobel; the discoverer of Dynamite. Six prizes are awarded annually for (*i*) Chemistry, (*ii*) Physics, (*iii*) Medicine, (*iv*) Literature, (*v*) Peace and (*vi*) Economics—started since 1969.

   The following Indians so far have been awarded these prizes:

   (*i*) Dr. Rabindra Nath Tagore (1913) for his *"Geetanjali"*.
   (*ii*) Dr. C.V. Raman for Physics in 1929.
   (*iii*) Mother Teresa for Peace in 1979.
   (*iv*) Prof. Amartya Sen in 1998 for Economics
   (*v*) Kailash Satyarthi for Peace in 2014.

   In addition, four non-resident Indians have also been awarded the Nobel Prize. They are:

   (i) Hargobind Khurana for Medicine in 1968.
   (ii) Subramanian Chandrasekhar for Physics in 1983.
   (iii) Venkatraman Ramkrishnan for Chemistry in 2009.
   (iv) Abhijit Vinayak Banerjee for Economics in 2019.
2. **Gandhi Peace Prize:** The government instituted this Rs. 1 crore prize on the lines of the Nobel Peace Prize in 1995. It is the highest Civilian International award by the Govt. of India.
3. **Magsaysay Awards:** The Ramon Magsaysay Award, named after a Philippines President, who died in an air crash in 1957. It carries a gold medal, a certificate and US$ 50,000. It is awarded on August 31, every year.
4. **Oscar Award:** This prestigious award of film world is given annually by 'National Academy of Motion Picture Arts & Sciences' of America.

☛ Highest Honours of Some Countries

Country	*Highest Honour*
India	Bharat Ratna
Pakistan	Nishan-e-Pakistan
Kuwait	Mubarak-Al-Kabir Medal
Saudi Arabia	Shah Abdul Aziz Medal
Argentina	The Order of Sona Martin
Nicaragua	Augusto-Caesar Sandino Order
Vietnam	The Order of the Golden Star
Hungary	The Order of Banner
Britain	Member of British Empire, Victoria Cross
Japan	Order of Moulovenice Sun
Denmark	Order of Diana Brog
France	Legend of Honour
America	Presidential Medal of Freedom
Germany	Pore Lee Merit Iron Cross
The Netherlands	Netherlands Lion

MULTIPLE CHOICE QUESTIONS

1. Lima is the capital of:
A. Peru B. Chile
C. Argentina D. Uruguay

2. Saina Nehwal plays which of the following games?
A. Lawn Tennis B. Badminton
C. Chess D. Swimming

3. Who among the following is also called 'Bharatendu'?
A. Harishchandra B. Premchand
C. Jayashankar D. Vidyapati

4. How many rings are there in the Olympic flag?
A. 6 B. 5
C. 4 D. 8

5. Which of the following is situated in Paris?
A. Statue of Liberty
B. Eiffel Tower
C. Victoria Memorial
D. Leaning Tower of Pisa

6. The man, whose gums bleed, requires:
A. Vitamin C B. Vitamin D
C. Vitamin B D. Vitamin A

7. National Anthem 'Jana-gana-mana' was composed by:
A. Rabindranath Tagore
B. Bankimchandra Chatterji
C. Madam Cama
D. Surendranath Chatterji

8. Gateway of India is located in:
A. Mumbai B. Delhi
C. Hyderabad D. Kolkata

9. Which is the most ancient Veda?
A. Atharvaveda B. Yajurveda
C. Rigveda D. Samveda

10. C.R. Das is also popularly known as:
A. Chacha
B. Mahatma
C. Deshbandhu
D. Deenbandhu

11. Whose samadhi is at Shaktisthal?
A. Mahatma Gandhi B. Indira Gandhi
C. Kasturba Gandhi D. Jawaharlal Nehru

12. Who of the following was the first speaker of the Lok Sabha?
A. G.S. Dhillon B. G.V. Mavalankar
C. Hukum Singh D. K.S. Hegde

13. Who is the author of the book 'Glimpses of World History'?
A. Abul Kalam Azad
B. Jawaharlal Nehru
C. S. Gopalan
D. S. Radhakrishnan

14. Chilka lake is situated in:
A. West Bengal B. Andhra Pradesh
C. Odisha D. Tamil Nadu

15. Indo-Pak border is known as:
A. Durand Line B. McMohan Line
C. Redcliffe Line D. Line of Control

16. Which of the following is called a 'red planet'?
A. Saturn B. Venus
C. Jupiter D. Mars

17. The first nuclear test was conducted in India in the year:
A. 1973 B. 1974
C. 1975 D. 1976

18. The first Satellite of India sent to space, was:
A. Bhaskar B. Rohini
C. Aryabhatta D. Apple

19. Night blindness is caused by the deficiency of:
A. Vitamin B_1 B. Vitamin C
C. Vitamin A D. Vitamin E

20. Light from the Sun reaches Earth in about:
A. 2 minute B. 4 minute
C. 8 minute D. 16 minute

21. Subrato Cup is related to:
A. Badminton B. Hockey
C. Football D. Polo

22. Who started the Bhoodan movement?
A. Jayaprakash Narain
B. Vinoba Bhave
C. Morarji Desai
D. J.L. Nehru

23. The first railway in India was started in the year:
A. 1835 B. 1853
C. 1875 D. 1958

24. Who is the Supreme Commander of the armed foces?
A. President
B. Vice-president
C. Prime Minister
D. Defence Minister

25. National tree of India is:
A. Mango B. Neem
C. Banyan D. Lotus

26. The dance form 'Mohiniattam' hails from:
A. Kerala B. Punjab
C. Karnataka D. Tamil Nadu

27. Dada Saheb Phalke Awards are given in the field of:
A. Journalism B. Literature
C. Sports D. Cinema

28. Daulat Beg Oldie, a well-known airstrip for supply of provisions to the armed forces is located in:
A. Arunachal Pradesh B. Ladakh
C. Andaman Islands D. Sikkim

29. How many Fundamental Rights are in our constitution?
A. 5 B. 6
C. 7 D. 8

30. Who was the first Prime Minister of India?
A. J.L. Nehru
B. Mahatma Gandhi
C. Dr. Rajendra Prasad
D. Lal Bahadur Shastri

31. Areawise, which among the following is the largest state of India?
A. Uttar Pradesh B. Rajasthan
C. Madhya Pradesh D. Bihar

32. Populationwise, which one among the following is the biggest state of India?
A. Uttar Pradesh B. West Bengal
C. Maharashtra D. Bihar

33. The age of retirement of a High Court Judge is:
A. 65 years B. 62 years
C. 60 years D. 58 years

34. Lord Buddha was born at:
A. Pataliputra B. Ujjain
C. Rajgriha D. Lumbini

35. Surat is situated on the bank of river:
A. Tapti B. Godavari
C. Narmada D. Bhima

36. Which country is called 'The Sugar Bowl' of the world?
A. Cuba B. India
C. USA D. China

37. Which Indian State is often called the heart of India?
A. Uttar Pradesh B. Punjab
C. Madhya Pradesh D. West Bengal

38. The highest rank in the Indian Army is of:
A. General B. Major General
C. Captain D. Brigadier General

39. The Army Headquarters is in:
A. New Delhi B. Kolkata
C. Pune D. Patna

40. Vatican City is the residence of:
A. Pope B. British Queen
C. French President D. Cyprus President

41. The largest populated country in the world is:
A. India B. China
C. Russia D. USA

42. 'Land of White Elephant' is the surname assigned to:
A. Japan B. Thailand
C. Bhutan D. Nepal

43. Wimbledon is associated with:
A. Bridge B. Hockey
C. Golf D. Tennis

44. Ranji Trophy is associated with:
A. Tennis B. Cricket
C. Badminton D. Hockey

45. 'Lion of Punjab' is the nickname assigned to:
A. Bipin Chandra Pal
B. Lala Lajpat Rai
C. Sardar Ajit Singh
D. None of these

46. Pt. Ravi Shankar was specialised in playing:
A. Flute B. Sarod
C. Shehnai D. Sitar

47. Mahabharata was written by:
A. Ved Vyas B. Valmiki
C. Tulsidas D. None of these

48. The United Nations Day is observed annually on:
A. November 14 B. October 24
C. October 2 D. October 30

49. Garba, a popular folk dance, is associated with:
A. Rajasthan
B. Andhra Pradesh
C. Himachal Pradesh
D. Gujarat

50. Famous Hindu Pilgrimage Amarnath is in:
A. Uttar Pradesh
B. Madhya Pradesh
C. Jammu & Kashmir
D. Andhra Pradesh

51. The words 'Satyameva Jayate' are taken from:
A. Hitopadesh
B. Mahabharata
C. Rig Veda
D. Mundaka Upanishada

52. The wheel on the middle strip of the National Flag has:
A. 24 spokes B. 20 spokes
C. 48 spokes D. 18 spokes

53. The first Nuclear test was under-taken in India in the year:
A. 1975 B. 1974
C. 1973 D. 1977

54. Which State is known by the name of 'Mountain State'?
A. Arunachal Pradesh
B. Himachal Pradesh
C. Sikkim
D. Punjab

55. The smallest state (in area) of the Indian Union is:
A. Kerala B. Tripura
C. Punjab D. Goa

56. The earliest of the holy books of the Hindus is:
A. The Gita B. The Ramayana
C. The Mahabharata D. The Vedas

57. Sanchi in Madhya Pradesh is famous for:
A. rock-cut temples
B. cave paintings
C. stupas
D. Ashoka's rock edicts

58. 'Jatakas' are the sacred books of the:
A. Vaishnavas B. Jains
C. Buddhists D. Shaivas

59. The Ist woman president of United Nations General Assembly was:
A. Margaret Thatcher
B. Vijaya Laxmi Pandit
C. Eleanor Roosvelt
D. Sirimavo Bhandaranaike

60. Out of a total strength of 15, the number of permanent members of the UN security council is:
A. Four B. Ten
C. Eleven D. Five

61. The noted work of Surdas is:
A. Krishna Charit B. Sursagar
C. Sukhsagar D. Bhagwad Gita

62. 'Panchatantra' was written by:
A. Vishnu Sharma B. Ved Vyas
C. Valmiki D. Tenali Ram

63. Fuehrer is the nickname of:
A. Mussolini B. Rommel
C. Napoleon D. Hitler

64. Egg is a rich source of:
A. Vitamin C B. Fats
C. Hormones D. Protein

65. Penicillin is discovered by:
A. Karl Landsteimer
B. Alexander Fleming
C. Paul Muller
D. W. Murdock

66. Kuchipudi dance originated from:
A. Punjab B. Rajasthan
C. Andhra Pradesh D. Karnataka

67. India's anti-tank missile is:
A. Agni B. Prithvi
C. Akash D. Nag

68. The largest fresh water lake in India is:
A. Dal Lake B. Wular Lake
C. Pushkar Lake D. Bhatkal Lake

69. 14th November is celebrated in India as:
A. Health Day
B. Women's Day
C. Children's Day
D. Indira Gandhi's Birthday

70. Which Commission replaced the Planning Commission in 2015?
A. NITI Aayog B. NIYAM Aayog
C. NAGRIK Aayog D. Jan Aayog

71. The Indian Military Academy is situated in:
A. Pune B. Dehradun
C. Patna D. Jabalpur

72. Which state was formerly known as Mysore?
A. Karnataka B. Tamil Nadu
C. Maharashtra D. Madhya Pradesh

73. Hirakud Dam is built across the river:
A. Bargi B. Ramganga
C. Krishna D. Mahanadi

74. The State in India with the largest coastline is:
A. Tamil Nadu B. Gujarat
C. Andhra Pradesh D. Maharashtra

75. Days and nights are caused due to the earth's:
A. rotation B. revolution
C. gravitational pull D. nearness to the sun

76. Rickets is a disease which is caused by the deficiency of:
A. Vitamin A B. Ribaflavin
C. Vitamin C D. Vitamin D

77. ELISA tests is done for the detection of:
A. Cancer B. AIDS
C. Diabetes D. None of the above

78. The famous Gandhian, who was also known as the "Frontier Gandhi" is:
A. Liaqat Ali Khan
B. Yusuf Khan
C. Khan Abdul Ghaffar Khan
D. Abdul Wali Khan

79. Ladakh become a Union Territory in:
A. 2017 B. 2018
C. 2019 D. 2020

80. The minimum age for casting vote in India is:
A. 18 years B. 21 years
C. 22 years D. 19 years

81. Which country awards the Noble Prize?
A. USA B. India
C. Russia D. Sweden

82. The highest civilian award of India is:
A. Padma Vibhushan
B. Padma Shri
C. Bharat Ratna
D. Ashok Chakra

83. Who is known as Father of India's "White Revolution" and "Operation Flood"?
A. Dr. Verghese Kurien
B. J.B. Kripalani
C. Baba Amte
D. Har Gobind Khorana

84. 'Durand Cup' is associated with:
A. Hockey B. Cricket
C. Football D. Badminton

85. Koneru Humpy is well known as a:
A. Table Tennis player
B. Swimmer
C. Chess player
D. Football player

86. The only state of India—in which gold mining is being carried out is:
A. Tamil Nadu B. Bihar
C. Goa D. Karnataka

87. Which is known as the "City of Lakes"?
A. Hyderabad B. Udaipur
C. Chennai D. Bengaluru

88. 'Godaan' was written by:
A. Mahadevi Verma
B. Prem Chand
C. R.K. Narayan
D. Mahaveer Prasad

89. Corbett National Park is situated in:
A. Gujarat B. Uttarakhand
C. Madhya Pradesh D. Asom

90. Bhakra Nangal Dam is built on which river?
A. Ravi B. Beas
C. Chenab D. Sutlaj

91. What is the tenure of the members of Rajya Sabha?
A. 5 years B. 7 years
C. 6 years D. None of the above

92. The phrase "The Nightingale of India" is associated with:
A. M.S. Subbulakshmi
B. Sarojini Naidu
C. Indira Gandhi
D. Lata Mangeshkar

93. Who is regarded as the great law giver of ancient India?
A. Kautiliya B. Manu
C. Panini D. None of these

94. Which Indian President held office for two consecutive terms?
A. Dr. Zakir Hussain
B. Pratibha Patil
C. R. Venkataraman
D. Dr. Rajendra Prasad

95. The maximum strength of the Rajya Sabha is:
A. 250 B. 270
C. 325 D. 545

96. Milkha Singh is normally associated with the following discipline:
A. Poetry B. Politics
C. Athletics D. Mountaineering

97. Who among the following transformed the Shivaji and Ganapati festival into a national festival?
A. Lala Lajpat Rai
B. Bal Gangadhar Tilak
C. Veer Savarkar
D. Gopal Krishna Gokhale

98. Akbar's mausaleum is situated at:
A. Mumbai B. New Delhi
C. Sikandara D. Sasaram

99. Who is Medha Patkar?
A. Singer B. Dancer
C. Painter D. Social Activist

100. Who was the Guru of Kabir?
A. Ramanuja B. Ramananda
C. Vallabhacharya D. Namadeva

101. "Swaraj is my birth right and I shall have it?" Who said it?
A. Aurobindo Ghosh
B. Mahatma Gandhi
C. Subhash Chandra Bose
D. Bal Gangadhar Tilak

102. Mao-tse-Tung was the leader of the Communist Movement of:
A. Burma B. Malaysia
C. China D. Mongolia

103. Anna Hazare is known for:
A. Watershed Development
B. Rural Education
C. Tribal Development
D. Co-operative Development

104. Eden Garden, a famous cricket stadium, is located in:
A. Kanpur B. Kolkata
C. Jamshedpur D. Pune

105. 'Merdeka Cup' is associated with:
A. Golf B. Football
C. Squash D. Hockey

106. Which one of the following is the longest river in the world?
A. Amazon
B. Yangtze-Kiang
C. Nile
D. Mississipi-Missouni

107. Which of the following is a cash crop?
A. Wheat B. Rice
C. Maize D. Sugarcane

108. Who was the first President of India?
A. Mahatma Gandhi
B. Dr. Rajendra Prasad
C. Sardar Patel
D. Dr. Jakir Husain

109. AIDS disease is caused by:
A. Virus B. Sexual Contact
C. Bacteria D. Protozoa

110. Eco mark is given to Indian products that are:
A. pure and unadulterated
B. rich in protein
C. environment friendly
D. economically viable

111. The Arjuna awards are given to outstanding persons in the field of:
A. Science B. Sports
C. Social Services D. Literature

112. The Bhartiya Jnanpith award is given to:
A. Sports persons B. Scientists
C. Coaches D. Creative Writers

113. Which is the national game of China?
A. Football B. Cricket
C. Table Tennis D. Kabaddi

114. Who among the following sportsmen is called the 'Magician of Hockey'?
A. Dhyanchand
B. Dhanraj Pillai
C. Pargat Singh
D. Baljit Singh Dhillon

115. The name of Novak Djokovic is associated with this sport:
A. Tennis B. Cricket
C. Chess D. Basketball

116. Who among the following is the writer of 'Anand Math'?
A. Harindra Nath Chattopadhyay
B. Rabindranath Tagore
C. Mulk Raj Anand
D. Bankim Chandra Chatterjee

117. The Capital of Mizoram is:
A. Imphal B. Shillong
C. Kohima D. Aizwal

118. Who was the founder of Mughal Empire in India?
A. Akbar B. Babur
C. Humayun D. Timur

119. What is the old name of Iran?
A. Salisbury B. Sians
C. Vienna D. Persia

120. Who is called 'Frontier Gandhi'?
A. Abdul Gaffar Khan
B. Maulana Azad
C. Satishchandra Dasgupta
D. Mahatma Gandhi

121. On which river the city of Srinagar is located?
A. Beas B. Chenab
C. Ravi D. Jhelum

122. Who composed the 'Bande Mataram'?
A. Bankim Chandra
B. Aurobindo Ghosh
C. Rabindranath Tagore
D. Mukunda Das

123. Wimbledon known for lawn tennis courts, is in:
A. Washington D.C. B. Paris
C. Rome D. London

124. Sunita Williams is a:
A. Tennis player B. Novelist
C. Politician D. NASA Scientist

125. VAT is a:
A. Tax B. System
C. House D. Rule

126. Which of the following is the smallest ocean of the world?
A. Pacific B. Indian
C. Atlantic D. Arctic

127. Which of the following river is known as 'Sorrow of Bengal'?
A. Damodar B. Gandak
C. Kosi D. Sone

128. Abhinav Bindra is a distinguished athlete in which of the following games?
A. Swimming B. Weightlifting
C. Shooting D. Archery

129. Which state is regarded as the land of five rivers?
A. Gujarat B. Assam
C. Chhatisgarh D. Punjab

130. Which of the following states has the largest size of population?
A. Uttar Pradesh B. Madhya Pradesh
C. West Bengal D. Maharashtra

131. The 'Chipko Movement' is related to:
A. Wildlife preservation
B. Forest Conservation
C. Scientific agriculture
D. Deforesation

132. The chemical name of 'Common Salt' is:
A. Sodium Chloride
B. Sodium nitrate
C. Ammonium Chloride
D. Calcium Chloride

133. The National Stock Exchange is located in:
A. New Delhi B. Mumbai
C. Kolkata D. Chennai

134. In India Union Budget is always presented in the Parliament in the month of:
A. February B. March
C. April D. December

135. Santosh Trophy is associated with the game of:
A. Cricket B. Football
C. Hockey D. Tennis

136. 'LBW' is the term associated with the game of:
A. Cricket B. Hockey
C. Tennis D. Football

137. Which planet is nearest to sun?
A. Jupiter B. Mars
C. Mercury D. Venus

138. The H.Q. of UNO is located at:
A. Geneva B. New York
C. Paris D. Washington D.C.

139. 'Gidda' is the folk dance of which state?
A. Odisha B. Punjab
C. Rajasthan D. Nagaland

140. Who is the Chairman of NITI Aayog?
A. Prime Minister B. President
C. Vice-President D. Governor

141. Who was the first Nobel Prize winner of India?
A. C.V. Raman
B. Mother Teresa
C. Rabindra Nath Tagore
D. S.C. Bose

142. Seismograph is used in the study of:
A. Earthquake B. Moon
C. Floods D. Tides

143. Which is the highest literate state of India?
A. Kerala B. Mizoram
C. Sikkim D. Arunachal Pradesh

144. Where are the Caves of Ajanta located?
A. Odisha B. Kerala
C. Maharashtra D. Madhya Pradesh

145. The Bodo language is spoken in which of the following states?
A. Mizoram B. Tamil Nadu
C. Assam D. Arunachal Pradesh

146. EURO is a:
A. Currency B. City
C. Group D. River

147. Who founded Sikhism?
A. Guru Govind Singh
B. Guru Ramdas
C. Guru Nanak Dev
D. Guru Hargovind

148. Human Rights Day is celebrated on:
A. 10 December B. 1 December
C. 4 December D. 3 December

149. The 'first lady' of the Indian Silver Screen is:
A. Madhubala B. Devika Rani
C. Durga Khote D. Nargis Dutt

150. Who said, "You give me blood, I will give you freedom"?
A. Mahatma Gandhi
B. Subhash Chandra Bose
C. Bhagat Singh
D. Bal Gangadhar Tilak

151. Dhyanchand was associated with which sports?
A. Badminton B. Hockey
C. Tennis D. Football

152. 'Raja Harishchandra', an early Indian film, was produced by:
A. D.G. Phalke B. Ashok Kumar
C. Ardeshir Irani D. Dilip Kumar

153. Teratali is the folk dance of:
A. Kerala B. Rajasthan
C. Madhya Pradesh D. Tamil Nadu

154. Sarnath is in the state of:
A. Kerala B. Maharashtra
C. Gujarat D. Uttar Pradesh

155. Who has scored highest number of runs in test cricket?
A. Allen Border
B. Sachin Tendulkar
C. Brian Lara
D. Sunil Gavaskar

156. The great law giver of ancient times was:
A. Ashoka B. Arya Bhatt
C. Manu D. Vatsyayana

157. Who wrote the famous song 'Saare Jahan Se Achcha Hindustan Hamara'?
A. Sahir Ludhianvi
B. Sir Sayyad Ahmad Khan
C. Muhammed Iqbal
D. Bahadur Shah Zafar

158. The first Indian to win Nobel prize was:
A. C.V. Raman
B. Rabindra Nath Tagore
C. Hargobind Khorana
D. Amartya Sen

159. Citrus fruits are rich source of vitamin:
A. B B. C
C. K D. A

160. The fourth estate is:
A. Press B. Property
C. Metals D. Tax

161. Which part of the body is affected by the disease called 'rickets'?
A. Lungs B. Skin
C. Intestines D. Bones

162. The first woman to be the speaker of Lok Sabha is:
A. Vijay Lakshmi Pandit
B. Sarojini Naidu
C. Indira Gandhi
D. Meira Kumar

163. How many litres of blood a normal human adult body contains?
A. 5-6 litres B. 10 litres
C. 15 litres D. 2 litres

164. Which of the following is not a Veda?
A. Upanishada B. Rigveda
C. Atharvaveda D. Samaveda

165. What is the name of the northern most state/UT in India?
A. Rajasthan B. Jammu & Kashmir
C. Gujarat D. Himachal Pradesh

166. How many colours are there in our national flag?
A. Two B. Three
C. Four D. Five

167. On what date is Republic Day celebrated?
A. 15 August B. 26 November
C. 26 January D. 15 June

168. Meenakshi Temple is located in which state?
A. Tamil Nadu B. Kerala
C. Maharashtra D. Himachal Pradesh

169. When did the First World War Start?
A. 1914 B. 1918
C. 1939 D. 1921

170. 'Red Fort' is located in which place?
A. Delhi B. Amritsar
C. Puri D. Bijapur

171. The first Indian to go into space is:
A. Rakesh Sharma
B. Ramesh Sharma
C. Rajesh Sharma
D. Rohit Sharma

172. Salarjang museum is at:
A. Hyderabad B. Mysore
C. Bengaluru D. Delhi

173. The Flag on half pale represents:
A. War B. National Mourn
C. Defeat D. Victory

174. 'Palk Strait' separates India from:
A. Pakistan B. Sri Lanka
C. Bangladesh D. Nepal

175. What did the Lactometer instrument measures?
A. Purity of milk
B. Atmospheric pressure
C. Temperature
D. Energy

176. Ayodhya is situated on the bank of which river?
A. Yamuna B. Ganga
C. Saryu D. Gandaka

177. Who is called the iron man of India?
A. Sardar Patel
B. Mahatma Gandhi
C. J.L. Nehru
D. Subhash Chandra Bose

178. How many are the numbers of bones in human body?
A. 200 B. 206
C. 210 D. 218

179. Which of the following is not a capital of any state:
A. Lucknow B. Meerut
C. Bhopal D. Dispur

180. Who is known as Lok Nayak?
A. Chitranjan Das
B. Bal Gangadhar Tilak
C. Madan Mohan Malviya
D. Jay Prakash Narayan

181. Who is the first Indian woman to Climb Mount Everest?
A. Bachendri Pal B. Raksha Yadav
C. Subhash Yadav D. Kalpana Chawala

182. In which state Bhakra Nangal Dam is situated?
A. Punjab B. West Bengal
C. Andhra Pradesh D. Maharashtra

183. What is the capital of Maharashtra?
A. Bhubneshwar B. Patna
C. Hyderabad D. Mumbai

184. Who was the second Prime Minister of India?
A. Lal Bahadur Shastri
B. Indira Gandhi
C. Morarji Desai
D. Rajiv Gandhi

185. Who is known as father of computer?
A. Bill Gates B. Charles Babbage
C. Alon Euning D. John Euning

186. Who is called the Father of our Nation?
A. Mahatma Gandhi B. Jawahar Lal Nehru
C. Rajendra Prasad D. Sardar Patel

187. Which language is spoken in Kerala?
A. Tamil B. Kannada
C. Telugu D. Malayalam

188. What is the name of the Capital of France?
A. Paris B. Berlin
C. Stockhalm D. Freetown

189. Which state has the longest coast line?
A. Gujarat B. Maharashtra
C. Andhra Pradesh D. Odisha

190. Thomas Cup is associated with which sport?
A. Lawn Tennis B. Badminton
C. Cricket D. Football

191. Famous Sun Temple is located in which state?
A. Odisha B. Gujarat
C. Maharashtra D. Uttar Pradesh

192. Who is the head of a state in India?
A. Governor B. Chief Minister
C. Home Minister D. Prime Minister

193. What is the name of Samadhi of J.L. Nehru?
A. Raj Ghat B. Shakti-Sthal
C. Shantivan D. Vijay Ghat

194. Who was George Washington?
A. First President of USA
B. First Prime Minister of UK
C. First President of Russia
D. First Prime Minister of France

195. When is the Army Day?
A. 15 January B. 15 February
C. 15 March D. 15 April

196. 'Kathmandu' is the capital of:
A. Malaysia B. Nepal
C. Singapore D. Sri Lanka

197. Which is the most populated city in India?
A. Delhi B. Kolkata
C. Greater Mumbai D. Chennai

198. Which country use TAKA as their currency?
A. Pakistan B. Nepal
C. Iran D. Bangladesh

199. Which city is called Pink City?
A. Jaipur B. Bangaluru
C. Kolkata D. Hyderabad

200. Light from the Sun reaches Earth in about:
A. 2 minute B. 4 minute
C. 8 minute D. 16 minute

201. 'Yangon' is located in which country?
A. Myanmar B. Sri Lanka
C. Pakistan D. Japan

202. Shortage of which Vitamin causes scurvy?
A. Vitamin 'A' B. Vitamin 'B'
C. Vitamin 'C' D. Vitamin 'D'

203. 'The Bible' is a holy book of which religion?
A. Hindu B. Mohammedan
C. Sikh D. Christian

204. 'Nasik' is located in which state?
A. Maharashtra B. Uttar Pradesh
C. West Bengal D. Odisha

205. How many players are there in a cricket team?
A. 9 B. 10
C. 11 D. 12

206. What was the old name of Sri Lanka?
A. Ceylon B. Babylon
C. Yangoon D. None of these

207. What is the name of the first woman Prime Minister of any country?
A. Indira Gandhi
B. Benazeer Bhutto
C. Sirimavo Bhandaranaike
D. Margaret Thatcher

208. Who was the founder of Jain religion?
A. Rishabhadeva
B. Gautam Buddha
C. Swami Vivekanand
D. Ram Krishan Paramhans

209. Who is the first Indian woman IPS officer?
A. Kiran Bedi B. Ela Bhatt
C. Kiran Desai D. Kiran Walia

210. Who discovered the sea route to India?
A. Vasco-di-gama
B. Kepler
C. Captain Cook
D. Copernicus

211. The Dalal Street is at:
A. Delhi B. Mumbai
C. Chennai D. Kolkata

212. Who was the founder of Bangladesh?
A. Sheikh Mujibur Rehman
B. Khalida Zia
C. Moh. Irsad
D. Jiaur-Rehman

213. What is the name of the capital of Kerala?
A. Shimla
B. Jaipur
C. Bhubaneshwar
D. Thiruvananthapuram

214. 'Mettur Dam' is constructed on which river?
A. Sutlej B. Mahanadi
C. Cauvery D. Krishna

215. Viswanathan Anand is associated with which sport?
A. Tennis B. Badminton
C. Chess D. Mountaineering

216. What is produced at Sindri?
A. Watches B. Fertilizers
C. Crude oil D. Steel

217. Who gave the slogan 'Jai Hind'?
A. Subhash Chandra Bose
B. Mahatma Gandhi
C. Sardar Patel
D. J.L. Nehru

218. 'Evereday' is a famous brand of:
A. Torch Cells B. Sewing machine
C. Tea D. Soap

219. 'Usha' is a famous brand of:
A. Watches B. Fertilizers
C. Steel D. Sewing machine

220. Which is the last month of National Calendar of India?
A. Chaitra B. Phalguna
C. Ashadha D. Sawana

221. Sariska Sanctuary is located in which state?
A. Assam B. Kerala
C. Gujarat D. Rajasthan

222. Who said, "Independence is our birth-right; we shall seize it."
A. Bal Gangadhar Tilak
B. Bhagat Singh
C. Ram Prasad Bismil
D. Subhash Chandra Bose

223. The term 'Duck' is associated with:
A. Chess B. Volleyball
C. Golf D. Cricket

224. Supreme Court in India was established in Calcutta (Kolkata) in:
A. 1771 B. 1774
C. 1775 D. 1776

225. The name of India's first aircraft carrier is:
A. INS Nilgiri
B. INS Himgiri
C. INS Kukri
D. INS Vikrant

226. Who is known for Narmada Bachao Andolan?
A. Parvati Devi B. Medha Patkar
C. Rama Bai D. Gaura Devi

227. Who was first Mughal ruler in India?
A. Babar B. Akbar
C. Jahangir D. Humayun

228. Satellite Launching Station Sriharikota is located in which state?
A. Andhra Pradesh
B. Karnataka
C. Kerala
D. Madhya Pradesh

229. 'Vihar' is the place of worship of which religion?
A. Hinduism B. Buddhism
C. Sikhism D. Jainism

230. In which state birth place of Mahatma Gandhi 'Porbandar' is situated?
A. Maharashtra B. Rajasthan
C. Gujarat D. Madhya Pradesh

231. Jama Masjid, the biggest mosque in India is located in:
A. Delhi B. Lucknow
C. Hyderabad D. Bengaluru

232. Which is the biggest Planet?
A. Mercury B. Jupiter
C. Mars D. Venus

233. What is the name of first satellite, launched by India?
A. Bhaskara B. Rohini
C. Apple D. Aryabhata

234. Who invented telephone?
A. Samual Morse B. K.C. Gillet
C. G. Marconi D. Graham Bell

235. C.K. Naidu trophy is related to:
A. Hockey B. Football
C. Cricket D. Badminton

236. 'Bully' term is related to which sport?
A. Football B. Hockey
C. Badminton D. Cricket

237. Nandan Kanan wild life sanctuary is in which state?
A. West Bengal B. Asom
C. Odisha D. Kerala

238. Which is the longest irrigation Canal of India?
A. Sarda Canal
B. Grand Anicut Canal
C. Hijli Canal
D. Indira Gandhi Canal

239. Oscar awards are associated with:
A. Literature B. Science
C. Sports D. Films

240. Hari Prasad Chourasia is a renowned player of:
A. Tabla B. Sarod
C. Flute D. Sitar

241. DTH (Direct to Home) is related to:
A. Television B. Telephone (hand)
C. Mobile Phone D. Internet

242. The Bhilai Steel Plant is located in:
A. Chattisgarh B. Madhya Pradesh
C. Odisha D. Jharkhand

243. The President of India can nominate to the Rajya Sabha:
A. 6 members B. 9 members
C. 12 members D. 15 members

244. The Nilgiris are part of the:
A. Eastern Ghats B. Western Ghats
C. Vindhyachal D. Tamil Nadu Hills

245. Who among the following has been called the 'Father of Indian Unrest'?
A. B.G. Tilak B. G.K. Gokhale
C. S.C. Bose D. Mahatma Gandhi

246. The historic 'Dandi March' is associated with:
A. Boycott of elections
B. Violation of 'Salt Law'
C. Hindu-Muslim Unity
D. Abolition of Untouchability

247. Who was the first man to go into space?
A. Alexei Leonov B. Dennis Tito
C. Yuri Gagarin D. Charles Dickens

248. Which country is called 'Land of Rising Sun'?
A. Japan B. Norway
C. Switzerland D. Australia

249. Where was India's first underground nuclear explosion conducted?
A. Pokhram B. Sriharikota
C. Balasone D. Udaipur

250. Taj Mahal is in the state of:
A. Kerala B. Maharashtra
C. Gujarat D. Uttar Pradesh

251. The President of India holds office for a period of:
A. 6 years B. 5 years
C. 4 years D. 7 years

252. The judges of the Supreme Court are appointed by the:
A. Prime Minister of India
B. Speaker of the Lok Sabha
C. President of India
D. Ministry of Law & Justice

253. Currency notes in India are printed and supplied by the:
A. SEBI B. FICCI
C. IFCI D. RBI

254. The smallest planets is:
A. Venus B. Mercury
C. Jupiter D. Earth

255. Which planet is known as a blue planet?
A. Mercury B. Venus
C. Jupiter D. Earth

256. Which is the crop of the longest duration?
A. Gram B. Millet
C. Barley D. Sugarcane

257. About .... of the earth's surface is covered by water.
A. 60% B. 70%
C. 79% D. 55%

258. Capital of which of the following states of India is not situated on the Bank of river?
A. Bihar
B. Telangana
C. Uttar Pradesh
D. Madhya Pradesh

259. Who was the first Muslim President of India?
A. Dr. A.P.J. Abdul Kalam
B. Fakhruddin Ali Ahmad
C. Dr. Zakir Hussain
D. None of these

260. How many bits are there in one byte?
A. 8 B. 1
C. 2 D. 1024

261. The Konark temple in Odisha is dedicated to:
A. Lord Indra B. Lord Rama
C. The Sun God D. None of these

262. The Kanha National Park, tiger reserve, is located in:
A. Uttar Pradesh B. Madhya Pradesh
C. Rajasthan D. Punjab

263. Supreme Command of all the three wings of the armed forces is vested in the:
A. Prime Minister of India
B. President of India
C. Chief of Army Staff
D. Defence Minister

264. In size, India is .... largest country in the world.
A. seventh B. second
C. third D. tenth

265. Telegraph was invented by:
A. Enhorse B. Morse
C. Graham Bell D. Rontgen

266. Famous Leaning Tower of Pisa is in:
A. Italy B. Greece
C. Cyprus D. Turkey

267. China's sorrow is:
A. Hwang Ho B. Tigris
C. Irewadi D. Cantaon

268. Jojila pass is in:
A. Rajasthan B. Ladakh
C. Uttar Pradesh D. Punjab

269. Bangladesh came into existence in December 1971. Formerly it was known as:
A. East Bengal B. Banga
C. Brahmadesh D. East Pakistan

270. The largest in the world in respect of Area is:
A. China B. India
C. Russia D. USA

271. 'Silly point' word is connected with:
A. Tennis B. Cricket
C. Hockey D. Football

272. In which game the term 'Tee' is used?
A. Chess B. Golf
C. Billiards D. Snooker

273. Charak was a renowned:
A. Historian B. Physician
C. Minister D. Astronomer

274. Who founded the Indian National Congress?
A. W.C. Bannerjee
B. A.O. Hume
C. Sardar Patel
D. Subhash Chandra Bose

275. Olympic Games are held every ....
A. 2 years B. 4 years
C. 5 years D. 6 years

276. What is the name of capital of Iraq?
A. Baghdad B. Tehran
C. Rome D. Tokyo

277. Delhi is located on the bank of which river?
A. Ganga B. Yamuna
C. Gomati D. Tapti

278. Varanasi is located on the bank of which river?
A. Krishna B. Shipra
C. Ganga D. Yamuna

279. 'Aizawl' is the capital of:
A. Nagaland B. Mizoram
C. Manipur D. Meghalay

280. What is the capital of Chhattisgarh?
A. Raipur B. Jabalpur
C. Bastar D. Bhopal

281. Mount Abu hill station is in which state?
A. Madhya Pradesh B. Rajasthan
C. Maharashtra D. Himachal Pradesh

282. Holy place Rameshwaram is in which state?
A. Andhra Pradesh B. Bihar
C. Tamil Nadu D. Gujarat

283. Badrinath is in which state?
A. Uttarakhand B. Haryana
C. Gujarat D. Odisha

284. Who was the first Vice-President of India?
A. Dr. Zakir Hussain
B. V.V. Giri
C. Dr. S. Radhakrishnan
D. G.S. Pathak

285. McMohan Line divided:
A. India-China B. India-Pakistan
C. India-Nepal D. India-Bangaladesh

286. 'Panditji' is the Nick Name of:
A. Jawaharlal Nehru
B. Lal Bahadur Shastri
C. Subhash Chandra Bose
D. Bal Gangadhar Tilak

287. 'Pravada' is a famous newspaper of which country?
A. Russia B. America
C. Britain D. China

288. 'Kangaroo' is a national emblem of which country?
A. America B. Australia
C. Italy D. Japan

289. Which is the largest continent of the world?
A. Asia B. Africa
C. Europe D. North America

290. I.S.I. is a intelligence agency of which country?
A. India B. Britain
C. Pakistan D. Nepal

291. Tripitaka is a holy book of which religion?
A. Jew B. Buddhism
C. Jainism D. Parsi

292. Tuberculosis is a disease caused by:
A. Bacteria B. Virus
C. Protozoa D. Malmu

293. Which of the following causes AIDS?
A. Rubella virus B. Vanicella Virus
C. HIV D. None of the above

294. Varahamihira was a great:
A. Poet B. Philosopher
C. Astronomer D. Astrologer

295. The earliest of the holy books of the Hindus is:
A. The Gita B. The Ramayana
C. The Mahabharata D. The Vedas

296. India is a:
A. Secular State B. Bilingual State
C. Communist State D. Capitalist State

297. To contest election for the office of Vice-President of India, the Candidate must have completed the age of:
A. 40 years B. 35 years
C. 30 years D. 45 years

298. Who is known as the father of Indian Atomic Energy or Nuclear Research:
A. Dr. Homi Bhabha B. Vikram Sara Bhai
C. C.V. Raman D. Dr. Bhatnagar

299. What is "hotline"?
A. A telecommunication link
B. An electric wire
C. Hard disk
D. Modem

300. Who discovered that the earth moves round the sun?
A. Newton B. Galileo
C. Copernicus D. All are true

301. Which city is called the 'City of Seven Hills'?
A. Oslo B. New York
C. Tokyo D. Rome

302. Cuba is nicknamed as:
A. Cockpit of Europe
B. Hermit Kingdom
C. Land of the Golden Fleece
D. Sugar Bowl of the World

303. The biggest gold producing country in the world is:
A. USA B. Russia
C. China D. None of these

304. Vatican City is the residence of:
A. Pope B. British Queen
C. French President D. Cyprus President

305. National Defence Academy is located in which state?
A. Maharashtra B. Punjab
C. Andhra Pradesh D. Uttar Pradesh

306. The biggest port in India is:
A. Vishakhapatnam B. Mumbai
C. Tuticorin D. Kandla

307. The headquarters of the World Bank are at:
A. Manila B. Washington
C. New York D. Geneva

308. The disease 'beri-beri' is caused by the deficiency of:
A. Vitamin A B. Iron
C. Vitamin B D. Iodine

309. Who presides over meetings of Rajya Sabha?
A. Prime Minister B. Vice-President
C. President D. Speaker

310. The Swaraj Party was founded by:
A. Motilal Nehru and Chittaranjan Das
B. Chandrashekhar Azad
C. Motilal Nehru and Tilak
D. Jawaharlal Nehru

311. Judges of Supreme Court hold office up to the age of:
A. 56 B. 62
C. 60 D. 65

312. Light year is a unit of:
A. Light B. Time
C. Distance D. Intensity of Light

313. The three primary colours are:
A. Violet, Black, Blue
B. Yellow, Orange, Red
C. Blue, Yellow, Red
D. Blue, Green, Red

314. The Census in India is done after a gap of every:
A. 5 years B. 10 years
C. 12 years D. 15 years

315. Which of the following awards is given for Excellence in the field of sports?
A. Kalinga Award B. Golden Pen Award
C. Arjuna Award D. Bharat Ratna

316. The oldest mountain in India is:
A. Satpura B. Nilgiri
C. Himalaya D. Aravali

317. Indian National Congress was established in:
A. 1880 B. 1885
C. 1906 D. 1905

318. Which of the following is related to Mathura?
A. Fertilizer
B. Leather
C. Petroleum Refinery
D. Chemical

319. Akbar built Ibadatkhana at Fatehpur Sikri to:
A. conduct mass prayer
B. hold darbar
C. hold religious discussions
D. hear public grievances

320. Animal with longest life is:
A. Elephant B. Dog
C. Crocodile D. Tortoise

321. Roger Federer is a famous:
A. Film actor
B. Author
C. Lawn Tennis Player
D. Cricketer

322. Dr. Amartya Sen is a famous:
A. Physicist B. Chemical Engineer
C. Psychologist D. Economist

323. Who was discoverer of America?
A. Columbus B. Cabral
C. Robert Peary D. S. Morse

324. Who was discoverer of Dynamite?
A. Alfred Nobel B. Otto Hahn
C. Dalton D. Moseley

325. Patna is located on the river:
A. Yamuna B. Hooghly
C. Ganga D. Sutlej

326. Surat is located on the river:
A. Tapti B. Kaveri
C. Shipra D. Krishna

327. 'Agartala' is the capital of:
A. Manipur B. Mizoram
C. Nagaland D. Tripura

328. What is the name of capital of Lakshadweep?
A. Silvasa B. Kavaratti
C. Port Blair D. Imphal

329. Kaziranga National Park is situated in which state?
A. Gujarat B. Tamil Nadu
C. Assam D. Karnatka

330. Famous Gir National Park is situated in which state?
A. Uttar Pradesh B. Uttarakhand
C. Gujarat D. Madhya Pradesh

331. Famous holy place 'Puri' is located in which state?
A. Odisha B. Uttar Pradesh
C. Uttarakhand D. Tamil Nadu

332. Famous holy place 'Kedarnath' is located in which state?
A. Uttarakhand B. Uttar Pradesh
C. Gujarat D. Mahdya Pradesh

333. 'Bodh Gaya' is situated in which state?
A. Jharkhand B. Bihar
C. Tamil Nadu D. Jammu & Kashmir

334. 'Rangaswamy Cup' is associated with which games?
A. Football B. Hockey
C. Table Tennis D. Rowing

335. 'Davis Cup' is associated with which games?
A. Lawn Tennis B. Cricket
C. Football D. Polo

336. Which country have biggest Army in the world?
A. USA B. China
C. Russia D. India

337. Which country is biggest in area in the world?
A. China B. Russia
C. USA D. Canada

338. Famous player Vishwanathan Anand is associated with which sports?
A. Chess B. Cricket
C. Football D. Tennis

339. South Gangotri is located in:
A. Antarctica B. Satpura
C. Willington D. Tamil Nadu

340. 'Republic Day' is celebrated on:
A. 26th January B. 15th August
C. 5th September D. 1st October

341. 'Shora' is the name of the parliament of:
A. Afghanistan B. Pakistan
C. Nepal D. Bangaladesh

342. Ras Leela, Yaosang and Lai Haraoba are the festivals of:
A. Assemese people
B. Manipuri people
C. Karbi people
D. Bodo people

343. Which is the Brightest planet in the Solar System?
A. Venus B. Mercury
C. Jupiter D. Saturn

344. Which is the highest mountain peak in the world?
A. K-2 B. Kanchenjunga
C. Mount Everest D. Makalu I

345. Who is called 'Missile Man of India'?
A. S. Chandrasekhar
B. G.S. Raghavan
C. C.N.R. Rao
D. A.P.J. Abdul Kalam

346. Which city is called 'City of Palaces'?
A. Kolkata B. Mumbai
C. Jaipur D. Ahmedabad

347. Which city is called 'City of Nababs'?
A. Lucknow B. Mumbai
C. Patna D. Jaipur

348. 'Fire Temple' is a place of worship of which religion?
A. Jainism B. Jew
C. Parsi D. Sikh

349. 'Pravada' is a famous newspaper of which country?
A. America B. Britain
C. Russia D. China

350. 'Red Triangle' is a sign of:
A. Family Planning B. Medical Help
C. Danger D. Surrender

351. Ashoka belonged to:
A. Maurya dynasty B. Gupta dynasty
C. Kushan dynasty D. Saka dynasty

352. Kalibangan, the Indus Valley site is in:
A. Rajasthan B. Gujarat
C. Madhya Pradesh D. Uttar Pradesh

353. The Grand Trunk Road in India was got constructed by:
A. Ashoka B. Shershah Suri
C. Akbar D. Humayun

354. Who had founded the slave dynasty in India?
A. Qutb-ud-din Aibak B. Iltutmis
C. Mohammed Gauri D. Balban

355. What is Super Nova?
A. A black hole B. A dying star
C. An asteraid D. A comet

356. Where was Adi-Shankaracharya born?
A. In west Bengal B. In Andhra Pradesh
C. In Kerala D. In Kashmir

357. The founder of Islam was:
A. Prophet Mohammed
B. Khalifa Omaiyd
C. Omar
D. Osman

358. Raziah, the first lady ruler of India was the daughter of:
A. Qutub-din-Aibak B. Iltutmish
C. Yakut D. Malik Altunia

359. 'Chetak' was the name of the horse belonging to which king?
A. Shivaji B. Tippu Sultan
C. Umed Singh D. Maharana Pratap

360. When did the Second World War start?
A. 1941 B. 1937
C. 1939 D. 1945

361. What name is given to an imaginary line which divides earth in two equal halfs?
A. Latitude B. Equator
C. Longitude D. None of these

362. Paris is situated on the bank of river:
A. Seine B. Thames
C. Volga D. None of these

363. Which of the following lakes in India has the highest water salinity:
A. Wullar B. Chilka
C. Sambhar D. Dal

364. Where Indian's first cotton textile mill was established?
A. Surat B. Bombay
C. Madras D. Calcutta

365. The largest river of South India is:
A. Godavari B. Krishna
C. Mahanadi D. Kaveri

366. Which of the following is not a Kharif Crops:
A. Rice B. Maize
C. Bajara D. Wheat

367. Which of the following is not a Rabi Crops?
A. Wheat B. Gram
C. Rice D. Barley

368. Which of the following place is not related to railway manufacturing?
A. Varanasi B. Perambdur
C. Kapurthala D. Ludhiana

369. 'Father of History' is the name given to:
A. Herodatus B. Megasthenese
C. John Rey D. Ibn Batuta

370. In which state the 'Narora' Power Station is located?
A. Bihar B. Uttar Pradesh
C. Panjab D. None of these

371. Almatti Dam is situated on which river?
A. Tungabhadra B. Godavari
C. Krishna D. None of these

372. Jawahar Tunnel is located in which state/UT?
A. Assam B. Manipur
C. Jammu & Kashmir D. Punjab

373. Which of the following states has no coastline?
A. Odisha B. Maharashtra
C. Gujarat D. Mizoram

374. What is manufactured at Sindri?
A. Fertilizer B. Textiles
C. Watches D. Automobile

375. Black soil is best suited for the crop of:
A. Rice B. Wheat
C. Cotton D. Mustard

376. The quorum (minimum presence for proceeding) of Lok Sabha is:
A. 1/4 B. 1/10
C. 1/5 D. 1/2

377. The speaker if resigns, will send his resignation to:
A. President B. Vice-President
C. Deputy-Speaker D. Prime Minister

378. The President if resings, will send his resignation to:
A. Chief Justice B. Prime-Minister
C. Vice President D. Speaker

379. The minimum age for Governor is:
A. 30 years B. 35 years
C. 25 years D. 18 years

380. What is the age of retirement of a Judge of Supreme Court?
A. 55 years B. 58 years
C. 62 years D. 65 years

381. Which of the following is a land locked country?
A. Sudan B. Egypt
C. Bangladesh D. Afghanistan

382. The first secretary General of United Nations was:
A. Butrus Ghali B. Kafi Annan
C. U. Thant D. Trygvelie

383. The SAARC movement was launched for:
A. Regional cooperation
B. Military strategy
C. Cultural exchanges
D. Political alliances

384. Name the city in which Golden Temple is located?
A. Ludhiana B. Chandigarh
C. Amritsar D. Delhi

385. The first TV centre started in India in September, 1959 at:
A. Bombay B. Madras
C. Delhi D. Calcutta

386. Which of the following news agencies was the first to be set up?
A. Hindustan Samachar
B. Press Trust of India
C. Samachar Bharati
D. United News of India

387. Which of the following pair is wrong?
A. Teacher's day – 5 September
B. Aids day – 1 December
C. Labour day – 1 March
D. UNO day – 24 October

388. "Hey Ram" is written on the grave of which of the following leaders?
A. Mahatma Gandhi
B. Indira Gandhi
C. Lala Lajpat Rai
D. Bal Gangadhar Tilak

389. Where is the headquarter of Election Commission located?
A. Kolkata B. Chennai
C. New Delhi D. Mumbai

390. Which of this is not a state?
A. Jharkhand B. Goa
C. Mumbai D. Mizoram

391. Where Ranthambhore is located?
A. Uttar Pradesh B. Uttarakhand
C. Rajasthan D. Haryana

392. Which one of the following is the famous garden situated in the Rashtrapati Bhawan?
A. Budda Garden B. Lodi Garden
C. Mughal Garden D. Zoological Garden

393. Which of the following pair is wrong about award and their field?
A. Arjun Award — Sports
B. Dronacharya — Coaches of sports
C. Dada Sahib Falke — Film
D. Bhartiya Jnanpith — Medicine

394. Highest sports award of our country is:
A. Major Dhyan Chand Khel Ratna
B. Arjuna Award
C. Dronacharya Award
D. Indira Gandhi Award

395. Who is the first winner of Param Vir Chakra?
A. N.K. Jagannath Singh
B. CQMH Abul Hamid
C. Lt. Arun Khetrapal
D. Major Somnath Sharma

396. Which of the following Cup/Trophy does not belong to Tennis?
A. Wimbledon Cup B. Devis Cup
C. Fed Cup D. Derby Cup

397. To promote the Indian games Arjun Award was started in the year:
A. 1961 B. 1965
C. 1969 D. 1968

398. Derbi is associated with the game:
A. Horse riding B. Football
C. Cricket D. Tennis

399. 'Punch' is related with which of the event?
A. Boxing B. Volley ball
C. Kabbadi D. Football

400. Which of the following pair about the person and their contrary is wrong?
A. Kalidas — Vikramaditya
B. Tulsidas — Akbar
C. Amir Khusro — Allauddin Khilji
D. Ban Bhatt — Ashok

401. The last Governor-General of British-India was
A. Lord Wavell B. Lord Mountbatten
C. Lord Simon D. Lord Irwin

402. Some of the Princely States refused to join the Indian Union after Independence. Point the odd one out
A. Kashmir B. Junagarh
C. Hyderabad D. Gwalior

403. The great Indian saint who said, "There is neither a Hindu nor a Muslim: only man" was
A. Guru Nanak
B. Kabir
C. Sheikh Farid
D. Swami Vivekananda

404. The most important feature of the Indian culture is
A. its continuity
B. healthy attitude towards all life
C. toleration
D. unity in diversity

405. Home Rule Movement was started by
A. Bal Gangadhar Tilak
B. Mahatma Gandhi
C. Vivekananda
D. Annie Besant

406. The first country which recognised the emergence of Bangladesh was
A. Sri Lanka B. Soviet Russia
C. USA D. India

407. The Harappan civilisation belongs to
A. Bronze Age B. Neolithic Age
C. Paleolithic Age D. Iron Age

408. Hiuen-Tsang, the Chinese Pilgrim visited India during the reign of
A. Ashoka the Great
B. Chandragupta I
C. Harshavardhana
D. Chandragupta Maurya

409. Choose the correct pair
A. Ellora Cave—Saka
B. Mahabalipuram—Rashtrakutas
C. Meenakshi Temple—Pallavas
D. Khajuraho—Chandellas

410. Which Indian ruler conquered Java and Sumatra
A. Rajaraja Chola B. Rajendra Chola
C. Samudragupta D. Vikramaditya

411. Raja Rammohan Roy was the founder of
A. Arya Samaj
B. Brahmo Samaj
C. Ramakrishna Mission
D. Prarthana Samaj

412. The 1857 uprising failed mainly because
A. the British got the support of Gorkhas
B. the military supremacy of the British
C. lack of planning and leadership on the Indian side
D. betrayal of Indians

413. Fibre crops are
A. Jute, Sugarcane, Linseed and Rice
B. Cotton, Maize, Tobacco and Banana
C. Cotton, Hemp, Jute and Mesta
D. Hemp, Cotton, Maize and Saffron

414. The delta-forming rivers in India are
A. Ganges—Mahanadi—Narmada
B. Krishna—Ganges—Tapti
C. Cauvery—Ganges—Mahanadi
D. Narmada—Tapti—Krishna

415. Areawise, the biggest State in India is
A. Rajasthan B. Uttar Pradesh
C. Andhra Pradesh D. Arunachal Pradesh

ANSWERS

1	2	3	4	5	6	7	8	9	10
A	B	A	B	B	A	A	A	C	C
11	**12**	**13**	**14**	**15**	**16**	**17**	**18**	**19**	**20**
B	B	B	C	C	D	B	C	C	C

21	22	23	24	25	26	27	28	29	30
C	B	B	A	C	A	D	B	B	A
31	32	33	34	35	36	37	38	39	40
B	A	B	D	A	A	C	A	A	A
41	42	43	44	45	46	47	48	49	50
B	B	D	B	B	D	A	B	D	C
51	52	53	54	55	56	57	58	59	60
D	A	B	C	D	D	C	C	B	D
61	62	63	64	65	66	67	68	69	70
B	A	D	D	B	C	D	B	C	A
71	72	73	74	75	76	77	78	79	80
B	A	D	B	A	D	B	C	C	A
81	82	83	84	85	86	87	88	89	90
D	C	A	C	C	D	B	B	B	D
91	92	93	94	95	96	97	98	99	100
C	B	B	D	A	C	B	C	D	B
101	102	103	104	105	106	107	108	109	110
D	C	D	B	B	C	D	B	A	C
111	112	113	114	115	116	117	118	119	120
B	D	C	A	A	D	D	B	D	A
121	122	123	124	125	126	127	128	129	130
D	A	D	D	A	D	A	C	D	A
131	132	133	134	135	136	137	138	139	140
B	A	B	A	B	A	C	B	B	A
141	142	143	144	145	146	147	148	149	150
C	A	A	C	C	A	C	A	B	B
151	152	153	154	155	156	157	158	159	160
B	A	B	D	B	C	C	B	B	A
161	162	163	164	165	166	167	168	169	170
D	D	A	A	B	B	C	A	A	A
171	172	173	174	175	176	177	178	179	180
A	A	B	B	A	C	A	B	B	D
181	182	183	184	185	186	187	188	189	190
A	A	D	A	B	A	D	A	A	B
191	192	193	194	195	196	197	198	199	200
A	A	C	A	A	B	C	D	A	C
201	202	203	204	205	206	207	208	209	210
A	C	D	A	C	A	C	A	A	A
211	212	213	214	215	216	217	218	219	220
B	A	D	C	C	B	A	A	D	B

221	222	223	224	225	226	227	228	229	230
D	A	D	B	D	B	A	A	B	C
231	232	233	234	235	236	237	238	239	240
A	B	D	D	C	B	C	D	D	C
241	242	243	244	245	246	247	248	249	250
A	A	C	B	A	B	C	A	A	D
251	252	253	254	255	256	257	258	259	260
B	C	D	B	D	D	B	D	C	A
261	262	263	264	265	266	267	268	269	270
C	B	B	A	B	A	A	B	D	C
271	272	273	274	275	276	277	278	279	280
B	B	B	B	B	A	B	C	B	A
281	282	283	284	285	286	287	288	289	290
B	C	A	C	A	A	A	B	A	C
291	292	293	294	295	296	297	298	299	300
B	A	C	C	D	A	B	A	A	C
301	302	303	304	305	306	307	308	309	310
D	D	C	A	A	B	B	C	B	A
311	312	313	314	315	316	317	318	319	320
D	C	D	B	C	D	B	C	C	D
321	322	323	324	325	326	327	328	329	330
C	D	A	A	C	A	D	B	C	C
331	332	333	334	335	336	337	338	339	340
A	A	B	B	A	B	B	A	A	A
341	342	343	344	345	346	347	348	349	350
A	B	A	C	D	A	A	C	C	A
351	352	353	354	355	356	357	358	359	360
A	A	B	A	B	C	A	B	D	C
361	362	363	364	365	366	367	368	369	370
B	A	C	B	A	D	C	D	A	B
371	372	373	374	375	376	377	378	379	380
C	C	D	A	C	B	C	C	B	D
381	382	383	384	385	386	387	388	389	390
D	D	A	C	C	B	C	A	C	C
391	392	393	394	395	396	397	398	399	400
C	C	D	A	D	D	A	A	A	D
401	402	403	404	405	406	407	408	409	410
B	D	B	D	D	D	A	C	D	B
411	412	413	414	415					
B	C	C	C	A					

★ ★ ★